The Gentleman's Daughter

The Gentleman's Daughter

Women's Lives in Georgian England

Amanda Vickery

Yale University Press
New Haven & London

Copyright © 1998 by Amanda Vickery

Designed by Gillian Malpass

Printed in Great Britain

Library of Congress Cataloging-in-Publication Data

Vickery, Amanda.
The gentleman's daughter: women's lives in Georgian England/by Amanda Vickery.
p. cm.
Includes bibliographical references and index.
ISBN 0-300-07531-6 (hbk. alk. paper)
1. Women–England–History–18th century.
2. England–Social conditions–18th century.
3. Gentry–England–History–18th century.
I. Title. HQ 1599.E5V47   1988   97-45792
305.42'0942–dc21   CIP

A catalogue record for this book is available from
The British Library

Contents

Acknowledgements

Tʜᴇ ʀᴏᴀᴅ ғʀᴏᴍ Pʀᴇsᴛᴏɴ ᴛᴏ Pʜ.D. is paved with clichés, but my gratitude is no less heartfelt for its predictability. At Penwortham Girls' Grammar School, my history teacher, Alison Gibson, singled me out and encouraged me, while my parents, Derek and Renée Vickery, made every sacrifice that I might, as the adage has it, go Down South. At nineteen, in London, I was lucky enough to come across Professor Penelope Corfield. She was inspiring as an undergraduate tutor, alternately soothing and bracing as a Ph.D. supervisor, and is now unfailingly helpful as a colleague, but still shrewd as a critic. She will blush, but I salute her.

Institutions that have supported my career thus far and whose financial aid I happily acknowledge include the E.S.R.C., the Institute of Historical Research, Churchill College, Cambridge, and Royal Holloway, London University. Most recently, I enjoyed the Helen Bing fellowship at the Huntington Library, San Marino, California, and an Ahmondson-Getty fellowship at the Clark Library, U.C.L.A. My blissful stay in California was infinitely enriched by Helen Bing's remarkable kindness and the friendship of Shelly Bennett, Tom Cogswell, Karen Kupperman, Amy Myers, Jack Myers, Kate Norberg, Jenny Stine and, above all, Roy and Louise Ritchie.

In researching this book I have drawn heavily on both local and national record offices and the patience of their archivists. The following archives have all kindly permitted me to quote their manuscripts: the Lancashire Record Office, Preston; the Lancaster Public Library; the Wigan Record Office, Leigh; the Borthwick Institute of Historical Research, York; the Yorkshire Archaelogical Society, Leeds; the West Yorkshire County Record Office, Bradford; the West Yorkshire County Record Office, Leeds; the West Yorkshire County Record Office, Wakefield; the North

Yorkshire Record Office, Northallerton; the Cheshire Record Office, Chester; the Cumbria County Record Office, Carlisle; the Corporation of London Record Office; the Guildhall Library, London; the Westminster Public Library; the Essex Record Office, Chelmsford; the Kent Record Office, Maidstone; the Tyne and Wear Record Office, Newcastle; the Public Record Office, London; and the Huntington Library, San Marino, California. In particular, I must single out the kindness of Mrs Diana Parker of Browsholme, who permitted me to use the manuscripts in the Parker of Browsholme deposit in the Lancashire Record Office, alerted me to unused documents left at Browsholme, allowed me to photocopy countless manuscripts and was very helpful in advising my of illustrations. Two archivists and scholars who have been more than generous with their local knowledge and unpublished work are Faye Oldland of the Pendle Heritage Centre and Brett Harrison of the West Yorkshire Record Office at Leeds. I am grateful to all.

For references, suggestions, critical readings and intellectual fellowship, I am deeply indebted to Jonathan Bate, Kelly Boyd, Mike Braddick, Amanda Craig, Anne Goldgar, Helen Hackett, David Jarvis, Lawrence Klein, Alison Light, Rohan McWilliam, Charlotte Mitchell, Roy Porter, Naomi Tadmor, Pat Thane, the anonymous readers of Yale University Press and especially Joanna Innes, who has read my work many times over and found supporting examples too numerous to acknowledge in the notes. Successive generations of students on the Royal Holloway Women's History M.A. course have also helped shape this book with their questions and comments. For help with illustrations I must thank Mr John Aspinall of Standen, Madeline Ginsburg, the Hon. Mrs Jackson, Mr Harry Matthews, Mr Stephen Startin, Mr and Mrs John Warde of Squerries, Paul Langford who suggested the cover picture, and particularly Neil Holland, who heroically stepped in at the last minute to sort out my photography crisis. Yale University Press has proved a model publisher. Celia Jones's copy editing has been careful and helpful, while my editor Gillian Malpass has cheered me with her sustained commitment to the book and a remarkable attention to detail throughout.

Yet history is not everything, and it must be admitted that life is more fun than work. For disregarding my academic guise, I want to thank my oldest friends Gregory Battle, Jill Farrington, Neil Holland, Elizabeth Muir and all those wonderful girlfriends who have come after. The completion of this book coincided with the birth of my fearless daughter Hester and is competing with a complicated second pregnancy as I write, so to neglect to mention the unstinting support of my G.P., Fred Kavalier, the Camden midwives and everyone who has helped me at the University

College Obstetric Hospital would feel perverse. In time-honoured tradition, my biggest debt is acknowledged last. John Styles has banned the gushing and detailed acknowledgement that I have been perfecting over the years. Still, if life with two demanding women resembles an uphill struggle, then he has nobly put his shoulder to the wheel. This book is for him.

Note on the Text

ORIGINAL SPELLING, PUNCTUATION AND capitalization has been retained throughout. Abbreviation of 'the', 'that', 'which' and 'would', among a host of other nouns and verbs, was universal. Where the text is hard to follow these contractions have been rendered in full in square brackets.

The bibliography and biographical index contain details of most primary and secondary sources cited, and therefore abbreviations for these works have been used throughout in the notes; references to those works not included in the bibliography or biographical index are given in full in the notes at their first appearance in each chapter. Unless otherwise stated, the place of publication is London.

Facing page: Map of Lancashire and Yorkshire showing the principal towns and villages mentioned in the text.

LANCASHIRE

Liverpool
Ormskirk
Wigan
Bolton
Manchester
Preston
Clitheroe
Browsholme
Burnley
Colne
Slaidburn
Gisburn
Settle
Slyne
Lancaster

YORKSHIRE

Rydal
Kendal
Skipton
Bingley
Bradford
Halifax
Wakefield
Hooton Pagnell
Doncaster
Pontefract
Selby
Skipwith
Thorp Arch
York
Harrogate
Otley
Horsforth
Leeds
Scarborough

Key

———— County boundaries

· · · · · · · Boundary of the
parish of Whalley

N

0   20 miles

Introduction

IN 1820 GEORGE III DIED, the first iron steamship was launched, Shelley published *Prometheus Unbound* and an unremarkable middle-aged woman took stock of her past. She took out her old letters, burning some and arranging others, and thereby the ghosts of a decorous life materialized before her: 'These letters brought back many events, but above all marked the progress of time & how it sweeps into its course over friends over feelings – our hopes & fears – We here see man in a mirror – they appear as when they pass by mere reflections.'[1] It is from just such disconnected reflections that *The Gentleman's Daughter* is wrought. The letters, diaries and account books of over one hundred individuals from commercial, professional and gentry families form the basis of this book. Collectively, I have labelled this social group 'the genteel'. It is the relayed hopes and fears of the women of these families, the merchants' daughters, the solicitors' wives and the gentlemen's sisters, that are the central focus. To read the letters of the long dead is to summon up a veritable army of apparitions; to be bombarded with the complexities and particularities of countless comfortable lives lived outside the spotlight of history. So how is the historian to marshal all this teeming detail? What artful categories will create order from the chaos of the individual and the everyday? How should we write the history of the proper and the prosperous?

The answer for many has been to offer a narrative of decline and fall, using women's manuscripts to illustrate a tale of increasing female passivity and ever-tightening domestic encirclement. In fact, it is almost impossible to open a book on wealthier British women between the sixteenth and nineteenth centuries that does not offer a catalogue of declining female options; but, worryingly, what is presented as the key period of deterioration depends upon the author's own chronological specialism. In the sixteenth and early seventeenth centuries, so Alice Clark famously argued in 1919, the wives of craftsmen and manufacturers made a substantial contribution to the family enterprise, since the home and workplace were usually one. Gentlewomen were active in household and estate management, public affairs and even government; but as the century wore on, the rapid increase of wealth permitted the wives of prosperous men to withdraw from productive activity. In parallel, the spread of capitalistic organization concentrated manufacturing on central premises – separating the home and workplace, with devastating consequences for female enterprise. Once production left the home, the wife was divorced from her husband's trade and lost the informal opportunity to learn his skills. Creative housekeeping fell into decay. In contrast to their hardy and resourceful Elizabethan grandmothers, the moneyed ladies of the Restoration were distinguished only by their 'devotion to idle graces'.[2]

This resonant tale of the descent of seventeenth-century propertied Englishwomen into indolence and luxury has been frequently reiterated.[3] Most of these accounts rest on the curious assumption that the performance of heavy manual labour is intrinsically empowering for women, so therefore the relief from drudgery saw women automatically devalued by society. Lawrence Stone, for instance, leaves us in no doubt about the frivolousness and futility of a woman's life once she had vacated the dairy and laid down the distaff:

> Wives of the middle and upper classes increasingly became idle drones. They turned household management over to stewards, reduced their reproductive responsibilities by contraceptive measures, and passed their time in such occupations as novel reading, theatre going, card playing and formal visits . . . The custom of turning wives into ladies 'languishing in listlessness' as ornamental status objects spread downwards through the social scale.[4]

Some have built on the tale of woman's divorce from useful labour to assert that the early eighteenth century saw the 'new domestic woman' step forward to take the hand of the new economic man:

> With the eighteenth-century glorification of 'Man' came a radical narrowing of women's participation in and contribution to productive and social life, and a drastic diminution of women's stature. It was not merely a relative decline. Pre-capitalist woman was not simply relatively eclipsed by the great leap forward of the male achiever; she suffered rather an absolute setback.[5]

Scholars of English literature have tried to chart the construction of domesticated femininity, although there is a certain confusion as to whether the new domestic woman was the epitome of bourgeois personality, or was an ornament shared by the middling ranks and the landed. Whatever her social background, it is agreed that the sweet domesticate was created 'in and by print'. The most impressive study of early eighteenth-century periodicals concludes that 'during the eighteenth century, as upper and middle-class Englishwomen increasingly began to participate in the public realm of print culture, the representational practices of that print culture were steadily enclosing them within the private sphere of the home'.[6]

Another influential body of writing on women's history assumes that it was the years 1780–1850 that saw the rise of 'separate spheres'; years, it is argued, during which the everyday worlds of men and women were definitively separated, as a result of industrial capitalism and the emergence of a class society. Propertied men came to exult in the public sphere of business and affairs, safe in the knowledge that domestic femininity kept the home fires aflame. Meanwhile, privileged women abandoned all enterprise, estate management and productive housekeeping to their servants in order to devote themselves to decorative display. Thus, Mrs Average led a sheltered life drained of economic purpose and public responsibility. Cramped by custom, corset and crinoline, she was often a delicate creature, who was, at best, conspicuously in need of masculine protection, and, at worst, prey to invalidism and hysteria. And yet she abjured self-indulgence, being ever attentive and subservient to the needs of her family. Only in her matronly virtue and radiant Christianity did she exercise a mild authority over her immediate circle. She was immured in the private sphere and would not escape until feminism released her.[7]

As a story of change, this saga could be undermined at many points,[8] but possibly the most damaging weakness is the fact that all these accounts, irrespective of the period they pin-point as the key moment of change, rest unquestioningly on the assumption that a thundering commercial or industrial revolution created a new gender order, indeed *the* modern gender system, in the very era under consideration. So, if the literature is read as a whole, it is hard to avoid the impression that the spheres definitively separated and the new domestic woman was born in virtually every century since the end of the Middle Ages. Like the insidious rise of capitalism, the collapse of community, the nascent consumer society and the ever-emerging middle class, the unprecedented marginalization of wealthier women can be found in almost any century we care to look. When confronted with the numerous precedents, nineteenth-century historians of this phenomenon may claim that early modern developments represent

only the germ of what was to come on a grand scale for the Victorian
middle class. But the obvious problems of periodization which result
cannot be brushed aside with the explanatory catch-all of 'uneven development'. The problem is exemplified if we try to reconcile arguments
about early modern Norfolk with assertions about nineteenth-century
Suffolk.[9] Are we to believe that women were driven out of a public sphere
of production and power in one district in the seventeenth century, while
just over the county border the same development was delayed by well
over a hundred years? Surely uneven development of this magnitude
would have raised some contemporary comment, or at the very least
female migration? The determination of authors to claim that the single
turning point in gender history conveniently occurred in the period of their
own book means that chronological inconsistencies continue to abound.
They will persist until the quest for *the* instant when modernity began is
acknowledged to be fruitless.

In any case, the apocalyptic economic revolution so often invoked as the
deep cause of the trouble, does not look quite so earth-shattering in the
light of new research. Startling, all-consuming transformation may live on
in the textbooks and the imagination, but a convincingly revised
economic history has stressed the distinctively gradual growth of commerce and manufacturing in Britain since at least the fifteenth century.
Furthermore, a closer look at the operation of early modern businesses
raises doubts about the conviction that female enterprise decayed substantially between 1700 and 1850. First, it is clear that the explanatory power
given to the notion of the separation of the home and workplace is unwarranted. If industrial change had involved a simple linear transition from
family workshop to factory then certainly this process could have been
devastating, but, as D. C. Coleman remarked in another context, there
were many key early modern enterprises which simply could not be
performed in a cottage by husband, wife and children. In mining, ship-
building, iron smelting, pottery firing, glass blowing, paper making, soap
boiling, fulling wool and so on, the place of work was of necessity divorced from bed and board from the very inception of the industry.
Moreover, the factory was far from being the normal unit of production in
the mid-nineteenth century.[10] Economic change followed many roads and
did not arrive at a single destination. Second, when we consider those
businesses that women pursued in their own right, continuity is again
more apparent than change. Studies of fifteenth-century York and seventeenth-century London reveal a picture not so different from the 1851
census, with urban women already clustered in the so-called feminine
trades: petty retail, food and drink, and textiles. One would search long

and hard for significant numbers of female goldsmiths, blacksmiths, cabi-
net-makers, curriers and so on at any point in British history. Interestingly,
single women were prominent amongst rentiers, investors and money
lenders, suggesting that wealthier women had long found trade an unappetizing option.[11] But if female withdrawal from active involvement in a
business was a likely consequence of increasing family wealth then any
study of an expanding business, be it in fourteenth-century Norwich,
seventeenth-century London or nineteenth-century Birmingham, would be
likely to show a reduction over three generations in the *formal* participation of female members of the owning family. Of course, only genuine
comparative research will substantiate this suggestion, but it is already
clear that a lost golden age of prestigious, highly profitable and wide-
ranging female work is a chimera.[12]

A second area of critical weakness for the domesticity thesis concerns
the interpretation of contemporary commentary. Much weight has been
placed upon an apparent increase in texts grumbling about unemployed
womanhood, a muttering which grew to a clamour from the 1690s. A
flashy villainess swanked across the pages of plays, commentaries and
complaining sermons: the London woman who scorned productive labour
for the sake of consumerism and indulgence. However, the redundant
woman of the Augustan period, languishing on her sofa, may not have
been as novel a creature as the indictments suggest. More likely, it was her
flamboyant habits that were new and public, rather than her actual lack of
gainful occupation. It could even be argued that such criticism was merely
another symptom of the general moral panic of the late seventeenth century about the decline of Spartan virtue and the rise of luxurious corruption, rather than evidence of any new social group or practice. After all, in
their fears about the vicious consequences of wealth, writers fell back
upon stereotypical images of devouring, unreasonable womanhood,
images that were as old as Eve herself – something which suggests we
might better view such accusations as testimony to the persistence of male
anxieties, rather than a simple guide to female behaviour.[13] Of course,
scholars of print might also suggest that the rising tide of complaint and
conduct literature owes far more to the relaxation of censorship after the
failure to renew the Licensing Act in 1695 than it does to the outbreak of
a new disease called female parasitism.

If this flowering of public discussion was not necessarily a simple reaction to the mass female abandonment of active enterprise, was it subsequently responsible for the creation of an entirely new model of feminine
behaviour? Did the *grande peur* about female ostentation and publicity lead to the inscription of a new pattern of virtuous, domesticated

womanhood? To be sure, many scholars have detected a growing emphasis on women's innate moral superiority and a declining preoccupation
with uncontrollable female sexuality in Augustan literature. Backed by an
authoritative survey of advice literature written between 1670 and 1750,
Fenela Childs argues that cloying idealization set in from 1700, although
she stresses the obvious but important point that visions of female nature
had for centuries oscillated between impossibly pure and irredeemably
depraved.[14] Similarly, Marlene Legates suggests that we should not overestimate the novelty of eighteenth-century views of women. She argues
that chastity and obedience were ancient prerequisites of the ideal woman,
that a belief in woman as redeemer was as old as courtly love, that positive
views of marriage had co-existed with explicit misogyny in classical and
humanist thought, and that even the sentimental themes of love, marriage
and virtue under siege had a long pedigree. Legates concludes that the
eighteenth century saw not so much a dramatic break with past assumptions about the good woman, as a compelling dramatization of her
traditional predicament.[15] Indubitably, eighteenth-century literature con-
tains much that nineteenth-century historians might identify as 'domestic
ideology', yet these themes were far from revolutionary. The dialectical
polarity between home and world is an ancient trope of western writing;
the notion that women were uniquely fashioned for the private realm is at
least as old as Aristotle.

   It is important to remember that periodicals, novels, sermons and conduct books contained many other ideological messages. Jean Hunter's
examination of the *Gentleman's Magazine* (the most widely read and
successful of all eighteenth-century journals) reveals much less celebration
than one might expect of the joys of life within the narrow confines of
domestic office. As she concludes, 'if three out of every four writers who
touched on the woman question bemoaned the plight of women and
suggested concrete reform measures, perhaps the traditional, conservative
ideal of woman had less widespread support and more opposition in the
eighteenth century than has been thought'.[16] Even the prevailing didactic
lectures and venomous attacks were probably subject to multiple or selective readings. Who can say how the female reader received the exaggerated
complaints in the *Gentleman's Magazine* of July 1732 'that women were
seeking to supplant men in some of their prerogatives. They were wearing
breeches, riding astride, shaking hands, ordering men to get the coffee
rather than serving them as they should, carrying pistols, and even taking
the initiative in love affairs.'[17] Can we assume that all readers recoiled with
fastidious horror at such an excitingly Amazonian prospect? Furthermore,
sermons and satires were hardly the only publications on the market,

and female taste might be just as eclectic as male. The female reader could study sermons preaching domesticity in one mood and philosophies praising active citizenship in another. Take the example of Mary Chorley. In 1776 in Lancaster this ten year old admired the *Life of William Penn*, as one might expect of a Quaker, but she also thrilled to the rigorous public spirit of Plutarch's heroes – 'Publicola was the most virtuous citizen and greatest general Rome ever had. He was tried at the expense of the public.' By thirteen she was gasping at the goodness of Richardson's *Sir Charles Grandison* (1754) – 'Oh what a noble man Sir Charles Grandison is I do think . . .' – and laughing at the drolleries of *The Expedition of Humphry Clinker* (1771).[18] We should not presume without evidence that women (or men) mindlessly absorbed a single didactic lesson like so many pieces of unresisting blotting-paper. Nor should we see the promulgation of domesticity as cast-iron proof that women were domesticated. Viewed from another perspective, the increased harping on the proper female sphere might just as easily demonstrate a concern that more women were seen to be active outside the home rather than proof that they were so confined. In fact, the broadcasting of the language of separate spheres was almost certainly a shrill response to an expansion in the opportunities, ambitions and experience of Georgian and Victorian women – a cry from an embattled status quo, rather than the leading edge of change.

Is 'separate spheres' useful as description of women's lives? Did the wives and daughters of eighteenth-century elites resemble domestic angels, confined to a private sphere? Certainly it is incontrovertible that the majority of eighteenth- and early nineteenth-century ladies were primarily associated with home and children, while gentlemen controlled the majority of public institutions. Indeed in no century before the twentieth did women enjoy the privileges that nineteenth-century feminists sought – the full rights of citizenship. Public life for Georgian gentlemen invariably assumed the taking of office, but there was no formal place for their wives in the machinery of local government. However, this rough division between private and public could be applied to almost any century or any culture – a fact which robs the distinction of its analytical purchase.[19] If 'separate spheres' boils down to the observation that women are obliged to spend more time at home with children while men appropriate greater institutional recognition and reward, then separate spheres is an ancient phenomenon, which is certainly still with us. These deep-seated and enduring inequalities are to be deplored, but they do not capture the specificities of gender relations in a particular social group, country or century.

Of course, biological and familial imperatives governed the chief roles available to women in professional, commercial and gentry families, as they long had done. Ladies' lives resembled a stately progress through recognized stations – maid, wife, mother and, if she was lucky, widow, dowager and grandmother – with different duties and liberties attached to each role. Each stage had its own frustrations, but in their difficulties women told each other to bow to the will of providence and do their duty. Indeed, it was a commonplace that the strict performance of duty generated a degree of secret pleasure, and ladies were relentlessly tutored on how to reach and enjoy the moral high ground: 'You must also learn to be satisfied with the Consciousness of acting Right', counselled Lady Sarah Pennington, 'and look with an unconcerned Indifference on the Reception every successless Attempt to please may meet with,' while Eliza Haywood promised 'Sweet indeed are the reflections, which flow from a consciousness of having done what virtue and the duty owing to the character we bear in life, exacted from us . . .'[20] Women's own letters and diaries do suggest that many did their duty to a round of inner applause, finding a certain exaltation in it. Ladies accepted patriarchy in theory, although, strikingly, the assertion of male authority often proved much more acceptable and manageable coming from fathers than from husbands and brothers. Still, when wronged, genteel women rarely questioned the justice of the gender hierarchy; rather they bemoaned the fact that their menfolk departed so sorrily from the authoritative masculine ideal. That said, none of the women studied here expected to endure tyranny, or in contemporary terms an 'Egyptian bondage', and they were fully conscious of what was owing to their dignity and rank. While not above the occasional exhibition of an almost theatrical feminine inferiority when petitioning for favours, the habitual self-projection of most was of upright strength, stoical fortitude and self-command. To be mistress of oneself was paramount – genteel ladies aimed to be self-possessed in social encounters, self-controlled in the face of minor provocations, self-sufficient in the midst of ingratitude, and, above all, brave and enduring in the grip of tragedy and misfortune. Abject feminine servility was the ineradicable mark of the kitchen maid not her employer.

For most genteel women, the assumption of their most active material role coincided with marriage, when they became the mistress of a household. Thereby, the administration of the household, the management of servants, the guardianship of material culture and the organization of family consumption fell to their lot. Most were well prepared for this deluge of responsibility; in girlhood, many had copied and seconded their mothers, others heeded advice that they should begin a reference manual on matters material to the running of a house. A lady's work was managerial, but in this she resembled her husband. Gentlemen did not, after all, harvest corn or weave cloth themselves, but instructed servants, labourers and apprentices to do it for them: 'To manage well a great Family', acknowledged Richard Steele in 1710, 'is as worthy an Instance of Capacity, as to execute a great Employment . . .'[21] Even as conduct literature advocated female softness and obedience in one chapter, in another it minutely tutored privileged women on the exercise of power.

Yet the household and family were not the limit of an elite woman's horizon. Nor was the house in any simple sense a private, domestic sphere. Indeed, the idea that the home was a refuge insulated from the social world is one that would have perplexed the well-established in this period. Genteel families were linked to the world in a multiplicity of ways, as kinsfolk, landowners, patrons, employers and as members of the elite. All these social roles were expressed through a variety of encounters which took place in the home. Open-handed hospitality was still crucial to the maintenance of social credit and political power, and, as mistress of ceremony, the elite hostess might wield considerable practical power from the head of her dining-table. The women at the heart of this study presented themselves to the world in the mantle of politeness. Politeness was a tool which a well-born woman could use to extend her reach: she could use the language of politeness and civility to encourage heterosexual sociability, to demand social consideration and to justify criticism when this was denied. The accusation of vulgarity was as significant as a weapon to undermine male posturing and masculine brotherhood, as it was a device to disparage the less socially favoured. A polite lady also laid claim to wider cultural horizons through reading and exchanging periodicals, pamphlets, papers and novels, through letters, and through cultural consumption on an unprecedented scale. The domesticates of the morning were the polite adventurers of the afternoon.

It is hard to overestimate the impact of what has been termed the English urban renaissance on the scope of privileged women's social and cultural lives. The mushroom-growth of cultural institutions in late seventeenth- and early eighteenth-century provincial towns – assembly rooms, concert series, theatre seasons, circulating libraries, clubs, urban walks and pleasure gardens, and sporting fixtures – inaugurated an entirely new public, social terrain which celebrated, indeed depended upon, active female involvement.[22] By the 1730s in most large towns it was possible for wealthier women to pursue a host of public activities and yet remain well within the bounds of propriety – as even the most fastidious observers understood it. From the early eighteenth century to the early nineteenth century the core of public entertainment remained remarkably constant.

However, by the end of the period the opportunities for institutional participation had expanded markedly. During the late eighteenth century there was a proliferation of charitable institutions through which women could garner a new kind of public standing and radiate something of that public spirit revered by their brothers. The institutionalization of fashionable benevolence constructed altogether new arenas for the expression of female conviviality and officiousness. Far from being eclipsed as the eighteenth century progressed, the public profile of privileged, provincial women had never been higher. The saga of progressive female incarceration is as inconsistent with the social history of the eighteenth century as it is incompatible with the new history of the indefatigable Victorians.[23]

My rejection of the conceptual vocabulary of 'public and private' and 'separate spheres' deployed so extensively in women's history rests above all on the fact that it has little resonance for the prosperous women studied here. In so far as they categorized their lives, they singled out their social and emotional roles: kinswoman, wife, mother, housekeeper, consumer, hostess and member of polite society. To make sense of their existence they invoked notions of family destiny, love and duty, regularity and economy, gentility and propriety, fortitude, resignation and fate. Hence, women's own writings suggest that the dominant historiographical debate about elite women's lives has been misfocused, curiously negligent of those women's own concerns; distinctions of limited significance have been over-emphasized, while central preoccupations have been missed altogether. To be sure, we can never definitively know what women writers took for granted, but if we are to construct an account in which they might at least recognize a reflection, we must take seriously the terms they actually used. Of course, only an antiquarian would limit analysis entirely to the historical actors' own conceptions of events, but historians must give those conceptions very serious consideration to avoid the most crass anachronisms. In identifying absences and silences we must be cautious. It is futile to berate Georgian women for 'failing' to perceive their limitations. It is also worth considering what we are measuring these past lives against; for instance, a typical letter written by one woman to another in our period might agonize over a child's illness, exchange local news and society gossip, offer opinions on literature and politics and request information about servants, fashions and consumables; perhaps, by modern standards, a touch parochial in its details. However, read this letter against the archetypal missive sent man to man in the same era and it looks like a national editorial, for a man's letters often chiefly concerned his own illnesses, minor matters of law and local administration, and above all sport – effectively summarized as my gout is still bad; here is the gun dog I promised you; have you finished the will? Of course, genteel men had more opportunities than the letter through which to ventilate their intellectuality, but it is deeply questionable whether genteel women's mental horizons were any more hidebound than men's, even though their economic and political power was obviously much more circumscribed. Yet I would do these families a disservice if I set too much store by the factors that divided husbands and wives and neglected to mention the powerful experiences and convictions which they held in common. All shared an unassailable belief in the social consequence and intrinsic authority of the propertied; most were united in a sense of history and of place, of stoic philosophy and unenthusiastic faith; and many were welded together through heartfelt loyalty and love, bearing together the tragedies of what remained, in their own eyes, a hard life.

This book does not present a history of Everywoman; it offers a study of genteel women strongly anchored in the hills of the north of England. Yet because of the nature of their correspondence networks – northern women received copious post from letter-writers dispersed across the country, and concentrated in some numbers in London – claims to a broader viewpoint can also be made (see Appendix 1 for sources). It must also be said that the experiences of one particular woman, Elizabeth Shackleton (1726–81), dominate the book because of the astounding rich-ness of her manuscripts: amidst literally thousands of letters she received and wrote, thirty-nine minutely detailed diaries document Mrs Shackleton's life over a nineteen-year period from 1762 to her death in 1781. However, while Mrs Shackleton's records are unparalleled in their range and detail, they are far from extraordinary in their content: elements of her experience and value system can be found across scores of other women's manuscripts. In effect, the diaries constitute that intact Delft platter (to borrow a metaphor) which allows us to identify and make sense of the shattered fragments scattered across other collections and archives.[24] Still, the book is not an exhaustive account of all aspects of female experience, but a concentrated examination of the concerns that privileged women were prepared to commit to paper (two topics that were virtually never canvassed, for instance, were spirituality and sex). This book quite consciously uses the categories which emerge in women's own writings. Thus, female experience is carved up by the multiple roles they played. In the playing, these roles could be constraining, but a proper performance drew its own psychological and social rewards. For the women at the heart of this study considered themselves profoundly con-ventional. They were hostile to errant duchesses, adulterous wives, female fraudsters and pregnant servants, holding to the view that the woman who set the world at naught was very far gone. It is hard to imagine them ever smiling on the likes of a feminist writer such as Mary Wollstonecraft, a mannish lesbian such as Anne Lister or a fashionable adulterer such as Georgiana, Duchess of Devonshire. What follows then is a study in seemliness; a reconstruction of the penalties and possibilities of lives lived within the bounds of propriety. Yet, as it will emerge, even the bounds of propriety were wider than historians have been apt to admit.

I

Gentility

THE PROVINCIAL WOMEN AT THE HEART of this study hailed from families headed by lesser landed gentlemen, attornies, doctors, clerics, merchants and manufacturers. As a group they described themselves as 'polite', 'civil', 'genteel', 'well-bred' and 'polished'. As brides they aimed to appear 'amiable and accomplished'. Yet they did not pretend to be members of 'the quality', the people of fashion, the cosmopolitan beau monde or the *ton*, although they were not above harping on their exalted acquaintances among the nobility or the antiquity of their lineage when they saw fit. Their possessions were contrived to have a genteel effect, rather than a dazzling elegance, and their entertainments aimed at generous liberality not sumptuous magnificence. The pomp and splendour of a crested coach, six horses and equipage was beyond their grasp. As a shorthand description, I have labelled this group 'the polite' or 'the genteel'. While polite manners could be practised at lower social depths and amplified at greater heights,[1] this label captures the moderate social eminence I wish to convey, combined with an emphasis on outward behaviour, while not prejudging an individual's source of income. This choice of terms also reflects the findings of Paul Langford on the collaboration of 'the landed gentry and the upper elements of bourgeois society . . . When they did so they constituted that category of the indisputably "polite", which in the last analysis forms the closest thing to a governing class in Georgian England.'[2] Above all, I have deployed these labels because 'the polite' and 'the genteel' are the only terms consistently used by the women studied here to convey their social prestige. They had no recourse to a vocabulary of 'upper', 'middle' and 'lower class'.[3]

However prominent the polite in Georgian social observations, this social stratum has not been well served by recent historical investigation.

One element of it, the English lesser gentry, has hardly been researched at all and is usually written off as 'parish gentry', or smothered under the conveniently elastic label 'aristocracy'.[4] Commercial and professional elites have received more attention, but too often they are simply assumed to occupy a place in the social hierarchy one step below a monolithic landed upper class.[5] Some of the work on the commercial world has highlighted the massive gentry recruitment to prestigious trades and the extent of intermarriage between the landed and mercantile elites. However, many such studies are designed to establish the Georgian origins of a cohesive nineteenth-century middle class and its cultural identity. Consequently, they exhibit little interest in exploring the extent of sympathy between the upper echelons of that emerging middle class and its landed neighbours. Thus John Smail's painstaking search for the origins of middle-class culture in Halifax leads him to argue that in the eighteenth century the northern middling sort defined themselves against the neighbouring gentry: 'On the whole, although individuals within this group might aspire to become gentlemen, the middling sort recognized the social superiority of the gentry and the profound cultural gulf that separated them from the landed elite.' A prudential bourgeoisie is perennially contrasted to an aristocracy that is mad, bad and dangerous to know. Thus, Davidoff and Hall's account of middle-class formation in Suffolk, Norwich and Birmingham from 1780 to 1850 sets much store by the 'oppositional culture' of the late eighteenth-century middle class, arguing that they forged their collective identity in conscious contrast to an aristocracy that is itself caricatured as thoroughly profligate, indebted, licentious and dissipated. Despite the enormous numbers of lesser gentry, certainly well over ten thousand families in contrast to the two to three hundred that comprised the nobility in this period, their role in this epic battle of commercial versus aristocratic mores is virtually never mentioned. By implication, the lesser gentry should be subsumed into one camp or the other: either they represented the lesser echelons of aristocracy, somehow sharing the world view of noble families with one hundred times their income, or they should be seen as rural rentier bourgeois. As things stand, the lesser gentry inhabit a social no-man's land, apparently lying low while the shots of a cultural war whizzed overhead.[6]

At the level of the parish, however, the image of a profound cultural gulf yawning between the local elites of land and trade bears little resemblance to the teaming interactions of the marriage market and the dining-room. What follows is a detailed case study of elite social contact rooted in one particular area for which rich records survive. Let us turn to the moors and valleys of the Pennine north; in particular to the enormous parish of

Whalley, which embraced the towns of Colne, Burnley and Clitheroe.[7] The land to the south of Pendle Hill was known for its poor soil, heavy rainfall and long-established textile manufactures. Its economy was heavily dependent on making cloth long before the period covered by this book and was to continue so long after. In the course of the eighteenth century production expanded and the types of cloth produced changed radically. These changes were partly a response to the introduction of new power machinery that is conventionally associated with the term Industrial Revolution. Neverthless, before 1830 work in the area's textile industries continued to be performed mainly by hand. A large number of independent clothiers produced woollen cloth in the sixteenth and seventeenth centuries, but from the early eighteenth century the production of woollens was increasingly superseded by the manufacture of worsteds under the putting-out system. The construction of a Piece Hall in 1775 was concrete proof of Colne's success in worsted marketing. In 1781 Colne and Rochdale were considered more important markets for worsted cloth than Manchester.[8] However, from the 1780s cotton manufacturing was on the ascendant. The mechanization of cotton spinning made work for an army of hand-loom weavers. The shift was recognized by Aikin, visiting Colne in 1795: 'The trade formerly consisted in woollen and worsted goods, particularly shalloons, calamancoes and tammies, but the cotton trade is of late introduced, the articles consisting chiefly of calicoes and dimities.'[9] By the 1830s the area had become what it was to remain into the mid-twentieth century, the northern frontier of the Lancashire cotton district.

 For all their economic buoyancy, eighteenth-century Colne and Burnley were remote from larger towns and the major north–south trade routes. In 1750 the area had no turnpike roads whatsoever and the inaccessibility of this Lancashire frontier was a proverbial joke. All this was shortly to change. A turnpike trust was established in 1755 for the building of a new road between Bradford and Colne (known as the Blue Bell turnpike), transforming the treacherous journey over the Pennines, or 'the alps' as they were locally dubbed. By 1770 Colne and Burnley had become local nodes in the turnpike network, with improved roads from Colne to Skipton, Keighley and Bradford and from Burnley to Halifax, Manchester and Preston.[10] A Navigation Act authorizing the cutting of the Leeds to Liverpool canal was passed in the late 1760s, but the canal did not reach Colne until 1796.[11] These improvements opened up the area to outsiders and increased the mobility of natives, although in 1824 Baines still regretted that 'there is in this tract much fine romantic scenery which, as it is at a distance from any of the principal roads of the kingdom is less visited than it deserves'.[12] In the modern tourist imagination, of course,

1 Piece Hall, Colne, Lancashire, 1950. It opened in 1775 as a market place for worsteds, though it was largely supplanted by the Halifax Piece Hall (1779) and the rise of cotton manufacturing. The Piece Hall also functioned as the local assembly rooms and hosted a gala series of oratorios and balls in August 1777. It was demolished in 1952.

2 Emmott Hall, near Colne, Lancashire, c.1990. This rare photograph depicts the home of the gentry family of Emmott. A large hall, originally built around 1600, its classical frontage was added in 1737, with new sash windows introduced in the cross wings at the same time. It was demolished in 1968.

these blasted moors will eternally represent the outer reaches of 'Brontë country'.

If the parish of Whalley was remote from polite resorts it was not in want of polite families. A host of well-established families inhabited the valley of the Lancashire Calder; their lasting monuments are the wealth of modest mansions still standing in the vicinity of Burnley and Colne. Dispersed at two- or three-mile intervals across the valley's lower slopes, most of these gentry residences had originally been built in the sixteenth or seventeenth centuries, sometimes by prosperous yeomen, sometimes by the then smaller number of local gentry. In the course of the eighteenth century few entirely new gentry houses were erected, but most of the gentry's existing residences were substantially rebuilt to incorporate up-to-date interior schemes and symmetrical frontages with some classical detailing (see plates 2, 6 and 8, for example).[13] With their dynastic pretensions, dignified halls and landed estates, the lesser gentry constituted the enduring heart of polite society in north-east Lancashire; they were well acquainted with each other and frequently intermarried. However, land was not the only litmus test of politeness. On equal terms with local lesser gentry were a number of professionals and their families. The doctors William St Clare the elder and William St Clare the younger, for example, acted as both friends and physicians to the northern gentry for over fifty years. That clerics, lawyers and doctors should be *personae gratae* in polite society is hardly surprising, given that many of them were themselves substantial landowners and the sons of gentlemen. Indeed, many prominent barristers on the northern circuit were not only the sons of gentlemen, but their principal heirs. In addition, the personnel of elite society extended to commercial families. Often such families were related to the landed gentry, something which was especially likely among the so-called genteel trades such as woollen merchant, wine merchant, wholesale draper and so on. Thus, local polite society incorporated minor gentry, professional and mercantile families; their enmeshed relationship is perhaps the most striking feature of family history in the Pennines. Indeed, many families were so 'hybrid' in status, that it seems artificial to assign them a single occupational label. Let us consider in detail the careers and contacts of three northern families who have left copious records: the Parkers, the Barcrofts and the Horrockses.

The Parkers of Alkincoats exemplify the links between the northern gentry and the textile trade. John Parker (1695–1754) was a scion of the Yorkshire gentry, who made his way as a London linen-draper, and married the daughter of an Essex merchant. In 1728 he inherited the Parker estate through a half-brother and so became master of Browsholme

3 Arthur Devis, *The Parker Conversation Piece*, 1757. Edward Parker and his wife, Barbara, née Fleming, are shown on the terrace at Browsholme Hall, near Clitheroe. The stables, horse and groom to the right of the picture, along with Edward Parker's spurs and tilted hat, all allude to his sporting interests. However, the landscape in the background owes more to Claude than the topography of the forest of Bowland.

5 (*facing page bottom*)   Alkincoats Hall, near Colne, 1896. This large Pennine house on the outskirts of Colne, Lancashire, was built in the seventeenth century, refronted in the 1720s or soon after and modernized again in the 1750s. Elizabeth Parker came here some months after her marriage to Robert Parker in 1751. In his own estimation, Alkincoats was 'a comfortable Convenient House but not grand'. The house was demolished in 1958.

4   Browsholme Hall, near Clitheroe, 1808. Though a London linen-draper, John Parker inherited this Yorkshire estate through a half-brother in 1728. The *Gentleman's Magazine* described
the house as an 'old magnificent chateau, an extensive and venerable pile'.

Hall in the West Riding, close to the Lancashire border, and of substantial farm lands worth almost five hundred pounds in annual rent.[14] His only daughter married her second cousin Robert Parker of Alkincoats (1720–58), and removed thirteen miles across the county border to Alkincoats in Lancashire. Robert was hardly the glittering matrimonial prize that Elizabeth's family had hoped for, unable to support her in the 'splendour & elegance' they had envisaged.[15] Her relatives complained about his small fortune (the Alkincoats estate comprised only 160 acres and yielded a comparatively modest £290 per annum in rent[16]), arguing 'that a Coach & 6 was preferable to a double Horse'. Robert Parker himself conceded to his bride, 'I can't make a large jointure, keep a coach & deck you out in pomp and splendour'. Nevertheless, Robert Parker was an acknowledged gentleman and county office holder, and, as he reasoned, 'we shall have a sufficient competency, wch . . . will make us breath in [the] world'.[17] He initiated rebuilding work at Alkincoats in 1751–2 in preparation for his bride's residence, intending, in his own words, to 'make it a comfortable Convenient House but not grand'. Judging by friendly reactions, he succeeded in his aim, Elizabeth Parker being teased by richer friends that hers would be a 'a good, though odd house'. As her best friend remarked, she had elected to 'live in a narrow Compass to pass your days with the man you love'.[18]

Robert Parker's premature death in 1758 left her a widow at thirty-two, with three small sons under five. After seven years of widowhood, however, Elizabeth Parker sensationally eloped to Gretna Green with John Shackleton (1744–88) of nearby Stone Edge, Barrowford. This local woollen merchant was an outrageous eighteen years her junior; twenty-one years old to her thirty-eight. By her actions Elizabeth forfeited her brother's society for at least six years and was barred from the Browsholme threshold. Thomas Parker, the son and heir, came into the estate upon his majority in 1775. Despite a mooted career in the church or the army, he took up no profession. Upon his marriage in 1779 to the nineteen-year-old heiress Betty Parker of Newton Hall, Yorkshire, his mother removed definitively to John Shackleton's newly built mansion, Pasture House at Barrowford. At his death in 1788 John Shackleton's will reveals a substantial landowner bequeathing numerous copyhold properties in the Lancashire and freehold lands in the nearby West Riding. Although acreages are not recorded, he had at least thirty-three tenants.[19]

Elizabeth Shackleton's younger sons turned, like their grandfather before them, to the textile trades in London. To their mother's distress, they were found to lack the intellectual capacity for university and the Church. In 1770, aged fifteen, John was bound as apprentice to a draper on

6 Pasture House, near Colne, Lancashire, 1977. This mansion was built for the manufacturer John Shackleton in 1777 in the height of modern fashion. The house exhibits some Palladian effects; the semi-circular windows are thought to resemble those at Chiswick House.

Fleet Street, although Elizabeth Shackleton had first to arrange the sale of a wood to raise the fee. Two years later, with yet more deft accounting, Robin was apprenticed to a wholesale hosier, Mr Plestow of Bishopsgate, London. In May 1779 the two brothers set up together as hosiers in partnership with Mr Plestow amid a shower of blessings from their mother, but John Parker later took the name of Toulson, in order to inherit property from his distant relatives, the Toulsons of Skipwith, ten miles south of York, where he ended his days as a landed gentleman. Thus, for generations the land/trade 'boundary' was crossed and recrossed by individuals in the same family.[20]

By contrast, the history of the Barcrofts of Noyna throws more light on the links between the gentry and the professions – in this case, the army and the law – and also on the floating status of the unmarried gentlewoman in lodgings. The Miss Barcrofts were the offspring of the prominent barrister John Barcroft of Gisburn and the Lancashire heiress Elizabeth Barcroft.[21] At their father's death in 1782, the five Miss Barcofts inherited a meagre one thousand pounds between them and a younger brother. One sister married a Colne lawyer and another a Colne gentleman, but the three remaining girls never married, vacillating for decades between lodgings and family. By 1834, as spinsters and widows, all the sisters were again living together in middle-aged sisterly society at Park House in Colne.[22] The Miss Barcrofts lost both of their brothers in the 1790s. The heir, Captain Ambrose William Barcroft, perished in a shipwreck in 1795, leaving an infant daughter Ellen, who was reared by her Barcroft aunts in Colne. In 1816 the heiress Ellen Barcroft married a second son, Edward Parker, who practised as a solicitor in Selby. In 1832 Edward Parker inherited Alkincoats and Browsholme through his elder childless brother and abandoned the law.[23] Here again, the distinction between the gentleman and the professional was far from clear. To what single social category should this family be assigned?

The social mingling that characterized genteel society also came to embrace the families of at least some of the wealthier factory-masters of the area. The Horrocks cotton dynasty hailed from the Bolton area in southern Lancashire. John Horrocks began his career in textiles as a master putting out raw cotton to hand-spinners in the vicinity of Bolton. (Quaint tradition has it that he employed his three younger sisters winding yarn on paltry pay, and when they struck for better wages he bought them off with new silk dresses.) In January 1791 he rented a small warehouse in Preston and began manufacturing muslin, leaving his elder brother Samuel in control of the Edgeworth business. Thereafter, his Preston enterprise developed very rapidly. By 1798 he had erected six factories, a hundred workmen's cottages in New Preston and had established a London office. Phenomenal success crowned his efforts – the business made a profit of £55,000 in 1799 alone – enabling him to enrich his kinsmen whom he integrated into the enterprise. At his premature death in 1804, at the age of thirty-six, John Horrocks left an estate worth £150,000.[24]

Backed by their glorious wealth, the Horrockses sought to entrench themselves socially and politically. In 1796 John Horrocks unsuccessfully contested Lord Stanley's seat in the parliamentary election of that year; in 1798 he became a captain in the Royal Preston volunteer force; in 1801 he established his young family at Penwortham Lodge, his specially commissioned mansion overlooking the Ribble a mile outside the town; and in 1802, by virtue of an electoral pact with the Whig Earl of Derby, he achieved the status of Member of Parliament. In the same year his brother Samuel Horrocks became Mayor of Preston. Traditionally seen as the more stolid brother, Samuel Horrocks nevertheless consolidated the business, served as MP for Preston from 1804 to 1826, and erected a fashionable neo-classical mansion in the town to house his large family.[25] The marriages of the Horrocks offspring illuminate the social choices of the 'Cottontots': John's son Peter abandoned business and married into the Kent gentry. Of Samuel's brood, Sam, the son and heir, followed commercial convention and married the daughter of his father's business partner. The younger sisters moved in the outer orbit of the Lake Poets, and eventually married into the professions. The eldest daughter, Eliza Horrocks, married into the county gentry, wedding Charles Whitaker of Simonstone in 1812 – an officer and a gentleman. Well pleased with the match, Samuel Horrocks made a settlement of three thousand pounds in his daughter's favour, and Whitaker installed his bride at Roefield, a handsome town house in Clitheroe on the banks of the River Edisford.[26] Although, in a famous (and possibly apocryphal) anecdote, one prominent resident found Preston 'no longer a fitt place for a gentleman to live in' when John Horrocks was served before him at the fish market, the Horrocks family could hardly claim to have been shunned by a snobbish county, given their marriages and political successes.[27] If a cultural war was being waged, then half the county was shamelessly fraternizing with the enemy.

Relations between land, trade and the professions were not, of course, simply a matter of intermarriage, but also of daily social interactions. A similar pattern of interpenetration emerges in the everyday social world revealed in diaries and letters. Elizabeth Shackleton's diaries record in fastidious detail her daily encounters with friends, neighbours, business associates, social inferiors and kin over a nineteen-year period. To analyse her social contacts, two years have been selected, documented by five diaries. The three diaries for 1773 reveal Elizabeth Shackleton's social life when mistress of Alkincoats, Colne, and the two diaries devoted to 1780 illuminate her social calendar when living at Pasture House, Barrowford (see Table 1, p. 394).[28]

One of the striking features of Elizabeth Shackleton's social interactions is the heavy preponderance of her kin. Well over a third of social occasions and exchanges involved family members. Kin were particularly prominent at dinner-parties, in gift exchanges and in correspondence (almost half of all the letters Elizabeth Shackleton sent or received were from or to her kin). The majority of contacts with her kin involved her sons.[29] Only a tiny number of diary entries record contacts with her brother and sister-in-law, Edward and Barbara Parker of Browsholme, a pattern explained by Edward Parker's disapproval of his sister's second marriage, and the resulting social punishment visited on her in particular.[30] Given Edward Parker's chilly treatment of his sister, the enhanced significance of wider kin is hardly surprising. Of Elizabeth's wider kin, the physician's widow

Ann Pellet maintained greater claims to gentility than schoolmaster's wife Bessy Ramsden, although both were the daughters of London merchants and both married into the professions.[31] But the majority of Elizabeth Shackleton's blood kin belonged to the gentry both in the opinion of her contemporaries and by the standards of current historical investigation. Of the sixteen individuals related to Elizabeth Shackleton who encountered her or corresponded with her in 1773 and 1780, four were engaged in trade and three associated with the professions, while the remaining nine drew their income principally from land.

Given the bias towards land among Elizabeth Shackleton's kin and their central role in her social life, it is hardly surprising that well over a third of all Elizabeth Shackleton's social encounters embraced at least one individual from the landed gentry. However, even when her kin are excluded, the gentry still figure prominently. Elizabeth Shackleton's entire corpus of diaries and letters testify to (at the very least) a nodding acquaintance with every established landed family in north-east Lancashire, though not all of them register in the two years selected. Moreover, confirming genteel status for spinsters and widows is difficult, so a total of twenty families is almost certainly an underestimate of Elizabeth Shackleton's gentry frienships. Of course, a snapshot of two years, while showing where Elizabeth's warmest relationships lay, will not of its nature demonstrate the breadth of her acquaintance, but by ranking gentry families according to the frequency of contact, the key players in Elizabeth Shackleton's social life emerge. Her close circle was made up of well-established neighbouring families, such as the reputable Waltons of Marsden Hall and the aspiring Cunliffes of Wycoller; and Yorkshire families such as the fox-hunting Wiglesworths of Townhead and the elegant Listers of Gisburn Park. Her outer circle included grand county families like the Townleys of Royle and the Starkies of Huntroyde, with whom she enjoyed only very occasional personal contact, although her sons were regularly invited to their dinner-tables.[32] But what place did such families occupy in landed society as a whole? Clearly, they all lacked titles. (The Listers were ennobled in 1794, after her death, as a consequence of the political manoeuvrings of the Portland Whigs.) Elizabeth Shackleton was not on visiting terms with noble families, not even with the holders of lesser titles such as knights or baronets. This absence may have been a function of locale, as baronets were thin on the ground in north-east Lancashire, but it also reflects on her wealth and status. Progressive downward mobility through both her marriages distanced her from her brother Edward Parker of Browsholme and his exalted associates. As the heir of 'a truly ancient and respectable family' living in an 'old magnificent chateau, an extensive and venerable pile', as the *Gentleman's Magazine* eulogized, Edward Parker enjoyed great standing in the wider county and the north, as well as in his immediate neighbourhood. He married the daughter of a baronet, 'a prudent choice . . . to keep up the dignity of his family which few in this Giddy Age thinks of', and was thus related in the female line to the nobility of Yorkshire, Westmoreland and Cheshire. Both Edward Parker and his son John were listed on the Commission of the Peace (the official register of eligible men from which the magistracy was drawn) for the West Riding of Yorkshire, while John Parker became MP for Clitheroe in 1780. Edward Parker's was certainly the milieu of the greater gentry, while his sister's social horizons were, by comparison, decidedly parochial.[33]

Nevertheless, most of the gentlemen of Elizabeth Shackleton's acquaintance held some county office. Thirteen of the twenty gentry households, outside her kin, who graced the pages of her social calendar in the years 1773 and 1780, had menfolk listed on the Commissions of the Peace for Lancashire, or Yorkshire, or both. The minimum property qualification for this office was landed property worth at least a hundred pounds per annum, the basic threshold of gentry status according to Robert Walpole in political debate in 1732.[34] However only six of these families, the Butlers, Claytons, Ferrands, Pattens, Townleys and Waltons, produced a Deputy-Lieutenant for their county, an office which carried the higher property qualification of two hundred pounds per annum and greater social prestige, and again only six of the families, the Claytons, Starkies, Townleys, Pattens, Waltons and Parkers of Cuerdon, boasted an officer in the militia.[35] Similarly, those who were registered as having five or more male servants in the servant tax returns for 1780 were drawn from the same group of prominent county families: the Listers, Claytons, Starkies, Townleys, Pattens, Waltons and Parkers of Cuerdon. The remainder of Elizabeth Shackleton's gentry acquaintance were taxed on only a couple of servants, or escaped the tax altogether – a full seven households evaded the commissioner.[36] A good number of Elizabeth Shackleton's gentry circle, indeed many of those to whom she was closest, fell below the more demanding thresholds of gentry substance.

A less exclusive means of gauging the minimum wealth and status of these families is afforded by the records of the Bradford to Colne (Blue Bell) turnpike from 1755 to 1823. The basic qualification for a Blue Bell trustee was the possession of land worth at least a hundred pounds per annum. Twelve of the twenty gentry families who associated with Elizabeth Shackleton in 1773 and 1780 served as trustees.[37] Thus, if the records of the Commission of the Peace and the turnpike are used in combination,

7   Carr Hall, near Burnley, Lancashire. The house was the property of the
Townleys, but came to the Claytons by marriage in 1755. The Claytons belonged
to the county gentry, providing deputy-lieutenants and militia officers for Lancashire and being registered as having five male servants in the servant tax returns
for 1780. They were wealthy enough to decamp to Bath for the Season. Carr was
demolished this century.

virtually every family in Elizabeth Shackleton's network is encountered,
confirming that most of her genteel friends were worth at least a hundred
pounds per annum.[38] Although she regularly encountered those families
who easily passed the higher property qualification for Deputy-Lieutenant, she was not on intimate terms with them. Therefore, while clearly in
contact with the principal county families, her inner circle was made up of
local lesser gentry.

Moving from those families who lived principally on rents, 18 per cent
of the social interactions Elizabeth Shackleton recorded in her diaries
(family members excepted) involved a man who practised a profession,
or his kin.[39] (In only one case, that of a Bradford teacher 'Schoolmistress
Wells', do we meet a professional woman.) However, it is important to
remember that there is considerable overlap in personnel between the
gentry and professional categories. Some individuals could be claimed by
either camp – an unremarkable fact given the porosity of the boundary

between gentry and professionals.[40] Eliminating those individuals who had qualified in a profession, but did not practise, it emerges that Elizabeth Shackleton interacted with fourteen professional families in 1773 and 1780. She had the most contact with the barrister John Barcroft of Clitheroe Castle. In this case, however, the intensity of interaction was a consequence of family business dealings rather than simple friendship. In 1773 John Barcroft advised the Parker family on at least thirty-four occasions, in letters, over dinner and during overnight visits, on the civil and legal ramifications of a complicated land purchase. But in 1780, with the sale completed, he and his wife met Elizabeth only once. Other professionals she encountered had more ambiguous claims to gentility. She entertained and corresponded with the lawyer Shaws of London and Colne, a stream of curates who officiated at Colne Parish church, the Slaidburn and Barrowford schoolmasters, and three local doctors and their wives.[41]

Over a third (229) of all the non-kin exchanges recorded by Elizabeth Shackleton involved an individual who was in trade. Even when business letters, calls and meetings are stripped out, there remain 190 exchanges with men and women who derived their principal income from commercial activity. However, as the case of the lawyer John Barcroft has already indicated, it is important to remember the extent to which Elizabeth Shackleton's encounters with all social groups had a 'business' element. In practice, offering a visiting professional some refreshment (as well as a fee) in return for his advice, differed little from the hospitality lavished on the milliner and mantua-maker. Similarly, notes written to local gentlewomen requesting information about the availability, skills and terms of fresh servants had as much of a business purpose as any letter written to a London merchant concerning the fine print of an apprenticeship. Nevertheless, in the case of tradespeople, an attempt has been made here to differentiate intrinsically social correspondence from business letters, and 'quintessential hospitality' from that which accompanied an immediate financial transaction, in an effort to establish as unambiguously as possible the participation of commercial families in polite sociability.

Nearly a third of all the 'quintessential hospitality' offered by Elizabeth Shackleton at both Alkincoats and Pasture House incorporated tradespeople,[42] but, of course, Mrs Shackleton did not consider herself to be on terms of equality with everybody she had to tea, supper and dinner. She encountered the retailer Betty Hartley on over twenty-two occasions in two years, more times than she met or heard from many of the gentlewomen of her acquaintance. Yet in the diaries that record these occasions, Betty was often designated 'Betty Hartley Shopkeeper' in a rather smug acknowledgement on Elizabeth Shackleton's part that hospitality was no natural enemy of hierarchy. Still, there was an important social difference between a retailer who received tea and condescension and a genteel wholesaler who met Elizabeth Shackleton on terms of near equality, if not superiority. A distinction between 'the genteel Trades, all those which require large Capitals' and 'the common Trades' had powerful purchase throughout the period.[43] Drawing a distinction between upper and lesser trades, it emerges that bankers, merchants, manufacturers and the like accounted for over half of Mrs Shackleton's social encounters with trades-people, while retailers and craftspeople were involved in only a third of such interactions.[44] Nevertheless, this analysis undoubtedly underesti-mates the number of merchants and manufacturers on visiting terms with the gentry, not to mention the number of gentleman who carried on an enterprise which has left no historical record. Outside the big towns, which published directories of tradesmen, smaller merchants and manu-facturers are notoriously hard to identify.

In 1773 and 1780 Elizabeth Shackleton's diaries reveal she had dealings with at least sixteen families (outside her kin) engaged in upper trades.[45] Nearly half of all upper trade contacts listed in the diaries involved one commercial clan: the Bulcocks of Bishopsgate and Borough High Street, London, and Colne, Lancashire. This family ran a tailoring busi-ness in Colne and another branch of the family operated as wholesale haberdashers at three outlets in London.[46] They sold John Shackleton's callimancoes and helped place out the Parker boys as apprentices; in return John and Robin Parker took on a younger Bulcock as their own apprentice, and Elizabeth Shackleton supervised the education of the young Nancy Bulcock who became a milliner (and ultimately married a London hatter). In similar fashion, practical considerations governed the measured friendship which grew up between Elizabeth Shackleton and the textile wholesalers to whom her sons were apprenticed: the hosier Mr Plestow of Bishopsgate, London, and the draper Mr Brome of Fleet Street, London.[47] Of the upper tradespeople closer to home, many were every bit as wealthy as the local gentry and met Elizabeth Shackleton on terms of social equality, if not financial superiority. The Leaches of West Riddlesden Hall, Yorkshire, for instance, were rich and socially promi-nent. The merchant Thomas Leach owned extensive estates in the West Riding, mined and shipped coal, and opened Bradford's first bank in 1777.[48] The Wilkinsons of Maize Hill, London, and Broad Bank, Colne, were able to bid £23,000 for a local farm and kept a handsome carriage – something many of Elizabeth Shackleton's landed friends were unable to do. Moreover, of the local commercial families Elizabeth Shackleton regu-

larly encountered, seven produced one or more men who met the hundred
pounds per annum property qualification to become trustees of the Colne
to Bradford turnpike.[49]

In addition to polite networks of gentry, professional and greater commercial families, Elizabeth Shackleton was integrated into neighbourhood
networks which incorporated farmers, artisans and labourers, many of
whom were her tenants. That this was so should be no surprise. Small
farmers and producers supplied her intermittently with foodstuffs and
household goods, and local labourers and craftsmen found occasional
employment in her house and the estate. In addition, the local community
purchased her butter and rabies medicine. Most of the community could
expect to receive some basic hospitality under Elizabeth Shackleton's roof,
when bills and rents were paid, work delivered, grievances aired, patronage dispensed and so on. As a result, 11 per cent of all Elizabeth
Shackleton's recorded interactions with non-kin involved a servant, a
tenant, a farmer, a worker or some combination of the four, although
many of her encounters with the poorer sort in her locality may have gone
unrecorded.

The place Elizabeth Shackleton held at the junction of various networks
is thrown into relief when her social interactions are analysed by region
(see Table 1, p. 394). She participated in the social life of her immediate
neighbourhood, engaging, as seen, with those who were manifestly her
social inferiors in fulfilment of the needs and responsibilities of a local
landowner. She socialized with many Lancashire merchants and professionals, but knew fewer such families from over the Pennines. Greater
contact was maintained with mercantile and professional families in the
metropolis, although in most cases these links were a function of pre-
existing local connections and kinship. At the same time, however, she
participated in a gentry network which bridged the Pennines, yet this
network was essentially northern and provincial. Elizabeth Shackleton
enjoyed no social relationships with the London-based elite, and played no
role in elite culture at a national level.

Moving from Elizabeth Shackleton to the other major gentlewomen
in this study, an analysis of social interaction of equivalent precision is
thwarted by the lack of documentation. The only means of establishing
the social networks of Eliza Whitaker and the Barcroft sisters is through
their surviving correspondence. As Table 2 (p. 395) makes clear, manuscript letters are hardly a perfectly designed source. By comparing Elizabeth Shackleton's correspondence network as revealed in the diaries with
that which can be reconstructed from her surviving letters alone, it
appears that those manuscript letters which survive do not necessarily

represent the full spread of a correspondence. Letters from kin, for example, are over-represented in the archives, although this is hardly surprising, given that most family collections were sorted by descendants for storage in old chests and dusty attics. Nevertheless, the proportions are not sufficiently divergent to render an analysis of social contacts based on surviving correspondence entirely meaningless. Handled with sufficient caution, statistics based on surviving letters can form the basis of some suggestive comparisons.

Table 2 summarizes the social characteristics of those correspondents who can be identified from the surviving letters of Elizabeth Shackleton, Eliza Whitaker and the Barcroft sisters. The proportion of gentry correspondents is broadly similar in each case, as is the proportion of letter-writing kin. Significant contrasts emerge in three areas: the social profile of non-gentry correspondents, the residence of all correspondents and their sex. The evidence of the surviving letters is at its most problematic where social profile is concerned, because of the large proportion of correspondents in the Whitaker and Barcroft networks for whom reliable status information has not been found. Nevertheless, the high proportion of upper tradespeople in the Whitaker network is striking and significant.[50] In the light of Eliza Whitaker's own family background in manufacturing, this high proportion is not surprising. In the Barcroft network, on the other hand, the proportion of correspondents in trade appears rather low. Yet this is probably a reflection of the difficulty of identifying smaller merchants and manufacturers in rural areas.

The Parker, Barcroft and Whitaker networks varied in geographical scope. The Parker network naturally stretched into the West Riding of Yorkshire, since the majority of Elizabeth Shackleton's kin resided just over the border. Indeed, much Parker property was scattered about Craven in Yorkshire and John Shackleton's textile dealing took him to the Yorkshire worsted towns. The Parker's London links have already been explained. The preponderance of Yorkshire correspondents in the Barcroft network is unremarkable in a family from the east Lancashire border. However, the Yorkshire bias was reinforced by the fact that the Miss Barcrofts resided in Otley, just north of Leeds, for some years. The Whitaker network offers a regional contrast, being drawn most heavily from Lancashire itself, and particularly from Preston, Bolton and Liverpool. In social terms, Eliza Whitaker was oriented to the west and south, unlike most of her immediate neighbours who looked east into the West Riding of Yorkshire. Or, from another perspective, the Parker and Barcroft networks could be said to reflect the geography of the worsted industry, while the Whitaker network reflected that of cotton. Undoubtedly, Eliza Whitaker's Preston upbringing and Bolton antecedents explains the bias towards central and south Lancashire. There was also a family presence and company office in London, which accounts for her metropolitan letters. The links between Eliza Whitaker and her scattered correspondents in the south of England are more mysterious. It is possible that these women were Lancastrian by origin and that the emergence of a national marriage market accounts for the diaspora. Another plausible explanation is that these women met at a boarding school which drew from a national pool.[51]

Individual variations notwithstanding, some concluding generalizations can be made. All these women were members of the lesser gentry (at least by marriage), all were intimate with the same Lancashire families and all were enmeshed in a tissue of friendships which embraced the upper trades and professionals. Too often the manuscripts of Georgian commercial families have been studied without reference to the surviving records of their landed neighbours. By reading the personal papers of commercial families in conjunction with those of the landed gentry, a neglected aspect of the pyramid of local society is revealed. In social and administrative terms, east Lancashire was dominated by landed gentry, polite professional and greater commercial families – a local elite who exhibited considerable cohesion. Their incomes, whether in rents, fees or profits, were broadly comparable. The menfolk of these families tended to be educated at northern grammar schools, not southern public schools, particularly so in the early to mid-eighteenth century.[52] They served together on local turnpike commissions and were listed side by side on the Commissions of the Peace for Lancashire and Yorkshire. In addition to their shared role in administration, landed gentlemen, professional gentlemen and gentlemen merchants stood shoulder to shoulder on the grouse moor and riverbank. They combined for hearty, exclusively male meals, notably pre-expeditionary breakfasts and formal dinners at local inns. Meanwhile, their wives exchanged information on print and politics, local news, servants, prices and fashions, recipes and remedies, child-bearing and child-rearing. Whole families encountered each other at dinner-parties and ate off similar mahogany dining-tables – most of them bespoke from the same rising firm of craftsmen, Gillows of Lancaster.[53] These families employed a bevy of female servants, yet most of their households were sufficiently unassuming to escape the tax on male servants levied in 1780. All were mobile on horseback, by one- or two-horse chaise, or by hired post-chaise, for to have one's movements dependent upon the whim of others was anathema to respectable independence, or, as one anxious mother put it in 1731, 'may look low in the eye of the world'. Nevertheless, few genteel families could afford the great status symbol of a crested coach and six horses – the possession of which was a universal shorthand for worldly wealth and social prestige.[54] Nor did genteel families expect to decamp to London for the Season.

Intellectual sympathy across the elite was pronounced. Establishment prejudice, Whig and Tory, and unenthusiastic Anglicanism is everywhere apparent. Nevertheless, both polite Dissenters, such as the gay Quakers and genteel Methodists could be absorbed into the elite, since the most significant religious faultline in the county ran between Protestants and Catholics, not between the different brands of Protestantism. Mrs Shackleton, for instance, saw a smattering of her circle embrace Methodism in the 1770s, and although she was far from impressed with the growth of the 'methodistical tribe' and thought it imprudent for her son John to marry the Methodist Miss Dawson, she did not cut off social contact. Moreover, she regularly entertained the Ecroyds of Edge End, a prominent Quaker family involved in the textile trade. By contrast, two local gentry families with whom Elizabeth Shackleton had virtually no contact were the Tempests of nearby Broughton and the Townleys of Townley, both of whom were Catholic. Indeed, of the latter she sniped in 1779, 'Mr Townley of Townley raising 500 men to fight the combined fleets. Will a Roman Catholick fight for England or France?'[55] Faced with a common enemy, Anglicans and wealthy Dissenters could unite in the name of Protestant gentility.

Of course this local elite did not exist in a vacuum. Gentry and professionals were often linked by blood and friendship to the supreme county families; many commercial and gentry families had relatives struggling in lesser trades. All of these factors led to minute discrimination within the local elite itself – by their associations were they known – but snobbery was not a powerful enough solvent to separate into distinct landed, professional and commercial fractions families who had so much else in common. However, was the social cohesion of landed, professional and commercial families peculiar to north-east Lancashire? After all, the parish of Whalley is not England. Different social relations may have prevailed in areas without a large lesser gentry presence, a long history of manufacturing, or with a different religious history. Yet because few historians have concerned themselves with the lesser gentry, the case studies which would settle the issue are scarce. This is not to suggest, on the other hand, that north-east Lancashire was aberrational. Far from it. One of the distinctive characteristics of English social structure according to eighteenth-century foreign travellers was the extraordinary interpenetration of land and trade. De Saussure noted in 1727, 'in England commerce is not looked down upon as being derogatory, as it is in France and Germany. Here men of good family and even of rank may become merchants without losing caste. I have heard of younger sons of peers, whose families have been reduced to poverty through the habits of extravagance and dissipation of an elder son, retrieve the fallen fortunes of their house by becoming merchants...'[56] Moreover, cultural homogeneity has been stressed by many eighteenth-century historians, notably those unhampered by a prior commitment to a tale of Victorian middle-class emergence.

From the Restoration, finds R. G. Wilson, the merchant oligarchy in Leeds had more in common in terms of social life with Yorkshire gentry than with humbler Leeds clothiers. Merchants enjoyed a similar income to the lesser gentry, and had a comparable taste for luxury goods and fashions:

> There was a uniformity of upper-class taste and design in Georgian England, which saved the rich from the censures of vulgarity that were later levelled against the leaders of the new industrial society. There was no division between north and south, no clash between the gentility of the aristocracy and the barbarity of urban society . . . Before 1780 there was one pattern of living, that manifested by the aristocracy.

This style of living set the gentlemen merchants apart from the self-made in the town, since 'the barrier was not one of wealth but of social form'.[57] Many achieved 'a country life in business' on the northern fringes of the town, and a healthy proportion sank their profits in a country estate and set about founding a landed dynasty, that being the peak of merchant ambition, according to Wilson. Many factors, therefore, eased the integration of lesser gentry and mercantile society: common business ventures (transport and mining), the exchange of financial services, a shared role in county administration and economic ties that were consolidated by intermarriage. This social and cultural integration can be found elsewhere if the search is made. Even John Smail concedes (rather at odds with his overall thesis) that 'the evidence from Halifax amply confirms that the boundary between the commercial and professional elites and landed society was not very clear'. At least some members of the Halifax commercial elite supped, rode and intermarried with leading county families.[58]

A similar story could be told further afield. The potentially lively social intercourse of commercial, professional and landed elites in eighteenth and early nineteenth-century Nottingham is demonstrated by the diary of Abigail Frost Gawthern (1757–1822), the daughter of a grocer and the wife of Nottingham white-lead manufacturer. After her husband's death in

1791, Gawthern managed the works until 1808, when it was sold off, and administered considerable property in the town and surrounding countryside. Her daughter married a captain in the 100th Regiment of Foot in 1812. Of Gawthern's social position, Adrian Henstock concludes,

> Her circle of relatives and friends embraced members of all classes from the titled families, the county gentry, the clergy and visiting army officers, to the attorneys and respectable tradesmen, all of whom constituted Nottingham Society in this period and whose boundaries were often fluid. In her later life, Abigail Gawthern was both a Nottingham manufacturer and a county landowner.[59]

The comparative inclusiveness of polite society in the provincial south is revealed by the diaries of James Oakes, one of the wealthiest manufacturers and bankers in Bury St Edmunds, Suffolk. Through his mother, Oakes was related to the Suffolk gentry and, through his father, to wealthy cotton merchants and dyers, whose sons went on to become barristers in London. Oakes's sisters married prosperous Liverpool merchants and when he visited Liverpool and Manchester, he was entertained by both mercantile elites and northern gentry. Like other prominent men in Bury, Oakes could claim a common cultural background with the gentry; he belonged to the same clubs and libraries, pursued a similar interest in agriculture and inventions, painting and architecture, entertained as liberally and enjoyed the same public assemblies and private parties. Oakes and his ilk also shared the burden and prestige of local administration with the neighbouring gentry and aristocracy: he served as County Treasurer, Receiver-General of the Land Tax, Deputy-Lieutenant, Justice of the Peace and as a regular member of the Grand Jury. All of which leads his editor Jane Fiske to conclude, 'Bury society was comparatively open. There was no discernible line between urban and country gentry.' On the other hand, 'it was a finely graded society in which men were very conscious of status. . . . [and] Oakes always made a distinction between gentlemen in which he included himself, and the middling or trading sort and the lower orders.'[60] Thus, again, the crucial social divide was seen to run between genteel commerce and retail trade, between the polite and the vulgar, not between land and trade as such.

Nor is it likely that Bury was an oasis of social mingling in an otherwise snobbish south-eastern waste, given R. G. Wilson's recent research on the uniformity of polite taste in commercial Norwich and gentry Norfolk.[61] By 1700 in Northamptonshire, Alan Everitt tells us, the majority of younger sons from gentry families turned to the Church or to trade in the metropolis, while daughters were more likely to marry a London merchant than a local gentleman.[62] On finally reaching London, confirming evidence can be found amongst the papers of the patriciate. Nicholas Rogers's account of the 'big bourgeoisie' in Hanoverian London, stresses their social confidence and the polite culture they complacently shared with the gentry. They should not be seen as desperately emulative of the landed aristocracy he suggests, rather as secure possessors of urban gentility: 'Refinement was not the exclusive preserve of landed culture. Merchants employed fashionable architects, portrait artists and statuaries; rubbed shoulders with the gentry at the local assembly rooms and spas; joined them at the races and the hunt; and invited them to share in the annual round of civic convivialities.'[63]

The social cohesion of landed, professional and gentry families was not necessarily the universal experience, but it was nevertheless widespread in the eighteenth and early nineteenth centuries. Of course, this engagement was not without its tensions. Satires disparaging the aspirations and pretensions of trading families circulated widely, and a political language that characterized land and commerce as enemies was certainly available, although its popularity fluctuated.[64] There were obviously instances when political conflicts were aligned along a land/trade divide, but these were

8   Standen Hall, Clitheroe, Yorkshire. The austerely elegant seat of Serjeant John Aspinall, a gentleman barrister on the northern circuit, who acted against the interests of the Parkers of Browsholme and the Listers of Gisburne Park in the disputed Clitheroe election of 1781. Elizabeth Shackleton suspected he had taken a bribe to 'enable him to make a Portico or add a Venetian window to the Beauties of Standen'.

relatively few in the mid-eighteenth century, when social commentators often emphasized the shared interests of the comfortably off. As Bob Harris reports in a slightly different context, 'In 1753, the essay-paper the *Protester* defined the "middle ranks" as the "Gentry, the Liberal Professions and the whole mercantile Interest". William Beckford's often-quoted definition of the "middling people of England" it is worth recalling, included country gentlemen and yeomen, as well as manufacturers and merchants.'[65] Undoubtedly the political tensions between land and commerce increased towards the end of the eighteenth century, and it is possible that manufacturers, unlike rentiers and financiers, became progressively frozen out of land-based polite society as the nineteenth century advanced. Indeed, it is Wilson's contention that while the Yorkshire elite could easily absorb greater merchants in the eighteenth century, it drew the line at manufacturers in the nineteenth. Certainly, a literary distinction between genteel merchants and vulgar manufacturers had popular currency throughout the period. The commentator and cleric Josiah Tucker, for example, distinguished in 1757 between 'farmers, freeholders, tradesmen and manufacturers in middling life and . . . wholesale dealers, merchants and all persons of landed estates . . . in genteel life'. Meanwhile, novelists sympathetic to trade made heroes of merchants at the expense of new manufacturers. Nevertheless, the experience of the Preston cotton manufacturers John and Samuel Horrocks, whose children married into clerical and Domesday families, suggests the continued inclusiveness of Lancashire high society in the 1810s and 1820s and beyond, a feature which has been remarked by other studies of the county.[66]

It has been customary to imagine the gentry, the professions and the upper trades as distinct strata of the social hierarchy. It makes more sense, however, to see each as a thread in the complicated texture of genteel society – a woven fabric or an intricate cobweb being more exact metaphors to conjure social structure and social relations in the provinces. In parochial terms, the lesser gentry, the genteel trades and the respectable old professional families constituted the local elite. In national terms, contemporaries thought of them as the polite, below the quality, but occupying a comfortable eminence from which to patronize the vulgar. These were the women who, in Eliza Haywood's understanding, were not 'placed so high as to have their actions above the Reach of Scandal', but those 'who have Reputations to lose, and who are not altogether so independent, as not to have it their Interest to be thought well of by the World'. They belonged to 'the Little Gentry', who went 'in such Crowds to all Places where their Superiors resort . . .'[67] While these families were linked by a web of kinship to the great, it would be mistaken to see them as simply fawning junior members of a monolithic upper class. Their relation to the greater gentry and nobility was ambivalent: fascinated admiration, deferential respect, scandalized horror, amused condescension and lofty disregard can all be illustrated from the manuscripts of the genteel.

The genteel read of the scandalous activities of London-based lords and ladies with an appalled and untiring fascination, but strongly defined themselves against such outrageous self-indulgence. Pamphlets such as *The Court of Adultery: A Vision*, which satirized 'Tonish' excesses and censured the likes of 'Chats—H's sprightly dame' (the Duchess of Devonshire), were read with general satisfaction. Dissertations on metropolitan immodesty were relished: 'I recd a long and an entertaining letter from Mrs Ramsden of the present Indecent, Fashionable meetings of the conspicuous, Great Ladies of this Isle, fie for shame.'[68] Even those on visiting terms with the great, tempered their deference with a little humour. Mrs Parker of Cuerdon gently satirized her titled guests even as she struggled to honour them: 'tho' I could not place Lady Egerton's Bum upon so rich a Sopha as she had at Home or Give Her so Elegant a dinner as she wou'd have had at Heaton House the best I coud procure for her was at her service.' She took every opportunity to point out arrogant perversity, such as that of Lady Jane Clifton, who refused an invitation to a Preston assembly with the excuse 'Because the Ladies dress their Heads so High and she woud not dress hers so – Good Lord what a Reason – but she is a woman of quality'. With equal wry amusement, Miss Fanny Walker made fun of the 'vastly formall' London company at a Yorkshire house-party when she entertained 'three of the longest chinned familys that ever was seen'.[69] The old provincial families flattered themselves that they could see the real worth behind fine feathers, broad acres and smart connections. Most would have enjoyed the dry proverb Elizabeth Shackleton transcribed into her diary in 1768: 'How wise was nature when she did dispence a large estate to cover want of sense'.[70] Nor did the genteel automatically seek marital alliances with the fashionable: the mercantile Stanhope clan tried to talk their rich heir Watty Spencer Stanhope out of buying a London house as they feared he would surely end up marrying an expensive 'Woman of quality'.[71] Snobbery did not lead the lesser gentry automatically to associate themselves with the values of the fashionable aristocracy. Provincial gentility had rewards of its own. As Ann Pellet counselled her niece on the superior fortunes of the Browsholme family, 'tho their grandure at *present* may seem a little more conspicuous – yet . . . a constant uniform life generally produces more solid happiness to a family than all the Glorious fatigues of dress & equipage'.[72] Genteel society has a distinct history. It is to women's role in this that the discussion now turns.

9 'The Assignation', from the *Lady's Magazine* (1772), depicting the thrill of clandestine correspondence.

2

Love and Duty

THE WALK TO THE ALTAR was the most decisive a lady was ever to take. For all but the most privileged, or the most desperate, there was, quite literally, no going back. As marriage was 'a thing of the utmost consequence', involving 'so material a Change of Life',[1] the awful significance of a woman's choice loomed very large. As the wary Mary Warde put it on the occasion of her cousin's marriage in 1742, 'No Woman of understanding can marry without infinite apprehensions, such a step inconsiderately taken discovers a Levity and Temper that is allways displeasing to a looker on . . . & if the woman has the good fortune to meet with a man that uses her well it is being happy so much by chance that she does not deserve it'. In short, the reckless bride risked bondage to misery. When the worldly Miss Warde herself resolved on 'taking the most Material Step in Life' three years later, her letters were replete with solemn reflections: 'you cannot imagine how infinitely serious it makes me, a temper naturally thoughtful & diffident of itself cannot be otherwise on such an occasion, & the leaving my Father & Brother is more painfull then I will attempt to express, or perhaps a steadyer mind would feel . . .'[2] Of course, a match well made was a bed of contentment for the partners, the tap-root of stability in a household, a firm promise for the lineage and a secure bulwark in the defensive networks of the kindred. At best, marriage could offer a sustaining union of bodies and souls, as conventional blessings so often envisioned. After all, according to the Book of Common Prayer, one of the express purposes of marriage was to promote the mutual society, help and comfort of the partners. Well-wishers routinely testified that the union of man and woman offered the greatest happiness this side of the grave; that mutual love would bear couples up through all the trials of life. Needless to say, the keys to earthly paradise were not given to all, and those without might endure thirty years or more in matrimonial purgatory. The petty irritations, inconveniences and denials to which the married women was heir were carefully noted by observant spinsters: 'really there is so much Care in a Married State & fiddle faddle in most Men's Tempers that I Esteem myself vastly happier in having nothing to do with 'em . . .' Spectacularly disastrous marriages were sufficiently publicized to lead even the decorous to liken wedlock to the 'Dreadful noose'.[3] The vagaries and varieties of marital fortune were too conspicuous to be ignored.

Contemporaries were convinced of the determining role of 'temper' and 'disposition' in marriage; a belief in the significance of personality which novels only reinforced. Amiability, generosity and good sense recommended the pleasant husband. Yet these pleasant qualities were hardly distributed equally amongst the male population, so a shrewd evaluation of a suitor's character was crucial. Friends and family drilled young women on the monumental importance of making their marital beds such that they could lie in them for a lifetime: 'When you are of an age to think of settling,' Elizabeth Kennedy urged her daughter in 1801, 'let your affections be placed on a steady sober, religious man, who will be tender and careful of you at all times . . . Do not marry a very young man, you know not how he may turn out; it is a lottery at best but it is a very just remark that "it is better to be an old man's darling than a young man's scorn".' Altogether conventional in her advice, Kennedy did not neglect to mention the material underpinnings of connubial bliss, reminding her daughter 'that when poverty comes in at the door love flies out at the window'.[4] A prudent and considered choice was of the essence if a girl was not to be architect of her own misfortune.

Not that young lovers were expected to decide alone, listening only to the promptings of their urgent hearts. We should be suspicious of the entrenched argument that the eighteenth century saw the substitution of the arranged marriage with the romantic betrothal, not least because the artificial dichotomy of cold-blooded arrangement versus idyllic freedom makes a mockery of the wide spectrum of courtship practices which have been identified in the early modern period. The seventeenth-century family was not so uniformly cold-blooded as Lawrence Stone has suggested, nor was the eighteenth-century one so universally romantic.[5] Among the seventeenth-century nobility, upper gentry and urban plutocracy, parental decisions usually governed choice, although formal consent was always sought. Less preoccupied with dynastic imperatives, the lesser gentry allowed their children more initiative and privacy in courtship. Among the propertied middling sorts, parental consent was useful, but not decisive for sons, but across all social classes, early death robbed many parents of the opportunity to arrange their children's future. A good match satisfied a range of criteria, including family advancement, the ideal of parity, character and affection. Of course, the relative importance of these factors varied – piety might count for more with a Puritan gentleman than with an Anglican peer – but strategic considerations weighed heavily with most propertied parents, from the dynastic elite to the modestly prosperous, and often in the calculations of their more conformist children. Mutual affection which crowned an advantageous match was a welcome blessing, but immoderate passion leading couples to disregard other criteria was thought near-insane. Nevertheless, manuscript evidence of heady, romantic expectation among the wealthy abounds, surfacing in courtship correspondence as early as 1400. Wronged lovers complained of lovesickness in the Stuart church courts, and the torture of frustrated passion brought many patients to the consulting rooms of the celebrated early seventeenth-century physician Richard Napier.[6] The eighteenth-century romantic novel did not arrive upon the discursive scene wholly unanticipated.

However, this is not to deny the extraordinary eighteenth-century proliferation of literature which glamorized romantic experience. The early eighteenth century has been isolated as a key period of innovation in prescriptions for manners, a period when courtesy writers began to dwell at some length on the naturalness of female virtue, the benefits for men of female company and the positive pleasures of matrimony and domestic life.[7] The mid-eighteenth century saw the phenomenal success of the novels of sensibility, which glorified the supposedly female qualities of compassion, sympathy, intuition and 'natural' spontaneous feeling, while neglecting the cardinal virtues of reason, restraint and deference to established codes and institutions. But new idioms do not necessarily connote new behaviour. This literature may have exaggerated young people's expectations, but hope and experience are different creatures as parents and pamphleteers monotonously cautioned. It may be that the titled elite (on the basis of whose papers most arguments are made), developed more of a taste for the sugar-frosting of romance on their political and dynastic alliances, but love hardly carried all before it. Nobles who threw away All For Love remained the deluded exception, for as the wits put it 'Love in a cottage? . . . Give me indifference and a coach and six.'[8] Noble endogamy was still emphatically the norm, only now parents sought to achieve by education and an exclusive marriage market that which had previously been enforced by fiat. After all, if young people met only suitable companions, they would assuredly make a suitable, free choice. So it was that

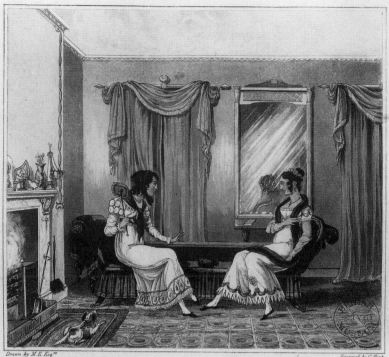

Drawn by M.E. Esq.ʳᵉ   Engraved by G. Hunt.

THE CHOICE OF A HUSBAND.

EMMA

"Tell me dear Anna. if you can
What you most admire in Man,
That you & I for once may see
If we can both in taste agree."

ANNA

"Admire my dear; I scarce can tell,
The creatures are all very well;
But all to Plutus homage pay,
As he endures, so worship they!"

EMMA

"Softly. I think you're too severe,
Sure there are some who worth revere
Speak briefly, now explain to me
The character approved by thee."

ANNA

"An open heart a generous mind,
To be well bred not too refined,
In judgment good, in reason clear,
In friendship firm, in love sincere."

EMMA

"And is this all my thoughts enquire,
This sort of man your hearts desire,
Me thinks theres something still to say,
Now try your skill to paint him pray."

ANNA

"Well then I'd have a pleasing face,
A form not void of manly grace,
Possess'd of wit, from satire free,
Polite to all, & kind to me."

EMMA

"Oh Yes, & he must have a heart
To bear misfortunes' cruel smart,
A heart that feels anothers woe;
A hand that freely can bestow."

ANNA

"Religion must his Soul inspire,
That more than all I should desire;
Confirmed by that Esteem shall last,
When youths gone by, & beauty's past"

EMMA

"Just such a swain should we e'er find,
Adapted is to Annas mind;
Just such an one should e'er I see
Be honored. lov'd. obey'd. by me."

ANNA

"His mind we've drawn, pourtrayed his face,
But were the original to trace
Is what I'd thank you to display,
And I will due attention pay."

EMMA

"We both may fortunes children prove,
Her smiles may all our fears remove;
Nay dont despair or think it vain,
For such a man we may obtain."

ANNA

"But should your early hopes be blighted,
And should you be by fortune slighted,
Say, can you live a single life,
And envy not the name of Wife?"

EMMA

"Yes rather than a Clown I'd wed,
A fool, a fop, or one ill bred,
Through life I single would remain,
Twill spare my heart full many a pain."

ANNA

"Your choice my Emma, I commend,
And hope your future hours you'll spend,
From lifes tyrannic influence free;
I know you wish as well to me."

Pub.ᵈ by Pyall & Hunt. 18. Tavistock Street. Covent Garden.

10   'The Choice of a Husband', c.1825.

Drawn by M.E.Esq.   Engraved by G.Hunt.

THE CHOICE OF A WIFE.

Two men of Ton. no matter what
Their Titles were. for I've forgot.
So just shall give each christian name.
Which for this once may do the same.

Charles then was one, a rakish blade,
Of mettle high and when arrayed
For war or love, he was a match,
For man or woman a fair batch.

Tom is the short for Thomas, so
Shall stand here, & if't sounds low,
The fault is not with me or you,
For such a name is not so new.

Well then, for shortness' sake we'll call.
The other hero stout and tall,
Tom only, which will well agree,
With his frank nature as you'll see.

The Hummums' hotel clock had struck
The hour of Twelve. but 'twas the luck
Of yawning Serviters to wait.
Which most of them, love not. but hate.

'Twas true most Bloods had then retired,
But with one thought two men were fired,
Being no other than these two
Who paused, then talked till all was blue.

But I'd forgot almost the cause,
Which brought these worthies to a pause,
As quaffing Regents punch they sat,
In rational and friendly chat.

"Dash it cried Tom, a sober thought,
Within my precious brain is wrought,
No less than what a wife should be,
To suit such lads as you and me."

Charles upon hearing Tom, quick said,
"Out with it man, or I'll to bed,
Perhaps some lady young and gay,
Most fond of Routs, but more of Play."

"You have not yet my friend guess'd right,
So try again." "A Gretna's flight,
Perchance with one, whose upmost thought,
Would be the weighty dowry brought."

"Again you're wrong, the number three
May prove more near" "Well let me see:
One who had spirit to upbraid
When you from home too late had stay'd."

"No, no, cries Tom you're further off,
Such wives as those would be my scoff,
Now hear my thought upon the choice,
Then say if I have not your voice."

"Good looks of course, of lady mien,
Now for the mind: O let it teem
With noble sentiment and feeling,
To o'erlook faults, my anguish healing."

"This speaks whole volumes Charles cries out,
She'd put my follies to the rout."
"Such then's the wife returned his friend
"Who would retain me to life's end."

Pub.d by Pyall & Hunt, 18, Tavistock Street, Covent Garden.

11   'The Choice of a Wife', c.1825.

when the seventeen-year-old Lady Catherine Cecil gave her hand to Viscount Perceval in 1737, she assured him that she would not have agreed to an arranged marriage: 'She told him, among other things, that she would have refused the Earl of Berkeley and the Duke of Leeds if they offered.'[9] A little more romance in the aristocratic drawing-room was hardly a social revolution in the making. Nor did genteel matchmaking suddenly become a thrilling free-for-all either. The propertied did all they could to ensure that their children planted their affections in prudent soil. As Pollock has astutely observed 'it is uncoerced consent which lies at the heart of our marital system not unconstrained choice'.[10]

One-dimensional accounts of marital motivation that present families making a clear-cut operatic choice between love on the one hand and lucre on the other crudely reduce the intricacies of human choice. For surely the strategic and the emotional are blended in all of us? Human motivation rarely boils down either to pure, disinterested emotion or to scheming, material strategy.[11] In any case, that the eighteenth century witnessed a great surge of romantic emotion which washed away all mercenary stains is unlikely in the extreme. In 1790s ladies' debating societies were still deliberating 'In the Marriage State, which constitutes the greater Evil, Love without Money, or Money without Love?'[12] All but the most quixotic parents urged their offspring to make a sensible match, and as Elizabeth Bennet archly remarked in 1813, 'Where does discretion end, and avarice begin?'[13] Simple choices are the essence of romantic tragedy, or a staged debate, but rarely are they the basis of decision-making in life. Wealth and rank had an intensely romantic, as well as mercenary, appeal.

If eighteenth-century choices are allowed to be complex, so eighteenth-century lovers must be allowed to vary. There was no single model of romantic presentation. There was, however, something of a standard, fashionable repertoire, as humourists enjoyed pointing out. Thus, Oliver Goldsmith mocked preening pretensions in his sketch of the history of courtship:

> The lover in the reign of King Charles was solemn, majestic and formal. He visited his mistress in state. Languished for the favour, kneeled when he toasted his goddess, walked with solemnity, performed the most trifling things with decorum and even took snuff with a flourish. The beau of the latter part of Queen Ann's reign was disgusted with so much formality, he was pert, smart, lively; his billet doux were written in quite a different stile from that of his antiquated predecessor; he was ever laughing at his own ridiculous situation; till at last, he persuaded the lady to become as ridiculous as himself. The beau of the third age,

in which Mr Nash died, was still more extraordinary than either; his whole secret in intrigue consisted in perfect indifference. The only way to make love now, I have heard Mr Nash say, was to take no manner of notice of the lady, which method was found the surest way to secure her affections.[14]

Jocular use of the romantic conventions of the 1730s was made by a Miss Marthae Taylor on a coach trip, when she and three other ladies teased an 'old bachelor' with their flirtatious attention. 'For my part I did not scruple to mimic all the arts of his sex . . . Today I addressed him in the languishing vein, tomorrow in the heroic; now I speak my passion with a certain plainness and simplicity of style, by and by I adorn it with all the flowers of rhetoric and garnish of gesture that my sportive fancy could suggest, nor were gentle airs or soft poetry omitted . . .'[15] Similarly, Eliza Haywood in her novel *The History of Miss Betsy Thoughtless* (1751) mocked the romantic addresses of a range of suitors, from the blunt sailor who offered 'I can weather out any storm to come at you', to the designing imposter who oiled 'Divine Charmer . . . you are the empress of my heart, – the goddess of my soul . . . Words cannot describe the ardency of my flame.' And so on. The courtier, the beau, the rake, the fool, the villain and the man of honour all had their own vocabularies. 'What a romantic jargon is here?' concluded Miss Thoughtless, unimpressed.[16] Thus, a range of rhetorical options was comfortably in place before the rise of literary sensibility and romanticism.

Despite the appealing array of courting characters, the demands of Georgian gentility were such that matchmaking amongst the propertied remained a lengthy and complicated process of negotiation involving a range of family and friends, rather than a simple matter of beating hearts and lovers' vows. The issues at stake are perhaps best conveyed by the close analysis of the correspondence surrounding the making of an eighteenth-century marriage. Eighty-one letters written between 1745 and 1751 by Robert Parker of Alkincoats and Elizabeth Parker of Browsholme map the long road to marriage amongst the northern gentry. The protracted negotiations are most revealing in the exposure of power relations and gender strategy: the interplay of paternal commands and filial entreaties being basic to the Parker negotiations, although even individual decision-making was far from straightforward. Elizabeth Parker was profoundly ambivalent in the face of parental opposition, revealing the tension between the will to wed and the will to obey operating in a single breast – a reminder of the extent to which a woman could identify with the principles of her elders. Robert Parker's letters are enlightening in their recourse to a range of voices, from the courtly to the desperate, through which he hoped to prevail upon his lady love. But whether dignified or despairing, the language Robert Parker used a-wooing also suggests some of the pleasure courtship held for women. For a sweet interval the tables were turned; as men coaxed and petitioned while women sat in judgement.

Robert Parker's courtship campaign lasted at least seven years, enduring many intermissions and revivals. His advances had been firmly and repeatedly discouraged by Elizabeth Parker's family in the 1740s, and his friends urged him to abandon his hopeless suit: 'after ye usage you have mett wth nothing could be imputed to you, if you did make advances elsewhere.' Still his hopes had not been extinguished; this was his 'old love . . . not be forgot.'[17] In May 1751, after a silence of three years, Robert Parker resolved to bid again for Miss Parker's hand. He was thirty-one years of age, his father was dead and the match was his own to make. But how was he to go about reopening his suit? Under ordinary circumstances, he might contrive an encounter with his sweetheart at a public assembly or ingratiate himself in the home of a mutual acquaintance. Once on a cordial footing he might call on her in the bosom of her family.[18] With proximity guaranteed, a pretender could then introduce the courting strategy advocated in the humorous *Ladies Dictionary* of 1694. This manual advised the fashionable suitor to mobilize all his parts to secure the affections of his lady-love. If sufficiently enraptured a young woman might then be prepared to apply to her mother, harrying the older woman until she yielded her consent. Once won over, it should be left to the mother's discretion 'to mould the father into a complying temper; as best able to deal with him'.[19] Unfortunately for Robert Parker, chance meetings on the moors of the remote Lancashire–Yorkshire border were improbable, assemblies were rare and he had long since been barred from visiting Miss Parker at home. Thus, he was limited to regenerating affection through a third party or by letter. Robert faced guaranteed paternal opposition and with Elizabeth's mother long dead there could be no hope of maternal intercession. The need to engage his sweetheart's advocacy was paramount. In the event, he renewed his campaign with a written proposal, secretly delivered by a visiting gentleman sympathetic to his suit.

On the face of it, Robert's opening volley reads like the innocent relation of news to an old acquaintance:

After this long silence I make no doubt but you willl be greatly surprized to receive a Letter [from] me, but you may remember [when] I had the Pleasure of spending a few Happy Hours [with] you, [that] I always promised to let you know before I attempt'd to make my Addresses to another, [which] now I am determined upon, & my Choice meets [with] the approbation of several of my Friends, [therefore] I hope you'll excuse it;

but the style is deceptive. This was an incendiary, designed to inflame an old love and frighten her into action. Nevertheless, Robert Parker could ill afford to hurt Elizabeth Parker's pride, so he followed up with fulsome reassurances: 'You can't but imagine after [what] has passed betwixt us but that this Resolution is forced and . . . that I have nothing but wretchedness and Misery before me . . . dear Miss Parker . . . give me leive to hope [that your last decision] & Severe decree is not irrevocable.' The rest of the letter used the conventional language of proposal, familiar from the popular letter-writing manuals of the period. Invariably, when the perfect gentleman correspondent disclosed a sincere and honourable passion, he diffidently stressed his own unworthiness, in contrast to the estimable qualities of his chosen object.[20] Robert Parker was no different. He presented himself as supplicant, 'a humble servt and sincere admirer'. In emphasizing his subservience to Elizabeth's wishes, he flatteringly accentuated her power over him and her gracious condescension:

> [Therefore], Madam, to my Conduct & Character I only appeal but not insist upon, willing rather to submitt my self to [your] Compassion [from] yr Tribunal I must expect my doom . . . but dear Miss Parker, dwell long upon the Assurances I have given you, & upon the Secret protestations I have made of devoting my whole to yr Pleasure, of making it subservient to yr inclination & be assured that honour and sincerity was always my Intention.

Respectfully he invoked the memory of intimacies and promises. Throughout he was at pains to demonstrate his sincerity and honour. As a stoic, he would bear her decision:

> give me some small returns of mutual affection, & the greatest Monarch on Earth will envy my Felicity, but if you are determined, (wch. I flatter myself you are not) in such a Manner as to render me [the] most unfortunate the most abject and Miserable Wretch in the Creation, I shall kiss the Hand [from] whence I recd the Blow.[21]

Having stressed his capacity for self-control, he ended with a request that Elizabeth condescend to a clandestine meeting at eleven o'clock that night.

A well-judged combination of threat and promise, the letter had the desired impact. No evidence survives of Elizabeth's private reaction, and the secret meeting was refused, but guarded encouragement was extended by letter. Although Elizabeth's reply was crisp, a disdainful reference to her rival indicated that Robert had hit his mark:

> Sir . . . As I intend to apply to my Father once more on yr account, will take the first opportunity of declaring my sentiments . . . when I know my father's resolution, will inform you. If you think this will be the Least delay to your present Intentions begs it may be no hindrance, but follow your Inclinations. I am sir your most obliged Humble Servant E. Parker.[22]

This terse declaration did not satisfy Robert Parker. If Miss Parker was lukewarm or irresolute then there was little hope she would prevail. The ideal respondent declared herself 'a warm and zealous advocate' from the outset. Injecting some urgency into the proceedings, Robert promptly wrote again reminding her of

> how I am pressed by some Friends to wait upon another Lady and the necessity of doing it in such a Time . . . I know you will accuse me much [about] my forwardness; but consider dr. Parky, the Life I have [spent] for 3 years last past, consider my Necessity of having a partner in my Family; also [what] an advantagious thing now offers, & I dare venture to say you will think my Resolution just especially as I have no assurance but [what] you gave me yesterday . . .[23]

Through emotional blackmail, Robert pressured Elizabeth to 'determine in my favour' and bring her powers of persuasion to bear: 'It must be fm yr. Resolution & wont'd good nature [that] I must expect my Happiness or Misery.' The identity of the other contender never emerges, perhaps she was fictitious, but, as Robert had intended, the spectre of the rival sufficiently stiffened Elizabeth's resolve. Four days later all is summarized in an innocuous note:

> I have spoke to my father who intends to desire your Company at Browsholme in a little time, he dos not seem so greatly averse to my Intentions as I imagined but when you meet you'll be better inform'd how matters are. I flatter myself you'll not make a bad use of this declaration, nor I be deceived in the good opinion I have of you.[24]

This formal exchange of letters represents a terse debate with three issues in play: power, duty and honour. If power is defined as the ability to control individuals and events, an unsuitable lover who lacked influential kin was all but impotent. Under such circumstances, everything turned on the daughter's advocacy, so Elizabeth Parker had to be persuaded to use all her eloquence on her widowed father. This father–daughter axis was more than a commonplace of social commentary or a flattering opening gambit. Elizabeth Parker was a noted intercessor in family disputes. In 1753 London relatives called on Elizabeth to reconcile her father and brother, at odds over a settlement negotiation: 'God will reward the glorious peace maker', encouraged her Aunt Pellet: '[Your uncle] & all other friends think tis in your power (more than all them put together) to prevail with your dear pappa . . .'[25] In recognition of Elizabeth Parker's skill in mediating patriarchal authority, her betrothed was prepared to take a secondary role in the protracted marriage negotiations: 'The Management of this Affair I must leave entirely to you . . .' In the course of their long amour, Robert Parker had often requested her advice and relied on her judgement: '[I] expect a Line in [the] meantime to know how our affair goes on, & likewise how I am to behave . . .' He often appealed to her domestic statecraft: 'do not fail using all arguments yr Rhetorick is master of in my behalf', being certain that it must be from 'yr good Management' that success would ultimately issue.[26] Exactly how Elizabeth Parker managed her father is hinted at in a reference to subsequent paternal obstruction: 'My father . . . condemns me greatly to be in a hurry and it was with much difficulty that he let me write for my Cloaths, nay even the Morning he set out almost insisted on not sending my letter, and when he was so positive about it I began to fear that his [commands] would have got the better of my entreaties. But at last he consented . . .'[27]

Robert Parker's gratitude is also suggestive: 'I can't too much extoll yr good nature in Pleading my cause in so moveing & Pathetick a manner to yr Papa.'[28] Whatever John Parker's commands, it was widely recognized that his daughter's entreaties could sway him. A pathetic performance was designed to soften the stern certainties of patriarchal dictate. Nor was this daughter's influence unusual. The sponsors of Hardwicke's Marriage Act of 1753 (which, among other things, outlawed the marriage of minors without parental consent) railed against paternal tenderness, deploring the fact that fathers were 'too apt to forgive' their eloping daughters, unable to bring themselves to inflict the appropriate financial punishment. By this view, the father's susceptibility to the influence of his girls was a social problem which threatened the preservation of property.[29] The darling daughter was patriarchy's Achilles heel.

However antipathetic to modern sensibilities, female pleading (to entreat, to mould, to determine, to prevail) was seen as legitimate policy in a society habituated to hierarchical relationships. As Lord Halifax notoriously enlightened his daughter in 1688, 'you have more strength in your *Looks*, than we have in our *Laws*, and more power by your *Tears*, than we have by our *Arguments*'.[30] In fact, it was the exhibition of abject weakness

12   'Modern Love: Courtship', 1782.

13   'Modern Love: The Elopement', 1782.

14 'Modern Love: The Honeymoon', 1782.

15 'Modern Love: Discordant Matrimony', 1782.

which was the key to a successful petition. When letter-writing manuals spelled out the language to use on an obdurate father, vulnerability and sorrowing submission were all to the fore; a defenceless maiden professed herself poised to fulfil the most peremptory commands driven by 'the most inviolable Duty to a Father, who never made the least Attempt before to thwart the inclinations of his ever obedient Daughter'.[31] The prospect of so much quivering helplessness was contrived to bring out the benevolent paternalist lurking in almost any patriarch. Consequently when an unappetizing marriage was mooted for Frances Burney in 1775, the appalled twenty-one-year-old 'wept like an infant', ate nothing all day and finally after supper threw herself at her father's feet, wailing 'I wish for nothing only let me Live with you!' Such tearful tactics were routine amongst the genteel. When Betty Atkinson wanted her uncle and guardian John Stanhope to give his consent to her marriage in 1766, she appealed to his pity and his affection, apologizing for her cowardliness in writing, not speaking: 'but why should I be so fearful to the kindest of uncle's who never did refuse me anything I ask'd . . .' Atkinson laboured her obedience throughout: 'I . . . will rely intirely upon your judgement in this as well as all other cases.' Although she favoured her Mr Jones above all other men, she assured her uncle, 'I wou'd rather drag on life in Solitude than incur your displeasure'. Rather than remonstrating with her uncle, Betty Atkinson promised to comply unreservedly with his commands, even if it cost her a lifetime of drear unhappiness. Thus, her wretchedness would be on his conscience: could he live with such guilt?[32] Not that these strategies of perfect, if miserable, obedience always met with success. Though Frances Burney got her wish, Betty Atkinson was denied, but then Charles Burney was an egotistical musician susceptible to flattery while John Stanhope was a flinty advocate on the northern assize circuit, finely attuned to, if not inured to the calculated phrases of petition and appeal.

Trained as a linen-draper, not a lawyer, and noted for his paternal affection, the force of John Parker's determination eventually dissolved in his daughter's tears. Given Elizabeth Parker's vaunted ability to soften her father's authority, it remains a mystery why she had not prevailed with him before. Robert Parker had experienced 'so many Obstinate refusals' and despaired that the 'Circumstances wch chiefly weigh [with] Old People are no better'.[33] John Parker was unwilling to lose his only daughter and the sole mistress of his household to the Parkers of Alkincoats, the poorer, cadet branch of his own family. Although some suspicion of Robert Parker's character is apparent, the smallness of his fortune was the principal objection to him. As Robert ruefully reflected, 'Every Parent takes [the] utmost care to marry his child [where there] is Money, not

considering Inclination wch is [the] only plea for Happiness . . . Yr Papa
no doubt may marry you to one [that] will make large settlements, keep an
Equipage & support you in all Grandeur Imaginable . . .'[34] But no sudden
windfall promoted this staunch swain in 1751. Nothing material had
changed, so perhaps resolution had been previously lacking on Elizabeth's
part. She may even have prolonged the courtship for strategic reasons, for
the girl of the period was cynically advised to 'keep herself at a genteel
Distance, lest the Conquest afterwards might be reckon'd cheap'. She was
continually warned against those 'Easy Compliances' that 'extinguish the
Desire of Marriage'.[35] Perhaps Elizabeth Parker's delays even bespeak a
reluctance for marriage itself. On the basis of the love-letters exchanged by
nineteenth-century Americans, Ellen Rothman and Karen Lystra have
both argued that it was common for women to secure an engagement, but
repeatedly to defer the wedding. Moreover, Lystra found that betrothed
women liked to throw several obstacles in a lover's path, eventually
orchestrating some deciding crisis to test the mettle of their men and to
reconcile themselves to the enormity of the commitment they had to make.
Women as well as men had to survive the self-inflicted 'crisis of doubt'.[36]
In Elizabeth Parker's case, defying her father went against the grain, while
dutiful behaviour generated satisfactions of its own; what Ann Pellet
described as 'that peace and tranquillity of mind which is the result of all
good actions'.[37] Not that Elizabeth Parker wanted to lose her dashing
suitor either. Indeed, for an extended period in the 1740s, she had been
able to combine a thrilling, clandestine romance with the outward observance of her father's orders. She never took up Robert Parker's suggestions
that they marry without consent. In short, she had not been forced to
choose. She conceived of love and duty as countervailing principles. At the
ripe age of twenty-five (already a few months older than the average
bride),[38] the threat of losing Robert Parker to another was worth an
attempt to bring the two principles into equilibrium. She felt obliged 'to
collect all that little Rhetorick I am Mistress Off and have had a difficult
task to satisfie my Duty and my love, not to please the one without
offending the other. I hope to God I have now accomplished both and that
it may be for our Happiness . . .'[39]

   While the genteel girl of Georgian England may have engineered delays
and deferrals like her American cousin, all these had to precede the
betrothal, thereafter it was in her interests for matters to be settled with
the utmost expedition. Engagements which collapsed at the settlement
stage tainted a woman's reputation, so publicity in the nervous months
between the promise and the wedding was a mixed blessing for elite
brides.[40] As Hugh Kelly warned in 1767, 'of all the stages in a woman's

life . . . none is more dangerous as the period between her acknowledge-ment of a passion for a man, and the day set apart for her nuptials'.[41] In Elizabeth Parker's case, cautiousness was compounded by Robert Parker's admission that he had been on the point of proposing to another. The wary maid had to be convinced of his sincerity. Only when she had gained preliminary consent from her father and negotiations were set in motion did she feel at liberty to make what Robert Parker called a 'Generous & Polite declaration'.[42] Elizabeth Parker conceded,

> after what has pass'd between us now I think I may own absence has not Lessen'd my esteem for you . . . I still trust to that honour, I always thot you [possessed] off, so do not deceive me it wo'd be an unpardonable crime as I assure you I have no view or desire but to be happy so if your sentiments are chang'd generously declare yourself for nothing sho'd tempt me to proceed in an affair of such material consequence if our inclinations varied in the least . . . P. S. Sure it is a needless caution to desire not to let anybody see this, I hope to see you soon.[43]

These early letters offer yet another illustration of that old historical cliché, the different meaning of honour for men and women. A gentle-woman's honour lay in the public recognition of her virtue, a gentleman's in the reliability of his word. Throughout the courtship correspondence Elizabeth played on Robert's honour; exhorting him to stand by his decla-rations and to behave like the gentleman he professed himself to be. Robert in reply, struggled to present himself worthy of Elizabeth's trust, 'be assured [that] I have no Intention or design of making a bad use of the sincerity & Confidence you repose in me', and in return for such a momen-tous favour claimed the least he could pledge was 'good Nature [with] Sincere and Honourable behaviour' for the rest of his life.[44]

A month after his written proposal Robert Parker received a formal invitation to Browsholme. At this key breakthrough, what Elizabeth Parker called 'a revolution in our affair', she wrote with excitement, 'my Felicity . . . can better be conceived then represented and more may be learnt from your Imagination than my pen.'[45] Thereafter, the lovers settled into a more assured period of courtship and Robert was free to visit Elizabeth at home. Negotiation was no less intense, but now the lovers presented a united front to the kindred. Elizabeth Parker still orchestrated all communication between her father and lover, warned Robert Parker to mind his behaviour to her friends and relatives, and continued to represent the couple's interest in the trudge towards settlement. 'Pray my dear Parky', urged Robert, 'forward every thing [with] the greatest expedi-tion.'[46] In this second stage of courtship, the all-important family friends had to be reconciled to the match – demonstrating that what Martin Ingrams has termed the 'multilateral consent' of all interested parties was still crucial to a successful conclusion.[47] As representative of Elizabeth's maternal relatives, Aunt Pellet remained convinced that Robert was too modest a catch, repeating 'her old argument that a Coach and 6 was preferable to a double Horse'. Only this time, Elizabeth Parker refused to submit: 'Aunt Pellet seems miserable at my determination tho' hopes time may bring her to reason.' Edmund Butler of Kirkland Hall, a respected elderly relative, who had killed off Robert's chances in the 1740s, continued to raise objections. Robert's gentlemanly stoicism was tried over the four months of negotiation. He was still nervous that 'yr relations will twart me [with] every obstacle, will arm themselves [with] every real and imaginary obstruction to my happiness', that his 'Old & Worthy *Friend*' Butler would represent his 'character & Circumstances' in such a 'Lively Colour' that all would be lost.[48] However, by late summer the Butler camp (who seem to have had a candidate of their own) gave up resistence. As the end came into sight, agitated suspense evolved into pleasurable anticipation. Public recognition could now be welcomed.

> Our Gentlemen returned in high good humour, drank your health, wish'd our happiness, wondered at Butlers delay & said ten thousand kind things [which] you may believe was no small comfort to your faithful E. I'm in hopes our felicity is now begun and that we may find (as a recompense for what we have known) that LOVE like VIRTUE is its own reward.[49]

Four months of intricate financial negotiation were brought to a close on 21 September 1751, when the Parker marriage settlement was at last drawn up.[50] This crucial hurdle cleared, the couple were married by special licence ten days later. A campaign of at least seven years duration had ended in well-won victory.

The Parker courtship correspondence lays bare the power play that underpinned even a respectable gentry match. Even in the supposedly sentimental century, an estimable love-match could be subject to considerable delay and constraint, confirming the unhelpfulness of a sharp distinction between freedom and arrangement in matchmaking. Indeed, hardly a settlement is mentioned in Georgian social correspondence without comment on the dawdling pace of business; though few were as frank as Frederick Mullins, who protested in 1747 that 'my taking of the charming Phoebe' was unnecessarily delayed by the trustees of his marriage settlement. But then, they were 'not so eager for a f—k as I am'.[51] However, the Parker courtship was long even by contemporary standards. For years family and friends opposed the match on the grounds that Robert Parker was too dingy a prize. For his part Robert acknowledged their concern, but reasoned 'The arguments . . . are very Natural, but in my Opinion not Satisfactory, because many things ought to be dispenced [with where there] is a mutual Passion . . .'[52] For her part, Elizabeth Parker equivocated and prevaricated, unable to bring herself to disoblige her father, but equally unwilling to let Robert go. Of course, in pursuing a clandestine courtship Elizabeth Parker could have claimed some impeccable literary models and may have been inspired by her reading to persevere. Moreover, prolonging an affair in secret was a not uncommon scheme for a daughter who lacked the rebelliousness for elopement.[53] Wearing one's family down with tearful obstinacy posed limited risk to reputation and security. When at last John Parker relented, he must have abandoned all hopes that his daughter would marry a great gentleman. Perhaps the real test here was that set by the Parker family for Elizabeth. Seasons in London, Preston and Pontefract had not borne romantic fruit. The persistence of her affection could not be in doubt. In courtship Robert enjoyed more freedom of manoeuvre than Elizabeth. Although he could not guarantee acceptance, he was at liberty to investigate, choose and offer. What is more, the whimsical letters exchanged among bachelors suggest that matchmaking was seen as an adventure, an exhilarating test of luck and skill. Robert Parker grandly compared himself to the skilful mariner whose craft was only truly tried on a tempestuous ocean; and attested repeatedly that he welcomed difficulties as an opportunity to prove his mettle. In fact, Eliza Haywood suspected that the perseverence of many a male lover proceeded principally from 'an ambition of surmounting difficulties', not from passion at all.[54] In short, courtship was an invigorating challenge to manhood. Unquestionably, men enjoyed greater rhetorical licence in the art and mystery of courtship. It was inappropriate for a woman to confess her sentiments until convinced of her suitor's intentions. Moralists deplored the pretender who tried to secure prior assurances of love before he made his offer – a cynical policy, aimed, it was said, at circumventing the woman's right to refuse.[55] Elizabeth Parker's early letters reveal the circumspection required of an unmarried woman. Demure reticence was obligatory, all peacock display was expected of the male.

For the most part, Robert Parker presented himself in the role of the plain-speaking man of honour. Above all, he vowed his suit was sincere. He scorned flattery, dissimulation and the 'Cant Phrases' of his 'great *neighbours*', defining himself against those who revelled in empty language. Thus Robert Parker disavowed all claim to rhetorical skill: 'But why [should] I torture my Invention for Eloquence I shall never be master off; & I utterly disclaim all pretentions to [the] latter willing rather to be miserable for ever, [than] gain my happiness by unjust means . . .' The proof of his sincere affection lay precisely in his verbal restraint: 'You will Injure me very much, if you do not think me a truer friend & admirer [than] any Romantic Lover.'[56] Reticence as a rhetorical device had wide currency. The love-letters an Exeter surgeon George Gibson wrote to Anne Vicary in the 1740s could almost be mistaken for Robert Parker's. Gibson rejected 'artifice and dissimulation' and professed himself an enemy to 'violent protestations', while his 'esteem and affection . . . was not produced of a sudden, but is the effect of a long and intimate acquaintance'. Similarly, Charles Pratt, a rising young barrister on the home circuit, emphasized the reason and moderation of his love for the heiress Elizabeth Jefferys at mid-century. He scoffed at romantic affectation, stressed his true love for a woman of sense and urged a resolute cheerfulness in separation.[57] All three men drew here on a modish suspicion of rapturous and exaggerated emotion. The elevated 'half Theatrical, half Romantick' style of late seventeenth-century lovemaking had been effectively ridiculed by the influential Richard Steele in 1712. A man should bring 'his Reason to support his Passion' argued Steele, and in his own love-letters to Mary Scurlock he struck out against rhetorical excess: 'I shall affect plainnesse and sincerity in my discourse to you, as much as other Lovers do perplexity and rapture. Instead of saying I shall die for you, I professe I should be glad to Lead my life with you . . .'[58] By 1740 a self-conscious affectation could be laid down in some quarters as an emotional law. 'The Motions of an honest Passion, are regular and lasting . . .', decreed Wetenhall Wilkes, 'its Elegance consists in Purity, and its Transports are the result of Virtue and Reason. It never sinks a Man into imaginary Wretchedness, nor transports him out of himself; nor is there a greater Difference between any two Things in Nature, than between true Love, and that romantic Passion which pretends to ape it.'[59] Violent raptures and extravagant praises were to be suspected, for flash-fires burned out fast.

Yet for all that Robert Parker disclaimed the hackneyed postures of overheated romance, he was not above striking melodramatic attitudes himself when circumstances absolutely demanded it. At the first refusal in April 1746, Robert Parker declared himself ready to undergo the 'severest Pennance' and assured his love '[Were] I to be plunged into the lowest Pit of despair, my Passion [would] still Emerge, all the Powers upon Earth are not able to stifle it. The Moon will sooner cease to move round her orbit, the earth round its axis than I to admire Pure Hippocrisie.' When

Elizabeth Parker first admitted that Robert's affections were returned, the revelation had 'so great Influence ovr my spirrits, [that] I [could] not help appearing in confusion'. So, after the fact, he summoned up some lyricism to convey his ardour: 'the poet I am sure had not half [the] sense of my affliction [when] he says Parting is worse [than] death & c.' And when his affair met with seemingly unconquerable reverses, as here when Elizabeth Parker broke off the secret engagement in 1746, he could be driven to headlong prose: 'Our parting, Parky I must never forget, but [that] was nothing to [what] I have undergone since, upon [your] telling me we must never meet again upon [that] head. For God sake, Parky, write & comfort my spirits [with] hopes at least, till you are made happy in anothers arms.'[60] His performance of the role of honest, plain-speaking, true lover was far from seamless, though he did manage to convey the impression that his lapses were the result of genuinely overpowering emotion not an expression of cynical flattery.

Crucially, he was sensitive to the flimsy purchase of a letter: 'Consider, Parky, tho I have numberless well wishers, yet I have no Proxy no Advocate or Confidant near you in my Absence, nothing in the world but [this] slip of Paper, wch can but convey a Poor Epitome of my Passion.' He brooded 'upon ye danger of abs[cence]'. Therefore he reminded her again and again of that which was unwritten: the powerful assurances and reassurances of their secret 'evening conferences', which had so many times brought his affair back from the brink. His practice in the 1740s had been to visit Elizabeth Parker incognito after the Browsholme household was abed, tarrying with her for two or three hours, departing before dawn to complete the three-hour ride back to Alkincoats unrecognized.[61] Once he even tried to engineer a secret nocturnal meeting when both were house guests at Kirkland Hall, but farcically was foiled by uncertainty as to which was her chamber. When despondency or doubt threatened to weaken Elizabeth Parker's resolve, Robert Parker rushed to her side to fortify it. With what face-to-face intensity he persuaded her of his good faith, we shall never know, but of its ultimate effectiveness we cannot doubt. The letter, in the end, was possibly not the most potent weapon in the artillery of his persuasions. But his protestations, whether written, verbal or perhaps even physical, are redolent of the gratifications for women inherent in courtship. In supplication, Robert Parker dramatized the power Elizabeth Parker had gained over him through love. As he said himself, 'a more submissive Slave breaths not Vital air'.[62] No wonder a woman might seek to prolong the season of her supremacy.

*   *   *

After the excitements of the wedding came the monotony of the marriage; for 'Wedding puts an end to wooing . . .' as the *Ladies Dictionary* dismally put it. Men got up off their knees and, metaphorically at least, women got down on theirs. The young bluestocking Elizabeth Robinson considered it a general rule that marriage turned the obsequious lover into the imperious husband. Richardson's Pamela was appalled at the 'strange and shocking difference' for brides when 'fond lovers, prostrate at their feet' were transformed into 'surly husbands trampling on their necks'. While Arabella in the *Gentleman's Magazine* thought the engaged woman should be forewarned in plain English that 'when she has entirely given up her Fortune, her Liberty and her Person into [her husband's] keeping, She is immediately to become a *Slave* to his Humour, his Convenience, or even his Pleasure, and that she is to expect no more Favour from him, than he in great Condescencion thinks fit to grant'.[63] They had a point. The legal, institutional and customary advantages of manhood were legion, while a virtual industry proselytized the relative duties of the married female. 'You must lay it down for a Foundation in general, That there is Inequality in the Sexes' was George Savile's firm counsel in 1688.[64] For all the sweet idealizations of gentle womanhood that the next century produced, few self-appointed moral pundits found another base upon which to ground a vision of marriage and family. Obedience remained the indispensable virtue in a good wife. Marriage may have been celebrated as a cosy partnership across a wide range of media, but it was still an unequal partnership in the eyes of most commentators. Genteel wives took it absolutely for granted that their husbands enjoyed formal supremacy in marriage. After all, even the haughtiest bride vowed before God to love, honour and obey.

However, it is possible to overstate the case. Even in the supposedly authoritarian seventeenth century, advice literature emphasized the *mutual* duties of husband and wife. Husbands were enjoined to offer kind consideration in return for wifely obedience and both partners were expected to conciliate and forbear. It is also worth noting that advice about the inner workings of these unequal partnerships was often written by inexperienced boys and bachelors who could claim no personal understanding of power behind closed doors.[65] So how far real partnerships resembled the ideal hierarchy remains an open question. Historians who seek an answer have ultimately to wrestle with the complicated relationship of gender power and conjugal love. It has been argued for the seventeenth century that the actual balance of power in a particular relationship depended upon the interplay of a variety of factors: wealth, prior property agreements, relations with kindred, age, skills, personality and attractiveness. The extent of conjugal compatibility and affection is seen to play a determining role in marital power relations. As Vivienne Larminie observed in the case of the Leicestershire Newdigate family, much depended upon a woman's 'individual capacity to attract and therefore influence or dominate [her] husband'.[66] Again and again, diaries, letters, wills and eulogies testify to the long-standing expression of love within marriage. Of course, the extent, or typicality, of warm conjugality even among the propertied cannot be established, but references abound in sufficient quantity to lead Keith Wrightson to posit 'the *private* existence of a strong complementary and companionate ethos, side by side with, and often overshadowing, theoretical adherence to the doctrine of male authority and *public* female subordination'.[67] This common-sense suggestion has much to recommend it, although it would be a mistake to see the existence of affection in marriage as *a priori* evidence for greater equality between the sexes. Defoe may have preached that 'Love knows no superior or inferior, no imperious Command on the one hand, no reluctant Subjection on the other . . .',[68] but demonstrably, love could thrive within starkly unequal relationships. Certainly love sometimes empowered a woman to lead her husband by the nose, but it might just as easily encourage her to swoon submissively in his masterful arms. Love was no enemy to hierarchy; one need look no further than fairy tales for proof that inequalities of power might infuse a relationship with greater romantic and erotic charge. So even if Lawrence Stone's dubious assertion that love in marriage was on the increase could be proved, the impact of love on marital power relations would still be wildly unpredictable.

One of the hardest areas for historians to explore is that of ordinary sexual and emotional relationships. Inevitably the most intimate thoughts and feelings go unrecorded. What follows is a discussion of five marriages based largely on letters exchanged by the couples themselves, but in one case on the letters a couple despatched to a relative in conscious celebration of their union. It is not claimed here that letters offer a window on the totality of matrimonial discourse. They represent only one of the myriad voices with which men and women addressed each other. Moreover, as a genre in its own right, the letter is subject to particular conventions and constraints; formal models in letter-writing manuals and epistolary fiction abounded. So letters are not in any simple sense an unmediated expression of the self, but, on other hand, our public performances are no less significant than our secrets. In fact, public performance was not as uniform as might be expected from the rigid and unchanging advice laid out in the available guide-books. Obviously the generic similarities are there, but far more striking is the variety of conjugal idioms in play in the Georgian era.

The Gossips of Thorp Arch expressed an extraordinarily tender companionship in their letters. The correspondence of the Stanhopes of Leeds conceded a respectful affection; that of the Parkers of Alkincoats a dignified love. The letters the Ramsdens of the Charterhouse sent to a cousin broadcast a jolly domesticity, while the Whitakers of Simonstone used their letters to ventilate some po-faced and prosy romanticism. The plot to a successful marriage may have broadly similar, but every couple wrote a different script.

The earliest marriage studied here, that of the Gossips of Thorp Arch, was one of the most emotionally expressive when it came to written prose. In material terms, it was also a splendid match. William Gossip inherited a fortune from his successful mercer father and through his marriage to the heiress Anne Wilmer in 1731 acquired estates in Yorkshire and Essex. Together William and Anne Gossip set about founding a dynasty and embarked upon the construction of a country seat.[69] Yet their marriage was as securely founded in affection as it was shored up with fashionable bricks and mortar. William Gossip never left his wife's side without complaint. Even after fifteen years of marriage, he lamented a separation: 'heartily tired of being so long absent from my dearest life. I am now entered upon the fifth week of my exile – this will be the longest separation we ever yet have had.' He struggled to cover the breach with pen and ink:

16   Thorp Arch Hall, Wharfedale, Yorkshire. The fashionable seat of the rising Gossip family, designed by the Yorkshire architect John Carr in the 1750s. The family fortune was amassed by William Gossip's father, a West Riding mercer. Gossip himself was both a J.P. and Deputy-Lieutenant for the county. Of William Gossip's sons, one went to Edinburgh to study medicine, while the rest were apprenticed as hosiers in Leicester.

17   Philip Mercier, *William Gossip of Thorp Arch*, 1745.

'I can't help persecuting my dearest nanny with my letters whenever I have
a spare moment on my hands. My heart will open itself towards the object
of its desires.' The comfort he found in her arms was never far from his
thoughts, and his bed was cold without her. 'I am just going to tumble into
a solitary bed, & dream if I can of my Dear', he wrote in April 1734; 'My
little flock are all well & fast asleep as I hope I shall be immediately, for I
am just going to my Solitary Bed where I have nothing to do but sleep', he

18   Philip Mercier, *Anne Gossip of Thorp Arch*. 1745.

complained in August 1746. After twenty-six years of marriage, in 1757 he still teased 'as for a bed you shall be welcome to half of mine without a compliment'.[70] Anne Gossip was no less appreciative of her husband. She dated 'all my happeness and sattisfaction' from the day of her marriage, and caring for him was her first concern: 'I don't want to stay hear, if you who I love a thousand [times] better than myself or anything in this world, are ill and want me at home.' She too invoked the comfort of the matrimonial mattress: 'I wish I had my poor Dear in his own bed with me. I think you would be beter . . .' An unembarassed physical intimacy is a remarkable feature of their correspondence. When his bad shoulder ached, William Gossip longed for his wife's 'dear hand to coax it a little', while Anne Gossip confessed 'I am fright'd about your Bowels', and reported the state of her own troublesome piles. Warts and all they loved each other. William looked about him in fashionable company in London and still 'saw none I liked half so much as my old wife. Don't blush, you know I hate flattery.' To enjoy 'the repose of my own fireside' was his dearest wish.[71]

A more united couple it would be hard to find. Both strove to make the other happy. Which is not to say, however, that the Gossips were blithely unconventional when it came to the division of labour and authority. Their understanding of gender roles was utterly traditional. William Gossip praised his wife as a devoted mother and frugal housekeeper. His life was more mobile and more public than her's, but Anne Gossip deputized for him on the estate when necessary (paying the land tax, the window tax and so on), as had long been a sanctioned practice. William never quarrelled with her management. On the occasions when he asserted his authority, he offered respectful suggestions rather than orders: 'I don't write this with an intent you should blindly follow my opinion herein, but I think this point is neglected.'[72] Through William Gossip's respect and affection, and perhaps her own acceptance of prevailing norms, Anne Gossip wore her subjection lightly. Still they did not set romantic self-gratification on a pedestal; both were devastated when their son and heir, George, married in secret and beneath him. The pretty daughter of a Halifax mantua-maker was not their idea of a catch for a wealthy hosier. Indeed William Gossip reached out to punish the imprudence in his will.[73] Love was no justification for a rash, demeaning choice.

The handsome Leeds merchant Walter Stanhope delayed marriage till almost forty. Legend has it that he cut a romantic swathe across the North, breaking at least one aristocratic heart with his casual indifference. 'Long did the gay, the gen'rous Stanhope reign Unmov'd by Beauty, free from Love's soft chain', versified an observer on the occasion of his wedding in 1742. But both his wife and baby son were dead by 1747, and just two years later he married again. His second wife was the twenty-seven year-old Anne Spencer of Cannon Hall, and theirs has been described as an ideal economic alliance, uniting a leading professional-mercantile family with a landowning family busy in the industrial production of iron.[74] It was also a match of loyal attachment. Walter Stanhope showed concern for 'My dearest Nanny', 'my poor wife', in childbed, anxiety about her health in general, solicitude for her comfort and routinely bought her presents when he went away. Still this couple never elaborated on their intimacy in their letters. They undoubtedly missed each other when separated, but their acknowledgements of this were always terse: 'I want much to hear from you', Walter conceded at the end of a letter in June 1757. By that August he admitted, 'I begin to wish for our meeting, for realy the house does not look right without you'. 'I do assure you I have thought it long', Anne Stanhope returned.[75] Though profoundly committed to each other, the Stanhopes disapproved of emotional exhibitionism and considered it a duty to quell any self-indulgent sadness. So it was that Walter chided his wife for a momentary weakness: 'I have not had [the] least uneasyness since I left you, but [the] tenderness at parting, wch gave me pain, least you should not behave as you ought to do, & by that means detriment your health.' While Anne apologized for her lapse: 'I'm sorry my behaviour shd have given you so much ineasiness, but you'll excuse it, when I tell you I have been in good spirits ever since Bror Will brought me word of you performing yr first days journey so well.'[76] On the whole, Anne Stanhope, who came from a powerful Yorkshire family and produced the requisite heir, presented herself as capable and collected, delivering her requests and receiving instructions with confidence. In this she contrasted starkly with her sister-in-law Barbara Stanhope, who could not tolerate the routine absences of her barrister husband and made a sorry spectacle of herself in letters: 'ded [you] but know how uneasy I have bene sence you left me I am sure you wood petey me', she wept in 1726 'my hart is so full I cannot right half I wood for sheding tears . . . I am going to Horsforth today: but not to finde you thear, is intolerabel. I know not how to bear it . . . ten thousand times Dear Jacke thy Duteyfull Wife tell Death.'[77] Even if neither Walter nor Anne Stanhope was given to conjugal rhapsody, theirs was a respectful union and this matron did not feel the need to abase herself at her husband's feet.

As a married man with the obstacles of courtship behind him, Robert Parker was no longer expected to launch into declarations of courtly supplication and petitions for his wife's every favour. Nevertheless, Robert Parker proved to be a loyal husband, who identified with his wife's interests and beliefs. In courtship, he had 'vowed the most religious Observance to [his betrothed's] commands', and when newly married he still made light-hearted, but no less gratifying, play of courting her good opinion: 'I got Home . . . on Sunday & was a good Boy in following yr directions by going to Church . . .' Both Parkers had anticipated happiness and companionship in marriage; Robert sought a 'partner', while Elizabeth was 'anxious . . . to share every circumstance in this life' with her betrothed. Once wed, they still set store by conjugal togetherness and were doleful in separation:

> I must own my dear Parky [that] I hardly ever part'd fm you [with] greater reluctance [than] yesterday occasion'd by yr dejected looks and uneasiness [about] it & it took such hold of my spirits [that] I [could] not sleep at all; so that if I do not recover soon shall but have a dull journey; however will use all endeavours to make absence agreable; & begs my dear Parky for this time will do [the] same, wch will be a satisfaction [when] we meet to dear Parky yr. Sincere and Loving Husband Robt Parker.

Writing 'in bed' one Wednesday morning he sent his 'compts to the stale virgin', and in complaining of insomnia confessed to emotional and physical need:

> I am just got out [from] Bed; [where] I went last night abt 10 in hopes to have found some rest; but in Vain for in dosing, tumbling & Reflection I have spent all the night nay even that before; so [that] I can now fairly say [with]out flattery or dissimulation, [that] I have no rest but [when] [with] you & no pleasure [when] absent [from] you . . . I long to be [with] you but am apprehensive can't relieve myself till Saturday, so [that what] can't be cured must be endured.

Every expression of the pain of parting, however, carried a coda that one had to make the best of a bad job. When Elizabeth confessed to any lowness of spirits herself, Robert urged her to bear up and throw off her melancholy. The cheerful resignation Robert Parker sought to achieve in matters matrimonial, was consistent with his stoical response to disappointment in general; in short, 'Misfortunes must be made [the] most of & Bore [with]'. Thus, he remained suspicious of emotional self-indulgence and excessive romantic display.[78]

By contrast, the Ramsden marriage was nothing if not a performance. The Londoner Bessy Parker was the sister of an Essex manufacturer and a London stationer. After her marriage sometime in the late 1750s she set up home at the Charterhouse School, in Charterhouse Square, where her husband the Reverend Ramsden was an usher. The Ramsdens were virtually never separated, and any letters they exchanged between them have not survived, so the reconstruction of their marriage is based on the comments they offered for the admiration and entertainment of outsiders. Verily, the letters they sent to their northern cousin in the 1760s and 1770s are one long advertisement for the delights and drolleries of family life. William Ramsden wallowed in domesticity; whether it be watching his children play, his wife perform household tasks, or simply the arrival of his dinner: 'here comes Supper (Dinr I should say) Smelts at Top, 'Sparagus at Bottom, a smiling Wife – Who'd be a king?' Bessy Ramsden was equally versed in the vocabulary of cosy intimacy and artless pleasure: 'to morrow three weeks we brak up again for a month. Deary is looking out for some snug Country Box to carry me & my Lambkins to Grass . . .' Predictably, they hated to be apart: 'all the World goes to Margate', sighed the Reverend, 'but to me it proved a very insipid spot because I had left the Sweetener of Life behind, for Bessy was obliged to stay at home to nurse.' Bessy Ramsden declared herself 'melancholy' without her husband and confidently assumed others would feel the same: 'my Wife wonders how her loving Cousin cou'd trust her Deary so far from home. She & hers having never yet been twenty miles asunder & but two nights separated since they first became one flesh.'[79]

Yet the syrup was also salted with humour. Reverend Ramsden variously described his wife as 'the Baggage', 'yr broad bottomed cousin', 'a trumpery woman', 'My Duchess', 'Dame Bessy', 'My Eve' and 'My Better Half'. Bessy habitually referred to her spouse as 'Mr R.', 'My Good Man', or 'Deary'. Both Ramsdens produced wry narratives recounting their tiffs and revelling in resentment. In fact, hardly a letter from the Reverend was sent that did not contain a dissertation on Bessy's features and foibles, from her big bottom, terrible handwriting and distaste for bathing, to her scolding tongue and social exuberance, in particular her weakness for gallivanting out to play. In truth, he congratulated himself on her independence – 'mine Madam is a *saucy Hussy*, not to be imitated by you Obedient Wives' – and rather welcomed the role of the beleaguered husband, carrying out his wife's orders with a certain long-suffering relish:

> thirty long miles have I rode this afternoon through Clouds of Dust all the Way on one of my Wife's fiddle faddle Errands to Farmhill forsooth to fix the Christening day with my Lady Godmother.

> Madam at her Departure left me a hundred things to do, with strict Instructions to follow Her by Tea Time; which to be sure I must obey.

> Oh! . . . did you but know what a Baggage she grows . . . But I dare not complain. And here she commands me to stop . . .[80]

The conscious satisfaction the Ramsdens derived from almost every aspect of their relationship can perhaps be attributed to their late marriage. William Ramsden was at least fifty years old when he came to wed. Bessy Ramsden herself offered maturity as an explanation for their deliberate management of home life: 'we go by clockwork which I [know] you will think very formal stuff but then you will say it [is] not to be wonder[ed] when a old maid . . . [has] married an old Bachelor which of the two I am at a lost to tell which [is] the worse . . . *but happy are they when they come to gether*.[81] Whatever the cause of such connubial comfort, it is clear that not only did the Ramsdens enjoy each other, they also relished the theatrical performance of matrimony itself – dramatizing squabbles and intimacies with equal ease. This was the correspondence which tried hardest to shed charm on the mundanities of marriage. Yet for all the purring domesticity, this was also the marriage which nurtured the most mobile and extrovert wife.

The mundane was not valorized by the young Whitakers of Simonstone, a newly married couple of the 1810s who expected their emotions to take elevated flights. The alliance between Eliza Horrocks of Preston and Charles Whitaker of Simonstone united a cotton lord with the Lancashire gentry, but strategic concerns were as nothing compared with the power of love, or so their letters imply. Like many eighteenth-century couples before them, the Whitakers confessed to a mental struggle between reason and emotion. However, in their case this was a manifestly unequal struggle, feeling consistently outstripping self-control. Their letters lurched from declaration to declaration: 'I shall *not often* feel disposed to leave you', wrote the twenty-three-year-old Eliza to Charles in the first year of marriage in 1813, 'I really seem quite an unmarried miss, having neither my husband to speak to, or a house to attend to. I adore my dependence. I hope ever shall I have reason to do so for that will ever insure the happiness of both.' Ensconced with her father's family, Eliza waxed prolix on the pain of separation, the great void she felt and wondered if it was all worth it, since life was so short – strong stuff considering she was only away just over a week. Receiving no reply from Charles, Eliza wrote again dramatizing her fretful longing:

Do my dear soul let me hear from you. I am a sad anxious creature at the best of times you know, though I do think I have in some degree got the better of this troublesome sensation by dint of constant exertion against it. We are a merry party but still there is something so dear at home I cannot banish it from my thoughts however I reason with myself. Tonight we heard a horse . . . & immediately ran to the door & to my great disappointment it was Robert May of Ramsbotham come to see us.

The importance of the marital bond was constantly stressed. Eliza and her aunts longed for 'our better halves'. Without men they were incomplete.

Charles, Love said tell you that when once you get me home again shall not stir from your side so you know what to expect . . . I have had all the aches and pains I endured in our courtship, when you were out of my sight. I have too much affection for myself to endure the same feelings again if I can avoid it. I do not admire my widowed state. My Aunt R. and I have the same feelings on the subject. She sighs every now and again when we are alone 'Oh my dear Robbins bless you I wish you were here.' I feel the same but suppress the speech and try to console her.[82]

All this wifely devotion did not fall on deaf ears. Back at Roefield (their villa in Clitheroe), enjoying the grouse shooting, Charles endeavoured to reply in the same ardent tone. As Eliza presented herself as yielding and dependent, so he reciprocated with delight in his dear little wife, his precious jewel. However, Charles Whitaker was no master of the genre, shifting from plodding protestations back to a chattier idiom with palpable relief:

My dear creature, return you many thanks for your goodness in writing to me, it causes me so much delight. Thankful indeed do I feel that I am possessed of so amiable and best of creatures. Like the lady whom being asked respecting her jewels . . . might explain these my children are the purest and most valuable of all my jewels in you I find the saying realized. Poole and Clark have gone upon the moors this morning . . . I have preferred remaining at home that I might have a little chat with you.

Through images of possession and protection, however muddled, Charles affirmed his devoted attachment: 'Oh my dear creature, how truly glad I shall be to have you home again. Be not surprised if I ever trust you from me again. Pray burn all my letters that no mortal eyes may see them. I have ordered all the walks in the wood to be swept clean and I hope to have everything in order at your arrival . . .'[83] Ernest in tone and laboured in expression, these letters suggest that the young Whitakers had an investment in the ideal of ardent romantic emotion. Perhaps it was not enough for them to be simply loving in marriage. It appears that they wanted to be desperately, awfully in love, and love for Eliza Whitaker meant melancholy languishings and swooning submission. She wanted to adore her dependence on her solicitous young husband. Charles Whitaker treasured his 'dear little wife'. The language of feeling they deployed was pregnant with allusions to tender mastery and pleasurable surrender.

However, for all this language of Big Man and Little Woman, the

Whitaker marriage was no different in practicalities to those that preceded it. For all the implication that love was a miraculous force blending two souls, it was not powerful enough a solvent to dissolve the customary distinctions between man and wife. Eliza Whitaker was an assiduous housekeeper, a resourceful, supportive kinswoman, a cultural consumer of some pretension and later an irreproachable mother. Charles Whitaker was as absorbed in field sports and county administration as any of his predecessors. Eliza Whitaker may have represented herself as a vulnerable, little woman in letters to her husband, but it does not follow that she behaved as such with others. Moreover, what was said to express throbbing feeling in separation was perhaps not expected to apply to everyday life. Furthermore, her quiverings may not have survived the honeymoon years of marriage. In fact, the play on charming subservience may have been cynically conceived in the first place, for Eliza and her Horrocks sisters were certainly criticized on precisely this count by a sharp-eyed acquaintance:

all the stories of the Ladies feigned illness &c are well known – even little Annes are all put on, they say, & not one of the sisters are free from the charge of using these means, of gaining their ends & working upon the feelings of father and husbands – alas! alas! one had need be ashamed of ones sex – & tell yours to beware – for there is a beautiful lady in this . . . neighbourhood who can to serve her turn hold herself stiff & motionless as in a trance for 24 hours!![84]

Perhaps Eliza Whitaker turned her swooning dependence on and off like the proverbial tap.

Demonstrably, conjugal idioms varied across the period. Some of this variety must be attributed to temperament and context – one would hardly expect the same vocabulary from a twenty-three-year-old newly-wed as from a fifty-year-old father of four – yet linguistic models derived from letter-writing manuals, essays and novels also played a role, even if their dominance was incomplete. A neo-classical reserve tempered the protestations Robert Parker and Walter Stanhope were prepared to commit to paper in the 1740s and 1750s. Doubtless they agreed with Richard Steele, who thought marriage should be regarded as an everyday matter, and found it preposterous when women were 'treated, as if they were designed to inhabit the happy fields of *Arcadia*, rather than be Wives and Mothers in old *England*'.[85] Almost certainly they inherited the belief, still strong across the North today, that the trumpeting of marital affection is embarassing and anti-social: 'tis indecent, to be always slabbering, like a couple of Horses nabbing one other.'[86] By contrast, the Ramsdens

considered themselves a liberal couple and were encouraged in their expressiveness by their reading of Samuel Richardson: 'You may laugh at
your humble servant if you please for I am not ashamed of my passion,'
wrote Bessy Ramsden in 1762, 'you know Sir Charles says a woman
should never be ashame[d] of owning a passion for a worthy man.'[87] A
romantic faith in the authenticity and desirability of emotional transport
can be detected in the leaden Whitaker exchanges. In fact, they moved on
the fringes of the Lake Poets, so they may have drunk of such ardour at the
source.

Admittedly, the mechanism by which a literary ideal informs private
writing, the much touted 'inter-textuality' of literary studies, is notoriously difficult to substantiate. Evidence on the reception of texts is exceptionally hard to secure. However, occasional remarks are revealing of the
ways in which enthusiasm for the Romantic or sentimental message may
have shaped female discourse, witness a teenage Lancaster Quaker con-
fiding her reactions to Richardson in the 1770s: 'We have begun to read Sir
Charles Grandison. I admire much the character of Miss Harriet Byron. I
dislike as much Mr Greville and Fenwick as I love her . . . How I was
affected by Miss Byron being carried from the masquerade by sir
Hargrave'; 'Miss Byron O how she will be afflicted when [Sir Charles]
goes to Bologna.' Mary Chorley quickly moved from sympathizing with
the novel's characters, to musing on her own sensibility: 'I really am at a
loss to know what to say in my transactions. I think if I were to open my
heart like Miss Byron and Miss Jewson the contents would fill a room.'
Literary formulae could have a stunning impact on personal expression.[88]
Yet, of course, fiction itself is hardly a monovalent force driving lovers
down a straight road to the emotional expressiveness of the late 1960s.

It would be incautious to use these cases to construct a neat chronology
of dignified restraint giving way to romantic release in the written expression of love. The Gossips were as cosy in the 1730s as any *gemütlich*
Victorian couple; Barbara Stanhope as helpless and abject in her love in
the 1720s as any heroine of a Gothic romance. More plausible is Marilyn
Butler's thesis that politeness and passion were rival, not successive, philosophic and emotional ideals. Certainly, the 1760s and 1770s represented
the sentimental heyday, when a group of committed writers displayed an
optimistic interpretation of unpolished human nature of a piece with their
liberal sympathies. Much of their confidence in subjectivity and sensation
was inherited by the radical novelists of the 1790s, though unsurprisingly
the same decade witnessed a conservative literary reaction 'attacking the
cult of self in politics, psychology and ethics'. In fact, by the early nineteenth century, a moderate language of love was again fashionable in

exalted literary circles.[89] Competing emotional conventions had long been in play; fashions rose and fell, but they always had their competitors and contenders.

However, amidst the different patterns of happy marriage, some common threads can be drawn. What all these successful marriages shared was a division of role and responsibility mutually agreed by man and wife. For these were dutiful, proficient women. All but Barbara Stanhope did the expected thing and supplied a quiverfull of heirs for the lineage. Their competence in the household and authority over servants was recognized and respected. Male prerogatives were taken for granted, but not pushed to their limit. As far as can be gathered from letters, none of these husbands expected blind obedience in every detail of domestic life. William Ramsden, for one, relished a little insubordination in his lively wife; it amused Robert Parker to fulfil his wife's teasing commands; while William Gossip couched his orders as respectful suggestions. Unequal partnership was workable if a wife observed the general proprieties and a husband tempered his authority. Clearly, wedding put an end to wooing, but, fortunately for these couples, was 'the beginning of solid and substantial love'.[90] The letters of all these couples bespeak the tight bond of marital alliance. All these men and women managed to convey the impression that their married life was a shared endeavour; that together they would bear the revolutions of fate.

*　　*　　*

It is not my purpose to suggest that the Georgian era was a golden age in the history of marriage. For every harmonious union described a parallel example of stale boredom or harsh discord could be offered. Conjugal disillusionment and disregarded loneliness were staples of eighteenth-century commentary, and the monotony of marriage was inadvertently publicized by many an authority. Weetonhall Wilkes warned that 'There is great Discretion requir'd to keep Love alive after Marriage; and the Conversation of a married Couple cannot be agreeable for Years together without an earnest Endeavour to please on both Sides.' The observant lap-dog Pompey the Little noted in 1751, 'there is this little Misfortune attending Matrimony, that People cannot live together any Time, without discovering each other's Tempers. Familiarity soon draws aside the Masque, and all that artificial Complaisance and smiling Good-humour, which make so agreeable a Part of Courtship, go off like *April Blossoms*, upon a Longer Acquaintance.'[91] But anticlimax was not the worst a woman had to fear. The potential for violence and cruelty in marriage can be glimpsed from the horrible complaints of the aggrieved

minority who felt compelled to seek redress in the church courts, and from
the depositions generated when noblemen sued their wives' lovers for
financial compensation (the common law suit of 'criminal conversation'),
and pursued the ultimate dissolution of a parliamentary divorce. Complete marital failure was not unheard of.

Of course, divorce by act of parliament was prohibitively expensive and
exceptionally rare; between 1670 and 1857 there were only 325 divorces in
England, all but four of these obtained by men. Annulments were always
staggeringly unusual, and to gain a legal separation in the church courts,
divorce *a mensa et thoro* without the right to remarry, a female petitioner
had to prove adultery as well as life-threatening cruelty. However, there
were doubtless numerous private deeds of separation drawn up, and
informal 'divorce' through desertion or mutual agreement must have been
widespread. Still, the social prohibitions against informal separation were
powerful, and the penalities faced by an estranged wife could be grim.
Without the safeguard of a carefully worded deed of separation, a wife
still suffered all the legal disabilities of *couverture*: any income from real
estate, any future legacies or earnings, all personal property and total
control of the children could be claimed by a vindictive husband. What is
more, in strict legality, a wife could not leave her husband's house without
his permission and an affronted spouse had the law on his side if he chose
to drag his wife back.[92] Only the most desperate, or the most protected,
woman could countenance leaving a marriage on such terms. Understandably then, court records describe only the tip of a possible iceberg of
everyday misery. This final section examines two case studies of marital
breakdown which never reached the ecclesiastical court. The marriage of
Elizabeth Parker and John Shackleton (covering the years 1765–81) is
compared with that of Ellen Weeton and Aaron Stock (1814–22). Both
cases are suggestive of the miseries women might endure with no obvious
legal remedy. In the absence of a husband's goodwill and a family's
support, the potential vulnerability of a woman's position comes into crisp
focus.

Elizabeth Parker's happy marriage to Robert Parker of Alkincoats was
shortlived. He died in 1758 at the age of thirty-eight, leaving her alone with
three sons under five. But her increasingly jolly widowhood of seven years
came to an end in July 1765, when she eloped to Gretna Green with a local
woollen merchant John Shackleton. He was twenty-one years old to her
mature thirty-eight. Why she married him is not recorded for posterity,
but it cannot have been anything other than her own free choice to do so.
In financial terms, she had no one to please but herself. However, she still
had to answer to friends and family, which probably explains her scandalous elopement. When presented with the *fait accompli*, her outraged

brother Edward Parker broke off personal communication with his sister for years.[93] This was an inauspicious beginning to sixteen years of progressively unhappy marriage, the details of which are recorded in the diaries Elizabeth Shackleton kept from her marriage to her death. Doubtless affectionate, at least on Elizabeth's side, this match was far from advantageous. Indeed it was positively degrading – a fact which alienated powerful kin and exaggerated her reliance on the goodwill of the man she had chosen. Sadly she had founded her happiness on cracking clay.

For the first seven years of her marriage Elizabeth Shackleton recorded no instances of serious matrimonial strife. By contrast, the diaries written between 1772 and 1781 catalogue the steady worsening of relations during the last nine years of marriage. Coming so late in the marriage, the Shackletons' difficulties cannot be seen as simply the conventional problems of early marital readjustment. Elizabeth Shackleton's principal complaint against her husband was his heavy drinking. John Shackleton's drunkenness was first recorded, without comment, in July 1771, when a servant from Alkincoats found him stumbling back from a nearby farm, having lost his way, his silver buckle and his stock. Thereafter, Mrs Shackleton enumerated her husband's drinking sessions with disapproval. From 1772 John Shackleton expressed dissatisfaction with his wife and his marriage, of sufficient note to reach the pages of Elizabeth Shackleton's diary: 'Mr S. very Cross. Never pleas'd at what I say nor do.' It is hard to say whether discontent fostered his drinking habits or *vice versa*, but whatever the root cause, complaints about his ill-nature and savage temper increased during the 1770s. John Shackleton subjected his wife to verbal abuse: 'Mr S: so cross, so rude, so in humanly ill natured as wo'd amaze, swore most horribly indeed at me.' Amidst general curses, he issued malicious threats. In May 1773 he threatened to make a sale and leave, publishing her discredit in the 'Publick papers'. In 1776 he claimed he would freely give a hundred guineas for a divorce, and in 1778 declared his antipathy was so intense, he was prepared to die. 'Mr S. further said he wo'd destroy himself I was . . . nought to him, he co'd not live with me. Nor wo'd not. He quite hates me, dos not like me. He behaves most cruelly to me. I had a most shocking night. Cry'd and fretted.' Once installed in his own home, Pasture House, Shackleton threatened bodily to throw his wife out, knock her head against her ribs, and to send for his father 'to keep me orderly & to comfort him in his great trouble & to rule such an Ungovernable Bitch as myself . . .'[94] He was not a happy man.

The incidence of physical abuse followed a similar pattern to that of verbal violence, first registering in January 1772 when Mrs Shackleton tersely recorded, 'Mr S. coming rude, threw water on me & vulgar to a degree'. In July of the same year Shackleton threw a great lump of hard crust in her face, bruising her lips and loosening a tooth. Provoked by an imagined slight in September 1773, he broke up a family card game throwing his wife out of her chair and breaking a saucer. By the late 1770s he had graduated to direct assaults, striking his wife with his fists, bloodying her nose and mouth. By 1780 he had taken to his wife with a horsewhip. Even in her last and fatal illness, John Shackleton did not forbear: 'he struck me violently many a time. Took the use out of my Arm, swell'd from my Shoulder to my wrist, the skin knock'd off at my elbow in great Misery and pain he afterwards got up & left my bed, went into a nother room pritty Matrimonial comforts god Bless and help me.'[95]

Virulent hostility is laid open in Elizabeth Shackleton's diaries, but do they provide the whole story? Of course not. Local tradition holds that John Shackleton kept a diary of his own, but this document has long since disappeared, so at his side of the story we can only guess. It is also possible that Elizabeth Shackleton used her diary to comment on just the negative aspects of her marriage, not to encompass the whole. Perhaps her diary functioned principally as an escape valve, wherein she rehearsed her version of events during occasional disputes? By this view, their contents might reflect only the extraordinary aspects of marital interaction not its day-to-day character. However, even were this the case, infrequent conflict of such magnitude has important significance in its own right; the Shackletons were at odds over fundamentals not superficial specifics. As it was, however, the diaries did not fulfil an occasional confessional function. They grew out of the daily record-keeping of genteel housewifery. Comments on Mr Shackleton, good and bad, are woven into a tapestry of commentary on, among other things, the servants, housekeeping, local and national news, the family and, inevitably, the weather. Nevertheless, it is possible that the increasing incidence of recorded strife in the later 1770s represents not a real increase in quarrels, but rather Elizabeth Shackleton's use of a large journal in addition to her traditional pocket diaries. She now had more space to fill with evidence of her mistreatment. But it seems more likely that the intensification of strife was a genuine reflection of an ominous shift in the balance of power between the couple. By 1780, apparently their worst year together, the Shackletons were living in John's own mansion, Pasture House. Elizabeth Shackleton was fifty-two years of age, all-but toothless and habitually ill. At thirty-six John Shackleton had no heirs and was suffering from attacks of gout. Both his confidence and ill will seemed to increase in his own house. Still, it would be wrong to see the diaries as a testimony to unremitting emotional travail. Mrs Shackleton gratefully accepted any sign of goodwill or penitence on the part of her husband. She continued to pray for his health and a blessing on his ventures. But these were brief periods of remission between bouts of drinking and aggression.

Given the extremity of her marital difficulties, what was Elizabeth Shackleton to do? Separation was not absolutely inconceivable amongst her social circle, since an old friend had parted from 'her Drunken Hog' of a husband in 1779 on account of his drunken cruelty and alehouse debts. But temperamentally Elizabeth Shackleton was no friend to single women and she looked upon the desperate Mrs Knowles as an outlaw. All of which suggests that she herself could not countenance the social suicide of a judicial separation. Probably the risk of scandal was deterrent enough, for she found the prospect of exposing her marriage to public scrutiny an odious one. All references to John Shackleton in Elizabeth Shackleton's social correspondence indicate that in vindication of her decision to elope, she had represented him to the world as the perfect gentleman. The fact that she noted with embarrassment an altercation witnessed by her polite neighbours and his public humiliation in a tenant's house suggests her pride on this score.[96] A less drastic measure was to call upon the intervention of wider kin. But if anything, the situation was aggravated rather than tempered by John Shackleton's father. Christopher Shackleton of Stone Edge was himself an habitué of the alehouse and a day at Stone Edge preceded several of John Shackleton's outbursts, so Old Shackleton may well have fuelled his son's sense of grievance. Certainly, the father–son conference of 1773 designed to bring home the dangers of drink had no perceptible impact.[97] Under different circumstances, Elizabeth might have appealed to her powerful brother. Although reconciled to Edward Parker of Browsholme in 1775, to call on his aid she would have to denounce Shackleton as a vulgar brute. Her failure to do so demonstrates her reluctance to lose face. In any case, such an admission would only confirm Edward Parker's worst prejudices and jeopardize the fragile reconciliation so recently achieved. Eventually, in 1780 she compromised, calling upon the mediation of her son, Thomas Parker: 'My own dear Tom came here this forenoon to hear the disputes betwixt myself and Mr S. Mr S. made me into the vile offender, himself the person illused. He the upright. Myself the guilty. Time Time will shew.' The outcome of arbitration was indecisive. They did not part, nor did the arguments cease. Weakened by illness, Elizabeth confided prayers and grim resignation to her diary. In 1781 she read a prophetic proverb in the printed preface to her last diary: 'That honest Poverty is better than rich Roguery is a Maxim, which though many will not allow, is nevertheless a true one; for like a dead Wife it brings a man peace at last.' Her last diary entry ends on a characteristic note of mournful dignity. 'A wet close day, my foot most shocking painful, about one Mr S. & I went off to dine at good old Alkincoats good luck to us.'[98] She was buried a week later in Colne Church. Shackleton remarried the next year.

Ellen Weeton's reflections and letter-books provide a more extreme example of matrimonial breakdown in Lancashire in the early nineteenth century. No evidence survives of the courtship of the thirty-seven-year-old governess and thirty-eight-year-old manufacturer, nor any record of how the pair met. Miss Weeton first mentioned the Calvinist widower Aaron Stock only two weeks before she married him, when she requested her brother Tom Weeton's opinion of Aaron Stock. (Stock leased a Wigan factory from Tom Weeton's mother-in-law.) Tom Weeton stood to gain a hundred pounds at his sister's marriage or death, by the terms of their mother's will. Whatever his personal knowledge of Aaron Stock, he must have reassured his sister, since the wedding took place in September 1814, when Miss Weeton 'resigned my prospects of future happiness or misery for this life, into the hands of another' and her legacy into the hands of her brother.[99] The Stocks embarked upon married life in Aaron's house at the back of the factory, but moved to polite Standishgate once Aaron Stock's enterprise, bolstered by his wife's modest capital, began to prosper. Within ten months of marriage, they had a daughter of their own. Nevertheless, even these early months were inharmonious, judging by occasional letters of the period transcribed into her copybook and a retrospective narrative written in 1822.

Ellen Stock struggled from the outset to establish her authority in the household, but was thwarted by her stepdaughters and disloyal servants. In 1816 Mrs Stock described her husband's earlier behaviour in terms of 'wayward humours', 'ill-treatment' and 'tyranny'. In the same year reported strife led an old friend Bessy Price to wonder aloud if lengthy spinsterhood had rendered Ellen Stock incapable of that wifely servitude which guaranteed harmony. On the contrary, Mrs Stock insisted in June 1816, it was '*firm, judicious* opposition' not 'abject submission' which elicited better treatment. By this method, Ellen Stock achieved ten months of uneasy equilibrium. By November 1816, however, relations had deteriorated to the extent that Ellen Stock was contemplating leaving her husband and taking up teaching again: 'My husband is my terror my misery! and I have little doubt, will be my death', she confided to Bessy Price.[100] For a brief period in the summer and autumn of 1817 Ellen Stock recorded enjoying a 'degree of domestic comfort': her baby daughter provided much diversion, her stepdaughters were cordial, the servants respectful and Aaron Stock prepared to be peaceable. However, amity gave way to strife by Christmas 1817. Events took a public turn in the new year, when Ellen Stock was physically turned out into the street and had to seek shelter from her brother in nearby Leigh. After two nights in Leigh, brother and sister returned to Wigan to effect either a reconciliation or a negotiated separation. Neither was satisfactorily achieved since Ellen Stock would not agree to Aaron Stock's terms:

> Mr Stock wants me either to remain at home pennyless, as an underling to his own daughter, or to be kept by anyone that will take me. I cannot agree to such a reconciliation, or such a separation, whilst he has plenty of money. I am obliged totally to withdraw myself from any domestic affairs, in obedience to my husband's orders; to live in an apartment alone; not to sit at table with the family, but to have my meat sent to me; and amuse myself as I can.[101]

Later the same month Ellen applied to her lawyer brother again cataloguing her grievances: Stock rebuffed all attempts at affectionate contact, kept her totally without money, made her eat the servant's fare or go without, informed servants of household affairs long before their mistress, encouraged his daughters to conduct the house as they saw fit, periodically ordered her out of room and house, and ridiculed her face and figure.

Tom Weeton's intervention two days later brought only temporary respite. Subsequent letters of recrimination indicate that on at least four occasions between the summer of 1818 and February 1822, Ellen Stock was forced to flee the house with Mary, taking refuge with neighbours in Wigan and friends across the north-west. Each flight ended in ignominy; financial pressure forcing her miserably back to Aaron Stock. In 1819 Stock demoralized his wife still further by relegating her to the back quarters of the Chapel Lane factory and sending Mary to boarding school. Thereafter, he restricted Ellen's access to her daughter and intercepted her letters. Between 1820 and 1822 Ellen Stock was assaulted by her husband, threatened with the lunatic asylum and twice arrested at her husband's instigation. Fearing she would be murdered or transported if she stayed and finding it increasingly difficult to procure clothes and even food in exile, Ellen Stock eventually agreed to an unjust deed of separation signed in early 1822.[102]

Not unnaturally, Ellen Stock's manuscripts offer the case for her own defence. Autobiography represented a self-proclaimed effort to win her daughter's sympathy: 'it is surely proper that my daughter should be acquainted with the truth . . . It is for my little Mary principally I write this.' To acknowledge such partisanship, however, is not to suggest that Ellen's account had no foundation in events (the assaults and arrests have been checked against local court records and found to be accurate), rather it alerts us to the inevitable partiality of her narrative. In her letters and autobiography, she represented herself as a blameless wife, beset by the unwarranted abuses of a tyrant. As proof of proper conjugality on her own part, Ellen Stock cited the dedicated mending of Stock's oldest clothes, a chore she hated, and the cheerful relinquishing of all her property save a lump sum of twenty-three pounds pocket money. Ellen maintained throughout that the attempt to please was my 'daily and hourly study'.[103]

When still a spinster Miss Weeton had disapproved of *Lord Chesterfield's Letters to his Son* (1774), because of the author's contempt for matrimony. She believed men and women should marry their social equals in order to achieve harmony and balance. From her criticisms of her then employer Edward Pedder, it is clear she believed the ideal husband was a dignified 'senior partner' who protected and esteemed his wife. The ideal wife was industrious and dutiful, yet more than a mere 'shirt-and-pudding-maker'. Although appalled at Edward Pedder's despotic abuse of his young bride, the governess still counselled submission: 'I say it is a disgrace to the dignity of the female character for any woman to strive to become master in her husband's house', and could not condone Mary Pedder's flight to her father.[104] But unequal partnership was no more palatable in her own case, partaking more of naked tyranny than benign paternalism: 'He that should nourish, cherish and protect me . . . he is the man who makes it his sport to afflict me, to expose me to every hard-ship to every insult.' In negotiating her husband's authority, Mrs Stock deployed all her persuasions, but quickly learned that Aaron Stock was not susceptible to influence: 'no powers of rhetoric will work upon him . . .' She began to feel that 'a severity so everlasting' justified some resistance. Drawing on her experience in the Pedder household, she developed a new strategy, outlined here in June 1816:

> The man who rules by tyranny, can never be obeyed by affection; he is submitted to from fear, and delights in abject submission; it gratifies the pride of his heart to see everyone trembling around him. But mark! the tyrant in power, is ever the slave when humbled; he knows no medium, and the only way of living peaceably with him, is . . . not to be afraid of him; for tyrants are always cowards.[105]

Unfortunately, this 'judicious opposition' met with a modified success for ten months only. As Ellen Stock came to recognize her powerlessness ('My late exertions have only been like the weak struggles of a drowning insect, and if I cannot be rescued I must inevitably sink!') her written response to suffering wavered between stubborn indignation, a struggle to attain a state of Christian resignation and outright spiritual despair: 'My life, my strength cannnot sustain me much more.'[106]

A traditional tactic open to the persecuted wife was to call on the intervention of kin and the censure of public opinion, but if Aaron Stock's four siblings sympathized with their benighted sister-in-law, then they lacked the spirit to intercede, as her plaint reveals:

> if a few individuals would interest themselves for me, the fear of what the world may say, would induce Mr S. to treat me with more appearance of kindness. But he overawes all who come near him . . . Although many despise him, none dare shew any disrespect in his presence; and whilst they shew him so much outward attention, it is tacit encouragement to his tyranny at home.[107]

In sum, Ellen Stock's manuscripts conjure a public opinion critical of blatant marital oppression, but ambivalent about personal intervention. She was taken in and supported by a neighbouring doctor and his wife and found a late servant willing to testify to Aaron Stock's 'cruel usage', yet most observers seemed to think that active mediation fell to kin.

Ellen Stock threw herself on her brother's mercy and moderate success greeted her attempts to shame him into action. It was perhaps the threat of local scandal which motivated his initial efforts. 'I would not, at this time, have applied to you' wrote Ellen in January 1818, 'had it not been frequently said to me "Why do you not apply to your brother? As he lives so near, it is his duty to protect an only sister from the ill-usage of an unkind unfeeling husband".'[108] However, Tom Weeton's half-hearted intercession did little to deter Aaron Stock. In all probability Weeton simply desired that the affair be kept quiet, while his sister had long been convinced that only the 'arm of the law' would ensure Stock kept to his promises. Although a solicitor himself, Tom Weeton refused to defend his sister's interests in negotiation of the deed of separation, pleading his fear of inordinate expenses and that supporting her case would lead Aaron Stock to give up the lease on his mother-in-law's premises. He refused to act as her bondsman. Astoundingly, he chose to act for his brother-in-law instead, apparently encouraging Stock to even harsher terms and advising him to insist that Ellen Stock sign the deed heard read but unseen. Thereby, Mrs Stock unknowingly limited herself to seeing her daughter just three times a year and agreed never to visit Wigan, or to live within a two-and-a-half-mile radius of the town, in return for a yearly income of seventy pounds. Ellen Stock never forgave such 'unbrotherlike conduct', relieving her feelings in a twelve-thousand-word narrative sent to Tom Weeton in 1822 (which provides much of the detail of this account) castigating him for his conduct throughout: 'Your cruel neglect was the astonishment of great numbers in Wigan, who said you would even be quiet if I were in murdering.'[109] The confederacy of husband, brother and lawyer shows patriarchy at its most cruel and crushing.

The Shackleton and Stock relationships provide ample evidence of the negative potential of marriage for women in our period. Although John Shackleton only threatened what Aaron Stock carried through, the two cases bear interesting similarities. Both the Shackleton and Stock marriages represented a second attachment for one of the parties, and both households contained stepchildren, whose presence inevitably complicated the creation of trusting, domestic unions. Both Elizabeth Shackleton and Ellen Stock felt their role as mistress to be in jeopardy, fearing their authority over servants was being undermined and, at times, experiencing miserable isolation in their own households. Yet, whatever the cruelty they suffered, neither woman questioned the validity of marriage, nor the principle of patriarchal authority, rather they mourned the fact that their husbands bore so little resemblance to their masculine ideal. Both automatically looked to their male kin for relief, only to find them distant and ineffectual, or sadistically obstructive. Both cases reinforce the general conclusion that faced with determined oppression, a wife who lacked powerful, sympathetic kin or interested neighbours could expect little formal redress. Stylistically, Ellen Stock's account differs from that of Elizabeth Shackleton in the degree of cohesion the aspiring authoress imposed on her retrospective narrative and the extent to which she reflected on her own apparently spotless marital conduct. Obviously, Ellen Stock's degradation outstripped anything suffered by Elizabeth Shackleton, who was released by death not divorce from bed and board. Ellen Stock's accusations of the 'cruelty' she met with from 'a monster of a husband' may sound extreme or even crazed, but appear a standard feature of the rhetoric of matrimonial breakdown when judged against the records of the church courts. When Lancashire and Cheshire women filed for a separate maintenance in the Chester Church Court in the later eighteenth century they made familiar allegations of barbarous behaviour: accusing their husbands of denying them sufficient victuals, clothing and other necessaries of life; showing hatred, aversion and physical brutality; threatening to murder or maim; and keeping company with prostitutes and adulteresses. Indeed, when Margaret Hunt examined separation suits at the London Consistory Court in the years 1711 to 1713, she found that in half the cases, husbands had threatened to commit their wives to a house of correction or the madhouse. In fact, looking at in another way, an awareness of the acceptable grounds for a legal separation probably structured Ellen Weeton Stock's narrative, which unfolds like a deposition.[110] Clearly, we should add the deposition to the novel and the letter-writing manual in any further consideration of the rhetorical models which informed the language of marriage in our period.

The perfect genteel alliance was both prudent and affectionate. Exactly how prudent a choice should be was open to interpretation, however. Possibly opinions on this matter differed most strongly from the contrary vantage-points of youth or age. Yet we would be naive to assume that young suitors themselves did not find their hearts beating faster at the prospect of 'a most accomplished young lady, with a handsome fortune', or even 'an agreable young lady with a genteel fortune',[111] while money and magnificence were conducive to passion in many a female breast. Even one of literature's most ardent heroines, Austen's Marianne Dashwood, who claimed in 1811 that wealth and grandeur had nothing to do with happiness, could not conceive of marrying without a 'competence' of about two thousand pounds a year, to support 'a proper establishment of servants, a carriage, perhaps two, and hunters'.[112] The length of a man's rent-roll remained the ultimate aphrodisiac. Of course, families with fortunes to consider did not hand over their daughters to any old adventurer. Male suitors had to plan a romantic campaign with military precision; its skirmishes and reverses welcomed by the confident as a thrilling trial of their masculine audacity. No one expected courtship to be the work of a moment. Even for the perfectly matched, courtship always culminated in tedious financial negotiation, in which the interests of the parties were usually represented by their legal guardians; a device which at least meant that young lovers could project all mercenary motives on their elderly representatives. Courtship, settlement and marriage remained bywords for bargain and sale throughout this period.

For all that, courtship was the supreme adventure for an agreeable young lady with a genteel fortune. Perhaps for the only time in her life, a woman was the absolute centre of attention, and often the protagonist of a thrilling drama. Many walked a tightrope of romantic excitement: imprudent encouragement smacked of filial disobedience and could end in disinheritance and disaster, but a fastidious decorum might dishearten a suitor and lead to aching disappointment. Nevertheless, however interesting a woman's dilemmas, her star was never higher and the girl of family, fortune and character could make a career of her coming out. The eponymous heroine of Elizabeth Haywood's *Miss Betsy Thoughtless* (1751) rejoiced in her reign: 'As the barometer is governed by the weather, she said to herself, so is the man in love governed by the woman he admires: he is a meer machine, – acts nothing of himself, – has no will or power of his own, but is lifted up, or depressed, just as the charmer of his heart is in humour.' Is it to be wondered that the lively Betsy preferred entertaining a 'plurality of lovers' and savouring the triumph of 'awing the proudest into submission', to settling down with the first man of virtue who came along?[113]

Yet, the sought-after maiden exercised only a 'short-lived tyranny', as
Mary Wollstonecraft warned. Few men expected to carry the elaborate
homage and tedious forms of courtship into marriage. Indeed, the vil-
lainous suitor of Haywood's *Betsy Thoughtless* was only biding his time,
having 'armed himself with patience, to submit to everything his tyrant
should inflict, in the hope that it would one day be his turn to impose
laws . . .'[114] And therein lay the rub. For all the poetry of courtship, marriage remained a social and economic contract written in sober prose, so
many a bride was doomed to disillusionment. 'How soon is the painted
Scene changed', reflected the clear-eyed Arabella, 'and the same Woman,
that just now personated a *Lady* is anon to be a *Waiting-maid*, a *Cook* and
a *Nurse*: And well it is, if after all she can gain the Applause and Approbation of her Proprietor.'[115] So whether a woman was content in marriage
turned in large measure on her ability to resign herself to the traditional
roles, responsibilities and relationship of husband and wife. As a philosophical Anna Larpent reminisced in 1800: 'I have been married 18 years
today I have had my roughs & smooths but the former chiefly arose from
expecting too much.'[116] Not that an automatic desire to rebel against
matrimonial convention should be assumed. Many women exhibited a
craving to do their duty as ardent as any hunger for narrow, personal
gratification. For, as Ann Pellet observed, 'there is certainly a secret
pleasure in doing what we ought, tho' perhaps one don't meet with a
suitable return'. In fact, 'the consciousness of doing right' in the face of the
most extreme provocation seems to have offered some women a near-
mystical satisfaction in their matrimonial martyrdom.[117] Doubtless the
highest conception of happiness for some was the knowledge that they had
pleased their husbands: 'To a slave's fetters add a slavish mind,' requested
one cynic, 'that I may cheerfully your will obey.'[118]

Still, marriage was not all sacrifice and submission. The deferential
utterance is not an unerring sign of a deferential spirit, as Georgian men
were only too aware. Wives, like servants, might only offer 'eye-service' –
a superficial deference which masked a contemptuous heart. As E. P.
Thompson has reflected, 'The same man who touches his forelock to the
squire by day – and who goes down in history as an example of deference
– may kill his sheep, snare his pheasant or poison his dogs at night.'[119] Lip-
service to masculine dominion abounds in genteel correspondence, but
some playfulness is also apparent. Wives made arch references to their
formal subjection, as here, where Jane Scrimshire signs off a letter: 'my
Husband sends you His best wishes not forgetting your worthy *Master*',
and Bessy Ramsden mocks her schoolmaster husband: 'then comes home
my Lord and Master for his breakfast which must not be delay[ed] a

moment . . .'[120] In fact, some brides seemed to exult in the fact that they had a husband to order them about in the first place. The self-possessed Anne Parker of Cuerdon, for one, liked to dramatize her matrimonial encounters, advertizing her gracious submission to the great, northern gentleman she sought to tame:

> Now for an Account of what I saw at our Races which Entre Nous I woud have left & gone to Visit my friends at a Distance but my Robin Absolute (upon my hinting to him with Great Submission) my inclination of being absent mutterd an Ejaculation which sounded so Like Swearing I was half frightened & then told me in plain English He insisted upon my being at the Races & I might Invite any Company I chose to have with me at Cuerdon at that time. I believe I Pouted a Little for Softening his Voice he added I beg as a favor you will Stay the Races & you shall Visit who you Please afterwards. I then made Him a very Pretty Curtsey & said to be sure Mr Parker as you have an Inclination for me to be at the races I shall oblige myself for going to them on those terms (nicely said was it not).

Anne Parker's complaints about 'Mr Husband' had the unmistakable air of self-congratulation: 'To be sure I was born to be Contradicted (oh! foh! how I stink of Matrimony).'[121] Perhaps she sought to exaggerate his bluff jurisdiction the better to spotlight her own civilizing mission, for the softening power of female influence was an article of eighteenth-century common sense and a point of covert female pride.

A clever woman managed to assert herself within the paradigm of male supremacy and female subjection, it was often suggested. Lord Halifax's thoughts on the bride's empire of tears were endlessly recycled in eighteenth-century print. *A Picture of true Conjugal Felicity* of 1765 offered the example of the mild, agreeable Amanda, who consecrated her life 'to the full discharge of her relative duties' and put her excellent husband Manley so at ease, that she was able 'to enjoy the amiable female privileges of ruling by obeying, of commanding by submitting, and of being perfectly happy from consulting another's happiness'. Their harmonious marriage represented 'strength and softness blended together'. While Manley 'must soften to be happy', Amanda 'must subdue by obedience'. Presumably Amanda's fluffy charm settled on Manley's authority like a smothering blanket. Rousseau offered the same assurance that a woman could govern the governer: 'Woman's empire is an empire of gentleness, skill and obligingness; her orders are caresses, her threats are tears. She ought to reign in the home as as a minister does in a state – by getting herself commanded to do what she wants to do.' The stern law lord Henry Home reiterated this creed: 'A man indeed bears rule over his wife's conduct: his will is law. Providence however has provided her with means to bear rule over his will. He governs by law, she by persuasion. Nor can her influence ever fail, if supported by sweetness of temper and zeal to make him happy.'[122]

Of course, such advice was far from radical in its intentions, but it nevertheless identified a comfortable fiction that many women lived by: 'I am glad [women] can find, in the imaginary Empire of Beauty, a consolation for being excluded every part of Government in the State', despaired Lady Mary Wortley Montagu in 1737.[123] If beauty alone failed to do its work, then a more drastic tactic was the exaggerated fulfilment of given orders, the parade of excessive obedience rather than open defiance, by which means a woman might expose the tyranny of an authority figure. Fanatically dutiful daughters threatened to sacrifice themselves on the altar of paternal dictate and good wives were not above the ostentatious exhibition of their bondage. Thus, when Mrs Elizabeth Montagu's husband refused her permission to visit a friend, she assented to his order, but proposed to decline the invitation citing his refusal as her specific reason. Her embarassed husband then relented and said she could go for three days. Not satisfied with this small concession, Montagu insisted that he frank the letter that contained her explanation:

> You would have laughd if you had seen the gravity with which he frank'd a cover for ye letter which I said I was to write to acquaint her with his denial, he thought I shd repeat my request, point du tout, I took the cover with great indifference & was determined either to have my pleasure or give a signal mark of my obedience to his noble exertion of prerogative.

Although Elizabeth Montagu shamed her husband into giving her the full permission she desired, that she was reduced to such schemes at all rankled painfully: 'Do you not admire these lovers of liberty! . . . I am not sure that Cato did not kick his wife.'[124] If Elizabeth Montagu was to wear her chains, then the world would hear them rattling.

However, the universal efficacy of non-confrontational tactics was by no means guaranteed. Ellen Weeton was dubious from the outset: 'I have often read of the experience of others, and have seen a few instances myself, where the accommodating spirit began and remained on one side, without having any softening influence on the other, but on the contrary, *increased* its *malignity* by indulgence . . .'[125] Even the most pathetic petition will not melt a heart of stony indifference, so ultimately a wife was still dependent upon the warmth of her husband's goodwill. Obviously, some men were more liberal in outlook than others. The London schoolmaster William Ramsden refused to imitate 'Adam a very shabby Fellow; who, to excuse Himself, was for laying the Blame on his wife', and thought Lord Chesterfield's letters unsuitable reading for his sons because of the misogynistic images of women therein.[126] On the other hand, the Leeds merchant Walter Stanhope, while a dutiful husband, advertised none of this effortless enlightenment. Philosophic beliefs apart, men varied in their susceptibility to female persuasion. 'I know by Experience', wrote Jane Scrimshire in 1756, that 'when Old Men Marry Young Women there is no Bounds to the influence they have over them'.[127] Since female influence was conditional on character and circumstance, its extent varied wildly. Elizabeth Parker managed an indulgent father and devoted first husband with relative ease. However her second husband was immune to polite persuasion and was beyond caring about losing her love and good opinion. Similarly all Ellen Stock's rhetoric could not moderate Aaron Stock's commands nor stay his fists. After all, a man's right to chastize his wife was enshrined in common law. Both women found to their cost that influence was no substitute for power.

Marriage carried the potential both for harmonious licence and for miserable servitude, as it long had done. The patriarchal and the companionate marriage were not successive stages in the development of the modern family, as Lawrence Stone has asserted, rather these were, as Keith Wrightson has sensibly argued, 'poles of an enduring continuum in marital relations in a society which accepted both the primacy of male authority and the ideal of marriage as a practical and emotional partnership'. Feminine deference and sexual submission hardly vanished from a young man's wish list: it is striking how many dissatisfied Victorian husbands still directed their wives to the uncompromising words of the marriage service.[128] Before Victoria, elite women sought prudent, affectionate matches, that they might share in the prestige and the pleasures of genteel family life. Emotional warmth was a reasonable guarantee of considerate treatment, while a pragmatic choice maintained or improved one's position in the world and secured the long-term support of family and friends, whose backing it was wise to preserve against the possibility of male authoritarianism. Thus, the key to a successful match lay in the balancing of these two elements. In a non-divorcing society, the Georgians fostered the prudent romance, for in Samuel Richardson's words, 'Love authorized by reasonable prospects; Love guided and heightened by duty, is everything excellent that poets have said of it'.[129]

3

Fortitude and Resignation

IN THE SPRING OF 1754 Elizabeth Parker's indulgent father John Parker lay dying at Browsholme of a 'paralytick disorder'. Heavily pregnant with what would be her first surviving child, Elizabeth was not deemed fit to make the thirteen-mile journey to sit at his bedside. In consequence, her husband Robert went in her stead, leaving his agitated wife awaiting news and letters by messenger. Concerned for his wife and the fragility of life in the womb, Robert wrote back 'I must own absence [with] the certainty of yr Condition & Fretfulness, gives me particular and great uneasiness'. 'Pray my dear hoop up yr spirits', he entreated from John Parker's deathbed.[1] Perhaps he nursed a lurking fear that maternal shock would impress itself upon, and thereby deform, the foetus, but given his degree in medicine and Elizabeth's recent failure to carry a child to term, perhaps his fears were more straightforward. Whatever his misgivings, he prayed for her composure: 'consider [the] Situation you are in, for by uneasiness you may not only endanger yourself but the little poor things, and as these shocks are only [what] happens in all Familys & Fulfilling the great Law of Nature am almost convinced you will be that Philosopher not overmuch to regard them.'[2]

Robert Parker was not alone in his fears and exhortations. Elizabeth's Aunt Ann Pellet wrote from London calling upon her to recognize that the obligations of a mother-to-be outweighed those of a grieving daughter. Mrs Pellet believed that in prudence Elizabeth should avoid the deathbed lest the confrontation leave too strong an impression on her mind. Instead, since 'all your present trouble is from that Power which cannot err', she begged Elizabeth to bear her sorrow 'with that submission which is due from a [Chris]tian hero': 'consider the great injury you will do the dr Baby as well as [your]self & family if you should grieve immoderately especially since . . . we are sure you know your duty much beyond the generality of our sex.'[3]

Such sentiments were not confined to interested parties and moral guardians. Jane Scrimshire who was a long-standing friend, close in age, worldly and a young mother herself, also wrote in philosophic vein preaching resignation:

> Arm yourself my Dear Friend against the impending Blow. Reflect those unborn & nearest to you will Suffer by your Affliction you have a Husband that I make no Doubt will supply the Place of father by a Double Portion of Tenderness . . . if you were bringing into the World a Fatherless Being how much worse wo'd yor [present] Situation be & yet it has been the fate of many. You have a Good husband & that is all Relations in One.[4]

John Parker died that March. Elizabeth Parker clearly reassured the family with a relatively calm acceptance of her loss, since Aunt Pellet recorded her 'great satisfaction' at 'how well! you Madm know your Duty which consequently leads to the vertue of resignation to the unerring dispensations of Providence'. Elizabeth Parker was safely delivered of a son and heir twenty-three days later, amid a flurry of letters of congratulation and relief. Aunt Pellet hoped Elizabeth would be 'so sensible of her *present blessings* as to forget all *past troubles*'.[5]

Sixty years later a comparable crisis galvanized the women of the Whitaker network. In February 1814 the health of Robert Robbins, a London barrister and father of four was failing fast, to the obvious distress of his Lancashire-born wife Anne Eliza Robbins. Mary Whitehead, her elder sister, rushed from Preston to Lincoln's Inn Fields to offer comfort and support – a service deemed particularly necessary since Anne Robbins was 'in the family way', six months pregnant with her fifth child. By early March Robbins was dead and his wife utterly prostrated with grief. She was nursed through the immediate shock of her bereavement by her capable sister. Two London friends kept the household afloat and supervised the children. Lancashire kin were sent regular bulletins on the widow's mental state.[6] After two days delirious with grief, Anne Robbins found the strength to write to her niece, revealing her agonized struggle to bear Robbins's death with proper Christian resignation:

> The lord above only knows how extreme [my feelings] are and as it is *his* will to afflict me – so deeply he will I fervently hope restore my mind to some composure 'ere long. I ought to remember that through my *heavy* and *heart breaking* trial he *bears* me up and that I cannot better

recommend myself to his favour than to submit with resignation and obedience to all his dispensations . . . Oh Sarah can you judge of my anguish or how agonizing my feelings must be when I reflect that my beloved husband is no more! It is like a frightful dream and requires more than human fortitude to bear it with proper composure. My poor dear children . . .[7]

Her kindred were shocked by her plight and did not attempt to play down the magnitude of the tragedy. Anne's parents believed 'the loss of such a husband [is] almost irreparable, but we must all submit to the will of the almighty'.[8] Eliza Whitaker rushed to London, despite her own ill health, in order to console her aunt in this disastrous spring. As the confinement approached, 'a great test', the older children were farmed out to the London friends. On 31 May 1814 Anne Robbins was safely delivered of a daughter.

Eliza Whitaker must have alerted her Lancashire friends to Anne Robbins's plight, since details of the drama reverberated throughout the Whitaker network in the spring of 1814. Intense sympathy for Mrs Robbins was widely expressed. She had been deprived of both her husband and a father for her small children, at a time when she could least afford the loss:

I am not at all surprise[d] at your going as Mrs Robbins wishes it, Poor Woman, in such a dreadful State that she requires every consolation . . . I think no situation can be more dreadful than hers, indeed if she had expected the extent I do not think she could have prepared her mind in any way to bear so great a loss . . .

. . . even if your aunt had not had much great suffering I should fear for her, in her confinement. She must be so worn out by grief . . .[9]

Resignation was seen to be the only course open to the widow, though she was considered better equipped than most to endure and submit, by virtue of her distinctive piety: 'from her religious mind she will better enabled to undergo suffering'.[10] Above all, the women of the Whitaker network were convinced that, in time, Mrs Robbins would find comfort in her children ('the many blessings she has left behind') and consolation in her role as a mother.[11] Recovering from labour, Anne Robbins found 'so much cause for *thankfulness*', because her 'bodily sufferings' had been comparatively slight. She assured her concerned nieces that she had 'acquired a degree of composure . . . once thought impossible', and was exerting herself against grief for the sake of the children. Asking after a Lancashire subscription

for an afflicted widow, Mrs Robbins preached the sermon she herself
had received: 'Poor Mrs Johnson how much has she occupied my
thoughts, her situation is indeed truly *pitiable*, God grant it may improve
and that she may recover to perform her duty to her Children with *placid
satisfaction . . .*'[12]

The letters generated by these two crises reveal the Anglican vernacular
of the 1750s and 1810s. In response to bereavement both the Parker and
Whitaker networks expressed an uncomplicated, unenthusiastic spirituality, preaching resignation to the irreparable and grateful acceptance of
available consolations. At her father's death Elizabeth Parker was urged to
reconcile herself to that which happened in all families: the inevitable
succession of the generations. However, at the premature death of a young
husband, the Whitaker network could make no appeals to the reassurance
of the natural. Luckily, Anne Robbins was noted for 'religious feelings',
which were expected to provide mysterious solace beyond the comprehen-
sion of ordinary churchgoers. Nevertheless, both the Parker and the
Whitaker networks invoked God's providence as the arch determinant of
life's joys and afflictions and to which it was wise to be reconciled. The
woebegone were routinely directed to the book of Job.

Beyond their general assumptions about life and death, these crises also
convey the particular fears surrounding pregnancy for the expectant
mother and the unborn child. They testify to the place of pregnancy and
childbirth in female culture. Pregnancy was first and foremost a woman's
drama, a period of special vulnerability and a subject of shared female
concern.[13] Pregnancy, confinement and children were everyday themes of
women's letters across the centuries. In moments of tragedy it was female
kin who were believed best qualified to advise and assist. For, as the
celebrated midwife Sarah Stone put it, 'there is a tender regard one
Woman bears to another, and a natural Sympathy in those that have gone
thro' the Pangs of Childbearing; which doubtless, occasion a compassion
for those that labour under those circumstances, which no man can be the
judge of.'[14] The Parker and Whitaker correspondents shared an over-
arching conviction that a woman's *raison d'être* was motherhood. The
Parker crisis gave rise to explicit prescriptions of female duty, while the
Whitaker letters carried tacit assumptions about woman's natural role.
Whether her role was believed to be entirely natural or enjoined and
learned, in 1750 as in 1820 a married woman was primarily a mother,
before she was a daughter or a sister. Whether, in the final analysis, a
woman's obligations to her children were seen to outweigh the claims of
her husband is a more difficult question. Given paternal expectations and
dynastic pretensions, conflict between the role of good wife and good

mother was probably comparatively rare. Yet the fragmentary evidence that exists on the issue suggests the potential for tension. A case in the Chester church courts is suggestive on this point. One of the very few admissions of female retaliation in marital conflict was justified by the claim that the children had been injured by their father.[15] By implication, outraged motherhood justified the abandonment of wifely submission. However, this rare privileging of maternal duty over patriarchal respect apart, it appears that no absolute hierarchy of roles was conventionally agreed amongst the genteel. Nevertheless, maternity was one of the defining features of most women's lives throughout the period, as doubt-less in all periods.

The institution of motherhood has been the subject of historical contro-versy. Historians of the family, of women and of medicine have all offered sweeping analyses of the place, power and emotions of mothers over time. It is the history of the family, and in particular of childhood, which provides the most widely known chronology. In brief, it has been claimed that the early modern period was a miserable time to be a child: no allowances were made for immaturity, discipline was rigidly enforced, warmth and affection were absent. Thus, parenting was cold and distant business; infant mortality left mothers unmoved since 'maternal instinct' had not yet been invented. In the eighteenth century, so the story goes, a revised view of children emphasized their innocence and unique individu-ality, permissive child-care regimes were established, parents displayed benevolent affection and women became 'natural' mothers. From here, parent–child relations steadily progressed to the apparently happy families of liberal modernity.[16] Unsurprisingly, this thesis has been pretty thor-oughly dismantled by a new generation of scholars. The story proved at its weakest in the presentation of unremitting misery and severity in the seventeenth-century family – a picture which was laughably easy to dis-prove using letters, diaries and depositions, which revealed widespread emotional investment in children.[17] By contrast, the vision of Augustan improvement has proved harder to dislodge among non-specialists, who tend to see the decline of swaddling, wet-nursing and so on as the advent of mother love.[18] However, in stressing the continuities in good parenting from around 1600 to the present, the revisionists unwittingly invoked 'instinct' as an historical constant, implying that the force of 'nature' is immutable and inescapable – an uncomfortable suggestion for historians and feminists alike. Nevertheless, it is surely possible to accept that some elements of human experience are remarkably enduring without either endorsing an anti-feminist agenda, or suggesting that the family remains utterly the same down through time.[19] The core of parenthood may indeed be biologically determined, but it is also framed by changing social and economic institutions and understood through a history of changing ideas and social values.

Women's history, by contrast, has long been firmly committed to a vision of the cultural construction of motherhood.[20] Consistent with the conventional wisdom that separate gender spheres emerged in the later eighteenth century is the notion that between 1780 and 1850 women became newly defined as moral mothers, virtuous guardians of the nursery and domestic hearth.[21] A very similar argument tying the exaltation of motherhood to the development of capitalism ('the counterpart to land enclosure at home and imperialism abroad') is also current amongst scholars of eighteenth-century literature, although the phenomenon is usually back-dated to the middle decades of the eighteenth century. So eighteenth-century motherhood was 'a newly elaborated social and sexual identity for women', which, in tandem with the novel concept of 'bourgeois womanhood', redefined women as asexual beings and colonized the female body for domestic life.[22] This old story has been freshly bolstered by Laqueur's argument that a new model of gender difference triumphed among medical theorists from the late seventeenth century, a model which emphasized the extreme physiological contrasts between men and women's bodies, supplanting the classical view derived from Galen which had emphasized the anatomical similarities – the vagina was but the penis inverted, and so on. By 1700 women were no longer seen as less evolved versions of men, rather as innately different beings with a distinct nervous system and separate set of biological impulses.[23] Thus, Anthony Fletcher concluded a recent synthesis with the statement 'the ideology of difference made possible the positive and idealised notions of domestic nurturance and emotional warmth which gave the wife and mother her place in society'.[24] Motherhood as a social role was an eighteenth-century invention.

Is this plausible? After all, whether ordained by God or determined by nature, motherhood was a virtually inescapable institution for married women throughout the centuries. Research on the maternal ideals and practice of earlier periods suggests that eighteenth-century consecrations of natural motherhood were far from unprecedented. Judging from Patricia Crawford's analysis of seventeenth-century advice manuals, the ideal good woman had long been the good mother. Breast-feeding was justified by examples from nature; instances of infallible maternal instinct had anecdotal currency; and a mother's inability to love her offspring could lead to the diagnosis of insanity. Seventeenth-century women set great store by their maternal experiences and used their maternity to claim authority. Victorian mothers would have no difficulty in recognizing the gender roles described here: 'the rearing of children under seven was women's work and it was their natural function. Men in turn were expected to exercise authority over their families, to support them financially and to play a role in the education of older children.'[25] So far, so familiar.

How convincing then is the argument that the eighteenth century saw the discovery of organic difference between men and women? Academic medical theory apart, there is plenty of evidence that men and women had seen themselves as quintessentially physically different from each other for centuries. The long-standing taboos surrounding menstruation, for instance, bespeak an enduring vision of woman as the mysterious other – unclean and in lifelong thrall to her unpredictable womb.[26] Nor can a belief in natural feminine virtue be confined to the eighteenth century. Fenela Childs argues that although a fresh wave of cloying idealization set in from about 1710, the idealization of women was nothing new; visions of female nature had oscillated for centuries between the virtuous and the vicious. For all the early eighteenth-century praise of female purity and softness, there was no change whatsoever in the fundamental qualities expected of women. Whether the vision of the Madonna or the Magdalene was uppermost in male imaginings, the same modest demeanour was prescribed for women.[27]

All of which is not to deny the sheer glamour of the images of tender motherhood which proliferated in eighteenth- and early nineteenth-century media, but it is to suggest that these precedents should raise suspicions about a case which argues from silence for ideological revolution. What distinguishes the eighteenth-century discourse of motherhood from its predecessors is not a sudden idealization, but rather the overlaying of a range of secular celebrations on the ancient religious solemnizations. When Samuel Richardson singled out the breast-feeding mother in *Sir Charles Grandison* (1753–4), one of the most popular novels of the century, he presented a traditional duty in a haze of beguiling limelight. Witness the scene when the once naughty Lady G. is surprised with her babe at the breast by her estranged husband:

Never was a man in greater rapture. For lady Gertrude had taught him to wish that a mother would *be* a mother: He Threw himself at my feet, clasping me and the little varlet together in his arms. Brute! said I, will you smother my Harriet – I was half-ashamed of my tenderness –

Dear-est, dear-est, dear-est Lady G. – Shaking his head, between every
dear and est, every muscle of his face working; how you transport me!
– Never, never, never, saw I so delightful a sight![28]

As the mother who determined to *be* a mother gained in romantic profile,
so fashionable maternalism presented fresh rhetorical opportunities.
Feminists exploited the discourse of maternity for political ends. In 1697
Mary Astell cited the mother's crucial influence over men in childhood as
reason enough to support any scheme to improve female education. Provincial mothers joked that their healthy production of able-bodied boys
was a patriotic act, geared to 'enlarging his [majesty's] forces both by sea
& land', and eighteenth-century actresses carefully accentuated their
maternity to refurbish their reputations.[29] But the rhetorical claims of
motherhood were not unlimited, after all, the divorced wife always risked
the loss of her children however exemplary she had been in the nursery.
Further, while the ecstatic embrace of maternal romance may have made
for compelling reading, or artful self-promotion, sentimental glamour is
not the mantle which attached to motherhood as most genteel women
described it. The experience was too cruel, unpredictable and unremit-
tingly physical to be decently covered by such a sugary wrapping.

For modern women, childbirth and child-rearing is usually the key
collision between them and the medical establishment, which probably
accounts for much of the contemporary interest in this encounter in centuries past. While there are many useful individual studies of contraception,
wet-nursing, maternal breast-feeding and so on, the most cohesive and
polemical interpretation of the confrontation between female patients and
male practitioners has been offered by those who dispute traditional
accounts of the glorious rise of scientific medicine. To this end, it is argued
that childbirth was a female domain in early modern England. Mother-to-
be, midwife and gossips combined to make labour a ritualized affirmatory
experience from which men were excluded. Some would go so far as to
claim the lying-in chamber as a site of collective female resistance to
patriarchal power.[30] Given such a positive vision of 'traditional' childbirth, the eighteenth-century man-midwife or surgeon can only be seen as
a villain who displaced the midwife, de-ritualized the ultimate rite of
passage and generally imposed his authority upon women in an effort
to establish professional identity. By this view, the patriarchal victory
over teeming women and traditional midwifery reached its zenith in
nineteenth-century obstetrics, with its careerism, unnecessary and often
dangerous interventionism, and profoundly unsympathetic ethos.[31]

That the medical profession established itself between 1660 and 1850 is not in question. In addition, most social historians would accept that the delegitimization of the skills of the midwife was a function of this rise, and few would claim the obstetrician as an unambiguous life-saver.[32] However, some scholars would be less inclined to celebrate the joyousness of the birth experience before the efficient use of the forceps, podalic version, antiseptic, antibiotics and analgesia (despite the much-cited reassurance that probably as many as twenty-nine out of thirty births were spontaneous and uncomplicated, and that the vast majority of women looked happily forward to 'a safe deliverance'.) [33] Others refuse to see women as simple victims of male professionals, incapable of an informed choice about their own welfare. The notion that the obstetric surgeon was but one conspirator in a wider patriarchal plot has been questioned most directly. Reconstructing the contemporary debates around the rise of the man-midwife, Roy Porter reveals a vocal strain of husbandly horror. He conjures a substantial section of male public opinion in the later eighteenth century which did not regard female employment of male accoucheurs as a victory for men, rather 'as a chapter in the emergence of female licence, and an insidious challenge to male authority.'[34] Indeed, it is in female choices not male, Adrian Wilson argues, that we should seek the explanation for the rising stature of the man-midwife at mid-century. As mothers became aware that a male practitioner could deliver a living child in an obstructed delivery (without resort to the gruesome hooks and crochets), they called on them earlier in labour and more frequently. The fact that these emergency practitioners soon eclipsed the traditional midwife at even straightforward births amongst the fashionable, he attributes to the desires of polite accomplished ladies who sought to distance themselves from the old-fashioned collectivity of midwifes and gossips in the name of fashionable gentility. Thus, 'the making of man midwifery was the work of women'.[35] Simplistic conspiracy theories are also impugned by Judith Lewis's thoughtful work on the decisions made by pregnant noblewomen between 1760 and 1860. For these ladies of quality the accoucheur was almost invariably the practitioner of choice. Indeed, he proved a useful ally to his patient in her battles with convention, duty and demanding relatives; 'their voice of authority could be used to approve or disapprove much that women wanted to do – or avoid doing'.[36] Nor should we take it for granted that professional–client relationships before the obstetrician were automatically harmonious, given the recorded evidence of conflicts between mothers, midwives and gossips in the early modern lying-in chamber.[37] It is quite possible that the rich female collectivity romanticized by some was experienced as an alarming and oppressive cacophony by young mothers struggling to exercise their own maternal judgement. Community was not without its costs. In any case, it seems anachronistic to indict mothers for feminist betrayal if they chose a practitioner of the opposite sex, or failed to entertain half the village at the bedside.

Important as these debates are, the questions posed derive largely from late twentieth-century anxieties and conflicts about birth, motherhood and childhood. One can almost hear the echo of modern slogans – pregnancy is not an illness, male intervention is problematic, breast is best, and so on. This may go some way to explaining why seventeenth- and eighteenth-century mothers often appear in tabloid guise, as either cold, unnatural sophisticates, or communitarian, breast-feeding heroines. But our battles were not necessarily theirs. This chapter reconstructs maternal desires and difficulties in the terms set out in their own letters by genteel women in the Georgian period. It offers a varied picture which allows for human diversity, indecision and ambivalence, pleasure as well as pain. Overall, the discussion emphasizes the impact of childbirth – seen as both natural fulfilment and an inescapable duty – on genteel women's private lives and public profile. The sentimental prestige of parenthood and a celebration of the pet-like appeal of the progeny is detectable, yet far more striking are the sheer blood and guts of bearing and raising children. When a woman conceived she was launched on a roaring wave of fate. No one could predict how easily she would bear pregnancy, how safely she would deliver, how robust would be her infant, or how long and healthy the life of her child. Cumulatively the discussion stresses the mammoth emotional, physical and social costs of that passage: a studied resignation and willed endurance helped women pay the price. Christian stoicism was the philosophy of the genteel mother, just as inner strength and self-control were the qualities that defined eighteenth-century adult manhood. However, to be brave in suffering and resigned to the weight of one's biological burdens is not necessarily to be supine in the face of custom and authority. Mothers were particularly suspicious of medical opinion when it came to deciding what was best for their children: the feeding of infants and the inoculation of children were two fields over which the doctor's word was far from law. Experience gave women credentials of their own, but despite the measureless emotion and energy spent on children, women never described motherhood in terms of work. For all that genteel women were positively immersed in the business of child-bearing and child-rearing, they lacked a vocabulary with which to grasp the character of their reproductive labour. Trifling fears, pestering interruptions and a thousand little nothings were the inadequate phrases called upon to describe the infinite practical demands of motherhood. The sum and substance of motherhood lay in multitudinous details.

For fertile women, motherhood could absorb almost all reserves of physical and emotional energy for at least a decade, and was an anxious backdrop for a lifetime. The 'average' mother in this period bore six to seven live children. It was a truth universally recognized that a childless marriage was a sad marriage and most mothers paid lip-service to this maxim.[38] Yet recitations of the trials and disappointments that children brought threatened to subvert the assumption. Female ambivalence about dutiful motherhood found its most explicit expression in the letters of the Whitaker network. In 1814 newly wed Eliza Whitaker shared what appear common apprehensions with her young husband:

> My aunt has had a letter from Mrs Morgan . . . the subject you may guess. She gives many reasons why we should not be anxious to possess a family, She says she was 3 or 4 yrs before the birth of her daughter, which was an ecstasy of delight to herself and her husband. The little creature sickened and a month after its birth died, and for many months they were miserable and wished they had no family. How little we know whether the attainment of our wishes will bring us happiness.[39]

Eliza Whitaker's early failure to conceive was appreciated by her friends, but given her comparative youth, women correspondents were unperturbed, as Elizabeth Addison's ambiguous commiseration indicates:

> I should be one of those to rejoice with you, if your illness proceeded from the *common cause* for once they come they are such a comfort, though I cannot help feeling thankful to have escaped so long. I should like to have several more yet if I had my choice. I do not know if I dare to choose to have them, but I am a terrible coward even in trifles.[40]

The burden of such counsel was clear enough. A mother paid for the comfort of children in anxiety and pain.

The manuscripts of the Parker, Barcroft and Whitaker networks are littered with references to unfortunate women who had undergone a fatal labour; expectant mothers could not but be acquainted with the potential hazards they faced. 'I attempt to be Witty in vain,' wrote Jane Scrimshire in 1749, 'as at this [moment] the Bell is tolling for the funeral of poor Mrs Wilkinson who Dyed in Childbed last Friday . . .'[41] Recent revisionism may stress that the average woman ran only a 6–7 per cent risk of dying in her reproductive career, and was as likely to die by infectious disease or accident, but such statistics do not justify the claim that childbirth was seen as an insignificant cause of death. Even by the revised figures, perinatal complication was probably the single most common cause of death in women aged twenty-five to thirty-four, accounting for one in five of all deaths in this age group. As the expert says himself, in a large village a woman might see a contemporary die in childbed every third year.[42] But statistics, in themselves offer only a tangential guide to meaning and *mentalité*. Even today, when the risks of sudden infant death in England are a moderate one in four hundred, it is hard to find a new mother who has not walked to the cot with a fleeting dread. Human fears are rarely based on a rational calculation of probabilities, but on the appreciation of the gravity of the possible outcome. In any case, statistics, good or bad, were unknown to eighteenth-century women; they would have judged the possiblities on the basis of anecdotal report. Doubtless, all pregnant women knew of someone who had died in childbed, and no one could guarantee that they would not be the next. Expectant mothers had limited control over the quality of their labour, could do virtually nothing to prevent an unborn child becoming obstructed by the head, and, as Linda Pollock has remarked, they had many long months to contemplate the event.[43] Unsurprisingly, morbid fears surface in the letters of Georgian women, as they do in seventeenth-century documents. While pregnant in the 1750s Jane Scrimshire grimly joked about the new polite fashions she would adopt 'If I Live till Spring', and morosely observed 'I hear of nothing but Dying'.[44] Indeed, it was still not uncommon for pregnant women to prepare themselves for death to the extent of drawing up conduct letters for children, yet unborn or still in leading strings. As one gloomy expectant mother prophesied in 1801, 'My dearest child, When this is delivered unto you, the hand that writes it will be mouldered in dust'.[45] Even without the mortal risks (however 'low'), labour was a painful and often prolonged ordeal for both mother and unborn child. In consequence, it was an extremely forbidding prospect; a point under-lined by Jane Scrimshire's plaint of 1756: 'I do assure you I dread the approaching time very much as I suffer'd so greatly before & I am afraid Mr Scrimshire will be oblig'd to be at York about that time.'[46] Even if, on the basis of rational calculation, a pregnant woman might resolve not to worry about the comparatively small risk to her own life, she could still be prey to anxiety about the pain and physical trauma of birth and not unnaturally about the health and wholeness of the child in the womb. Tragically, Jane Scrimshire's eldest daughter was born blind. Experienced mothers often dreaded repetitions and the consequences for their children, first-time mothers feared the unknown.

In addition to mental misgivings, the Parker and Whitaker correspondents catalogued the attendant physical discomforts. Surprisingly, however, there is but one surviving reference to nausea – a dramatic sign which now looms so large in the popular impression of early pregnancy. Perhaps vomiting was seen as both normal and healthy given the universal reliance on purging as a prophylactic and general cure-all. In any case, more striking to eighteenth-century letter-writers were the accompanying melancholy, aches and immobility of pregnancy. Elizabeth Parker, Jane Scrimshire and Eliza Whitaker all complained particularly of lameness. In fact, the gamut of side effects endured by Eliza Whitaker in 1816 ran to headaches, abdominal pain, dizziness, fainting fits and palpitations.[47] Emotional confusion, blunted concentration and depressed spirits were routinely associated with pregnancy. 'Do all in yr power to keep up your spirrits', Ann Pellet urged her niece, 'for the want of spirits is the greatest misery that can be felt this side of the grave.' In fact, she claimed her own '*labour* was but a triffle when compared to weak nerves'. Similarly, John Parker bolstered his pregnant daughter: 'I am glad my Dr you keep up yr Spirits, which is [the] only thing to support us in this life . . .'[48] In the 1750s Jane Scrimshire was plunged into despondency and felt her powers of concentration slip away: 'My abilities decrease & I have no more notion of Penning a smart letter than I now have of making a smart cap . . . both body and mind disorder'd but have never been well since I came from Harrogate & what is worse my complaint is of the *Encreasing* kind & nothing but time can cure . . .'[49] In the 1810s an unusually torpid Elizabeth Addison felt unequal to polite conversation and even her lifeline – letter-writing: 'I cannot bear the thought of being among strangers . . . you know my awkward bashfulness at all times. But when I am in my present way it is doubly perceptible . . . I shall write no more for I am in a sad, stupid humour, this hot weather stultifies me.'[50]

By the third trimester of pregnancy, several women within the Parker, Barcroft and Whitaker networks were practically immobilized and thereby socially isolated. The pregnant Elizabeth Parker felt she could not stir from Colne; a Leeds merchant's wife, Mrs Ridsdale, had to catch up with her friends after a winter's 'long Confinement'; while Mrs Addison of Liverpool admitted, 'I was so entirely confined to the house for the two months before that I could not even walk around the garden & I have always been active to the last before'.[51]

Of course, the experience of pregnancy differed from woman to woman, and as the last comment suggests, from pregnancy to pregnancy. A useful leavening is provided by the robust commentary of schoolmaster's wife Bessy Ramsden. In the 1760s and 1770s she suffered little or no discomfort, was resolutely humorous throughout her four pregnancies, and even contemplated 'the fatal moment' with apparent equanimity. Although incommoded by her sheer size, she refused to forgo the pleasure of visiting, shopping and card-playing in the metropolis.

> I am determined not to stay at home any Longer till I take to my bed; which I am at a loss to say when to expect the fatal moment. I give it out to my friends that I shall not give caudle till the first week in Feb[ruary] but they all say it is impossible I should waddle about till that time I am such a monster in size; and indeed I am under great apprehensions I shall drop to pieces before I am ready for the little stranger . . .[52]

While Bessy Ramsden was supported throughout life by her good humour and high spirits, she was also lucky, for, beyond a certain point, ease or discomfort in pregnancy were outside a woman's control. Only Eliza Whitaker recorded the receipt of treatment for her side-effects and this attention was essentially a by-product of her doctor's efforts to avoid the miscarriages to which she was believed prone.[53] Most other women were simply prescribed a good dose of resignation, since ante-natal indisposition was seen as a relatively unimportant symptom of 'carrying on the Great Cause of Nature'. The inevitability of female suffering was ancestral. It was simply 'the penalty entail'd on our sex by our G.mother'. In fact, ill health in the pregnant mother was long seen as a good omen, proof of a thriving foetus within. Thus, Elizabeth Shackleton smugly reported of her pregnant daughter-in-law: 'Mrs P. was sick a good sign.'[54]

That women's letters are so rich in references to pregnancy is testimony to a shared female concern with the business of motherhood. Female well-wishers reassured and advised, expected to be told exactly when the 'little stranger' would arrive (women estimated the date of their confinement with varying degrees of success), were interested in the details of pregnancy and eagerly awaited news of the birth. Practical preparations for the confinement fell to the expectant mother. Women decided where to be confined; some returned to their maternal home or a well-serviced centre like Preston; others requested the company of their close female kin in the marital home. However, the evidence is too sparse to establish one standard practice. By contrast, the wives of peers usually arranged to be confined in London, where midwives and recovery nurses had the best reputations.[55] Once installed, the mother-to-be attempted to prepare the household and procure a nurse and/or nursery maid. While inured to worry about matters medical, Bessy Ramsden admitted 'I sleep in fear of Consequences', having fallen behind on domestic preparations, with 'yet a new bed to make up for the ocasion, which is to be made at home, beside a Thousand odd matters'.[56]

Of all practical arrangements, procuring a practitioner to assist at the birth and a nurse to attend in the aftermath were considered the most pressing. Medical historians have dwelt on the rivalry between midwives and surgeons or men-midwives, while the northern manuscripts reveal that local physicians were also common assistants at the birth. Elizabeth Parker in the 1750s, Bessy Ramsden in the 1760s, Beatrix Parker in the 1770s, Betty Parker in the 1780s, Eliza Whitaker in the 1810s and Ellen Parker in the 1820s were all attended by local physicians – many of whom came from genteel families and who knew their patients socially. From the fragmentary evidence that exists most of these appear to have been booked appointments for the doctor to call at the onset of labour, without a midwife in support.[57] Only Eliza Whitaker's letters evidence the ante-natal care of an advance call. Meanwhile, Jane Scrimshire in fashionable Pontefract made a seemingly controversial decision and opted for a man-midwife, as she confirmed in a letter of 1756:

> My mother inform'd you right that I am determin'd to have a Man Midwife but am quite unsettled who the Individual is to be, whether Thomits of Doncaster Street, Lucas or a Mr Cockill of this town, who has begun to practice since Lucas. Pray who have you fix'd on [?] Whoever it is I heartily wish you good Success . . .

Indeed, she cannot have been alone in her choice, at least in Pontefract, for judging by Jane Scrimshire's tart remarks Lucas's stock was clearly rising: 'Lucas is in high degree as Man Midwife, he don't so much as smile [now].'[58]

The fact that there was enough custom in Pontefract to support three men-midwives as early as the 1750s is interesting in itself. It has been customary to look on the mid-eighteenth century as the period when male midwifery was established in metropolitan anatomy schools and teaching hospitals, while the expansion of provincial practitioners has been dated much later. The evidence also does not marry with the received chronology regarding the character of professional involvement at the birth. Guided by the historiography, we would expect mothers in the 1750s and 1760s to be delivered as a matter of course by midwives, only calling in a man and his forceps in emergency. However, male professionals were already the practitioners of first resort for the majority of the genteel women who recorded their arrangements. Clearly, the polite already pre-ferred the ministrations of a presentable professional over the traditional collective participation of midwife and old women. However, this is not to say that polite matrons were lured away from a rich neighbourly collectivity by suspicious husbands. An important negative finding is the absence of a single instance of reported tension between mother and father-to-be over the choice of birth assistant. Dispute, discussion and persuasion is confined to the letters women exchanged amongst themselves. Correspondingly, when William Hunter advised aspiring accoucheurs on how to make a good impression at a lying-in, he strongly advised the assiduous cultivation of the mother's friends, but made no reference at all to consultation with the father.[59] Of course, genteel mothers were surrounded by servants, so they did not need a bevy of neighbours to cook, clean and look after the family during the lying-in. Nevertheless, they still relied on the support of female kin and close friends. Pregnancy and birth still engendered female collectivity, albeit one gathered on narrower social terms.

Women in the Parker network, in particular, encouraged their pregnant kin to make full use of available medical expertise, their own advice was seen as a supplement not an alternative to academic authority. Ann Pellet (herself the widow of a president of the Royal College of Physicians) showed no loyalty to practitioners of her own sex; pronouncing herself 'much pleased that [Mrs Scrimshire] designes to follow your prudence in choosing to be assisted by a Docr, rather than an ignorant old woman'. She was a firm supporter of the doctor who attended her niece, and encouraged Elizabeth Parker to follow his 'directions in every *point*', implying that her previous miscarriage could have been avoided. She hoped 'you'll manage better than you did last; by giving Dr Clayton more timely notice that he might be of greater service to you'. On her own homely authority, Aunt Pellet entreated her niece to air her linen properly, not to drink too many cooling drinks, not to go riding and to have 'a friend with you during yr approaching confinement'.[60] In sum, there is no evidence of female hostility to professional medicine. Overall, whether genteel women plumped for physician, surgeon or midwife they enjoyed a considerable degree of personal choice.

Women rarely appear to have committed the details of their labour to paper. At any rate, no detailed accounts of childbirth have survived in the northern records. Only laconic references to delivery can be found in the Parker correspondence: Jane Scrimshire had 'a very severe time', Bessy Ramsden mentioned the 'History of my Groaning &c', while Elizabeth Shackleton commiserated with her daughter-in-law: 'My sister Parker tells me she never saw so large a child . . . You wo'd feel for that. I often think how you went on – Thank God it is over. I Hope this child will be a comfort & make amends by grace & every Virtue what you suffer'd for him . . .'[61] Given such glancing mentions of labour and birth, the practical business of the lying-in chamber remains obscure for most. However, one disturbing and graphic account remains, which bears repetition in full here because of its rarity and because of its horror – an account of birth that stunningly demonstrates the physical and emotional trauma that a woman, whatever her rank, might have to undergo. In June 1739 Anne Gossip laboured in agony for forty-nine and a half hours, and with a stoicism barely imaginable suffered her dead baby to be torn apart within her and removed in pieces. A nightmare in the fullest sense, this episode was recorded with almost dispassionate clarity by William Gossip her devoted spouse:

about 2 in ye Afternoon my dear A.G. fell into a most painfull tedious & dangerous Labour; she was not [delivered] before Jun 14 about ½ an hour past three in ye afternoon. The child a Boy was dead & lay cross for the birth, with his arm forward, which made it necessary (I suppose it's Death being not then perfectly known) to turn it in order for a more natural posture. But unfortunately in the Operation, the Child flew so high up, & the womb was so much contracted for want of the water, which had broke in a very large quantity 2 days before & continued from thence to run away perpetually that the surgeon could not possibly lay hold of it again, with any firmness, after 3 severall efforts to no purpose, which my pore Dear bore with a patience, resolution & resig-nation that was truly surprising I prevailed upon Mr Dawes to sit down once more & try if he cd not by ye help of his Instrument tear ye child in pieces & bring it away in [that] manner. The Event answered beyond expectation, after a tedious & terrible operation in which the surgeon was sooner tired with afflicting her than she with Suffering, His Spirits & Strength were quite exhausted, whilst hers continued fresh & vig-orous under such torments as it is surprising how human Nature could subsist under it He rose from his knees to refresh himself & then returning to his business broke into the abdomen of ye Child with his Instruments, & thence extracted the bowels & other viscera & broke of part of ye ribs, this evacuation made room in ye Uterus for him to insinuate his hand between the belly of ye child & the sides of the collapsed womb, by which means he got hold of ye feet of ye child which were turned quite upwards almost as high as the diaphragm & thus with all the violence he durst use for fear of breaking the child in the back which was much weakened by the Crosse of ye ribs, he happily under ye Providence of God extracted the remains of his mangled Carcass, except the arm which first present itself, & which had been cut of as soon as the Childs Death was preceived. Its shattered remains were buried near ye rest of my Children in . . . St Martins Church in Coney Street York.[62]

Of course, a grotesque ordeal was not the universal experience, yet the potential for it haunted most. A crescendo of anxiety and hope was almost invariably experienced by the family of the labouring mother. Let the following account of an uneventful London labour penned by an exhausted mother-in-law in 1821 stand for the many apprehensive households:

I knew you would kindly desire to hear how our dear Invalid Recovered. Thank God! She is as well as we ought to expect, considering the sufferings she went thro' for two days & a half, she was wonderfully supported, her spirits & good humour never failed, except when nature was quite exhausted. The anxiety has been almost too much for her husband & Myself, I am going for a few days to my sister Leghs to strengthen my Nerves . . . Altho' I have not named it, yet I am a very proud Grandmother, the sweet Girl is already my darling, tho' till her Mother was safe, I did not care at all whether the baby was dead or alive indeed so great was my indifference about it and anxiety for my Daughter, that when told she was safely delivered, I went out of the house without looking at it or asking if it was Well, or Perfect. I must make it up by future love. I rejoice in its being a girl, Tom is too young a man to have a son treading on his heels, and wanting his estate before he is ready to part with it.[63]

After the birth, it was the female kin or the father (by his wife's directions) who communicated the good news to their kin and consequently it was to them that the first congratulations were often addressed. When they did eventually take up their pens, genteel mothers expressed their profound relief and thankfulness for God's great mercies. To have safely delivered 'a fine living child', endowed with all its 'Senses Limbs & Faculties', marked with no disfigurement, was a blessing indeed.[64]

Genteel women appear to have recognized the traditional lying-in period of about four weeks, as Bessy Ramsden's relief confirms: 'thank God I had a very good Lying in, for had not an hour's illness the whole month and my Littel Boy as well as myself.' However, the post-natal period was still seen as a period of risk to the mother as well as the baby, unsurprisingly given the significant dangers of puerperal fever, haemorrhage, thrombosis and, perhaps above all, milk-fever – given the traditional habit of keeping the baby from the breast until the flow of colostrum had ceased. So ardent prayers were offered for a safe recovery and remedies exchanged to prevent hardness or soreness in the breasts and looseness in the bowels.[65] Yet, if the mother was relatively well and the baby thriving, this was a period of pleasurable recuperation and polite celebration. There is no indication of post-partum disappointment if the babe was not a son and heir; indeed the only positive preference which surfaces in genteel correspondence is for girls, although this may be because most of the matrons studied here had plenty of boys.[66] Presents were received for the new-born, godparents were sought to stand as sponsors at the christening and names were chosen; more often that not being family names, 'shewing the respect that's due'.[67] Bessy Ramsden gave small parties for her gossips to drink the spicy potion caudle. In fact, this was such a customary accompaniment of labour and lying-in, that 'giving caudle' served as a euphemism in the Ramsden letters for giving birth. For Bessy Ramsden, and doubtless for other successful mothers, lying-in was a well-earned excuse to leave off domestic duties and enjoy the fruits of their labour. William Ramsden's letters reveal his sunny spouse basking in bustling attention:

> thank you . . . for remembring so kindly the Good woman in the straw, hitherto all has gone exceedingly well, the Baggage looks sleek and saucy; the Brat fat and healthy . . . I wish the next Week over that I may resign the *Keys* of my *Office*, for indeed most heartily am I tired of being *both Mistress & Master* . . . Madam has got her [Chamber] full of Gossips this afternoon one of whom is a Reverend Dockter of Divinity. Pray do the Ladies of Lancashire take the *Benefit of the Clergy on the like Occasions*? half a score . . . at least I have been call'd up, since this scribble was begun.[68]

What remains unclear is the stages by which elite women emerged from the lying-in chamber, and whether they observed the traditional sequence of first lying prone in bed, sitting up in bed after one week, moving around the chamber after two, keeping to the house after three, and finally after four or five weeks emerging for the ritual purification and thanksgiving of churching.[69] For genteel matrons, no absolute ban on mixed-sex sociability or leaving the house is detectable, although female kin recommended that 'the good woman in the straw' keep warm, take care, limit company and late nights, and avoid larking and jaunting about. In the 1750s Elizabeth Parker received many cautions from Aunt Pellet: 'As this month is the most precarious, she begs Mrs Parker will be very careful of taking cold & desires her not to be too venturesome.' By the 1760s and 1770s Elizabeth Parker was offering exactly the same advice to Bessy Ramsden, as William's acknowledgement reveals: 'Thank you for all . . . your most friendly Cautions against catching Cold &c tis the very Doctrine that has been preached to us by all the Matrons of [Charterhouse] & cannot therefore fail, I hope of being put into Practice.'[70]

Understandably, rates of recovery of strength and spirits varied from woman to woman. After the traumatic birth and death of her infant son in 1757, Barbara Parker lay near death herself and had mourning to add to the tedium of convalescence. In the same decade Jane Scrimshire endured 'low spirits' for at least four months after birth and commiserated with Elizabeth Parker who suffered for six. By contrast, the fortunate Bessy Ramsden enjoyed miraculous recoveries in both 1764 and 1768, boasting not half an hour's sickness in either case. The Mancunian Bertha Starkie got 'pure well' after the birth of her first baby in 1769, yet her sister still hoped 'she won't breed till she [has] got a little more Strength'. The Liverpudlian Elizabeth Addison regained her health and figure very quickly after her confinement in 1816, but admitted 'my nervous head will not allow me to take very great liberties with it'. Ellen Stock left Wigan in June 1815 to convalesce in Southport but 'laboured under so great a depression of spirits that my recovery was slow'. In 1824 Ellen Parker's confinement almost killed her and she took six months to recuperate in Selby, during which time four of her brood were farmed out to their great-aunts in Colne.[71] The possibility of post-natal melancholy was widely recognized and the experience of it acknowledged by the sufferers. It is estimated today that between 50 and 80 per cent of mothers will suffer a fleeting bout of 'the blues' shortly after birth, between 7 and 30 per cent will endure a more prolonged post-natal depression and a blighted 0.1–0.2 per cent will be assailed by puerperal psychosis.[72] However, low spirits were by no means inevitable; biological experience could bear quite differently on different women despite their shared cultural assumptions and similar background.

Moreover, the rate of recovery both physical and emotional also varied for individual women from confinement to confinement. In 1749 Anne Stanhope's post-partum sufferings put her family to 'a great deal of concern'. The doctor was called in and she was bled repeatedly, but fortunately her husband the Leeds merchant Walter Stanhope was able to report 'in all our hurry abot its Mama, we have had no care, nor trouble' with the baby. A later birth was much less physically damaging to the mother. In March 1753 Stanhope was thankful that 'never any body coud have a more easy & speedy delivery, than she had'. Catastrophically, however, the infant began to fail within days of birth and to compound the family's distress, the elder boy Watty was seized with 'convulsion fits' heralding the onset of smallpox. A wretched Walter Stanhope feared his wife was 'not recovered enough to bear such a shock'. However, by April 1753 he was able to report 'your sister has been low this day or two', in the sombre aftermath of the baby's funeral, but 'in other ways she is [purely] recovered'. Conversely, in 1783 Betty Parker of Alkincoats was less well after the birth of her second child than after the first because 'her labour was rather more severe than before'. Her doctor gave strict instructions to keep her quiet and cool which he hoped would 'abate the fever and danger that usually ensue'. Uncharacteristically, the widowed Anne Robbins retrieved her wits and strength very shortly after her fifth delivery in 1814 and, unusually for her, was able to name her daughter almost immediately. Still grieving for her barrister husband, however, her spirits took months to revive.[73] Even for seasoned matrons the aftermath of birth remained hard to predict.

Once safely delivered, the neonate had to be sustained. Well before the birth elite women had decided whether they themselves would breast-feed the baby, and depending upon that decision had hired a nursery maid or found a wet-nurse. Such decisions have assumed a totemic role in many accounts of eighteenth-century motherhood. Somewhat perversely, Stone and Trumbach have both used the incidence of maternal breast-feeding as an index of blooming mother love in the period, by implication indicting all those apparently unloving mothers who bottle-feed today.[74] Growing expectations that the ideal mother would breast-feed her own babies have been routinely remarked throughout the period 1600–1850, but whether a precise chronology can be constructed on the basis of propaganda is questionable. However, rigorous study by Valerie Fildes of all the available options verifies that the national trend over the period was one of increasing dissatisfaction with the alternatives to mother's own breast-milk.[75] What this meant for practice at the local level at any particular point in time is another matter. While acknowledging the direction of change, Judith Lewis finds a striking diversity in infant feeding among the fifty noblewomen at the heart of her study. Despite an increase in maternal breast-feeding from 1760 to 1850, no single custom prevailed.[76] What a national increase in maternal breast-feeding says about the complexities of maternal emotion for individuals also remains obscure. In fact, when eighteenth-century ideologues urged the 'natural duty' of breast-feeding, their principal lure was that the practice was beneficial to the mother's health.[77] The exact meaning of breast-feeding to a nursing mother or concerned father awaits further research.

In the genteel families studied here, discussion of feeding decisions is confined to the letters women exchanged with women. Paternal preferences seem all but irrelevant. Yet the issue was undoubtedly charged with emotion. Jane Scrimshire betrayed an anxious need to be confirmed in her own decisions when she told Elizabeth Parker 'I sho'd be glad to know whether you intend the Little one to suck or not I Hope you do', and repeatedly asked 'you have never said whether he suck'd or not Pray let me know your next'.[78] The female decisions recorded here roughly correspond with a decline in wet-nursing, but the revealed trend is by no means decisive. In the 1730s in York Anne Gossip breast-fed her babies. In the 1740s in Leeds Anne Stanhope employed a 'thorough, healthy good natured girl' to serve as a live-in wet-nurse, as did Elizabeth Parker in Colne in the 1750s. Jane Scrimshire also opted for a wet-nurse in this decade, but sent her babies out of Pontefract to be suckled.[79] In the 1760s the Londoner Bessy Ramsden breast-fed all her babies herself. In the 1780s Betty Parker's first-born was 'obliged to be brought up by the spoon as his mother has not Milk for him', provoking the grandmother's disapproval: 'God bless him he has already experienced his Disappointments what a pitty he co'd not have the breast.' However, she had the grace to concede 'his uncle name sake was brought up by hand & he is no Skeleton'.[80] In the 1810s Ellen Weeton had to abandon breast-feeding through illness and employ a live-in nurse. Elizabeth Addison suckled her babies, while the widowed Anne Robbins found relief and consolation in being a successful nurse. This is not to imply that between the 1730s and the 1820s women made a simple, once and for all choice between wet-nursing, artificial feeding and the breast, swayed only by contemporary medical opinion. As three of the preceding examples suggest, by no means all women were able to breast-feed, whatever their convictions.

The earliest account of the suckling and weaning of babies is that of Jane Scrimshire, who left a nursing record for the two youngest of her three children, Jenny, Tommy and Deborah. Born 19 June 1753, Tom Scrimshire was nursed away from home. He came back for at least two visits; his mother received regular reports and recorded her satisfaction. Tom was put into short coats in December 1753, he cut his first tooth in February 1754, and at nine months his mother began 'to think of Weaning in about a Months time as the Learned say they shod never suck Less than half a year, not beyond a Whole year'. In September 1754, at fifteen months, he returned to the family for good. Deborah Scrimshire, however, was nursed away for a mere five months. Born in May 1756, when she came home for a visit in November her mother was loath to part with her, whatever the opinion of the learned. 'Debby has been at Home these two months' wrote Jane in January 1757, 'her Pappa says nothing about her Going, so I shall not. She has got two teeth . . .' It appears that the babe was promptly weaned, but the wet-nurse was subsequently hired as nursery maid.[81] It should go without saying that the mere fact of wet-nursing is no proof in itself of maternal indifference or callous neglect.

Bessy Ramsden nursed her four children, Billy, Betsy, Tommy and Dick herself. 'As I am a nurse,' she reported in 1768, 'I take great care of myself and drink porter like any fishwoman.' But breast-feeding was not without its difficulties and side effects. Dame Bessy suffered headaches, loss of concentration and diminishing sight all of which she attributed to nursing, yet she was determined to persevere: 'I have been almost Blind & am still dim sighted. It tis Thought that suckeling is the occasion of it, but I don't care to give a hearing to that subject, as my littel Tommy shall not Loose his comfort, Tho' his Mama's peepers suffer for it.' Nevertheless, Bessy Ramsden was evidently conversant with the positive benefits of her practice:

> My Littel Boy has not for this three week been from my Bed or lap half hour at a time. For to my shame (Tho' happy it was for him) I still suckel him. therefore dear Madam do not take it into your head that I am in an increacing way for thank God I am not.

Either she drew on the widespread belief in the contraceptive power of prolonged lactation, or she acknowledged the conservative prohibition against intercourse while breast-feeding. Either way, she registered a desire to delay weaning and control her own fertility.[82] Weaning, however, might also have been postponed for its own sake, for it was seen as an arduous transition, traumatic and very dangerous for the child and possibly hazardous for the breast-feeding mother:

> Betsy is to be shod tomorrow & in a month will I hope be able to run alone: but what will you think when I tell you she is not yet Weaned. how to set about it is more than I know: this may serve to shew that some of your suspicions are Groundless & that the number of your relations is not Likely to encrease soon at least at the Charterhouse.[83]

Women were not unaware of expert opinion and fashion, yet the decision to commence weaning could be swayed by contingent factors. In 1756 Jane Scrimshire had Deb weaned before the six-month 'minimum' simply because she wanted the infant home. Women's ambivalence on the issue of weaning had not waned by the early nineteenth century, neither had the vagaries of circumstance. Ellen Weeton had her daughter Mary weaned earlier than she would have liked because of the nurse's uncivil conduct: 'I am sorry to wean the child so soon, but the nurses conduct has been so very reprehensible, that I must part with her. She has behaved well to the child, and had she been but commonly civil to me in any degree trusty I would have kept her some months longer'.[84] In 1813, well aware of current medical opinion, Elizabeth Addison consciously delayed weaning her ten-month old baby boy. Perhaps she breast-fed in order to avoid another pregnancy, for her fears of childbirth were intense: 'I nurse him yet,' she declared, 'notwithstanding the fashion of weaning at 3 or 4 months.' Three months later, only outright conflict with medical authority forced her hand: 'I have at last weaned [my little boy] much against my inclination,' she reported, 'but I was persuaded to it or at least ordered to do it, by Mr Shuttleworth when he attended John.'[85] Whatever the timing, however, 'the arduous task of weaning', like teething, was a source of considerable anxiety to both parents across the eighteenth century, as indeed it had been in earlier centuries. Still these northern remarks offer considerable evidence to support the contention that infant feeding was an area of considerable female autonomy, women being prepared to resent and resist medical opinion which did not suit their own inclinations. As James Nelson complained in 1753, 'the precise Term of a Child's sucking is a point much controverted, particularly among Ladies, but nothing ascertain'd'.[86]

*   *   *

In the elite family the care of and responsibility for young children fell principally to the mother, supported by a nursery maid. Even with the help of a servant, it is evident women found their responsibilities all-consuming, leaving little or no time for the pleasures and activities of spinsterhood or the honeymoon years. What is less clear, however, is the precise division of labour between a mother and nursemaid. It would appear plausible that maids performed the menial tasks such as cleaning, washing, making children's meals and sewing, while mothers amused, educated and disciplined their children. But here evidence is at its most fragmentary. Bessy Ramsden felt her nursery maid had enough to do without needlework, consequently she spent the evenings trying to catch up with her making and mending, and bewailed 'it is not without Constant imploy that I can keep them out of Raggs'. Yet Bessy was undoubtedly an extraordinary employer. She fully expected her friends to expostulate, 'What, don't her maids do the needel work?'[87] In the 1780s Betty Parker employed a full-time nurse, who was supposed to be with the infant at all times, enabling the mother to continue a comparatively lively local social life. Half a century later Ellen Parker declared when a mother of one, 'I have not a regular nurse girl, only an occasional assistant when busy'. But in the 1820s, with a growing brood of five she was forced into reliance on

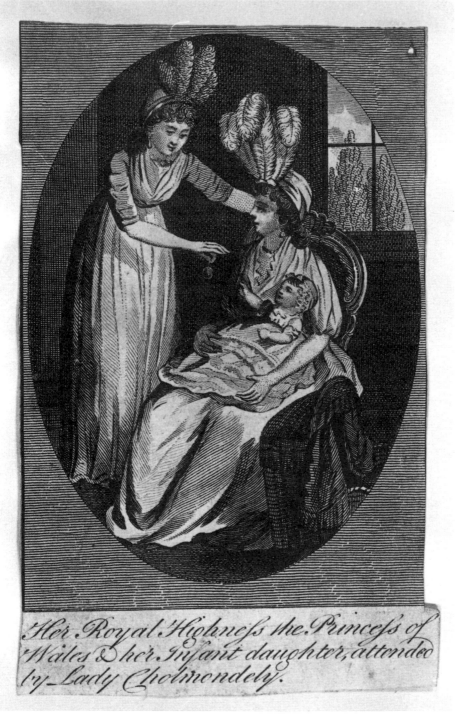

Her Royal Highness the Princess of Wales & her Infant daughter, attended by Lady Cholmondely.

19 'Her Royal Highness the Princess of Wales & her Infant daughter, attended by Lady Chomondely', 1797. Royal maternity is celebrated in this image of the unfortunate Princess Charlotte as a babe in arms, born in 1796. The young princess died lingeringly in childbed in November 1817, aged twenty-one, an event that registered in the letters of countless ladies that year.

MORNING DRESS.

20 'Morning Dress', depicting an affectionate mother and child, from *Ackermann's Repository of Arts* (1810).

21   'Goodnight', 1808, depicting another indulgent mother.

a regular maid, something which proved a chronic source of anxiety. She feared some women were too feeble to manage the turbulent spirits in her nursery, while others she suspected of neglect and outright cruelty when her back was turned.[88]

This is not to imply that elite mothers spent only an amusing couple of hours each evening with their offspring. Nursemaids were seen as a supplement to the mother, not a replacement. Children were routinely described as companions and mothers took seriously their role as educators and entertainers. In the 1770s Bessy Ramsden was reported reading the new play to her brood and she presided over the staging of a play. In order to see how 'her Bratts *behave* themselves' and because she still had 'a Taste for tweedledum & tweedle dee', she accompanied them to children's parties and private balls and took 'the tribe' out on jaunts to Greenwich and Kensington. In fact, Mrs Ramsden claimed (not with unvarnished truth as it turned out) that for the sake of taking the children out into the sunshine, she had given up visiting entirely.[89] Anna Larpent consciously saw herself as a teacher. She set aside 'stated times for regular study even in infancy'; and devised a rigorous programme of domestic reading for her yawning young sons. Countless afternoons were spent escorting them round educational exhibitions and panoramas. Larpent took issue with much fashionable educational theory, disagreeing with Maria Edgeworth on many points and boasting subsequently,

> I never found my children troublesome – I always tried to feed their minds as well as their bodies . . . by encouraging observation & interest in what they see. & by early giving them an idea of getting information . . . I was always ready to hear them read spell &c. A good nurse should always be ready to suckle her child. A good mother should always be ready to feed its mind.[90]

In the 1810s, although never believing she was 'calculated for a School Mistress', another Londoner, the widow Anne Robbins, taught her children reading, writing, spelling, Latin grammar, accounts and geography.[91] A complete maternal performance, from which many women drew much pride, could be intellectually as well as practically demanding.

Even for the employing classes, the social constraints of child-rearing were very real. If the different roles of men and women were discussed in relationship, men were associated with important matters and women with children: 'I hear Mrs Parker is confined by the natural effects of matrimony and yourself by the workmen', wrote Ned Parker to his cousin Robert Parker in 1754.[92] Motherhood devoured almost all reserves of physical and emotional energy for, at the very least, a decade of a fertile woman's life. Ten years of Elizabeth Parker's life (c.1753–62) were absorbed by pregnancies and caring for children under five; Jane Scrimshire spent eleven years so employed (c.1751–61); and Bessy Ramsden thirteen (c.1763–75). All three women became poor correspondents for this period of their lives. Indeed, Jane Scrimshire prophesied in 1752 that Elizabeth Parker's long, witty letters would soon be a thing of the past: 'therefore Dear Mad'm pursue it as long as you're able for I have a Strange Suspicion that when you become a Mother & a Housekeeper you'll be as bad as some other people . . .' And sure enough Mrs Scrimshire was soon able to tease the young matron: 'I am not at all surpriz'd you don't answer your Correspondents as punctually as you used to Do.' But Scrimshire had to make similar amends herself, pleading maternal responsibilities: 'I ought to have thank'd my dear Mrs Parker last post for the many Civilitys & favours we Recd at Alkincoats but a thousand Petits riens that happens in Familys prevented me giving myself that pleasure and you a Journal of our travels.'[93] No born correspondent, Bessy Ramsden's letter-writing lapsed almost completely in the 1760s, since husband William was prepared to maintain the correspondence on her behalf. William completed her half-finished letters and made her excuses: 'Mrs R. was called up to her Nursery or she woud not have left off so abruptly.' Her occasional letters are testament to constant domestic interruption: 'My littel folks are making such a noise that I cannot tell what I write.' It was not until 1773 that she felt in a position to contemplate devoting time to letter-writing:

> my time is always imployed and if I do take a pen I always meet with some interrupsion – but I hope now to mend – as I have Lay'd by my cradle I shall have more time and be quite a fine Lady, thank God the Barns [are] now . . . out of the way in the nursery . . . My little folks are now pestering me [for] their Tea, so shall conclud.[94]

In fact, motherhood was so well associated with a decline of social intercourse that a lazy, but unmarried correspondent was able to jest, 'would you advise me to be married and then I can get my mother in law to write *all* my letters, for when I am Breeding, therefore consequently sick, it will be a good excuse to save myself the trouble'. Mary Warde complained when a distant correspondent mounted the altar: 'it was very elegantly said by Orinda to Poliarchus that the Marriage of a Friend is the Funeral of Friendship.'[95] Once embarked upon a maternal course, married women had only limited time and creative energy to invest in anything beyond household and kin; a point forcibly made by an extraordinary woman, Hester Thrale, when criticized for her incomplete record of Doctor Johnson's sayings:

> little do these wise Men know or feel, that the Crying of a young Child, or the Perverseness of an elder, or the Danger however trifling of any one – will soon drive out of a female Parent's head a Conversation concerning Wit, Science or Sentiment, however She may appear to be impressed with it at the moment: besides that to a *Mere de Famille* doing something is more necessary & suitable than even hearing something; and if one is to listen all Eveng and write all Morning what one has heard; where will be the Time for tutoring, caressing, or what is still more useful, for having one's Children about one: I therefore charge all my Neglect to my young one's Account . . .'[96]

As new mothers, genteel women became less mobile and their time for company was radically reduced. Although Jane Scrimshire and Elizabeth Parker longed to meet 'to Compare notes about our young ones', they reconciled themselves to the indefinite postponement of cross-county visits while carrying and nursing their infants. Bessy and William Ramsden never embarked on their long-discussed trip to Lancashire and Yorkshire.

Initially, the long journey north was thought too much for the babies and later plans were scotched by the children's numerous illnesses. In 1768, breast-feeding her third child, the ever-gregarious Bessy Ramsden complained that she had only got out of the house three times since her confinement. She felt obliged to pay a promised visit, 'but the Lord knows when, for I find full imployment in my nursery'.[97] Still, as time went on, a semblance of pre-children social life was re-established. Deputizing a willing husband or trusted servant for a few hours, cards, tea, assemblies and oratorios might again be enjoyed in polite urban centres like Preston, Pontefract, York and London. For the women of the remote Whalley parish, however, polite sociability depended upon considerable mobility and long visits. Elizabeth and Robert Parker made at least one tour alone together without their children, though not without detailed progress reports from the children's nurse; and, after at least a five-year delay, the Scrimshires made the trip from Pontefract to Colne in the summer of 1757. With much planning, packing and determination, it was possible for an older family to be fairly mobile. By the late 1760s the Ramsdens were escaping the disease-ridden capital every summer to tour about the home counties and south coast in two post-chaises, and once Elizabeth Parker's sons went to school and she purchased an all-weather carriage, her friends anticipated a resumption of local jaunting.[98]

The surviving records for the later period confirm the foregoing account of maternal mobility and freedom. In 1816 both Eliza Whitaker and Anne Robbins complained that 'family concerns' had eaten into letter-writing time.[99] In the same year Elizabeth Addison wrote wistfully about her lapsed oil painting in terms strikingly similar to those used by the harassed Bessy Ramsden of the 1760s: 'I fear it will be a long time before I can resume my studies in that way, for whenever I fix to begin something occurs to employ my time – more than ever, Surely when my 3 little boys go into trousers then I can begin.'[100] The picture which emerges from the Barcroft network is an altogether consistent one. Ellen Parker's letters had a familiar tendency to end abruptly: '[Elizabeth] . . . is crying to Mama to nurse her, *therefore* you will excuse a short, hasty & uninteresting letter.' After worried complaints about her erratic correspondence, Ellen Parker had to impress upon her querulous aunts the real limits on her time: 'recollect there is only myself to superintend our domestic concerns and with them, my Nursery and frequent additions to my Family I have not always at my command the [grea]test part of a Morning or afternoon, which is the time my *lengthy* epistles generally occupy.' However, from the same pen comes a reminder that even the arguably closeted mother of the 1810s and 1820s was prepared to persevere when determined. Taking advantage of the improved road and coach network across the Pennines, Ellen Parker travelled alone in 1817 from Selby to Colne (forty-five miles away) to introduce her baby son Ambrose to her Colne aunts. She refused to find the journey an inconvenience and was determined not to be confined to a nursery on arrival, asking for 'an old clothes basket – *There must be one with a handle too, to carry* [Ambrose] *about in.*'[101] Throughout the period, the smothering potential of maternity is fully evident; nevertheless women's efforts to surface were as vigorous in the 1820s as in the 1750s and earlier.

After childbirth itself, life-threatening illness was the supreme trial that parents faced. Contagion circulated all about eighteenth-century parents, invading their nurseries and doubtless their nightmares. As inevitably as the ripening of the fruit, epidemics of dysentery, typhoid, enteric fever, spotted fever, putrid fever and smallpox (to name but a few) scourged the cities and towns of Georgian England through late summer to the first frosts. Diptheria and typhus raged in the winter. The emotional cost of illness was dear to both parents; the father's panic was as conspicuous as the mother's anguish when the lives of beloved babies hung in the balance. Yet, of course, the full burden of nursing fell to the mother. Indeed, most letters relating the facts of family illness to the kindred were written by men, as women could not be spared from the bedside. The extent to which a mother's role was interchangeable with that of sick-nurse is demonstrated here by the correspondence of the London Ramsdens. That the metropolitan experience was not necessarily exceptional is confirmed by the tragic history of the Gossip family of Skelton, Yorkshire. The experience of both families bears detailed reconstruction here to convey one of the monumental concerns of adult life. Witnessing the acute suffering of one's children was a virtually universal ordeal, capable of obliterating every other thought in the head of the near-helpless parent, yet, strangely, it is a test which merits barely a sentence in many accounts of genteel life and philosophy.

A startling (though not necessarily comprehensive) record of children's illness and the toll on the family is provided by the Ramsden letters between 1764 and 1774. 'A Married Life I find is full of cares', sighed Bessy Ramsden in August 1764, reporting the two weeks she had just spent nursing her fevered daughter Betsy. Unbeknownst to her, this lament heralded a decade of intermittent sickness in the Charterhouse nursery. From October to December of that year Mrs Ramsden attended both Betsy and her brother Billy who had contracted smallpox. Under the circumstances, William Ramsden feared his wife would nurse herself ill, but was proud to report that she 'performed her Part like an experienced

Matron'. When the two children caught the measles in December 1765, William had to complete Bessy Ramsden's abandoned letter explaining 'one or the other [of her children] are upon her lap almost all day long'. The next year the children apparently recontracted measles from the Charterhouse schoolboys; Bessy was busy in the nursery for the whole month of December. The year 1767 was a particularly gruelling one. When the Charterhouse matron was dismissed that year, Mrs Ramsden found herself responsible for the welfare of 'about fortty boys . . . to make mend wash & nurse when sick', besides the care of her own family. Her own children suffered a series of undiagnosed illnesses, were repeatedly taken to the doctor and bled. William reported Bessy (herself pregnant and ill) had not 'a hand, or even a finger to spare'. She spent at least three weeks in October so completely confined to the nursery that at the first signs of recovery she was wild to get out of the house.[102]

When Tom, the new baby, caught the whooping cough in June 1768, the Ramsdens received the advice of two physicians, 'besides good women's nostrums in abundance.' Bessy Ramsden spent a fearful fortnight in February 1769, 'wholly taken up with her own little boy'; Tom was so ill the Ramsdens prepared to lose him. In fact, the worst was yet to come. In May 1770 Billy contracted scarlet fever, which then spread from Betsy to Tom and from him to the new baby Dick. With all four children 'set on fire' throughout the summer holidays, William had to second Bessy in the sick-room. 'In all my Distress,' declared William, 'Providence has [been] very indulgent to me by sparing her Health.' In September 1772 the family fled the smallpox which had broken out next door, but to no avail, as the two youngest boys succumbed. Tom was left scarred, while Dick suffered upsetting recurrences until April 1773:

> Mrs Nurse has held up a Miracle, many a time has my heart ached for Her while the Mind was on the Stretch between Hope and Fear, the machine kept a going; tho' I coud perceive it wearing down daily. The worst was to be apprehended when we came to *ruminate* on what was past.

By 1774 Bessy Ramsden could justifiably say 'they have now thank God, gone thro all the deseases that children [are] liable too', while William Ramsden concluded in more poetic vein, 'what bitter Sweets are these Olive branches.' Obviously the London experience could be extreme, as the Ramsdens acknowledged, waxing dramatic on the infections swirling in the air of the metropolis and the importance of rural escape in high summer. Yet, illness could still scythe through the provinces. Seventy children were reported dead in the Colne smallpox epidemic of 1776, while 'prodigious numbers' were carried off in a further outbreak in 1782.[103]

The large Gossip family of Skelton and later Thorp Arch was mortified by disease in the middle decades of the eighteenth century. Anne Gossip bore eleven children between 1732 and 1745, but only three outlived her. Harrowingly, four treasured babes died in their mother's arms before seeing a second birthday; an infant boy was stillborn; a fine boy was lost aged eleven; and two sons perished in their twenties. Friends and relatives sympathized with 'the constant fears' plaguing 'poor Mrs Gossip', for the threat of mortal illness hovered over this newly landed family like the mythical sword.[104] When William Gossip was away from his wife and 'our little flock', he turned his eyes homeward in an ecstasy of hope and dread. In June 1746 Gossip was alarmed at Buxton when naught but silence met the six letters he had despatched; was something the matter with the children? – he could not help but wonder. In 1750, when Anne Gossip was again separated from her husband and one of her sons, she also needed constant reassurance: 'I long to know how you and poor Jack do.'[105] Terrible decisions had to be taken to preserve the children. In August 1746, when one son threw off a mild strain of smallpox with comparative ease, Anne Gossip decided to expose the other under the supervision of an apothecary in Ripon. To her terrified dismay the dreaded 'pestilence' took a vicious hold. William Gossip despatched letters of support and advice by every other post: 'I heartily pity my dearest life, who I am sure must have been in a terrible fright for my poor Willy: God almighty bless and pre-serve you both, & give blessing to the means used for his Recovery.' Happily, in this instance, 'God almighty's mercy & goodness' along with Anne Gossip's 'tender care' restored the little boy. By October a relieved father found cause for cautious optimism: 'I hope now the fruit season is over, my lads will recover their good looks . . .'[106] But as we already know, further affliction awaited this doomed family. Nineteen years and many unrecorded tragedies later, William Gossip groaned 'Will our misfortunes never end!' His son Tom had fallen into fits, Wilmer was delirious, Randy was 'almost paralysed to death' and his own stoic philosophy was near exhausted. 'I wish I could send you a line of comfort but I cannot with any truth . . . I am yr almost heart broke W. Gossip'. As he concluded, 'a melancholy catalogue indeed.'[107] Providence did not temper the wind to these Yorkshire lambs.

The Gossips saw their worst nightmares realized, but in their anxieties they were not unusual. In Pontefract Jane Scrimshire worried about childish 'distempers', whether her children fell ill or not. Her social life was similarly curtailed, not only by the sick-room, but by the mere risk of infection. After the death of a friend's child from a 'bad sort' of measles, Michael Scrimshire went alone to visit his relations in Bradford, as his wife refused to leave her children for longer than a night. Mrs Scrimshire also had to warn off Elizabeth Parker from visiting Pontefract, on account of infection, 'I Can't *in Conscience* Conceal we have the Smallpox within two doors of us', and when trying to lure her back insisted 'we're Clear of all Distempers except the Consumption and that not a *Bodily* Complaint'.[108] In the event, the visit was cancelled because of illness in the Parker nursery. Meanwhile, regular bulletins issued from the northern grammar schools on the incidence of disease among the boys. When a 'filthy distemper' broke out at Bradford Grammar School in 1757, Anne Stanhope refused to take her son back to school until she had been over herself to confirm 'that they are all thoroughly clear'.[109]

Half a century later maternal preoccupation with sick children and the sinister stirrings of infection in the locality were still standard themes of women's letters and diaries. When her children were ill at home in the 1790s, Anna Larpent suffered 'extreme anxiety' and attendance at the sick bed 'emply'd every moment of my time, every thought of my mind'. Meanwhile, her household business went undone and presumably her journal unwritten until somewhat later. 'The utmost care being necessary claimed my attendance on the child, altho he was certainly gradually recovering, yet I can enter on no employment, for he was still in the lowest anxious state.' At school the risk of infection was ever-present; the irruption of fever at the boys' school in Cheam provoked a frantic dash to withdraw the children.[110] Ellen Parker's experience in the 1820s was analogous to that of Bessy Ramsden in the 1760s. Despite the fact that her children were vaccinated for smallpox, scarcely a month went by without one of her numerous children succumbing to, or recuperating from illness. Her letters catalogue dangerous coughs, irruptions in the face, outbreaks of typhus fever and Ellen's chronic fear and fatigue, which of course she dismissed with the traditional female selflessness: 'my little indisposition merely proceeded from a slight cold and the broken rest & anxiety the baby occasioned, but was altogether so trivial . . .'[111] In the same decade, the Greene family apprehensively experimented with inoculation for smallpox convinced of the inefficacy of vaccination, only to see their darling baby daughter suffer horribly. Together they struggled to rationalize the decision they had taken: 'The inefficacy of Vaccination in preventing small pox daily experience shews, the Medical Men who were Strenuous in its Favor, are now at a dead Pause, Dr Pope, our friend at Staines, has six nieces just recovering from the small pox all of them were vaccinated some years ago.'[112] Yet, however many times a child's life hung in the balance, even a single vigil at the bedside was intensely real to its mother and father.[113] For to be a parent was to be keenly exposed to the vagaries of fate.

Still, child-rearing was not unremitting misery, it was widely recognized that caring for children could be profoundly rewarding and highly amusing. Self-conscious domesticity was no invention of the early Victorians. A studied maternity was relished by Jane Pellet in the 1750s who sent kisses to 'little Marmouset (as lady G. Calls it)', emulating the tender, blushing motherhood which redeems the lively Charlotte Grandison in *Sir Charles Grandison*. The satisfactions inherent in the most routine aspects of family life were proclaimed again and again by the Ramsdens of the Charterhouse in the 1760s and 1770s: 'On my left hand sits Madam darning of stockings, on my right is our heir apparent reading the News; Betsy is making a Cap for her Doll, Tom and Dick are playing at Marbles on the carpet. To say more of Ourselves will be needless.'[114] The fascinations of child-rearing were canvassed as readily at the end of the period: 'I hope your little treasure and may I say your little *companion* is going on well,' wrote a friend of Eliza Whitaker's in 1816, 'engaging your attention by a thousand interesting little ways, he is just growing into the fascinating age.'[115] Proud parenthood radiated from the young mothers and fathers of the Greene clan in the 1820s: 'Willm & Ann are so proud of their little Girl, that they seem almost jealous of the Group that are advancing to put her nose out of joint. He, in the pride of his heart said the other day "They'll none of them have a nicer child than ours" They will all think the same of their own, I dare say.'[116] Ellen Weeton Stock's letter-books leave no doubt that she lavishly cherished her dumpling of a baby girl:

> My little Mary improves, and is the delight of all; she is just 16 months old. She does not say a word yet, notwithstanding which, she has a thousand little engaging actions. Her hair is very light, and curls all over her head like a little mop; and she is all over so fat and so soft. I have many a kiss in the course of the day, and many a laugh at her little droll ways; her father would be quite lost without her, and I am sure, so should I. I wish I had another . . . but hush! don't tell.[117]

From the first, Mary Stock provided her parents with sensual compensation for their disastrous marriage. Abundant affection and sentimental pleasure were widely expressed by genteel parents. Yet for all the sentimentality, the more compelling impression which emerges from their manuscripts is one of gritty emotional endurance. The cumulative impact of reading letters and diaries written in both joy and affliction is to bring home the sheer stamina upon which these parents had to draw. Yet there is no evidence whatsoever that fond parents gave of themselves partially and warily with one eye on the bills of mortality and the other on a comfortable old age. Lawrence Stone's assertion that high infant and child mortality cauterized parental affection is doubtful, and his belief that 'the value of children rises as their durability improves' highly questionable. Few Georgian parents could stem self-sacrificing emotion when confronted with a stricken child: 'Most willingly wou'd I make a pilgrimage barefoot as far as my legs would carry me, to get the poor little Fellow cured', supplicated Reverend Ramsden in 1772. It was not for nothing that Dr Johnson listed 'tenderness, parental care' as one of his dictionary definitions of love.[118]

*   *   *

The production and rearing of children had a transforming effect on genteel women's lives, all but obliterating their past selves and public profile, but the vista from the conjugal bed was far from clear. Established pregnancy was as unpredictable in its outcome as it was inexorable in its progress. The biological bore quite differently on different women. True, biology was mediated by culture: it was the custom of denying the neonate colostrum which could lead to starvation in an enfeebled infant and often milk-fever in the mother. Yet physical factors beyond a mother's immediate control often determined family fortunes – the breadth of her pelvis, or the outbreak of an epidemic were not directly subject to the dominion of discourse. When medicinal waters failed to give Barbara Stanhope a child, she had come to the frontier of culture's power over nature. Needless to say, the notion that aspects of biological experience lay beyond human management would not have surprised the genteel. That the hand of God was seen to determine so much is testimony enough to their powerful sense of culture's limits. Submission to one's natural lot was the keynote of genteel maternity. From smallpox to shirt-making, the epoch of motherhood is minutely catalogued in women's records, but rarely is the totality of maternity put into words and never is it questioned. But then motherhood was not a discrete event, or the work of a day, it was the quintessential labour of love which knew no clock and spent itself in endless small services, a thousand little nothings. In its boundless details, mothering swamped genteel matrons even as it defined them.

This chapter has focused on the trials and pleasures of motherhood, in an effort to recreate one of the dominant employments of genteel women, but all this should not be taken to imply that a father's feelings for, or involvement with his children was negligible. William Ramsden's paternal satisfaction gushed from his pen in 1763, writing

> from the arm of my Wife's easy Chair, a Situation I wo'd not change [with] the King of Prussia: no, nor (with a Man a Million more times to be envy'd) with George the 3rd king of Grt Britain: my good Woman at the same time with Glee in her Eye, contemplating her little Boy, who also in his turn seems as happy as this World can make him, only [with] his Leather Bottle. Pardon this Gossip, Good Madam Parker, but the Air of a Nursery is Infecting.[119]

Ramsden often took sole responsibility for his children in the evenings when his more sociable wife skipped out to card-playing parties and, in a crisis, seconded her efforts in the sick-room. William Gossip was, in his own words, a 'very affectionate papa', to whom the expression of tenderness came easily. Willy was his 'dear Jewel', while Jack was his 'Poor Rogue' of whom he quipped 'he does provoke me sometimes, yet I think I love him too'. Of his suffering Wilmer, he asked 'Does he take notice of my not being with him? I am afraid the dear creature should think himself neglected by me.' Moreover, Gossip preached to his sons what he practised himself: 'my dear needs never be ashamed of showing affection to your relations'; apparently with some success, as his adult son George refused to take a foreign army posting, for fear that he would miss seeing his children grow up.[120] Across the northern networks, male correspondents dwelt with anxiety and pride on developmental hurdles cleared and crises overcome. Paternal investment could be profound.

Nevertheless, the supreme responsibility for babies and young children always devolved on the mother. When his children were around Ramsden found it difficult to think, work or write letters, witness his recorded speech when petitioned to write an overdue letter: 'now Bessy says he how can you be so unreasonable: I that have always so much Busness upon my Hands; and besides you are always Bring[ing] your Brats in the way; that I cannot settel to any thing for them.'[121] Similarly, William Gossip occasionally superintended at least some of his brood during his wife's absences, but he also recorded the disabling distraction of infantile needs: 'Fathy is by me, & keeps such a perpetual Clack, that you must excuse me if I blunder. I can't get her to hold her tongue – at last we are silent . . .'[122] In the end, as he freely acknowledged, it was the unfailing consistency of Anne Gossip's 'tender care' (along with God's mercy) which stood between her blighted babies and eternity.

The inequities of labour notwithstanding, the letters of eighteenth-century parents demonstrate the all-important reality that men and women experienced with one mind. The shared emotional capital invested in children shines out of the letters men and women exchanged. In their children, men and women were tied indissolubly to each other. In them they saw blended blood and shared destiny. Ultimately, we see the shocking precariousness of that destiny. The death of a child was a grievous loss, in the face of which common catastrophe parents had little choice but to draw deep on their stoical reserves and attempt to submit like proper Christians. Announcing the death of the 'rare thumping lad' he himself had delivered twelve years earlier, Dr William St Clare told the unsuspecting father,

> this, my dear Sir, must be considered as one of these afflicting trials, these awful warnings which are inflicted to remind us that the present is not intended to be a state of perfect happiness. There is nothing [I can write in] consolation which your own fortitude and Christian resignation will not more readily suggest.

The same belief in the sustaining power of a deliberate fortitude is found in comforting praise Walter Stanhope sent his wife Anne, who had lost three of her four children in infancy, 'I am glad to find . . . that you have behav'd with prudence in these melancholy schemes, so as not to throw yourself down.'[123] Again and again, parents struggled to resign themselves to their losses and to bear up under misfortune, clinging to the belief that their sacrifice fulfilled some divine purpose, that they had not surrendered their infants in vain. Mercifully, they did not see a child's death as a particular punishment for their own sins because the God who presided over the Georgian Church of England was not an especially wrathful deity. Instead, parents simply tried to accept a bereavement as a divine mystery. However, it would be wrong to suppose that the much-parroted language of resignation means that parents were easily reconciled to child mortality, then or earlier. Men and women brought exactly the same spiritual equipment to bear in the event of an adult's death. The bereaved were routinely urged 'to submit with the greatest Resignation to whatever the hand of providence inflicts on us, & to persuade ourselves it is for our Good in some Respect or other . . .'[124] When Abigail Gawthern lost her 'dear Eliza' to the whooping cough, she tersely recorded 'it pleased God to release her, to the inexpressible grief of her father and mother'. In an addendum replete with unspoken pathos, she noted 'she was two years and a half and six days old'. Maternal loss might be no less agonizing for the absence of hysterical expression, or the 'sable trappings of woe', for, as Mrs Gawthern herself later wrote, 'heartfelt and unaffected grief turns with disgust from the hackneyed display of ostentatious sorrow'.[125] If anything, the prevalence of the vocabulary of Christian endurance speaks to the unutterable power of parental grief, not to its weakness, suggesting rather the abysmal depths of misery into which men and women might sink if ever they relaxed their grip on the rafts of courage and resignation. Contemporaries feared the thundering force of parental grief, and maternal anguish in particular was recognized as a 'species of savage despair'.[126] Moreover, desolation could snuff out a mother's own life and her overlasting soul, so to survive grief was seen as an act of will. Thus, a studied fortitude was a crucial necessity once embarked on the parental course. For, as parents, men and women stood side by side, watching the unfathomable waters of providence lapping ominously and relentlessly at their undefended feet.

THE

L A D I E S

MOST ELEGANT AND CONVENIENT

POCKET BOOK,

For the YEAR 1776.

CONTAINING

Amongst a great Variety of useful, ornamental, and instructive Articles, the following:

The necessary Pages for Engagements, Memorandums, and Expences, ruled in a more plain and familiar Manner than any yet adapted for the Use of the Ladies; Poetical Address to the Ladies: Holidays at the different Offices; Remarkable Days in the Year; Prose Address to the Ladies; A Letter from her present Majesty to the King of Prussia; Poetry; Favourite New Songs sung at the public Gardens; Country Dances; Marketing and Interest Tables; Rates of Coachmen, Chairmen, &c. &c.

Compiled at the Request of several Ladies of Quality.

Printed for J. WHEBLE, No. 22, Fleet-Street; and sold by J. BEW, in PATER-NOSTER ROW.

22   Title-page from Elizabeth Shackleton's Pocket Diary of 1776.

4

Prudent Economy

The Management of all Domestic Affairs is certainly the proper
Business of Woman; and unfashionably rustic as such an Assertion
may be thought, 'tis certainly not beneath the Dignity of any Lady,
however high her rank, to know how to educate her children, to
govern her servants, to order an elegant Table with Oeconomy, and
to manage her whole family with Prudence, Regularity and method
(1761).[1]

I must assert that the right of directing domestic affairs, is by the
law of nature in the woman, and that we are perfectly qualified for
the exercise of dominion, notwithstanding what has often been said
to the contrary . . . Experience is wholly on our side; for where-ever
the master exceeds his proper sphere, and pretends to give law to
the cook maid as well as the coach man, we observe a great deal of
discord and confusion . . . But when a woman of tolerable good
sense is allowed to direct her house without controul, all Things go
well; she prevents even her husband's wishes, the servants know
their business and the whole family live easy and happy (1765).[2]

The Domestic oeconomy of a family is entirely a woman's province,
and furnishes a variety of subjects for the exertion both of good
sense and good taste. If you ever come to have charge of a family,
it ought to gain much of your time and attention (1774).[3]

THE WRITERS OF ADVICE LITERATURE groomed genteel women for the
exercise of power. The effective government of servants had long
been seen as an essential duty. Women were tutored on the careful choice
and moral regulation of servants, on the rewarding of the industrious and
the expulsion of the immoral. They were told to sustain their sway
through the exhibition of judicious reason, and were cautioned not to

weaken their authority through capricious direction or over-correction. Like good kings, good mistresses had no favourites and did not stoop to familiarities. Instead, they were to exhibit that general courtesy and good breeding which generated universal respect and affection. On this depended the credit and happiness of a family. A virtuous female superintendent was an indispensable member of the genteel Georgian household.

For their part, gentlemen bestirred themselves to ensure that a kinswoman presided over their housekeeping. Thus, when Robert Parker lost his last close female relative in April 1748, among many letters of condolence, he received advice of a downright sort: 'There's nothing for you now but marrying,' wrote his friend and business partner, 'don't think of keeping house with servants, in my opinion there's few to be trusted.' But of his pressing domestic needs Robert Parker required no reminding. He had to cry off both entertainments and administrative duties for want of a housekeeper, because his grandmother's death 'has left me a family to manage, which I am not ye least fit for & what to do with them and myself God knows.' Within a month he had had enough: 'I am already tired of Housekeeping, but don't know how to help it.' Similarly, in 1742 the Lancastrian William Stout was heartily relieved to have his niece undertake the management of his household. His brother Josias Stout was served by their mother in this capacity, until she grew too infirm, when she 'was urgent upon him to marry, he not being willing to keepe house with a servant'. The Yorkshire widower Thomas Birkenshaw made no bones of the fact that he needed a wife to run his household in the late 1770s as his servants were ruining him:

> I found that servants and housekeepers were not to be trusted, I had no grandmother, no mother, no sister . . . upon whom I might rely, and who might in good measure, supply the place of a wife, in taking care of my children and looking after the concerns of my family. I had it not therefore, in my choice . . . to marry or not to marry. No imperious necessity, arising from the state of my family, required me to get a wife as speedily as possible. During the state of my widowhood, for want of a wife in the house when I was absent, I had already suffered to my own knowledge, to the amount of forty or fifty pounds at least, by downright thievery, so that continuing as I was, I had no prospect before me but ruin.

Male desire to have a relative as housekeeper appears unabated in the later period, and indeed the Victorian widower's recourse to the services of his dead wife's sister was proverbial.[4]

Demonstrably, when gentlemen dabbled in the marriage market they hoped to procure a bride as prudent and economical as she was charming and genteel. The manufacturer Edward Parker had second thoughts about his favoured damsel, a Miss Holt, whom he had visited three times at home and gallanted to a play, when he discovered her extravagance. By contrast, the self-made William Gossip found in his bride an unpaid housekeeper as dutiful and continent as any paragon of Protestant pre-scription: 'for sure no woman of your fortune was ever less expensive.'[5] A clear appreciation of female management skills is apparent in a host of masculine manuscripts. When John Parker pleaded with his unmarried daughter to return from one of her jaunts in 1749, his increasing reliance on her superior administrative powers was made explicit:

> Dr Child I shall be glad of yr Company at home for I know not how we goe on; for Peggy & Tom doe nothing but play the Foole togeather from morning to night & she is very heedless, & [what] with workmen & serv[ants] this house as I now grow into years is quite above my hand to manage therefore [should] be glad if I could draw myself into a narrow[er] compass & spend my remaining days in quiet & ease . . .

Similarly, when Anne Stanhope was away at her sister's, her husband Walter Stanhope grew impatient for her return, pleading his helplessness: 'ye house does not look right without you & I am no way qualified for housekeeping.' In fact, a strict division of authority was eagerly embraced by most genteel husbands. Witness William Ramsden in 1770, com-plaining of overwork during his wife's lying in: 'I wish the next Week over that I may resign the *Keys* of my *Office*, for indeed most heartily am I tired of being both *Mistress & Master*.' Indeed, cuckolded husbands who brought the common law action 'criminal conversation' against their wives' lovers, often claimed additional financial compensation for the loss of their house manager.[6]

As the mistress of a household, the genteel bride tasted of administrative power and exuded quasi-professional pride. While betrothed in the summer of 1751, Miss Elizabeth Parker of Browsholme anticipated her household responsibilities with officious excitement. Her letters were pep-pered with questions about Alkincoats, her future marital home, and she commissioned her friends and servants to bring her further information. She was particularly concerned with Robert Parker's rebuilding scheme and offered frequent opinions on the renovations. She asked to be in-formed of his design, and made specific suggestions: 'Pray let no conveniency be lost that you can make by way of Cupboards & Closets, for they are usefull in a family . . .' Throughout, she was opposed to false economies: 'for I know by experience if repairs in old houses are not done effectually they are a continual expense.' Miss Parker could not resist chivvying her betrothed about the pace of improvement, encouraging him to stick to his plans and avoid the distractions of company. 'I am very angry with you to jaunt about at this rate. I imagine you have laid aside all thoughts of yr house. Tho' you neglect it, its much my care, which I esteem a pleasure.' She grew proprietorial about Alkincoats, praying that God would grant prosperity to both the present owner and 'the owner elect', as she styled herself. In fact, her promptitude laid her open to mockery. When Miss Parker pointedly inquired of a Lancashire gentleman how he could think of inflicting his company on Robert Parker, hard at work at Alkincoats, the friend 'made answer that I was a saucy Miss and wonder'd what business I had to give myself airs, for that my share at present in [Robert Parker's] house was no more than a Goose co'd sit in.'[7] Impatience to wield authority over a household is palpable.

The status and satisfaction to be drawn from genteel housekeeping is clear from the praise paid the mistress by observant women, as here in an approving sketch of the young charmer who had induced her clerical lover to renounce a college fellowship to marry her: 'Certainly his looks do her great credit – and her good sense knows how to become the prudent domestic Wife in which character she shines as much as when in her Boudoir surrounded by her various collection of shells, feathers, and paintings of her own performance.'[8] The credit gained through housekeeping can also be judged by the regret at its passing. Resigning the post of mistress could be traumatic, as William Stout's mother found at Lancaster at the beginning of the eighteenth century. Though she herself had urged Josias Stout to marry, actually handing over the reigns of power proved unpleasant: 'But when the young wife came to housekeeping, my mother thought to have some direction in that, more than the young wife (who had been her father's housekeeper) would allow; which made their mother uneasy.'[9] Similarly, when Mrs Shackleton surrendered the management of Alkincoats to her daughter-in-law in 1779, she could not hide her pique and sense of rejection, as here when ostensibly disavowing any interest in possible mismanagement: 'God knows what all their great big Maids are doing at Alkincoats in their absence. That is nothing to me.' She could not refrain from belittling Betty Parker's efforts 'in the housekeeping way'. Mrs Shackleton noted in May 1779 that Alkincoats was under poor stewardship, 'all in sad Confusion', and she held her daughter-in-law directly responsible: 'I think Mrs P. should not molest [Tom's] things & Mrs P. to blame.' Later the same month Betty Parker further alienated her mother-in-law, by offering her a damp bed with dirty linen on an overnight visit.

Within a year, however, the new Mrs Parker began to redeem herself with conspicuously dutiful and dignified housekeeping. 'My good Daughter is a most exceedingly Good Wife, she ruffled her Husband a shirt & always is Industrious and manages with prudent Oeconomy.'[10] Like Elizabeth Shackleton, Betty Parker learned how to nourish her reputation through good housekeeping. Even letters from the missish Eliza Whitaker bespeak a gentlewoman's investment in, and protection of, her housekeeping role. Here she fishes for compliments from her young husband, hoping her invaluable contribution to the household and the happiness of its master will be missed:

> I am only fearful of your being so much at your ease in the company of your friends that you will be in no hurry for my reappearance in my domestic capacity. I make no doubt but you are an excellent house-keeper, but as I do not wish you to become very knowing in that way as I am rather anxious about the good order of my maidens, be so good as to tell the coachmen to start in the curricle between 4 & 5 o'clock on Sat morning.[11]

Female management was an established institution with recognized symbols and ceremonies endorsed by both sexes. Yet for all that, female administration has received scant attention from the historians, perhaps because its most skilful exponents self-consciously expunged any impression of laborious attention. As Hester Chapone put it, 'the best sign of a home being well governed is that nobody's attention is called to the little affairs of it'. By the mistress's sleight of hand 'all goes on so well of course that one is not led to make remarks upon anything, nor to observe any extraordinary effort that produces the general result of ease and elegance that prevails throughout'.[12] Were domestic details to obtrude, then the spell of regulation and refinement would be broken and those who advertised their pains were vulnerable to disdainful mockery. So it was that the Quaker Betty Fothergill, an opinionated journal keeper, derided in 1769 those women who made household management 'their constant theme in all companies who are unfortunate to fall in their way', and approved an acquaintance who, though a 'a remarkable good manager of her family', happily 'does not make that parade with it others do whose whole knowl-edge is centred in domestic concerns.'[13] The genteel housekeeper never went about her work with fanfare and bustle, but used art to conceal her industry. The advertisements of successful female management were subtle, possibly too subtle for the proper acknowledgement of posterity.

To be fair, historians have long recognized the contribution of the sixteenth- and seventeenth-century elite mistress, only her enterprise is usually seen as another feature of the world we have lost. 'At the beginning of the seventeenth century,' observed Alice Clark, 'it was usual for the women of the aristocracy to be very busy with affairs – affairs which concerned their household, their estates and even Government.' The management of the country estate was often left to the mistress for months at a time, while the master was away at court, or at war. As a wedding sermon promised, a good mistress had much to offer. She is like a merchant's ship, for 'she bringeth her food from far . . .' This paragon is portrayed as energetic and enterprising: 'thro her Wisdom and Diligence great things come by her; she brings in with her hands, for, *She putteth her hands to the wheel* . . . If she be too high to stain her Hands with bodily labour, yet she bringeth in with her Eye, for, She overseeth the *Ways of her Household* . . . and eateth not the Bread of *Idleness*.' In consequence of the discipline of 'productive' and 'creative' work, these sturdy housekeepers were respected comrades, notable for their initiative, resourcefulness, bravery and wit. But not for long. By the Restoration, the spread of wealth meant that the 'stern hand of economic necessity was withdrawn' from elite housekeeping, so ladies could devote themselves 'to spending money and the cultivation of ornamental qualities'. Creative housekeeping decayed, the mistress's skills atrophied, and the idle wife emerged in all her parasitic glory.[14] Housekeeping became redefined as housework – that time-consuming drudgery which is best left to servants. Thus, between 1600 and 1850, it is often assumed, traditional housekeeping fell into a decline, thereby transforming prosperous housewives into inconsequential decorations and poorer respected workers into degraded skivvies.[15]

This account of the decay of housekeeping has done little to illuminate the responsibility, activity and prestige of the eighteenth-century housekeeper, largely because the extent of home production has been made the litmus test of the 'creativity' of housekeeping. If a woman did not make butter or cloth then her contribution is seen to be negligible or merely decorative. To recover the full content and meaning of the housekeeping over the *longue durée*, this over-emphasis on a single element of women's work, 'production', must be countered. As Laurel Ulrich has said with regard to eighteenth-century America, it is time historians abandoned the spinning wheel as the ultimate icon of women's work, and in pursuit of a more inclusive analysis of work in the house she suggests an alternative symbol – the pocket:

> Much better than a spinning wheel, this homely object symbolizes the obscurity, the versatility and the personal nature of the housekeeping role. A woman sat at a wheel, but she carried her pocket with her from

room to room, from house to yard, from yard to street . . . Whether it contained cellar keys or a paper of pins, a packet of seeds or a baby's bib, a hank of yarn or a Testament, it characterized the social complexity as well as the demanding diversity of women's work.[16]

In a similar spirit, two different symbols for genteel housekeeping are proposed – the house keys and the ladies' memorandum book. The bundle of keys which jangled at a lady's waist was an obvious emblem of female domestic authority, subject, as an object, to its own fashions in the eighteenth century. Less familiar is the pocket memorandum book; yet this was both the means and the emblem of female mastery of information, without which the upper hand was lost and prudent economy obliterated. These pocket-sized memorandum books survive in virtually every English archive, packed with notes and accounts: from the number of bacon flitches hung in an attic, to the terms of a servant's contract. For they were everyday handbooks on the running of a house. They were the tool of the literate and the lasting record of the 'business' that tied the genteel housekeeper to her writing desk every morning. Mentors like Hester Chapone advised young girls to prepare just such a manual on huswifery:

> Make use of every opportunity you can find, for the laying in some store of knowledge on this subject, before you are called upon to the practice; by observing what passes before you, by consulting prudent and experienced mistresses of families and by entering in a book a memorandum of every new piece of intelligence you acquire. You may afterwards compare these with more mature observations, and you can make additions and corrections as you see occasion.[17]

Had women not recorded the details of management as instructed, then much of the evidence for this chapter on the nuts and bolts of genteel housekeeping would not exist. Take Elizabeth Shackleton's domestic memoranda. From the early 1770s her pocket diaries were roughly divided into 'Letters to Friends and Upon Business', 'Remarkable Occurrences' and 'Ordinary Occurrences, Memorandums & Accounts'. They were cross-referenced to each other, older diaries, letters, accounts and receipts and were often subsequently annotated. Some contained printed marketing tables and guides to casting-up wages, expenses and taxes; all of which demonstrates that the diaries were designed to be consulted on a regular basis. It is the evidence of systematic use combined with rich commentary on the organization of provisions, property and personnel within the household, which together indicates that the diaries functioned as a set of personal reference manuals on the mechanics of keeping house.

They catalogue the regime of the mistress housekeeper. At the core of genteel housekeeping in the seventeenth, eighteenth and nineteenth century was vigilant administration. 'She bringeth in with her Eye, for, She overseeth the *Ways of her Household.*' A lady's work was managerial.

An inevitable component of genteel administration was the management of servants. Yet to look to the leading authority on eighteenth-century servants for a sense of the mistress's responsibility might be misleading. J. J. Hecht's national study of 1956 takes as its paradigm the noble household, an elaborate structure which could incorporate over thirty distinct male posts and about ten female positions. This platonic hierarchy assumed an executive division of upper servants, who oversaw the minutiae of management: a house steward who hired and disciplined the servants, a housekeeper who kept the household accounts, a clerk of the kitchen who bought provisions and served as guardian of supplies, a butler who administered the distribution of wine and plate, a groom of the chambers who was responsible for the maintenance of furniture, and so on.[18] Together these household generals might make it possible at least, for a noblewoman to personify Lord Halifax's apparition of 'an empty airy thing' who sails 'up and down the House to no kind of purpose', looking 'as if she came thither only to make a visit'.[19] However, the aristocratic household with its formal ceremonies, ancient retainers and exalted female figurehead, cannot be expected to mirror the power relations and division of labour in the modest mansions of the genteel. Noble households represented only the very tip of the iceberg of servant employment. A steward's list for Lord Rockingham's mansion at Wentworth Woodhouse, for instance, registers a veritable army of eighty-one servants.[20] By contrast, genteel families often managed with less than ten. In fact, the tax on male servants of 1780 reveals that numerous genteel households were too unassuming to attract the attention of the enumerators, while those grander northern establishments which drew the taxman's eye still boasted only between five and eight male servants. Elizabeth Shackleton's own commentary suggests an ideal complement of about seven live-in servants – a number favoured by modest landowners nationwide, such as Francis Sitwell in the 1730s, Henry Purefoy between 1735 and 1753, Sanderson Miller in 1748 and George Betts in 1784. The rich and upwardly mobile Gossips of Skelton employed only six servants and a boy in the 1730s, though they added a butler and postillion in the 1750s, when William became Deputy-Lieutenant for the county. When a friend of Mrs Shackleton's considered retiring from the world, he contemplated living 'humbly with a small Establishment of two Women & one Man Servant'. So while a staff of seven might seem enormous by modern standards, by contemporary standards it was respectably genteel though still unpretentious.[21]

Genteel households were too small to sustain an executive division of upper servants who marshalled the lower ranks, so the genteel house-keeper had to lead from the front. Few senior female servants stayed long enough to liberate the elite mistress from the pressing demands of day-to-day supervision. Indeed, to say that female servants constituted a su-premely unreliable workforce is to offer a fatuous understatement. Serv-ant numbers, particularly female servant numbers, giddily fluctuated. Given the poor rewards and the considerable demands and humiliations of service a tendency to abscond is hardly surprising. However, looking at it from an employer's perspective, hardly a week went by when a mistress might not be reeling from a servant's flight, arranging emergency relief, procuring replacements or training new applicants. In fact, in the time-consuming co-ordination of the endeavours of permanent staff, emer-gency staff and day labourers, the mistress-housekeeper was less the gracious chatelaine than she was an impresario of staffing. Yet even in periods of relative stability, genteel mistresses felt compelled to undertake the constant surveillance of their property and provisions, and the minute supervision of the work and behaviour of their live-in staff. Characterized by stark inequalities of rank and power, combined with mutual depend-ence, which sometimes fostered affinity but often nurtured antagonism, the mistress–servant relationship was hardly an unalloyed pleasure for either party. Elite women had to work harder to bolster their authority than one might expect; as they ailed and aged some felt mastery slip from their grasp and found their dependence on insubordinate and flighty girls to be their aching Achilles heel. Bitterness in the face of apparent ingrati-tude is a testament to the evaporation of the ideal of a well-ordered hierarchy of loyal, deferential servants who cheerfully did their bidding. The government of servants was a full-time job.

Of all the mundane trials a gentlewoman faced, by far the most tedious was the acquisition and retention of honest, loyal and efficient servants. These could be acquired through placing advertisements in the press, attending hiring fairs, or applying to metropolitan register offices, but over whelmingly the most popular means was personal recommendation. Employers devoted quantities of ink to the free exchange of relevant information. In the case of Alkincoats, servants were drawn from up to a sixteen-mile radius of home. In the 1760s Mrs Shackleton had fruitlessly extended her enquiries to London, but was told 'yr VIRGINS are as scarce a commodity here as in the country'.[22] Appendix 5 details the letters Eliza-beth Shackleton recorded sending or receiving in pursuit of servants in the

1770s. Most striking is the predominance of women among her informants: seventeen women, as opposed to four men and one family. The male
informants (a miller, steward, innkeeper and a purveyor of medicine) all
had experience of employing servants and met a wide spectrum of working
people. Her female informants comprised both genteel ladies of her
acquaintance and tradeswomen. Shopkeepers, mantua-makers and milliners are revealed as important intermediaries between two worlds of
women. The absence of even a single landed gentleman is revealing about
the division of labour in polite households. Co-operation between women
was the basic mechanism of this informal employment agency. Letters
devoted to gathering and exchanging information about the local labour
market abound in the manuscripts of genteel women.[23] The search for
domestic servants was a characteristically female quest which they had to
pursue for a working lifetime.

The servant hierarchy in the genteel household bore little resemblance
to the exact and elaborate model sustained by the nobility. Elizabeth
Shackleton may well have cherished a vision of a finely graded domestic
hierarchy wherein qualified servants performed distinct roles. The system
she had managed at Browsholme incorporated under-cooks, gamekeepers,
stewards and so on, but in a more modest establishment and faced with
chronic staff shortages, she was sentenced to perpetual compromise. In her
efforts to procure women servants, she referred to the posts of cook-
housekeeper, kitchen maid, dairymaid, housemaid and chambermaid.
However, in practice, she used the titles of 'chambermaid' and 'housemaid' interchangeably, and servants were known to offer themselves as
cook, housekeeper and chambermaid. Moreover although a cook-
housekeeper was preoccupied with the preparation of food, she was also
expected to clean and sew. In practice, the labour of the kitchen maids,
chambermaids and dairymaids overlapped. Mrs Shackleton's report of
September 1770 on the brief career of an inadequate servant illuminates
the versatility expected of an 'upper maid': 'She set off from here on
Thursday morning September ye 13th on her feet in a hurry. She co'd
neither sew, wash, Iron or get meat. She has left behind her as a specimen
of her work a shirt part done of Will's which Was her Employment nine
days.'[24] Evidently, female servants were expected to be maids of all work.
Male appointees lacked specific titles. There is no reference, for instance,
to an Alkincoats groom, coachman, valet or footman, though her menservants doubtless performed some of these services. Under ideal circumstances, the Shackleton household was serviced by four maids and
probably three menservants.

Of course ideals do not translate into reality without unremitting exertion. Detailed analysis of servant employment in a single year reveals an everflowing river of unpredictable women servants pouring through the household. In the year 1772, twenty-nine women servants worked in some capacity at Alkincoats. Of this number, the length of employment can be calculated with some confidence for twenty-five women.[25] Close analysis of their careers reveal three distinct forms of service: live-in servants hired on a permanent basis, live-in servants hired on a temporary basis, and day servants who came to perform a particular service or to top up a reduced workforce. Of the twenty-five women cited above, fourteen were theoretically employed on a permanent live-in basis. Yet ten of them worked for less than thirty days and, of the remaining four, Hannah Atkinson, dairymaid, stayed for six weeks, Ellin Platt for nineteen weeks, and Molly Vivers the housekeeper for twenty-four weeks. The only permanent presence was that of the twelve-year-old Nanny Nutter, who worked in a general capacity at Alkincoats for over three years. But even Nanny ran away in September 1772 and had to be brought back by her father. Was this an unusual state of affairs? Was Mrs Shackleton a particularly unrewarding or difficult employer? After all, as Chapone averred, 'those who continually change their servants and complain of perpetual ill-usage, have good reason to believe that the fault is in themselves, and that they do not know how to govern'.[26]

Be that as it may, Mrs Shackleton was an altogether unexceptional employer when it came to financial remuneration. Between 1762 and the mid-1770s, her cook-housekeepers received five pounds a year in wages, all other maidservants were paid four guineas a year. Such wages were slightly lower than those offered by the substantial northern gentry, but they were on a par with those dispensed in many genteel households, and substantially more generous than those offered by some local manufacturers, such as the Heatons of nearby Ponden Hall.[27] Her servants could not complain that their wages were exceptionally meagre. More likely, the volatility of Mrs Shackleton's servants is a reflection of the rich local opportunities for less demeaning work in textile manufactures. Nevertheless, the absence of continuity in the servants' hall was certainly not unique to east Lancashire. Jane Scrimshire condoled with her friend on the loss of servants, 'I know what it is to lose one that is used to one's ways', and complained herself of tiresome disruption: 'this Transition in my Family has disconcerted me greatly as I have a prodigious dislike to Strange Faces . . .' The Gossips saw a stream of cooks pass through their household, and Mrs Gossip 'would not willingly have [a maidservant] under four and twenty, for she has already found the inconvenience of young giddy girls'. The Lancaster widow Jane Pedder was too busy to write to her son in June 1780 because of the aggravation of changing and training servants. Meanwhile, in Preston in the 1810s Jane Horrocks had to cancel her holiday on account of her father's disintegrating staff: 'The house I am ashamed to say is in a filthy State & likely to remain so till we get a fresh supply of servants.'[28] Further afield, Earle finds that well over half his sample of female domestic servants in London between 1695 and 1725 had served twelve months or less in one place, and reminds us that Samuel and Elizabeth Pepys engaged at least thirty-eight servants between 1660 and 1669. Hecht also emphasizes that instances of lengthy service were exceptional. He cites the Purefoys who employed at least thirty servants in ten years, and identifies a similar turnover in the households of Anthony Stapley a Sussex gentleman, John Baker a lawyer and Parson Woodforde in Norfolk. Meanwhile, back in the north, at Wentworth Woodhouse, Jane Holmes finds that though the upper servants might have borne a resemblance to the lifelong retainers of patriarchal fantasy (four servants served over twenty years), a rapid turnover of lower servants was the norm.[29] As the eighteenth century progressed, servants' wages steadily climbed and opportunities multiplied. The labour market worked to the advantage and independence of female servants. Unusually lucky was the employer who did not have to improvise strategies for dealing with transient personnel.

How did Elizabeth Shackleton cope with her ever-shifting labour force? When staff shortages loomed, she immediately sent off batches of letters in pursuit of permanent replacements. Yet young women servants tended to abscond rather than giving and working out notice, and re-employment could take up to a month while references were gathered and terms negotiated. Something had to be done in the interim. The available employment data for 1772 reveals that Mrs Shackleton bridged the inevitable gaps in her permanent workforce by employing emergency labour. Seven women were engaged on a temporary basis in 1772 to live and work at Alkincoats for a designated brief period. Looking at servant employment across all her diaries from 1762 to 1781 uncovers the existence of a pool of local women upon which Elizabeth Shackleton drew *in extremis*. Take two local examples. Lucy Smith of nearby Priestfield was employed on an intermittent basis from 1767 to 1778; in 1772 she worked at Alkincoats for eight short periods (on average eleven days) and six individual days. Although Susy Smith was considered an extravagant cook-housekeeper when in permanent employ in 1771, she was employed intermittently until 1777; in 1772, she came in twice overnight and worked for two periods of eight and nineteen days. Through her correspondence and by word of mouth, Mrs Shackleton kept her finger on the pulse of the provincial labour market against the day when she was servantless. She managed to procure 'the good cook' Molly Hargreaves from Hellifield (eleven miles away) for two short periods in the autumn of 1772, because she heard that Molly was between jobs. On occasion, she even poached or leased servants from other employers for the emergency period. For example, Betty Platt arrived on 11 May 1772, promising to 'help us till I can meet with a servant in the upper place'. She left twelve days later as her employer could spare her no longer. Chance remarks indicate that Elizabeth herself was also prepared to loan out her female servants for an afternoon.[30] Obviously she was not alone in the need to improvise.

Close analysis of the diaries for 1772 reveals another category of female servant. In addition to permanent and emergency live-in staff, Elizabeth Shackleton paid women to come for the day, usually to perform a single service. Thus, in 1772 five women were employed on this basis. Women were paid by the day to work in the kitchen and dairy, coming in to make the butter, to help get the dinner and to bake for both ordinary and special occasions. The duties traditionally associated with a housemaid were regularly discharged by casual workers, engaged to do a day's ironing, heavy washing, or sewing and mending. The intimate services of a chambermaid were fulfilled by local women when necessary, including the 'getting up' of personal linen, packing up of clothes, assisting with dressing and undressing, washing feet and even cutting toe-nails. However, day servants represent a complex category. Some day workers were sent for at moments of crisis and are indistinguishable from the emergency labourers discussed above. Other women workers offered particular skills, such as specialist sewing, starching or baking, and could routinely be called upon. In consequence, the tasks performed by specialist day servants were in many cases identical to those performed by local tradeswomen, as in the case of Betty Shaw, who 'came to make me up two Dress'd & two undress'd Caps – As she's esteemed a Profficient in that way & just arrived Piping Hot from Manchester'. The availability of skilled day labour afforded Mrs Shackleton some flexibility as an employer, although bringing in extra labour could create its own tensions, particularly if the daily worker was seen to trespass upon a permanent worker's domain: 'sent for Nancy Crooke to make the Butter. She denyed me, said she was Busy & did not like to do it as the Maid might take it amiss – at last she came, very saucy & Sulky.'[31] 'Personnel problems', in the modern euphemism, were not the least of Mrs Shackleton's irritations in her attempts to orchestrate the work of the different categories of female servant under her roof.

What of men's labour in the household? Returning to a close analysis of

one year, the Shackletons may have employed as many as four menservants in 1772. These four are all referred to by their Christian names
only (Isaac, Will, Jack and Matthew) and no titles are given, although
evidence from elsewhere in the diaries reveals that Will was William
Brigge, her husband John Shackleton's apprentice, while Matthew was
probably less of a servant and more of a handymen attached to
Shackleton's wool business.[32] Mrs Shackleton had little cause to advertise
for menservants because they were more static than their female counterparts and this fact alone may account for the absence of any discussion of
her theoretical requirements in male household servants. Will, for example, lived with the family for some eleven years and Isaac for at least eight.
Of course, the silence in the letter-books on the subject of male servants
might also mean that the hiring of men was a gentleman's preserve.
Certainly, the majority of the male servants' contracts which can be found
in the diaries were recorded in the early 1760s, when Elizabeth was still a
widow. Along with the virtual absence of official titles, such as chaise
driver, butler or groom, there is no evidence to suggest rigid specialization
among male household servants. If a female employee was a maid of all
work, then a male servant was certainly a jack of all trades. Throughout
his long career, Isaac was recorded making medicine, brewing, delivering
letters, accompanying female servants, driving the wool cart, cleaning the
chaise and harness, clearing rubbish, moving stones, spreading soap ashes
and farrowing. Moreover, William Brigge's apprenticeship does not seem
to have excused him from domestic duties. He delivered presents, accompanied servants, collected provisions, sold medicine and brewed ale. On
several occasions, he accompanied Thomas Parker to the Lancashire and
Yorkshire races dressed in a new livery, so he could also be called upon to
appear as footman/valet for the day. Over and above her permanent staff,
Elizabeth Shackleton also paid a gardener to come in twice a week, and the
unmarried Tom Parker employed a huntsman.[33]

    In many instances, the tasks performed by menservants blurred into
those performed by local tradesmen, craftsmen and agricultural
labourers.[34] Inside Alkincoats itself, tailors were often employed for heavy
sewing, mending upholstery and pack sheets, and cutting stays and petticoats; the barber called to cut hair and alter wigs. Local tradeswomen also
made home calls and must have laboured alongside the maids. Seamstresses came in to make up and mend batches of caps, handkerchiefs,
ruffles, petticoats, shifts and shirts, and gowns were often fitted at home
by the local mantua-makers. Demonstrably, the genteel household was a
toiling hive of male and female paid labour, dispatched by permanent live-
in staff, emergency live-in staff, emergency day labourers and regular day

labourers. Consequently, in its staffing the household functioned like most eighteenth-century commercial enterprises. In the acquisition, co-ordination and direction of a range of different workers, the managerial effort of the genteel mistress-housekeeper was akin to that of a putting-out master or gentleman farmer, and far removed from the received picture of the unruffled lady of the manor.

If the logistics of hiring servants were complicated, more knotty yet were the intricacies of daily government. The construction and mainte-nance of a mistress's authority over her servants could not be taken for granted; a point reinforced by the detailed printed advice on the preserva-tion of supremacy and widespread warnings about a lack of innate defer-ence in the servile. ('Eye service', a superficial deference masking a resentful, contemptuous heart, remained a particularly disturbing possi-bility.) That the modest eminence on which the mistress stood could be deeply undermined was well understood by the genteel. It was a proverbial adage that employers had to decide early whether they were to manage their servants or be managed by them: 'A Mutiny in the House with Servants', groaned a weary Elizabeth Shackleton in 1780. Forty-odd years later, a relative of Sarah Tatham's dared not leave her new, but superan-nuated antiquary of a husband alone with his cantankerous old house-keeper for fear of the ground she would lose: 'I wish she could have a littel change of scene But she is afraid of Mrs Cooks ascendancy over him if she comes to stay here.' Joanna Gossip was equally insecure in her power and authority. Mourning the ruination of her vegetable crop in 1814, she regretted 'had I been able to do superintend my affairs as I used to do this had not happened'. In the frailty of eighty, she had little choice but to delegate to careless servants, 'yet I dare not stir from ye fireside & my maid [assured] me that they wod be safe. I had no alternite [sic] but believe her report . . .'[35] The upper hand once lost was not easy to regain. The compe-tent government of servants and household required energy and vigilance.

Not surprisingly, eighteenth-century employers went out of their way to obtain 'sober, steady and industrious' labour in the first place. (Elizabeth Shackleton and Anne Gossip also specifically sought servants who were not Roman Catholic, and Mrs Gossip also drew the line at Methodists since they went to too many meetings.) Early nineteenth-century employers continued to seek servants who possessed the 'qualifications of honesty, sobriety and respectable carriage towards [their] superiors'.[36] Yet all were constantly disillusioned by domestics who proved pert, drunken and dubious. As an informant of Anne Gossip's put it, 'good servants are very scarce, bad ones people better be without'. Of course, the 'servant problem' was an ageing chestnut even in 1700. Ann Pellet's complaint of

1756 that 'the times are very bad . . . on servants' has a timeless ring to it. Indeed, Jane Scrimshire was as vexed and plagued about maids in the 1750s as Jane Pedder in the 1780s and the Horrocks sisters in the 1810s. Genteel women saw servants as an irretrievable thorn in the flesh – 'no doing without those necessary Evils.'[37] Doubtless their maids returned the compliment.

Elizabeth Shackleton, for her part, attempted to enforce certain standards of behaviour among her workforce. She esteemed and rewarded servants whom she thought 'civil', 'diligent', 'labourous', 'honest', 'sensible', 'agreeable', 'proper looking', 'good like', 'clean looking', 'handy' or possessing 'good hands'.[38] Male and female servants alike were censured for being extravagant, dirty, clumsy and dishonest, but men were more likely to be accused of drunkenness and licentiousness and women of impudent language and carriage. But both men and women were denounced for that great sin against hierarchy – taking liberties. Unlike some other employers (such as Parson Woodeforde), Mrs Shackleton made no formal allowance for tea, coffee and sugar in her servants' contracts, yet they helped themselves to these high-status provisions regardless. Mrs Shackleton was infuriated when she surprised her cook drinking full-cream milk, and was 'much vexed' to discover old Luce Smith 'sciming Milk Bowles & drinking the Cream . . . sorry there is no more trust to be put in People'. The expropriation of illegitimate perquisites threatened both Elizabeth Shackleton's authority and her economical regime, a dual challenge which is made explicit in a note of 1779: 'found Betty Crooke Makeing Coffee & breaking white sugar to drink with it – Servants come to a high hand indeed. What will become of poor House Keepers?'[39] Mrs Shackleton was equally alarmed by verbal insubordination. The diaries are peppered with complaints that the servants were insufficiently docile and deferential. Black Betty Walton was described as 'saucy dirty & Ungovernable'; Sally Crooke was thought 'a beast of a woman', equipped with the 'vilest, most brutish tongue'; and Betty Crooke was dubbed 'a saucy vulgar woman'.[40] But for all their vulgarity, Mrs Shackleton was painfully dependent on them – and therein lay the rub.

Genteel households could not function without servants, yet as we have seen lower servants were strikingly independent and mobile; the risk of losing a good character reference seems to have worried them not a whit. Mrs Shackleton attained her full complement of staff for only short-lived idylls and within a matter of days could see her maids dwindle in number from four to one and on desperate occasions to zero. In December 1775 she reported 'a dark day in great distress for want of proper women servts.

Not one But Nelly now'. In August 1776 she lamented 'Betty after supper run away to Blakey. No servants all at an end'. In December 1778 she complained '[Mary Foulds] went today left me without a servant in her Place'. In June 1780 she wailed, 'Mary Crooke went to a Wedding. Nobody left as a woman servant in this house. God help me what will become of me.' In September of that year she despaired, 'I am now in a pritty plight. Not one woman in this House. God Grant I may be so fortunate as to live and go on better if it be his Blessed Will. No Bread in the House.' Mrs Shackleton could not have been more conscious of her painful dependence on paid labour. Thus, she was prepared to tolerate a deal of bad behaviour from competent servants. Impudence alone was not enough to merit dismissal, at least not in the last, vulnerable years of Elizabeth Shackleton's life. Even the departure of the insolent Betty Crooke was regretted in March 1780: 'I am sorry to part with Betty, as I have not yet heard of a person that is proper to serve me. My years and Infirmities require a staid knowing diligent woman.'[41] Repeated drunkenness on the part of Isaac and William Brigge, though disagreeable, did not warrant expulsion. The discovery in June 1772 of a 'Courtship . . . of the warmest kind' between William Brigge and Ellin Platt did not result in the sacking of either servant, although Ellin ran away a week later and so removed half the problem. Similarly, Isaac's 'amour' with Nanny Driver was tolerated. However, in 1779 Isaac's dalliance with Susy Smith reaped the whirlwind in the guise of Susy's mother. Incensed, Peggy Smith descended on Pasture House 'like a distracted woman' and dragged her daughter away, declaring that Susy 'sho'd not have Isaac. She wo'd be her end before she sho'd bear her Bastard in Barrowford workhouse.' In the full glare of local publicity, Isaac had to go.[42] Yet, Isaac's departure notwithstanding, it is striking how many 'freedoms' Mrs Shackleton was prepared to tolerate in her efforts to maintain a full complement of workers. It appears she committed one of the employers' venal sins, tolerating bad men because they were good servants. Immaculate delicacy was a luxury she could not afford.

The mistress–servant relationship was nothing if not complex and paradoxical. Relations with some female servants were characterized by fondness and intimacy, with others by distance and antagonism. The emotional possibilities and limitations inherent in the relationship are amply demonstrated by the three-year career of the adolescent maid, Nanny Nutter, to whom her mistress devoted an entire pocket diary. Nanny Nutter entered the Shackleton household as a girl of twelve, the daughter of a neighbouring tenant farmer, well known to the family. Little commentary exists on her work role; she was noted footing and knitting stockings, and taking her work home for the day. Yet after three years, she was sufficiently qualified to be engaged as a chambermaid at nearby Carr Hall. There is no evidence that Nanny Nutter was paid a yearly wage, however Elizabeth Shackleton laid out £3 8s. 1d. on clothes for Nanny in 1773, £3 11s. 1d. in 1774 and £4 0s. 2d. in 1775. So, at the very least, Nanny received a return for her services worth approximately four pounds per annum, roughly the wage of a housemaid. Formal remuneration apart, Nanny Nutter was indulged with numerous trinkets and accoutrements: a Halifax ribbon, a gauze cap with a spider thread lace border, a black silk laced handkerchief, a pair of old dimity pockets, an old worked muslin apron, a red and white handkerchief, an old mob, a yard of scarlet ribbon, and a pair of single lawn ruffles being but a selection of her mistress's offerings.[43]

A quasi-parental concern infused Mrs Shackleton's dealings with the maid. Elizabeth Shackleton herself made shirts and shifts for Nanny, as she did for her own sons. Mrs Shackleton recorded Nanny's illnesses and noted what was almost certainly the onset of the menses, in October 1773, when Nanny was fifteen years and four months: '29th – on this day Nanny Nutter began to be unwell for the very first time.'[44] Relations were sufficiently intimate for mistress and maid to share a bed, and although this practice was far from unusual, it was still meaningful enough to warrant special mention in Elizabeth Shackleton's diary on 9 March 1772: 'Nanny Nutter lay with me for the first time.'[45] The maid was also taken on pleasure outings into Yorkshire and was encouraged to visit her family regularly, often showing off her new clothes in the process ('on this day Nanny Nutter put on her new stays and strip'd Callimanco gown & went home'), bearing gifts from Mrs Shackleton to the Nutter family.[46] From Elizabeth Shackleton's perspective, this appears an affectionate and lenient regime. Doubtless she considered herself a very generous employer.

Nanny Nutter's perspective goes unrecorded, though her actions do not suggest grateful loyalty to an irreproachable patron. After all, servitude was servitude. Nanny Nutter absconded from Alkincoats on at least four occasions. In September 1772 her father brought her back. In January 1773 messages sent to her sister and her parents were sufficient to induce her unaccompanied return. In December 1774 she was again returned by her father, but in September 1775 she ran away for good: 'While I & Mr S. were both from home, Nanny Nutter threw her clothes out of the Red room window and run home. Keep her there.'[47] This tendency to take flight was hardly unusual among Elizabeth Shackleton's servants. Nanny Nutter's youth and the proximity of a family refuge may have been further catalysts. On the other hand, Mrs Shackleton complained that Nanny was growing wilful, describing her as 'very Impertinent' and 'saucy', though 'a fine girl if she pleases', while Nanny Nutter circulated stories of ill usage, as Mrs Shackleton discovered in December 1774:

> Mr Shackleton and his father was a hunting. Old John Barret told Keyser Shackleton that Nelly Nutter had told him that I had so near throatled her daughter Nanny as to near hang her. John Nutter went to enquire about it. Went to Stone Edge that night & said his Daughter sho'd not stay any longer here . . .

In the event, John Nutter was easily pacified, though this may say less about his daughter's credibility than about his own financial circumstances: 'John Nutter came here in a rage for to take Nanny Home for here she sho'd not stay he was soon appeased – was glad to leave her where he found her. Tho' most likely his Poverty not his Will consented.' Either way, the cause of Nanny Nutter's unhappiness with Alkincoats and its mistress is unfathomable. What is beyond doubt, however, is that Mrs Shackleton's relationship with Nanny was charged with strong emotion. The diary entries recording the maid's final departure and re-employment are infused with bitterness: 2 September 1775: 'Nanny Nutter run away – There may she remain forever'; 5 November 1775: 'Nanny Nutter went to be chamber Maid at Carr. an ungratefull lying girl.'[48]

It could be argued that Nanny Nutter's career represents a special case. Certainly no other servant in Mrs Shackleton's employ warranted an entire diary. Nevertheless, when William Brigge 'walked of with his box & cloaths & left a Pack of Malt in the Tub' in August 1777, Mrs Shackleton was caught on the raw again, wondering how a boy who had grown up at Alkincoats could so betray her – 'a Generous Deed after being brought up here & lived near ten years'. When Will repented his action three months later, Elizabeth Shackleton refused to see or re-employ him. Thus rejected, he enlisted in the 19th Regiment on Christmas day. Even servants of relatively short standing could gall Elizabeth Shackleton with their ingratitude: 'Betty Spencer run off without leaving a word to any person. Left all the cloaths to dry & Iron – an Impudent Dirty Slut. Never shall she have any favour from me . . .' At Pasture House, in the last four years of her life, Elizabeth Shackleton clung to her female servants with a pathetic sense of her own vulnerability. Her needs, both physical and emotional, are palpable in her response to the arrival of Molly Blakey – 'I gave [her] my old black mode silk Cloke because I thought she was poor & came to me when I was desolate & quite without any help.'[49] In her loneliness, Mrs Shackleton endowed her relationship with selected servants with a condescending sentimentality.

On the other hand, the sentimental content of mistress–servant relations should not be seen as evidence that Elizabeth Shackleton sought to dissolve the social distinction between governess and governed. To be sure, her expectation of a befitting gratitude amongst the servile was supremely hierarchical. Her attention to social differentiation could be minute and her resentment of disloyalty implacable. Elizabeth Shackleton considered her servants beholden to her; an assumption shared by her contemporaries, like the Leicester hosier Thomas Gossip who was irked that his selfish maid Mary had the temerity to put her own happiness before his convenience, when she 'very foolishly threw herself away into the hands of a soldier without giving me the least notice'.[50] Indeed, when elite masters and mistresses harped on the thanklessness of servants it led at least one contemporary observer to conclude, 'They think highly of what they bestow, and little of the service they receive; they consider only their own convenience, and seldom reflect on the kind of life that their servants pass with them . . .'[51] Of course, a formidable sense of social and moral superiority was dyed in the genteel wool. When Mrs Parker of Cuerdon heard from a servant that a relative was ill, she hardly knew whether to credit the report, since 'it is only a Verbal Account from the Unintelligible Mouth of a Servant'.[52] Patently, this county gentlewoman could not comprehend the full humanity of her servants. It is also worth remembering that mistresses were empowered by common law to use physical correction on these dependents. A Mrs Burnall who had gone too far in beating her maidservant was hissed at by the crowd on leaving the assize court in Nottingham.[53] Elite employers took superiority as a birthright.

Even the possession of docile and devoted servants did not relieve genteel women of the obligation to labour in their households, although the ambiguity of elite commentary on the matter combined with the tendency to take the presence of servants for granted make it hard to ascertain with certainty how much physical drudgery a genteel mistress took upon herself. Elizabeth Shackleton's diaries, for instance, do not differentiate systematically between everyday tasks performed by her alone, tasks performed with the aid of servants, and those performed exclusively by servants under their mistress's supervision. Consequently, interpretations may vary of daily entries such as 'spent the day cleaning and scowering', though most readers would concede that to make such a statement, the mistress must have been closely involved in labour of this kind. Certainly, there is no evidence in the northern manuscripts to suggest a gentlewoman lost caste through heavy-duty housekeeping. In fact, Mrs Shackleton wrote most approvingly of hard-working ladies, as here in December 1780 at Pasture House: 'Alice Waddington a most usefull Visitor. She strip'd of her Ornaments and best Attire & helpd washd & Iron.'[54] Moreover, chronic staff shortages of the kind experienced by the Shackletons would have undermined even the most determined efforts to attain decorative idleness. No upper servant remained long enough to become truly accountable for the smooth running of the household and thereby relieve Elizabeth Shackleton of active supervision. A significant degree of co-operation between mistress and servants, markedly in food preparation and laundry, has also been noted in Meldrum's study of smaller establishments in early eighteenth-century London.[55]

The genteel mistress was hardly engaged in back-breaking toil, nevertheless the pattern housekeeper was determined that all be clean, neat, regular, well ordered and economical, a determination which translated into energetic attention to household operations. To guarantee that household tasks were done well, the elite mistress had to be on hand to direct and assist. In order to judge the quality of the work performed, she herself had to know how to sew a straight seam, clean a piece of silver, churn good butter or harvest sweet vegetables. 'The proper discharge of your domestic duties,' argued Lady Sarah Pennington, necessitates 'a perfect knowledge of every branch of Household Oeconomy, without which you can neither correct what is wrong, approve what is right, or give Directions with Propriety.' Hence, Pennington urged her daughter, 'make yourself Mistress of the Theory, that you may be able, the more readily, to reduce it into practice; and when you have a Family to command, let the Care of that always employ your principal Attention, and every part of it be subjected to your own Inspection'. Even Rousseau's meek Sophie, who gladly substituted for the domestics when necessary, had principally learnt their multifarious functions because 'One can never command well except when one knows how to do the job oneself'.[56] Just as prudent economy had many branches, so an elite housekeeper understood many skills. Her reach embraced the ordering and cleaning of the physical household, the production of clothes and household goods, husbandry and provisioning, and the making and dispensing of medicine. Her responsibilities were wide-ranging even if her drudgery was minimal.

The elite mistress managed her household property like a museum curator administering her collection, for the neatness and order of a house and furniture was a quintessential feature of genteel economy, a mark too reflective of character to be left entirely to the unexacting care of servants. Consequently, when Anne Gossip sent a box of new purchases home, she asked for the unpacking to be delayed until she could orchestrate it: 'I had better be there when they are unpack'd ye can't know where to find anything.'[57] Precise attention to the physical arrangement of the household is minutely documented in Elizabeth Shackleton's pocket diaries:

> On Saturday June the 14th I Bot of old John Pollard four yards & a half of Blanketing at 18 pr yd, cost 6s and nine pence It is marked 1771 W.J.G. I design'd it for Will's and Isaac's bed in the Gallery But afterwards thot it best upon consideration to let [it] be put upon the bed next the window in the Nursery. So I have marked it nursery.[58]

When new commodities entered the household, whether bought, made or received as gifts, it was the mistress-housekeeper who decided their eventual destination. Mrs Shackleton often wrote of 'putting things in their places', 'taking possession' of cupboards and 'regulating' their contents. The diaries are littered with reminders of the whereabouts of individual items, and with *ad hoc* inventories of cupboards and boxes. When her sons left property in her willing charge, she wrote up minute catalogues in duplicate. She prided herself on safe, efficient storage and took palpable pleasure in her ample cupboards. In a well-regulated household, the mistress-housekeeper could literally itemize the physical contents of a house and knew exactly where to lay her hands on a particular object.[59] Hence, when loyalist women petitioned the British government after the American War, they were able to present minute inventories of furniture, plate and kitchen utensils lost to the rebels, something most male claimants were unable to do – 'a Variety of Articles' being the best that one male refugee could recollect.[60] How his wife would have sighed for those forgotten goods.

Domestic inspection and reorganization was routine for the genteel housekeeper, witness Mrs Shackleton detailing the 'regulation' of her linen one November morning in 1768: 'I removed the Chest out of the red room in the Gallery & took all the linnen out of the linnen draws over the fireplace into the nursery & put the linnen draws near the fireplace in the red room in the gallery as they stood to damp before.'[61] Mrs Shackleton monitored the condition of the household goods and kept a record of breakages, wear and tear, the mending of broken bits and the regular servicing of utensils. In genteel households cupboards were well-ordered, sheets crackled with starch and the utensils shone, for chipped cups, blunt knives, dirty linen and domestic disarray were all visceral emblems of the slattern; they announced the presence of a neglectful, indolent and probably sluttish mistress to her shuddering guests. Conversely, when Boswell encountered a lady of quality who had sacrificed herself in marriage to a rich, greasy old man, he felt nauseated: 'She looks to me unclean . . . like a dirty table-cloth.'[62]

A well-regulated household was a clean household, for 'nastiness' would deprive a family of polite company. What exactly constituted an acceptable level of cleanliness in eighteenth-century terms is hard to assess, but it is apparent that even an undemanding definition assumed constant work. Although Alkincoats was refurbished in the 1750s and Pasture House was a completely new building, both houses were plagued by inefficient chimneys and leaking roofs. Mrs Shackleton engaged John Smith to sweep the chimneys ('a most dirty do'), yet this did not remove the threat of dangerous fires in the store room and parlour chimneys, an occurrence reported in 1771, 1774 and 1775. Heavy rain also created chaos. With dismal regularity Mrs Shackleton awoke to find Alkincoats flooded with water, the fireplaces belching smoke and 'a great deal of damage done'. The situation was no better at Pasture House: 'A deluge at Barrowford, this house Every room smokes like a Kiln. The water runs down the Chinies and swims upon all the Floors.'[63] Under such circumstances keeping an eighteenth-century household even moderately dry and orderly was an arduous and unending task.

The work involved in meeting Mrs Shackleton's standards of cleanliness is suggested by her bulk purchases of castile soap and the variety of dusters and cleaning rags mentioned in the dairies, including 'china cloths', 'a cloth for to wipe the leads', 'knife cloths' and 'tin cloths'. Reference is made to the intermittent whitewashing, cleaning out of rooms and polishing of plate in anticipation of visitors. Elizabeth Shackleton associated herself with laborious tasks: 'I wash'd all the China Pots & c in the Store room which was extremely well clean'd out – a very troublesome Job am glad it is over so safe and well. It answers the pains and looks very clean nice and well . . .'[64] But whether she actually got her hands dirty remains a mystery. Mrs Shackleton's use of the personal pronoun is ambiguous, witness three references to a common household task: 'We scowered all the Pewter & cleand all the things in the Kitchen'; 'We scowered all the Pewter cleaned Coppers & Irons'; 'a very fine day. The maids scouring pewter'.[65] In each case, Elizabeth Shackleton may have meant that while her maids toiled, she stood by to direct and encourage. But even if the role she performed was essentially supervisory, she was unquestionably an interventionist superintendent, who at the very least had her own ideas about the best way to scour pewter. Mrs Shackleton certainly led the battle to keep the dirt at bay and was mortified when overwhelmed: 'such a house for dirt as I never saw. It quite hurts me to see this good old place so deplorably nasty.' The public pride she drew from running a clean household can be inferred from her humiliation in defeat: 'What a nasty drunken beastly house for a stranger to clean . . .'[66] Clean-

liness was powerfully associated with gentility. Nevertheless, the exemplary mistress who ensured the decent order of her house was expected to
conceal her efforts behind cloak of gracious nonchalance, lest she radiate
'the air of a housemaid' and thereby discomfort her husband and her
guests. Her aim was to contrive that a visitor took neatness and order for
granted and remained blind to the scrubbing, washing and polishing she
daily orchestrated.[67]

Of all the tasks associated with 'keeping house', one of the most productive, in a simple economic sense, was the making up and maintenance of
personal and household linens. The diligent mistress claimed this as part
of her domain, although it was a domain whose boundaries were shifting
in the course of the eighteenth century. At the turn of the seventeenth
century it was common for women of the lesser gentry in the north to
organise the manufacture of linen, and sometimes woollen cloth for
household use. Gentry women would superintend the spinning of textile
fibres into yarn by their female servants and contract with jobbing weavers
in their neighbourhood to transform that yarn into cloth. This kind of self-
provisioning only supplied a proportion of the household's textile requirements, with an emphasis on the coarser textiles, but it nevertheless
constituted a significant responsibility for gentlewomen. There is no evidence of this kind of household self-provisioning of textiles in Elizabeth
Shackleton's voluminous diaries, and it appears to have largely died out in
other northern gentry households by the second half of the eighteenth
century, as they came to rely entirely on an ever-expanding supply of shop-
bought cloth.[68] Gentlewomen were largely responsible for purchasing this
cloth, and they continued to be responsible for processing it once bought,
particularly for cutting out and sewing linen cloth into sheets and handkerchiefs, shirts and shifts. It should not be assumed, however, that this
switch from partial self-provisioning to dependence on retail supply
resulted in less work for gentlewomen. Time saved in organizing the
manufacture of cloth may simply have been eaten up by shopping for
larger quantities or more diverse qualities of cloth, by ever-more demanding standards of needlework, or by other tasks unrelated to textiles.

As had been the case with household spinning at the end of the previous
century, the elite mistress of the second half of the eighteenth century
expected to administer more sewing than she performed herself, yet her
own practical ability was vital to effective production. As Dr Gregory
lectured the elite seamstress, 'the intention of your being taught needlework, knitting and such like, is not on account of the intrinsic value of all
you can do with your hands, which is trifling, but to enable you to judge
more perfectly of that kind of work, and to direct the execution of it in

others.'[69] At Alkincoats, fabric was regularly bulk purchased, extra labour brought in and the family's new linen made up in enormous batches under Elizabeth Shackleton's supervision. But she herself sewed and labelled many ruffles, stocks, neckcloths and handkerchiefs for her menfolk and favoured servants, for a lady's plain-work was an attractive symbol of her dutiful ministration to the needs of her family. Sheets, pillowcases, blankets, towels and napkins for family and servants were all cut, stitched and labelled by Elizabeth Shackleton: 'Made two pairs of sheets, one pair for the red room marked R.R. and a diamond, the other pair with a diamond red for my own bed.' The first making was only the beginning of the story, many an afternoon was spent 'busy mending old shifts, shirts and sheets'.[70] Outdated or faded gowns were often unpicked to the original 'whole breadths' and 'pieces', and sent to be re-dyed in Manchester or London, while old linen was laboriously maintained and adapted. For Elizabeth Shackleton's was a thrifty regime, wherein every last scrap was utilized; a virtue she liked to broadcast. She reproved her improvident married son precisely for his failure to save fabric pieces: 'I asked [Tom] for a piece of cloth to make me a Pincushion. He told me he had none. I said he sho'd keep bits. If they had not done so at Newton, how co'd the old Lady have made my own dear, nice, little [grandson] a pair of shoes.'[71]

Long after her sons left home, they continued to avail themselves of her services both managerial and technical. John and Robert Parker wrote from London requesting eleven new shirts without a qualm, while Elizabeth Shackleton was more than happy to oblige her sons. She told Robin in 1774 that she 'wo'd take particular care to have all his shirts done as he directed & desired his acceptance of the making of them'.[72] Mrs Shackleton revelled in her ability to be useful to her sons, urging them to bring home any shirts that required mending. Her efforts to make recompense with John Parker after a damaging quarrel are suggestive of the wider uses of her skills: 'I am Happy to have [John] here. Mended up slightly some shirts & night Caps, all his things much out of repair. God knows he will find it a great & expensive difficulty to renew them.' Even when theoretically head of an independent household, Tom Parker continued to resort to his mother over the matter of linens: 'Tom called . . . said he sho'd want a number of things in the Housekeeping way – Particularly Linnen. I might advise Miss Parker about things.'[73] Thereby he acknowledged Mrs Shackleton's accumulated expertise and authority.

Food was the most bountiful expression of genteel housewifery. Ladies recipe books, both printed and manuscript, detail a comprehensive interest in its production and processing. Elizabeth Shackleton was actively concerned with the running of the home farm. It seems unlikely (though not impossible) that Elizabeth Shackleton directed labourers in the fields, but she was still *au fait* with their labour. The letters she received from her first husband conveyed information about crops and livestock. In her widowhood, she ran the estate herself with the help of her brother's steward, and even after remarrying was directly involved in disputes with tenant farmers concerning their misuse of Parker land – contentious issues being the taking of rushes and timber, over-intensive ploughing and the laying of lime.[74] In her diary she noted the rhythms of the farming year: ploughing, lime burning and laying, hay-making, mowing and threshing, lambing, calving, sheep shearing and so on. She also coyly recorded the matings of livestock: 'A Mr Sheep came to visit our young Miss Lambs.' Throughout the 1760s and 1770s Mrs Shackleton discussed the farm animals in very possessive terms, writing of her 'little dandy cock and hen, which I value very much', 'my sweet little pigs', 'my good old handsome gander', 'my good profitable sow' and so on, and reporting tasks like 'set the old goose, March Wednesday ye 15th upon eleven eggs'. While such testimony is of limited value in ascertaining the full extent of her daily engagement in farm and estate management, it does at the very least confirm that this gentlewoman was no precious hothouse bloom withering at the first farmyard breeze. However, it may well be the case that her endeavours were usually concentrated in the immediate vicinity of the house. Abetted by her part-time gardener, Mrs Shackleton also tended a flower and kitchen garden, recording the prodigious yields of her apple and pear trees. When she moved to Pasture House, she sent away to a Pontefract nursery for moss, Provence and Portland roses, honeysuckles, gessamine and myrtles to establish her new garden.[75]

The diaries contain no evidence that crops or livestock were sent to market. Most produce seems to have been absorbed by the family or given away, with the exception of butter, which Mrs Shackleton sold at between fivepence and sevenpence per pound. Her customers were made up of neighbours, tenants and Colne traders. They either came directly to the dairy door to buy the butter, or had it sent by cart. Only occasionally was butter sent to Colne market to be sold. Looking in detail at butter sales in one year gives an idea of the scale of the dairying at Alkincoats. In 1776 Mrs Shackleton reported sending eight gargantuan pots of butter into the cellar. Of these, one pot was consumed by the family and the other seven were sold off at sevenpence per pound to neighbours. In all 496 pounds of butter was sold, bringing in £14 9s. 4d. in revenue. Thus, in relative terms, her butter trade was worth the annual wages of two to three maidservants.[76] It was a significant enterprise.

The complete and accomplished housewife was also an expert at the

'The Art of Preserving, and Candying. Fruits and Flowers, and making all sorts of Conserves, Syrups, Jellies and Pickles', as well as distilling and making artificial wines, perfumes, oils, musk balls and so on.[77] Certainly, Mrs Shackleton's year was punctuated by seasonal pickling and preserving on a liberal scale. May saw the fermenting of gallons of cowslip wine, July the making of currant jelly and the bottling of cherries, September the pickling of literally hundreds of cucumbers, October the sousing of onions, the preserving of damsons and gooseberries, and the perfecting of several varieties of ketchup. In addition to the processing of produce, Mrs Shackleton supervised her menservants in the brewing of ale and small beer and her maidservants in the home-curing of ham.[78] Stocking the larder with home-processed food and drink was the bread and butter of good housekeeping.

The scale of food processing was consistent with the overall tenor of Mrs Shackleton's provisioning. Many commodities were bought annually in staggering bulk, such as malt, flour, sugar, salt, wine, candles and soap. On arrival, these products were inventoried, labelled if appropriate, and put into storage. It was Elizabeth Shackleton and not the cook-housekeeper who monitored the amount of food in the household if the sheer number of inventories in her diaries are anything to go by.[79] Indeed, long after her removal to Pasture House, Mrs Shackleton continued to order the groceries for Alkincoats. In addition to the role of head-provisioner, Mrs Shackleton assumed the duties of a guardian of supplies. Minute testimony to her surveillance is provided by numerous, annotated inventories and her reaction to waste. The squandering of supplies on the part of careless or prodigal servants was condemned. This mistress prided herself on sound stewardship and resented any interference therein. Predictably, interference was yet another of Mr Shackleton's offences: 'Mr S. exceeding bad . . . as soon as ever he came down this morning he drank White Wine. S. threw that bottle down & another of red Port and broke them both, Sad terrible housekeeping indeed.'[80] Nowhere in the diaries, however, is there any suggestion or expectation that the mistress of the house would herself prepare food on a routine basis. Mrs Shackleton did make her husband a special cream cheese as a peace offering, but the power of the gesture lay in the exceptional character of her labour. A lady did not make family meals, instead she took pains to see that her cook joined 'Oeconomy with Neatness and Elegance' in the spreading of her tables.[81]

One of the most distinctive and traditional aspects of genteel housekeeping was the production and distribution of medicine. It is a commonplace that seventeenth-century gentlewomen saw the liberal dispensation of medicine and succour as part of their remit; a notable example being Lady Grace Mildmay and her herbal remedies.[82] As already noted, the female role of sick-nurse was long established, all but inescapable, and long enduring. Medicinal recipes remained a familiar currency of women's correspondence throughout the period. Moreover, informal medicinal philanthropy still survived here and there. For instance, Lady Lawson, wife of Sir Henry Lawson of Brough, in the North Riding of Yorkshire, had a local reputation among the poor in the 1750s for being 'skilful in medicines and bountiful in bestowing them', while in Denbighshire, Lady Wynne was eulogized in 1748 for a lifetime of relieving the poor with food, clothes and physick: 'a rare example in this extravagant and luxurious age'. In the Parker network, Barbara Stanhope was noted for 'the art of Quacking'.[83] Mrs Shackleton, for her part, was celebrated for the production of reasonably priced rabies medicine. She inherited a recipe and reputation for the making of rabies medicine from her first husband. Robert Parker (who studied medicine at Cambridge) and a Mr Hill of Ormskirk, Lancashire (apparently a merchant), had sold their 'Cure for Hydrophobia' throughout the 1740s and 1750s. Robert Parker's cure and public spirit was the subject of a letter to the *Gentleman's Magazine* in August 1753:

> One Mr Parker, a gentleman of considerable fortune near Colne, in Lancashire, has a certain and speedy remedy for that dreadful distemper [Hydrophobia] which I never heard to fail except once, which failure was occasioned by the persons own folly . . . There has been a great many hundreds cured by him, for which he takes no more than half a crown; I never heard he gave above one dose which always does the business; every patient is obliged to go to him for he gives it with his own hands, and will send it to nobody: indeed for a dog he will send it made up with a kind of paste.[84]

After Robert Parker's death in 1758, Elizabeth determined to perpetuate his public spirit, so she took over the production of the medicine and sold it at the modest price of a shilling a bottle.[85] In 1776 she passed the recipe on to her son John Parker, much to his satisfaction, but continued making the medicine right up to her death in 1781.[86] Unlike Robert Parker, if we are to believe the *Gentleman's Magazine*, she was prepared to send the mixture long distances, although consumers also came in person, or sent agents from far afield. Appendix 6 shows that the market for her medicine extended north and west to Westmorland, Cumberland and Scotland, north-east to County Durham, and south to Nottinghamshire and Derbyshire.

Elizabeth Shackleton enjoyed considerable provincial fame through her

medicine. The potion needed no introduction in 1777 to the readers of the
Leeds Mercury:

> A caution to the Inhabitants of Leeds, and the Neighbouring Villages.
> Within this fortnight past several dogs have gone mad in this town and
> neighbourhood, which have not only bit many other dogs, but what is
> more melancholy, no less than eighteen persons are now taking the
> Colne Medicine, having been bit also . . .[87]

Shackleton's reputation can also be deduced from the social character of
her custom, comprehending labourers, farmers and landowners in the
locality, and retailers, titled gentry and the nobility across the north.
Without straying from her medicine room, she enjoyed professional intercourse with the likes of Sir James Lowther, Sir George Saville, Lord
Scarborough and the Duke of Hamilton. By this emphasis, the medicine
business appears an exercise in modest enterprise, public spirit and, in
modern terms, networking. There is no evidence that Elizabeth Shackleton
actively exploited these exalted contacts, yet they must have reflected on
her social credit at home. But how did medicine production marry with
conventional huswifery? From a long historical perspective, the trade
appears a curious hybrid of ancient responsibilities and new commercial
practices. As noted, the elite housewife's talent for medicinal charity was
well established. This traditional inheritance perhaps accounts for the
'public-spirited' pricing system, and the readiness with which the widow
took over the job. On the other hand, the Parker remedy competed in a
world of heavily advertised patent medicines and undoubtedly benefited
from the commercial climate this advertising created, in particular an
increased readiness to trust a bottled potion brewed by a stranger. There
is no evidence that a paid advertisement was ever taken out in the northern
papers, but it is probable that word of mouth promotion lent the product
an important credibility which could only enhance the quality trade.
Indeed, satisfied customers applied again and again. In sum, if the prime
motive was the garnering of reputation, not profit, then Elizabeth
Shackleton's marketing strategy was well designed. Gratifyingly, for this
genteel housekeeper, messing about with pots and pans translated into
public renown.

Dedicated and fastidious though Elizabeth Shackleton might have been,
she was by no means an unusual housewife. The surviving records of
neighbouring landowners, the Listers of Gisburn Park, confirm an already
familiar picture of genteel housekeeping in the rural Pennines. Letters
written by Mrs Beatrix Lister and her daughter in the 1760s and 1770s
concern medicinal remedies, the making of curtains, sewing waistcoats,

the brewing of ale, the tending of bees and the grape harvest.[88] In fact, the evidence we have for the early eighteenth century suggests that the content of rural housekeeping was remarkably enduring. The anonymous account books of a Furness Quakeress written in the 1710s and 1720s, reveal her buying seeds for a kitchen garden, buying cherries and sugar for preserving, paying someone to gather and pickle mushrooms, bringing beehives from Penrith, making cushions and paying women to help with the washing.[89] Urban housekeeping, on the other hand, was further removed from husbandry, but the town and country contrast should still not be overstated. Between the ages of ten and thirteen, merchant's daughter Mary Chorley was taught the rudiments of housekeeping by her Lancaster aunts. In the 1770s she learned to bake, pickle, preserve, garden, make shirts, shifts and dresses, and to create homely remedies. In the same town in the 1780s clergyman's widow Jane Pedder made and mended her son's shirts, tended an urban kitchen-garden, and had a brew-house installed at her home in Bridge Street.[90] Moving further afield, however, it becomes immediately apparent that keeping house in some polite towns represented a different proposition. As the wife of a solicitor in fashionable Pontefract in the 1750s, Jane Scrimshire had no poultry yard, hotbeds or dairy to superintend. Similarly, Bessy Ramsden made no mention of keeping livestock or growing produce at Charterhouse Square between 1765 and 1780. Instead, she recorded her negotiations at the victualling office and bargain-hunting expeditions in the city. When Reverend Ramsden contemplated leaving London to take up a living in Cambridgeshire, Bessy Ramsden acknowledged her ignorance, telling her cousin 'you must come to teach me to Farm as I shall want a deal of instruction for a country Life'. Nevertheless, these friends shared many assumptions about the constituents of housekeeping, as indicated when Bessy wrote thanking Elizabeth for the gift of a home-cured ham: '[I] shall keep it to credit our kitchen, for I always think they are a[n] ornament and look like good housekeeping.'[91] Moreover, Bessy Ramsden not only performed all the family's sewing and mending, but had to do the same for forty Charterhouse schoolboys in the absence of the matron. As she tartly added 'I dout Mr R. never menson this particular'. Meanwhile, Jane Scrimshire was engaged in pickling, preserving and distributing medicinal recipes to her friends.[92] In short, while the exact content of housekeeping varied from country, to county town, to polite resort, to the metropolis, three common elements are identifiable: provisioning, sewing and rudimentary medicine. Of these three elements, it was the character of provisioning which was most dependent upon geography.

There is no evidence to support the theory that active housekeeping was in steady decline in these years, although, as noted for textiles, there may have been a shift over a much longer period in the composition of genteel housekeeping. This was a shift away from household production of raw materials and their manufacture towards final processing and management of a wider variety of goods purchased from retailers in a semi-finished or finished state. A shift from partial self-provisioning to greater reliance on retail provisioning was almost certainly characteristic of the supply of medicines between the late sixteenth and the early nineteenth centuries and may have been true of foodstuffs, although the long-term history of household food supply is a subject that has hardly been researched at all. What did not change in our period was the active and demanding nature of the mainly managerial role housekeeping required of genteel women.

In the 1800s Dolly Clayton used her pocket diaries in a similar fashion to Mrs Shackleton, recording meat purchases and bottling.[93] Letters written in the 1810s give partial insight into Eliza Whitaker's housekeeping. At the very least, her household activities comprehended the active supervision of extensive scouring and whitewashing, general provisioning, the preserving of food, the making of ketchup, and an experiment with keeping poultry. Her friend Mrs Bishop of Roby near Skelmersdale was an enthusiastic farmer, who kept Eliza Whitaker minutely informed of crop yields and livestock. Like Elizabeth Shackleton, Mrs Bishop both kept pigs and prided herself on frugality. She was proud to announce in 1812, 'we do not *waste even a* cabbage stalk. I inspect the curing of the bacon & (excuse boasting) it is excellent & much admired . . .'[94] In the 1810s and 1820s in Selby, solicitor's wife Ellen Parker sewed clothes for her children and talked of the time consumed by her duty to 'superintend our domestic concerns'.[95] In the same decades the Tathams lived in comparatively straitened circumstances in Southall, yet they enjoyed a prosperity of roses, lilies, lilacs and laburnums and boasted that their bountiful kitchen garden kept them almost completely in fruit and vegetables. In July 1819 Sarah Tatham was 'so much employd *now*' with preserving 'that Time outstrips me'.[96] Anna Larpent's 'domestic employments' in Regency London included settling the accounts, writing letters on business and regarding servants, cutting out shirts and shifts, knitting, looking over household linen and generally 'arranging family matters'.[97] Attention to detail remained the hallmark of the effective housekeeper: 'Various domestic businesses occupied me, not to be entered trivial in themselves, but necessary, the Atoms of which domestic duties are composed, which when formed in a Mass produce confusion if not attended to.'[98] Early nineteenth-century mistresses were every bit as 'busy in domesticities' and minute in their supervision as had been their forebears.

All the available commentary from the early eighteenth to the early

nineteenth centuries suggests that genteel housekeepers were interventionist household managers, who routinely performed specialist services
for their families, such as shirt ruffling and mending and who were prepared to participate in heavy-duty housekeeping when necessary. Under
ideal conditions, a mistress's labour was more managerial than manual,
but in this she was not alone. Gentlemen did not, after all, dig ditches or
pack cloth themselves, but instructed servants, labourers and apprentices
to do it for them. Had any of these families experienced a radical upturn
in their fortunes then perhaps a female withdrawal from all but decorative
housekeeping and nominal supervision might be expected. Increasing
wealth and a corresponding multiplication of servants would erode many
of the functions of the mistress-housekeeper. Yet only a tiny proportion of
the employer class could employ a vast army of servants with its own
executive division, and even those who could were not necessarily liberated from management, for, as the moralists often inquired, who shall
oversee the overseers, if not the mistress?

> It is with a family as with a common wealth, the more numerous and
> luxurious it becomes, the more difficult it is to govern it properly.
> Though the great are placed above the little attentions and
> employments to which a private gentlewoman must dedicate much of
> her time, they have a larger and more important sphere of action, in
> which, if they are indolent and neglectful, the whole government of
> their house and fortune must fall into irregularity. Whatever number of
> deputies they may employ to overlook their affairs, they must them-
> selves overlook those deputies, and be ultimately answerable for the
> conduct of the whole.[99]

Be that as it may, the experience of peers and plutocrats who enjoyed an
annual income in excess of three thousand pounds cannot be expected to
resemble the work practices of the families who lived on a modest three
hundred pounds a year. Such incomes were far too small to sustain the
specialized staff necessary to liberate a woman from constant domestic
attention. In any case, the difficulties gentlewomen faced maintaining a
staff of just four maidservants, meant few were at liberty to languish on
their couches.

Elite women may have softened towards selected servants, but they all
resented the upstart who tried to break down the forms of subordination.
Furthermore, they expected to preside over housekeeping and were keenly
resentful of encroachments on their authority. One of Mrs Shackleton's
many complaints against her husband was that he meddled with her
management. He berated her for reproving the servants and thereby

encouraged their insolence: 'Mr S. is quite cruel, ungenerous – takes the servants parts – Against me. He lets them abuse me scandalously & never contradicts them. All wrong I do. all right they do – God Almighty Bless Preserve & be with me.'[100] And thus he dangerously undermined her authority. From Elizabeth Shackleton's rancour, it can be argued that she expected to exercise absolute authority over female servants and over male servants when they worked within the house. One of Ellen Stock's many grievances against her cruel husband Aaron in the 1810s was his determination to suborn the servants, rendering her isolated, impotent but perhaps above all degraded, in her own household.[101] Sarah Cowper, the wife of a Hertfordshire baronet, acidly complained that her husband 'restrains me in all my due privileges': he rebuked her before servants for giving a neighbour flowers without his permission, he denied her custody of sheets and tablecloths, humiliated her before guests, objected to her tea and cocoa account and protected faulty servants. In sum, he prevented any administration on her part. Imagine her chagrin when she visited 'where they tell of ladies that manage their domestic affairs in such a manner as argues they have much power: then home I come a humble mouse gnawing on the thought that in forty years I have not gained the privilege to change a cook maid on any account whatsoever. Who can help being uneasy at these matters? Though I keep silence my heart doth burn within me.' The outrage felt by all three women suggests that John Shackleton, Aaron Stock and Sir William Cowper were all acting contrary to received assumptions about gender and authority. In fact, Sarah Cowper was adamant that established convention was on her side: 'I just now met with a note that tells the difference between a wife and a concubine. The wives administered the affairs of the family, but the concubines were not to meddle with them. Sure I have been kept as a concubine not a wife.' Even the Old Testament stressed that a wife was not a servant in the family, but a partner in its government. As the fictional Betsy Thoughtless concluded when her ungrateful husband demanded that housekeeping expenses and her servant's wages be met from her pin money, 'Is this to be a wife? – Is this the state of Wedlock? – Call it rather an Egyptian bondage; – the cruel task-masters of the Israelites could exact no more.'[102] Women anticipated allowing men all the rights of their place, but at the same time determined to maintain their own. They certainly could not countenance degradation in their own households.

A wife's authority was sanctioned by custom and case law. When Lancashire and Cheshire women filed in the Chester church courts for a separate maintenance, they repeatedly asserted the undermining of their authority over servants and domestic accounting as supporting testimony of male abuse. Moreover, the judges of the Victorian divorce courts were strikingly supportive on the frequent occasions when an aggrieved woman found herself 'entirely deposed . . . from her natural position as mistress of her husband's house.'[103] Ideally, a gentleman respected his housekeeper's contribution and did not trespass upon her household domain. In practice, he may not have been able to stop himself doing so, but by his actions he forfeited public sympathy and reputation. Beatrix Lister's reassessment of a vulgar, drunken guest in 1773, in the light of his esteem for his wife's housewifery, shows the reverse process at work: 'Ye only thing that [made] him the least tolerable was, his commending his wife as a notable good houskeeper, & took great [care] of his children and himself.'[104]

All the available commentary suggests that gentlemen and gentlewomen were seen to perform distinct work roles, with discrete areas of expertise and responsibility. Contemporaries stressed the momentous change in a woman's life when she became 'the mistress of a family', while even conservative prescriptive literature emphasized female dominion indoors, and directed advice to women on 'the government of servants'. It was widely accepted that the post of mistress could not be adequately filled by an upper servant. The desire for a prudent household manager had long been a real consideration in male courtship decisions and praise for a wife's competence was a traditional feature of the widower's eulogy. Not surprisingly, bachelors tended 'to set up housekeeping' with sisters or nieces wherever possible, while bereaved householders often called upon the services of their older daughters, or their dead wife's kin. For an effective housekeeper was a necessity, given the peripatetic life many sportsmen, administrators and businessmen expected to lead. When Robert Parker's grandmother and housekeeper lay dying, he was unable to fulfill his administrative responsibilities. 'I was summoned to Lancaster upon the Grand Jury, but cd not possibly go, as I had noone to take care of my Family. They say the judge is very severe upon the Non Appearance of jurors, if so Imagines I shall be fined . . .' And so he came to recognize just how much his peace of mind and public service rested upon his grand-mother's government: 'you are not a stranger [to what] advantage has accrued to me [from] her Civility, consequently must know how great my loss will be.'[105] A gentleman was expected to honour his housekeeper's authority. Most were only too happy to do so. Thus, the role of the dignified, efficient housekeeper was available to eighteenth and early nineteenth-century gentlewomen as a source of both personal satisfaction and public credit. For a house well regulated was a subtly burnished badge of decent gentility.

5

Elegance

GENTILITY FOUND ITS RICHEST EXPRESSION in objects. Indubitably mahogany, silver, porcelain and silk all announced the wealth and taste of the privileged. A shared material culture united polite families: almost anyone who was anyone in the North-West, for instance, be he lawyer, merchant or small landowner, bought his handsome, russet, dining-room furniture from the same workshop, that of the rising firm of Gillows of Lancaster. In the gleaming polish of these tables and chairs, visiting retailers and yeomen might discover something of the gloss they lacked. Yet, stylistically, Gillows furniture was characterized by a rather provincial fashionability, wanting the finesse of the Chippendales and the Linnells bespoken by the metropolitan elite.[1] Hence, the most imposing and expensive pieces of genteel furniture distinguished the polite from both the vulgar multitude on the one hand, and the ultra-fashionable quality on the other. In short, these mahogany objects embodied the social distinctions of provincial gentility.

However 'behold my social status' is not the only message Georgian possessions conveyed, as John Gregory alerted his daughter: 'You will not easily believe how much we consider your dress as expressive of your characters', he revealed, 'Vanity, levity, sluttishness, folly, appear through it. An elegant simplicity is an equal proof of taste and delicacy,' he dourly concluded.[2] That clothes expressed personality was a point which could also be made in lighter vein. Mrs Thrale's parlour games, for example, involved the likening of friends to types of silk (among other things). Thereby, Frances Burney was compared to 'a lilac Tabby', Sophy Streatfield to 'a pea Green Satten', Fanny Brown 'a Jonquil Coloured Lustring' and Dr Johnson a 'Marone'.[3] However, the eighteenth-century commonplace that objects had complex associations comes as something

of a miraculous revelation to historians. It has long been taken as read that
the motive driving all consumers was a simple obsession with keeping up
with the Joneses,[4] and if consumers in general have been seen as socially
emulative, then the queen of grasping, envious shopping is the female
consumer. Unquestioned belief in the shallow selfishness of female desire
has dogged historical discussion for decades.

Surprisingly, it was a satire of culture and attitudes in late nineteenth-
century New York, Thorstein Veblen's *Theory of the Leisure Class*, which
did most to influence the way historians characterized the elite woman's
role in the world of goods. According to Veblen, the lady of the 'leisure
class' played a crucial role in the performance of conspicuous leisure.
Innocent of paid employment, she was ultimate testimony to her husband's wealth and status, the clothes on her back the tangible proof of his
purchasing power. Her unpaid work, the 'painstaking attention to the
service of the master' and 'the maintenance and elaboration of the household paraphernalia', was a category of leisure, since these tasks were
'unproductive'.[5] In short, the leisured lady's economic *raison d'être* was
to consume and display what men produced, thereby driving her less
fortunate sisters to new heights of envious imitation. Veblen's pessimistic
interpretation of human motivation is apparent in Neil McKendrick's
explanation for expanding domestic demand and economic growth in the
eighteenth century. Though women's wages may fluctuate, apparently
their wants remain the same. Speaking here for every waged woman he
asserts, 'Her increased earning released her desire to compete with social
superiors, a desire pent up for centuries or at least restricted to a very
occasional excess . . . It was this new consumer demand, the mill girl who
wanted to dress like a duchess . . . which helped to create the industrial
revolution.'[6]

Thus we are left with the assumption that women are simply innately
covetous and congenitally wistful about the prospect of upward mobility
– an impression which is reinforced by traditional histories of the luxury
trades and, in particular, by historians of dress. Again, women's wants
and strategies are reduced to the need to ensnare a male and a compulsion
to keep up with, if not beat the Joneses, in the emulation of elite style. The
proof of this frivolous craving for elite modes and therefore social cachet
is found in travellers' reports, satirical social commentary and moralists'
diatribes, as here, when Aileen Ribeiro quotes the cynical satirist Bernard
Mandeville: '[The] poorest labourer's wife . . . who scorns to wear a
strong wholesome frize . . . will starve herself and her husband to purchase a second hand gown and petticoat, that cannot do half the service,
because forsooth it is more genteel.'[7]

Ancient prejudices have thus been passed off as actual behaviour. Meaningful research on women's consumption and material culture in the eighteenth century is conspicuous by its absence; a suggestive article by Lorna Weatherill stands virtually alone. By comparing the inventories of men and women (spinsters and widows), Weatherill discovered a higher concentration of decorative items among the possessions of single women, but concluded that the gender contrast was too muted to suggest a distinctively feminine material subculture. Yet, unfortunately, inventories cannot determine whether men and women attached different meanings to the same artefacts, something which must be ascertained if the question posed by Weatherill herself is to be answered: did men and women have different material values in the seventeenth and eighteenth centuries?[8]

Weatherill apart, most historians have dismissed women's dealings with material things as a 'category of leisure', domestic material culture as an arena of female vanity, not skill, and shopping a degraded female hobby, not unpaid work. Unnecessarily reliant on Veblen, historians have reproduced a sorely impoverished assessment of material culture; assuming that beyond their material function goods only convey information about competitive status and sexuality, and that consumables once possessed carry the same social and personal meanings for all consumers. Indeed, these ideas are so commonplace it could be thought that Thorstein Veblen had absolutely the last word on consumer motivation and the symbolic character of material things, which is demonstrably not the case. The last ten years have witnessed a massive rethinking of consumer behaviour in the fields of sociology, media studies and design history. Pierre Bordieu has questioned Veblen's bedrock assumption that social competition necessarily inspires imitation, since it could just as easily provoke differentiation. Bordieu's *Distinction* depicts a system whereby each class is actively distinguishing itself from other classes, in goods and lifestyle. Dick Hebdidge's work on subcultures and style presents evidence of the appropriation rather than the emulation of elite modes and symbols in the creation of solidarity among subordinate groups, while Jean Baudrillard has questioned whether material things have fixed meanings at all. Meanwhile, imaginative discussions of the meanings of material things have long been found in anthropological theory. Building on Marcel Mauss's dissolution of the gift/commodity distinction, anthropologists have asserted that while consumption is essentially social and relational, an awareness of comparative social status need not be competitive. So, in fact, having the same consumer items as the Joneses does not necessarily involve beating them, since a shared material culture is often a factor in social solidarity and cohesion. Mary Douglas and Baron Isherwood assert that the primary information goods convey is not status but character, stressing the importance of things in the construction of identity. Similarly, Daniel Miller has argued that however oppressed and apparently culturally impoverished, most people nevertheless access the creative potential of the unpromising material goods about them.[9] The impact of this writing is now being felt by historians, exhibiting an increased willingness to view consumption as a contribution to the creation of culture and meanings, and the general reassessment of consumption paves the way for the historical reclamation of the female consumer in particular.[10]

٭ ٭ ٭

As far as genteel women were concerned, shopping was a form of employment and one that was most effectively performed by women – note the language Elizabeth Parker used in 1751 to reprove her fiancé Robert Parker when, through careless procrastination, he bungled her commissions: 'you really are a proper person to intrust with business . . . the next time I employ you, you shall be more punctual.' Thereafter, Robert Parker appeared more mindful of his wife's instructions, apologizing from York in 1756 for silver buckles bought 'contrary to orders' and from Skipwith for some fancy hats, 'don't scold abt [the] latter, for cd not bear to see [the] plain'.[11] A very similar note of respectful apology was struck by William Gossip in the 1740s and 1750s: 'I have sent you what commisions I have executed, but I am afraid I shall never get all your locks as you would have them.'[12] Occasional marital disagreements over relatively minor consumption decisions illuminate the sexual division of labour as understood by genteel women. The delayed arrival of a hamper of produce from Pontefract in December 1753, prompted the following explanation from solicitor's wife Jane Scrimshire: 'I am sorry to hear your Apples were so long travelled . . . but things always happen wrong when Husbands will not hearken to their Wives for I co'd not persuade Mr Scrimshire to send them to Wakefield but now as far as the Dignity of a Husband will allow He acquiesces.' A month later Mrs Scrimshire admitted herself still 'extremely vexed' with Michael Scrimshire about the spoilt produce (and presumably the principle). Thereafter she 'wo'd not let him have any Management in sending [perishables]', and declared herself 'determined to have my own way this time'.[13] Jane Scrimshire's conviction that the management of consumption was a proper female concern is echoed in letters from Elizabeth Parker's cousin Bessy Ramsden. When despatching a box of elaborately patterned silks from London in 1764 ('in the very politest Fash[ion]'), Mrs Ramsden's apprehensions that they were '*too full* of work' for her cousin's taste were dismissed by her husband Reverend

Ramsden. Proved right, Bessy identified unwarranted male intervention as the source of the problem: 'Dear Cuzz, the Plot against your Peepers was not of *my* laying. The Patterns were of my *Husband's* chusing, to shew (as he says) his *Taste*. I tell him he had sufficiently shewn that before in his Choice of a – Wife.'[14]

A uniquely detailed reconstruction of the management and mechanics of consumption is permitted by Elizabeth Shackleton's thirty-nine diaries. As has already been pointed out, the diaries were divided into 'Letters to Friends and Upon Business', 'Remarkable Occurrences' and 'Accounts'. Unfortunately, for our purposes, the accounts were not an exercise in double-entry bookkeeping, being almost exclusively concerned with expenditure. If Elizabeth Shackleton kept a global account book (which seems likely) then it has not survived. Lost with it is the possibility of a precise correlation between income and expenditure over the life-cycle.[15] Not that Elizabeth Shackleton's accounts of expenditure were imprecise and unsystematic, far from it. The accuracy of her record-keeping has been verified by comparing the purchases of furniture from Gillows of Lancaster listed in the diaries and the relevant ledgers that survive for the firm.[16] Elizabeth Shackleton's furniture accounts were scrupulously exact in specification and accurate down to shillings and pence. In the case of furniture-buying, at the very least, the diaries offer an unerring record.

Among many other functions, the diaries served as a reference manual on the business of consumption and servicing a household. Mrs Shackleton kept a tally of the provisions, clothes and household goods she ordered from local retailers, usually with a note their quality or service-ability and price. When commissioning London relatives to purchase goods on her behalf, she sent remarkably detailed orders and specified how the proxy consumer was to be repaid and the means by which the purchases should be conveyed (either by coach, carrier or personally deliv-ered). All this information was duly transcribed into the diaries. When parcels and boxes of metropolitan products arrived, Mrs Shackleton listed their contents, registering how well they had survived the journey and whether they suited her taste. A general interest in the price, specification and availability of consumer goods is catalogued in the diaries ('Bought a small quantity of Mackrell at three pence a pound from Preston. I never saw any in Lancashire but once before'), while her correspondence reveals that she exchanged such information with her friends on a regular basis.[17] Although ultimate control of financial resources in the Shackleton mar-riage remains obscure,[18] there is no evidence that Elizabeth Shackleton felt financially constrained. The Shackleton marriage was riven with strife, yet there is no evidence of conflict over financial priorities, or Mrs

23 'The Haberdasher Dandy', 1818. Despite cultural preoccupation with the impulsiveness of consumer desire, most female consumers knew what they were about. Here the over-attentive male haberdasher fails to trick the calculating female customer into accepting short measure.

Shackleton's independence as a consumer. The household sustained only a handful of servants, and certainly was not grand enough to support a house steward, a clerk of the kitchen or an executive housekeeper to manage and monitor family consumption. The sheer quantity of consumer detail in Elizabeth Shackleton's diaries offers powerful evidence that outside the households of peers and plutocrats the daily *management* of consumption fell to women and with it control of routine decision-making. It must be for this reason that American patriots made such efforts to ensure female co-operation in the colonial boycott of British imports, particularly tea, in the 1760s and 1770s. Similarly, it accounts for why early nineteenth-century associations of British women found consumer boycotting an ideal political strategy.[19] Women enjoyed some recognized independence as routine consumers.

  Women jealously guarded their role as family consumers, but men were hardly untainted by the world of goods and fashion; rather, men and women were expected to consume different items and in different ways. When county business or commercial ventures took northern gentlemen to well-supplied or fashionable towns, they fulfilled their wives' commissions by proxy. They rarely returned from such trips without an additional parcel of toys, novelties and souvenirs. While Elizabeth Shackleton saw to the purchase of her sons' linens well into their twenties, they hunted for flashier items for themselves, expending much energy in pursuit of the perfect embroidered waistcoat for instance.[20] Undoubtedly, men considered themselves skilful consumers of particular types of commodity. When the Ramsdens fulfilled their cousin's commissions in 1765, Bessy Ramsden bought the 'Gowns, Caps, Ruffles and such like female Accoutrements', while William was accountable 'for the Wafers, Paper & Pocket Book'.[21] To be sure, the way spouses carved up their shopping lists must have varied from couple to couple – after all it would be remarkable if a schoolmaster had not been able to judge the quality of stationery. Similarly, John Parker's apprenticeship as a linen-draper and his subsequent endeavours in hosiery must have equipped him to deal in fashionable textiles and perhaps accounts for his growing importance to his mother as a proxy consumer in the later 1770s. The particularity of skill notwithstanding, it is surely significant that the remarkably uxorious William Ramsden was the only man in all the northern manuscripts who ever recorded going to market to purchase humdrum groceries. Other gentlemen, however, did occasionally concern themselves with the purchase and donation of higher status provisions, such as snuff, good tea, wine and barrels of oysters; and they were, of course, obsessively involved in the acquisition and distribution of game.

While husbands were not expected to interfere with the daily organization of household consumption, none the less it seems likely they retained ultimate sanction over extraordinary purchases requiring the outlay of considerable capital. For instance, in the once and for all furnishing of Pasture House in the 1770s, while Elizabeth Shackleton ordered small pieces of deal furniture from local craftsmen, it was John Shackleton who went to Lancaster to bespeak their mahogany dining-table and his name that appeared in the Gillows ledgers. Moreover, when her newly married son Tom Parker embarked on his first furniture-buying expedition, Elizabeth Shackleton recorded his departure with all the fanfare of a rite of passage: 'Tom going from Newton to Lancaster to buy new Mahogany Furniture. God Bless & Prosper with Grace, Goodness and Health all my own Dear Children . . .'[22] Although men bought many goods for themselves and certain commodities for the household, it was women who were principally identified with spending in the eighteenth-century imagination.

(Witness Eliza Parker teasing her father in 1796 from an auction, 'my Mamma says you are getting money today and we are spending a little of it'.)[23] The stereotypical distinction between the producing man and the consuming woman was endorsed by the regularity of female shopping. In sum, while substantive research on the differences between men and women's consumption remains to be done, the Lancashire manuscripts suggest the provisional conclusion that while female consumption was repetitive and predominantly mundane, male consumption was, by contrast, occasional and impulsive, or expensive and dynastic.[24]

Elizabeth Shackleton's diaries testify to the variety of ways commodities could be acquired. The Shackletons bespoke individual pieces (predominantly furniture and clothing) from Lancashire craftsmen and women. In the ordering of metropolitan goods, they relied principally on the taste and expertise of friends and relatives living in the capital. They commissioned goods on an *ad hoc* basis from neighbours and kin who happened to be visiting London or other polite centres, and went on intermittent shopping trips themselves to well-supplied northern towns, such as Preston, Warrington, Wrexham, Chester, Halifax and York. Local, everyday shopping was done in person in Colne, Barrowford, Burnley and Bradford, from retailers, producers and, very occasionally, hawkers. But Elizabeth Shackleton's social network was such that if she chose she could purchase fashionable metropolitan commodities with ease.

So how fashionable were Elizabeth Shackleton's purchases? In colloquial usage, 'being in fashion' indicates a general accordance with the modes and manners of the times, but also more specifically signals the possession of this season's model. If what historians of demand mean by fashion is the close shadowing of metropolitan high style, then Elizabeth Shackleton's engagement with fashion was very uneven. Even if the focus is restricted to those categories of goods which were at the very core of the eighteenth-century fashion system – furniture, tableware and clothing – the extent to which fashion influenced her purchasing decisions was different in each category. Elizabeth Shackleton's diaries are peppered with details of countless purchases, sufficiently detailed to enable the analysis of her purchases by their place of origin.[25] While household utensils, provisions and groceries were almost invariably obtained within the parish, furniture consumption was regional in scope. With the exception of one or two small pieces, all the new Shackleton furniture was purchased in Lancashire from craftsmen in Colne, Manchester and Lancaster. By stark contrast, the purchase of tableware was overwhelmingly biased towards the metropolis.

Elizabeth Shackleton evidently put a premium on polite china and silverware. Precisely why she did so is not made explicit in the diaries, however the pleasure she derived from exquisite tableware (she was devoted to tea parties, enjoyed examining her neighbours' new purchases, and even recorded which women snapped up the china at local house sales) probably reflects female investment in mealtime ceremony and domestic sociability. For all that, Elizabeth Shackleton was no leader of fashion. Unlike her gowns, tableware was only infrequently renewed. Few bulk purchases were made and these were prompted by 'necessity' not the dictates of changing fashion – upon first marriage, remarriage, removal to Pasture House and in response to breakages. Moreover, the letters Mrs Shackleton received from proxy consumers do not suggest a relentless pursuit of ultra-fashionable wares. Relatives made her aware of current modes and sometimes fashion constrained her choices – the tea-tray of china she sought in 1754 could not be had anywhere because of the rage for tea-boards. Similarly, in the 1760s she had to make do with a candela-bra decorated with Mars and Venus and not the branching flowers she requested, since the rococo had been superseded by neo-classicism in silverware design. Yet fashion also created unexpected opportunities for canny consumers. They had to decide whether 'to pay the fashion', since the preferences of the fashionable elite were seen to inflate the price of some goods and depress the price of others:

> the nanquen sort is most the present taste & consequently dearest, but as tis only blew & white . . . will not be thought so fine. However you may have a good, genteel, full sett (that is 42 pieces) for about 5 or 6 guineas – since the Beau Monde is chiefly for the ornamental China for Chimneys & brackets to adorn the room & sett out for entertainements . . .[26]

Certainly, the genteel liked to buy their tableware in London, but there is no evidence that they burned to drink their tea from the same cups as a duchess. They were satisfied with 'genteel' tableware and flattered them-selves that they were too sensible to be buffeted by the ever-changing winds of metropolitan taste.

Commentary on changing furniture design in Elizabeth Shackleton's diaries is conspicuous by its absence. Old-fashioned pieces were not traded in for modish novelties; indeed furniture was bought once in a lifetime and expected to last for generations. The Gillows mahogany bought new for Pasture House was impressive but not ultra-stylish. Anyone who wanted high design would betake themselves to a London showroom not a Lan-caster workshop.[27] Thus, when periodically re-stocking Alkincoats and Pasture House with high-quality household goods, the Shackletons appear

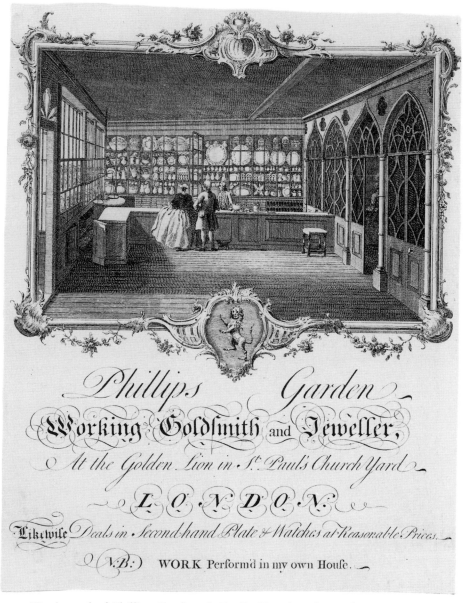

Phillips Garden
Working Goldsmith and Jeweller,
At the Golden Lion in St. Paul's Church Yard
L O N D O N.
Likewise Deals in Second-hand Plate & Watches at Reasonable Prices.
(N.B.) WORK Perform'd in my own House.

24 Trade card of Phillips Garden, St Paul's Churchyard, London, *c.*1750. A well-dressed couple is portrayed discussing a purchase of plate with a shopman in the enticingly fashionable, gothicized interior of a London goldsmith's shop.

Benjamin Cole.
at the Sun in St Pauls Church Yard
LONDON.
Imports & Sells all sorts of Cambricks,
Lawn, Macklin & English Lace, & Edgin,
Where all Merchants, Dealers &
Others may be Furnish'd, Wholesale or
Retail at Reasonable Rates.

25 Trade card of the London linen-draper Benjamin Cole, St Paul's Churchyard, London, *c*.1720. Throughout the eighteenth century, and probably long before, genteel women were accustomed to visit fashionable London shops unaccompanied by men. Here, well-dressed women, are shown poring over a display tray of lace placed on the counter by a female shop assistant. One woman customer sits on a chair near a pilastered doorway which opens on to a blazing fire in the back room. The interiors of fashionable shops were carefully designed to make shopping a comfortable and pleasurable experience.

to have purchased commodities which, although broadly fashionable, were not in the highest style.

When it came to dress, however, Elizabeth Shackleton prided herself on being *au courant* with 'the reigning fashions'. She had London newspapers sent up and regularly received informative letters from watchful friends in polite towns and London. These strategically located observers kept her posted on the modes and manners of 'the fine folks', 'the people of distinction', 'the better sort'. Their ability to provide such bulletins varied according to season, sociability and the visibility of 'the ladies of quality'. From Pontefract, 'this Capital of Politeness', Jane Scrimshire was best placed to answer Elizabeth's 'important questions about Negligees' when county families were in the town attending the winter assemblies.[28] Similarly, in London Bessy Ramsden had to attend public functions and arenas such as pleasure gardens, theatres and assemblies in order to identify up-to-the-minute modes: 'As for fashions I believe we must postpone them a little longer as it is too Early to tell what will be worn. I shall get all the information I can in the fashion way and let you know . . . excepting to the city assembly once this winter I have not been any where in Publick.'[29] So far, a model of the transmission of taste based on emulation theory is confirmed. Bessy Ramsden regarded London as the 'fountain head' of fashion, exhibited by an elite minority in arenas of social display, and to be sure Mrs Ramsden was a passionate spectator of any glamorous exhibition, as her husband never failed to point out. In 1766, the Reverend smirked at his wife's determination to view the queen's birthday court from the gallery:

> Possibly you may suspect this to be Curiosity to see the Fine Folks; not a bit on't, but only to enable her [to atone] . . . with your Ladyship for her past sins of omission by sending a Letter cramm'd full with such Glitterings, Dazzlings, Diamonds and so forth, as will almost put out your Peepers unless fortifyd by a pair of Spectacles, with the Glasses blackened as when we look at the Sun in an Eclipse.[30]

Bessy Ramsden was certainly a gossip and a lover of spectacle, yet she was not a straightforward emulator of the ladies of quality.

Bessy Ramsden mocked those aspirants to the beau monde who made themselves ridiculous for the sake of fashion, like a Miss Price who spent an afternoon stabbing insects to produce the current 'flea' colour, or a young bride whose ultra-fashionable trimming of wax strawberries melted in front of the fire. She reported the absurdities of high fashion with relish, describing monstrously oversized bonnets, headdresses of such towering height that ladies were obliged to sit on the floor of their coaches, and the

THE VIS•A•VIS•BISECTED•
OR THE LADIES COOP•

Pub. by Darly May 22 1776 Strand

26 'The Vis a Vis Bisected or the Ladies Coop', 1776. This satirical image perfectly illustrates Bessy Ramsden's description of ladies being obliged to sit on the bottom of their coaches to accommodate their monstrous headdresses. Mrs Ramsden may have seen a print on this theme. She certainly lived only a brisk walk from the printsellers of St Paul's Churchyard.

Duchess of Devonshire's habit of wearing a wax kitchen garden in her hair. Similarly, Ann Pellet laughed at the oversized hoops at court: 'a lady who going by another, tost her hoop so high that it entangled with the Diam[ond] flowers, &c in the next Lady's Head and had not some officious Gentleman come to their assistance we know not of what Direfull consequence it might have produced.' She enjoyed the discomfort of another unfortunate debutante who 'made a false step and kick't up her heels, Hoop, *and all*'. Likewise, Anne Parker of Cuerdon dashed off saucy reports about the Lancashire quality on parade in Preston: 'Miss Wall . . . [had] such an Enormous Quantity of Wool False Hair & c upon her Head that I Coud not help thinking if it was cut off t'woud Serve instead of a Wool Pack in the House of Peers for one of the Bishops to sit upon – poor Miss Wall. tis well she does not hear me for she wou'd not

27 'The Lady's Disaster', 1746, exposing the comic possibilities of large hoops. The theme is echoed in Ann Pellet's descriptions of embarrassing accidents with hoops in the same decade.

like perhaps to have a Bishops Bum placed upon her Noddle.'[31] Bulletins like these satisfied Mrs Shackleton's curiosity and enabled her to feel pleasantly scandalized: 'I recd a long and an Entertaining letter from Mrs Ramsden of the present Indecent, Fashionable meetings of the Conspicuous, Great Ladies of this Isle fie for shame.'[32] Evidently Mrs Shackleton contemplated the beau monde with a mixture of tantalized fascination and delicious disapproval.

While Elizabeth Shackleton's correspondents satisfied her general interest in fashion and the fashionable, they also answered specific inquiries concerning the making of negligées, nightgowns and sacks for wear in Lancashire. Her informants made suggestions based on a variety of criteria, recommending dresses that would be fashionable but also durable, versatile, attractive and appropriate to Elizabeth's age and modest height. Modes that originated at court might be rejected on aesthetic grounds – 'very ugly for all they are the Queen's', or in the name of modesty – 'it would not be thought decent for a widow with Children to show so much nakedness'. Extreme vogues were thought best confined to the peerage, who were accorded a degree of sartorial licence – 'the above is indeed the present tast and I am sorry to say much run in to by people of no rank'.[33] On the other hand, new designs might be more readily adopted if considered 'becoming', 'in character', 'prettiest for us Mothers', 'the Genteelest thing' or 'an Easy Fashion', while fabrics were chosen according to the time of year, in colours that would last. Efforts were made to match outfit to occasion. In the 1750s Ann Pellet suggested a long sack with a hoop for a formal wedding visit because it would look 'much more noble'.[34] (Although hoops were increasingly outmoded in everyday wear, they were still worn at official functions and at court.)

The relationship of fashion, age and decorum was hotly debated by the

28   'A lady in the Dress of the Year 1764', from Elizabeth Parker/Shackleton's Pocket Diary of 1765.

A Lady in the full Dress of 1772

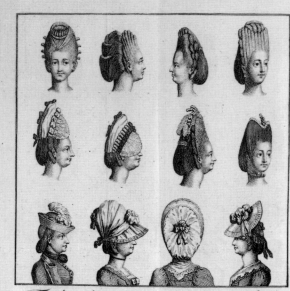

Twelve of the genteelest Head-dresses of 1772

29 (*above*) 'A lady in the Dress of the Year 1772', and 'Twelve of the genteelest Head-dresses of 1772', from Elizabeth Shackleton's Pocket diary of 1773.

Designed & Engraved for the Ladies New Memorandum Book.

Ladies of Quality in the most fashionable Head dresses

31 (*facing page*) 'A lady in the full Dress of the Year 1775', Frontispiece to Elizabeth Shackleton's Pocket Diary of 1776.

30 'Ladies of Quality in the Most Fashionable Headresses', from Elizabeth Shackleton's Pocket Diary of 1780.

genteel. Traditional pundits held that 'from a married woman engaged in family concerns, a more staid behaviour is expected than from a young woman before marriage; and consequently a greater simplicity of dress.'[35] For her part, Ann Pellet was not altogether pleased to see ladies of ninety years of age parading in flounced negligées, while Bessy Ramsden thought polonaises inappropriate for matrons and Italian nightgowns unsuitable for the old. However, Jane Scrimshire believed that it was behind the times to force older women to renounce fashion: 'I think I know you so well that I Can't help guessing at what thot will occur to you at this . . . [that] . . . a Marry'd Woman & a Mother of Children [should] talk of Dress but these my Dr Friend are Antiquated Notions & were you here you wo'd find Women of Sixty and Seventy just as anxious about [fashion] as formerly Girls were at 18.' The letters of all three women suggest that it was not only the young who were expected to dress modishly, but that different fashions were thought appropriate for different age groups. Dresses that suited 'the gravity of an elderly widow' were thought 'far [too] grave for a young wife'. Fashions were already targeted at 'young and middel age Ladies' as well as 'Elderly people'.[36]

Frontispiece.

A Lady in the full Dress of the Year 1775.

T. Cook sculp.

THE

LADIES

MOST ELEGANT AND CONVENIENT

POCKET BOOK,

For the YEAR 1776.

CONTAINING

Amongst a great Variety of useful, ornamental, and instructive Articles, the following:

The necessary Pages for Engagements, Memorandums, and Expences, ruled in a more plain and familiar Manner than any yet adapted for the Use of the Ladies; Poetical Address to the Ladies: Holidays at the different Offices; Remarkable Days in the Year; Prose Address to the Ladies; A Letter from her present Majesty to the King of Prussia; Poetry; Favourite New Songs sung at the public Gardens; Country Dances; Marketing and Interest Tables; Rates of Coachmen, Chairmen, &c. &c.

Compiled at the Request of several Ladies of Quality.

LONDON:

Printed for J. WHEBLE, No. 22, Fleet-Street; and sold by J. BEW, in PATER-NOSTER ROW.

Ten fashionable Head-dresses of 1786.

32   'Ten Fashionable Head-dresses of 1786', from the *Ladies Own Memorandum Book* (1787).

Elizabeth Shackleton and her friends both kept abreast of London fashion and exercised considerable discrimination. Engagement with fashion involved complicated decision-making; some designs were accepted *tout court*, some adapted for use in Lancashire, and others rejected out of hand. Mrs Shackleton was not a slavish imitator of elite modes, nor a passive victim of the velocity of fashion, for passive victims rarely exhibit a sense of humour, witness a satirical poem she transcribed:

> Shepherds I have lost my waist. Have you seen my body?
> Sacrificed to modern taste, I'm quite a Hoddy Doddy.
> Never shall I see it more, Till common sense returning
> My body to my legs restore, then I shall cease from mourning.
> For Fashion I that part forsook where sages plac'd the belly
> Tis lost and I have not a nook for cheesecakes, tarts or jelly![37]

London Pub by SW Fores N.3 Piccadilly December 1.1794

Shepherds I have lost my Waist!
Have you seen my Body?
Sacrificed to modern Taste,
I'm quite a Hoddy Doddy!
For Fashion I that part forsook
Where Sages place the Belly.
Tis gone — & I have not a nook
For Cheese cake, Tart, or Jelly!"

THE RAGE
or
Shepherds I have lost
MY Waist

Never shall I see it more,
Till Common Sense returning,
My Body to my Legs restore.
Then I shall cease from mourning:
Folly & Fashion do prevail
To such extreams among the Fair,
A Woman's only Top and Tail,
The Body's Banished God knows where!!!

33 'The Rage or Shepherds I have lost my Waist', 1794. A later version of the satirical poem
that Beatrix Parker of Marshfield gave Elizabeth Shackleton in the late 1770s.

Riding Drefs.   Full Drefs.   Undrefs.

Lady Torrington.   *Lady Archer.* ʃʃʃ   *Lady Waldegrave.*

34   Triptych, 'Lady Torrington', 'Lady Archer' and 'Lady Waldegrave', in Riding Dress, Full
Dress and Undress, *c.*1777.

How widespread was this equivocal relationship with high fashion? A
desire for precise *information* about new modes was widespread. Women
in the Whitaker, Barcroft, Dawson–Greene, Stanhope and Gossip networks all received regular fashion reports from female kin in the capital
and polite urban centres. However, a certain disdain for the absurdity of
metroplitan excess was *de rigueur* and a proper sense of the triviality of
fashion was often paraded. The worldly Mary Warde, for instance, complained about the need to 'sacrifice more time at the Toilet' when in
company, 'which I allways think sadly spent . . .', while Anna Larpent
declared herself resigned to the bore of dressing: 'a necessary tax on
time.'[38] Neverthless, most gentlewomen did aim at a general compliance
with metropolitan fashion in clothes, although adaptation for local use, in
keeping with the more relaxed decorum of the countryside, was very
common. The toning down of aristocratic designs was often preferred to
'a great deal of shew'; an impression which is confirmed by Anne Buck's
case study of the consumer choices facing southern provincial gentlewomen.[39] However, it does seems likely that this measured engagement
with London fashion was peculiar to the cautious wives of genteel merchants, professionals and lesser gentry. Peers, plutocrats and upper gentry

Ladies in the Dress of 1786.

35 'Ladies in the Dress of 1786' from the *Ladies' Own Memorandum Book* (1787).

Corbould, del.   Springsguth sculp.

Fashionable Dresses.

36   'Fashionable Dresses', from *Carnan's Ladies Complete Pocket Book for 1802.*

were sartorially much less inhibited (as were prosperous urban traders, according to Lorna Weatherill[40]), but many women were far more constrained. In her impoverished youth Ellen Weeton had suffered the ignominy of shabby garments, so her brother, a legal apprentice in Preston, could appear well dressed, and thereby lost several of her genteel acquaintances. In middle age she self-consciously adopted 'a neat, plain style of dress' consistent with her straitened finances and status as an unmarried governess. Although drawing puritanical satisfaction from her sartorial nonconformity, Ellen Weeton recorded the rude stares and 'severe insults and mortifications' she brought upon herself. In fact one of her friends refused to take her to church until she had ordered 'something fit to appear in' from the mantua-maker.[41]

Beyond its instrumental role, the exchange of information 'in the fashion way' had wider implications for feminine culture. Filling their letters with 'Fashions, Flounces & Flourishes', women shared doubts, advice and experience.[42] Basic to female relationships was the exchange of consumer services. Both Bessy Ramsden and Ann Pellet willingly fulfilled Elizabeth's fashionable commissions for 'tis allways a pleasure to serve our friends', sustaining relationships over two decades without a single meeting. ('Bessy is proud her Marketings gave Content . . . I verily believe she *did her best* and if at any time you would *highly oblige* Her, send Her *a Shopping.*'[43]) In a similar manner, Eliza Parker shopped for family and friends in Preston and York in the 1800s; Anne Robbins sent boxes of modish London clothes to her Lancashire nieces in the 1810s; and in the same decade Elizabeth Reynolds bought metropolitan goods on behalf of her female kin.[44] In practice, fashion had far more significance for a woman's relationship with other women than for her relationship with men.

❊   ❊   ❊

A genuine effort to explore women's relationship with the world of goods must move beyond the moment of purchase – a mere snapshot in the life of a commodity. In fact, Elizabeth Shackleton rarely recorded exactly why she purchased an item, but instead chronicled the way domestic goods were used and the multitude of meanings invested in possessions over time. In consequence, this second section is devoted to domestic material culture. It also sets bought commodities in the context of artefacts acquired by other means, such as inheritance, home-production and gift-exchange. The discussion examines the roles of artefacts in social practices: the maintenance of property was a constituent of genteel house-keeping, goods served as currency in the mistress–servant relationship, possessions were key props in inconspicuous ceremonies, but they also demonstrated polite conformity and were easy targets for social criticism. The discussion then proceeds to an elaboration of the range of meanings artefacts could embody.

The practice of housekeeping provided Elizabeth Shackleton with an esteemed role; her skills enabled her to remain useful to her sons and afforded a gratifying means of favourable comparison with other women. Nevertheless, in large part, housekeeping was a form of work which lacked an obvious and lasting product. Well-serviced clothes and domestic goods were in themselves rare and tangible proof of her labour. Wherever possible Mrs Shackleton prolonged the life of her semi-durable

possessions: 'I made me a work bag of my old, favourite, pritty, red &
white Linnen gown', and three years later, 'made a cover for the Dressing
drawers of my pritty Red & white linnen gown.' She took delight in
ingenious adaptation and thrift. 'I cut a pair of fine worsted stockings,
good legs & bad feet – to draw over my Stocking to keep my knees warm
– Like them much now they are made properly for the use.' Household
goods were valued for their fitness to purpose and for long years of trusty
service: 'to my vexation cross & rude Betty broke Mr S.'s pot that he has
had for his tea at Breakfast many years. She pore hot water init out of the
tea kettle & crack'd it all to pieces.'[45]

In addition to providing the architecture of her material role, goods
were part of the currency of the mistress–servant relationship. What was
Elizabeth Shackleton's to give and the servants' to take was subject to
negotiation and reinterpretation, as already noted, but a servant's right to
clothing was a particularly disputed issue – the confusion compounded by
the practice of occasional payment in kind and the provision of liveries for
menservants. Over and above payment, servants could expect discarded
clothing depending upon their mistress's mood.[46] Elizabeth Shackleton's
commentary suggests that these goods were offered in a spirit of gracious
patronage, not in recognition of the legitimacy of a customary perquisite.
However, if she hoped to foster deferential gratitude in her workforce,
Mrs Shackleton was constantly disillusioned. Unrepentant and ungovernable servants regularly packed up and threatened to be off 'with their
wardrobe'. Indeed, Elizabeth found that withholding a servant's belong-
ings could be a useful tactic in delaying their departure.[47] These domestic
servants have left no direct testimony, but from their mistress's records it
is obvious that they accepted new and cast-off clothes and trinkets, which
Mrs Shackleton believed them to value: 'Gave Betty [some] old Oratorio
Gauze that came of a white chip hat, it will make her very fine.'[48] However,
it is far from certain that wearing a lady's dress made a parlour maid look,
feel or be treated like a lady. To presume she wished she was a lady might
seem legitimate, but certainly does not follow from evidence that she
accepted a second-hand dress. After all, second-hand dresses could be
attractive simply because they had a high resale value. Moreover, the
efforts ex-servants made to retrieve their wages and wardrobe, including
the threat of legal action, suggest that clothing was seen as an important
part of their earnings, rather than merely the coveted equipment of social
emulation.[49]

One of the striking features of Elizabeth Shackleton's diaries is the way
in which she characterized almost all her possessions (clothes, plate,

kitchenware and linen) as either 'best' or 'common'. Common goods were those designated indispensable. Best goods were not necessarily new or fashionable. Neither does this best/common dichotomy neatly correspond with a public/private or front/back characterization of eighteenth-century domestic space. Elizabeth Shackleton drew on a conception of the occasion and the everyday to differentiate the ways things were used. The occasion may indeed have involved company and social display, but that did not define the event. Religious and sentimental observance both generated celebration, with or without an audience. Christian feasts called for special clothes, best tableware and thoughtfully arranged furniture. Family anniversaries were commemorated by private rituals involving new clothes and old treasures. On Tom Parker's twenty-fourth birthday, although he was absent and there were no visitors, his mother 'put on in Honour to this Good day my quite new purple Cotton night Gown And a new light brown fine cloth Pincushion [made of] a piece of coat belonging to my own Dear child, my own dear Tom, with a new Blue string'. On his twenty-fifth birthday she donned the same pincushion. Congratulating her youngest son on his birthday in 1777, Elizabeth Shackleton wrote 'I wish and better wish you my own dear love was with us . . . I have your valuable rings on my fingers, John's picture before me and my Bracelet on the table I write upon.'[50] Such intimate rituals emphasize the talismanic properties of material things and bear witness to the personal significance of inconspicuous consumption. Elizabeth Shackleton used material things to honour God and her family, to lend substance to her relationships and ultimately as reassurance in the face of death, witness her prayers in May 1779, in her fifty-third year: 'I now have only five teeth in all in my head. I left off my old stays & put on my best stays for Good. I left off my very old green quilted Callimanco Petticoat and put on my new drab Callimanco quilted petticoat for good. God Grant me my health to wear it & do well.'[51]

This is not to say that Elizabeth Shackleton was ignorant of social convention and the necessity for material and sartorial observance. Guests were usually treated to the best china and linen. When surprise visitors arrived at dinner-time, Mrs Shackleton 'made all nice as we co'd for our Guests. Used my handsome, new, Damask table cloth which looks most beautiful for the first [time]. Good luck to it, hope it will do well.'[52] When visiting herself, and in particular when attending dinner-parties and celebrations, Mrs Shackleton made a conscious and obvious effort: 'dress'd myself in my best A High Head & low Heels . . .'[53] She endeavoured to dress appropriately for the occasion:

> Mrs W. traild me through nasty dirtyvile back streets to [York] Minster, where we took several turns ... Mrs W. *would* have me put on my beautifull flower'd Muslin [which] was entirely [soiled] by the dust. Little wo'd have I done it had not she told me we were to have call'd upon Mrs Townend, for her to take me through all those nasty places in York a Hop sack wo'd have done ... [54]

Both in company and alone, her commitment to sartorial propriety ran deep. Social discomfort is palpable in this terse but revealing aside: 'Tom so cross, wo'd not let me have a cap out of the green room. I sat bare head a long time.'[55] Evidently, Elizabeth Shackleton's pride in wearing clothes appropriate to her companions, environment and occasion went beyond a simple desire to impress.

Mrs Shackleton's concern for proper ceremony, or informality, expressed in things was not confined to herself. Elegant dress in women, if combined with wifely decorum, merited a pleasant reference from Mrs Shackleton. She had nothing but praise for her nephew's wife, Beatrix Lister, and their neat, tasteful and elegant home, 'Chateau Marshfield'. She approved of various mansions she visited – 'made a long stop to reconitre [Mr Lascelle's] fine and elegant building' – and of the taste and civility of their owners – 'Mr Clayton who was as civil as possible showed me his Grounds Canals Garden & the House.'[56] Moreover, she was not an automatic critic of luxurious display. She had no quarrel with the glorious raiment of a local lawyer and his wife: 'Mr [&] Mrs Wainman came in good time to dinner. A very Agreable woman Elegantly dress'd. Diamonds & Pearls on her head. She is half gone with Child. A very Happy couple they are. Had a Handsome Carriage, Handsome Horses, Handsome Liveries – dark blue trim'd with silver ...'[57] However, she was quick to call into question the sartorial motivation of those she disliked. Things which demonstrated dignity, civility and elegance in her friends, could in others just as easily represent foolish pretension. Fashionable dress worn by women she disliked was immediately taken to be proof of feminine conceit and inconsequence, as was the case with the unfortunate Miss Clough, who was airily written off as 'a Fortune. A dressy person. Wears a very great Role.'[58] Nor was her contempt reserved for women. By 1779 Elizabeth Shackleton suspected that a neighbour, Owen Cunliffe of Wycoller, had been gossiping about her. She vented her spleen in a description of his ostentation and pretension:

> I knew that Cunliffe was at church this day in his Regementals, a *small* Captain, no Honour to the Royal Lancashire. Bro't his new Whiskey to Coln his new Man in his Elegant new Livery, red hair well powder'd,

two new Hunters. Can have a fortune by a Lady of £9,000 but thinks he deserves thrice that sum. – Cunliffe is too short too low – wants inches for a Captain.a Petit trop Petit Captain.[59]

When Sergeant Aspinall, a barrister on the northern circuit, acted against the interests of the Parkers of Browsholme and the Listers of Gisburne Park in the disputed Clitheroe election of 1781, Elizabeth Shackleton was furious. In her diary, she linked Aspinall's naked political ambitions with the architectural improvements recently undertaken at his seat, Standen Hall:

> That scrubby, Mean, underbred, lowlived, Ungrateful, Covetous, designing, undermining, Stupid, Proud Aspinall and his Large Wife May come to repent . . . He *within* these 30 years wo'd have esteem'd it a *Great* Honour and been Big of the application of being styl'd recorder of Clitheroe. What a wretch to behave so vilely to his most obliging, generous, worthy neighbours, Browsholme & Gisburne park . . . [He] most probably thinks Mr Curzon's Purse will enable him to make a Portico or add a Venetian window to the Beauties of Standen. What nonsense is he. Tho' like such a breed as he comes off . . . such *Little Men*.[60]

Clearly Mrs Shackleton did not disapprove of finery and elegant surroundings *per se*, or indeed of social status expressed in things. None the less, accusations of materialism, pretension and covetousness provided useful ammunition for criticism of those who did not know their place, had slighted her in the past or she simply disliked.

When it came to her own things, on the other hand, her professions of their personal value and associations were lofty and sentimental, as one might expect. Things for Elizabeth Shackleton were rich with memory:

> Wrote to my own dear Robert Parker, told him I was concerned I had told him I wo'd send the bible I had promised him, but that upon looking for it, found I had given it to my own dear Tom when he went to Winchester. But had sent him a good common prayer book [instead] given to me by Mr Cowgill of Emmanuel College, Cambridge who was there when his own good father was . . . I told him I would give him a ring that was made for my own dear mother, her hair under a crystal, the star round it all brilliants, worth ten guineas, which I beg'd he'd ever keep and wear for my sake . . . sent a piece of Brussels lace I promised him, desired he'd keep in remembrance of me.[61]

Even intrinsically mundane items testified to past relationships, or commemorated past events: 'My dear John gives me a full account of [Tom's] Wedding. Which letter I shall ever keep while I live.' Gifts were valued in themselves and as material proof of the kind thoughts of others: 'I esteem the ruffles very elegant and handsome, but what enhances the value to me is my dear Tom's most obliging remembrance.' Ever after, a gift prompted pleasant memories of the donor and the moment of giving, 'with his own dear hands'. Home-made presents were usually offered by women and were seen as time, labour and affection made concrete: 'I had the pleasure to recieve from Dear Miss Parker . . . a pritty green Purse with Spangles, her own work which I much value.'[62] Elizabeth Shackleton treasured items which had once belonged to people she loved, recording the wearing and mending of her mother's old shifts and the distribution of her first husband's clothing to his sons.[63] Certain possessions literally embodied something of the original owner, like the ring incorporating her dead mother's hair. Doubtless it was with one eye on being remembered herself that Elizabeth Shackleton set about creating a new heirloom, making extensive enquiries, five years before she died, for a craftsman 'who co'd do me an extreme neat Landscape in [my own] hair for my new Bracelet.' She also had a bracelet made up of hair from the heads of her three sons 'so as to shew all the hair distinctly'.[64]

Elizabeth Shackleton was not alone in ascribing meanings to inanimate objects. She drew on a shared awareness of the extra-material significance of things and in particular gifts. Tom and Betty Parker, for example, exchanged hair rings as love tokens during their courtship.[65] (However, Betty Parker's offences included sacreligiously cutting up the lace which had once belonged to Elizabeth's own mother and being insufficiently appreciative of Elizabeth's gifts.) The regular exchange of produce and trinkets was a significant currency in elite sociability. Elizabeth's estranged brother Edward Parker signalled his forgiveness in a gift and she appreciated the beginning of the thaw when she received 'a haunch of venison by the keeper of Bowland for which I gave him five shillings. This is the first present or taste I have had from Browsholme since I changed my name being six years.'[66] Shared awareness of extra-material meaning is most explicit in the case of painted portraits, which carried the most powerful human resonances and demanded remembrance of the sitter. When Elizabeth's sons Tom and John Parker were at odds, Tom's wife symbolically removed John Parker's portrait from her drawing-room and returned it forthwith to Elizabeth Shackleton. The mother cherished the abandoned portrait and recorded, 'On this day my own Dear John Parker's Picture was done up over the fire Place in the Parlour. I am truly Happy to see it there & think it dos great Honour to its Situation.'[67]

Things conjured the past and ensured continuity into the future. The completed purchase of large items of furniture, particularly in the last few years of her life, often occasioned a prayer, confided to her diary: 'John Hargreaves of Coln Edge brought my new Mahogany square tea table. I like it very well. God Grant Mr S. & myself to have good & long use of it.'[68] Evidently, heavy furniture felt reassuringly permanent and substantial, yet its arrival prompted the ailing Elizabeth Shackleton to contemplate her own mortality, perhaps because furnishing a house was characteristically associated with the beginning of married life rather than its end; this is how she recorded a furniture purchase the year before her death:

[Arrived a] . . . new Mahogany Dining Table from Messrs Gillows from Lancaster – it came quite safe & well not the least damage or scratch. It is in three parts. The middle a square and two ends which are half rounds all put together makes an elegant Oval. The Wood very handsome. 16 feet all very strong and made neat it cost the table only £5 5s Packing 3s 6d in all £5: 8: 6. good luck to it. Good luck using it & hope we shall all have our Healths & do well.[69]

The christening of a functional item was a private ritual: 'I wrote this [her diary] upon our new Oak table the very first time I ever did write upon it or use it – Good Luck attend me . . .'[70] The recording of first usage is consistent with Elizabeth Shackleton's pronounced awareness of the passage of time and the importance of the past and her memories in her everyday life.

Elizabeth Shackleton's sense of the family history and the continuity which Alkincoats represented was brought to its fullest expression when Tom Parker finally claimed his full inheritance, two years after his majority: 'Great alteration in this family . . . Tom was whole and sole master of Alkincoats.'[71] Quitting her marital home and household pre-eminence proved a drawn-out process. Mrs Shackleton immediately delivered all her diamonds and valuables into her son's hands. A year later she ritually handed over 'the keys of the Buroe where he wo'd find all the keys', a blatant act of resignation. Yet the final rupture did not come till 1779, when Tom married, at which point she definitively removed herself and her chattels to Pasture House: 'They all saw me come off Bag and Baggage. am Happy to leave good old Alkincoats my once Happy Home to my own Dear Dear Dear Dear Tom . . .'[72]

This spectacular loss of status was one she was prepared for and rationalized in what historians have often interpreted as stock gentry terms: the continuity of the family and the line, the importance of old traditions and the fundamental stability of the estate itself being of greater significance than any individual tenant. Thus, she deferred to and prayed for Tom and his new wife on their wedding day: 'Grant them Health & long life, Prosperity & comfort. May they enjoy Domestick Peace . . . May Good old *Alkincoats* Flourish in every degree. Long may the Usual Generous Hospitality Flourish within & without those *Walls* that ever did.'[73] Elizabeth Shackleton observed both the letter and the spirit of Robert Parker's will. Although she was miserable departing from her old home and experienced pangs upon its redecoration ('My poor, good, old yellow room. Transmogrified indeed into Elegance . . .'[74]), she remained convinced of the importance of inheritance and perceived herself as a guardian of property entrusted to, and on loan from later generations of Parkers:

> On this day I emptied all & everything belonging unto me out of my Mahogany Bookcase, Buroe & drawers. Given unto me by my own Tender, Good & most Worthy Father . . . My kind and most affectionate Parent. They were made & finish'd by Henry Chatburne on Saturday December the eighth one thousand seven Hundred and Fifty. I value them much but relinquish the valuable Loan with great Satisfaction to my own Dear Child Thomas Parker.[75]

Elizabeth Shackleton's records reveal the role of material things in a range of social practices. She presided over and performed the bulk of the day-to-day purchasing for her household and the maintenance of the goods therein. By extension, well-chosen and well-maintained possessions testified to her expertise and gratified her self-esteem. Eventually, many of these possessions served as currency in the mistress–servant relationship. Over and above their purely practical function, Elizabeth Shackleton's possessions both acted as crucial props in unobserved, intimate rituals and displayed her social status to the wider public. When slighted, she deployed the rhetoric of luxury and vanity to belittle the motives and material culture of her enemies. By contrast, her own world of goods was rich and complex. When self-consciously writing about her own possessions, she dwelt at length on their sentimental and talismanic associations. Growing frail, she contemplated the durability of the material in contrast to transience of flesh, hoping her heirlooms would guarantee remembrance. Ultimately, she drew reassurance from her belief in the continuity of the Parker family and estate and the importance of inheritance. Of course, Elizabeth Shackleton was a very privileged consumer. The very mahogany which carried family history down through time was itself an emblem of genteel status. Mrs Shackleton's property proved that she belonged to the local elite, and simultaneously distanced her from the likes

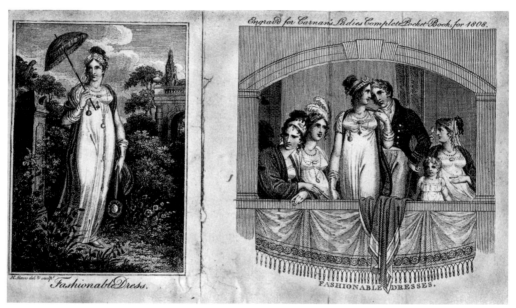

37 'Fashionable Dress' and 'Fashionable Dresses', from *Carnan's Ladies Complete Pocket Book for 1808.*

of Betty Hartley Shopkeeper, but social differentiation through material possessions is a subtly different phenomenon to social emulation.

Elizabeth Shackleton updated her wardrobe for her own gratification and for social propriety. She doubtless would have agreed with the likes of Lady Sarah Pennington who decreed, 'a Compliance with Fashion, so far as to avoid the Affectation of Singularity is necessary, but to run into the Extream of Fashions, more especially those which are inconvenient is the certain proof of a weak mind . . .'[76] Nevertheless, a subterranean pleasure may have been derived from the display of London modes to Lancashire society, yet only once in her entire correspondence was an item recommended on those grounds. In an effort to reconcile her suspicious cousin to some ostentatious fabrics, Bessy Ramsden exploited the language of emulation: '[The Silks] were to be shure vastly pretty and the extraordinary trouble in the working of 'em will be amply repaid you in the Envy & c they will excite among the Misses of Coln.'[77] Granted, Elizabeth Shackleton adopted some stylish innovations which originated at court, but that did not necessarily mean she admired the 'Ladies of Quality' or wanted to be the Duchess of Devonshire. Besides, even if an item was originally bought for the express purpose of dazzling east Lancashire, it could in time become a repository of memories or a grateful reward: 'I gave Betty Cooke my strip'd & sprigg'd muslin Apron above Thirty years in my Possession.'[78]

It is also important to recall that not all categories of goods were equally susceptible to fashion. Metropolitan chic was more highly prized in clothing than in tableware, in tableware than in furniture and in furniture than in kitchenware. Nor did fashion obliterate all other associations. Elizabeth Shackleton's hair jewellery offers an explicit example of the possible coexistence of different systems of meaning. Constituted of human hair, such ornaments were potent extensions of the self. They were bequeathed to loved ones as heirlooms and were exchanged by lovers as tokens of mutuality and romantic esteem. Private associations notwithstanding, they also signalled an engagement with high fashion, enjoying along with other 'love ornaments' a massive vogue in the later eighteenth century.

Even if the new clothes, tableware and furniture bought by Elizabeth Shackleton were all broadly fashionable in form, their form neither expressed the full range of her motivations nor did it dictate the function these goods performed for her. Elizabeth Shackleton's records testify to the sheer diversity of meanings it was possible to attach to possessions. Of course, meanings were not absolutely rigid, since objects accrued different connotations according to use and context, yet some general patterns can be observed. Large or expensive items, bought new or inherited, were suggestive of history and lineage. The reassuring permanence associated with substantial pieces of furniture was akin to that conveyed by the built environment: furniture, carriages, roads, bridges and houses were all blessed in similar terms by Elizabeth Shackleton.[79] Unsurprisingly, pieces of clothing and accoutrements expressed individuality, promoting the remembrance of original owner or donor. Kitchen utensils were valued for trusty service, ingenuity and sometimes novelty, while china and tableware signified genteel ceremony and pleasant sociability.

Of course it is possible that Elizabeth Shackleton was an isolated material obsessive, but this seems unlikely, given the corroborating references which can be found in other manuscripts. While demonstrating their expertise as fashionable consumers, Elizabeth's friends also sent her sentimental gifts, for, as Jane Scrimshire remarked, '*small presents* Confirm friend[ship]'. Bessy Ramsden used the language of remembrance to recommend her offerings – 'I have taken the liberty to enclose a cap which you will do me Great Honour to except. It is by way of your seeing what Trimming will be wore in the second mourning. I do desire that you will wear it for my Sake and not put it up in Lavender.' A preoccupation with family history expressed in things can be found in Ann Pellet's letters.

When Elizabeth was pressed to raise an apprenticeship fee, she asked permission to sell the diamond stay-buckles given by her Aunt Pellet. Mrs Pellet authorized the sale with the following proviso: 'I . . . only beg you'll never give them out of your *family*, as I had [them] many yrs, was yr dear Grandmamma's – Mrs Scrimshire seem'd to entertain some hopes of my giving them to her, but I never once design'd it as t'wod be very unnatural to give [them] out of my family.'[80]

Although the breadth of commentary on consumption and property found in Elizabeth Shackleton's diaries is unparalleled among surviving Lancashire manuscripts, elements of her value system can be found in the records of other women outside her acquaintance.[81] But this is not to argue that every woman's relationship with material culture was the same. Elizabeth Shackleton was in her forties and fifties when she wrote the diaries, a younger woman might have ranked the purchase of novelties over the conservation of old treasures. Furthermore, a custodial attitude to property might be peculiar to the experience of widowhood and trustee-ship. Not all women had Elizabeth Shackleton's opportunity to develop a housekeeping, curatorial ethos in their dealings with things. Sentimental materialism, along with mahogany furniture, may have been a luxury many women simply could not afford.

The diary and letters of Ellen Weeton lend themselves to an analysis of consumer motivation in terms of the pursuit of social acceptance, envy and wishful thinking: 'If I were rich enough to buy furniture, and to take a house and keep a servant, I could have as much society – highly respect-able – as I could wish.' Nevertheless, amongst the palpable social anxiety and preoccupation with respectability, sentiments of striking similarity to Elizabeth Shackleton's are revealed. Ellen Weeton made every effort to pass on domestic expertise to her daughter by letter, urging Mary Stock to practise measurement, cutting out and sewing and sending minute accounts of her purchases, 'for you will never be fit to be a housekeeper unless you know the value of most things in daily use'. Concerned to provide her daughter with a sense of family history, Ellen sent a bundle of humble heirlooms, cataloguing their past associations:

The green ribbon is part of a box-full my mother (your Grandmother Weeton) once had; they were taken in a prize which my father captured during the American war . . . I am thus minute, my Mary, that you might know something of the history of your mother's family . . . The piece of patchwork is of an old Quilt, I made it above 20 years ago . . . The Hexagon in the middle was a shred of our best bed hangings . . . they were Chintz . . . which my father brought home with him from one of his voyages . . .[82]

Even where things were coveted for social status, this does not preclude the simultaneous existence of more complex responses to material things. Social emulation and conspicuous consumption are useful concepts accounting for purchasing motivation under certain circumstances, but as portmanteau descriptions of eighteenth- and early ninteenth-century consumer behaviour and material culture they are dangerously misleading. Certainly the language of luxury and longing was available to and occasionally deployed by contemporary consumers, yet this was only one vocabulary among many. Wedgwood china figured in genteel material culture, but took its place alongside an assemblage of other artefacts equally important to their owner: inherited cabinets, family portraits, christening cups, favourite old teapots, home-made purses, scraps of faded gowns, and locks of hair set in gold. Material culture before Victoria will not reduce to a shallow search for competetive status in goods.[83]

One final question remains: to what extent could these material values be seen as distinctively female? Only further investigation of male consumption will truly clarify this. Nevertheless, recent research on the wills of both sexes suggests marked gender differences in attitudes to commodities once possessed. Women's records consistently reveal a more self-conscious, emotional investment in household goods, apparel and personal effects. On the rare occasions when male testators particularized their personal property they usually referred to tools or livestock.[84] Exactly why this should be the case is in question, although possible answers come readily to hand. A gentlewoman was far more likely than her brothers to inherit personal property, while real property (land) tended to be reserved for male beneficiaries. As a result, most women had only movable goods to bestow.[85] Denied access to the professions and public office, women could not pass on the invisible mysteries of institutional power or professional expertise to their descendants. A gentlewoman's skills were characteristically embodied in that 'unskilled' arena, the household.[86] Small wonder if, in consequence, she turned to personal and household artefacts to create a world of meanings and, ultimately, to transmit her history.

6

Civility and Vulgarity

IN THE DOG DAYS OF 1778 a gentry family reopened their Pennine mansion for the shooting season. To mark their return the Waltons of Marsden Hall threw a sumptuous dinner for a clerical couple, for the local doctor and for their old friend Elizabeth Shackleton. All was elegantly arranged and the small company feasted on a cornucopia of 'rich fruit' from the Waltons' hotbeds and orchards: pineapples, peaches, nectarines, pears, plums, currents and gooseberries lay on the supper table in profusion. At the end of the evening, Mrs Walton dispensed choice treats. She handed over the vermicelli she had been commisioned to buy for her friend in York, gave a myrtle as a gift and loaned out some some fashionable pamphlets: *The Court of Adultery a Vision* and *An Interesting Letter to the Duchess of Devonshire*. 'A most Elegant dinner', concluded Elizabeth Shackleton with approval, 'Very much made off', she smiled. Thus the Waltons were received back into the genteel community with warmth and ease.[1]

The public significance of home-based hospitality has long been recognized by early modern historians. Indeed, it is something of a truism that the seventeenth-century family was a resoundingly public institution and the large country house a centre of influence and patronage, the stage on which a gentleman dramatized his power and magnanimity to his locality. In the words of Henry Wotton's *Elements of Architecture* of 1624, 'Every man's proper Mansion house and home [is] the theatre of his hospitality, the seat of self-fruition'.[2] While the sad passing of good, old, rural hospitality which embraced all comers be they rich or poor, friend or stranger, was a proverbial seventeenth-century lament, social largesse nevertheless remained the hallmark of the gentleman and gentlewoman at home. Although Stone and Ariès have controversially argued that elite families became increasingly inward-looking over the course of the eighteenth century,[3] most studies of the eighteenth- and nineteenth-century gentry and nobility, stress that open-handed hospitality was still crucial to the maintenance of social credit and political power. Landed families recognized, at least in principal, an obligation to 'treat' their dependants, while exerting themselves to sustain convivial relations with their equals and superiors.[4] Moreover, there is also a suggestion that Tory families in particular breathed new life into country liberality, 'A true English Hospitality' in the context of eighteenth-century political patronage.[5] As mistress of ceremony, the elite hostess might wield considerable practical power from the head of her dining-table, a phenomenon which reaches back well into the sixteenth century and lived on in the nineteenth.[6] Certainly, the idea that the home was a refuge insulated from the social world is one that would have perplexed the rural gentry in this period.

That social exchanges in homes have a 'public' function is also basic to newer perspectives on sociability in America. Accounts of mid-nineteenth-century urban manners demonstrate that the middle-class parlour was the platform upon which a self-disciplined performance was enacted, stage-managed by the watchful Victorian hostess.[7] Recently, historians of American visiting have used their material deliberately to question the public/private dichotomy so widely deployed in women's studies. Research by Dallet Hemphill, for instance, on the Byzantine rules for social visits in ante-bellum conduct literature reveals that visiting was conceived of as a ritualized mixed-sex activity taking place on a terrain under feminine jurisdiction. Thus, she posits the existence of 'the social sphere, an intermediate sphere between the public and private worlds. The social sphere was an important arena for intermingling between the sexes . . . It was in some ways a female sphere, but it was neither private nor domestic.'[8] By its very nature, sociability resists the categories of public and private, for its very function is to integrate the two.

Historians of eighteenth-century Britain and Europe have become preoccupied with the operation of this social world and its new behavioural code 'politeness'. Built on continental traditions of civility, politeness was theoretically at odds with medieval conceptions of all-inclusive hospitality, since it justified the exclusive sociability of the well-bred, and distanced the vulgar. Nevertheless it assumed that dining-rooms and parlours were fitted for social traffic and cultural debate. After all, it was Addison's famous ambition to bring 'Philosophy out of Closets and Libraries, Schools and Colleges, to dwell in Clubs and Assemblies, Tea-Tables and in Coffee Houses'.[9] The early eighteenth-century periodicals, pre-eminently the *Tatler*, *Spectator* and the *Guardian*, celebrated polite con-

versation among educated men and rational women as the golden mean
between pedantry on the one hand and gossip on the other. And it is the
possibilities for women inherent in this edifying, conversable heterosexual
sociability which recent studies have emphasized, playing down the more
constraining definitions of female purpose which can also be found in the
same periodicals.[10] While English polite conversation never granted to
women as significant a role as did the French salon tradition,[11] it nevertheless assumed the refining influence of women on the conversable world. By
this view, 'politeness' was a way of conceptualizing an unofficial public
sphere to which privileged women could lay legitimate claim.

   The theoretical content of eighteenth-century politeness has been
closely studied through the examination of courtesy literature. Eighteenth-
century writers on manners inherited the concerns of Castiglione and Sir
Thomas Elyot, whose own tenets can be traced, like so much in western
culture, to Athens and Rome. At bottom, Augustan manners were
founded on Aristotelian moderation and Cicero's conception of 'decorum'
– the notion that an individual's behaviour should vary according to his or
her sex, social rank, occupation, age and immediate circumstances. Both
philosophers endorsed the stoic code as hammered out by Epictetus. Not
only did the citizen have a duty to use reason to restrain appetite and
passion, but he ought to cultivate an indifference to pleasure and pain,
eschewing all outward emotional display. To the classical legacy must be
added that of seventeenth-century France. Salon civility or *honneteté*
stressed the pleasing of others, especially women, by cultivating the arts of
conversation. All these ideas were synthesized by English writers under
the umbrella concept of 'good breeding', the most coherent expression of
which is John Locke's *Some Thoughts Concerning Education* of 1693.
However, by the 1730s the term 'good breeding' had fallen into disrepute,
its currency debased by association with modish superficiality. In its place
came 'politeness', which inherited the manners associated with good
breeding, but not the philosophic seriousness of its originators.[12]

   What attitudes and practices did good breeding and politeness comprehend? Good breeding was intimately linked with education and nurture,
conveying a sense of rounded personality, a cultivated understanding and
a thorough knowledge of ceremony. Its lynchpin was the assumption that
outer manners were the reflection of inner civility. Civil virtue was the
product of a proper sense of self combined with goodwill towards others.
Thus manners were not empty gestures, but the sincere expression of an
ethical code. Politeness had been applied to manners from at least the
1710s, but implied a greater emphasis on external conduct at the expense
of inner qualities. Interestingly, the polite model was not the aristocratic

Plate 2.

B. Dandridge Pinx.

L. P. Boitard Sculp.

According to Act of Parliament.

38   A woman demonstrating the gesture 'To GIVE or RECEIVE', from F. Nivelon, *The Rudiments of Genteel Behaviour: An Introduction to the Method of attaining a graceful Attitude, an agreeable Motion, an easy Air and a Genteel behaviour* (1737).

Plate 4.

B.Dandridge Pinx:

L.P.Boitard Sculp.

According to Act of Parliament.

39   A man demonstrating 'The Complement RETIRING' from F. Nivelon, *The Rudiments of Genteel Behaviour: An Introduction to the Method of attaining a graceful Attitude, an agreeable Motion, an easy Air and a genteel behaviour* (1737).

40   H. Gravelot, untitled lady, 1744.

41　H. Gravelot, untitled gentleman, 1744.

courtier, but the simple gentleman and gentlewoman. (From the tone and content of the advice, it appears that courtesy writers targeted the greater gentry.) The gentleman should maintain his rank through his manners: assuming an air of personal dignity, the appearance of easy assurance, a controlled deportment, the repression of emotional display, the assumption of distinguished speech, and by proper decorum in his relations with the world in all its various degrees. In similar fashion, the gentlewoman should be distinguished by an air of dignified ease and graceful control, taking care to treat others according to their status. In addition, she was encouraged to be clean, to adopt nice table manners and foster the art of diverting conversation. But her gentility, did not provide exemption from the rules for Everywoman, above all, she was to be modest and chaste.[13]

The practical application of contemporary theories of politeness is richly elaborated in Elizabeth Shackleton's diary. Probably no other source offers such a vivid, detailed and possibly petulant account of genteel sociability. It makes possible a reconstruction of the processes of home-based sociability and an elaboration of the language used to assess social behaviour in which it is apparent that the historians' perceived dichotomy between a private, interior home secluded from a public, exterior world is inadequate in the consideration of both of space and attitudes. The late eighteenth-century genteel home was not in any simple sense 'off-stage', nor were basic assumptions about the conduct of social relations abandoned, like muddy boots, at the front door. Sociability both in and out of the house was evaluated in the same terms – terms derived from the courtesy tradition of civility and politeness. Further, if the genteel home was a stage, then it was one with many different settings which could accommodate everything from elite conviviality to the dispensation of patronage and the conduct of business, from mixed sex companies to congregations of men. Of course, individuals occasionally engineered private or secret encounters in their own houses, secluded from the gaze of an audience. In Elizabeth Shackleton's first courtship, her suitor Robert Parker pleaded for the chance of a clandestine interview in her chamber: 'I waited last night, Parky, till three a clock in hopes of spending an Hour wt you in private . . .', but failing that he petitioned for leave to spend 'a dinner or an Evening [with] you publickly'.[14] Yet most so-called 'private' encounters in the genteel home were exclusive social gatherings, for a powerful contrast was routinely drawn between the vulgar and the select, between inclusive sociability open to all and discriminating parties accessible to the few. It should be noted that in both these usages of public and private, the historian's distinction between a female home and a male world was *not* the dichotomy at work.

A 'boundless hospitality' was a hereditary characteristic of the Parkers of Browsholme celebrated the *Gentleman's Magazine*,[15] and Elizabeth Shackleton certainly bestirred herself to maintain something of that liberality which bespoke her ancestry. While she could not compete with the likes of Warde of Squerries, Kent, who entertained an estimated 7,000 of his country neighbours on strong beer to celebrate Admiral Vernon's (premature claims of) success at Cartagena in 1741,[16] Mrs Shackleton's diaries testify nevertheless to a certain festal lavishness. As mistress of Alkincoats Hall and later Pasture House, she kept a table 'publick' or invited 'a mixed multitude' to dine on days of local festivity, such as the village sports day and on an appointed day after Christmas.[17] Tenants were offered drinks or sometimes dinner on rent day, and 'tenants wives' were invited to elaborate tea parties. Sheep-shearers, hay-makers, mowers and stonemasons were treated with alcohol and a fiddler in the servants' hall at the end of their labours. Family anniversaries inevitably involved some gesture of inclusion to the immediate community. On Thomas Parker's sixteenth birthday the tenants were treated to boiled beef, plum pudding and quantities of ale. On his twenty-first birthday in 1775 over a hundred people (including the tenantry) sang and danced at Alkincoats to the tune of a fiddle till four in the morning.[18] And when the British took New York in 1776, Tom Parker sent five shillings for a toast at the Arms and John Shackleton sent two shillings and sixpence to the ale house to pay for a round of drinks. In addition, local children came to Pasture House to toss pancakes on Shrove Tuesday and could expect the odd coin or piece of produce to come their way at momentous points in their lives, such as christening or breeching. The local colliers were given a dole of two shillings every Christmas. With a similarly conspicuous face-to-face charity, Elizabeth Shackleton interested herself in local women in childbed, visiting them, sending pitchers of gruel or gifts of old linen. The blending of charity and sociability suggested by some diary entries does conjure the memory of the older ideas of hospitality outlined by Felicity Heal, however there is a striking departure from medieval good lordship. The Parkers and the Shackletons were suspicious of strangers and felt under no Christian obligation to shelter all-comers. Even a visitor claiming kinship, displaying privileged knowledge of the family and bearing eight woodcocks by way of open sesame was suspected to be an impostor, refused hospitality and shown to the alehouse to spend the night.[19] Good, old hospitality had to be reconciled with polite exclusivity.

The personnel of polite society in the North have already been introduced. That these families were known to and accepted by Elizabeth Shackleton was a function of geography and birth. Few experienced a formal moment of entry into the local elite. For strangers and incomers, however, social acceptance was not guaranteed. Known family connections, or the personal recommendation of a mutual friend smoothed an outsider's path. Both worked to the advantage of the young Owen Cunliffe of Sheffield, who moved into the area in the 1770s having inherited Wycoller through his uncle. It was his good fortune to meet John Parker in London who engineered his speedy introduction:

> The bearer of this is Mr Cunliffe who has often expressed to me the pleasure he should have in your acquaintance . . . I hope to hear you frequently spend time together . . . I imagine he will often pay you a visit at Alkincoats where I dare say he will meet with a hearty welcome from my mother & Mr Shackleton to the usual run of their table.[20]

Thereafter, Mrs Shackleton was prepared to be complaisant: 'saw young Mr Cunliffe at Church, seemingly a civil Man.'[21] Social acceptance was achieved only by degrees. The formal procedure is made explicit in a letter anticipating the arrival of the Bulcock family from Wapping: 'I am not fond of Cultivating new Acquaintance at my time of day. It is rather a disagreeable Circumstance but will send Compts when I know they are come to Langroyd and if we approve them upon knowing will make Neighbours of them & shew them civility.'[22] If visitors did not meet with unqualified approval, then a chilly civility might ward off further advances: '[My cousins] came here from Mr Claytons of Carr where they were cooly look'd on & their Invitation very slight.'[23] However, there is no evidence that Elizabeth Shackleton ever sent her servants to say she was not at home, or that she used that great nineteenth-century weapon 'the cut'.

Sending compliments, essentially brief messages, was the most basic form of polite notice, and required some acknowledgement in return. A large acquaintance could be maintained with occasional visits and the regular exchange of compliments via servants or tradespeople. Compliments were sent by way of introduction and welcome, to inquire after health and journeys, to take leave, to decline invitations, to offer congratulation and condolence, and to express gratitude for hospitality, gifts or compliments. It behoved the elite to broadcast these messages across the county: 'Mr Lister sent his own servant from there with a letter from him and compliments to the whole family at Cuerdon. Civil, Polite, Well judged & shewd Mr Lister, what he is – the Gentleman.' And protocol demanded reciprocity: 'Ralph Wilson the fish man from Coln Brought neither letter nor message after our enquiries of Mrs Parker of Browsholme. Very surprizing and extremely disrespectfull as Tom from his fall required the same.'[24] Few elite families escaped this ceaseless traffic. The newly married Mrs Mary Clayton complained in 1745 of 'the infinity of Compliments & Civilitys one is on such an occasion necessitated to pay & receive', while Anna Larpent observed in 1790 that 'writing notes on business, civility &c' was one of 'the Taxes of London society'.[25] Although a pointed failure to return compliments was one way to allow acquaintance to cool, conversely, association could be warmed into friendship through the exchange of visits, gifts and parties. Intimates and favourites might stay overnight or make lengthy sojourns.

Mrs Shackleton did not differentiate between ceremonious and friendly visits, although the distinction was certainly available in the period. Beau Nash expected 'ladies of quality and fashion' to make 'a visit of ceremony' on arrival or departure from Bath, and this formal means of honoring acquaintances was soon to be a common device of nineteenth-century etiquette.[26] Duty visits were hard to evade. Both family and friends were expected to keep up a decent level of social exchange and could be rebuked for their inattentiveness. Jane Scrimshire complained that the young Elizabeth Parker had not eaten mutton, drunk tea or even left a bit of card at her door in Pontefract since she married. Ann Pellet protested that her nephew Edward Parker of Browsholme 'has not behaved polite enough to keep within the bounds of common civility for he has never stay'd an hour . . . but once *at first*, since they have be'n in town, tho' the ladies have be'n several times'. Even a common civility demanded a high level of social exchange within the network.[27]

Contemplating her impending departure to Pasture House in 1777, Elizabeth Shackleton declared 'when I leave Alkincoats, I feel I must have no Connections with the world'.[28] Because of Elizabeth Shackleton's advancing age, illness and her relegation to what was in effect a dower house, one might expect a decline in formal sociability in her later years. Yet, in fact, a quantitative analysis of her social encounters in 1773 and 1780 reveals the opposite trend. Encounters with individuals other than co-resident kin and servants jumped from a total of 150 a year in 1773, to 226 in 1780. This increase in recorded activity may be a function of better data, since Elizabeth used an additional large journal each year from 1777 to her death, yet internal evidence suggests a real increase in social events. With Elizabeth Shackleton's physical separation from her eldest son Thomas Parker and his household, unrecorded family meals were translated into formal sociability. Thus, in 1780 37 per cent of social events involved kin, while in 1773 a family member had participated in only 9 per cent of such occasions. Evidently, the two miles between Pasture House and Alkincoats were but a short step to an old woman determined to maintain her hold on her son and to establish relationships with her two infant grandchildren. As should already be evident, the most abiding figures in Mrs Shackleton's social life were her close kin; a finding consistent with those of similar network studies from previous centuries.[29]

In both Alkincoats and Pasture House, sociability revolved around meals and hot drinks and therefore was concentrated in certain rooms. Shreds of commentary confirm that some spaces were deemed more appropriate to polite guests than others. The kitchen was the place of first resort for common visitors. At her grand-daughter's christening dinner, Mrs Shackleton noted that there was both a raft of elite guests and a large 'kitchen company' of attendants.[30] John Shackleton's male visitors were sometimes given dinner in the kitchen, and his drinking with his workers seems to have taken place there and in the servant's hall. On those occasions when drunken festivity spilled into the parlour, Mrs Shackleton recorded her disapproval. Toasts were raised and impromptu drinks were taken in the kitchen by gentry visitors on occasion, but the most well-used social space at both Alkincoats and Pasture House was the dining-room. From the late seventeenth century the most expensive and ostentatious goods in genteel houses were no longer to be found in the bedroom, but in the dining-room. The dining-rooms of both Alkincoats and Pasture House glowed with Gillows mahogany in the 1770s: 'The new Dining Room looked very handsome. Good, Gentele, warm & Comfortable.' After dinner, polite guests withdrew to the parlour where they eventually took tea and supper. Favoured female guests were sometimes invited into the bedroom to examine new clothes and fabrics – a distinct mark of familiarity. Not that rooms like the dining-room or the parlour were simply and always public and formal. Elizabeth Shackleton consciously increased or lessened the level of formality, by using different accoutrements; the diaries show her varying the use of tableware according to occasion and company. Hence her disappointment when she made fuss and fanfare to little effect: 'the only Company that did come to dinner here was my own Dear Tom, Messrs Turner & Swinglehurst. Our nice table & cloth spread for a very little to do.'[31] Interior spaces, could be more or less public, more or less formal, according to the arrangement of furniture and tableware, the level of ceremony and the status and number of the guests. Thus, Mrs Shackleton noted the arrangement of a public table, and her surprise to find her kitchen was 'very publick' with a stream of unexpected visitors.

Home-based sociability comprehended a variety of different encounters and transactions: some of these social exchanges mingled the sexes, some did not, some of these encounters presupposed conviviality among equals, others were built around the gracious dispensation of condescending hospitality. Returning again to the quantitative analysis of the hospitality Elizabeth Shackleton extended in 1773 at Alkincoats and 1780 at Pasture House, it emerges that each meal had a slightly different character (see Table 3, p. 396). As a social event, breakfast was a manly meal. Breakfast guests were predominantly male and near social equals, usually sharing an early meal with the gentlemen of the house as a precursor to a joint sporting or business expedition. (However, hearty breakfasts of cold meat and ale were served as late as eleven o'clock on occasion.) Dinner was an elaborate meal served mid- to late afternoon.[32] It was the encounter most likely to integrate guests of both sexes, although at over half the dinners the guests were exclusively male. It was also the meal most associated with the extended family (particularly Sunday dinner) and with celebration and festival. The Shackletons catered for their yeomen neighbours and trades-people, and even labourers and servants on occasion, gatherings Elizabeth routinely described as 'a mixed multitude'. But usually the dinner was a forum for her polite acquaintance drawn from land, trade and the profes-sions. Most often a select company sat around the substantial mahogany dinner table and admired the damask tablecloths, the silver candelabra and the genteel blue and white dinner service ordered specially from London. On those occasions when ladies were present, it is unclear whether they withdrew after dinner, leaving the men to their toasts. Prob-ably the practice of allowing elite men a little licence for three quarters of an hour or so was simply taken for granted. Certainly, most remarks on the subject have been gleaned from the notes of foreign visitors.[33] Yet if there was a female withdrawal, there had to be a subsequent reunion, as tea, coffee and often supper were served to remaining guests later in the evening. By contrast, supper parties were much less exclusive, usually involving local men, often social inferiors, unencumbered by wives and daughters; which suggests that supper was an informal affair, stripped of the ceremonies of dinner. It may also be that women were not expected to host supper parties: 'My friend [William] of Roughlee came & chatted at supper time. A late hour of visiting to such an old woman.'[34]

The tea party was one of the most socially inclusive events in Elizabeth Shackleton's social calendar, involving anyone from a Justice of the Peace to the mantua-maker. Tea parties were not in themselves an exclusively female affair. Any impromptu visitor, male or female, might benefit from the basic ceremony with kettle, teapot, china and silver. Although the Shackletons used 'tea-time' to designate the late afternoon, it appears that hot drinks were drunk at any time of day. However, it was tea that Elizabeth Shackleton was most likely to serve to exclusively female com-pany. Male guests were more often entertained with dinner or supper.

Moreover, the special fascination teaware held for women betokens their particular investment in this social activity.[35] In fact, it has been argued that the ritual performance of tea-drinking constituted one of the key expressions of ornamental femininity, and that the tea table was the 'place where the upper-class female body was disciplined to participate in a narcissistic display of availability'.[36] Undoubtedly, tea-drinking was a *sine qua non* of ladylike sociability, whereby gentlewomen showed off their manners and porcelain, but it was also the forum for business dealings in the widest possible sense. Elizabeth Shackleton produced her china in a spirit of patronage for the benefit of ex-servants, the mothers of her servants and her tenantry: 'all the Tenant's Wives Invited to drink tea. They were civilly Entertain'd. Had wine, coffee, tea, muffins, toast, Punch and great pieces of Iced rich Plumb cake.'[37] Hot drinks fuelled a gentle-woman's dealings with tradeswomen. Tea was routinely served at the haberdashers and mantua-makers. In fact, Betty Hartley Shopkeeper's hospitality was so widely recognized that in 1775 she was given the affectionate title of the 'Queen of Boston' by her customers. Moreover, when mantua-makers, seamstresses and shopkeepers came to call at Alkincoats and Pasture House, dresses were fitted, orders and instructions given, finished work received, and trinkets purchased all to the accompaniment of tea.

> Molly & Betty Hartley drank tea & suppd here, gave Molly a pair of corded ruffles to make for Mr Parker.

> Betty Hartley Shopkeeper drank tea and suppd. Bot a new black short apron.

> Betty Hartley came to tea. My son paid her. Her bill in full to this day. £2:17.[38]

Ladies offered tea in the parlour to social inferiors in much the same way as gentlemen bought ale in the tavern, to lubricate the process of giving orders and doing business. Tea facilitated the process of exchange.

The other social engagement in the home which was particularly associated with women, although not always confined to them, was the card party. By far the commonest form of home entertainment was cards; a recreation which enjoyed a massive vogue in the mid-eighteenth century. Elizabeth Shackleton played at whist, commerce, quadrille and sometimes backgammon with both guests and family. From Pontefract, the unlikely Metropolis of Politeness, Jane Scrimshire professed in the 1750s 'the Days are so short there is little to be done but Eat, Sleep & play at Cards' and the winter weather so atrocious that the company in town could only manage to travel 'from one Card Table to another, wch nothing but a Sick Bed prevents'. Bessy Ramsden nursed a similar addiction throughout the 1760s and 1770s, being out some nights from six till ten in the evening, leading her husband to report that 'wicked Housekeeping and vile Card playing murders all ones Time'. Meanwhile, even in semi-retirement Ann Pellet could be tempted to join small gatherings for 'a little snug party at Whist' or 'her little innocent parties of Quadrille'.[39]

Card-parties, tea-parties and visiting in general were widely associated with women in the satirical imagination. Building on an ancient critique of gadding women, moralists waxed monotonous on the unfortunate trade of female visiting. Visiting drew women from their duties and encouraged idle chat or worse scandal. 'The D. take the fellow as first invented card playing,' William Ramsden memorably concluded, 'visiting and visited is the whole of a Woman's Life in London.'[40] Doubtless this feminine sociability had considerable vigour and visibility. Fascinatingly, Mary Chorley's diaries demonstrate that for little girls visiting was a treasured performance of female adulthood. She learned the rituals of sociability first as a form of play, but graduated within two years from make-believe ceremonies to the real thing. At ten years of age, in 1776, Mary Chorley noted 'Nell & Maria came & we played at visiting', but by the age of twelve she recorded, 'It being my birthday I had many young ladies to drink tea with me', and at thirteen, 'Went to Elhill to drink tea. We danced three hours in the evening, we spent a delightful afternoon.'[41] However, the conventional scenario of tinkling tea cups and female tittle-tattle, should not be allowed to obscure the frequency of male visiting or the range of genteel interactions. The exchange of compliments, gifts, visits and meals between elite families sustained the horizontal ties of polite friendship. Vertical relationships within the community were fostered through gracious hospitality dispensed on designated days, or confined to the common parts of the house. Male association was reinforced over pre-expeditionary breakfasts, while dinner fed polite, conversable couples. Genteel families were linked to the world in a multiplicity of ways, as kinsfolk, landowners, patrons, employers and as members of the elite. All these social roles were expressed through a variety of encounters which took place in the home.

Having reconstructed the substance of sociability, the discussion now turns to a consideration of the meanings attached to social conduct by one sensitive commentator. It explores those manners thought perfect and those found wanting. Elizabeth Shackleton's diary bristles with the adjectives 'polite', 'civil', 'genteel', 'well-bred', and 'polished', and this reliance on the language of civility to describe best social practice makes clear her debt to early eighteenth-century courtesy literature. She and her circle drew deeply on the early eighteenth-century vocabulary of Addison and Steele. They exchanged copies of the *Tatler* and the *Spectator* (works famously admired by ladies), quoted readily from Richardson's *Sir Charles Grandison* (1753–4) and debated the content of Chesterfield's *Letters to His Son* (1774). So much for the theory. What did civility mean in practice for Elizabeth Shackleton? She had a conventional appreciation of decorum, protocol, elegant ease, polite conversation and amiable consideration between men and women. She expected to be treated with the respect which was due to her ancient lineage, or in her own words 'proper for her consequence', and the consideration due to one of her 'age and infirmities'. Therefore, it seems that those who showed her overt respect and kind consideration were, *ipso facto*, polite.

That she clung to this gratifying way of judging the civility of others is made clear in her positive descriptions of social encounters. A successful evening in the autumn of 1778 took place at Langroyd Hall, where the Shackletons, Tom Parker and a local gentleman Mr Whitaker enjoyed tea and a 'a very neat & pritty supper'. Mrs Shackleton noted that she was dressed out in her best satin, that the host Mr Bulcock lent her the *Works and History of Flavius Josephus* and that her son Tom accompanied her home in the chaise. 'Civily Entertaind much made on', was her verdict on the event. Fluent praise was lavished on a wedding visit to her newly married nephew John Parker and his bride Beatrix Lister, at Marshfield, their elegant villa in Settle. Mrs Shackleton found the house beautiful, tasteful and neat, the table splendid and their new plate magnificent. Her fellow visitors were accomplished and she enjoyed recitals on the piano, harpsichord and John Parker's playing of the guitar. Of the young Parkers she concluded, 'nothing co'd exceed the friendly Civility with which they recd us'. However, it was also possible to be 'most civilly Entertain'd' by those lacking gentry status. At Roughlee (the home of a local cabinet maker), Elizabeth Shackleton was satisfied by the wide choice of wines, tea and fruit laid out, and by the basket of apples and the beautiful nosegay with which she was presented. Similarly, she commended a card party at Broadbank (the second house of a London merchant), since the house was 'very clean & neat', a sumptuous dinner was laid on and the subsequent entertainment was 'all conducted with great Decency and good order'.[42]

Elegant dinners had a recognizable set of components. The tables groaned with unusual delicacies or wholesome produce. The other guests were socially exalted and amiable, or suitably well behaved and courteous. Mrs Shackleton and the company were dressed according to the occasion and all proceeded with propriety. Often, she bore away a gift or a loan to savour subsequently and was gallantly conducted home. Doubtless, she enjoyed all these elements in themselves, but it is also apparent that she welcomed the respect for her person that the ceremonies and courtesies also demonstrated. Not unnaturally, she relished being singled out for attention and 'obliging kindness', being 'much made on', or cherished, in Dr Johnson's definition of the word. After an evening of such warm civility, Elizabeth Shackleton felt valued and ease with the world.

It is apparent that Mrs Shackleton believed civility to issue most naturally from those of superior birth and breeding. Her praise for friends and acquaintances demonstrates the way that manners had an affinity with rank, witness her obsequious reception of hospitality from a leading member of the county gentry: 'Myself, son and Mr S. all dined at Royle. Civily received much made of. Great good manners from generous Mr Townley,' and the associations with exalted status she made in praise of a helpful Lawyer: 'Mr Wainman behaved like a Prince. Honourably like a Gentleman and Genteley.'[43] Yet as we have seen, she could appreciate the civil behaviour of those she considered beneath her. Furthermore, while those without gentle birth could through cleanliness, neatness, regularity and unaffected generosity achieve a civil entertainment, friendly civility was not always forthcoming from those she considered her superiors. Elizabeth Shackleton was watchful of her dignity and quick to resent a slight. When she was not singled out for attention, she could be querulous: 'My Bror just civil no great joy to see me'; 'No enquiring after poor me all night'; 'I came all by myself. No one with me. Small notice of poor me. All things change.'[44] When openly insulted she was implacable. She never forgave the *arriviste* Cunliffe of Wycoller for having the temerity to patronize someone of her lineage: 'Mr Cunliffe was most Sneakingly submissive to me. I told him of the Condescension to the wife of a shabby Tradesman. Bid him ask his Relations Walmesley & Shaw of Preston if I disgraced the Acquaintance of Cunliffe. I knew what he was. Bid him enquire after me.'[45] Feelings often bruised by perceived social neglect or condescension, Mrs Shackleton had a tendency to harp on the pretensions of the local gentry, sneering at their 'formal grandeur', their 'pomp and suite' and their 'great fuss over fine folks', laying the charge of haughty conceit by way of revenge. By the rule of decorum, pomp, grandeur and magnificence were the proper attributes of noble hospitality, the appropriate expression of genteel hospitality being the more restrained elegance and liberality. So, through her choice of adjectives, Mrs Shackleton charged her neighbours with ideas above their station and smirked at their impertinent affectation.

On the other hand, Elizabeth Shackleton herself could be punctilious about the precisions of etiquette. A newly arrived commercial clan, the Bulcocks of London, demanded a degree of respectful notice from this ailing gentlewoman because of their known local connections, but they did not meet with her approbation and were pronounced 'a most free & easy family – Very impertinent, very Intruding'. Their major sin was arriving unannounced and uninvited, late in the evening upon only slight acquaintance: 'Never let me know she was to come. An entire stranger . . . put me much out of my old beaten road & quite overturn'd all my Schemes & Engagements.' In like manner, two trading couples, the Conyers and the Brindles, lacked an appropriate sense of polite distance and insisted on dropping in unasked: 'Much put out of the way by the arrival of Mrs Conyers & Betty Brindle that moment after we had dined.' They made far too free with Mrs Shackleton's hospitality leading her to complain, 'I wonder they did not shame to call so often . . . making this house just like a publick one.' She presented herself wearied by these flagrant breaches of protocol, 'I hope I shall not have the fatigue of vulgar intruding people this week as I had the last',[46] perhaps because she lacked an effective strategy (between the simple measure of withholding further invitations and the extreme step of having the servants see them off the premises) for excluding those insensitive to etiquette. A frosty demeanour sent a clear message only to the tactful. However, to emphasize Elizabeth Shackleton's punctiliousness is not to suggest that she strove for excessive formality in her interactions. A starched formality was emphatically not the desired effect, since Richard 'Beau' Nash had done so much to make 'Gothic haughtiness' appear old-fashioned and absurd. Dignified ease and cheerful friendship were the hallmarks of modern, effortless elegance. Yet this was a delicate balancing act, the distance between 'elegant and easy' and 'free and easy' being very small indeed.[47]

The practice at the heart of polite sociability was conversation. The whole purpose of conversation was positively to please other people, yet the art had to be well-judged. Elizabeth Shackleton was gratified by encounters which proved 'very Chatty & good' or 'Chatty, Civil & most Agreable', but could vilify acquaintances for their garrulousness if she so chose. Talkativeness in those she considered her inferiors was particularly irksome. The chatter of Mrs Fielden, the mantua-maker, was pronounced 'tiresome and disagreeable'. The discredited Mrs Knowles subjected Elizabeth Shackleton to 'an unmerciful clack her tongue never stood still. She let in go on most sillyly wo'd permit no one else to talk. It was very hot and disagreeable.' Smoking like a kiln all the while, 'Mrs Knowles has dedicated all this day to Sir Walter. She has reeked it away.' Predictably, the uppity Mancunian Mrs Cunliffe proved a formidable chinwag: 'a great talker a high head & her hair very rough . . . [she and her husband make] a quere pair and Uncouth.'[48] But it was William Hargreaves of Roughlee, a local cabinet maker, who seems to have had all the conversational vices: he raised an uncongenial topic, was over-talkative and over-zealous, he did not display good nature or consideration for his hosts and he undoubtedly did not know when to stop: 'Call'd here about 5 staid till 11 at night. Brawl'd & talk'd upon Religion. A most terrible Argument. Am not of his opinion, an Ignorant man. Much fatigued, quite ill with with his discourse & noise.'[49]

What the Methodist William Hargreaves manifestly failed to do was please his hostess. He exhibited none of the courtesy and deferential gallantry of the ideal gentleman. The pattern gentleman was under an obligation positively to please women, extending to a lady of equal rank that respect usually due to a social superior. He was advised to keep a check on his language, raillery and disputatiousness in the presence of ladies.[50] Indeed, it was a commonplace of courtesy literature that the company of accomplished women was itself crucial to the production of civilized masculinity. Yet, in practice, unpolished masculinity seemed to pose a chronic threat to polite sociability as the conduct books understood it. In practice, amiable consideration between men and women was often conspicuous by its absence.

Elizabeth Shackleton detected a want of delicacy and respect in many men of her circle. Lawyer Shaw almost suffocated her with his tobacco smoke over breakfast, while the unmarried Tom Parker, who must have fully appreciated his mother's disapproval did the same. He also let a gun go off in the parlour and often stormed out on to the moors or hunting field 'very saucy and cross'. John Parker also exhibited a churlish lack of manners on occasion: 'John took possession of my chair, read the newspaper, never spoke, went away from here immediately after he had got his breakfast – very uncivil, underbred Behaviour indeed.'[51] And her nephew, John Parker, was lacking in *savoir-faire* before the fragrant Beatrix Lister got to work on him. As an unmarried young blood, he left dilapidation in his wake, romping about Alkincoats as if it was inn: 'My nephew makes this an entire Hotel – spoils books, tables & all sorts of Furniture . . . I wish my nephew was safe & well at Browsholme. He dos make such violent, monstrous hurrys.'[52] Moreover as male sociability was usually propelled by alcohol, drunken disorder was latent in almost all evening gatherings of gentlemen, as even her positive comments testify: 'all our Gents returned safe from the Wycoller Rout. No Quarrelling all Peace.'[53] When men were unaccompanied by their wives, some had a tendency to forget Addisonion niceties: 'Whitaker Riotous to a degree. Barton Dumb.

Cunliffe Moralizing. Shackleton sulky, quarellsome, Cross.' In liquor, some proved coarse and offensive; if Elizabeth Shackleton was not already abed, then such behaviour quickly drove her there: 'Most terrible drinking & quarrelling. George Ormerod very abusive. Mr S. set up till five a clock in the morning.'[54]

Although Mrs Shackleton did not disapprove of alcohol *per se* (she noted the oddity of a male visitor who drank only water), and enjoyed dinners in her husband's company at the White Bear, she deplored the vulgarity which the alehouse seemed to encourage in gatherings of men, as two characteristic incidents from 1774 show:

> Cunliffe last Thursday at the White Horse meeting, very rude to Dr Midgely, told him his [daughter] was a W—r, & common to all – very polite Behaviour, Generous & like the Oxonian that professes the gentleman.

> A great bustle at the Hunting meeting at the Hole in the wall dinner at Coln this day . . . where I fear my Good and Civil son did not receive treatment that was Proper for his Consequence. But Hottentots not Men when assembled together.[55]

In particular, Elizabeth Shackleton disapproved of the promiscuous social mingling which the alehouse licensed: 'Mr Emmott made himself very Popular in the Hole in the Wall great Chamber, it being the Bull Bate. He appeared very Loving with his own Maids – treated them & the rest of his servants with tea & coffee at Petty's afterwards. Had a Dance with them. So much for a tiptop Education.'[56] In like manner, cockfighting and bull-baiting were deprecated because of the informal social mingling they promoted, not because these sports were seen as barbarous. Quite simply one rubbed shoulders with too much mean company.

If Elizabeth Shackleton expected considerate encounters with well-bred gentlemen, she was most spectacularly disappointed in her husband. In fact, the diary presents him as the absolute antithesis of the polite partner, his varied offences revealing the myriad rules of civility in the breach rather than in the honouring. Throughout the 1770s John Shackleton sought escape from and compensation for the problems of his marriage in hunting, shooting and fishing. To this end, he habitually left the house before his wife had emerged from the bedroom and only returned well after dark, fortified by liquor. When he was in the house, he often refused to acknowledge his wife by word or gesture. Of course, his behaviour only made matters worse, fuelling the chagrin of his wife who smarted at such blatant discourtesy:

Mr S., James Wilson & Tom went by 7 a fishing to Arncliffe. Tom did come upstairs to wish me a good day, but Mr S. never did, nor spoke to me. He was too Happy with his pot companion old Hargreaves of the Laund, who came quite drunk from Coln & made a noise as was abominable. Too rude to describe.

In his boorish disregard ('Mr S . . . Despises me as if a washer woman.'[57]), Shackleton set an appalling example for his three stepsons, something Elizabeth Shackleton frequently bemoaned, and he encouraged none of that cheerful heterosexual sociability she craved: 'He is very unmanerly, not much calculated for a Matrimonial Life.' Sadly, her unmarried sons followed Shackleton's lead and indulged their homosocial pursuits to the hilt: 'Kind usage from Sons to a mother & a Husband to a wife. Each following their own Diversion.'[58]

Although excessive alcohol consumption was a fact of life, it behoved a gentleman to confine its effects to appropriate settings, something John Shackleton manifestly failed to do. Consequently, his behaviour was seen to jeopardize attempts to run an efficient, creditable household. Indeed, he periodically got servants and workmen so drunk in the daytime that they could not continue their work. He was often unfit for business himself in the morning and was ignominiously led home and put to bed by his dependants on numerous occasions: 'Not a regular house. The Master so much given to Drunkenness.'[59] Of course, controlled drinking with inferiors under suitably hierarchical conditions could be approved as proper hospitality, if the host retained his self-possession, but control was hardly Shackleton's watch-word. He behaved with an unpardonable licence towards his social inferiors, getting outrageously drunk on a persistent basis with his tenants, sheepshearers, masons and servants at taverns in Colne and in the servants' hall at Alkincoats and Pasture House. Not infrequently, he inappropriately allowed such 'vulgar company' into the parlour, thereby invading Elizabeth Shackleton's polite sanctum. After the sheepshearing in 1780, the diary records, 'all drunk in the servants Hall and most Beastly so in the parlour. Great noise & reeking. tho' free from riots.' The next day the diary recapped: 'Atkinson wo'd come into the parlour last night & sit with Mr S: all the shearers with the piper John Riley were most horridly drunk. A quantity they did drink. They all went about four this morning. What a nasty, drunken, beastly house for a stranger to clean . . .'[60] This over-familiarity with social inferiors was a very serious failing, for by his actions John Shackleton undermined his claims to proper respect and brought the gentility of his household into question. It was not for nothing that the conduct writers warned employers, 'Familiarity breeds contempt'.[61] Conversely, John Shackleton could prove ungracious when called upon to offer proper patronage, slighting a boy who came to toss a pancake on Shrove Tuesday 'Never down stairs all day. Sad Housekeeping. Mr S. quite rude, no charity, he knows nothing of it.'[62] In his base familiarities, he obliterated both polite exclusivity and condescending hospitality.

Quite apart from this lack of decorum, which undermined Elizabeth Shackleton's social standing in the world, he also inflicted physical and verbal violence on his ailing and unhappy wife as we have seen: 'never saw him so rude, vulgar, nor so drunk. He took his horse Whip to me.'[63] On occasion, he sabotaged his wife's ceremonies, smashing wine bottles and china, turning over the card table and disrupting all play. He also interfered with the exchange of customary courtesies: 'Mr & Mrs Walton were so kind as to send Harrison to enquire after my heath. Thinks myself greatly obliged to them. I wo'd have sent today to have enquired after them, but Mr S: wo'd not let me. He Cursed & D—d swore no servant of his sho'd run about the country with such foolish messages . . .', and once threatened that she should be denied the use of his horses.[64] By no stretch of the imagination could the behaviour of this surly drunkard be described in terms of Addisonian consideration or Chesterfieldian fastidiousness. John Shackleton utterly disgusted his wife on several occasions: 'he shits in bed with drinking so continualy'; 'The gentleman came home near 12 at noon & Sans Ceremony went snoring to clean bed – where he farted and stunk like a Pole Cat'; 'Most exceedingly Beastly so to a degree never saw him worse – he had made water into the fire.' In the full glare of humiliating publicity he made plain his complete want of physical restraint: 'Mr S was very sick & spew'd Abundantly. Sat in Tom Brindle's House upon the Long Settle before the fire & exposed himself as Publickly as he co'd . . . a very nasty, dirty, stinking creature.' No wonder that his wife once concluded 'Mr S. like a Brute. No Man.'[65] The descriptions of John Shackleton's inconsiderate, unmannerly, wild, beastly, barbarous, brutish, nasty, dirty, odious, hideous, stinking, horrid, rude, surly, cross and vulgar behaviour seem to have exhausted all the adjectives in his wife's overworked stock. His assault on Elizabeth Shackleton's world of dignity and distinction could not have been more complete.

This is clearly only one narrative – the assault of bestiality upon refinement – in a shared story. Nothing survives of John Shackleton's view, nor of any independent criticism of his behaviour. How might John Shackleton have interpreted the struggle? Perhaps he saw himself simply protecting his manly pleasures? Perhaps he saw Elizabeth Shackleton's polite rules as so many artificial constraints on nature. After one offensive episode, he did report that his father thought Elizabeth 'a great hypocrite', so he may have cherished a belief in the sturdy authenticity of masculine excess. From his perspective, perhaps politeness was made up of so many insincere conventions: hypocrisy glorified into virtue, for it was certainly a continuing concern of the writers of courtesy literature that without inner goodwill, a polite performance could so easily become a sham, a veneer of polish concealing cynical self-interest.[66] However, this is not to imply that men represent honest and unselfconscious pleasure while women are bent upon its repression, for John Shackleton's excess was undoubtedly as constructed as Elizabeth Shackleton's control – a point made by a notorious pundit of politeness, Lord Chesterfield:

> The character which most young men first aim at is, that of a man of pleasure; but they generally take it upon trust; and instead of consulting their own taste and inclinations, they blindly adopt whatever those with whom they chiefly converse, are pleased to call by the name of pleasure; and *a man of pleasure* in the vulgar acceptation of that phrase, means only a beastly drunkard, an abandoned whore-master, and a profligate swearer and curser.[67]

Nevertheless, one does wonder what John Shackleton stood to gain from such debauched conduct. Perhaps it reinforced his masculinity amongst his male peers and dependents? As a code, politeness was always in danger of collapsing into effeminacy. While mixed company guaranteed civilization, too much time spent in the company of women alone was seen as effeminizing. Real men had somehow to strike a mean between an ill-bred vulgarity on the one hand and simpering affectedness on the other. In his boorishness, John Shackleton could never be accused of continental foppery – a proof which may have been important to the merchants he caroused with. It is also worth noting that men enjoyed much more licence than did women to create solidarities through excess, as moralists like Jeremy Collier made clear: 'Obscenity in any Company is a rustick uncreditable Talent; but among Women 'tis particularly rude. Such talk would be very affrontive in Conversation, and not endur'd by any Lady of Reputation.'[68] However, given the high value put on status and self-control in eighteenth-century discourses on elite masculinity, John Shackleton had much more to lose through his humiliating lapses in dignity. If, as E. P. Thompson has suggested, the display of dignified manners was part of the studied performance of cultural hegemony, then Shackleton substantially jeopardized his social and political authority by his lack of restraint,[69] – and unlike a roistering lord he could claim no intrinsic noble worth through blood. If anything, mercantile and

manufacturing elites stood in greater need of the genteel social graces to
sustain the connections crucial to the quality trade. For instance, Richard
Greene, a merchant-adventurer, put down his failure in the tea business
precisely to his inability to cut a dash in Calcutta: 'Indeed my [dear] sister
I am so unpolished a shrub that I am ashamed of my awkward appearance when I am in Gentele company and I woud Actually give 100£
sterling could I even make a bow, but as I never had any expence thrown
away on me for that purpose, I therefore must walk in a path below that
which by birth I am intitled to in short I look upon it that the want of a
little adress has been some thousands of pounds out of my pocket.' Politeness, not vulgarity, was crucial to commerce. So, in fact, Shackleton's
conduct achieved nothing for him but the sour triumph of sharing out that
misery he experienced in a marriage with an ailing, all-but toothless
woman, seventeen years his senior. Possibly then his vulgarity was simply
a destructive expression of impotent rage.[70]

An unresolved problem is the extent to which the struggle here between
restraint and excess was distinctive to this one unhappy couple. After all,
civility and vulgarity may have been banners behind which two unusually
unhappy spouses fought their matrimonial battles. Happier couples
doubtless effected a better reconciliation between the rugged and the
refined. Still, the argument that home-based, mixed-sex sociability nour-
ished marriages and respectability while all-male, ale-house sociability
reduced them certainly had a long-standing currency among moralists.[71]
The notion that men were rough diamonds in need of refinement was
widespread. Even the young Lancaster Quaker Mary Chorley used the
secular vocabulary of civility to criticize a graceless kinsman: 'Today my
cousin Ford behaved in a very manner [sic] to me. He flatly contradicted
me thrice. I think he wants a great deal of polishing.'[72] Variants of the same
struggle over polite ceremony can be found amongst unhappy couples.
The early eighteenth-century diary of a Hertfordshire baronet's wife,
Sarah Cowper, offers a useful comparison. Sir William Cowper, for instance, rebuked his wife 'before servants for giving my neighbour a few
flowers without his allowance', retained custody over tablecloths and
sheets, thus humiliating Lady Cowper before guests, and made dinner
parties so agonizing for onlookers that the county gave them a wide berth:

> Sir W. hath so ordered matters that at table we see not the face of a
> gentleman or woman in age but the most despicable people one can
> imagine, because none that wants not a dinner cares to see the uneasi-
> ness we are in . . . If I carve . . . he bids let them help themselves, if I let
> alone he calls on me to do it, and if I put them upon calling for a glass

of wine, he saith sure they best know their own time . . . and so on in every like instance. In very solemn fashion I have desired him not to have me perpetually under correction, but to no purpose. He persists even before my sons which makes me chagrined and uneasy that they should see us so silly.

The consequence of this humiliation, Lady Cowper complained was to make the household 'the epitome of hell'. Where the authority of genteel femininity was scorned amongst the servants 'the sins of men as cursing, swearing, whoring, cheating . . . the devil of envy, wrath, hatred, malice, lying reigns here without due control'.[73]

Elizabeth Shackleton's use of the language of civility was profoundly derivative. Polite ideals had extensive currency in the eighteenth and early nineteenth centuries.[74] Even the journals of the unfortunate Lancashire governess Ellen Weeton are revealing in their manipulation of the discourse of civility. Weeton openly accused her sister-in-law of deploying a forbidding formality that left her socially paralysed, 'apprehensive of forgetting some little ceremony, or transgressing some rule of etiquette', a strategy inimical to true politeness. Yet Miss Weeton demanded if not kindness, than at least a 'common civility' from her employers, for 'unless I were degraded something below human, I never would submit to haughtiness, tyranny and ill-temper', and was gratified when she was 'very politely received' and made to feel 'at home, and quite comfortable'.[75] Interestingly, Weeton's journals impart a greater preoccupation with the minute rules of etiquette than is apparent in Shackleton's diaries, an anxiety about externals which could be function of the acute vulnerability of her social position, or a comment on the nineteenth-century codification of politeness, yet she still found in civility a comparable justification for resistance.

Nor was an investment in civility and the derogation of vulgarity confined to northern women. In the 1760s the lawyer Thomas Greene was enraged by the undignified conduct of his uncle, and particularly appalled by the want of consideration shown his mother. If it continues, Greene warned his mother, 'we shall be under the necessity of discarding him in his old age . . . I will hear no Death-Bed repentences . . . So if he do continue to prefer drinking, and being a *great Man*, amongst a Parcel of Taylors & Coblers, to living soberly with you and me, let him follow his Inclination & take the Consequences for his wages.'[76] Parson Woodforde disapproved of his brother's cockfighting precisely because it brought him into contact with vulgar company: 'quite lowlife sort of people, much beneath Jack.' Similarly, Parson George Woodward despaired of his gauche and churlish younger brothers: brother Jack had no polite conversation whatsoever, despite his travels, 'for his curiosity seems to be little more than that of a stage coachman' who interested himself only in roads, food, drink and landlords; while, in 1755 brother Tom ate the household out of meat, heedless of all the niceties of polite convention – 'I asked him once, how he managed about suppers, as he never eat cheese or apple pie; he said if he did not happen to be where there was meat, he often eat no supper at all, but smoked his pipe instead of it'. Given this heroic lack of refinement, Woodward contrived to get his brother out of the way when the Warden of All Souls and his wife came to visit '(to speak the truth) I did not much care to show them such an uncouth relation of mine'. In the event, Tom invited himself to dinner with a local farmer and his mother and happily smoked all night.[77] No suave urbanity for those who shirked the responsibilities of patriarchy.

Of course, Elizabeth Shackleton's perspective was a distinctive one. As she ailed and aged, she waxed pathetic, believing herself spurned and disregarded at every turn. Awareness of her social descent through marriage probably sharpened her insecurity and bred a defensiveness about her social reception. Painful illness no doubt increased her sensitivity: 'the treatment I meet with from all sides as I grown into years almost breaks my Heart and my legs swelling more & more.' Doubtless she was not an easy companion herself, nor necessarily a dispassionate commentator on the incivility of others: 'When we went to bed I went into John's room & told him I wonder we did not hear from Roben. He snappd & was very rude. Said he had most probably his reasons for not writing. I am sure I have not offended. They are unkind & uncivil to me.' After the gentle rebukes she ventured to offer her intimates for various small slights, she seemed genuinely astonished to find them suddenly 'Humpy Grumpy', 'quere' or 'upon reserve'.[78] Yet it is in this very hypersensitivity that the real value of the diary lies for historians. In her irritation and unhappiness Elizabeth Shackleton exploited a conventional language to the full. Her perspective demonstrates the broad range of discursive uses to which civility could be put, some uses altogether unanticipated by Addison and Steele.

Reliant on the rules of decorum, which decreed that inferiors should know their place, civility and politeness were hardly useful tools for everywoman, but for genteel ladies, civility offered an eminent vantagepoint from which to patronize men and male sociability. When Elizabeth Shackleton complained 'the friendships of the present times like those described by Addison are oft Confederacies in vice or Leagues of Pleasure',[79] she enlisted the essayist in support of her critique of

Shackleton's social selfishness. But this vocabulary could be extended even further to derogate the masculine world of local associations, for, in Mrs Shackleton's immortal words, gentlemen were 'Hottentots, not men, when assembled together.' In all likelihood, she here drew on Addison's cautionary tale of the unfortunate Hottentot who was brought to England and 'polish'd out of his natural Barbarity: But upon being carry'd back to the Cape of *Good Hope* . . . he mix'd in a kind of Transport with his Country-men, brutalized with 'em in their Habit and Manners, and wou'd never agen return to his foreign Acquaintance.'[80] Lacking the temporizing effects of female company at their meetings in local taverns, Mrs Shackleton observed, men threw off the mantle of civilization and revealed themselves as primitive barbarians. She thus tied the progressive evolution of civilized society to the presence of female company. Similarly, when John Shackleton got lost on the moors in 1779 trying to follow the high sheriff's official cavalcade to Blackburn on a beribboned horse, and his wife scorned his 'Inconsiderate, wild, extravagant doings', by extension she disparaged the self-important ceremonies of county administration. While no radical, she was ambivalent about inflated masculine rituals: after an impressive description of the three hundred or more gentlemen riding two by two behind the high sheriff, she loftily concluded of 'this Grand Parade . . . so much for worldly ambition'. Although gratified that her son had a seat in the high sheriff's coach, her patronizing comment, 'it will make him esteem'd of Consequence', indicates a certain personal superiority to such a pompous demonstration of status.[81] While Addison and Steele had explicitly linked heterosexual conversation to the advance of human society, it is unlikely that they had envisaged politeness as a tool to undermine the dignity of local government.

Elizabeth Shackleton's story is one of valiant politeness all but over-come. Ultimately, therefore, it presents a poignant study in repeated failure. But, by default, her perspective suggests the practical benefits which might accrue to elite women from the consolidation of polite codes of behaviour. Civility and politeness validated mixed companies where elite women were valued and 'made much of'. It allowed the possibility that old and ailing women be given social consideration and justified their indignation when respect was denied: 'I neither can nor will bear this treatment. It is neither proper nor suitable to my Infirmities nor years.'[82] In theory, at least, civility protected elite women from brutal oppression, for 'when the pale of ceremony is once broken', wrote another Lancashire diarist, Dolly Clayton, in 1783, 'rudeness and insult soon enter the breach'. Samuel Johnson may have scoffed that *Chesterfield's Letters to His Son*, 'teach the morals of a whore and the manners of a dancing master',[83] but

from the female perspective even a dancing master is a preferable companion to a disobliging bedfellow or an ill-mannered brute.

Elizabeth Shackleton did not see the domestic interior as a complete
refuge from the social world. She held cherished ideals about the conduct
of social relations which were not shrugged off once she entered the
stillness of her own parlour. In the idiom of the conduct-book writers,
genuine politeness was not a formal suit only to be worn when the circumstances of ceremony demanded it. Rather, it was a garment that should
never be laid aside, and which ought to be worn lightly and gladly, as if it
were no encumbrance. Inside and outside, Elizabeth Shackleton contrived
to achieve decorum, protocol, elegant ease, polite conversation and,
perhaps most important of all, an amiable consideration between men and
women. Both in what they reveal about the use of space and the evaluation
of behaviour, Elizabeth Shackleton's records give the lie to the notion that
the walls of the house constituted the frontier between public and private
worlds.

Sociability tied the individual to their many communities. Through the
exchange of compliments, gifts, dinners and teas with other elite families,
the genteel reaffirmed their gentility and maintained a wide polite
acquaintance. Through condescending hospitality they asserted their position as masters and mistresses of servants, as patrons of local businesses
and as responsible landowners, but the doors of country mansions were
not to be left open to the multitude like the gates of Ranelagh and Vauxhall. Elizabeth Shackleton designated days for 'publick' entertainment,
when Alkincoats and Pasture Houses were open and common to all, but
by their very existence, these occasions bring to mind the rest of the year,
when these mansions were open only to select company on invitation.
Public festivals remained very distinct from polite dinner parties. Indeed,
Mrs Shackleton once invited her polite neighbours the Waltons to one of
her feast days, but alerted them in advance to the fact that they would have
'to sit down with a mix'd Multitude'.[84] They declined the invitation.
Under ideal circumstances, sociability was engineered according to the
rules of decorum. Dependants were to be entertained in the 'common'
parts of the house, obviously the servants' hall and the kitchen. Casual
callers and presentable traders received tea from the common tea set, with
an appropriate level of formality in the dining-room or parlour. Elite
guests could expect to see the same rooms decked out in the best linen, best
china and silverware, and behaved accordingly. When, in practice, visitors
forgot polite correctness and made too free with her hospitality, Mrs
Shackleton complained of the fatigue of vulgar, intruding people, silently
accusing them of treating the house as if it were a public one. But in

invoking the term public, the dichotomy implied here is that between vulgar publicity and polite selection, not between the archetypal male public sphere and a female cloister. Sociability was one of the means by which the public was regulated in the home. Ideally, it was regulated in ways that married with cheerful, domestic companionship and polite distinction, for Mrs Shackleton had a vision of matrimonial pleasure which involved ceremonies and civilities, not the abandonment of all social effort in an orgy of self.

7

Propriety

IN MARCH 1741 Miss Mary Warde rattled off a long list of her diversions for the information and, presumably, the envious admiration of a country cousin:

> You enquire after our Diversions, Last Night finished the Ridottos, you know three is the constant Number I was at them all. I love to meet my Friends & seeing a greater Number, at that place than any other, makes me prefer that Gayety to all the rest. Plays are this winter in great Esteem. We have at the Old House two [antick dancers] that are very extraordinary in their way . . . at Covent Garden the Barberini shines, as a dancer, but quite of another kind . . . at the same house acts Mrs Woffington, the finest woman I ever saw, & what is almost incredible she is as Genteel a young Fellow & in Mens Cloths esteemed as an Actress better then in her own. Musick is at a low Ebb. Next winter we are promised a good Opera, tho' Oratorios & Concerts are very frequent which with very many private assemblys, & the Park in a Morning (where I generally Walk) fills up the round of making us very busy with nothing to do.[1]

Despite her disclaiming self-mockery, Mary Warde was not, of course, lacking things to do in the mid-eighteenth-century city.

Much has been made of the eighteenth-century elaboration of commercialized leisure in London and subsequently the regions – what Ann Pellet called the 'variety of new diversions which the town [devises] to gather the company to Publick Places'.[2] However, there is still a surprising vagueness and confusion about the extent of female participation in the overtly commercial high culture which characterized Georgian England. Most recently, historians influenced by Jürgen Habermas have chosen to

42 (*facing page*)   Detail from 'Prospect of a Noble Terras Walk', York, *c*.1756 (plate 55).

characterize the new leisure culture as a component of the 'public sphere', 'a forum in which the private people, come together to form a public, readied themselves to compel public authority to legitimate itself before public opinion'.[3] For this was a civil society which came to occupy the cultural space vacated by a weakened court and an indolent church, to which governments might be called to answer.[4] However, some have read Habermas's concept of the 'bourgeois public sphere' quite literally, as the foundry wherein middle-class cultural identity was forged.[5] One of the most recent surveys of eighteenth-century cultural history, by Ann Bermingham, invokes Habermas to reinstate the traditional view that the public sphere was a bourgeois creation, increasingly closed to women and constructed in opposition to the private domestic sphere: 'The public represented in this discursive and commercial space . . . imagined itself to be polite, rational, moral and egalitarian. In universalizing this self-image of enlightened rationality as well as its discursive and institutional forma- tions, the bourgeoisie empowered themselves and disempowered those whom the discourse excluded or opposed . . . (the rural, the illiterate, the poor, the non-European, the women and children.)'[6] By contrast, Law- rence Klein appeals to Habermas in discussion of the same issues, but to legitimize the opposite conclusion – that the public sphere of rational critical discussion which mediated between state and family, offered and validated a public role for women.

Of course, the term 'bourgeois public sphere' echoes the vocabulary of public and private spheres long deployed in feminist rhetoric and women's history. The received wisdom of women's history holds that there was once a far distant time when middling and propertied women enjoyed higher public status, but this modest gleaming of female public life was soon snuffed out by capitalism and the forces of reaction. Thus, R. J. Morris reflects on the assemblies, debating societies and ladies' associa- tions of the 1770s: 'There was a brief glimpse of female public action in the public sphere before the flood tide of evangelicalism swept the gender frontier back into the private and domestic.'[7] Moreover, it is a cliché of recent scholarship that any well-dressed woman out and about, ran the risk of being taken for the ultimate public woman, the sexual street- walker. The cultural street-walker had to wait, it is argued, till the 1880s and the department store to make her debut.[8]

So were women excluded from the emergent commercialized high culture that characterized the eighteenth century, or 'merely' from its political expression? Were they culturally active at the beginning of the eighteenth-century and not at its close? Was a female public life seen as tantamount to prostitution? Certainly, an impression of female ascendancy at eighteenth-century cultural congregations has long been conveyed by social historians. As Langford concludes, 'women not only shared fully in the literary and recreational life of the day but seemed positively to dominate it'.[9] Yet, for the most part, the extent of female engagement with this new culture has been either asserted or denied. Either way it has rarely been systematically researched by historians. Much more has been done by scholars of English literature to reconstruct the role of women as cultural producers and latterly as consumers of print, but, unfortunately, to date there is no comprehensive survey of the public venues to which women were drawn and institutions in which they participated. Hence, there remains an extraordinary mismatch between the precision of the conceptual claims made about women in public and the exceeding murkiness of historical knowledge. What follows is, therefore, a necessarily wide-ranging and schematic reconstruction of the potentialities of public life for polite women in Georgian England.

The selection of venues for discussion here is guided by the definitions of public life offered by eighteenth-century women themselves. For Mary Warde in the 1730s 'the publick' incorporated the diversions and resorts frequented by the quality: 'If Publick can Entertain I believe you will find the Wells as Gay & Splendid as they ever can be as the Inhabitants will certainly Exert themselves on the appearances of their Royal Highnesses.' For Betty Ramsden going out 'in Publick' in the 1760s and 1770s involved a visit to the theatre, the assembly, the pleasure garden or a trial.[10] Similarly, the Lancaster widow Jane Pedder's recitation of 'Publick Places' she frequented on a London visit in 1786 comprised the playhouse, the oratorio, the Tower, Bank, St Paul's museum, and the Chapel Royal.[11] Lady Mary Wortley Montagu maintained that assembly rooms provided 'a kind of public education, which I have always thought as necessary for girls as boys', while in *Sir Charles Grandison* (1754), Richardson's Lady Betty expressed her delight in public places – meaning masquerades, ridottos and the inevitable Vauxhall and Ranelagh.[12] In this formulation, then, the public was made up in large part of the comparatively new sites of commercialized leisure – assemblies, oratorios, theatres, promenades and pleasure gardens – venues which could be penetrated for the price of a ticket and where the great world could be encountered in almost all its variety. But these public venues were not primarily associated with an emergent bourgeoisie, far from it, rather, they were identified as the principal haunts of the people of fashion, the quality, the beau monde. The presence or the promise of royalty and nobility guaranteed the popularity of a venue with genteel spectators. Thus, the chapter first considers the royal court, before embarking on an examination of the opera, the theatre, the concert, the criminal and civil courts, the assembly, ridotto, masquerade and the pleasure garden. Then discussion turns to the woman walker abroad in the city, on promenades, shopping trips and cultural excursions. Finally, this section considers institutional participation looking at the church, charitable associations, intellectual clubs and print. Although the chapter concedes that 'much of the public sphere . . . was seen as potentially compromising for women, a zone whose very attractions were its dangers and which could only be entered with caution and restraint',[13] it argues that this is by no means the whole story. Women of honour trafficked numerous public venues without the least criticism and used simple strategies to protect their reputations at more risqué diversions. In their thousands, they sallied forth in the armour of conscious virtue. Viewed as a whole, the female public world was both larger and much less menacing than historians have often allowed. Overall, if a cultural renaissance was in progress, then appointment diaries suggest that genteel women took their participation in it absolutely for granted.

If one of the key pleasures of metropolitan public life was the witnessing of royalty, nobility and greater gentry at close quarters, then the ultimate spectacle was obviously the royal court. After Whitehall burned down in 1697 the focus of court display was St James's Palace. Great 'public' festivities were held at court on the monarch's birthday, and on the anniversary of the accession and coronation, while smaller drawing-room assemblies were held every week in the Season (De Saussure in 1725 preferred those held on Monday and Friday evenings, to those on Sunday afternoons 'as more ladies attend them'[14]). The royal family was also to be seen at prayer in the Chapel Royal – a conventional stop on tourist itineraries for over a century. Indeed, for all that the vigour and prestige of court society was in relative decline, and the fact that the pageantry of royal ceremonial varied from monarch to monarch, the 'splendid appearance' of royalty and nobility, was still greedily beheld by the genteel at every opportunity. In 1740 Mary Warde revelled in the celebrations for the Princess of Hesse's wedding, frequenting the drawing-room before the wedding, viewing the royal family at supper, watching the bride undressed in her apartment, and enjoying the next day a splendid drawing-room audience and after it a crowded ball of bejewelled duchesses 'amongst as much Finery as can be Imagined'.[15] Despite an avowed disdain for pomp and circumstance, the genteel lawyer Thomas Greene went to join the company at St James's Palace on Coronation day in September 1765:

it being the Coronation Day his Majesty of Course expected the Nobility & Gentry to wait upon him at Court . . . therefore I scoured up

New LADY's MAGAZINE.
Published by Alex. Hogg at the Kings Arms, N.16 Paternoster Row, May 1786.

Dodd delin.   Noble sculp.

View of the BALL at St James's on the celebration of HER MAJESTY's BIRTH NIGHT. Feb. 9. 1786. which was opened by their Royal Highnesses the Prince of Wales & the Princess Royal.

43   'View of the Ball at St James's on the Celebration of Her Majesty's Birth Night February 9 1786', from the *New Lady's Magazine*.

my sword (which has never had an airing since it came to England) & being equipped with that & a Bag-Wig I sallied forth in a Sedan Chair to St James & went to Court amongst all the great Folks, you may be sure I summoned all my Impudence upon the Occasion but I was determined for once to see that nonsensical Farce, which is nothing but idle Ceremony, tho' it may be what is necessary.[16]

Nonsensical farce or no, Bessy Ramsden made no secret of her desire to feast on every morsel of the royal pageant. Her triumph was to procure a place in the gallery to view the queen's birthday court in 1766 and to have 'had the honour of being with Her [Majesty] & the Children in their own Apartments' on coronation day in 1773. Similarly, a visitor who scrutinized the royal family at prayer mused, 'I like the Queen much; her appearance is not at all majestick but there is in her mien Countenance and behaviour (for I have had several opportunities to observe it) so much sweetness, affability & condescension that it is impossible to see her often without loving her'.[17] For all the cultural mediocrity of the Hanoverians, an unflagging interest in the court and royal festivity is suggested by the letters of visitors and natives alike.

Outside the court, the most prestigious commercial entertainment and strongest concentration of sheer aristocratic glamour was to be found at the opera. For historians, the emergence of the London opera, particularly Italian opera at Sir John Vanbrugh's King's Theatre in the Haymarket ('English opera' with spoken interludes could be enjoyed at Covent Garden and Drury Lane), represents the cultural elaboration of Whig oligarchical power. The King's Theatre was established and largely administered by noblemen and gentlemen until the late eighteenth century, but even when handed over to professional management, Italian opera retained its social cachet. William Weber has calculated that in 1783 two-thirds of the male subscribers were, or had been, MPs or peers of the realm. The opera became another setting for the playing out of party politics from the highly visible front boxes. Moreover, Weber calculates that of the 354 subscribers to boxes, there were 49 peers, one peeress and 44 wives of peers.[18] Even if not possessing boxes in her own right, a lady's presence, dress and deportment could be the subject of detailed commentary. Consequently, the female profile was as high, if not higher than the male. Indeed, the Countess Spencer wrote to her daughter Georgiana Duchess of Devonshire in 1782, to warn her that she had been seen too much at the opera in the company of the Prince of Wales, prompting rumours of romantic and political entanglement: 'When, dear Georgiana, shall I see you out of scrapes that injure your character? If you and your sister would but give up the Opera or any public place this one winter, on the just pretence of nursing your children, how easily might all this [adverse publicity] still be avoided.'[19] However, there were spatial distinctions to be drawn within the opera theatre. There were five levels of boxes, the fourth and fifth being the least exclusive. For the first fifty nights of the season the boxes were privately subscribed for, after which a second, less fashionable subscription was opened and more boxes were made available to the general public. Ladies could purchase tickets by the night for the pit, provided they wore evening dress, or for the galleries. In Fanny Burney's instructive novel *Evelina, Or a Young Ladies Entrance Into the World* (1778), when the eponymous heroine made her debut at the opera, she sat in the pit, 'where every body was dressed in so high a style, that, if I had been less delighted with the performance, my eyes would have found me sufficient entertainment from looking at the ladies . . .' and afterwards mingled with ease in the coffee-room; but on her second outing with her vulgar cousins she was put out to find herself ensconced in the uppermost, one shilling gallery. Throughout the eighteenth and early nineteenth centuries the most exclusive and stylish seats remained those in the prominent front boxes. For the genteel the constant attraction of the opera was the exhibition of glittering aristocratic femininity; even the serious-minded Anna Larpent was not immune from compulsive staring at the audience, as she confessed of a night at a comic opera at the King's in 1797: 'But what with Staring at ye spectacle & Company for 4 hours I got sick & dizzy . . .'[20]

Equally alluring, though less concentratedly aristocratic, was the theatre. Despite waves of reformist effort aimed at suppressing the theatre, it had never succumbed. In fact, the argument that plays were as conducive to virtue as to vice was often rehearsed, and in some years play-going was claimed to be a more fashionable pursuit than opera-going.[21] The London theatres, prominently the Theatre Royal, Drury Lane, Covent Garden (built 1732–3) and the Little Theatre in the Haymarket, which had their share of rougher custom, were nevertheless frequented by the quality and royalty, whose showy presence added to the enticements of these establishments for the less socially favoured.[22] Indeed, given the fact that London auditoria were as brilliantly lit as the stage itself, it is hardly surprising that sections of the audience might find themselves as closely scrutinized as the paid performers. Mrs Larpent was quite explicit about the object of a visit to Covent Garden in January 1793: 'We went to see the Royal family at the play'; although, as it transpired, the king and queen stayed away from their favourite theatre as the news of the guillotining of Louis XVI had just come in. When eventually Mrs Larpent coincided with the royal family at Covent Garden in 1795, she had a sufficiently clear view of the Prince of Wales's box to record a detailed description of the enraptured expressions of the unremarkable Princess of Wales, the boredom of her 'bloated, sodden' husband and the officiousness of Lady Jersey, who hovered in attendance on the prince 'with the air of a Persian Concubine'.[23] From the letters written by provincial visitors, it is clear that a night at one of the London theatres was experienced in terms of magical transport, as in this description of a dramatic performance at the Opera House penned by the dazzled Ellen Barcroft in 1808:

> it was scarcely possible when seeing Mrs Siddons . . . [as Margaret of Anjou] to persuade oneself that she did not really feel the passions attributed to that haughty Queen. The beauty of the house did indeed surpass my most sanguine expectations. In the centre of the ceiling was

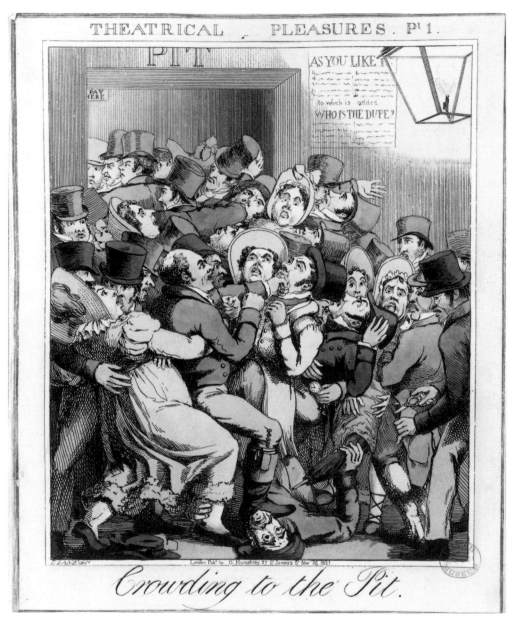

44 'Theatrical Pleasures, Crowding to the Pit', 1821.

45 'Theatrical Pleasures, Contending for a Seat', 1821.

a beautiful emblematic painting & the same in the front of every box. The beauty of the scenes, together with the brilliancy of the chandeliers made the whole appear like enchantment.[24]

As with the opera, contemporaries drew sharp distinctions about status and sexual propriety based on a viewer's position in the auditorium. At Drury Lane the observant Evelina drew a distinction between 'the most conspicuous' and the 'most private part of the house'. When Margaret Pedder saw Mrs Jordan in *The Country Girl* at the same theatre in 1786, she paid six shillings and sat in a front box, whereas James Boswell had lolled cheerfully in the pit at Drury lane with Oliver Goldsmith and his drinking companions in 1763. As at the opera, the upper boxes or green boxes were seen as the proverbial 'flesh market'.[25] Taken together, metropolitan plays, players, audience and *mise-en-scène* constituted a crucial component of the town talk so beloved by country cousins. But the social pleasures of the play should not be allowed to overshadow the aesthetic engagement of the female audience, which could be thoroughgoing. After all, it was due to the campaign of the aristocractic Shakespeare Ladies Club, formed in 1736, that John Rich and David Garrick reintroduced Shakespeare to the repertoire. This (largely) anonymous group has been credited with the permanent reform of literary taste. At the time they were praised for bringing morality back into fashion; their championing of Shakespeare against both raunchy Restoration plays and foreign imports, such as Italian opera, was celebrated in the name of virtuous patriotism – 'a truly public Spirit'.[26]

Provincial theatre flourished by mid-century, with the proliferation of town companies (the first at Norwich, York and Bath), the construction of new purpose-built auditoria in county towns, market towns and provincial resorts, and the success of touring companies. Few were the towns by the late eighteenth century which had not glimpsed the likes of Sarah Siddons or mounted a voguish play. Take the county of Yorkshire by way of example. In a typical season between 1769 and 1803, the actor-manager Wilkinson Tate took his acting troupe on an annual circuit of the Yorkshire theatres, including performances in York (January to May – Spring Assizes), Leeds (June to July), Pontefract (August), York (August – Race Week), Wakefield (September – Race Week), Doncaster (October – Race Week) and Hull (November to December).[27] He obtained cash in advance by selling box subscriptions for each town's season, but relied on bespoke performances requested by the likes of the Honourable Lady Carolina Herbert (Wakefield, 22 September 1775), Lady Armitage (Wakefield, 20 September 1776), 'The High-Sheriff and the Gentlemen of the grand Jury' (York, 16 March 1782) and 'the Ladies and the Gentlemen of the Card

Assembly' (York, 25 April 1782) to swell his coffers, since the advertise-ment of a grand presence tended to draw a wider audience of gawpers. The most exalted aristocratic patronage was to be had during the Wakefield and Doncaster race seasons. Subscribers could also lease a seat in the pit for the season, although there were cheaper nightly seats to be had as well in the first and upper galleries. By this means even towns like Leeds (which Wilkinson dismissed as 'little better than a Botany Bay for actors') could offer a fashionable array of new comedies, old tragedies and popular entr'acte entertainments, such as *tableaux vivantes*, a medley of songs, comic dances and pantomime romps. In just a single season in 1771 the New Theatre at Leeds mounted productions of Shakespeare's *Romeo and Juliet* (1597) and *King Lear* (1605), Rowe's, *Tamerlane* (1702), Young's, *The Revenge: A Tragedy* (1721), Vanbrugh and Cibber's, *The Provoked Husband* (1728), Hull's, *Royal Merchant: An Opera* (1768), Colman's, *The English Merchant* (1767) and his *The Portrait* (1770), Kelly's, *A Word to the Wise* (1770) and Cumberland's *The West Indian* (1771) for the edification of a 'a numerous and polite audience'.[28] Moreover, women made up an opinionated section of the polite audience for provincial theatre as their letters and diaries amply testify.[29]

Private theatricals performed by the great, at their height in decades between 1770 and 1810, drew intense public interest in the period. In fact, in the publicity accorded them and the sheer size and social range of the invited audience, many private theatricals were often only 'private' in the narrow sense that the cast were not paid professionals. Audiences of 150 were not uncommon; spectacular performances at Blenheim, Richmond House and Hinchingbrook were reported to have depressed winter book-ings at Bath. However, if the professional actress was an ambiguous figure still vulnerable to the imputation of prostitution, then amateurish flaunting cast a reputation for demure dignity in a dubious light, to put it mildly. The donning of disguise and the doffing of decorum might be thrilling for the participants, but it could be disquieting to attentive observers, as novels such as Jane Austen's *Mansfield Park* (1814), Maria Edgeworth's *Patronage* (1814) and Fanny Burney's *The Wanderer* (1814) dramatically demonstrated.[30] Yet perhaps the very shattering of the ideal of modest female reserve was politically calculated in the first place. In a brilliant new study, Gillian Russell reminds us that 'many leading Whig families were identified as enthusiastic thespians; in this respect amateur acting can be regarded as part of a repertoire of behaviour – including libertine flamboyance, female exhibitionism, and the cultivation of public celebrity – that was used to define the Prince of Wales's party in defiance of the "Farmer George" probity associated with the King'. Russell argues that private theatricals were not only an important expression of country-house paternalism, but also a mechanism for the consolidation and enactment of social alliances amongst the political elite, an arena in which women glittered centre stage in conspicuous contrast to their negligible role in more traditional fora. Thus, in April 1787 a private performance of *The Way to Keep Him* at Richmond House occupied so many parliamentarians that a motion in the House of Commons had to be deferred.[31] Of course, the modest family theatricals mounted by the gentry lacked the political punch and the titillating excitement of these aristocratic extravaganzas. Minimal publicity, a small audience, a suitable play and senior family members *en costume* put the stamp of innocent diversion on family play-acting. Still, an unsated interest in more outrageous productions remained widespread amongst the genteel.[32]

Musical entertainment of all forms enjoyed a roaring vogue in the eighteenth century. The aforementioned Italian opera, spearheaded the development of the musical stage, while commercial concerts and music festivals were promoted in London from the 1670s. Borsay has unearthed evidence for at least a dozen towns experimenting with a public concert series by the 1760s, and a small but growing number of provincial music festivals in the cathedral cities. Taking Leeds again by way of exemplar, the evidence of newspaper advertisements suggests that the concert, in particular, was a well-established constituent of the cultural scene in the 1760s and 1770s, probably because of the appointment of William Herschel as director of public concerts in 1762. Leeds offered an annual autumn programme of subscription concerts of the works of Bach, Giardini, Boccherini and so on in its New Concert Hall, on Vicar Lane, and at the Old and New Assembly rooms in these decades. There were also a large number of single performances of organ and choral works mounted by local churches: Handel's *Messiah* and his *Judus Maccabaeus*, and Purcell's *Te Deum* and *Grand Coronation Chorus* being perennial favourites. In Leeds, as elsewhere, the Church remained an important provider of public music. Unsurprisingly, the concert audiences tended to be genteel and mixed sex, and the concert may therefore be seen as another new and vibrant cultural form which added further breadth to the social horizons of polite provincial women in the period.[33]

Staged spectacles of all kinds flourished in the eighteenth century, from militia reviews to ladies' processions, from firework displays and magic shows, to the exhibition of 'freaks' and dancing dogs, but perhaps the unlikeliest spectacle which coined a profit was the trial. The awful theatricality of the criminal courts was much remarked on by contemporaries as well as modern historians, while the civil courts which dealt with

46 'York Music Festival', 1824. This was a four-day festival to raise money for the York county hospital and the Hull, Leeds and Sheffield General Infirmary. Clearly women predominated in the audience. Ellen Parker of Selby for one was transported by a similar concert in the Minster in 1823: 'It was the "Messiah" & no words can describe how beautiful was the singing & grand the Choruses . . . there were 1500 applications for tickets . . . The gallery was filled with grandees–chiefly (the Ladies) in small bonnets.'

interpersonal disputes presented an enduring fund of scandalous anecdote. On the northern circuit, the biannual assize courts at Lancaster and York and the annual sittings at Durham, Newcastle, Carlisle and Appleby offered the drama of capital trials to an eager public of men, women and children, as well as the gathering of the county in the host town for the accompanying race meetings, public assemblies and private parties. Although the thirteen-year-old Mary Chorley was too young to attend the Lancaster assize ball in 1779, the opportunity to witness the judge's triumphal entry and the posturing showmanship of the barristers in action offered thrills aplenty: 'went to court and was much [amused] with hearing the lawyers plead. Mr Lee indeed a most provoking man for he is always in the right.' However, the audience's thirst for spectacle was not always gratified. Susannah Gossip wrote from York with apparent disappointment in 1729, complaining 'We had but little business at our assize only one man executed for murdering', although she took solace in the presence of at least eighteen noblemen in town for the races and Lord Carlisle's ball.[34]

The trials that did most to gratify the prurient were those involving the rich and celebrated, a higher concentration of which were staged in the London courts. Although the Old Bailey was not an everyday site of gentry traffic, *causes célèbres* such as the Rudd–Perreau trial for forgery in 1775, or the trial of the Earl of Ferrers for the murder of his steward in 1760 drew elite women in droves. Lord Lovat's trial for fraud, for instance, prompted an unseemly scramble for tickets, presumably dispensed by an opportunistic porter: 'all the young ladies are now wishing for tickets to be at Lord Lovats tryall for no bodys pity seems great for him they can go with less concern . . .'[35] Voyeurism was so pronounced in the intricate Rudd–Perreau case that when the apparently well-born Mrs Rudd and the Perreau brothers were committed for further examination, 'the public office in Bow-Street was so crowded with genteel people, that the magistrates thought it most prudent to adjourn to Guildhall, Westminster'. Ultimately, 'the solemnity, that was with so much propriety assumed by the bench on this occasion, joined to the plaintive tone of Mrs Rudd's voice; the artless manner in which she told her story, and the decency of her whole deportment, produced a scene so truly pathetic, as to draw tears from many of the spectators'.[36] More thrilling still were the civil suits for 'criminal conversation' and divorce. They offered, as the published *Trials for Adultery, Or The History of Divorces* promised, 'a complete History of the Private Life, Intrigues and Amours of many Characters in the most elevated sphere'.[37] Bessy Ramsden, for one, could hardly contain herself at the prospect of a ticket to witness the trial of the Duchess of Kingston for bigamy at Westminster Hall in 1776.

> There is nothing talk off now but the preparations for the Trial of the Duchess of Kingston. We had some ladies hear the other day who are to be at it . . . They are to go at seven o clock in the morning. It must be a fine sight . . . I think was a Ticket to be offered to me I would not have the prudence to refuse it.

> The Late Duchess of Kingston seem[s] to be forgoten all ready. When Her trial is printed which is now in hand, she will I suppose be renew[ed] again in convasation. Don't you think I had great self-denial in not going to the Trial When I tell you I had three offers?[38]

47 'A Perspective View of the Inside of the Grand Assembly Room in Blake Street', 1759. Burlington's magnificent new assembly rooms at York (opened in 1732) were said to outshine those of Bath.

Through print, letters and hearsay the polite could take a horrid pleasure in the sensational details, even if they had not witnessed the cross-examination first hand. Scandalous trials and notorious or glamorous criminals added spice to polite conversation throughout the period.

The supreme arena of polite leisure was the assembly – an evening gathering accommodating dancing, cards, tea and, perhaps above all, talk. While the precise origins of the assembly remain obscure, their popularity in the early eighteenth century is manifest in bricks and mortar. London and the spas led the way in the building of assembly rooms, but the provincial towns of the north were not slow to follow. Assemblies were mounted in custom-built or customized public rooms in Leeds and Liverpool from at least 1726, in Preston from 1728, in Sheffield and Scarborough from 1733, in Whitehaven from 1736, in Beverley from 1745, and in Manchester and Hull well before mid-century, while Burlington's magnificent new assembly rooms at York (opened in 1732) were thought to outshine those of Bath. When the new assembly rooms were opened in Leeds in 1777 a 'most brilliant appearance of Genteel company' attended the first ball, and 'upwards of 200 gentlemen and ladies present, who all appeared to be competitors for politeness of behaviour, gentility and complaisance' were congratulated by the *Leeds Intelligencer*. From the first, assemblies were synonymous with female diversion. A definition of the assembly in 1751 stressed both its social exclusivity and its mixed-sex constituency: 'A stated and general meeting of the polite persons of both sexes, for the sake of conversation, gallantry, news and play.'[39] Orchestrated heterosexual sociability was the *raison d'être* of the assembly.

The power and prominence of women at eighteenth-century assemblies were remarked upon again and again. Although some resorts boasted an official master of ceremonies, in many towns a band of gentlewomen and noblewomen were styled the 'Governors' of the assembly and often one of their number was singled out as reigning 'Queen' of the assembly. From the 1720s a committee of titled ladies, including Lady Panmure and Susanna, Countess of Eglinton, oversaw the conduct of the Edinburgh assembly rooms and 'agreed upon certain rules' of conduct and ceremony. At mid-century Miss Nicky Murray wore a gold medal as badge of her position as 'Lady Directress'. Only in the 1780s was the management of protocol handed over to a male steward. Female management was equally to the fore in Derby, where a succession of lady patrons demonstrated their command of book-keeping and social discrimination, as an entry in the account book for 4 August 1752 indicates: 'Delivered up the Assembly room to the right Honourable the Countess of Ferrers, who did me the great honour of accepting it. I told her that trade never mixed with us ladies.' Strikingly, not only were the assembly rooms at Almacks run by a female committee, but the new Almacks gambling club set up in 1770 allowed female members the right of nomination and veto of prospective male members. Mrs Boscawen recorded that 'Lord March and Brook Boothby were blackballed by the ladies to their great astonishment'. Women's prestige at 'the exclusive temple of the *beau monde*' was routinely remarked upon. As late as 1821, men about town still complained about the necessity of being on their best polite behaviour at Almacks before 'the *fastidious* PATRONESSES, that parade up and down here, as the arbitresses of fame and fortune.'[40]

Of course, the assembly was not the sole possession of the nobility and their intimates. Some gatherings were more exclusive than others, subscription balls were more select than all-inclusive public balls, but generally the stalwarts of the provincial assembly were the lesser gentry, the professions and the genteel trades. And nationwide, dancing masters acted as impresarios, mounting countless small assemblies for their pupils to which a wide spectrum of respectable parents was drawn.[41] The Doncaster assemblies of the 1740s were regrettably not noted for 'grand appearances'. In the 1760s the Mrs Wilson who was Queen of the Lancaster assembly had taken lodgings in town rather than submit to the expense of refurbishing the family house in Kendal. A fine appearance she may have had, but broad acres and a considerable fortune were obviously lacking. In 1780 Mrs Owen Cunliffe, the daughter of a Manchester manufacturer, presided over a small Colne ball and, lacking noble consequence, was dismissed as 'The Little *Queen*' by the acid Elizabeth Shackleton. In the 1790s a mere Mrs Shaw presided over the Otley assemblies and saw 'everything conducted with due decorum'. It was gentility, not nobility, which formed the backbone of these provincial congregations, as a no less delighted Eliza Parker reported of the July assemblies in early nineteenth-century Preston: 'we have been very Gay a great deal of Genteel company is in Town . . . The first Assembly was a very good one and tonight is expected a brilliant meeting. I never saw so much dress required at Preston before.' Meanwhile, London had its more modest assemblies, like the assemblies for the City of London and the Borough of Southwark patronized by Bessy Ramsden in the 1760s and 1770s.[42]

Whether an assembly was ultra-fashionable or respectably genteel, commentators again and again drew attention to the high visibility of women and, unsurprisingly, the presence of young marriageable women by the score. Mary Warde noted of the assembly at Bury St Edmunds in 1740, 'it has for a great many Years been famous for the number of pretty Women that the neighbouring Countys send to it . . . I fancy you have seen the Duke of Graftons & Lord Herveys daughters . . .'[43] To some observers not only did women seem prominent in the ritual performance of the assembly, they appeared positively bumptious with power. Certainly this was Eliza Haywood's horrified assessment of the 'Air of Boldness' with which some fine ladies stormed public Assemblies:

> They do not walk but straddle; and sometimes run with a Kind of Frisk and Jump; – throw their enormous Hoops almost in the Faces of those who pass by them; – stretch out their Necks, and roll their Eyes from Side to Side, impatient to take the whole Company at one View; and if they happen to see anyone dress'd less exactly, according to the Mode,

48a (*above*) and b (*facing page*)   *Cuerdon Masquerade*, 1822, two watercolours by Emily
Brookes. This select fancy-dress ball was part of the 1822 Preston Guild celebrations, a famous
civic festival which took place every twenty years, drawing visitors from across the north.

than themselves, presently cry out, – *Antiquity to Perfection! – A Picture
of the Last Age!* – Then burst into a Laugh, loud enough to be heard at
two or three furlongs distant.[44]

Whether enshrined in the rule book or not, the assembly was associated
with collective female influence. It was not for nothing that the election-
eering Walter Spencer Stanhope was warned before the by-election of
1784, 'The Hull Assembly . . . is composed of a set of partial proud
people . . . you must . . . be all things to *all* the women.'[45]

The assembly spawned a host of variations, including the masquerade,
the ridotto (a combined concert and assembly) and the ridotto al fresco
staged in public rooms and gardens, and the musical party, the rout and
the drum hosted in private households. Contemporary definitions of these
myriad forms of social congregation routinely assumed female participation, indeed most saw heterosexual sociability as the very essence of
the event, as here where Smollett defines the drum in 1746, 'A riotous
assembly of fashionable people, of both sexes, at a private house, consisting of some hundreds; not unaptly stiled a drum, from the noise and
emptiness of the Entertainment.'[46] As with the assembly, the fashionable
private party was associated with female performance and pleasure. As the
fourteen-year-old Ellen Barcroft engagingly concluded after the sand-
wiches, jellies, tarts, procession and dancing of a London rout in 1808,
'Mem[o]. Spent a most delightful evening indeed'.[47]

The aforementioned ridottos and masquerades were a marked feature

of London social life, drawing men and women in colossal numbers, but these gatherings enjoyed a scandalous reputation in some quarters and their voguishness was often cited as evidence that young men and women were on the road to debauchery. Concern lay with the sheer size and anonymity of these promiscuous gatherings. A ridotto at Vauxhall Gardens in May 1769, for instance, was attended by roughly ten thousand people. Similarly, *The Times* estimated that because of the mistakenly low price of admission a mixed bag of sixteen hundred people attended a masquerade at the Opera House in February 1798 and, unfortunately, 'the freedom of conversation which is allowed in these motley meetings, became, on this occasion, indecent ribaldry and licentiousness.' By the rules of the masquerade, absolute anonymity had to be respected and introductions were dispensed with. Addison in 1701 reported that 'the women either come by themselves or are introduced by friends who are obliged to quit them upon their first entrance to the conversation of anybody that addresses them.' *Mist's Weekly Journal* may have claimed soothingly in 1718 that 'there is absolute freedom of speech, without the least offence given thereby', but in the eyes of many the abandoning of decorum combined with strict anonymity was a recipe for social and sexual chaos. The Bishop of London preached a sermon against masquerades in 1724 and George II made an ineffectual attempt to have masked balls suppressed.[48] Yet the dismay of the desiccated did little to dent the popularity of these fashionable social congregations. The Swiss businessman Johann Jacob Heidegger established the commercial success of the masquerade at the King's Theatre, Haymarket, in the 1730s and 1740s (between operas), admitting all-comers with twenty-seven shillings for the ticket and the appropriate costume. Subsequently, Vauxhall, Ranelagh and the Dog and Duck gardens in St George's Fields, Southwark, became famous for their masked Venetian balls, as did the Pantheon in Oxford Street, opened in 1772 ('all the world goes to see this new outlandish Place, Kings, Queens, Duchesses, Countesses & commoners . . .'[49]), and Carlisle House in Soho Square in the 1760s, under the auspices of Mrs Teresa Cornelys. Even this notorious diversion could be reconciled with polite exclusivity: Jane Pellet noted in 1748, that 'all people of *taste* have Plays & Masquerades at Home. There was last Thursday the Grandest Subscription Masquerade that was ever know. It is said there was not a Jewel in Town but what was there . . .'[50]

While the masquerade was a diversion associated with the metropolis, indeed it was one of the key emblems of cosmopolitan excess, fashion took it out to the provinces. Two masquerades were offered at the Preston Guild celebrations of 1742 (a civic festival held every twenty years), although a rather proper Miss Richardson, a Yorkshire gentlewoman, used them to advertize northern superiority to such a disreputable diversion: 'I believe there was the least Company at them, indeed I had not the Curiosity to go . . .' In fact, as early as 1722 a comedian at the Preston Guild had urged the bachelors in the audience to seek a virtuous local bride 'averse to wanton serenades, To midnight Balls and *London Masquerades*'.[51] Nevertheless, a grand masquerade held in January 1779 by Edwin Lascelles at Harewood House near Leeds was enjoyed by 'some of the nobility and a great number of the neighbouring gentry' without any negative comment from the Leeds papers, but private masquerades, with their hand-picked guests and ritual unmaskings, never produced the same erotic *frisson* as the anonymous public gatherings. In Pontefract in 1755, when there was masquerading all over town, Jane Scrimshire could detail the costumes of a whole raft of guests in advance.[52] In a melée of sailors, harlequins, ballad singers, fools and columbines she would have no trouble identifying her friends; thus were the mysteries of the masquerade cleared away to meet the demands of provincial gentility. So much for social and sexual chaos.

The most public of the public places where women and men congregated was surely the pleasure garden, the most famous of which were in London: Vauxhall, Ranelagh, Marylebone and Kensington. Vauxhall Gardens on the south bank of the Thames in Lambeth was reopened to the public in 1732 by Mr Jonathan Tyers for ridottos al fresco on summer nights. A wooded twelve-acre grove, Vauxhall offered picturesque alleys and covered colonnades to stroll in and clearances dotted with classical columns, alcoves and temples in which to tarry. With glittering lights

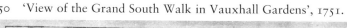

49 'A General Prospect of Vauxhall Gardens', 1751.

50 'View of the Grand South Walk in Vauxhall Gardens', 1751.

*A View of the Company in
Vauxhall Gardens.*

51 'A View of the Company in Vauxhall Gardens', 1779, from *Carnan & Newbury's Pock*
Book.

A View of the Company at the Pantheon, Oxford Street.

52 'A View of the Company at the Pantheon, Oxford St', 1779, from *Carnan & Newbury's Pocket Book*.

strung among the trees, it had an orchestra and an area for dancing. The evening's entertainment usually opened with a courtly promenade down the main walks, the ladies in full evening dress and the gentlemen carrying their hats. Then followed a concert and a chicken supper in one of the supper boxes decorated with the paintings of Francis Hayman and others. Vauxhall's chief rival was Ranelagh, in Chelsea, which opened in 1742 and rapidly became the more fashionable resort. As Jane Pellet reported in 1743, 'Among the people of Tast le Delicatesse I think Ranelagh is now the darling pleasure for the sake of Mr Sullivan, who sings the Rising Sun & Stella & Flavia'.[53] By reputation Ranelagh was more exclusive, but less exciting than Vauxhall. After paying half-a-crown for admission, a visitor was at liberty to wander about the garden admiring the Chinese buildings, the canal, the bridge and to take a circuit round the Rotunda, an enormous circular hall designed for a high-profile parade. By the 1770s it was considered fashionable to arrive at the Rotunda as late as eleven or twelve.[54]

These metropolitan gardens had a tremendous capacity and admitted virtually anyone who could afford the price of the ticket, so the size of the throng and the dangers latent in the mob were close to the surface in the written reactions of polite visitors. To celebrate the proclamation of the Peace of Aix-la-Chapelle in 1749, 'a new way of entertaining the publick with a jubilee masquerade' was devised at Ranelagh, expected to draw 'Millions of people' and an 'a bundence of people come from France, Italy and Holland'.[55] One visitor, the lawyer John Spencer, reported with amazement that 'the crowd of people in the park was greater than you can possibly imagine & what is very surprising there was not in the least riot or disturbance of any kind all the evening'; despite the fact that the fireworks display caused one of the grand pavilions to ignite.[56] Being a popular resort for both the likes of Frederick Prince of Wales and the well-dressed prostitute, the pleasure garden, particularly Vauxhall Gardens, conveyed the spice of danger amidst the glory, but demonstrably the gardens were also visited by respectable married couples and family parties. Polite, agreeable entertainment was to be had if one kept to the lighted path, in the company of known acquaintances. Dr Johnson reportedly believed Ranelagh to be altogether 'a place of innocent recreation'.[57] Outside London, town pleasure gardens, such the Spring Gardens in Leeds (in existence from at least 1715) or the Spring Gardens in Bath (from 1742), had less racy reputations, drawing a more socially homogenous custom.[58]

A high-profile promenade was also to be had along one of the numerous custom-built walks laid out in London and the provinces in the late seventeenth and early eighteenth centuries. The most prestigious perambulation was to be enjoyed on the London Mall, constructed by

A VIEW IN KENSINGTON GARDENS, DURING THE PERFORMANCE OF THE MILITARY BAND

53 'A View in Kensington Gardens During the Performance of the Military Band', from *Poole's Cabinet of Fashion and Repository of Literature* (1827).

54 These ladies admiring potted plants appear in the untitled frontispiece to *Marshall's Ladies Fashionable Repository* (1827).

Charles II in 1660, where the quality were to be observed on summer evenings and winter afternoons in their charming 'undress'. Although one of the avenues on the Mall was reserved for the royal family and their friends, virtually anyone could join the cavalcade in the other carriage-ways, so the walk became synonymous with the moving of multitudes. De Saussure reported in 1725, 'the park is so crowded at times that you cannot help touching your neighbour. Some people come to see, some to be seen, and others to seek their fortunes; for many priestesses of Venus are abroad, some of them magnificently attired, and all on the look-out for adventures.'[59] The appeal for some was akin to that of a colossal beauty parade, as here, where a maudlin Sir Richard Philips sighs in 1817 for the bewitching beauties of yesteryear:

> My spirits sunk and a tear started into my eyes as I brought to mind those crowds of beauty, rank and fashion which used to be displayed in the centre Mall of this park on Sunday evenings. How often in my youth had I been a delighted spectator of this enchanted and enchanting assemblage! Here used to promenade for one or two hours after dinner, the whole British world of gaiety, beauty and splendour. Here could be seen, in one moving mass, extending the whole length of the Mall, 5,000 of the most lovely women in this country of female beauty, all splen-didly attired and accompanied by as many well-dressed men.[60]

Town walks in the provinces fulfilled the same exhibitionary function. The Pantiles in Tunbridge Wells (laid out in 1638), Avenham Walk in Preston (1690), the 'New Walk' in York (1730s) and the Grand Parade in Bath (1740s) are all famous examples of formal walks laid out as places of polite resort.

That genteel women walked the town and city streets of Georgian England cannot be in doubt. Indeed, foreigners attributed the unattractive size of English women's feet to their prodigious taste for exercise.[61] When ladies were not sauntering along an elegant tree-lined parade, they were taking more purposeful walks in fashionable shopping districts. London's superior shopping was renowned across Europe. The most stylish shops were to be found on the Strand, Pall Mall, St Paul's Churchyard and, latterly, on Bond Street. In 1725 De Saussure was entranced by the attrac-tive shops on the Strand, Fleet Street, Cheapside and Cornhill, 'where the choicest merchandise from the four quarters of the globe is exposed to the sight of the passers-by. A stranger might spend whole days, without ever feeling bored, examining these wonderful goods.'[62] London shops were often open until ten at night, but the afternoon was the most popular time for conspicuous consuming. Christian Goede, a German visitor in London

55 'Prospect of a Noble Terras Walk', York, c.1756. Another of York's facilities for polite recreation, this walk was laid out in the 1730s by the City Corporation.

between 1802 and 1804, noted that the West End was busiest between one and three, when the ladies purchased luxury goods in Bond Street and 'the gentlemen pass on horseback up and down the street to see and be seen. [The] foot-pavement is so perfectly covered with elegantly dressed people as to make it difficult to move.'[63] But in May 1808 Ellen Barcroft contrived to miss the carriage trade despite having spent half a day at large in the city: 'We were out at least 5 hours walking in different parts of the town. We were in Bond st but the fashionable had not made their appearance.'[64] A stroll around the better London shops was a standard feature of most tourist itineraries, male or female, just as a shopping spree was a crucial element of a trip to town in the provinces. Shops offered pleasures for the eye, but also opportunities for refreshment and relaxation, one of the most famous venues of the 1790s being Harding, Howell and Co. on Pall Mall, which had four departments on the ground floor and a room above where customers partook of wine, tea and sweetmeats. Even in Colne, local ladies and gentlemen collected at Betty Hartley's general store for tea, 'to be tempted with her fashionable and elegant assortments from London'.[65] Shopping was well entrenched as a public cultural pursuit for respectable women and men long before the advent of Selfridges and Whiteleys. Shops and showrooms were acceptable sites of mixed sex congregation from their very establishment. When, in 1711, Lady Mary Pierrepont and Edward Wortley surveyed the available spaces for a romantic rendezvous, both Cortelli's Italian Warehouse and Colman's toyshop were mooted spots. The urban voyager and female pleasure-seeker was no invention of the 1880s.[66]

Cultural tourism was a mainstay of the genteel life out of doors. Both the tour and the day-trip were popular diversions throughout this period, incorporating the viewing of a catholic range of sites. 'How-to' manuals for patriotic travellers were published throughout the eighteenth century, encouraging the observation and investigation of everything from field systems to local birth rates.[67] Tourist attractions fell into five main categories: the commercial exhibition, scenes of natural beauty, architectural wonders, industrial sites or feats of engineering, and impressive institutions. Thus, in addition to predictable visits to county seats and pretty views, genteel tourists examined bridges and factories, hospitals and almshouses. Elizabeth Shackleton fancied herself a connoisseur of domestic architecture and the rural picturesque, but she also found time to ride out to view the new turnpike road, the Leeds cloth hall, the new locks on the Leeds to Liverpool canal at Bingley, and went to watch poor children winding silk. She also regretted having missed Mrs Walton's outing to view the Peels' cotton printing factory at Church.[68] In the 1770s Mary Chorley was taken to admire Preston and Liverpool docks, a paper factory, a coal pit, a picture gallery, a china auction, an army exercise and the opening of the Lancaster assize. On a visit to London in 1786 Margaret Pedder relished all the traditional metropolitan attractions, but also attended the Foundling Hospital, Greenwich Pensioners' Hospital, the Magdalene and a meeting of sons of clergy and charity at St Paul's, making charitable donations at three of these institutions. In the 1790s Mary Chorley's own daughter Sarah Ford of Lancaster catalogued her visits to a furnace, a sugar house, a rural powder mill, the new Lancaster canal and the aqueducts at both Preston and Lancaster. Ellen Barcroft's sojourn in London a decade later, also incorporated edifying visits to Christ's Hospital, Greenwich Hospital, the Fishmonger's Almshouses, St Paul's meeting of the sons of the clergy, and the Magdalene chapel where she heard a sermon on charity. Judging by a rapt description of the steam-powering of Derby Infirmary penned in 1813, the female fascination with both engi-

56   An untitled
illustration of two
ladies in a phaeton,
from *Heideloff's
Gallery of Fashion*
(1794).

neering and worthy institutions still ran deep in the early years of the
nineteenth century.[69]

A traditional, but enduring forum for genteel women's public lives was
the established church. Women bulked large and opinionated in eighteenth and early nineteenth-century congregations, although for many
apparently observant Christians a Sunday service offered a taste of the
pleasures of this world as much as a prospect of the next, something which
can quickly be deduced from advice to young women on their attendance:
'Regard neither the Actions or Dress of others,' urged lady Sarah Pennington, 'let not your eyes rove in search of Acquaintance, but in the Time
of Divine Service avoid as much as possible, all complimental civilities, of
which there are too great an intercourse in most of our Churches; remember that your only business there is to pay a solemn Act of Devotion to
Almighty God . . .'[70] But compliments and felicitations would not be extinguished. Susannah Gossip met her friends 'with all imaginable civility'
at church every day in York in the 1730s. Elizabeth Shackleton had exemplary religious credentials, having been confirmed into the Anglican
church by the Archbishop of Canterbury at the Tower of London, but she
still passed far more comment in her diary on who she met at church and
how they looked, and on church-seating disputes, than on the content of
the sermon. Mary Warde sacrilegiously invoked the country pulpit as a
byword for 'Dull Discourse', and, of course, many a romantic fire was lit

by looks sizzling across the pews. A Mr Town in the *Connoisseur*
revealed the voiceless but eloquent byplay of the congregation, when he
sought to curtail the loud socializing of the theatre: 'The silent courtship
of the eyes, ogles, nods, glances and curtsies from one box to another may
be allowed them the same as at Church, but nothing more.'[71] We would be
naive to ignore the social appeal of the local church, especially in those
small towns and villages which lacked alternative public venues.

Even in the decades when Evangelical reaction was at its height, social
considerations could weigh as heavily as the spiritual with genteel Anglicans. In 1805 in Nottingham Abigail Gawthern took strong exception to
the new curate 'a most disagreeable vulgar voice and a drunken man',
while Eliza Whitaker's circle offered running commentaries on pulpit
performances in the manner of a theatre critic: 'Isaac Austen preached at
the old church this morning . . . he beat the cushions most unmercifully
and had not a good voice.'[72] In fact, the Horrocks sisters seemed to have
toured the Preston churches on the look-out for the liveliest young man at
the lectern. In clear contrast, serious study of sermons was made by Mrs
Anna Larpent, who always assessed those she heard in terms of form,
content and delivery and, if thought-provoking, reflected at length on their
significance for her. But whatever motivation was uppermost, the letters
written by Anglican women about their churches are suffused with the
assurance of social ownership, although none of the women studied here
condoned the indecorous spectacle of female preaching. Let Beatrix
Lister's horrified response to what she termed a Shaker meeting in the
1770s speak for all the women of her stripe: '[the meeting] had preaching
enough to satisfy any reasonable people. A woman that had folly sufficient
to make herself ridiculous held forth about an hour. She was quite frantic
& in my opinion so far from making me laugh that upon me it had a very
different effect, after this we soon made our escape with a resolution never
to visit the meeting again.'[73] Genteel religiosity stopped far short of enthusiastic public exhortation.

The proper public expression of a gentlewoman's religious energy was
the charitable association. Informal, individualized charitable giving was a
long-standing aspect of elite stewardship, a Christian obligation entailed
by the possession of property. Yet alongside this old tradition, often
championed by devout women, grew up the great eighteenth-century associative charities directed by men, such as the Foundling Hospital and the
Marine Society. Comparable charities and self-help associations sprang up
in most prosperous provincial cities.[74] Less is known, however, of the
increasing number of provincial societies set up and run by women. In the
absence of systematic research, scattered instances must suffice to suggest

57   'A Nottingham Card Party', 1797.

58   'A Polite Congregation', 1797, depicting with satirical zest the unspiritual pleasures of church-going in a provincial town.

the potential range of early female associative life. Take the Bedale Ladies Amicable Society begun in 1783: essentially a self-help association set up to relieve its 123 members, in illness, disability and old age, it also offered the pleasures of participation in club life. A president and two stewards were appointed every six months, as was a clerk, 'which may be male if thought proper by the society', along with a standing committee of seven members to transact business. The members met on the last Saturday of every month, except December, between six and nine in the evening at rented club rooms and paid eightpence into the communal box. On club nights the ladies were each given a ticket which they could exchange for a glass of wine or a pint of ale. On feast days the members processed into church together to hear a sermon upon the occasion. All its members were demonstrably women of 'sober life and conversation', but some were in greater need than others. Doubtless the likes of the Honourable Mrs Pierce, Mrs Jane North and Mrs Ann Burgess (unlike those members rendered without a title) attended in a spirit of gracious patronage, or Christian responsibility, or even female solidarity, rather than financial expectation. Beyond its immediate monetary benefits, membership of such a society offered women the gratifications of institutional importance. By 1820 few were the provincial towns which lacked new public platforms for female right-doing. Certainly, archival evidence survives for female societies in York, Bradford, Leeds, Whalley, Wakefield, Carlisle, Workington, Hawkshead, Chester, Liverpool – and doubtless elsewhere.[75]

For the particular gentlewomen whose lives have been studied in detail here, involvement in a self-proclaimed society with the full panoply of officers, rule book and annuities was a comparatively late development. No such affiliation can be found in the records of Elizabeth Shackleton, Jane Scrimshire, Bessy Ramsden, Ann Pellet, Mary Warde, Anne Stanhope or Anne Gossip, but by 1819 the Southall circle were members of a society which mounted ladies' booths at local bazaars, the proceeds to go the poor. In 1820 Mrs Tatham reported from Southall that 'Miss Frith . . . is going to busy herself in a penny club' that aimed to help clothe poor children. She stressed the novelty of this particular development, 'This idea is from [Edmonton] where it has answered extremely well', and the inherent possibilities for purposeful female recreation, 'Mary likes occupation only in her own way – it gives a little consequence and will employ her mind which as she has nothing to do but for herself, may be of service.'[76] In 1820 the sixty-two-year-old Mrs Anna Larpent was an officer and regular attender of her local female friendly society which was held in the parish vestry, was involved in the administration of a local school, operated a soup kitchen for poor children, did some workhouse and parish visiting, and sewed simple items for 'Mrs Porter's charity repository'. While Mrs Larpent had always been a devout, observant Christian, comparing the diaries she wrote in 1790, 1800, 1810 and 1820 it is striking how many more formal 'opportunities' she had 'of being useful' in her last years.[77] Hence, while some historians have stressed the extent to which respectable women were marginalized in nineteenth-century associative life, what is more remarkable from the eighteenth-century perspective is the extraordinary explosion in the number of philanthropic ventures authored and administered by women. As F. K. Prochaska has concluded of the early nineteenth-century boom in 'feminized' philanthropy, 'The welling up from below of female power produced, among other things, the rapid growth of district visiting, with its emphasis on the moral and physical cleansing of the nation's homes; the prominence of institutions for servants, widows and "ladies"; the application of the family system in orphanages, ragged schools and other institutions; and the expansion of children's charity.'[78] The public lives and profiles of genteel women were certainly enhanced by the nineteenth-century multiplication of organizations which gave a little consequence.

Beside the improving society in eighteenth-century England, blossomed groups for the furtherance of particular literary, antiquarian or scientific interests, along with clubs set up for sheer conviviality. In 1750 the novelist Edward Kimber estimated that 'perhaps Twenty Thousand people in London' met every night at clubs. Although little substantive research has been done on participation in such societies, first impressions suggest that, formally at least, the majority of these were within the purview of men.[79] However, at this early stage of research it would be unwise to pronounce too emphatically on the dearth of a public intellectual life for women. In fact, suggestive new research by Donna Andrew using newspaper advertisements has uncovered a hitherto unsuspected number of female debating societies and mixed debating societies operating in London in the 1770s, 1780s and 1790s. A bracing cocktail of debates was on offer, from the question 'Does an uncorrupted Senator, or an able general, render the greatest Services to the State?' (14 March 1780, Oratorical Academy, Mitre Tavern) to 'Does the clause of Obedience in the Marriage Ceremony, bind a Wife to obey her Husband at all times?' (12 November 1798, Westminster Forum).[80] Not that women's public speaking met with universal approval: *The Times* of 1788 maintained that 'the debating ladies would be much better employed at their needle and thread, a good sempstress being a more amiable character than a female orator'. To little avail: there were at least forty-eight sets of rooms in the metropolis hired out to mixed or ladies' debating societies in this period, Andrew finds.

However, debating societies in general, like combinations of all kinds, did fall foul of Pitt's 'terror' (the government-inspired persecution of political radicals) in the autumn of 1792; only societies debating non-political topics endured.[81] Nevertheless, the popularity and scope of debating societies is suggestive of the potentialities of a public culture both rational and entertaining to which metropolitan women could lay claim. Further research must test the vitality of this culture in the provinces, although it is already clear that there were 'female coffee-houses' and conversation clubs sprinkled about the growing cities and resorts.[82] It remains to be seen whether debating societies (male and female alike) revived in the more relaxed legal climate of the 1820s.

Interestingly, however, when we return to the particular genteel women who are our focus, intellectual societies are not referred to in letters and diaries until the early nineteenth century. It is plausible that provincial ladies attended local events such as the Leeds lectures on oratory in August 1776, or the Auricula Society's grand show at Wakefield in April of that year, but mentions of formal membership are missing. From the 1810s; however, it is another story. Book societies had been set up by Eliza Whitaker in Clitheroe, Alice Ainsworth in Bolton, by 'A. B.' in Preston and probably by Sarah Horrocks in the same town by 1816. A letter written by Alice Ainsworth in pursuit of a treasurer for her society, reveals that these female clubs incorporated formal (if unpaid) officers, and thereby echoed the organization of male associations. Taste ran not only to novels, but also to biographies, travelogues and improving tomes. Some societies were more serious minded than others; Alice Ainsworth's Bolton circle, for instance, sustained both a French and an English club and disdained popular literature, for, as she explained, 'we do not tolerate the common novels of the day'. By contrast, 'A. B.' complained that her Preston society stocked little other than novels and altogether too few of those; she found both Mrs West and Madame d'Arblay's works disappointing.[83] Female club life was in full flower in the provincial north by 1820.

This evidence for an early nineteenth-century institutionalization of female intellectual life is suggestive, in that it directly contradicts the chronology of increasing domestication so entrenched in nineteenth-century women's history. However, it must be observed that these societies formalized something long practised on an informal basis. Elizabeth Shackleton borrowed books from friends and lent her own books widely, noting the title and date of the transaction in her pocket book.[84] Moreover, recommendations for and commentaries on reading-matter were a common currency of women's letters throughout the period. Mary Warde

found a 'beautiful simplicity' in the second volume of Richardson's
Pamela (1740–41); Ann Pellet thought both his *Clarissa: Or the History of
a Young Lady* (1748) and Fielding's *The History of Tom Jones* (1749)
'vastly entertaining'; Jane Scrimshire subscribed to local publications and
adopted phrases from *Sir Charles Grandison* (1754); William Ramsden
affected the whimsical style of Laurence Sterne and coined the nickname
'Tristram Shandy' for his cousin Elizabeth; and an affronted Bessy
Ramsden asked for an opinion on offensive passages in *Lord Chesterfield's
Letters to His Son* (1774).[85]

Genteel female readers enjoyed unprecedented access to the public
world of print. In the period 1640–1750, 81 per cent of women among
gentry and professional families in the counties of Yorkshire, Cumberland, Westmorland and Northumberland are thought to have possessed basic literacy skills. Therefore the percentage of gentlewomen
unable to engage at some level with print by the nineteenth century must
have been negligible. No evidence exists of classical erudition in the letters
studied here, and comparatively few of the ladies discussed were sent away
to school,[86] so no claim is made that women were equal participators in
exalted intellectual debate. Yet the proliferation of periodicals which
translated ancient concerns in amusing, and manageable essays can only
have increased female access to the basic agenda of high culture and
politics.[87] Even little girls could reflect on the classical themes of stoicism
and public virtue by reading Roman texts in translation – a thirteen-year-
old Quaker was soul-stirred by her reading of Plutarch in 1779: 'We are
reading the Life of Cauis Marius. O what a noble general he is, how he
bore up under so many troubles as he had to go through in that small
island.' An aristocratic schoolgirl revealed her admiration for the Spartan
virtues to her patient mother in 1771: 'I am very much entertained with
reading the Account of the Ancient Britaines how luxury is increased
since those times, for their diet was spare & mean being barks & roots of
trees . . . [etc etc].'[88] Whether the daughter of a Quaker merchant or an
Anglican lord, girls, like boys, could be inspired by the austerities of
history. Unquestionably, the rhetorical nuts and bolts of public debate
were available to literate women in the period.

The analysis of one woman's engagement with print culture is instructive in the demonstration that even from a comparatively remote area in
the Pennines, it was possible and desirable to keep abreast of national and
local politics, fashion and cultural debate. Elizabeth Shackleton kept a
long-standing account with a London cousin, for the regular despatch of
London papers. After his death the account was taken over by the obliging
William Ramsden, who promised 'a Dish of Politicks every Post-Day'. By

this means Mrs Shackleton kept up with the business of parliament, receiving Saturday's news by Tuesday morning. Her taste in print journalism can be deduced from occasional remarks in her correspondence and letter books. From at least 1764 she read the *London Chronicle*, but in 1766 she was recommended the *Whitehall* over the *Chronicle*, 'as a political or rather a party Paper'. After 1768 she took the *St James Chronicle* or the *British Evening Post* on a regular basis. On an *ad hoc* basis, she also received unnamed magazines from London friends and occasional travellers, and her pocket diaries all came equipped with thirty-odd printed pages of useful knowledge and fashionable comment. In addition, she possessed several volumes of *The Spectator*, which she lent out to friends and neighbours. From 1772 she also took a Leeds paper, but she did not specify whether it was the *Leeds Intelligencer* or the *Leeds Mercury*. Although she found the paper unsatisfying in terms of national news, it offered the closest approximation of local journalism and carried approving commentary on her efficacious Rabies medicine. Occasional diary entries reveal that she had access to other papers bearing Preston and Manchester society news, but these journals may have been borrowed rather than bought. Mrs Shackleton copied into her diary the contents of pamphlets on subjects such as the utility of labour-saving machinery or the qualifications of prospective local MPs ('Mr Stanley [is] unacquainted not only with our Provincial manners, our internal Polity, Our Commercial Interests, our relative connections with our Trading Powers in the great Map of foreign & domestic Commerce, but he is even unaquainted with himself') and declared the pleasure she derived from evenings spent discoursing upon literature, history and politics. She may not have gleaned her gossip from a coffee house, but she was certainly an attentive and discriminating member of that general public addressed by both the *Leeds Intelligencer* and the *St James Chronicle*. The reader who wept over the fate of Clarissa Harlowe was equally capable of fuming about the progress of the American war, or applauding the release of John Wilkes.[89] Even a reader at some distance from a polite resort, could be an engaged member of that general public addressed through print.

*   *   *

The potentialities of female public life should by now be apparent; but it would be misleading to neglect the factors that shaped cultural access for individuals – wealth, sex, age and geography.

The 'provincial urban renaissance' notwithstanding, there were wide geographical variations in the availability of fashionable, commercialized leisure. The public venues that the polite so complacently colonized were essentially urban, the most famous were metropolitan and the majority were only truly open or fashionably frequented in the season. The London season coincided with the royal family's residence at court and ran from November to May, or, as Ann Pellet put it, when 'old winter will collect the whole within our Grand Metropolis where tis [said] will be various amusements to regale every new fancy for the present age'.[90] Breezy bulletins from town catalogue the profusion of polite entertainments available every winter. However, by early summer the quality had moved on in search of rural refreshment, roosting on their country estates or in lodgings at a provincial resort. Those left behind in the depopulated city were to be pitied: 'but surely the Town is a dreadfull place when Empty, & in the midst of summer when the Country is so very delightfull.'[91]

Of course, numerous provincial cities and county towns had their own winter season of assemblies, plays and oratorios. York, the radiant capital of northern gentility was specifically designed to rival the attractions of London, Bath and Tunbridge Wells. Susanna Gossip proudly boasted in 1730 that the new director of the Long Room, Lord Burlington, 'proposes to make it ye most compleat place of entertainment in England'.[92] Even lesser northern towns could be surprisingly lively. In Pontefract in the 1750s Jane Scrimshire reported with pleasure on flourishing assemblies, an election ball, a mayor's ball, a ball in honour of the king's birthday, a masquerade, a music meeting, plays such as Hoadley's *The Suspicious Husband* (1747) staged three times a week and an endless round of card parties taking place in 'this Metropolis of Politeness'. In the severe winter of 1756 Jane Scrimshire found the Pontefract playhouse the warmest place in town because of the charcoal fires glowing in the pit.[93]

Moreover the shire towns enjoyed a mini-season, often accompanied by horse races, during the Assize Week or even the Quarter Sessions, and local festivals and national anniversaries invariably launched a flotilla of civic events and commercial entertainments in public-spirited towns. For example, two weeks of festivity crowned the Preston Guild held every twenty years. In 1742 a visitor reported that the 'entertainments was quite handsome and Genteel, everything that the season cou'd afford, there was approx two setts of players, an assembly besides Private balls and two masquerades . . . I never so great a Crowd of good Company as there was at the assembly, the room is but small, and there was four Hundred and forty five Tickets taken out.' Yet, even in ordinary years, Preston's Race Week was noted for its 'very Genteel' assemblies, 'fill'd with Well Looking Men & Well Dress'd Women'.[94] The spas typically had summer seasons: the earliest established one at Tunbridge Wells extended from May to

59 Moses Griffiths, *Harrowgate Wells*, 1772. From the 1750s to the 1820s and beyond the northern gentry and commercial elites drew benefit from the waters of Harrogate.

60 John Raphael Smith, *Chalybeate Well*, (Harrogate), 1796.

A TRIP TO SCARBOROUGH A.D. 1783.

61   'A Trip To Scarborough A.D. 1783'. From as early as the 1720s, genteel northern visitors collected at Scarborough for their health and for the love of society. By the 1820s, other northern seaside resorts such as Cleethorpes, Blackpool and Lytham had become popular also.

October; the season at Bristol Hot Wells ran from late April to late September; while early eighteenth-century Bath had two seasons – in the spring and the autumn – but the resort became so popular as to have year-round appeal.[95] The northern health resorts quickly came into their own. Buxton early boasted established social ceremonies and a constant flow of northern gentry, as the gouty William Gossip lugubriously reported to his wife in the summer of 1746. By the 1770s a 'Genteel Post-Coach' was laid on from Leeds to Harrogate, twice a week, for the June season.[96] The development of the seaside resorts from the 1720s shadowed the growing popularity of sea bathing, and the tradition of taking an annual summer holiday was well established by the later eighteenth-century – a fashion which prompted the further growth of cultural institutions in those resorts favoured by the genteel. As early as July 1727 Barbara Stanhope noted a 'great deal of company' including a sprinkling of nobility gathered at Scarborough, and a visitor there in the summer of 1733 noted dancing every night.[97] Throughout the period the spas maintained a reputation for accommodating a high-profile female public life. The Dean of Gloucester was appalled to find in 1783 that women at Bath were sufficiently embold-ened to make advances to men. In sweeter vein, Elizabeth Reynolds testi-fied 'for ladies there cannot be another place so well calculated'.[98]

Despite the greater distribution of commercial entertainment, access to urban delight was not uniform. A comparison of Elizabeth Shackleton's social calendar with that of her most diligent correspondents reveals the cultural impoverishment of life in north-east Lancashire relative to other parts of the county, or nearby Yorkshire. Colne, Burnley and Clitheroe could not boast of a town walk, a pleasure garden, a concert hall or a theatre. An analysis of the decade 1770–80 reveals a smattering of public events, but the area could support nothing approaching a season of assemblies and music meetings. A 'dancing ball' was held at Colne in February 1773; Clayton and Cunliffe hosted a dance at the Red Lion Inn in January 1777; in September 1778 there was a dancing-master's ball in Colne; in October 1779 an assembly in Burnley; and, finally, in the spring of 1780 a children's ball was given by the Colne dancing master.[99] Easily the highlight of the decade was the opening of the Colne Piece Hall in August 1776 with its accompanying oratorios and balls. Dresses were made long in advance, handbills advertising the programme were kept as souvenirs, flowers and ribbons specially purchased. Of the oratorio, Mrs Shackleton reported, 'We all was most agreably entertained. Had fine singing, Good Musick, Gentele Company, good Regularity and order. Mr Johnson a fine singer, Miss Radcliffe a good singer. The Choruses Noble.' The festivities drew 'a number of well dress'd people from Burnley, Halifax, Leeds, Keighley, Manchester and all the neighbourhood', and happily 'these Entertainments was Conducted with the greatest Regularity, Peace & quiet. Several Soldiers kept Guard at the bottom of the steps not the least Riot nor no accident happen'd.' Of course, the ink spilt on this 'Grand Jubilee' testifies to its rarity: 'such *Doings* at such distance from London, but seldom happen and must therefore be the more *Marvellous*.'[100] And while nearby towns mounted comparable events and festivities, these were not annual celebrations but individual events, such as the jubilee which accompanied the opening of the canal locks at Bingley in 1774 or the inauguration of the Halifax Piece Hall in 1779. For regular events, it was crucial to make the journey to a northern provincial capital or resort, for the countryside in winter could be cheerless with just a pack of cards for diversion.

The attractions of an urban winter season were a determining influence on the movements of the wealthy. Like the nobility, the greater gentry flocked to London with the frosts.[101] Prominent county families like the Listers of Gisburn Park and the Parkers of Browsholme, who aspired to glitter on a national stage, spent several seasons in London. For a family with sufficient means, motivation might be simple boredom with country life, as a casual letter from Edward Parker to his nephew Tom indicates:

'The weather of late has been so Stormy and the neighbourhood of Browsholme so destitute of society that I think this may be as good a reason for [a] trip to the South perhaps as any other.'[102] Northern families with means might rent or even own a town house in York, Manchester, Pontefract or Preston, but modest families exploited what property or family connections they had or found themselves left behind to the society of 'squires, parsons' wives, visiting tenants or farmers'.[103] There is no evidence that Elizabeth Shackleton ever rented a house in town, but she and her first husband occasionally exploited the hospitality of relatives within striking distance of the brilliant assemblies of York. Thomas Parker's unmarried daughter Eliza managed to taste the sweets of the season by staying with friends and relatives in Preston, Liverpool and Selby throughout the 1800s. Having been brought up to urban bustle and company, Eliza Whitaker of Roefield was not prepared to forego it, returning with her husband to Lark Hill, Preston, for family gatherings and winter music meetings.[104] However, not all genteel families were destined to enjoy even an intermittent public life. The unfortunate Mrs Ridsdale saw all hopes of fashionable urbanity evaporate when her husband's Leeds business went bankrupt. They had little choice but to accept the tenancy of a small farm from a kinsman and to embrace the joys of rural seclusion in Wensleydale. Gallantly, Mrs Ridsdale told her friends that she was 'perhaps as happy in the *Shade* as many *lustring* in the *Sunshine*', and tried not to dwell on the amenities she had given up: 'were I to live in the World again it might only produce regrets that perhaps it is as wise to forget the recollection of.'[105] The Ridsdales' hard lesson was that below a certain financial threshold it was simply not possible to pursue a public life in the polite sense of the word. Similarly, Barbara Wiglesworth knew that her prospective groom could not keep her in style. He 'lamented that prudence forbade his keeping a carriage & c. As splendour was never a part of my gratification or much gaiety we shall live in a quiet domestic manner & not see much company.' Many were the brides who had to reconcile themselves 'to a retired, rather than parading life', for want of means.[106]

Wealth apart, consumption of urban culture and fashionable leisure among genteel women was patterned on the life-cycle. Children were expected to be innocent of urban dissipation, those ripe for marriage cautiously at the centre of it and those with family responsibilities well above it. The assemblies, plays and pleasure gardens of Georgian England were first and foremost stalls in the marriage market. If a young woman's romantic ambitions outstripped the confines of the parish, then she had to be seen 'in public' at the nearest town offering reputable entertainment. If her family were ambitious for a handsome match, then braving a season in York, Bath or, better still, London was the surest strategy. Once the genteel young woman was suitably married and had a house, servants and children to manage, the traditional assumption prevailed that she would retire gracefully to her domestic duties and recontent herself with the local horizon. (By contrast, the nobility and greater gentry were seen as public families born to live in the great world, so their wives were not allowed the liberty of retiring from the beau monde.) Of course, in fact, the polite did not so easily abandon their cultural pretensions, but the impetus behind their cultural consumption was considerably diminished. Young matrons were inevitably hampered in their journeyings by the never-ending needs of the nursery, but as women aged and parental responsibilities lightened, many re-emerged in the dignified role of chaperon. However, illness and frailty eclipsed the public lives of others.

Take the varying cultural engagement of Elizabeth Shackleton between the ages of nineteen and fifty-six. The letters she wrote as the unmarried Miss Parker in the 1740s effervesce with youthful cultural confidence. She enjoyed a reputation for wit and taste, and as 'Parkerissa' exchanged fashionable literary anecdotes and town talk with 'Pelletiana', her friend and kinswoman Jane Pellet. In 1746 Parker's long-awaited plan 'to Launch into the *Grande Monde* & make such an Eclat as will dazzle all Beholders . . .' came to fruition. Together the teenagers toured the metropolitan arenas of display ('this part of the world is the Quintessence of Politeness') and sampled race meetings, assemblies and card-assemblies in Preston, Pontefract and Wakefield, teased about being 'such excessive Gadders abroad' as they did so.[107] However, as a decorous young mother in the 1750s, Mrs Parker resolved to stir abroad with her babies as little as possible, despite her aunt being in 'Hopes you'll go often abroad than formerly when the turnpike roads are finish'd which the Yorkshire gentleman boast much of lately'. Once married, she never made another trip to London and hardly ever went to Preston, Lancaster or York; she certainly gave up all pretence of pursuing an urban season. But as widow Parker, with her children away at boarding school, she purchased a chaise in 1762, marking a new era as her friends acknowledged: 'now you can have no excuse for staying at home as your little family are absent and a carriage to convey you in all weathers'. It was this more active local social life which led to her second marriage in 1765 (itself achieved by an exciting dash to Gretna Green). Galvanized by her second attachment, Elizabeth Shackleton occasionally accompanied her young husband on wool-buying trips in the first years of their marriage, thereby enjoying diversions such as luxury shopping in the Chester Rows and a charity concert in the cathedral. By the 1770s her health and infirmity began to get the better of her; with the exception of an excursion to York in 1781 in a friend's coach, Mrs Shackleton confined herself to very infrequent day trips within a fifteen-mile radius of home. In 1777 she refused for months to leave the house at all, because 'the smallpox was so general'.[108]

As every reader of Jane Austen knows, proper young girls grew up in a certain social seclusion, before they 'came out' around the age of fifteen or sixteen. Precisely how much seclusion was good for genteel girls was subject to interpretation. Some exposure to good company and knowledge of the world between seven and fourteen, believed Mrs Delany, was crucial to the formation of a gracious manner and a discriminating approach to pleasure; punctilious parents often allowed their adolescents to attend only private balls and school balls, leaving public assemblies and the resorts till the first assault on the marriage market, yet others let their offspring join the romantic fray from as young as thirteen.[109] Contemporaries relentlessly associated urban congregations with the making of matches. In the 1720s Defoe sneered that the daughters of the gentry 'carry themselves to market' at the newly established assemblies.[110] Indeed, the teasing of the young implied that they went to town with no other view. The sly John Aspinall tried to lure the unmarried Elizabeth Parker to Preston in 1746 with the advertisement 'we have a great many fine Gents in Lac'd Coats and Cockades, and surely if there was nothing else to induce you a Marquis and two Lords ought to be sufficient, the first of them intends to give a Ball . . .' The unmarried John Spencer had to leave his packing to shrug off his sister-in-law's enquiries: 'your surmises about matrimony are groundless I had no such motive for a London Journey.'[111] In 1747, on the eve of the Chester races, Robert Parker was teased about his 'very fancy' new clothes: 'Thus Equip'd you may likely make a Conquest of a Cheshire Lady.' Yet such pleasantries were not so wide of the mark. The next year Robert Parker freely declared he was off to Wakefield races in deliberate pursuit of a wife. When Elizabeth Parker and Jane Pellet attended the same races in 1749, Ann Pellet happily procured the necessary silks for them, hoping that the silver gauze would aid their 'conquests' of 'Southern beaus', admitting her great matrimonial 'expectations'.[112] That the urgency of alliance was the key motive for visiting a public resort could not have been raised more explicitly than in 1727, when the sheepish Sir Ralph Standish was forced to admit failure to his mother: 'I am sorry to find [your ladyship] can't think of my coming down as I came up, single; its in vaine for me to think of getting a wife in towne for theres none to be seen there, and I cannot resolve to go to any of their houses.'[113] The trip to town was synonymous with the pursuit of a spouse.

Public venues were notorious sites of sexual spectatorship, both male and female. Newspaper advertisements appealed to young men and women spotted in public to allow or encourage further advances. In her cautionary *Letters Moral and Entertaining* (1728), Elizabeth Singer Rowe had a repentant swain recount his harassment of a young bride: ' I took all handsome opportunities to follow and converse with the fair Cleora . . . I attended her coach, her chair, haunted her at publick places, ogled, star'd, sighed and practised all the modern fopperies of love.' In the same spirit Lady Mary Wortley Montagu described Sir John Vanbrugh in quest of a wife at York in 1713: 'Tis certain he keeps Mondays' and Thursdays' market (assembly days) constant . . . I believe last Monday there were 200 pieces of Woman's flesh (fat and lean) . . .'[114] Comparatively unconstrained social intercourse between the unmarried was one of the tantalizing possibilities that public venues promised. When Walter Spencer Stanhope renewed his advances by letter to Miss Pulleine in 1783, he picked up where he had left off in a pleasure garden: 'A whole fortnight has passed since I was so cruelly interrupted in attempting to speak it at Ranelagh.' In urging his beloved to hear his suit, he laid out the romantic geography of London.

> Oh! Miss Pulleyne! What a moment of Suspense and Fearfulness is this! Might I venture to presume to call in Hertford Street this morning – if it were only to make or bring you some franks – it would be less in the Public Eye. Or may I flatter myself with the Hopes of seeing you in the Park or Gardens this morning, or at the Exhibition, or at Sir Ashton Lever's, or at the Opera this Evening, or in St James's Park?[115]

Even the sophisticated Mary Warde brought herself to suggest that young men were one of stellar attractions of the urban round, when she reflected on the inconveniences of the war of Austrian Succession: 'I apprehend Men will be very Scarce in all Publick Places; many of the Idle ones will visit their friends in Flanders & the officers that are obliged to be there will be visibly missed . . .' In 1743 Jane Pellet obviously linked the 'lost bloom' of St James's Park to the absence of eligible partners out of season: 'no Body goes there now but old maids and half pay officers.'[116]

Whether the moralists liked it or not, if a gentlewoman was to marry well then she had to be seen on the national marriage market, or at the very least on the regional circuit. It was precisely for this reason that the sensible Reverend George Woodward advised his stepsisters not to remove to what is now rural Oxfordshire:

> What you say with regard to the obscurity of the place is true enough; it is but an indifferent one for young ladies to shine in; nor can they

indeed (as you go on to observe) shine in any advantage, till like the
moon they are gilded and replenished with the cast off beams of a
setting sun; and then perhaps, like what the poets feign of that same
amorous orb, they'll meet with some Endymion or another, and take
him to their arms.[117]

His whimsical language was a flimsy cloak for his naked assessment of the
exigencies of romantic campaign. Certainly a deal of parental anxiety
about public arenas was disingenuous. Most parents knew full well what
they were doing when they towed their prize daughters from assemblies to
plays: 'What can be more indelicate' asked Wollstonecraft 'than a girl's
coming out in the fashionable world? Which, in other words, is to bring to
market a marriageable miss, whose person is taken from one public place
to another, richly caparisoned.'[118] In fact, genteel parents were less concerned with sexual exhibitionism *per se*, than they were apprehensive
about the qualifications of the young men who had seen the show.

Marriage, in theory, liberated women from the burden of chaperonage.
In *Pompey, the Little* (1751), a dog's eye view of polite society, the flighty
Cleanthe admitted that '*we Girls* are under so many Restraints, that one
must wish for a Husband, if it be only for the Privilege of going into public
Places, without Protection of a Married Woman along with one, to give
one Countenance'. Still the burden of constraint that decorous women
laboured under has not been thoroughly weighed. While it is clear that a
lone maiden entering a commercialized entertainment would be regarded
by many as an easy prey, or worse, young ladies probably enjoyed more
freedom in other settings than we have been accustomed to think,
although it is difficult to gauge female freedom absolutely because the
privileged were inured to the presence of servants, and may easily have
taken their company for granted when noting the excitement of a solitary
expedition. Nevertheless, eighteenth-century novels suggest that genteel
girls walking in   airs aroused little criticism (Miss Betsy Thoughtless and
Miss Forward made pretences of going out together to the milliner and
mantua-maker in order to meet young sparks), and even the stiffest high
Victorians assumed that a lady could walk alone in parks and promenades
in the mornings, and elsewhere at other times if accompanied by a friend
or servant. Moreover ladies pocket diaries routinely printed the rates of
hackney-coachmen to enable their readers to combat 'the insolence and
impositions of coachmen, particularly to ladies', suggesting support and
sympathy for the single woman traveller.[119] More striking still, in 1748 the
young Jane Pellet took the brave step of leaving her stepmother's establishment and setting up in rented rooms on her own in Pontefract with just

a woman servant for protection. Her reputation survived unblemished and she soon married a rising young lawyer with county connections. Georgian girls did not labour under constant chaperonage.

Despite the conveniences of a permanent escort-service, many young matrons settled down to a period of self-conscious retirement once they docked in the safe-harbour of matrimony. 'Has Matrimony put a stop to all your rambles?' was the clichéd question asked of the bride Mary Stanhope in 1743. Yet this assumption was securely founded – in a surviving list of the nobility and gentry who appeared at the assembly rooms in York in 1789, married women without a daughter in tow were in a minority.[120] The extent of cultural engagement a new mother could easily enjoy without censure varied, as seen, with wealth and geography; an afternoon stroll to a London exhibition with babies in train, being a very different venture to an all-day cross-country drive in an open chaise to a distant assembly. But even given the same urban opportunities, women varied, of course, in their tastes and inclinations. Though married with four children, the unsinkable Bessy Ramsden still relished a little cultural panache, thirsting after court pageantry, salacious trials, the Pantheon and the playhouse, as well as romping at school balls, children's parties and city assemblies. At each remission of illness in her nursery, she left her husband in charge and swept off to the West End in pursuit of recreation: 'tonight Forsooth, She is frolicked away to the play.'[121] Yet the cultural consumption of another Londoner Anna Larpent stands in marked contrast. Although Larpent made countless uncomfortable appearances in the appropriate arenas of fashionable display as an unmarried girl in the 1770s, her diaries for 1790, 1800, 1810 and 1820, written after marriage to John Larpent, chart a solemn engagement with metropolitan culture. As wife of the censor of plays, Mrs Larpent maintained a discriminating interest in the licensed stage, but tended to avoid the hectic gaiety of large assemblies and places of public congregation (apart from church), preferring small family gatherings and private music parties. She made exceedingly few visits to the pleasure gardens which had so discomforted her as a girl, although this is not to argue that marriage and motherhood immobilized her – she religiously took daily exercise in the lanes and delighted in taking her children and later her grandchildren off to exhibitions and edifying spectacles – but it shifted the focus of her consumption decisively. As the mother of sons, she evidently felt no compulsion to shepherd them around the usual venues when they reached marriageable age.[122]

Chaperonage was an institution which offered an irreproachable public role to an older matron, albeit one played towards the back of the stage. One of Nash's 'Rules to be observe'd at Bath' promulgated in 1742 decreed

'That the elder ladies and children be content with a second bench at the ball, as being past or not come to perfection'. The lower profile of the middle-aged was similarly reported in 1814: 'The Assemblies of Nottingham are, as in all other places, the resort of the young and the gay, who go to see and be seen; and also of those, who, having played their matrimonial cards well in early life, are now content to sit down to a game of sober whist or quadrille.'[123] The widow Abigail Gawthern of the same town recorded a packed social calendar in the early years of the nineteenth century, taking time from the management of her lead works and properties to accompany her daughter Anna to local assize balls, races, plays and performances of choral works in local churches, to escort her to the resorts of Bath, Clifton and Weymouth and to parade her about the usual London landmarks: St James's Palace, Kensington Gardens, Vauxhall, the Opera, theatres, the British Museum, the Magdalene and the Foundling Hospital. That this was matrimonial strategy could not have been recorded more explicitly. She kept a business-like tally of with whom her daughter danced and the various proposals that resulted: 'At the assembly; Anna danced with captain Edwards, Mr Parker and Dr Marsden; P. said he should call the next day to declare his sentiments. Dec 15. Mr P. drank tea with us; he mentioned his strong attachment; refused on account of being as old again.' However, Mrs Gawthern was not without some scruples about public entertainments, drawing the line at a riotous militia ball and a ticketed masquerade: 'Gardiner called to offer Anna a ticket to the masquerade to go with some of his relations; I refused his offer not thinking it quite prudent, neither do I approve of that amusement.'[124] These omissions notwithstanding, the social life of a woman in her forties could be frenetic.

The social comforts of old age are here exemplified by the redoubtable widow Ann Pellet. Her own duties as chaperon despatched, Mrs Pellet lived a retired London existence with her paid companion Miss Bowen, lodging with quiet families in Ealing, Kensington and Westminster. She avoided routs, assemblies and so on because she was averse to 'a hurry' and acknowledged she was 'but little engag'd in the Beau Monde' and preferred hosts who kept '*no ill Hours nor any Fatiguing Pleasures*'. Still, she had a weakness for whist and was happy in the harmonious company of just enough genteel ladies to guarantee a 'Plurality of Card tables'. She relied on her old friends and acquaintances to come to her, as 'she very seldom stirs out, Partly from inclination and partly from fears which proceed from the continual Mischiefs & Robberies commited in the Streets in the Evenings'. Despite writing from Ealing, so near the 'Grand Metropolis', Mrs Pellet feared her household was 'Barren of Publick affairs'. Most of the town talk she retailed to country friends, she gleaned from the papers.[125]

While female cultural access and public profile varied with wealth, location and life-cycle, it was virtually never as extensive or as high as that of equivalent men. Gentlemen invariably held public office and the pursuit of institutional duties tended to throw men more in the way of commercial leisure than their wives.[126] Although the institutional life of the county was accompanied by a social culture in which women could take a part, it appears that unless they had a daughter to marry off they were unlikely to do so. Married men, on the other hand, enjoyed an easy sociability as a spin-off from their administrative duties. In the 1750s Michael Scrimshire of Pontefract often slipped away from legal matters to sneak in a day at the Doncaster and Wakefield races. Similarly, John Shackleton managed to combine a wool-buying trip with the Nottingham races in August 1780, and a spot of sea bathing at Heysham with his stint as a grand juror in 1778. Young merchants, manufacturers and professionals were clearly more constrained than inheriting gentlemen, but often travelled in the course of their business and could exploit their leisure time to advantage. For example, in the 1770s the apprentices John and Robert Parker successfully transformed their routine journeys from Lancashire to London into mini-tours, stopping off at Gloucester for music meetings and the like. Of course, throughout the period, the mobility of young men – from the continental grand tour to the local jaunt – stood in marked contrast to the limited peregrinations of provincial gentlewomen.[127]

Nor were male cultural tastes always in harmony with those of women. Male recreation had a dimension which might conflict with a female taste for urban diversion – sport. Sport was a recurring theme, *if not the dominant theme*, of the letters men exchanged with men and the sporting calendar was a powerful determinant of a man's movements, for the pursuit of prey was the archetypal prerogative of the gentleman. Those blood-sports popular with the northern families studied here comprised hunting foxes, hares and otters, coursing (pursuing hares with greyhounds), tracing (following a pre-set scent) and shooting moorgame (grouse), woodcocks and partridge. Moorland shooting was a constant feature of masculine culture in the rural north in the eighteenth and early nineteenth centuries.[128]

Although La Rochefoucauld asserted (on the basis of his Suffolk experience) in 1784 'women quite commonly in England take part in the shoot, and many of them are very good shots', none of the genteel women studied here ever wielded the gun. Still there were obviously occasional ladies noted for their marksmanship – the singular Anne Lister of Shibden for

62 James Northcote, R.A., *Grouse-shooting in the Forest of Bowland*, 1802, depicts hunting as a noble pursuit. The Lancashire hot-shots depicted here are William Assheton of Cuerdale Hall and the Revd T.H. Dixon Hoste. The forest of Bowland, like most of the Pennine moors, was famous for its rich shooting opportunities.

one.[129] Perhaps more common was the sportswoman who rode to hounds. Lady Mary Wortley Montagu's experience suggests a significant minority of huntswomen in Nottinghamshire in 1711 : 'I had a general Hunting Day last Tuesday, where we had 20 Ladys well dressed and mounted, and more Men. The day was concluded with a Ball. I rid and danc'd with a view of Exercise, and that is all – how dull that is!' Similarly, Mary Warde spent every autumn in the 1730s and 1740s out riding and hunting in Norfolk: 'I was seven hours a hunting this morning & rode hard enough to be extreamly tired . . .', although her gregariousness seems more to the fore than her blood lust: 'I meet a good deal of company Every Monday & Thursday Morning in the finest part of the Country, where a Pack of Hounds is the pretence. We ride hard or only saunter just as our Inclinations Engage us, to be Idle or alert.' But by her own admission, she was in a minority: 'We have a very large number of sportsmen & three ladies in our Hunt', and the meeting a particularly accommodating one: 'My notion of these sports is that it depends upon the company entirely. We had a gay set & two or three of the Gentlemen very Poetical.'[130] These

63   John Wootton, *John Warde and his Family*, 1735. The lively huntress Mary Warde can be seen on horseback to the left of the picture.

eighteenth-century Dianas were never numerous, as ambivalence about the propriety of female hunting was long-standing. Clarissa in *The Lady's Magazine* opined 'though hunting might be diversion used by the ancients, it is far from being a delicate one, or commendable in a modern lady'. No less a radical than Mary Wollstonecraft was prepared to endorse 'the exclamations against masculine women' when directed against 'their ardour in hunting, shooting, and gaming . . .'[131]

Despite the exceptional gentlewoman celebrated for her horsemanship, hunting had long been a proverbial expression of masculine competition and camaraderie. Certainly in the Pennines, local hunting songs of 1760s, 1770s and 1780s suggest a hearty culture of cocksure masculinity. Elizabeth Shackleton's scathing remarks speak to the display of braggadocio: 'Baron Cun-lif-fe his valet, groom & Hunters all in Parade & high Glory set out for Wigan Hunt.'[132] Although women often managed some indirect engagement with this sporting culture as dispensers of hospitality, male diversion could introduce a season of gender apartheid. Walton of Marsden, Townley of Royle and Parker of Browsholme went so far in 1775 as to purchase a hunting seat upon the Wolds in the East Riding, the gentlemen 'to join in Housekeeping & to go Hunt there this winter'. Mr

The Man that will not leave his bed
For sport so blithe & bonny,
We'll swear he hates fatigue & dirt,
And call him Macaroni

A FOX-HUNTING BREAKFAST

Pub.d 5.th May 1777. by W.Humphrey, Gerrard Street, Soho.

We'll wonder at his want of Taste,
Since nothing so bewitches
As living all the winter long
In Boots & Leather Breeches.

64 'A Fox-hunting Breakfast', 1777, affectionately satirises the earthy, masculine associations of field sports. An accompanying ditty suggests men who dislike hunting are Frenchified effeminates.

Lister left the north altogether in 1778 to reside at a hunting seat in Oxfordshire.[133] Whether men embraced outdoor pursuits as means to be with men, or as an excuse to escape domesticity and polite conversation is unclear. Perhaps they just preferred sport. As the hapless Ralph Standish Howard confessed in 1727, 'I long mightily to be in Lancashire again. Balls and operas and plays afford me no sort of pleasure in comparison with hunting and shooting . . .'[134] Diversions such as hunting, fishing and especially bull-baiting and cock-fighting brought gentlemen into contact with their social inferiors and freed them of the burden of polite heterosociality. As Elizabeth Shackleton complained of the chase, 'My son came home from Broughton Hunt where he sat up till three this morning afterwards went to Sleep in a nasty Alehouse at Marton. I like not these vulgar publick hunts . . .'[135] The gentleman whose love of rural sport could deprive his wife and daughters of urban pleasure and the sociability of her equals obviously had a life beyond routine caricature. No wonder so many women felt out of their element in the country where nothing might be talked of but 'The Militia, Farming & Justice business all day long'.[136] Indeed, to the green and giddy Betsy Thoughtless what was heralded as 'a happy tranquil manner of spending ones days', seemed in reality 'little better than being buried alive.'[137]

*   *   *

Women's letters and diaries brim with commentary on the array of public diversions from which they fashioned a cultural life. As we have seen, a woman's repertoire of pleasures varied according to her wealth, age, tastes and place of residence. Unusually lucky was the woman who enjoyed equality of access with her husband to the much vaunted Georgian delights. This much is constant. On the other hand, the sheer range of urban entertainments available in the provinces from the last decades of the seventeenth century in some areas and the early eighteenth century in others was regarded as a striking novelty. In 1722 Macky maintained that 'These assemblies are very convenient for young people; for formerly the Country Ladies were stewed up in their father's old Mansion Houses, and seldom saw Company but at an Assize, a Horse-Race, or a Fair'. With equal enthusiasm, John Ramsay of Ochtertyre recorded a 'wonderful change upon female manners in consequence of playhouses, assemblies and concerts'. Previously, 'the Scottish women made their most brilliant appearance at burials'.[138] Of course, it is possible that commentators exaggerated the extent of transformation the better to celebrate Augustan modernity, yet it does appear that the cultural institutions so well-established in spas and county towns by the early eighteenth century significantly broadened the social horizons of privileged women in the provinces. Sixteenth- and seventeenth-century rural existence could be boring to a proverb.[139] From the 1720s to the 1820s the scope of public entertainment remained remarkably constant. Social news exchanged among the Barcroft and Whitaker networks and among a younger generation of Parkers suggests that the core cultural institutions of the 1810s and 1820s were remarkably similar to their counterparts eighty years earlier. The Preston letters Eliza Parker wrote to her father Thomas Parker of Alkincoats in the 1800s present an altogether familiar picture of bride's visits, tea parties, charity balls, assemblies, race meetings, handsome dragoons, fashionable glamour and a dwindling allowance ('I can assure you we have done nothing but dress and undress all this week'[140]). On the pleasures of Preston, they could have been written by her grandmother. Of course, over the century the density of provincial facilities increased. By

1800, assembly rooms, theatres and clubs were no longer the monopoly of the county towns and resorts. However, the polite renaissance was never universal. While the improved road network may have increased access to several oases of politeness, the provincial north for instance still had its stretches of cultural desert, as Alice Ainsworth sighed of her home town, 'Bolton is *proverbially* dull just now'. In Haworth in the 1820s the Brontë's Aunt Branwell was said to have found the winter isolation of the Pennines very wearing after the cheerful visiting and lively society of Penzance.[141]

However, what emerges in sharper relief at the end of the period is the growing importance of an associative life for women, the extraordinary proliferation of institutions through which women could garner a new kind of public standing and radiate something of that public spirit revered by their brothers. Take the range of causes pursued by a typical anti-slavery activist of the 1830s and 1840s, retrieved by Claire Midgley. Ann Taylor Gilbert fulfilled all the duties incumbent on the wife of a Nottingham Independent minister, but she was also the leader of the women's anti-slavery society in the town, as well as the 'founder of refuge for "unfortunate" women, collector for a provident Society, member of a Committee for the Management of a Free Library, visitor to the Blind Asylum, superintendent of a Sunday School for young women, conductor of a cottage service for young women, and active in the Ladies Anti-Corn Law Committee . . .'[142] The ladies' debating societies may not have out-lived Pitt's 'terror', but the institutionalization of fashionable benevolence constructed altogether new arenas for the expression of female conviviality and officiousness. By the 1820s it was routine for ladies' pocket books to print in their opening pages long lists of the charitable institutions patronised by the truly fashionable. Not that the seriousness of purpose behind the many missions of Christian duty should be underestimated. Strikingly, the philanthropic impulse propelled the idealistic out of their safe meeting-rooms into squalid, disreputable and often frightening parts of town. In 1859 a Shrewsbury minister's wife recalled the struggle with her fear when first asked to do make unattended visits on Butcher Row. On encountering a group of men loitering outside the pub, she panicked and fled home to her husband: 'Being agitated, I burst into tears saying, "I cannot go out at night; it's no use trying". However next day I managed better.' As Anne Summers has concluded, the work of visiting was not just a dilettante fashion of passing free time, but an engagement of the self which involved the sacrifice of leisure and the development of expertise.'[143] The nineteenth century saw an expansion of the terrain of female action, not a diminution.

Assuredly, over the long run, individual cultural venues and diversions rose and fell in fashionable taste. The cultural *passeggiata* in St James's

Park fell away, but instead the nineteenth-century elite chose to ride the ring in Hyde Park. While the London pleasure gardens dwindled into variety venues and finally closed, the seaside promenade came into its own.[144] Apart from a handful of Regency revivals, the large public masquerade had fallen out of fashion by the 1790s, but court-sponsored festivity continued as did public dancing, now in the guise of charity balls.[145] Evangelical reaction may have dented the popularity of the theatre in some provincial towns (at least this is the argument made by many on the basis of Wilkinson Tate's recriminatory memoirs), but interestingly it seems not to have affected the discriminating enjoyment of the unimpeachable Anna Larpent, who actually rather enjoyed Mrs Inchbald's maligned *Lover's Vows* (1798): 'I cannot see the least Immorality in this Drama', she reported in 1800, 'On the Contrary the cause of truth & Virtue seem served by it.'[146] Public music and the opera survived virtually unscathed; and of course, the exhibition, the museum, panoramas and dioramas, the bazaar and the large department store took on even greater prominence for the later Victorians as places of female congregation and public promenade. Venues noted for female gatherings and heterosexual conversation in 1880s London included the British Museum reading room, mixed discussion clubs, galleries, tea shops, concerts and plays, and the craze for bicycling, tennis clubs, dramatics societies and garden parties had broadened the field of outdoor entertainment still further by 1900. Moreover, the respectable often walked unattended between one venue and another, leading Mica Nava to conclude that 'middle-class women were much closer to the dangers and excitements of city life than the notion of separate spheres would lead us to anticipate.'[147]

Comprehensive research on women and early nineteenth-century cultural space is lacking, but new investigations do not suggest the sudden eclipse of elite women's public lives. Important new research by Jennifer Hall on the audience for opera for instance, does not support the conventional narrative. Of the 1820s and 1830s, Hall concludes that elite women were particularly associated with the boxes, over the doors of which the names of the female proprietors were inscribed. Female physical prominence was accentuated by their tendency to sit at the front of the boxes, while men stood behind. Gentlemen, by contrast, enjoyed greater mobility in the opera house paying attendance at different the boxes and notoriously the green room, descending to the pit and the newly inaugurated stalls. Early in the century, respectable women did sit in the pit and the stalls on occasion, but risked having their reputations compromised by proximity to the prostitutes gathered there. However, by the 1840s the pit had become a more respectable choice for a reputable female opera-goer, although the ultra-fashionable still sought to display themselves on the first tier.[148] Against a backdrop of unsubstantiated assertion, such findings are suggestive of the weakness of the case which takes it for granted that privileged women were swept out of public space in the later eighteenth or early nineteenth centuries. There is little solid evidence to support the assumption that a great curfew was rung when the dewy Victoria ascended the throne.

On the other hand, none of this is to argue that female publicity was not a matter of long-standing concern and debate. The advance of commercialized leisure and public congregations did not pass without the wringing of hands. Promiscuous sociability in the company of strangers was anathema to this profoundly snobbish and hierarchical society, so those venues that promoted open access and anonymity were obvious targets for criticism; the indiscriminate mingling of legions accommodated by the sprawling pleasure gardens was seen as an invitation to vice.[149] But if the nameless hordes and trifling diversions to be found at the pleasure garden made moralists uneasy, the possibilities for disguise and deception inherent in the quintessential masquerade drove them to apoplexy.[150] It is not hard to see why so many moralists preached the unproblematic pleasures of private company, for it was in private company alone that a truly exclusive and predictable marriage market operated. Only in private company could the elite guarantee absolutely the qualifications of their companions.

It is important to emphasize, however, that not all public venues were tarred with the same gloomy brush – exhibitions, museums and edifying spectacles, the benefit concert, the church service, the friendly society, the small subscription assembly and the tragic play were rarely presented as perilous to virtue – and even the more risqué arenas such as pleasure gardens had their salubrious corners. The public world was large enough to admit of a range of diversions befitting a variety of moral tastes. As Goldsmith said of Bath, 'people of all ways of thinking, even from the libertine to the methodist, have it in their power to complete the day with employments suited to their inclinations'.[151] Similarly, the reformed Eliza Haywood brought herself to reason that 'Public diversions . . . may be enjoyed without prejudice, provided they are frequented in reasonable manner, and behaved at with Decency: – It is the immoderate Use, or rather the Abuse of anything, which renders the partaking of it a Fault.' Lady Sarah Pennington conceded, 'Diversions, properly regulated, are not only allowable, they are absolutely necessary to Youth, and are never criminal but when taken to excess', and no less a conservative than Dr Gregory acknowledged 'Every period of life has amusement which are natural and proper to it. You may indulge the variety of your tastes in these, while you keep within the bounds of that propriety which is suitable to your sex.' Even Richardson could be indulgent towards a women who loved to 'go to the public places', provided she was 'an excellent manager in a family' and 'earns her pleasures by her early rising'.[152] In effect, moral commentary acknowledged and accepted the female consumption of culture, but sought to minimize its worst excesses and to tutor women's cultural choices: improvement and business should come before pleasure, Fordyce's sermons should be read before Sheridan's plays, an assembly was preferable to a masquerade, the company of known friends should be favoured over the advances of complete strangers. Not that moralists singled out young women alone. It is important to recognize that such arguments were but an aspect of the pervasive contemporary anxiety about luxury which was seen to threaten both sexes. The immoderate cultural indulgence of both men and women was a cause for concern. Moralists certainly feared that women would be tempted from the path of domestic virtue by the tawdry delights of the town, but they also were apprehensive that men would be lured away from business, family responsibilities and rational endeavour,[153] note the anxious authorization to pleasure William Gossip afforded his hosier son in 1754:

> I am not at all ag[ains]t your subscribing to the Concert at Leicester, provided it is carried on by people of credit & fashion among you, & not merely by mercenary performers. Those hirelings are the very worst acquaintances you can make; I know the nature of the whole tribe of them. Jardini & his band after occasioning some disturbances in the family are all discoverd & gone from Bramham Park. If your Concerts are to be attended with dancing I think you would do well not to engage in that part of the diversion for the reasons you gave me when here. I hope you have more spirit than to subject yourself to more slights . . .[154]

Indeed, the ability to resist the lure of the pleasure garden and the play in particular came to symbolize a Spartan superiority to fashionable indulgence. The young lawyer Thomas Greene, at pains to demonstrate his iron resolve and modest entertainments to his sister, protested he'd 'Not been at Ranelagh since I was there with Mrs Wall, & but once since at Vauxhall. I go two or three times in a winter to see Garrick, & once or twice in a Summer to see Foote. I am generally in bed before twelve . . . From this you may judge of my Goings on & the Care I take of Myself.'[155] Likewise, Robert Parker restored his mother's good opinion in 1780 through his sobriety and restraint: 'Mr [Banastre] Parker says you are a downright Cit [citizen] Makes no doubt but you will be Ld Mayor. He co'd not prevail

65   The untitled frontispiece to the *Lady's Magazine* (1780). The polite female consumer is deliberating between folly (in the form of gambling) and wisdom.

with you Nor tempt you to go with him to Ranelagh. We was all glad to hear it & told him so.'[156]

Over and above this long-standing fear about the commercial assault on Spartan virtue, lay a set of pragmatic calculations about the promiscuous sociability which ticketed venues promoted. How to enjoy the benefits of a widened marriage market while facing none of the inherent risks was the dilemma which exercised the propertied. For their daughters to be admired in public by a nobleman was one thing, to be ogled by a penniless adventurer was quite another, and the resorts were famously 'crouded with Vulgars'. Even at Bath, Smollett's Matthew Bramble complained, 'a very inconsiderable proportion of genteel people are lost in a mob of impudent plebeians . . .'[157] Thus, warnings about the unsuitable mates lurking at commercial venues were the stock-in-trade of advice to young women entering the marriage market. Fanny Burney's *Evelina* famously reads like a handbook of the hazards of indiscriminate sociability for artless women. Virtually every time she ventured out to a pleasure garden, promenade, assembly or opera, the seventeen-year-old heroine found her-self preyed on by uninvited, plausible or vulgar strangers, although, of course, she was ultimately seen to advantage by the unimpeachable Lord Orville and ended her tour of urban resorts in matrimonial triumph. From the outset, a desire for the glittering possibilities of public congregation was balanced by fears of the encroaching hordes. Hence the continued attempt to demarcate exclusive space within arenas which could be penetrated by anyone who could afford a ticket. Hence the prevalence of devices which limited the access of the vulgar and preserved the gentility of culture: subscription, dedication, benefit and charity, as Jonathan Barry has pointed out.[158]

A clear preference for a select party over a commercial entertainment was a sure advertisement of a young woman's virtue. Being altogether a demure young woman, the teenage Anna Porter was aware of the distinction to be drawn between vulgar commercial leisure and selective polite culture and knew which the superior lady should prefer. At Ranelagh she remarked that she would have been more comfortably entertained at home with her friends 'than I was in all that hurly burly'. At the Pantheon she mused 'there is an emptiness, a lightness in all publick places', which she dreaded liking since it warped the soul and drew it from nobler pursuits. At the opera she exclaimed 'Surely the trouble and crowd of publick places is horrid!' And the day after an extremely agreeable dance at Lady Macclesfield's she found upon further reflection that she 'was fatigued & stupid & cried out on ye horrid effects of dissipation!' At fifteen years of age, Porter made the lofty observation that 'no pleasure equaled that of spending an Eveng in rational instructing conversation with sensible friends'.[159]

By far the most overworked dualism drawn on in discussion of leisure and culture was that of fashionable worldliness versus philosophical retirement, a 'hurry' versus peace, the gaudy town versus the rural glade. Urban ennui found expression in a self-conscious cult of rural retreat:

> From the Court to the Cottage convey me away
> For I'm weary of Grandeur & what they call gay
> Where pride without measure
> And pomp without pleasure
> Makes life in a circle of hurry decay
>
> Far remote & retired from the Noise of the Town
> I'll exchange my Brocade for a plain Russet Gown
> My Friends shall be few
> But well chosen & true
> And sweet recreation our Evening shall crown.[160]

After reciting the excitements of a dizzy social round, countless correspondents felt compelled to launch into unconvincing renunciations of the
urbane and cosmopolitan. At the Preston Guild celebrations of 1762, the
gentlewoman Mrs Wiglesworth attended four balls, four assemblies, plays
and a dinner at the Guildhall, but still protested, perhaps a little too
strenuously, 'I assure you I was quite Happy when I got home for my
Family & [the] Country is my delight, for that kind of hurrying Life would
be very disagreeable to me'. Still the pull of Preston was certainly strong:
'it was called little London, indeed if you had but Money you might see or
buy anything that was Pritty, but for all that I was very glad to see
Townhead . . .' Amidst the bubbling assemblies of polite Pontefract Jane
Scrimshire sighed 'I Long for a little retirement. I grow more & more tired
of Company one ought always to be on guard before . . .' Returning from
an extremely diverting season of 'crowded Balls & every amusement' at
Tunbridge Wells, Miss Warde mused on what she clearly believed to be
(or thought she ought to believe to be) the higher life of rural reflection:

> I am glad you were so well-entertained at Scarbro' Walking on the
> Sands & the Variety of Moss you speak of must be vastly amusing, it
> shews a just way of thinking to prefer that Solitary relief from Com-
> pany. I wish I could command one Equally so. I am very far from
> believing a Publick Life a happy one, or Capable of giving any real
> Satisfaction to the mind, but I own (tho' I never much wish for it), when
> I am entered into a scene of Gayety I have seldom the resolution to quit
> it in such a manner, tho' I never like many young People I know
> returned home with regret.

Even the desperate Isabel Carr, spurned mistress of Sir James Lowther,
longed foolishly for a 'little cottage' on her lover's Westmoreland estate: 'I
will live in a wood, or the middle of a Lake, or anywhere in the world, let
me be but near you', although she later saw the error of her ways and
likened rural banishment to colonial exile.[161]

However, it is worth emphasizing here that the avowed taste for a little
rural seclusion (however unconvincing) was not necessarily an acknowledgement of the power of domestic precepts, rather it was a nod to 'otium'
the Roman ideal of intellectual leisure. Originating in the rediscovery of
Horace, a cult of ostentatious solitude reached fashionable heights in the
grottoes and hermitages of the mid-eighteenth century and lived on in
Romantic ruralism. To achieve perfect happiness a 'man' needed space for
philosophical contemplation. Thus, a female prodigy who spoke several
languages and attended scientific lectures was touted in 1742 as 'quite a
Phylosophycal wise lady quite above ye pleasures of publick diversions

and follies of this town; tho' a very pretty woman . . .' In 1820 Lydia Boynton drew on the same conceptual armoury when she sought to reassure her future parents-in-law that she was no empty-headed socialite. She tried to banish their 'apprehension that a *Country Life* may prove dull & produce sensations of disappointment to me, after being accustomed to a London life', anxiously urging them 'to dispense all fears on that account – for the little knowledge and experience of the world I *possess* have taught me the transient pleasure & insufficiency great wealth & gaiety produce in comparison with the substantial enjoyments to be reap'd from rational houses & society.' She was appalled that they could think 'that I could for a moment drop a sigh of regret for the fluttering delusions of a Ball &c.'[162] In disavowing frivolity, women laid claim to rationality. In forswearing one public life they colonized another.

Conclusion

THIS HAS NOT BEEN A STUDY in nonconformity or rebellion. Propriety was the watchword of genteel women in Georgian England, and thus the majority were consciously resigned to the most enduring features of an elite woman's lot: the symbolic authority of fathers and husbands, the self-sacrifices of motherhood and the burdensome responsibility for domestic servants, housekeeping and family consumption. The fact that these elements were so abiding perhaps accounts for the extent of acquiescence – rebelling against roles that appeared both prehistoric and preordained would profit nothing. Resignation and accommodation were seen as the most sensible courses. That said, genteel women did not expect to live a life of grovelling subordination. Masculine authority was formally honoured, but practically managed; the dignity of genteel femininity demanded respect and courtesy; female stewardship of younger children, servants and housekeeping would brook little interference. Women were trained to allow a gentleman the rights of his place, but determined at the same time to maintain their own. At infringements of their jurisdiction, or humiliating instances of masculine tyranny, genteel women still boiled with indignation. After all, as members of the elite they partook, no less than their menfolk, of the haughty superiorities of wealth and rank.

In its essentials, this sketch of gender distinctions amongst the provincial elite could do service not only for the eighteenth century, but also for the seventeenth and perhaps even the sixteenth. But over these long-standing chords, newer themes sounded. The eighteenth century saw a sustained, secular celebration of romantic marriage and loving domesticity, alongside the institutionalization of a national marriage-market for increasing numbers of the elite through the London season and at the resorts; both developments heightened cultural preoccupation with the possibilities and problems of romantic choice. Yet for all the raised hopes and anxieties, most 'love matches' were still made within very strict limits. Admittedly, the father who dragged his unwilling daughter to the altar became seen as a gothic anachronism, but parents could achieve the same matrimonial ends through careful shepherding in and out of the more exclusive stalls of the marriage market and by inculcating a proper respect for position in their offspring. Indeed, the romantic appeal of rank and wealth hardly vanished, and few young lovers elected to live 'in a cell on love and bread and butter'.[1] In the event, the genteel sought matches that were as prudent as they were affectionate and the happiness of the outcome for the bride lay in the balance between the two.

Linked to the celebration of marriage was the growing sentimentalization of motherhood. Of course, the veneration of the mother is at least as old as the Madonna. Elizabeth I would hardly have represented herself as the Mother of her People if the role did not evoke positive associations, and the Puritans did much to promote the honour of breastfeeding in the elite. However, what distinguishes the eighteenth-century discourse of motherhood from its predecessors is the overlaying of secular hosannahs on the ancient religious solemnizations. Breast-feeding became an ultra-fashionable practice, eulogized in the most gushing manner in the novels of Samuel Richardson. But for all the sugariness of the proliferating representations of motherhood, the experience for most was not one of undiluted sweetness. Being a mother, against a background of disease and debility, remained a bloody, risky, uncontrollable and often gutwrenching experience, such that a painting of a cherub chasing a butterfly, or a description of a blushing nursing mother spoke only intermittently and even then superficially to the powerful feelings evoked. The Bible, and in particular the book of Job, still had more to say to most. The selfrepresentation commonest among genteel mothers was not that of a sighing, contented Madonna, it was rather that of a self-made pillar of fortitude and resignation, built to withstand the random blows of fate.

Against a backdrop of continuity and muted change, there were some striking departures. From the late seventeenth century the comfortably off in the provinces benefited from an extraordinary expansion and sophistication of their material and intellectual worlds. The import of such extra-European goods as tea and coffee, porcelain and chintz, the proliferation of new products like upholstered chairs, creamware dining services and printed wallpaper, and the rising expectations of domestic comfort that accompanied them made for the rapid elaboration of genteel material culture. As mistress of the tea-table or arbiter of family taste, the privileged eighteenth-century female consumer embraced the material enrichment of her world. Domestic processing continued on a prodigious scale, but eighteenth-century provisioning was increasingly a matter of orchestrating purchases from local, regional and distant suppliers and less a matter of manufacturing within the household. The eighteenth-century genteel household was less self-sufficient than its sixteenth or seventeenth-century counterparts.

In parallel, came the rise of politeness. This secular code of behaviour favouring easy and inclusive social intercourse within the elite, broadly conceived, was in the intellectual ascendant from the 1710s and found numerous adherents amongst genteel Anglicans and old Dissenters. Politeness, as expounded by Addison and Steele, meshed particularly easily with an unpained, inexplosive religion and a vernacular stoicism; it was a useful adhesive in the mixed society of provincial gentility; and it was particularly well received by ladies. The *Tatler* and the *Spectator* fostered and glamorized heterosexual sociability, thereby raising the prestige of those terrains which offered women a place beside their men, and the profile of the cosmopolitan gentleman who could do a woman honour. Not that politeness carried all before it; as much as a woman might want to promote a relaxed and dignified patriarchy, a man could be bent upon its disruption, as has been seen. Indeed, I suspect that a battle was waged for the soul of eighteenth-century gentility – with women, urbanites and upright patriarchs in one camp and unashamedly parochial sportsmen and irresponsible bachelors in the other.

Fuelled by polite ideals, the intellectual horizons of privileged, provincial women rolled majestically outwards in the course of the eighteenth century. To be sure, the most rapid increase in elite female literacy had occurred earlier, but what distinguished the eighteenth century was its dramatically expanding culture of female literariness. The pious soul-searching that inspired most seventeenth-century diarists is a distinctly muted theme in many eighteenth-century women's journals, leaving the page clear for sheer writerly virtuosity. In parallel, the near universal literacy of elite social networks and the elaboration of the daily and the cross posts (those between provincial cities) facilitated a immense intensification of female correspondence. The well-turned letter became an unavoidable performance of the long-standing female work of kin, but in addition it enabled unprecedented numbers of women to participate in worldly exchange and debate. It was in their tireless writing no less than in their ravenous reading that genteel women embraced a world far beyond the boundaries of their parish.

Entwined with the eighteenth-century revolution in print was the so-called provincial urban renaissance – another development which provincial women embraced with almost indecent alacrity. Where a Stuart lady might have experienced the occasional social thrill at the assizes, a horse-race or a fair in a provincial centre, by 1750, in the same town, her Georgian counterpart could rejoice in assembly rooms, concert series, theatre seasons, circulating libraries, daytime lectures, urban walks and pleasure gardens, in addition to regular sporting fixtures and the assizes; moreover, none of these arenas was off-limits to polite women. Indeed, the abundance of moral advice on proper female behaviour in public is itself a testament to the vividness of their presence. From the early eighteenth century to the early nineteenth century the central elements of public entertainment were notably enduring. The rising tide of religious Evangelicalism did not efface the woman in public, rather it reorientated the public life of the more serious-minded away from worldly entertainment towards good works. By the end of the eighteenth century, the institutionalization of fashionable benevolence had created altogether new platforms for female association and public action. By the early nineteenth century, although their family duties remained, the public profile of privileged, provincial women had reached unprecedented heights – and, of course, their numbers had increased. Because the growth in national wealth in the era of the classic Industrial and Agrarian Revolutions was distributed so unequally, it generated a great many more families possessed of the resources required to participate in the modes of life that constituted gentility, both in town and country. Many of them, probably most, aspired to do so, despite the growth in economic, social and denominational tensions within local elites between 1790 and 1830.[2]

This is not a story that sits comfortably with the accepted narratives and categories of English women's history, indeed, it is the very reverse of the accepted tale of progressive incarceration in a domestic, private sphere. Nor has the account had much to say about male appropriation of the public sphere. Instead, I have emphasized the concepts which animated genteel letter-writers and diarists not twentieth-century historians – in particular prudence and propriety, regularity and economy, politeness and vulgarity, fortitude, resignation and fate. Nevertheless, it would be blinkered to suggest that notions of 'public' and 'private' had no purchase in eighteenth and early nineteenth-century discourse. Yet even the most cursory sweep of Georgian usages reveals that the public/private dichotomy had multiple applications, which only sometimes mirrored a male/female distinction, and then not always perfectly.

A notional division of public and private which consigned women to domestic management and reserved policy to men had considerable hold on the eighteenth-century imagination. In a 'Letter to a New-born Child' written in the 1730s, Catherine Talbot counselled a female cousin, 'Let the men unenvied shine in public, it is we must make their homes delightful to them'.[3] William Wilberforce believed that women were naturally more disposed to religion than men, with the result 'that when the husband should return to his family, worn and harassed by worldly cares or professional labours, the wife, habitually preserving a warmer and more unimpaired spirit of devotion than is perhaps consistent with being immersed in the bustle of life, might revive his languid piety . . .'[4] And, of course, one would search long and hard for a pundit who did not believe that a woman's primary calling was matrimony and motherhood: 'Domestic concerns are the province of the wife', pronounced the Scottish judge Lord Kames in 1781, in a dour lecture outlining the conservative position on female destiny:

> To make a good husband, is but one branch of a man's duty; but it is the chief duty of woman, to make a good wife. To please her husband, to be a good oeconomist, and to educate her children, are capital duties, each of which requires much training. Nature lays the foundation: diligence and sagacity in the conductor, will make a beautiful superstructure. The time a girl bestows on her doll, is a prognostic that she will be equally diligent about her offspring.[5]

Ladies' advice literature always advocated energetic attention to household matters, and a substantial female investment in the home was taken for granted in genteel correspondence: 'We believe you to be too good a wife and too tender a mother to be often abroad, which certainly is the best means of preserving good order at home', Ann Pellet reminded her niece in 1757.[6] That boys would never be so domesticated was considered indisputable. In fact, a maternal preference for daughters was always explained by the commonplace that girls stayed at home: 'If a little Miss sho'd come, I hope 'twill prove a charming companion to you, which you cannot expect from the boys who will or sho'd spend most of their youth in schools.' Sixty years later Anne Robbins displayed identical reasoning (if in slightly heightened language) when reporting her satisfaction upon the birth of her baby daughter: 'Girls have more the power of being *home comforts* than boys and I hope she will prove one to [her] poor mother.'[7] Moreover, domestic life had many ardent female devotees who held that real happiness was found only at home. Predictably, the widow Ann Pellet subscribed to this view, wishing Elizabeth Parker 'a safe return to your own little castle where may you ever find the highest comfort this life affords (viz) the Riches of True Content'. Genteel writers routinely drew on the symbol of the hearth to suggest intimacy and security.[8] Yet, in practice, self-conscious domesticity and effective housekeeping did not automatically result in female seclusion. It is worth remembering that the most cloying celebration of home life which emerges in this book comes from the Ramsden household, whose mistress had an insatiable appetite for going out. Bessy Ramsden's letters advertised the cosy comforts of home and family, only to break off abruptly at the siren call of entertainment. As her husband concluded, 'thus far last night [went Bessy's letter when] . . . came the Coach to the Door and away whisked Madam to the Assembly as usual'.[9] A happy housewife and an incurable street-wife, Bessy Ramsden saw no inconsistency in relishing domesticity at one time of day and independent socializing at another. Nor was the Georgian home presented in women's own writings as a sanctuary from the social world.

It is crucial to stress also that there were constructions of the 'public' and 'private' which did not correspond at all to a distinction between male and female worlds. In fact, the typical usage of 'publick' in the writings of genteel women was that defined by Johnson as 'open for general entertainment'. Thus, when the young diarist Anna Porter listed all 'the publick places and private entertainments' she visited and enjoyed between 1773 and 1787, public places included the play, the opera, Richmond assembly and Ranelagh – all venues which could be penetrated by virtually anyone for the price of a ticket and where visitors could see and be seen. Private entertainments were attractively exclusive gatherings entered by invitation only. Therefore Jane Pellet was unabashed when a public ball 'for the *mob*' was cancelled on Twelfth Night in 1747, since she was honoured with an invitation from a duke to a fashionable ball in 'his private apartment'.[10] Genteel women played an active role, possibly even predominated, at both sorts of diversion. Clearly, a dichotomy between public and private was at work here, but the contrast drawn was that between the vulgar and the select, between inclusive sociability open to all and discriminating assemblies accessible to the few, emphatically not a distinction between a male world and a female home. The distinction between vulgar promiscuity and polite selection was a powerful key for the understanding of both commercial entertainment in urban resorts and social congregation in the genteel home. So it was that Elizabeth Shackleton designated days for 'publick' entertainment, when Alkincoats and Pasture Houses were open and common to all, when 'a mixed multitude' enjoyed her hospitality, but also complained about the common throng at a public ball in Burnley, 'but a vulgar affair & a quere mixd multitude'. To be sure, even exclusive gatherings of ten elite couples were still profoundly social, yet they remained engagingly 'private' in the eighteenth-century genteel imagination, since a guest would not have to sit down to dinner beside a chance stranger, and this was a crucial distinction, if there were many like Burney's Mrs Maple who was constitutionally unable to hold a conference 'with a person of whom she had never seen the pedigree, nor the rent-roll . . .'[11] The public and private in this usage related to the differentiation of rank not gender.

Literally hundreds of women, moreover, belonged to families that consciously conceived of themselves as public institutions. Public families, men and women included, were invariably eminent, titled and politically well-connected. They lived in the great world, constantly in the public eye, their doings reported in the public papers. For such families, the birth of an heir was a matter 'both of a happy private and public nature'. Public families sometimes neglected their wider responsibilities, by snobbishly opting for 'private weddings', to the disapproval of moralists.[12] Commentators tied themselves in knots deciding whether the ladies of these families belonged to public or private life. Thus, when Canning reflected on the death of the Duchess of Portland, his categories almost failed him: 'She was a good and almost a *great character*. I say *almost* because I do not know whether a woman in private life can fairly have that epithet attached to her.' Though obviously not a great statesman, she was virtually a national worthy. Similarly, Henry Ellison writing in 1781 was astonished at the 'distinguished reception which Lady [Ravensworth] met with at the Playhouse, the Audience applauding her as she entered, a compliment I do not remember to have been paid to any individual, not in a public character.'[13] The accolade testified to the publicity a lady of a great family enjoyed.

By contrast, private families lived out of the world, lacking the means to enjoy cosmopolitan, social success. Some gentlemen and ladies of means deliberately elected to live a life of retirement, consciously chosing groves and books over metropolitan prestige.[14] Many more were the men who acknowledged that because of their modest backgrounds and ambitions, they lived in private life. When a schoolmaster John Hodgkinson was offered a post of estate steward in 1791 he balked at his promotion to a higher sphere:

> I considered that I should be thrown into a more public life and into a society very different from what I had hirtherto mixed in. My life had so far been a secluded one compared with what was now opening out to me. I could not tell what effect this great change might make. My quiet and sober habits might be given up and others of a more dangerous tendency adopted. I troubled for my family and indeed for my own reputation.

Clearly it was possible for men to draw moral self-importance from a life lived outside the glare of high society and political intrigue. When Alexander Carlyle, a leading moderate minister, began writing in 1800 aged seventy-nine, he too disclaimed any part in a public sphere, describing 'the Humble and Private Sphere of Life, in comparison with that of many others, in which I have always acted . . .'[15] Now it may be that both of these men were primarily concerned to dissociate themselves from worldliness and corruption, yet it is still striking and significant that a schoolmaster and a minister, precisely the men nineteenth-century historians would expect to invest in the concept of a male public sphere, should so defiantly cling to a vision of the private character of their own lives. While noblewomen might glitter in the public sphere, the majority of men were relegated to, or rejoiced in the private shade.

Nevertheless, it must be acknowledged that in genteel society a gentleman's life had dimensions that his wife's did not; a fact which is given a rare canvassing in a letter written by Mrs Beatrix Lister to her son Thomas Lister MP in 1773. She was urging the taking of dancing lessons: 'I don't wish you to dance in publick, except it was quite agriable to you, but I think learning gives an ease to Carige & helps ye walking. Mr Spectator you know recomends it vastly tho' he realy values no man but for his publick Spirit, Justice & Integrity.'[16] Two kinds of public masculine performance are invoked here, the social commerce of the landed gentleman and the disinterested public service of the office-holder. Of the latter, provincial ladies could claim little share. From the exalted member of parliament or lord lieutenant for the county, to the worthy magistrate and respectable member of the grand jury, feckless was the gentlemen who had not found a platform from which to demonstrate his public spirit.[17] It was in the holding of office that the ideal of genteel adult masculinity inhered.

There were, nevertheless, ways in which women might lay claim to a certain public spirit through disinterested service to their local community, the county or the nation; Elizabeth Shackleton of Alkincoats, for instance, perpetuated her dead husband's 'publick spirit' by selling his celebrated rabies medicine at an affordable price.[18] Countless others promoted the common good through acts of charity. Furthermore, since political influence was largely a matter of property, the peeress and the heiress might simply assume certain rights and responsibilities irrespective of her sex, as Elaine Chalus, Linda Colley and Judith Lewis have pointed out.[19] Aristocrats were quite capable of pulling rank over gender if the need arose. When the Duchess of Queensberry led a squadron of ladies to storm the gallery of the House of Lords in 1739, she reportedly 'pished at the ill-breeding of a mere lawyer'.[20] Even if the dominant discourses of femininity were belittling, the reverence for rank, wealth and position remained overwhelming.

Not that female aristocratic power went uncontested. George Canning, for instance, deplored his aunt's tendency to take issue with him over matters of state and clutched at any hope of abatement:

> had no political differences – insomuch that I really thought Hetty had come to her senses, and seen that a woman has no business at all with politicks, or that if she thinks at all about them, it should be at least in a feminine manner, as wishing for the peace and prosperity of her country – and for the success and credit of those of her family (if she has any) who are engaged in the practical part of politicks.[21]

Thus he invoked the notion of the softly feminine foray into politics which was reiterated *ad nauseam* in Georgian and Victorian discourse; but, as some historians have pointed out, this patronizing concession offered a wonderful rhetorical opportunity which activists deployed to their advantage. When the Manchester Abolitionists appealed in 1787 for female aid in the *Manchester Mercury*, they promised that benevolent public action would be the ultimate expression of sensitive femininity, not its negation:

> If any public Interference will at any TIME become the Fair Sex; if their Names are ever to be mentioned with Honour beyond the Boundaries of their Family, and the Circle of their Connections, it can only be, when a public Opportunity is given for the Exertion of those Qualities which are peculiarly expected in, and particularly possessed by that most amiable Part of the Creation – the Qualities of Humanity, Benevolence and Compassion.[22]

Similarly, Linda Colley's female patriots used the rhetoric of feminine virtue to legitimize their actions: 'Posing as the pure-minded Women of Britain was, in practice, a way of insisting on the right to public spirit.'[23] Equally, female philanthropists mustered the rhetoric of domesticity to justify their non-domestic activities. In arguing that organized charity represented an altogether natural extension of female domestic duties, a form of 'social housekeeping', activists defeated the opposition with its own weapons. Sentimentalists like Ruskin handed rhetorical success on a plate when they mused, 'a woman has a personal work or duty, relating to her own home, and a public work and duty which is also the expansion of that', and 'wherever a true wife comes, [home] is always around her'.[24] In so far as the language of domesticity became more powerful and pervasive in the period covered by this book, then genteel women became increasingly adept at manipulating it to pursue a range of activities and assume a set of responsibilities outside the home. Indeed, the well-documented struggles of privileged Victorian women to participate more fully in institutional public life represented less a reaction against irksome restrictions, recently imposed, than a drive to extend yet further the gains made by their Georgian predecessors. Propriety might have made a tight-fitting suit, but it could worn in a far wider range of situations than we have been apt to think.

66   'The Patriotic Parting',
from the *Lady's Magazine* (1782).

Abbreviations

RECORD REPOSITORIES

BIHR	Borthwick Institute of Historical Research, York
CLRO	Corporation of London Record Office
CRO	Cheshire Record Office, Chester
CRO, Carlisle	Cumbria Record Office, Carlisle
ERO	Essex Record Office, Chelmsford
HL	Huntington Library, San Marino, Ca.
LPL	Lancaster Public Library
LRO	Lancashire Record Office, Preston
NRO	Northumberland Record Office, Newcastle
NYRO	North Yorkshire Record Office, Northallerton
PRO	Public Record Office, London
RCHM	Royal Commission for Historical Monuments
WPL	Westminster Public Library, London
WRO	Wigan Record Office, Leigh
WYCRO, Bradford	West Yorkshire County Record Office, Bradford
WYCRO, Leeds	West Yorkshire County Record Office, Leeds
WYCRO, Wakefield	West Yorkshire County Record Office, Wakefield
YAS	Yorkshire Archaeological Society, Leeds

JOURNALS AND MISCELLANEOUS

EcHR	*Economic History Review*
HJ	*Historical Journal*
HWJ	*History Workshop Journal*
P&P	*Past and Present*
UBD	*The Universal British Directory* (1791)
VCHL	*The Victoria History of the County of Lancaster*

Notes to the Text

Introduction

1 HL, HM 31201, Mrs Larpent's Diary, XI, 1820–21, facing f. 5.
2 Clark, *Working Life of Women*, pp. 14, 41, 296. Interestingly, Clark included the aristocracy and *nouveau-riche* businessmen in her category of 'capitalists' since the two groups approximated to each other in manners, see pp. 14–41.
3 Consider Amussen, *An Ordered Society*, p. 187; C. Hall, 'The History of the House-wife', in Hall, *White, Male and Middle Class*, pp. 43–71; George, *Women in the First Capitalist Society*, pp. 1–10; Hill, *Women, Work and Sexual Politics*, pp. 49–52, 78–80, 126–9, 245–9. On 'the restriction of women's professional and business activities at the end of the eighteenth century', see Pinchbeck, *Women Workers*, pp. 303–5. And on the ambition of the wealthier farmer's wife 'to achieve gentility' by having 'nothing to do', see pp. 33–40.
4 Stone, *The Family, Sex and Marriage*, p. 396. All citations refer to the 1977 edition.
5 M. George, 'From Goodwife to Mistress: The Transformation of the Female in Bourgeois Culture', *Science and Society*, 37 (1973), p. 6.
6 Shevelow, *Women and Print Culture*, pp. 5 and 1.
7 See W. E. Houghton, *The Victorian Frame of Mind, 1830–1870* (New Haven, 1957), pp. 341–93; M. Jaeger, *Before Victoria: Changing Standards and Behaviour, 1787–1837* (1956), pp. 113–30; M. Quinlan,*Victorian Prelude: A History of English Manners, 1700–1830* (New York, 1941), pp. 139–59. The classic work on vulnerable and cloistered femininity is M. Vicinus (ed.), *Suffer and be Still: Women in the Victorian Age* (Bloomington, Ind., 1972). The socialization of trainee domesticates is the theme of D. Gorham, *The Victorian Girl and the Feminine Ideal* (Bloomington, Ind., 1983) and F. Hunt (ed.), *Lessons for Life: The Schooling of Girls and Women, 1850–1950* (Oxford, 1987). On the inhibition of female sexuality and physical activity, read E. Trudgill, *Madonnas and Magdalens: The Origins and Development of Victorian Sexual Attitudes* (1976), pp. 65–78, L. Duffin, 'The Conspicuous Consumptive: Woman as Invalid', in S. Delamont and L. Duffin (eds.), *The Nineteenth-Century Woman: Her Cultural and Physical World* (1978), pp. 26–56, and H. E. Roberts, 'The Exquisite Slave: The Role of Clothes in the Making of the Victorian Woman', *Signs*, 2 (1977), pp. 554–69. On the rigid demarcation of public and private physical space, see A. Clark, *Women's Silence, Men's Violence: Sexual Assault in England, 1770–1845* (1987). That an emergent middle class built itself on the assumption of separate gender spheres is the argument of Hall, 'Victorian Domestic Ideology', and 'Gender

Divisions and Class Formation', both reprinted in id., *White, Male and Middle Class*, pp. 75–93 and 94–107. The most substantial restatement of the separate spheres thesis remains Davidoff and Hall, *Family Fortunes*.

8   See Vickery, 'Golden Age to Separate Spheres'.

9   Compare Amussen, *Ordered Society*, pp. 69 and 187, and Davidoff and Hall, *Family Fortunes*, pp. 272–5.

10 D. C. Coleman, 'Proto-industrialization: A Concept too Many', *Economic History Review*, 2nd ser., 36 (1983), pp. 435–48. See also R. Samuel, 'Workshop of the World: Steam Power and Hand Technology in mid-Victorian Britain', *HWJ*, 3 (1977), pp. 6–72.

11 See P. Earle, 'The Female Labour Market', and Goldberg, *Women, Work and the Life Cycle*. On the generation of income, see Earle, *The Making of the English Middle Class*, pp. 158–74, and Holderness, 'Credit in a Rural Community'. The constraints on female enterprise are richly elaborated in Hunt, *The Middling Sort*, and suggested by Simonton, 'Apprenticeship'.

12 Olwen Hufton was one of the first to question the validity of the decline-and-fall model of women's work, arguing that it rests on the dubious assumption of a lost egalitarian Eden which has proved elusive to empiral research: id., 'Women in History', p. 126. Her own narrative of change and continuity, 1500 to 1800, is much less dramatic, but her subtle, nuanced and multi-stranded story still convinces: id., *The Prospect Before Her*, pp. 487–508. Another important criticism of the golden age myth is Bennett, 'History that Stands Still'.

13 See Sekora, *Luxury*.

14 Childs, 'Prescriptions for Manners' (D.Phil. thesis), pp. 285–7.

15 M. LeGates, 'The Cult of Womanhood in Eighteenth-Century Thought', *Eighteenth-Century Studies*, 1 (1976), pp. 21–39.

16 Hunter, 'The Eighteenth-Century Englishwoman', p. 87.

17 *Gentleman's Magazine*, 58, pp. 222–4.

18 See LPL, MS 8752 (1776), 13 and 15 Dec.; MS 8754 (1779), 6, 21 and 29 April. A salutary development in this context is the attempt to recover the history of the reader herself. Two essays which contest the conventional image of the leisured reader passively ingesting eighteenth-century texts in private are Tadmor, 'In the Even', and Brewer, 'Reconstructing the Reader'.

19 See M. Z. Rosaldo, 'The Use and Abuse of Anthropology: Reflections on Feminism and Cross-Cultural Understanding', *Signs*, 5 (1980), pp. 389–417; and Kerber, 'Separate Spheres', pp. 18–19.

20 Lady Pennington, *Unfortunate Mother's Advice*, p. 65; Haywood, *Miss Betsy Thoughtless*, p. 370.

21 Bond, *The Tatler*, II, p. 444.

22 Borsay, *English Urban Renaissance*; Barry, 'Cultural Life of Bristol' (D. Phil. thesis).

23 For pointed criticism of the domestic angels thesis, see, *inter alia*, Branca, 'Image and Reality' and id., *Silent Sisterhood*; Peterson, 'No Angels in the House'; P. Thane, 'Late Victorian Women', in T. R. Gourvish and A. O'Day (eds.), *Later Victorian Britain, 1867–1900* (Basingstoke, 1988), pp. 175–208. The earnest enterprise and managerial skill of which Victorian women were capable is amply demonstrated by Prochaska, *Women and Philanthropy*; Summers, 'A Home from Home'. Ladies who displayed gumption, if not 'political correctness', are the subject of D. Birkett, *Spinsters Abroad: Victorian Lady Explorers* (Oxford, 1989), and Hammerton, *Emigrant Gentlewomen*. In fact, where historians have researched the activities of particular individuals and groups, rather than the contemporary social theories which allegedly hobbled them, Victorian women emerge as no less adventurous, capable and, most importantly, diverse a crew as in any other century. Read the excellent Jalland, *Women,*

Marriage and Politics; Caine, *Destined to be Wives*; and Peterson, *Family, Love and Work*.

24   This metaphor was deployed by Laurel Thatcher Ulrich in assessment of Martha Ballard's diary; see L. T. Ulrich, 'Martha Ballard and her Girls: Women's Work in Eighteenth Century Maine', in S. Innes (ed.), *Work and Labour in Early America* (Chapel Hill, NC, 1988), p. 72.

1   Gentility

1   See Klein, 'The Third Earl of Shaftesbury, pp. 186–214, and his imaginative 'Politeness for Plebes', pp. 362–82.

2   Langford, *Polite and Commercial People*, p. 76. However, Langford uses a portmanteau category of 'the middle classes' to group enormous swathes of the population.

3   This is not to say that the eighteenth century had no language of class, but it was one option among many and even when 'class' was preferred to 'ranks', 'sorts', or 'interests', a threefold classification was not the automatic choice: Corfield, 'Class by Name and Number'. Not that gentility had a cut-and-dried definition either, a point developed in id., 'The Rivals'.

4   In the standard account, Mingay, *English Landed Society*, three tiers of landowners are distinguished: peers, gentry and freeholders. Unlike many grand surveys that have followed, Mingay paid due attention to all three categories and noted the factors that cut across clear social distinctions: much overlapping of income, the fact that the younger sons of peers did not inherit a title and became *de facto* gentry, and the degree of intermarriage both across and outside landed society, which generated a complicated kinship web linking land with merchants, professionals and even with tradesmen. Compare this wide coverage with Beckett, *Aristocracy in England*, who includes the lesser gentry in his definition of 'aristocracy', but confines his discussion largely to the peerage. Studies which pay full attention to the gentry in the eighteenth century (unlike their seventeenth-century equivalents) are surprisingly scarce, but on the titled gentry see Roebuck, *Yorkshire Baronets*. Attention is given to the lesser gentry in Jenkins, *Making of a Ruling Class*, and Howell, *Patriarchs and Parasites*. Both these studies stress the interconnectedness of landed society and the close ties between land and trade. In Glamorgan, mining and metallurgical ventures brought the gentry into business partnerships with merchants, younger sons turned to trade in Swansea and Bristol, and in terms of marriage the mercantile heiress was a perennial draw. Furthermore, the gentry enjoyed an interdependent relationship with local professionals and were often related by blood to the clergy. In south-west Wales, the wealthier gentry were often blessed with rich mineral reserves which they mined religiously, but owing to economic isolation and unprofitable agriculture, 'the meaner sort of gentry' could be worth as little as £100–£400 a year; in fact, in terms of wealth some of them might be classed with small freeholders. They had to make do with local schools, not English public schools; they lived in modest residences some no larger than a substantial farmhouse, not the handsome and bustling mansions enjoyed by the prominent; and they were left to the locality when the 'great folk' decamped to London every winter. It was just this level that the Stones ignored in their attempt to debunk the notion that the upper echelons of landed society were open to outsiders from trade: Stone and Fawtier Stone, *An Open Elite?* By confining their discussion to owners of country houses of more than 5,000 square feet (in Hertfordshire, Northamptonshire and Northumberland), they exclude the very group from which, by their own findings, the majority of newcomers rose. The realistic outsider from trade probably aimed initially to penetrate the 'parish gentry', leaving it to later generations to

advance to county or national level. For critical responses, see C. Clay in *EcHR*, 2nd ser., 38 (1985), pp. 452–54; E. and D. Spring, 'The English Landed Elite, 1540–1879: A Review', *Albion*, 19 (1985), pp. 149–66. The openness of the elite has also been challenged by Cannon, *Aristocratic Century*.

5 Although there is no synthesis on a par with Mingay's, the middling sorts have become a focus of considerable historical interest in recent years. Political historians have moved beyond a focus on a patrician–plebeian struggle to emphasize the independence of middling political opinion. See, *inter alia*, Brewer, *Party, Ideology and Popular Politics*; N. Rodgers, *Whigs and Cities* (Oxford, 1989); and K. Wilson, *The Sense of the People: Politics, Culture and Imperialism in England, 1715–85* (Cambridge, 1995). The history of cultural and material consumption has brought the lifestyles of the middling sort vividly to the fore: Weatherill, *Consumer Behaviour*; Borsay, *Urban Renaissance*; and Barry, 'Cultural Life of Bristol' (D.Phil. thesis). The history of the professions is now being written: Holmes, *Augustan England*, Prest, *Professions in Early Modern England*, P. J. Corfield, *Power and the Professions in Britain, 1700–1850* (1995); Robson, *Attorney in Eighteenth-Century England*, and Porter, *Patients' Progress*. For case-studies of the provincial middling sort, see Smail, *Origins of Middle-Class Culture*; Wilson, *Gentleman Merchants*; Jackson, *Hull in the Eighteenth Century*; M. Hunt, *Middling Sort*; S. D'Cruz, 'The Middling Sort in Provincial England: Politics and Social Relations in Colchester, 1730–1800' (unpubl. Ph.D. thesis, University of Essex, 1990). The most substantial study of commercial families remains Earle, *Making of the English Middle Class*, but despite his ambitious title, echoing Edward Thompson's agenda-setting masterpiece, Earle sidesteps the conceptual debate on class and its 'creation' or otherwise. As a result, his conclusions are somewhat neutral, something which has limited the impact of his detailed research outside early modern social and economic history. Nevertheless, the book is a mine of information and offers a useful starting-point for long-term comparisons. For more on the metropolitan patriciate, see Rogers, 'Money, Land and Lineage'.

6 See respectively, Smail, *Origins of Middle-Class Culture*, p. 28, and Davidoff and Hall, *Family Fortunes*, pp. 21–2. One of the few historians to address the ambivalent position of the gentry is E. P. Thompson on the 'agrarian bourgeoisie', see id., 'Eighteenth-Century English Society', p. 162. Mingay estimates the number of families of mere landed gentlemen to have been between ten and twenty thousand. This is a conservative estimate based on an income range of £300 to £1,000 per year. See Mingay, *English Landed Society*, p. 26.

7 In 1781 the populations of Colne, Burnley and Clitheroe (including their surrounding townships) stood at 2,757, 1,890 and 830 respectively, and in 1801 at 3,626, 3,305 and 1,368: James, *Worsted Manufacture*, appendix, p. 40; and according to the 1801 census cited in Baines, *County Palatine of Lancaster*, I, pp. 620, 566, 612. The best history of the area remains Whitaker, *Original Parish of Whalley*. Additional information is in Carr, *Colne and Neighbourhood*.

8 In this, Colne followed the same economic trajectory as the adjacent textile areas of the West Riding of Yorkshire. In fact, historians of the textile industries consider the area to be an offshoot of the Yorkshire worsted field: Wadsworth and de Lacy Mann, *Cotton Trade*, pp. 88, 259, 278; Heaton, *Yorkshire Woollen and Worsted Industries*, pp. 271, 286, 311, 380; James, *Worsted Manufacture*, pp. 631–2. On textile-related occupations in north-east Lancashire, see N. Lowe, 'The Lancashire Textile Industry in the Sixteenth Century', *Chetham Society*, 3rd ser., 20 (1972), *passim*, and Swain, *Industry Before the Industrial Revolution*, pp. 108–48.

9 Aikin, *Description of the Country*, p. 279.

10 Compare the road maps for 1740, 1750 and 1770 in E. Pawson, *Transport and Economy: The Turnpike Roads in Eighteenth-Century Britain* (1977), pp. 137, 139, 140.

11   H. F. Killick, 'Notes on the Early History of the Leeds–Liverpool Canal', *Bradford Antiquary*, n.s., 1 (1900), pp. 169–238.

12   Baines, *Lancashire Directory*, I, p. 620.

13   For the history of rebuilding in this area, see Pearson, *Rural Houses*, pp. 118–25.

14   See the Parker pedigree, Appendix 3, p. 384, and *Genealogist*, n.s., 31 (1915), pp. 102–5. The rental was calculated from the entries for 1767, recorded in LRO, DDX 390 (1766–79), Account book of Thomas Stirling, Steward to Edward Parker of Browsholme. See also LRO, DDB 84/1 Browsholme survey book, which reveals that the Parkers owned pastures in seventeen townships in both Lancashire and Yorkshire.

15   LRO, DDB Ac 7886/239 (22 July 1748), M. Bowen, companion and secretary to A. Pellet, Great Ealing, London, to E. Parker, Browsholme: 'Oh! that my dear Parkie & Pell was so advantageously settled, how happy cod I be to see my two dr favourites live in Splendour and Elegance . . .' [Hereafter A. Pellet will be named as the author.]

16   Rental calculated from LRO, DDB/76/4 (1758–75), Trust Account of Thomas Parker. For confirmation of Robert Parker's landed qualifications, see also LRO, QSC/198, Commission of the Peace.

17   LRO, DDB/72/8 (16 June 1751), E. Parker, Browsholme, to R. Parker, Horrocksford; LRO, DDB Ac 7886/121 (c.1746), R. Parker to E. Parker. On the significance of a 'coach and six', see above, pp. 13, 41, 55.

18   For notes on the rebuilding, see LRO, DDB/72/23 (n.d.), R. Parker, Alkincoats, to E. Parker, Browsholme. Under Parker's aegis, a Gibbs-style surround was added to the main doorway and the mullioned and transomed windows on the ground and first stories were replaced by sashes. The interior was completely redecorated with new paper and wainscotting. Alkincoats was demolished in 1958, but its appearance is recorded in photographs, see RCHM, no. 33819, and its structure in surviving plans, see LRO, DDB/80/30, 'Plan of the principal floor of Alkincoats with the proposed additions and alterations'. An excellent discussion is provided in Pearson, *Rural Houses*, pp. 38, 39, 46, 49, 57, 118, 142a–b and pl. 94. For the remark about Elizabeth's social choices, see LRO, DDB Ac 7886/255 (10 Dec. 1748), J. Pellet, Pontefract to E. Parker, Browsholme.

19   LRO, DDB/22/3 (7 Sept. 1788), Will of John Shackleton, gent.

20   The failure of the Toulsons in the male line is documented by Skipwith church monuments, see Allen, *County of York* II, p. 38. The same tombstones record that John Toulson Parker was buried there in 1821.

21   Elizabeth Barcroft and her sister Martha were co-heiresses of the estate of Foulridge Hall and Noyna, comprised of 320 acres with a yearly value of £336: LRO, DDB/62/244 (1761), Survey of lands belonging to co-heiresses of Thomas Barcroft of Noyna.

22   Their co-residence is confirmed by a deed regarding turnpike shares: LRO, DDB/69/2 (1834). On the small inheritances of the sisters, see LRO, DDB/70/6 (1775), Will of John Barcroft of Clitheroe, gent., and LRO, DDB/70/9 (1815), Will of Matthew Wilson of Otley, gent.

23   For confirmation, see LRO, DDB/71/4 (1803), Apprenticeship of Edward Parker to Richard Swallow of Selby, and *Genealogist*, n.s., 31 (1915), p. 105. Further details are in Ten Broek Runk, *Barcroft Family Records*.

24   On the giant Horrocks, Miller and Co. in boom and depression, see Howe, *Cotton Masters*, pp. 9–10, 21, 25, 27, 316.

25   On Samuel Horrocks's unmomentous career at Westminster, see Thorne, *History of Parliament*, VI, pp. 247–8, and on his mansion, see Burscough, *Lark Hill, Preston*.

26   For biographical information, see J. Burke and A. P. Burke, *Genealogical and Heraldic History of the Colonial Gentry* (1891–5), p. 736, and LRO, DDPd 11/81 (1745–1804), Extract of Pedigree of Horrockses of Edgeworth and Preston. The Whitaker family had been associated with Simonstone township since 1300, though Simonstone Hall was built in the early seventeenth century, see RCHM, photograph

no. 33913, and *VCHL*, VI, p. 498. Whether Roefield in Clitheroe was owned or leased is unclear. It certainly was not the historic property of the Whitaker family; a letter to Mrs Helen Whitaker in the 1780s reveals that a Mrs A. Rigby was then in residence: LRO, DDWh/4/19.

27   Edgecombe, *Diary of Frances, Lady Shelley*, p. 3.

28   Appendix 4 discusses the construction of the data base, pp. 385–6.

29   Of interactions with her kin, 23 per cent concerned her eldest son Tom Parker of Alkincoats and his wife Betty, while 29 per cent engaged her younger sons John and Robert Parker, resident for most of this period in London. (If anything, these figures underestimate her sons' social role overall, since no social contacts with Tom Parker, apart from letters, have been recorded for 1773, when mother and son still lived in the same house.) If kin contacts are broken down by gender, the dominance of male kin is immediately revealed. 52 per cent of the total involved men alone, a large figure when compared to the 28 per cent which involved just women, and 20 per cent which incorporated both sexes. Yet, again, this pattern might be a function of the particularity of Elizabeth Shackleton's kin network: her mother and her mother-in-law (from both first and second marriage) were dead, she had no sisters or nieces, and her own daughter did not survive infancy. This negative effect becomes apparent when the gender breakdown of social contacts with non-kin is examined. Women alone figured in 34 per cent of non-kin interactions, men alone in 53 per cent and men and women in 13 per cent.

30   By contrast, over a fifth of all Tom Parker's social contacts in 1773, as listed in his mother's diary, involved his uncle and aunt. The sons were not implicated in their mother's disgrace.

31   See Appendix 2, pp. 360–61. Bessy Ramsden's brothers Tom and Ned, who do not appear in the sample diaries, were respectively a London stationer and an Essex manufacturer.

32   Numbers of encounters, in order of frequency, are as follows: Waltons of Marsden and Skipwith (94), Cockshotts of Park, Cockshotts of Bracewell and Cockshotts of Marley (33), Foulds of Trawden (18), Cunliffes of Wycoller (13), Wiglesworths of Townhead (11), Listers of Gisburn Park (8), Miss Cromblehome of Preston (8), Ambrose Walton of Carrybridge (6), Miss Elizabeth Parker of Preston (2), John Holgate of Breeze House (2), Butlers of Kirkland (2), Starkies of Huntroyde (2), Ormerods of Ormerod (2), Claytons of Carr Hall (1), Miss Dawson of Aldcliffe Hall, Lancaster (1), Benjamin Ferrand of St Ives, Bingley (1), Banastre Parker of Cuerdon (1), Pattens of Bank Hall (1), Townleys of Royle (1).

33   For Edward Parker's obituary, see *Gentleman's Magazine*, 65 (1795), pt. 1, p. 82. Gratification over his brilliant marriage is relayed in LRO, DDB/72/77 (7 Nov. 1753), A. Pellet, London, to E. Parker, Alkincoats. On his office-holding, consult PRO, C/234/44, Commission of the Peace for Yorkshire, 1762 and 1780.

34   Landau, *Justices of the Peace*, p. 161. The Lancashire Commissions of the Peace for this period contain, among others, the names of John Clayton (1777), Thomas Clayton (1814), Robert Cunliffe (1756 and 1766), James Foulds (1756), Robert Parker (1756), Thomas Patten (1777), Pierce Starkie (1756), Edmund and Richard Townley (1777), Thomas Townley (1756). The West Riding Commissions of the Peace cite Benjamin Ferrand (1762), James Foulds (1762), Nathaniel Lister (1762, 1780), Thomas Lister (1780), Le Gendre Starkie (1780), Banastre Walton (1762 and 1780), Ambrose Walton (1762) and James Wiglesworth (1762).

35   This may be an underestimate of the number of deputy lieutenants and militia officers in Elizabeth Shackleton's acquaintance, as the relevant Yorkshire records have not survived. For Lancashire, see LRO, QSQ/2/2–4, Property Qualifications of Deputy Lieutenants, 1757–1808; QSQ/3, Property Qualifications of Militia Officers, 1760–1803; and QSQ/4, Property Qualifications of Provisional Cavalry Officers, 1797–1808.

36   PRO, T 47/8 (1780), Tax on Male Servants. The returns were as follows: Listers (6),
     John and Thomas Clayton (4 and 1), Le Gendre Starkie (5), Edward and Charles
     Townley (5 and 3), Thomas Patten (7), Banastre Walton (8), Robert Parker of
     Cuerdon (6), Benjamin Ferrand (3), James Wiglesworth (2), Lawrence Ormerod of
     Ormerod (2), Henry Owen Cunliffe (1). No male servants are registered for the
     Cockshotts of Park, Bracewell and Marley, the Dawsons of Aldcliffe Hall, the Foulds
     of Trawden, the Cromblehomes of Preston, or the Holgates of Breeze House. Surpris-
     ingly, the Parkers of Alkincoats and the Shackletons of Pasture House are not regis-
     tered, even though it is clear from the diaries that these households employed at least
     two male servants. It may be that the assessors did not descend far below the level of
     the lieutenancy, or that families with trading interests could pass their servants off as
     apprentices and thus evade taxation. (I am grateful to Nicholas Rogers for sharing
     this material with me.)

37   See *Statutes of the Realm*, 28 Geo. II, *c.*50 (1755), and WYRO, Wakefield, RT 13/5,
     Minute Book of the Bradford–Colne Turnpike Trust, 1755–1823. In addition to
     Elizabeth Shackleton's first husband Robert Parker, her second husband John
     Shackleton and her brother Edward Parker, trustees included John Clayton, John
     Cockshott, Henry Cunliffe, Henry Owen Cunliffe, John Dawson, Benjamin Ferrand,
     James Foulds, John Holgate and John Holgate the younger, Thomas Lister, Robert
     Parker [of Cuerdon], Nicholas Starkie, Edmund Starkie, Le Gendre Starkie, Thomas
     Townley, Ambrose Walton and Banastre Walton.

38   Property qualifications indicate minimum not total income. Nevertheless, incomes
     between £100 and £300 were low by national standards. The political arithmetician
     Gregory King estimated in 1688 that a gentleman's family would enjoy an income of
     £280 per annum; the early statistician James Massie thought the lesser gentry worth
     between £200 and £600 per annum in 1759; while in 1801–3, the London magistrate
     Patrick Colquhoun believed the same families worth at least £700 per annum. Yet, it
     must be remembered that before the late eighteenth-century explosion in prices and
     land values the demands of northern gentility could be met with less rent than was the
     case in the south. Moreover, contemporary social tables are themselves a problematic
     source, see Lindert and Williamson, 'Revising England's Social Tables'.

39   The professional category has been subdivided into legal, medical, and clerical-
     educational occupations. Amongst these the law was clearly dominant. Social con-
     tacts with non-kin professionals and their families involved a lawyer on 60 per cent of
     occasions, a medic on 34 per cent and a clerical and/or teaching family in 6 per cent
     of cases.

40   Arbitrary decisions about categorization have been unavoidable. For instance,
     although a qualified barrister, Banastre Walton has been placed in the gentry camp,
     because there is no evidence that he ever practised at the bar. Conversely, Dr William
     St Clare of Preston and Grindleton, Serjeant John Aspinall of Standen Hall, Clitheroe,
     and Recorder John Barcroft of Clitheroe Castle and Noyna have all been placed with
     the professions, since not only did each practise, but also because they all built up a
     professional reputation. All three men and their descendants held county offices; John
     Aspinall was on both the Lancashire and the Yorkshire Commissions of the Peace and
     served as a Deputy-Lieutenant for the former, John Barcroft was on the Yorkshire
     commission; and William St Clare (the younger) and John Aspinall (the younger)
     were both officers in the Lancashire militia. The Lancashire records are LRO, QSC/
     204, 1766, and QSC/207, 1777; LRO, QSQ/4/1/1–15, 1797–8. And on Yorkshire, see
     PRO, C/234/44, 1762 and 1780.

41   Shackleton's contacts with professional families to whom she was not related were as
     follows: Lawyer and Mrs Barcroft (35), the Lawyers Jonas, Lawrence and Old Shaw
     (33), Dr and Mrs Midgely (17), Dr and Mrs Turner (15), Revd Wilson (1), School-
     mistress Wells (5), Revd Metcalf (4), Mr Sclater (3), Dr and Mrs St Clare (2), 'The

Bishop of Pendle' (2), Revd Johnson (1), 'The Barrowford Schoolmaster' (1), Lawyer Moon (1), Lawyer Aspinall (1).

42 Removing business calls and explicitly business meals from Elizabeth Shackleton's hospitality reveals 232 social interactions in her home in 1773 and 1780. Of these, 71 (31 per cent) involved a person in trade.

43 Nelson, *Government of Children*, p. 306.

44 Of 229 non-kin interactions which involved tradespeople, 128 (56 per cent) of the participants were engaged in an upper trade and 76 (33 per cent) in a lesser trade. The rest were mainly women whose status is uncertain.

45 Friends engaged in superior trades were the Plestows (hosiers) and Bromes (drapers) of London, the Bulcocks of London and the Bulcocks of Colne (haberdashers), Mr Hill of Ormskirk (genteel purveyor of medicine), the Leaches of Riddlesden (coal merchants), the Booths of Bradford (wine merchants), the Ecroyds of Edge End (textile merchants/manufacturers), the Hargreaves family of Heirs House (cotton manufacturers), the Sagars of Catlow and the Sagars of Southfield (cloth merchants), the Parker Swinglehursts of Trawden (worsted manufacturers), Mr James Wilson (tallow-chandler), Windles of Barnoldswick (merchants), the Wilkinsons of Maize Hill (merchants) and the banker Mr Nicholas Smith of Leeds.

46 The London haberdashery business carried on by Robert Bulcock of 28 Bishopsgate, James Bulcock of 85 Borough High Street and John Bulcock of 53 Borough High Street, is listed in numerous directories, see Appendix 2, p. 355. That this was a wholesale business is confirmed by a retailer's account book, see Kent Record Office, U 1823/35, A3, Daybook of a Draper and Haberdasher, Maidstone, 1768–73, f. 131: purchase from Messrs Bulcock and Co., Borough, 1770. I am grateful to John Styles for this reference.

47 Establishing the nature of business activities has been harder for other local families assigned to the upper trades. In the case of the Sagar, Hargreaves and Wilson families, applying a social label has not been easy. All these families were closely associated with the wool merchants John and Christopher Shackleton. The Sagar clan was of yeoman stock and lived in the ancient halls of Whitewalls, Catlow and Southfield. Nothing of their commercial activity could be guessed from official records, yet luckily Methodist hagiography records the zeal of William Sagar of Southfield, a cloth merchant. See Laycock, *Early Methodist Heroes*, p. 324. A Richard Sagar of Colne sold bays and callimancos to a firm of drapers in Newcastle upon Tyne in the 1750s: Tyne and Wear Record Office, Misc. Accessions 1431/1, Daybook of Goods bought by D. and W. Wholesale Drapers of Newcastle. On their halls, see Pearson, *Rural Houses*, p. 155, and Baines, *Lancashire Directory*, I, p. 620. Similarly, the Methodist Hargreaves clan incorporated a cabinet maker, while one branch inhabited the apparently genteel residence of Heirs House, yet they went on to establish one of the first cotton spinning mills in the district in 1784. Information on the 'ignorant and vulgar' Hargreaves family is in LRO, DDB/81/17 (1772), f. 49 and LRO, DDB/81/33 A (1778), f. 195. Another socially ambiguous tradesman was James Wilson. Described in some documents as a tallow chandler, he had the wherewithal to build himself a handsome mansion, and by 1824 the Wilsons of Heyroyd had risen sufficiently to feature in a published list of the Lancashire gentry. See Pearson, *Rural Houses*, p. 144, and Baines, *Lancashire Directory*, II, pp. v–xii.

48 Firth, *Bradford and the Industrial Revolution*, pp. 56–7.

49 Trustees associated in this analysis with trade include Christopher Bulcock, Henry Bulcock, John Bulcock, James Hargreaves, Thomas Leach of Riddlesden, John Parker Swinglehurst of Trawden, William Sagar of Catlow and William Sagar of Southfield, John Shackleton of Pasture House and James Wilson. Unfortunately, the turnpike records do not assist the positive identification of commercial men, only Thomas Leach is designated 'merchant', while known manufacturers such as the

Heatons of Ponden are styled 'gentlemen'. Refer to *Statutes of the Realm*, 28 Geo. II, *c*.50 (1755), and WYRO, Wakefield, RT 13/5, Minute Book of the Bradford–Colne Turnpike Trust, 1755–1823.

50 The very fact that reliable data on status cannot be found for certain correspondents suggests that most of the 'unknowns' were not from landed families; the gentry leave a greater historical mark than the lesser ranks. Given this, and the tenor of the letters in question, it is plausible that most of these correspondents came from commercial or professional families, although I have not assumed this in my calculations.

51 Although convention has it that the Miss Horrockses were educated at home by governesses, Eliza Whitaker talked of 'school fellows', and used girlish nicknames with at least one of her pen friends, see LRO, DDWh/4/29 (17 Aug. 1813), E. Whitaker, Edgeworth, to C. Whitaker, Roefield; LRO, DDWh/4/73 (13 Aug. 1814), M. Nichols, Bewdley, to same.

52 The northern counties rejoiced in reputable grammar and boarding schools. While statistical samples are lacking, it has been noted that the greater and lesser gentry of early eighteenth-century Northumberland, County Durham, Cumberland and Westmorland sent their sons to Newcastle Royal Grammar, Sedburgh, Hawkshead, St Bees and so on, although the famous southern public schools gained ground as the century progressed. See Hughes, *North Country Life in the Eighteenth Century: The North East*, pp. 341–67 and id., *North Country Life in the Eighteenth Century: Cumberland and Westmorland*, pp. 293–8. In the case of northern Lancashire and the West Riding of Yorkshire, polite families were served by Sedburgh, Bradford Grammar School and numerous smaller schools, but a growing trend towards the southern schools would be plausible. Until the 1780s the gentlemen merchants of Leeds sent their sons in great numbers to the Leeds Free Grammar School, thereafter most boys were sent further afield to both Dissenting academies and Anglican private schools: Wilson, *Gentlemen Merchants*, pp. 208–11. Similarly, Robert Parker of Alkincoats was educated at the Clitheroe school in the 1730s, while in the 1760s all his sons attended Bradford Grammar School, but went on to Winchester and a commercial academy at Northfleet. Robert's brother-in-law Edward Parker of Browsholme was sent in the 1740s to be educated at Bury St Edmunds, Suffolk, but he sent his own son to Eton. However, the published registers of Bradford and Sedburgh indicate that enduring loyalty to the northern schools should not be underestimated.

53 The shared material culture of gentility is particularly striking. Mahogany from Gillows was purchased by the John Shackleton of Pasture House, Thomas Parker of Alkincoats, Edward Parker of Browsholme, John Parker of Marshfield, John Aspinall of Standen, John Clayton of Carr, Miss Cromblehome of Preston, Robert Parker of Cuerdon, Banastre Walton of Marsden, William Barcroft of Clitheroe, Henry Owen Cunliffe of Wycoller, Thomas Lister of Gisburn Park, Le Gendre Starkie of Huntroid and Miss Moon, Richard Ecroyd and Oates Sagar of Colne. Refer to WPL, 334/51, Gillows Ledger 1769–75; 334/52, Gillows Ledger 1776–80; 334/53, Gillows Ledger 1781–90.

54 WYCRO, Leeds, TA Box 22/1 (17 May *c*.1731), S. Gossip, York, to W. Gossip, London. Elizabeth Parker purchased a chaise in the 1750s, but rode on horseback on occasion. She kept up the chaise as Mrs Shackleton, but was mortified when it was vandalized and by its increasingly dilapidated state 'a most unsafe shabby affair'. The Ramsdens of Charterhouse made do with a hired post-chaise for holidays in the 1760s and 1770s; Tom Parker bespoke a new dark green chaise with a crest in 1778, but he and his new wife also rode together. Of Mrs Shackleton's rich gentry friends, the Listers had a landau in London in the 1740s, the Waltons maintained a coach and four in the 1770s, as did the Starkies of Huntroyde. The Claytons of Carr and the sophisticated Parkers of Newton each bought a fashionable new coach in 1779. The wealthy London merchants, the Wilkinsons of Maize Hill, kept 'a handsome carriage'. A clear

signal about the significance of a carriage was sent by the Gossips of Thorp Arch – William Gossip purchased a post-chaise and hired a postilion-cum-groom when he was made Deputy Lieutenant for the West Riding in 1757. The unfortunate status of older single women is exemplified by the arrangements of a Miss Frith and Sarah Tatham in the Dawson–Greene network. In 1819 they kept a chaise at a local inn and borrowed a neighbour's pony to pull it when they wanted to go out; this being much a cheaper option than supporting a donkey, as they could afford neither the pasture nor the necessary manservant. Jane Austen, who kept a donkey carriage and two donkeys at Chawton, was attentive in her fiction to the inconveniences that the careful ranks faced. In Haywood, *Betsy Thoughtless*, p. 433, the heroine was chagrined that her Mr Munden claimed that his estate would not permit him to keep a carriage, and expostulated 'can you imagine I will ever marry to trudge on foot?' On the different types of carriage, see D. J. M. Smith, *A Dictionary of Horse-Drawn Vehicles* (1988), and on their use R. Strauss, *Carriages and Coaches: Their History and Their Evolution* (1912), pp. 147–75. For a case study demonstrating the potential social impact of carriage use, see Whayman, 'Modes of Sociability' (Ph.D. thesis), pp. 276–324.

55 LRO, DDB/81/35 (1779), f. 279. On Miss Dawson and the Methodists, see fos. 96, 177.
56 B. van Muyden (ed.), *Foreign View of England in the Reigns of George I and George II: The Letters of Monsieur Cesar De Saussure to his Family* (1902), pp. 215–16.
57 Wilson, *Gentlemen Merchants*, pp. 213, 215.
58 Smail, *Origins of Middle-Class Culture*, p. 200.
59 Henstock, 'Diary of Abigail Gawthern', p. 1.
60 Fiske, *The Oakes Diaries*, I, pp. 191–200.
61 Wilson, 'Towards an Economic History of Country House Building' (seminar paper).
62 A. Everitt, 'Social Mobility in Early Modern England', *P&P*, 33 (1966), pp. 67–8.
63 Rogers, 'Big Bourgeoisie', p. 453.
64 Raven, 'Image of Business' (Ph.D thesis); see esp. the case study of Mrs Gomershull of Leeds, pp. 281–317.
65 B. Harris, 'American Idols: Empire, War and the Middling Ranks in Mid-Eighteenth-Century Britain', *P&P*, 150 (1996), p. 140.
66 Tucker, *Instructions for Travellers*, p. 26; Joyce, *Work, Society and Politics*, pp. 1–50.
67 Haywood, *Female Spectator* (1745), I, bk 5, pp. 298, 269–70.
68 *Court of Adultery*, p. 24; LRO, DDB/81/36 (1780), unfol., see entry for 21 April 1780.
69 LRO, DDB Ac 7886/24 (n.d.), A. Parker, Royle, to Mrs Shackleton, Alkincoats, and LRO, DDB Ac 7886/280 (9 Jan. 1749), F. Walker, Whitley, to E. Parker, Browsholme.
70 LRO, DDB/81/7 (1768), f. 103.
71 WYCRO, Bradford, Sp St/5/2/5a (4 Oct. 1782), W. Stanhope, Brownberries, to W. Spencer Stanhope, Hull.
72 LRO, DDB/72/446 (13 Sept. 1755), A. Pellet, London, to E. Parker, Alkincoats. Ann Pellet also affirmed 'she wo'd not have a Great estate co'd it be purchased at so easie a rate as a wish since it is attended with nothing but vanity and vexation': LRO, DDB/72/77 (7 Nov. 1753), A. Pellet, London, to E. Parker, Alkincoats.

2 Love and Duty

1 WYCRO, Bradford, Sp St/6/1/99 (29 Nov. 1766), B. Atkinson, Horsforth, to J. Stanhope Esq.; LRO, DDB/72/188 (30 Sept. 1765), B. Ramsden, Charterhouse, to E. Shackleton, Alkincoats.
2 WYCRO, Bradford, Sp St 6/1/50 (8 Nov. 1742), M. Warde, Great Cressingham, to M. Warde, Hooton Pagnell; WYCRO, Bradford, Sp St 6/1/50 (16 April 1745), M. Warde, Saville Street, to M. Stanhope.

3   LRO, DDB Ac 7886/314 (3 Dec. 1749), J. Pellet, Pontefract, to E. Parker, Browsholme; and LRO, DDB Ac 7886/313 (2 Dec. 1749), A. Pellet, Ealing, to E. Parker, Browsholme.

4   CRO, Carlisle, D/Ken. 3/56/1 (c.1801), Conduct letter written by E. Kennedy. Kennedy's husband Daniel was a substantial landowner, who owned property in Ayrshire. He became Deputy-Lieutenant for Cumberland in 1810 and JP for the county in 1816.

5   The classic statement on the triumph of romance is Stone, *Family, Sex and Marriage*. According to Stone's schema, the early modern period witnessed the establishment of three successive family types: the late medieval 'open lineage family'; from 1530 the 'restricted patriarchal nuclear family'; and from 1640 the closed, domesticated nuclear family', a progression apparently caused by the decline of patriarchy and the rise of affective individualism. A more focused, but similar case, is offered by Trumbach, *Rise of the Egalitarian Family*. For surging sentiment across the Atlantic, consult Blake Smith, *Inside the Great House*. While a storm of criticism greeted Stone's argument from the outset (see E. P. Thompson, 'Happy Families', *New Society*, 41 (1977), pp. 499–501, and A. Macfarlane, in *History and Theory*, 18 (1979), pp. 103–26), substantive debate has been taken up by scholars of the sixteenth and seventeenth centuries, focusing on the creation and character of the so-called 'patriarchal family': Wrightson, *English Society*, pp. 66–88, and Houlbrooke, *English Family*, pp. 63–95. Nevertheless, Stone's case has had its supporters, notably Slater on the arranged mercenary marriages and chilly relations of the upper-gentry Verneys of Claydon House: Slater, 'The Weightiest Business', pp. 25–54; id., *Verneys of Claydon House*. Yet this too has been questioned. See S. Mendelson, 'Debate', *P&P*, 85 (1979), pp. 126–35, and latterly V. Larminie, *Wealth, Kinship and Culture: The Seventeenth-Century Newdigates of Arbury and their World* (Woodbridge, 1995). However for all the seventeenth-century critiques, Stone's eighteenth-century story has rarely been contested. Indeed, Stone has recently reaffirmed the rise of affective individualism in his widely read *Uncertain Unions*, *Road to Divorce*, and *Broken Lives*.

6   On decision-making, see Houlbrooke, *English Family*, pp. 73–8, and id., *English Family Life*, pp. 15–51. On self-conscious romantic culture in Stuart London, see Mendelson, 'Debate' (see n. 5 above), pp. 128–33. The symptoms of languishing lovers are recounted in Gowing, *Domestic Dangers*, pp. 174–7 and MacDonald, *Mystical Bedlam*, pp. 88–98.

7   For a wide-ranging review, see Childs, 'Prescriptions for Manners' (D.Phil. thesis), pp. 283–7. A shift from explicit misogyny to apparent veneration is identified in a miscellaneous assemblage of conduct literature and novels by M. Legates, 'Cult of Womanhood'. Margaret Hunt also argues that interest in women's moral influence was increasing over the eighteenth century, 'English Urban Families in Trade' (Ph.D thesis), pp. 240–55, but sees in this the triumph of Puritan-bourgeois expectations.

8   G. Colman and D. Garrick, *The Clandestine Marriage* (1766), I, ii.

9   Cited in Cannon, *Aristocratic Century*, p. 90. Nor did wealth and rank lose their allure. See Lewis, *In the Family Way*, pp. 17–56.

10 Pollock, 'An Action Like Stratagem', p. 492.

11 A tendency in modern social science to divorce the material from the emotional in the history of the family has been roundly criticized by H. Medick and D. Sabean (eds.), *Interest and Emotion: Essays on The Study of Family and Kinship* (Cambridge, 1984), pp. 1–27, and Thompson, 'Happy Families' (see n. 5 above), p. 501.

12 Andrew, 'London Debating Societies', p. 385.

13 J. Austen, *Pride and Prejudice* (1813; Oxford, 1970), p. 137.

14 Goldsmith, *Richard Nash*, pp. 74–5.

15 Recounted in Brophy, *Women's Lives*, p. 118.

16 Haywood, *Betsy Thoughtless*, pp. 104, 287.

17 LRO, DDB/72/485 and 480 (1748–9), Edward Parker, London, to R. Parker, Alkincoats.
18 In the 1720s the Lancastrian Catholic Ralph Standish came to London under orders to procure a wife, but he attended the requisite balls, operas and plays with little grace. When at last he built up an acquaintance with an obliging young lady, Miss Weston, he came to call and strolled in the garden with her and another lady. On finding himself at last alone with his object, he 'used all the art I am muster of without an open declaration', but was put off by 'a forbidding looke': WRO, D/D St C5/8 (2 March 1728), R. Standish Howard, London, to R. Standish, Standish Hall. In the 1740s the Essex manufacturer Ned Parker gallanted his sweetheart, a Miss Holt, to a play in the company of another unmarried woman and visited her two or three times at home before he considered pressing home his advantage: LRO, DDB/72/490 (c.1748), E. Parker, London, to R. Parker, Alkincoats. Almost forty years later, Walter Spencer Stanhope found the opportunity to propose to Mary Pulleine at Ranelagh: Stirling, *Annals of a Yorkshire House*, II, pp. 156–7. In the 1810s William Parker was regularly seen at the Preston balls, but when he proposed to Helen Aspinall he did so by secret letter. Unfortunately the contents were read by the bearer and broadcast across the county. The response 'was a deathblow to any further hope': LRO, DDWh/4/56 (8 May 1814), B. Addison, Liverpool, to E. Whitaker, London.
19 [HN], *Ladies Dictionary*, p. 498.
20 'From a Respectful Letter to his Mistress', in *Complete Letter Writer or Polite English Secretary*, p. 115. See also 'To the Fair Silvia' in *Ladies Miscellany*, p. 1.
21 LRO, DDB/72/1 (28 May 1751), R. Parker, Horrocksford, to E. Parker, Browsholme.
22 LRO, DDB/72/3 (1 June 1751), E. Parker, Browsholme, to R. Parker, Horrocksford.
23 LRO, DDB/72/4 (n.d.), R. Parker, Horrocksford, to E. Parker, Browsholme.
24 LRO, DDB/72/5 (n.d.), E. Parker, Browsholme, to R. Parker, Horrocksford. This must have been a significant admission, since Elizabeth retained a rough copy of her note.
25 LRO, DDB/72/82 (27 Dec. 1753), A. Pellet, London, to E. Parker, Alkincoats.
26 LRO, DDB/72/6 (9 June 1751), R. Parker, Horrocksford, to E. Parker, Browsholme; LRO, DDB Ac 7886/93, 103 and 142 (1746/7), same to same.
27 LRO, DDB/72/14 (3 Aug. 1751), E. Parker, Browsholme, to R. Parker, Alkincoats.
28 LRO, DDB Ac 7886/119 (n.d.), R. Parker, Alkincoats, to E. Parker, Browsholme.
29 Lemmings, 'Hardwicke's Marriage Act', p. 358; and see generally pp. 339–60.
30 Savile, *Lady's New Year's Gift*, p. 28. On the tradition of female petitioning, see Larmine, 'Marriage and the Family', p. 87.
31 *Accomplished Letter-Writer*, p. 123. A similar technique is demonstrated in *New Letter Writer*, pp. 19, 97.
32 Troide, *Early Journals and Letters of Fanny Burney*, II, pp. 146–8; WYCRO, Bradford, Sp St/6/1/99 (29 Nov. 1766), B. Atkinson, Horsforth, to J. Stanhope Esq.
33 LRO, DDB/72/4 (n.d.), R. Parker, Horrocksford, to E. Parker, Browsholme.
34 LRO, DDB Ac 7886/121 (c.1746), R. Parker to E. Parker. For further gloomy ruminations on the 'Misfortune of having a small Fortune' see LRO, DDB Ac 7886/119, 112, 93 (1745–6), R. Parker, Alkincoats, to E. Parker, Browsholme. The objections to Robert Parker on moral grounds are more obscure. He was reputedly involved in the second Jacobite rising, but given the Parkers' Tory sympathies this could even have counted in his favour.
35 Wilkes, *Genteel and Moral Advice to a Young Lady*, pp. 81–2.
36 K. Lystra, *Searching the Heart: Women, Men and Romantic Love in Nineteenth-Century America* (New York, 1989), pp. 157–91; E. K. Rothman, *Hands and Hearts: A History of Courtship in America* (New York, 1984), pp. 56–84.
37 LRO, DDB/72/171 (28 Oct. 1779), A. Pellet, London, to E. Shackleton, Alkincoats.
38 The mean age of marriage for noblewomen in this period was twenty-four years and

nine months: Hollingsworth, 'Demography', p. 11. Unfortunately, there are no demographic studies of the lesser gentry, but across the female population as a whole, the mean age at first marriage between 1750 and 1799 is also thought to be the same: Wrigley and Schofield, *Population History of England*, p. 255. Suffice it to say then that Elizabeth Parker must have been fully conscious of the passage of time.

39 LRO, DDB/72/10 (24 June 1751), E. Parker, Browsholme, to R. Parker, Horrocksford.
40 When financial negotiations surrounding the proposed marriage of Edward Parker to Barbara Fleming ground to a halt, the families were concerned because 'an affair so publick' unjustly tainted Barbara's reputation: LRO, DDB/72/82 (27 Dec. 1753), A. Pellet, London, to E. Parker, Alkincoats.
41 Kelly, *History of Louisa Mildmay*, p. 15.
42 LRO, DDB/72/9 (n.d.), R. Parker, Alkincoats, to E. Parker, Browsholme.
43 LRO, DDB/72/8 (16 June 1751), E. Parker, Browsholme, to R. Parker, Horrocksford.
44 LRO, DDB/72/6 (9 June 1751), R. Parker, to E. Parker, Browsholme.
45 LRO, DDB/72/10 (24 June 1751), E. Parker, Browsholme, to R. Parker.
46 LRO, DDB/72/11 (n.d.), R. Parker, Alkincoats, to E. Parker, Browsholme.
47 Ingrams, *Church Courts*, p. 136. On the long-standing and persistent importance of 'friends', see Tadmor, 'Family and Friend'; Gowing, *Domestic Dangers*, pp. 148-59; and D. O'Hara, '"Ruled by my Friends": Aspects of Marriage in the Diocese of Canterbury, c.1540-c.1570', *Continuity and Change*, 6 (1991), pp. 9-41.
48 LRO, DDB/72/8 (16 June 1751), E. Parker, Browsholme, to R. Parker, Horrocksford; LRO, DDB/72/12 (3 July 1751), E. Parker, Browsholme, to R. Parker, Alkincoats; LRO, DDB/72/23 (n.d.), R. Parker, Alkincoats, to E. Parker, Browsholme. On the weight attached to the opinions of relations, see LRO, DDB Ac 7886/115 (c.1746), E. Parker, Browsholme, to R. Parker, Alkincoats.
49 LRO, DDB/72/17 (13 Aug. 1751), E. Parker, Browsholme, to R. Parker, Alkincoats.
50 LRO, DDB/78/1 (1751), Parker Marriage Settlement.
51 A. P. W. Malcolmson, *The Pursuit of the Heiress: Aristocratic Marriage in Ireland, 1750-1820* (Belfast, 1982), p. 33.
52 LRO, DDB Ac 7886/119 (n.d.), R. Parker, Alkincoats, to E. Parker, Browsholme.
53 Baronet's daughter Elizabeth Moseley tried to preserve her clandestine affair with an unsuitable lawyer, Arthur Collier, at Bath and elsewhere, doing all she could to stave off a decisive confrontation with her parents: Stone, *Uncertain Unions* (see n. 5 above), pp. 68-77. Secretive encouragement in the face of parental opposition was also conveyed by the heiress Elizabeth Jefferys in the 1740s and a Mary Martin in the 1760s: Brophy, *Women's Lives*, pp. 83-5.
54 LRO, DDB Ac 7886/129 (18 Nov. 1746), R. Parker to E. Parker. The sense that courtship was essentially a game is also conveyed in LRO, DDB/72/476 (10 May 1748), E. Parker, London, to R. Parker, Alkincoats: 'It is to be hoped [that] at last some Damsel will take Compassion on us, for [the] very week Miss Plumb was married I had denial at two houses . . .' Haywood's suspicions are relayed in id., *Betsy Thoughtless*, p. 19.
55 *New Letter Writer*, pp. 45-7.
56 LRO, DDB/72/16 (n.d.), R. Parker, Alkincoats, to E. Parker, Browsholme; LRO, DDB Ac 7886/93 and 97 (1745), R. Parker, Alkincoats, to E. Parker, Browsholme.
57 Gibson's courtship correspondence is revealed in Hunt, 'English Urban Families' (Ph.D. thesis), pp. 256-9. However, Hunt attributes this language to a distinctively bourgeois taste for plain dealings, in contrast to upper-class linguistic excess. Non-bourgeois concern to live reasonable, affectionate, but self-possessed married lives is identified in Brown, 'Domesticity, Feminism and Friendship'. Pratt's correspondence is relayed in Brophy, *Women's Lives*, pp. 129-37. Moderation and reliability are also to the fore in the one letter of courtship Stone reproduces in *Road to Divorce*, pp. 59-60, written in 1755 by a Nottinghamshire cleric to his sweetheart's guardian.

Similarly, when the stranger Mr Jones bid for Betty Atkinson's hand in 1766, he too disdained 'employing artifice, or covert address' and stressed that his conduct had never deviated from that of 'the man of honour': WYCRO, Sp St/6/1/99 (c.1766), J. Jones, to J. Stanhope. Eliza Haywood also linked rhetorical restraint with masculine honour: 'Believe me, there is more true felicity in the sincere and tender friendship of one man of honour, than in all the flattering professions of a thousand coxcombs.' See id., *Betsy Thoughtless*, p. 174. For controlled language in the New World, consult Lewis, 'Domestic Tranquillity'.

58 D. F. Bond (ed.), *Spectator* (Oxford, 1965), pp. 197–8. For the love-letter, see G. A. Aitken, *The Life of Richard Steele* (1889), I, p. 174.

59 Wilkes, *Genteel and Moral Advice*, p. 83.

60 LRO, DDB Ac 7886/95 (20 April 1746), R. Parker, Alkincoats, to E. Parker, Browsholme; LRO, DDB Ac 7886/119 (n.d.), R. Parker, Alkincoats, to E. Parker, Browsholme; LRO, DDB Ac 7886/126 (c.1746), R. Parker, Preston, to E. Parker.

61 LRO, DDB Ac 7886/129 (18 Nov. 1746), R. Parker to E. Parker; LRO, DDB Ac 7886/112 (2 Sept. 1746), R. Parker, Alkincoats, to E. Parker, Browsholme. On the arranging of secret assignations, see LRO, DDB Ac 7886/97 (3 May 1745), R. Parker, Alkincoats, to E. Parker, Browsholme; LRO, DDB Ac 7886/122 (c.1746), R. Parker to E. Parker.

62 LRO, DDB Ac 7886/101 (1 July 1746), R. Parker, Alkincoats, to E. Parker, Browsholme.

63 *Ladies Dictionary*, p. 505; Myers, *Bluestocking Circle*, p. 92; *Gentleman's Magazine* (1738), VIII, p. 86.

64 Savile, *Advice to a Daughter*, p. 26.

65 On the reciprocal duties of man and wife, see Wrightson, *English Society*, pp. 90–92, and Houlbrooke, *English Family, 1450–1700*, pp. 96–8. Even Filmer, upon a wider reading, has proved much less 'patriarchal' than was previously thought: Ezell, *Patriarch's Wife*, pp. 129–44. According to Lawrence Stone, this prescriptive mutuality was novel and distinctively Puritan, giving rise to a new companionate ethos within marriage, discernible from 1660–1700. However, scholars of Christian prescription contend that Puritan conduct literature represents an amplification of, not a break with, pre-Reformation advice to the laity: Todd, 'Humanists, Puritans and the Spiritualized Household'; Davies, 'Continuity and Change', pp. 58–78. On the personal inexperience of the writers of Elizabethan prescriptive literature, see Wall, 'Elizabethan Precept and Feminine Practice'.

66 Larminie, 'Marriage and the Family'.

67 Wrightson, *English Society*, p. 92.

68 D. Defoe, *Conjugal Lewdness, &c* (1727), p. 25.

69 Harrison, 'Thorp Arch Hall'.

70 WYCRO, Leeds, TA 18/5 (30 Oct. 1746), W. Gossip, London, to A. Gossip, Skelton; TA 18/5 (16 Oct. 1746), same to same; TA 18/5 (25 April 1734), W. Gossip, Ware to A. Gossip, Ogleforth; TA 18/5 (8 Aug. 1746), W. Gossip, Skelton, to A. Gossip, Ripon; TA 18/5 (12 Dec. 1757), W. Gossip, Askam, to A. Gossip, Thorp Arch.

71 See respectively WYCRO, Leeds, TA 13/2 (n.d.), A. Gossip to W. Gossip; TA 18/5 (14 Oct. 1746), W. Gossip, Braintree, to A. Gossip, Skelton; TA 13/2 ('Tuesday'), A. Gossip to W. Gossip; TA 13/2 (2 Nov. n.y.), A. Gossip to W. Gossip; TA 18/5 (23 Oct. 1746), W. Gossip, London, to A. Gossip, Skelton; TA 18/5 (20 Oct. 1746), same to same.

72 WYCRO, Leeds, TA 18/5 (11 Aug. 1746), W. Gossip, Skelton, to A. Gossip, Ripon.

73 WYCRO, Leeds, TA 15/11/9 (25 Sept. 1763), W. Gossip's Will.

74 See H. Owen, *Stanhope, Atkinson, Haddon and Shaw: Four North Country Families* (1985), p. 70; R. G. Wilson, 'Three Brothers: A Study of the Fortunes of a Landed Family in the Mid-Eighteenth Century', *Bradford Textile Society Journal* (1964–5), pp. 111–21.

75 WYCRO, Bradford, Sp St/6/1/68 (13 June 1757), W. Stanhope, Birmingham, to A. Stanhope, Leeds; Sp St/6/1/75 (20 Aug. 1757), W. Stanhope, Leeds, to A. Stanhope, Sewerby; Sp St/6/1/57 (26 July 1757), A. Stanhope, Leeds, to W. Stanhope, Bath.

76 WYCRO, Bradford, Sp St/6/1/70 (11 June 1757), W. Stanhope, Derby, to A. Stanhope, Leeds; Sp St/6/1/69 (15 June 1757), A. Stanhope, Leeds, to W. Stanhope, Bath.

77 WYCRO, Bradford, Sp St/6/1/42 (1 Feb. 1726), B. Stanhope to J. Stanhope, Grays Inn. A similar note of apologetic submissiveness was sounded by two upper-gentry wives on early eighteenth-century Tyneside, though not all local ladies proved so timid: Levine and Wrightson, *Making of an Industrial Society*, pp. 314–18.

78 See respectively LRO, DDB/72/25, 34 (n.d.), R. Parker, Alkincoats and Trawden, to E. Parker, Browsholme; LRO, DDB/72/19, 29, 31, 36 (1751), E. Parker, Browsholme, to R. Parker, Alkincoats.

79 LRO, DDB/72/236, 75, 240, 298 (1770), W. and B. Ramsden, Charterhouse, to E. Shackleton, Alkincoats.

80 LRO, DDB/72/208, 236, 198, 220 (1767–70), W. Ramsden, Highgate and Charterhouse, to E. Shackleton, Alkincoats.

81 LRO, DDB/72/297 (n.d.), B. Ramsden, Charterhouse, to E. Shackleton, Alkincoats.

82 LRO, DDWh/4/27–9 (Aug. 1813), E. Whitaker, Edgeworth, to C. Whitaker, Roefield.

83 LRO, DDWh/4/31, 32 (Aug. 1813), C. Whitaker, Roefield, to E. Whitaker, Edgeworth.

84 Coburn, *Letters of Sara Hutchinson*, p. 346.

85 Bond, *Tatler*, II, p. 299.

86 *Ladies Dictionary*, p. 96.

87 LRO, DDB/72/173 (12 March 1762), B. Ramsden, Charterhouse, to E. Parker, Alkincoats.

88 LPL, MS 8753 (1778), f. 84; LPL, MS 8754 (1779), 16 Feb., 21 March. The impact of literary models on personal expression is also explored in Darnton, 'Readers Respond to Rousseau'.

89 M. Butler, *Jane Austen and the War of Ideas* (Oxford, 1975), p. 88.

90 *Ladies Dictionary*, p. 505.

91 Wilkes, *Genteel Advice*, p. 88; Coventry, *History of Pompey the Little*, pp. 23–4.

92 Ingrams, *Church Courts*, pp. 145–50, 171–188; Stone, *Broken Lives* (see n. 5 above); Hunt, 'Wife Beating'; Amussen, 'Being Stir'd to Much Unquietness'; Gowing, *Domestic Dangers*, pp. 180–231.

93 It remains unclear whether it was John Shackleton's immaturity or inferior circumstances which principally prompted Edward Parker's 'cold behaviour'. Either way, Mrs Shackleton was deeply hurt by her brother's behaviour. To Bessy Ramsden she had claimed his approbation was 'necessary to restore sunshine'. Bessy Ramsden tried to offer comfort when it became clear that 'friends' did not approve the choice: 'if Mr Shackleton's Circumstances were not equal to his merit the more Her [praise] who could be influenced by motives so different from the Sordid ones of a Selfish and ill-natured World': LRO, DDB/72/188 (30 Sept. 1765), B. Ramsden, Charterhouse, to E. Shackleton, Alkincoats. Who Elizabeth found to represent her interests in the drawing up of the marriage settlement is unclear. Although this document is mentioned in the diaries, it has not survived.

94 See respectively, LRO, DDB/81/13 (1771), fos. 62, 64; LRO, DDB/81/17 (1772), f. 75; LRO, DDB/81/20 (1773), f. 92; LRO, DDB/81/20 (1773), f. 4; LRO, DDB/81/29 (1776), f. 50; LRO, DDB/81/33A (1778), f. 60; and LRO, DDB/81/37 (1780), fos. 17 and 3.

95 LRO, DDB/81/17 (1772), fos. 15, 68; LRO, DDB/81/20 (1773), f. 97; LRO, DDB/81/31 (1777), f. 22; LRO, DDB/81/39 (1781), f. 204.

96 LRO, DDB/81/34 (1779), fos. 73–4; LRO, DDB/81/35 (1779), f. 279; LRO, DDB/81/20 (1773), f. 65; LRO, DDB/81/19 (1773), f. 74: 'We dined at Marsden. Made our Disturbances known to the family there.'

97   LRO, DDB/81/20 (1773), f. 38: 'C:S: dined here Reproved his son for Drinking. Who sets the bad example[?]'
98   See respectively, LRO, DDB/81/37 (1780), f. 203; LRO, DDB/81/39 (1781), fos. 13 and 231.
99   Hall, *Miss Weeton's Journal*, II, p. 134.
100 Ibid., p. 154. On disloyal and suborned servants, see pp. 141 and 153. For Bessy Price's counsel see, p. 145. On Aaron Stock's preceding behaviour and the hard-won truce, see p. 146.
101 Ibid., p. 159.
102 The deed itself has not survived. For her view of the document, see ibid., II, pp. 184–5.
103 See ibid., I, p. 3. For cross-reference to the local sessions rolls, consult ibid., II, pp. 178–9. For earlier official corroboration of Stock's violent temper, see also p. 140. On her 'daily proofs' of wifely dedication, see ibid, II, pp. 137 and 135.
104 Ibid., I, pp. 303, 239, 223, 277, 259–60.
105 Ibid., II, pp. 159, 141, 154, and 146.
106 Ibid., II, pp. 161 and 159.
107 Ibid., II, p. 161.
108 Ibid.
109 Ibid., II, pp. 184 and 180.
110 Hunt, 'Wife Beating', p. 19. Compare Hall, *Miss Weeton's Journal*, II, p. 140, and CRO, EDC 5, Consistory Court Papers, 1744–1809, especially the Calkin, Davenport, Hamilton, Nevett, Mainwaring and Green cases. I am indebted to Tim Wales for telling me about this material.
111 These are the stock phrases used to describe the brides whose weddings are reported in local papers. See for example, 'Extracts from the Leeds Intelligencer, 1763–1767', *Thoresby Society Publications*, 33 (1935), p. 186, and G. D. Lumb (ed.), 'Extracts from the Leeds Intelligencer and the Leeds Mercury, 1769–1776', *Thoresby Society Publications*, 38 (1938), p. 68.
112 Austen, *Sense and Sensibility*, pp. 78–9.
113 Haywood, *Betsy Thoughtless*, pp. 78, 247.
114 Wollstonecraft, *Vindication*, p. 121; Haywood, *Betsy Thoughtless*, p. 256.
115 *Gentleman's Magazine* (1738), VIII, p. 86.
116 HL, HM 31201, Mrs Larpent's Diary, III, 1799–1800, facing f. 196.
117 LRO, DDB/72/98 (Nov. 1754), A. Pellet, London, to E. Parker, Alkincoats.
118 'Woman's Fate, by a Lady', from the frontispiece of one of Elizabeth Shackleton's pocket diaries, LRO, DDB/81/36 (1780), f. 5; a republication of the anonymous poem 'Woman's Hard Fate' of 1733, retrieved by R. Lonsdale (ed.), *Eighteenth-Century Women Poets* (Oxford, 1990), p. 136.
119 See Thompson, 'Patrician Society, Plebeian Culture', p. 399.
120 LRO, DDB/72/152 (14 Oct. *c*.1756), J. Scrimshire, Pontefract, to E. Parker, Alkincoats; LRO, DDB/72/297 (n.d.), B. Ramdsen, Charterhouse, to same.
121 LRO, DDB Ac 7886/24 (n.d.), A. Parker, Royle, to Mrs Shackleton; LRO, DDB Ac 7886/22 (n.d.), A. Parker, Royle to Mrs Shackleton.
122 *The Scots Magazine* (1765), XXVII, p. 393; J.-J. Rousseau, *Emile, Or On Education* (1762; Harmondsworth, 1991), p. 408; Home, *Loose Hints*, pp. 229–30.
123 Halsband and Grundy, *Lady Mary Wortley Montagu: Essays and Poems*, p. 109.
124 The Montagu incident is related in Myers, *Bluestocking Circle*, p. 139. For another example of the use of 'overcompliance rather than remonstrance', see Brophy, *Women's Lives*, p. 91.
125 Hall, *Miss Weeton's Journal*, II, pp. 145–6.
126 LRO, DDB/72/298 (n.d.), W. Ramsden, Charterhouse, to E. Shackleton, Alkincoats; LRO, DDB/72/271 (n.d.), B. Ramsden, Charterhouse, to same.

127 LRO, DDB/72/139 (n.d.), J. Scrimshire, Pontefract, to E. Shackleton, Alkincoats.
128 Wrightson, *English Society*, p. 104; Hammerton, *Cruelty and Companionship*, pp. 100, 137.
129 Richardson, *Sir Charles Grandison*, pp. 400–01.

3   Fortitude and Resignation

1   LRO, DDB/72/50 (n.d.), R. Parker, Browsholme, to E. Parker, Alkincoats.
2   LRO, DDB/72/49 (n.d.), R. Parker, Browsholme, to E. Parker, Alkincoats. Popular medical theory held that foetal deformity represented the wages of sin, or the consequences of maternal imagination, see Blondel, *Power of the Mother's Imagination*. Twenty-five years later, the family still believed that maternal shock could deform a baby. Elizabeth Shackleton was relieved that her grandson was born without a 'mark [or] spot upon him', after her daughter-in-law had been frightened by a pet monkey: LRO, DDB Ac 7886/47 (*c.*1779), E. Shackleton, Pasture to B. Parker, Newton.
3   LRO, DDB/72/87 (21 March 1754), A. Pellet, London, to E. Parker, Alkincoats.
4   LRO, DDB/72/129 (28 March ?1754), J. Scrimshire, Pontefract, to E. Parker, Alkincoats.
5   LRO, DDB/72/88 (7 April 1754), A. Pellet, London, to E. Parker, Alkincoats; LRO, DDB/72/54 (25 April 1754), A. Pellet, London, to R. Parker, Alkincoats.
6   The rallying of the women is related in LRO, DDWh/4/130 (n.d.), M. Whitehead, London, to S. Horrocks, Preston; LRO, DDWh/4/42 (4 March 1814), S. Greaves, London, to E. Whitaker, Roefield; and LRO, DDWh/4/43 (10 March 1814), S. Horrocks, London, to same.
7   LRO, DDWh/4/132 (n.d.), A. E. Robbins, London, to S. Horrocks, Preston.
8   LRO, DDWh/4/41 (2 March 1814), J. and J. Horrocks, Edgeworth, to E. Whitaker, Roefield.
9   LRO, DDWh/4/49 and 64 (March–May 1814), B. Addison, Liverpool, to E. Whitaker, Roefield.
10 LRO, DDWh/4/59 (11 May 1814), C. Whitaker, Edinburgh, to E. Whitaker, Roefield.
11 LRO, DDWh/4/130 (n.d.), M. Whitehead, London, to S. Horrocks, Preston; LRO, DDWh/4/56 (8 May 1814), B. Addison, Liverpool, to E. Whitaker; LRO, DDWh/4/69 (6 June 1814), M. Whitehead, London, to same.
12 LRO, DDWh/4/117 (n.d.), A. E. Robbins, London, to S. Horrocks and E. Whitaker, Roefield.
13 Whether or not pregnancy was a period of special authority as well as vulnerability, as has been argued for early modern Germany, is less easy to determine. For this view, see U. Rublack, 'Pregnancy, Childbirth and the Female Body in Early Modern Germany', *P&P*, 150 (1996), pp. 84–110.
14 Stone, *Practice of Midwifery*, pp. xiv–xv.
15 See CRO, EDC 5 (1800–9), Lees v. Lees.
16 Read Ariès, *Centuries of Childhood*. Similar visions of a pre-modern nightmare are reproduced in De Mause (ed.), *History of Childhood*; Shorter, *Making of the Modern Family*, and Stone, *Family, Sex and Marriage*, pp. 113–27, 254–99.
17 For an exhaustive critique of the Ariès thesis using personal manuscripts, see Pollock, *Forgotten Children*. Wrightson had earlier rejected massive shifts in his *English Society*, pp. 108–18, as Houlbrooke did subsequently in *English Family, 1450–1700*, pp. 127–65. The testimony of kind and loving parents stands revealed in Houlbrooke, *English Family Life, 1576–1716*, pp. 101–97, and Macfarlane, *Ralph Josselin*, pp. 111–25. The methodological weaknesses of the Ariès case, in particular the crude inference

of modern meanings from past patterns of behaviour, are exposed in Wilson, 'Myth of Motherhood'.

18 See Plumb, 'The New World of Children'.

19 Pollock attempts to counter precisely these criticisms of her first book and thereby offer a revised agenda for the history of childhood in the introduction to her anthology, *Lasting Relationship*, pp. 12–13.

20 To this end, some feminists have embraced the unreconstructed Ariès thesis. In some eyes maternal instinct is an ideological device generated in recent centuries to keep modern women down. For a popular account, see Badinter, *Myth of Motherhood*.

21 Bloch, 'Ideals in Transition'; Davidoff and Hall, *Family Fortunes*, pp. 335–43.

22 Perry, 'Colonizing the Breast'.

23 Laqueur, *Making Sex*, pp. 149–54.

24 Fletcher, *Gender, Sex and Subordination*, p. 400.

25 Crawford, 'Construction and Experience of Maternity', pp. 13, 11–12, 28–9.

26 See the sceptical Roper, *Oedipus and the Devil*, pp. 16–18.

27 Childs, 'Prescriptions for Manners' (Ph.D. thesis), pp. 285–7.

28 Richardson, *Sir Charles Grandison*, p. 403.

29 See respectively Astell, *Serious Proposal to the Ladies*, p. 97; LRO, DDB/72/61 (22 March 1756), J. Scrimshire, Pontefract, to R. Parker, Alkincoats; and Crouch, 'Attitudes Toward Actresses' (D.Phil. thesis 1995).

30 A. Wilson, 'The Ceremony of Childbirth and its Interpretation', in Fildes, *Women as Mothers*, pp. 68–107. Wilson himself traces this interpretation to Davis, 'Women on Top'.

31 Eccles, *Obstetrics and Gynaecology*; Donnison, *Midwives and Medical Men*; Schnorrenberg, 'Is Childbirth Any Place for a Woman?'; Versluyen, 'Midwives, Medical Men and "Poor Women"'.

32 Widespread acceptance of this view is a testimony to the influence of Foucault's theories about knowledge and power on the social history of medicine, in particular his vision of the way professions construct and legitimize themselves by delegitimizing the knowledge of others. For chapter and verse, see M. Foucault, *The Birth of the Clinic: An Archaeology of Medical Perception* (New York, 1975).

33 A flavour of the debate can be tasted in D. N. Harley, 'Ignorant Midwives – a Persistent Stereotype', *Bulletin of the Society of the Social History of Medicine*, 28 (1981), pp. 6–9; A. Wilson, 'Ignorant Midwives, a Rejoinder', ibid, 32 (1983), pp. 46–9; B. and J. Boss, 'Ignorant Midwives: a Further Rejoinder', ibid, 33 (1983), p. 71.

34 Porter, 'Touch of Danger'.

35 Wilson, *Making of Man-Midwifery*, p. 192.

36 Lewis, *Family Way*, pp. 128, 151. Porter also stresses the doctor's role as ambivalent ally in matters clandestine, see his 'Touch of Danger', p. 224.

37 Wilson, 'Participant or Patient?' Exactly how this story of conflict marries with Wilson's later vision of collective solidarity at the bedside is unclear. See above p. 94.

38 Twelve parish reconstitutions suggest that between 1700 and 1749 the English family had on average 6.77 live-born children, and 6.92 children between 1750 and 1799: Wrigley and Schofield, *Population History*, p. 254. Gentry families probably bore fewer children, at least that was the case for the peerage. Noblewomen born before 1750 produced on average 4.51 children, those born between 1750 and 1774 had 4.91; those born 1775–99 had 4.98; and those born 1800–24 had 4.64: Hollingsworth, 'Demography of the British Peerage', p. 30. Infertility was usually blamed on a 'barren' wife. Amongst the genteel families studied here, Barbara Stanhope failed to conceive, which probably accounts for her trips to Scarborough to take the waters in the 1730s and 1740s. Unusually, the Parkers of Farmhill adopted a child in 1777. For female anxiety on this score, see Crawford, 'Construction and Experience of Maternity', p. 19, and id., 'Attitudes to Pregnancy'.

39 LRO, DDWh/4/28 (14 Aug. 1814), E. Whitaker, Edgeworth, to C. Whitaker, Roefield.
40 LRO, DDWh/4/124 (10 Nov. n.y.), B. Addison, Liverpool, to E. Whitaker, Roefield.
41 LRO, DDB Ac 7886/263 (8 Jan. 1749), J. Pellet, Pontefract, to E. Parker, Browsholme. Deaths in childbed are also noted in Henstock, 'Diary of Abigail Gawthern', pp. 49, 100 and 122.
42 R. Schofield, 'Did the Mothers Really Die?' Comparable estimates of maternal mortality drawn from early eighteenth-century Halifax are offered in Wilson, 'Perils of Early Modern Procreation'.
43 L. A. Pollock, 'Embarking on a Rough Passage: The Experience of Pregnancy in Early Modern Society', in Fildes, Women as Mothers, p. 47.
44 LRO, DDB/72/123 and 150 (1753), J. Scrimshire, Pontefract, to E. Parker, Alkincoats. For earlier examples, see Crawford, 'Construction and Experience of Maternity', p. 22; Pollock, 'Experience of Pregnancy' (see n. 43 above), pp. 47–9; Macfarlane, Ralph Josselin, p. 84; Mendelson, 'Stuart Women's Diaries', p. 196; and Laurence, Women in England, pp. 76–9.
45 CRO, Carlisle, D/KEN. 3/56/1 (c.1801), conduct letter written by E. Kennedy. Noble women frequently had new wills prepared and occasionally penned farewell letters to their husbands: Lewis, In the Family Way, pp. 74–5.
46 LRO, DDB/72/144 (19 Feb 1756), J. Scrimshire, Pontefract, to E. Parker, Alkincoats.
47 Side effects are discussed in LRO, DDB/72/142 (8 Dec. n.y.), J. Scrimshire, Pontefract, to E. Parker, Alkincoats and LRO, DDB/72/86 (21 March 1754), A. Pellet, London, to same; LRO, DDWh/4/113 (n.d.), Dr W. St Clare, to E. Whitaker, Roefield.
48 LRO, DDB/72/86 (21 March 1754), A. Pellet, London, to E. Parker, Alkincoats; LRO, DDB Ac 7886/78 (12 March 1754), J. Parker, Browsholme, to E. Parker, Alkincoats.
49 LRO, DDB/72/447 (13 Oct. 1755), J. Scrimshire, Pontefract, to E. Parker, Alkincoats.
50 LRO, DDWh/4/72 (31 June 1814), B. Addison, Liverpool, to E. Whitaker, Roefield.
51 See respectively LRO, DDB/72/158 (4 June n.y.), J. Scrimshire, Pontefract, to E. Parker, Alkincoats; LRO, DDB/72/1497 (23 March 1800), D. Ridsdale, Leeds, to E. Barcroft; LRO, DDWh/4/89 (29 Oct. 1816), B. Addison, Liverpool, to E. Whitaker, Roefield.
52 LRO, DDB/72/210 (11 Nov. 1767), B. Ramsden, Charterhouse, to E. Shackleton, Alkincoats. Monstrously bellied women appealed to William Ramsden's sense of the absurd. He thought that the overdue Mrs Jones of Snowhill resembled in both shape and size 'one of her husband's brandy butts', and mused aloud on whether Bessy's 'prominence' was a real 'Impediment': LRO, DDB/72/186 and 211 (n.d.), W. Ramsden, Charterhouse, to same.
53 The treatment Whitaker received from Dr William St Clare represented a variant of the lowering system aimed at calming a plethoric constitution, a 'habit' routinely associated with pregnancy. This 'excitement or irritability of [her] nervous system' was alleviated by early rising and moderate exercise, taking care on staircases and not to overheat. A dietary regime was thought unnecessary, but St Clare prescribed laxatives to avoid constipation. At the onset of pain or uneasiness, Mrs Whitaker was to lie down on the couch or bed, regularly shifting posture. When she felt intimations of miscarriage, he advised laudanum. Details are found in LRO, DDWh/4/92, 95, 102, 108, 111 (1816–21), Dr W. St Clare, Preston, to E. Whitaker, Roefield. Noble pregnancies received similar treatments, Lewis, In the Family Way, pp. 129–35. The contemporary view of pregnancy as a period of physiological imbalance is summarized in Peters, 'The Pregnant Pamela'.
54 For the quotations see repectively LRO, DDB/72/446 (13 Sept. 1755), A. Pellet, London, to E. Parker, Alkincoats; LRO, DDGr C3 (n.d.), M. Greene to Mrs Bradley, Slyne, Lancaster; LRO, DDB/81/35 (1779), f. 95. On the general acceptance of maternal indisposition, see Pollock, 'Experience of Pregnancy' (see n. 43 above), pp. 46–7 and Lewis, In the Family Way, p. 149.

55 Anne Stanhope sent for her sister in 1749, when her due date loomed. Similarly, in 1769 the unmarried Bridget Downes went to stay with her pregnant sister in Manchester and felt she could not leave for some months. Lady Egerton was reported returning to Heaton House for her confinement. Betty Parker chose to return to her mother's house in Newton for the births of at least two of her children in the 1780s. Eliza Whitaker was delivered of her first son at her old home in Preston. On the peerage, see Trumbach, *Rise of the Egalitarian Family*, p. 183, and Lewis, *In the Family Way*, pp. 159–62.

56 LRO, DDB/72/210 (11 Nov. 1767), B. Ramsden, Charterhouse, to E. Shackleton, Alkincoats.

57 The call to a male practitioner could be made in advance of the birth, at the onset of labour and in the event of emergency. The man-midwife might have seconded the efforts of a female midwife or replaced her altogether. Bookings could be made for all three calls: Wilson, 'William Hunter'.

58 LRO, DDB/72/144 (19 Feb. 1756), J. Scrimshire, Pontefract, to E. Parker, Alkincoats; LRO, DDB/72/445 (2 Jan. 1756), J. Scrimshire, Pontefract, to E. Parker, Alkincoats.

59 Wilson, *Making of Man-Midwifery*, p. 176.

60 Refer to LRO, DDB/72/82, 85, 86, 105, 118 (1753–6), A. Pellet, London, to E. Parker, Alkincoats.

61 LRO, DDB/72/146 (15 May 1756), J. Scrimshire, Pontefract, to E. Parker, Alkincoats; LRO, DDB/72/176 (3 April 1764), B. Ramsden, Charterhouse, to E. Shackleton, Alkincoats. There are a few Stuart narratives of birth: Mendelson, 'Stuart Women's Diaries', pp. 196–7. More modern reports can be read in Pollock, *Lasting Relationship*, pp. 34–8.

62 WYCRO, Leeds, TA 3/32, William Gossip's Memorandum Book, f. 113.

63 LRO, DDGr C3 (30 June 1821), M. Greene, Bedford Square, London, to Mrs Bradley, Slyne.

64 LRO, DDB/81/37 (1780), f. 33.

65 On Bessy's month, see LRO, DDB/72/214 (12 April 1768), B. Ramsden, Charterhouse, to E. Shackleton, Alkincoats. The postponement of breast-feeding until three or four days after birth is discussed in Fildes, *Breasts, Bottles and Babies*, p. 91, and deplored in Nelson, *Essay on the Government of Childen*, p. 47. For an example of a post-natal remedy, see WYCRO, Bradford Sp St 6/1/50 (12 April 1745), C. Sellwood, Billam, to Mrs Stanhope: '[This] Recpt I am going to write I had from Lady Northampton, she had it from [Dr] Rattclif. I never knew it fail in a Looseness wheather in a Lying In or at any other time . . .'

66 It is possible that the desire for a son an heir was so widely felt as to need no mention. Seventeenth-century gentlewomen expressed guilt when they failed to produce boys for the lineage, although girls could still be welcomed as proof of fertility: Crawford, 'Construction and Experience of Maternity', pp. 19–20, and Pollock, 'Experience of Pregnancy', pp. 39–40. However, a growing appreciation of daughters for their own sake amongst the eighteenth-century nobility is remarked by Lewis, *In the Family Way*, pp. 65–6.

67 LRO, DDB/72/90 (16 May 1754), A. Pellet, London, to E. Parker, Alkincoats.

68 LRO, DDB/72/234 (28 April 1770), W. Ramsden, Charterhouse, to E. Shackleton, Alkincoats.

69 For the traditional sequence, see Wilson, 'Ceremony of Childbirth', pp. 75–6. Highly ritualized confinements of four to six weeks were still common among the later eighteenth-century nobility: Lewis, *In the Family Way*, pp. 193–201. It therefore seems likely that genteel women observed at least a modified lying-in. Certainly, Mrs Betty Parker of Alkincoats was expected to spend a period of her recovery 'upstairs', see LRO, DDB Ac 7886/47 (n.d.), E. Shackleton, Pasture, to B. Parker, Newton. Interestingly, I have found only one specific reference to churching in the papers of the

genteel. Perhaps the dinner parties given after the christening were the polite equivalent.

70   LRO, DDB/72/62 (20 March 1756), A. Pellet, London, to R. Parker, Alkincoats; LRO, DDB/72/175 (26 Feb. 1763), W. Ramsden, Charterhouse, to E. Parker, Alkincoats.

71   See respectively, LRO, DDB/72/150 (16 Sept. 1756), J. Scrimshire, Pontefract, to E. Parker, Alkincoats; LRO, DDB/72/149 (30 Aug. 1756), same to same; LRO, DDB/72/176 (3 April 1764), B. Ramsden, Charterhouse, to E. Parker, Alkincoats; WYCRO, Bradford, Sp St/6/1/75 (22 Oct. 1769), B. Downes, Manchester, to A. Stanhope, Derfield; LRO, DDWh/4/89 (22 Oct. 1816), B. Addison, Liverpool, to E. Whitaker, Roefield; Hall, *Miss Weeton's Journal*, II, p. 139; LRO, DDB/72/1196 (21 July 1822), E. Parker, Selby, to E. Moon, Colne.

72   Laurence, *Women in England*, p. 80.

73   On the unfortunate Stanhope babies, see WYCRO, Bradford, Sp St/5/2/30 (10 Oct. 1749), W. Stanhope, Leeds, to W. Spencer, Cannon Hall; Sp St/6/1/64 (Feb.–April 1753), same to J. Spencer, Middle Temple, London. Betty Parker's labour difficulties are recounted in LRO, DDB/72/334 (4 Nov. 1783), Wm St Clare (the elder), to T. Parker, Alkincoats. Concern for Anne Robbins is relayed in LRO, DDWh/4/68 (2 June 1814), D. Bowyer, London, to E. Whitaker, Roefield, and LRO, DDWh/4/75 (16 Aug. 1814), S. Horrocks, London, to same.

74   Stone, *Family, Sex and Marriage*, pp. 271–3; Trumbach, *Rise of the Egalitarian Family*, pp. 197–235.

75   While the Duchess of Devonshire's promotion of breast-feeding amongst the fashionable in the 1780s is cited *ad nauseam*, seventeenth-century campaigns against wet-nursing are less familiar. For a brief discussion, see Crawford, 'The Sucking Child'. For a sobering exploration of the gulf between what women were told to do, what they thought they were doing and what they actually did, see Mechling, 'Advice to Historians on Advice to Mothers'. The general pattern is described in Fildes, *Breasts, Bottles and Babies*, pp. 98–134, 398–401.

76   Lewis, *In the Family Way*, pp. 209–12.

77   *Ladies Dispensatory*, vii.

78   LRO, DDB/72/128 and 136 (n.d.), J. Scrimshire, Pontefract, to E. Parker, Alkincoats.

79   WYCRO, Bradford, Sp St/5/2/30 (20 Jan. 1749), A. Stanhope, Leeds, to W. Spencer, Cannon Hall; WYCRO, Leeds, TA 18/5 (25 April 1734), W. Gossip, Ware, to A. Gossip, Ogleforth, York.

80   LRO, DDB/81/37 (1780), f. 28; LRO, DDB Ac 7886/47 (n.d.), E. Shackleton, Pasture, to B. Parker, Newton. Elizabeth Shackleton remained suspicious of artificial feeding on 'pobs', but was forced to acknowledge: 'they say he do's well on it'. Her scepticism was well-founded. Although artificial feeding became the fashionable alternative to maternal breast-feeding, it was often a lethal practice. Inappropriate foods, a contaminated water supply and dirty utensils often spelt gastro-intestinal disaster. The calamitous results of an experiment with dry nursing at the London Foundling Hospital in the 1740s were well publicized: Fildes, *Breasts, Bottles and Babies*, pp. 304, 400.

81   For Tom Scrimshire's babyhood, see LRO, DDB/72/124, 125, 128, 134, 135 (1753–4), J. Scrimshire, Pontefract, to E. Parker, Alkincoats. On Deborah Scrimshire, see LRO, DDB/72/156 (20 Jan. 1756), same to same.

82   For the quotations, see respectively LRO, DDB/72/214 (12 April 1768), B. Ramsden, Charterhouse, to E. Shackleton, Alkincoats, and LRO, DDB/72/295 (21 Sept. n.y.), same to same. On the mild contraceptive properties of lactation, consult McLaren, 'Nature's Contraceptive'. The desirability of limiting family size must have been a subject of discussion in the Ramsden household, given this quip of the Reverend's when his wife conceived: 'I wo'd it were the fashion with Children as with Kittens, viz. to keep no more than one can afford and to drown all the Superfluity': LRO, DDB/72/

217 (3 Oct. 1768), W. Ramsden, Charterhouse, to E. Shackleton, Alkincoats. The Ramsdens also debated taking to separate beds after the birth of their last child. A recent hypothesis offers abortion as a viable contraceptive method for women who sought to extend the interval between their labours, see Pollock, 'Experience of Pregnancy' (see n. 43 above), pp. 54–8. For a national account of contraceptive behaviour, consult McLaren, *Reproductive Rituals*, pp. 57–87. On the prohibition against sex, see Pollock, *Lasting Relationship*, pp. 53, 64.

83 LRO, DDB/72/183 (16 Feb. 1765) B. and W. Ramsden, Charterhouse, to E. Parker, Alkincoats. Similarly, William Gossip was anxious about the weaning of his 'poor babe': 'I hope your weaning of him has been attended with no ill consequences to either of you': WYCRO, Leeds, TA Box 18/5 (25 April 1734), W. Gossip, Ware, to A. Gossip, Ogleforth, York; as were seventeenth-century parents: Macfarlane, *Ralph Josselin*, p. 88. Fildes explains that contemporaries saw weaning as arguably the most dangerous period of infancy, linked to specific 'diseases' and even death. Moreover, it not only signified a change of diet, but also a change of station, from suckling to small child: Fildes, *Breasts, Bottles and Babies*, p. 351.

84 Hall, *Miss Weeton's Journal*, II, p. 141.

85 LRO, DDWh/4/124 and 40 (*c*.1813–1814), B. Addison, Liverpool, to E. Whitaker, Roefield.

86 Nelson, *Essay on the Government of Children*, p. 52. A similar impression is gained of the aristocratic experience: Lewis, *In the Family Way*, pp. 209–12.

87 LRO, DDB/72/264 (14 Oct. 1773), B. Ramsden, Charterhouse, to E. Shackleton, Alkincoats.

88 LRO, DDB/81/1506 (22 Dec. 1817), E. Parker, Selby, to E. Reynolds, Colne. Difficulties with her nursemaids are related in LRO, DDB/72/1196, 1208–9 (1822–5), same to E. Moon, Colne.

89 LRO, DDB/72/252, 269, 273, 281 (1770–75), B. and W. Ramsden, Islington and Charterhouse, to E. Shackleton, Alkincoats.

90 On the teaching of John and George Larpent, see HL, HM 31201, Mrs Larpent's Diary, I, 1790–95, fos. 19, 22. For expressions of educational philosophy, see HL, HM 31201, Mrs Larpent's Diary, III, 1799–1800, fos. 195–facing f. 196, 200, 207.

91 LRO, DDWh/4/88 (24 Aug. 1816), A. Robbins, Gloucester, to E. Whitaker, Roefield.

92 LRO, DDB/72/58 (25 Feb. 1754), E. Parker, London, to R. Parker, Alkincoats.

93 Browsholme Letters, uncatalogued (16 May 1752), J. Scrimshire to 'Mrs Parker, at Browsholme'; LRO, DDB/72/147 (24 June n.y.), J. Scrimshire, Pontefract, to E. Parker, Alkincoats; LRO, DDB/72/161(a) (17 Nov. *c*.1757), same to same.

94 LRO, DDB/72/178, 201 and 264 (1765–73), B. and W. Ramsden, Charterhouse and Highgate, to E. Parker, later Shackleton, Alkincoats.

95 LRO, DDB Ac 7886/10 (23 Sept. 1779), P. Goulbourne, Manchester, to B. Parker, Alkincoats; WYCRO, Bradford Sp St 6/1/50 (n.d.), M. Warde, to M. Stanhope.

96 Balderston, *Thraliana*, I, p. 158.

97 See LRO, DDB/72/134 and 445 (*c*.1755), J. Scrimshire, Pontefract, to E. Parker, Alkincoats; LRO, DDB/72/75, 222, 214 (1765–9), B. and W. Ramsden, Charterhouse, to E. Shackleton, Alkincoats.

98 See LRO, DDB/72/70 (2 Sept. 1756), Nurse Seedall, Alkincoats, to E. Parker, and LRO, DDB/72/69 (n.d.), T. Parker/Nurse Seedall, Alkincoats, to E. Parker; LRO, DDB/72/218 (29 Oct. 1768), W. Ramsden, Charterhouse, to E. Shackleton, Alkincoats; LRO, DDB/72/174 (16 Sept. 1762), B. Ramsden, Charterhouse, to E. Parker, Alkincoats.

99 LRO, DDWh/4/88 (24 Sept. 1816), A. Robbins, Gloucester, to E. Whitaker.

100 LRO, DDWh/4/89 (29 Oct. 1816), B. Addison, Liverpool, to E. Whitaker.

101 LRO, DDB/72/1508 and 1506 (1817–23), E. Parker, Selby to E. Reynolds, Colne; LRO, DDB/72/1528 (14 July 1817), E. Parker, Selby, to M. Barcroft, Colne.

102 See LRO, DDB/72/180, 181, 189, 195, 201 and 209–10 (1764–7), B. and W. Ramsden, Charterhouse and Highgate to E. Parker, later E. Shackleton, Alkincoats.

103 See LRO, DDB/72/216, 222, 237–9, 259, 258, 261, 269, 279 (1768–75), B. and W. Ramsden, Charterhouse, to E. Shackleton, Alkincoats. On provincial deaths, see Carr, *Annals and Stories of Colne*, p. 86.

104 WYCRO, Leeds, TA 13/1 (23 Oct.) S. Thorp, Cowick, to Mrs Gossip (the elder), York.

105 WYCRO, Leeds, TA 18/5 (3 Oct. 1746), W. Gossip, Stamford, to A. Gossip, Skelton; TA 18/5 (16 June 1746), W. Gossip, Buxton, to A. Gossip, Skelton; TA 11/4 (8 Aug. ? 1750), A. Gossip, York, to W. Gossip, Thorp Arch.

106 WYCRO, Leeds, TA 18/5 (1746), W. Gossip, Skelton, to A. Gossip, at Mr Thompson's, Ripon; TA 18/5 (8 Aug. 1746), W. Gossip, Skelton, to Master Gossip, Ripon; TA 18/5 (23 Oct. 1746), W. Gossip, London, to A. Gossip, Skelton.

107 WYCRO, Leeds, TA 18/5 (3 June 1765), W. Gossip, Thorp Arch, to Mrs Gossip, Leicester; TA 18/5 (9 July 1765), same to same.

108 On epidemics of fever, whooping cough and measles, see LRO, DDB/72/142, 150, 161 (1756–7), J. Scrimshire, Pontefract, to E. Parker, Alkincoats. On the perceived risks of infection, see LRO, DDB/72/158, 136, 149 (1756–7), same to same.

109 WYCRO, Bradford Sp St/6/1/57 (26 June 1757), A. Stanhope, Leeds, to W. Stanhope, Bath.

110 HL, HM 31201, Mrs Larpent's Dairy, 1, 1790–95, fos. 4, facing f. 5 and 6.

111 LRO, DDB/72/1598 (3 April 1823), E. Parker, Selby, to E. Reynolds, Colne; LRO, DDB/72/1198 and 1203–7 (1823–5), E. and E. Parker, Selby, to E. Moon, Colne.

112 LRO, DDGr C3 (23 Nov. 1821), M. Greene to Mrs Bradley, Slyne.

113 For example, the dates and circumstances of Tom Parker's life-threatening bout of smallpox were etched in his mother's memory. In 1777, at least twenty years after the fact, Elizabeth Shackleton recalled the crisis in her diary: LRO, DDB/81/30 (1777), f. 40: 'God make my own dear Tom ever thankful for the . . . mercies he received on this great day from almighty God . . . he came to the height of the small pox. My dear John was livid of it before and both did as well as my own dear Robert.'

114 LRO, DDB/72/132 (16 May 1754), J. Scrimshire, Pontefract, to E. Parker, Alkincoats; DDB/72/263 (14 Oct. 1773), W. Ramsden, Charterhouse, to E. Shackleton, Alkincoats.

115 LRO, DDWh/4/78 (1 May 1816), A. Ainsworth, Bolton, to E. Whitaker, Roefield. Similar expressions are widespread in the papers of the genteel. When the Miss Barcrofts of Colne informally adopted their orphaned niece Ellen in 1797, a friend assured the inexperienced sisters, 'she will be nice company for you and will beguile many an hour by her infantine tricks': DDB/72/1493 (26 Aug. 1797), B. Wiglesworth, Townhead, to E. Barcroft, Otley. When Ellen had children of her own, she regaled her aunts with fond progress reports, 'he talks of *Mamma* and *Bab-ba*, but I am not quite sure that he understands the *application* of the words': DDB/72/1505 (14 June 1817), E. Parker, Selby, to E. Reynolds, Colne.

116 LRO, DDGr C3 (*c.*1821), M. Greene to Mrs Bradley, Slyne.

117 Hall, *Miss Weeton's Journal*, II, p. 152; see also pp. 143–4, 169.

118 Stone, *Family, Sex and Marriage*, p. 264; LRO, DDB/72/258 (17 Oct. 1772), W. Ramsden, Charterhouse, to E. Shackleton, Alkincoats; Johnson, *Dictionary*, 'Love'.

119 LRO, DDB/72/175 (26 Feb. 1763), W. Ramsden, Charterhouse, to E. Parker, Alkincoats.

120 WYCRO, Leeds, TA, Box 18/5 (4 Nov. 1746), W. Gossip, London, to A. Gossip, Skelton; TA 18/5 (8 Aug. 1746), W. Gossip, Skelton, to Master Willy Gossip, Ripon; TA 18/5 (3 June 1765), W. Gossip, Thorp Arch, to Mrs Gossip, Leicester; TA 12/3 (1768), G. Gossip to W. Gossip, Skelton.

121 LRO, DDB/72/75 (30 July 1765), B. Ramsden, Charterhouse, to E. Parker, Alkincoats.

122 WYCRO, Leeds, TA 18/5 (1746), W. Gossip, York, to A. Gossip, Ripon.

123 St Clare announced the birth in LRO, DDB/72/492 (13 Feb. 1780), W. St Clare (the elder) to T. Parker, Newton, and the death in LRO, DDB/72/499 (22 Dec. 1802), same to same; William Stanhope's encouragement is in WYCRO, Sp St/6/1/68 (5 Feb. 1756), W. Stanhope, Leeds, to Ann Stanhope, Cannon Hall.

124 LRO, DDGr C1 (21 Dec. 1762), T. Greene, Inner Temple, London, to his mother. Phrases which abound in the correspondence of the bereaved and their commiserators include: 'we must endeavour to submit to the will of providence', 'joy and afflictions are both dispensed by the same divine providence, your own good sense will teach you to submit to the one as well as the other', 'who the lord loveth, he chastiteth and scourgeth', 'whatever is, is right'. An identical vocabulary is wheeled out in Richardson, *Sir Charles Grandison*, pp. 400–1: 'Yet even *this* Love must submit to the awful dispensations of Providence, whether of death or other disappointment; and such trials ought to be met with chearful resignation, and not to be the means of embittering our lives, or of rendering them useless.' A reliance on the language of resignation is also to the fore in the strategies used to cope with illness: R. and D. Porter, *In Sickness and in Health: The British Experience, 1650–1850* (1988), pp. 234–40.

125 Henstock, 'The Diary of Abigail Gawthern', pp. 52, 76.

126 This was Elizabeth Holland's description, cited in Porter, *In Sickness and in Health* (see n. 124 above), p. 80. Both the searing grief of seventeenth-century parents and the widespread fear that it might overmaster the sufferer if given full reign is noted in P. Seaver, *Wallington's World: A Puritan Artisan in Seventeenth-Century London* (Stanford, Ca., 1985), pp. 229–30, and Crawford, 'Construction and Experience of Maternity', p. 23. Of 134 cases of disturbing grief treated by the seventeenth-century physician Richard Napier, 58 were attributed to the death of child; 51 of these patients were mothers: MacDonald, *Mystical Bedlam*, p. 82. The elite of eighteenth-century Tyneside still found it a struggle 'to submit to what Povidence shall order', judging by Levine and Wrightson, *Making of an Industrial Society*, pp. 328–9. The 'paroxysms of panic' brought on by children's illnesses and the deep mourning of parents from the sixteenth century to the nineteenth is illustrated in Pollock, *Forgotten Children*, pp. 128–42.

4 Prudent Economy

1 Pennington, *Unfortunate Mother's Advice*, p. 27.

2 *Complete Letter Writer*, pp. 164–5.

3 J. Gregory, *A Father's Legacy to His Daughter* (1774; Edinburgh, 1788), p. 22.

4 LRO, DDB/72/475 (29 April 1748), W. Hill, Ormskirk, to R. Parker, Alkincoats; LRO, DDB Ac 7886/211 (March 1747), R. Parker, Alkincoats, to Edward Parker, London; LRO, DDB Ac 7886/216 ('Saturday Morn'), R. Parker, Alkincoats, to E. Parker, London; Marshall, *William Stout*, pp. 159, 233; Wright, *Thomas Birkenshaw*, p. 146.

5 LRO, DDB/72/490 (n.d.), Edward Parker, London, to R. Parker, Colne; WYCRO, Leeds TA 18/5 (23 Oct. 1746), W. Gossip, London, to A. Gossip, Skelton.

6 LRO, DDB Ac 7886/306 (9 Oct. 1749), J. Parker, Browsholme, to E. Parker, Birthwaite; WYCRO, Bradford, Sp St/6/1/75 (20 Aug. 1757), W. Stanhope, Leeds, to A. Stanhope, Sewerby; LRO, DDB/72/234 (28 Apr. 1770), W. Ramsden, Charterhouse, to E. Shackleton, Alkincoats; Stone, *Road to Divorce*, p. 293.

7 LRO, DDB/72/12, 7, 8, 15, 17, 14 (1751), E. Parker, Browsholme, to R. Parker, Alkincoats.

8   LRO, DDGr C3 (21 July 1819), S. Tatham, Southall, to Mr and Mrs Bradley, Slyne.
9   Marshall, *William Stout*, p. 159.
10 LRO, DDB/72/306 (n.d.), E. Shackleton, Pasture House, to J. and R. Parker, London; LRO, DDB/81/35 (1779), fos. 225, 229; LRO, DDB/81/37 (1780), f. 70.
11 LRO, DDWh/4/29 (17 Aug. 1813), E. Whitaker, Edgeworth, to C. Whitaker, Roefield.
12 H. Chapone, *Letters on the Improvement of the Mind Addressed To A Lady* (1773; 1835), p. 92.
13 Quoted in Brophy, *Women's Lives*, p. 120.
14 Clark, *Working Life of Women*, pp. 15, 39, 41. For other positive accounts of the housekeeper's domain, see Hole, *English Housewife*; id., *English Home Life*; and Bayne-Powell, *Housekeeping in the Eighteenth Century*.
15 Arguments about a decay of productive housekeeping between 1600 and 1850 are consistent with the decline and fall model of women's work which I have criticized elsewhere: Vickery, 'Golden Age to Separate Spheres', pp. 383–414. However, I am not arguing that housework was in any sense light work at any historical period. The grind of keeping a household supplied with water, heat, light, food and a measure of domestic comfort is demonstrated in Davidson, *Woman's Work is Never Done*. Sustaining a household with one or two maids of all work was still a slog for the Victorian housewife, see Branca, 'Image and Reality' and id., *Silent Sisterhood*. There is also a feminist interpretation of technological innovation in the household, contending that inventions did not liberate women, since men elevated standards of cleanliness and gentility still further, see Cowan, *More Work for Mother*.
16 L. T. Ulrich, *Good Wives: Image and Reality in the Lives of Women in Northern New England, 1650–1750* (Oxford, 1983), p. 34.
17 Chapone, *Improvement of the Mind*, p. 66.
18 Hecht, *Domestic Servant in Eighteenth-Century England* (1980), pp. 35–70. Before this there existed a unique article on the subject, Marshall, 'Domestic Servants of the Eighteenth Century'. Agricultural service has been better researched, A. Kussmaul, *Servants in Husbandry in Early Modern England* (1981). However, more broadly based researches are now beginning to appear: Holmes, 'Domestic Service in Yorkshire' (D.Phil. thesis); Meldrum, 'Domestic Service in London' (Ph.D. thesis); Seleski, 'Women, Work and Cultural Change'; Hill, *English Domestics*.
19 Savile, *Advice to a Daughter*, p. 72.
20 Cited in Holmes, 'Domestic Service in Yorkshire' (D.Phil. thesis), p. 48. Peter Earle argues that the employment of servants was virtually universal amongst the metropolitan middling sort and extended down even to lowly artisans: Earle, *Making of the English Middle Class*, pp. 218–19: His analysis of 176 households in two London, parishes (St Mary-le-Bow and St Michael Bassishaw) reveals that 56.8 per cent of households employed a single servant, 21 per cent had two, 11.4 per cent had three, 4 per cent had four, 4 per cent had five and 2.8 per cent had six or more.
21 See respectively Hecht, *Domestic Servant*, p. 7; Harrison, 'Servants of William Gossip', p. 135; and LRO, DDB/72/861 (30 March 1800), H. O. Cunliffe, Wycoller, to T. Parker, Alkincoats.
22 LRO, DDB/72/176 (3 April 1764), B. Ramsden to E. Parker, Alkincoats. Lancashire servants came from Padiham, Fence, Slaidburn, Grindleton and even Rochdale. Yorkshire women came from Keighley, Bracewell and Skipton. However, the preponderance of local surnames among her workforce (Blakeys, Crookes, Foulds, Hartleys, Hargreaves, Nutters, Sagers, Varleys) and, indeed, the absence of any comment as to their origins suggest that the majority of her servants were drawn from the nearby townships. Of course, some of these very local servants offered their labour unsolicited, coming to show themselves at Elizabeth Shackleton's back door or sending their parents to negotiate.

23   In the 1750s and 1760s Anne Gossip badgered her friends and kin across Yorkshire to inquire after servants for her. When John Spencer required a housekeeper in the 1760s it was his sister Anne Stanhope who pursued the necessary references for him. In the 1800s Betty Parker of Alkincoats asked her daughter Eliza Parker to investigate the availability of servants in Preston. In the 1810s Eliza Whitaker of Roefield broadcast inquiries across the county. Her sister Jane routinely interviewed the servants for her father's Preston establishment in the same decade. In the 1820s Ellen Parker of Selby asked her three Colne aunts Ellen Moon, Elizabeth Reynolds and Mary Barcroft if they could so assist her.

24   LRO, DDB/81/11 (1770), f. 85. For other examples, consult LRO, DDB/81/26 (1776), fos. 85, 91, 93.

25   These and the following calculations are based on daily entries in LRO, DDB/81/17 (1772), *passim*.

26   Chapone, *Improvement of the Mind*, pp. 94-5.

27   Chambermaids at Browsholme in the same period were paid £5 per annum, £1 more than at Alkincoats, see LRO, DDB/81/17 (1772), f. 46. At Burton Constable in the 1760s, the laundry and dairymaids were paid £6 and the cookmaid £5. However, the Gossips paid their cooks in the 1730s between £3 and 3 guineas, but by 1768 they paid a maid £4 1s.: WYCRO, Leeds, TA 12/3 (18 July 1768), L. Brown, York, to Mrs Gossip, Thorp; and Harrison, 'Servants of William Gossip', p. 135. The Heatons of Ponden Hall, a mere seven miles from Alkincoats, offered only 59s. a year. See WYCRO, Bradford, B 419, Account Book of Robert Heaton of Ponden, 1768-93 (I thank John Styles for this reference). The only published study of national wage rates can be found in Hecht, *Domestic Servant*, pp. 141-9. Hecht shows enormous variation in servants' wages, thus in the 1770s housemaids were paid anything from £4 10s. to 10 guineas; chambermaids between £6 and 10 guineas; dairymaids between 5 and 10 guineas; maids of all work between £4 and £10; cooks between £9 and 14 guineas; cook-housekeepers between 12 and 20 guineas. Back at Alkincoats, wage rates remained remarkably static from 1762 to the mid-1770s. The male servants (posts unspecified) whose contracts were mentioned received between 8 guineas and £9 a year, plus the supply of a frock waistcoat, breeches, hat and great-coat. Thus, they received at least twice as much as female servants. (In 1772, Mrs Shackleton considered the 'great wages' expected by the cook Molly Hargreaves of £8 10s. 12d. per annum to be unrealistic and excessive: LRO, DDB/81/17 (1772), f. 78.) From 1775 yearly wages crept up: maids being paid four and a half guineas and upper female servants 6 guineas. Unfortunately no male contracts were recorded for this later period, but a corresponding rise to £10 a year would be consistent. The few male employment contracts Elizabeth Shackleton recorded suggest that menservants received a livery in addition to their salary. By contrast, there is no evidence that maidservants were bought a specific wardrobe upon engagement. References to wage payments reveal that the cost of making garments for female staff was often deducted from their pay. However, extra services could be paid in kind. Nanny Nutter, for example, received a pair of black silk mittens in February 1773, in return for knitting a pair of claret silk and worsted stockings. Mrs Shackleton also lent her female servants money to purchase expensive investment items such as stays. From at least the early 1760s Mrs Shackleton launched an assault on the widespread practice among servants of taking tips from every household guest or 'taking vails'. (A national campaign against vails had been in operation from the 1750s.) But from the late 1760s her concern died away, as presumably did the practice. Mrs Shackleton probably paid the wages herself. Certainly, her pocket diaries contained printed marketing tables and gave advice on calculating yearly wages by the day: LRO, DDB/81/26 (1775), fos. 155-6 and LRO, DDB/81/20 (1773), fos. 13-18. In accordance with contemporary

convention, Elizabeth Shackleton engaged her permanent servants on a yearly basis. Permanent servants were given bed and board. Women servants slept in the nursery, male servants slept two to a bed in the gallery.

28 See LRO, DDB/72/161 and 149 (1756–7), J. Scrimshire, Pontefract, to E. Parker, Alkincoats; Holmes, 'Domestic Service in Yorkshire' (D.Phil. thesis), pp. 59–92, and Harrison, 'Servants of William Gossip', p. 141; LRO, DDPd/17/1 (6 June 1786), J. Pedder, Lancaster, to J. Pedder, Blackburn; LRO, DDWh/4/94 (Jan. 1817), J. Horrocks, Preston, to E. Whitaker, Roefield.

29 Earle, *City Full of People*, pp. 128–9 and Earle, *Making of the English Middle Class*, pp. 221–2; Hecht, *Domestic Servant*, p. 82; Holmes, 'Domestic Service in Yorkshire' (D.Phil. thesis), p. 102. Moreover, Meldrum has recently argued of lengths of tenure in London, 'that the norm, particularly for women, was a succession of relatively short stays in place after a settlement had been established': id., 'Domestic Service in London' (Ph.D. thesis), p. 39. Seleski also notes the eagerness of servants to change places, with apparently little fear of the consequences: id., 'Women, Work and Cultural Change', p. 150. Difficulties maintaining staff have also been observed of early eighteenth-century Northumberland and County Durham, see Hughes, *North East*, pp. 31–2. By contrast, Cumberland, 'the conservative North', was apparently blessed with exceptionally faithful domestics well into the late eighteenth century according to Hughes, *Cumberland and Westmorland*, pp. 116–17.

30 For the quotations, see LRO, DDB/81/17 (1772), fos. 49, 51. For other examples, see LRO, DDB/81/17 (1772), f. 31, and LRO, DDB/81/32 (1777), f. 90. Unfortunately, the mechanisms of this leasing system are uncertain; the movement of servants may represent altruistic co-operation between employers, or on the other hand could demonstrate that skilled servants were able to demand a busman's holiday.

31 LRO, DDB/81/35 (1779), fos. 48, 53.

32 LRO, DDB/81/28 (1776), f. 21–2: 'William Brigge was of age 21 years old and served his Apprenticeship to Mr John Shackleton he will have been here Eleven years next March.' Of the four men employed in 1772, there is definite proof that Will and Isaac lived in, while Jack probably did so since he was considered sufficiently part of the household to warrant having shirts made up for him. There is no evidence that Matthew lived at Alkincoats. He may even have been a servant of Christopher Shackleton's at Stone Edge: LRO, DDB/81/17 (1772), f. 26: 'Matthew at Stone Edge threw over the cart and broke it at Hellowells. A pack of Wooll a pack of Malt with other Materials went into the snow.'

33 For a range of Isaac's chores, see LRO, DDB/81/17 (1772), fos. 39, 42, 43, 48, 98. On William Brigge's duties, see LRO, DDB/81/17 (1772), fos. 64, 68, 78; On the gardener and the huntsman, see LRO, DDB/81/20 (1773), f. 35, and LRO, DDB/76/4 (1758–73), Trust Account of Thomas Parker (unfol.).

34 Non-servant workers on the home farm and estate included a tenant, John Spencer, who attended the family's horses; Henry Bradshaw, who kennelled the family's greyhound dog; the carpenter Emanuel Howarth, who constructed and repaired shelves, cupboards, doors and gates; the mason James Varley, who built yards, garden walls and the dog kennel; and a number of slaters, thatchers, hedgers, ditchers, mowers and sheep shearers were intermittently employed on the land and farm buildings. See LRO, DDB/76/3 (1758–67), Trust Account of Thomas Parker (unfol.) and LRO, DDB/76/4 (1758–73), Trust Account of Thomas Parker (unfol.).

35 LRO, DDB/81/37 (1780), f. 34.; LRO, DDGr C3 (11 Aug. 1821), S. Tatham, Southall, to Mrs Bradley, Slyne; WYCRO, Leeds, TA 18/6 (14 Jan. 1814), J. Gossip, Boston, to W. Gossip, Thorp Arch. Similarly, the Gossips' cousin Elizabeth Barker was unequal to management in the 1740s due to ill health 'for want of a good servant, ye care of her family seems to be too much for her.': WYCRO, Leeds, TA 13/1 (25 Sept. n.y.), S. Thorp, Cowick, to Mrs Gossip, York.

36   See WYCRO, Leeds TA 12/3 (8 July 1768), A. Wilmer, York, to Mrs Gossip, Thorp
     Arch, and LRO, DDWh/4/23 (26 Oct. 1812), N. Bishop, Roby, to E. Whitaker,
     Clitheroe. On religious qualifications among others, see LRO, DDB/81/28 (1776), f.
     79; Homes, 'Domestic Service in Yorkshire' (D.Phil. thesis), pp. 51–77; and Harrison,
     'Servants of William Gossip', p. 134.
37   See, respectively, WYCRO, Leeds, TA 12/3 (18 April 1768), E. Walker, Fairburn, to
     Mrs Gossip, Thorp Arch; LRO, DDB/72/113 (30 Nov. 1756), A. Pellet, London, to E.
     Parker, Alkincoats; LRO, DDB/72/149 (30 Aug. 1756), J. Scrimshire, Pontefract, to E.
     Parker, Alkincoats; LRO, DDB/81/35 (1779), f. 227. Complaints about the disruption
     caused by the frenzied turnover of household servants can be found in women's
     correspondence in any decade from 1720 to 1825. A selection is LRO, DDPd/17/1 (6
     June 1786), J. Pedder, Lancaster, to J. Pedder, Blackburn; LRO, DDWh/4/94 (Jan.
     1817), J. Horrocks, Preston, to E. Whitaker, Clitheroe; LRO, DDB/72/1506 (22 Dec.
     1817), E. Parker, Selby, to E. Reynolds, Colne. On this time-worn genre, see M. H.
     Perkins, *The Servant Problem and the Servant in English Literature* (Boston, Mass.,
     1928).
38   Consider LRO, DDB/81/37 (1780), f. 89; LRO, DDB/81/35 (1779), fos 54 and 208.
39   LRO, DDB/81/33A (1778), f. 110; LRO, DDB/81/35 (1779), fos. 257–8. For
     Woodeforde's allowances, see Beresford, *Diary of a Country Parson*, i, pp. 182, 236–
     7, 271–2. The Gossips of Thorp Arch also refused tea, see WYCRO, Leeds TA 12/3
     (18 July 1768), L. Brown, York, to Mrs Gosip, Thorp Arch.
40   LRO, DDB/81/37 (1780), f. 119; LRO, DDB/81/35 (1779), f. 118–19.
41   LRO, DDB/81/26 (1775), f. 116; LRO, DDB/81/29 (1776), f. 78; LRO, DDB/81/33A
     (1778), f. 61; and LRO, DDB/81/37 (1780), fos. 116, 187 and 36.
42   On Will's love-making, see LRO, DDB/81/17 (1772), fos. 62, 64. On Isaac's amours,
     consult LRO, DDB/81/20 (1773), f. 22, and LRO, DDB/81/35 (1779), f. 167–8.
43   On Nanny Nutter's work, LRO, DDB/81/15 (1772–5), fos. 26, 42; LRO, DDB/81/17
     (1772), f. 107. On her 'wages', see LRO, DDB/81/15 (1772–5), fos. 25–6, 31–2, 39, 41–
     2, 47; For gifts, see LRO, DDB/81/15 (1772–5), fos. 16, 24, 26, 44, 46, 56, 82, 86, 100.
44   LRO, DDB/81/15 (1772–5), f. 90a. See also f. 68.
45   LRO, DDB/81/15 (1772–5), f. 34. That female servants frequently slept with their
     mistresses while their masters were away is noted by Stone, *Road to Divorce*, p. 213,
     and Meldrum, 'Domestic Service in London' (Ph.D thesis), p. 173. The same has been
     said of France: S. Maza, *Servants and Masters in Eighteenth Century France: The
     Uses of Loyalty* (Princeton, NJ, 1983), pp. 184–6.
46   LRO, DDB/81/15 (1772–5), f. 72. For Mrs Shackleton's gifts of a brisket of beef, a
     piece of beef and a cabbage, a bottle of wine, 'some old things', half a crown for her
     sister, and some good rum, see fos. 30, 54, 60, 100, 104.
47   LRO, DDB/81/26 (1775), f. 89. See also, LRO, DDB/81/15 (1772–5), fos. 88, 22, 109,
     85.
48   See respectively, LRO, DDB/81/15 (1772–5), fos. 88, 109, 110, 85, 99. However, Mrs
     Shackleton was eventually prepared to forgive Nanny Nutter to the extent of
     returning her blue quilted petticoat, sending presents of cheese, beef and a new shift,
     and writing a reference stating that 'she was honest and had good hands'. See LRO,
     DDB/81/32 (1777), fos. 77–8, and LRO, DDB/81/33A (1778), f. 35.
49   LRO, DDB/81/32 (1777), fos. 68, 94, 104; LRO, DDB/81/35 (1779), f. 245; LRO, DDB/
     81/37 (1780), f. 191.
50   WYCRO, Leeds TA 13/3 (7 Aug. 1764), T. Gossip to W. Gossip.
51   Chapone, *Improvement of the Mind*, pp. 94–5.
52   LRO, DDB Ac 7886/18 (1 Feb. n.y.), A. Parker, Cuerdon, to E. Shackleton.
53   Henstock, 'Diary of Abigail Gawthorne', p. 31.
54   LRO, DDB/81/37 (1780), f. 267.
55   See Meldrum, 'Domestic Service in London' (Ph.D. thesis), p. 69.

56 Pennington, *Unfortunate Mother's Advice*, pp. 36–8; J.-J. Rousseau, *Emile or On Education* (1762; Harmondsworth, 1991), p. 394.
57 WYCRO, Leeds, TA 11/4 (n.d.), A. Gossip, York, to W. Gossip, Thorp Arch.
58 LRO, DDB/81/13 (1771), f. 51.
59 On the language of regulation, see LRO, DDB/81/37 (1780), f. 273, and LRO, DDB/81/33A (1778), f. 10. See the 'catalogue of the contents of R.P.s box with a lock and key in the nursery', enclosed in LRO, DDB/72/307 (28 Feb. 1777), E. Shackleton, Alkincoats, to R. Parker, London; and the lists on LRO, DDB/81/10 (1770), fos. 12–13. Mrs Shackleton took personal pride in well-designed cupboards – the machinery of her organizational regime; thus she recorded when Manuel the carpenter completed 'an Excellent Cupboard with two shelves Lock Key and button with other conveniences also three good, new Hooks at the out side for to hang birds on. He also altered the meat pulley to do right and well . . .': LRO, DDB/81/26 (1775), f. 117. At Robert Parker's death in 1758 Alkincoats comprised twenty-five rooms, divided up into fourteen family rooms, six servant and workrooms and five storerooms. His probate inventory refers to a storeroom, ale cellar, small beer cellar, bottle chamber and paper garret, while the diaries mention bureaux, linen drawers, cupboards in the medicine room, kitchen and parlour, a pewter case, and great boxes and chests in the nursery and bedrooms: LRO, DDB/74/14 (1758), Personalty of Late Robert Parker. Elizabeth Shackleton also commented approvingly upon the installation of special shelves, cupboards and even brass hooks for hats during the building and furbishment of Pasture House.
60 Norton, 'American Women in Peace and War', pp. 396–7.
61 LRO, DDB/81/7 (1768), f. 104.
62 Pottle, *Boswell's London Journal, 1762–1763*, pp. 64–5. Rousseau confirmed the correspondence between a woman and her objects, moving from Sophie's disgust at kitchen mess and soil to the assertion that 'cleanliness is one of the first duties of women – a special duty, indispensable, imposed by nature. Nothing in the world is more disgusting than an unclean woman . . .' See Rousseau, *Emile* (see n. 56 above), p. 395.
63 On the sweep, see LRO, DDB/81/22 (1774), fos. 37 and 117. On chimney fires, consult LRO, DDB/81/13 (1771), f. 106, and LRO, DDB/81/26 (1775), f. 80. On the floods, see LRO, DDB/81/26 (1775), f. 32, and LRO, DDB/81/33A (1778), f. 3.
64 LRO, DDB/81/37 (1780), f. 95.
65 See respectively, LRO, DDB/81/13 (1771), f. 98; LRO, DDB/81/29 (1775), f. 63; and LRO, DDB/81/31 (1777), f. 59.
66 LRO, DDB/81/33A (1778), f. 255; LRO, DDB/81/37 (1780), f. 188.
67 Pennington, *Unfortunate Mother's Advice*, p. 92.
68 For a broader discussion of this issue, see Styles, 'Clothing the North', p. 145, and, for a Furness case-study, Pidock, 'The Spinners and Weavers of Swarthmoor Hall'. This change was not confined to the north of England, although it may have occurred slightly earlier in the south.
69 Gregory, *A Father's Legacy* (see n. 3 above), p. 22.
70 LRO, DDB/81/22 (1774), f. 97. In May 1770, for example, she purchased seventy-seven yards of welsh sheeting: LRO, DDB/81/11 (1770), f. 53. She kept a record of the amounts of purchased and took note of the yardage needed for specific purposes: 'A piece of Irish cloth 25 yards long makes John Parker 8 shirts complete. And 9 pairs of sleeves. A piece of Irish cloth 25 yards long makes Robert Parker 9 shirts entirely complete. All this cloth yard wide.': LRO, DDB/81/14 (1772), f. 2. Batch production usually required extra labour to be brought into the household. Lucy Smith, Molly Bennet, Molly Hartley and Mary Shaw all came into the house in the 1760s and 1770s for this purpose. Lucy Smith was paid 3s. 10d. in 1773 for sewing three shirts for Christopher Shackleton; Molly Hartley was paid 19s. 3d. for making up seven shirts

for the Parker boys in 1775: LRO, DDB/81/20 (1773), f. 36 and LRO, DDB/81/26 (1775), f. 39. On occasion, local seamstresses took the fabric pieces home and returned some days later with the finished garment, but ordinarily this labour took place under Elizabeth Shackleton's roof and supervision. Mrs Shackleton also recorded rebinding the hems of her aprons, mending nightgowns and negligees under the armholes, putting new sleeves to old shifts and so on: LRO, DDB/81/31 (1777), fos. 32, 76; LRO, DDB/81/33A (1778), f. 52.

71 LRO, DDB/81/37 (1780), f. 208.

72 LRO, DDB/81/21 (1774), f. 37. On maternal attentions, see LRO, DDB/72/306-7 (1777), E. Shackleton, Alkincoats, to J. and R. Parker, London. For filial requests, albeit indirect, see LRO, DDB/72/328 (7 June 1774), J. Parker, London, to T. Parker, Alkincoats.

73 LRO, DDB/81/33A (1778), fos. 60, 246.

74 For examples, see LRO, DDB/72/29 and 42 (n.d.), R. Parker, Alkincoats, to E. Parker, Browsholme; LRO, DDB/81/7 (1768), f. 70; LRO, DDB/81/8 (1769), f. 95.

75 LRO, DDB/81/13 (1771), f. 92. Personal property in farmyard animals is expressed in LRO, DDB/81/7 (1768), f. 87; LRO, DDB/81/8 (1769), fos. 30, 87; and LRO, DDB/81/26 (1775), f. 55. On the kitchen garden and orchard, see LRO, DDB/81/4 (1765), f. 97; LRO, DDB/81/8 (1769), f. 99; and LRO, DDB/81/26 (1775), f. 91. The order for ornamental plants is recorded in LRO, DDB/81/33A (1778), f. 265.

76 These calculations are based on Mrs Shackleton's butter inventory for 1776: LRO, DDB/81/29 (1776), fos. 158-9. The variety of ways Mrs Shackleton engaged with her consumers can be sampled in LRO, DDB/81/11 (1770), fos. 49, 56; LRO, DDB/81/20 (1773), f. 41.

77 [Woolley], Accomplish'd Lady's Delight in Preserving, preface. See also [Shirley], Accomplish'd Ladies Rich Closet, preface.

78 For examples, see LRO, DDB/81/11 (1770), fos. 2, 92; LRO, DDB/81/17 (1772), fos. 46, 78; and LRO, DDB/81/33A (1778), f. 22.

79 Witness two typical examples of her stocktaking. LRO, DDB/81/7 (1768), f. 26: 'Hung our Bacon, two hams, two flitches, two shoulders, two cheeks – and two hams what we bought in March in the Market.'; LRO, DDB/81/32 (1777), f. 3: 'Mr Shackleton Bot five bottles of Catchup from Gargrave. Boild it over again . . . had 1.2.3.4. Brought from Alkincoats 1.2. bottles. So we have in all 1 2 3 4 5 6 bottles.'

80 LRO, DDB/81/37 (1780), f. 203. See also LRO, DDB/81/13 (1771), f. 15: 'My Provident, Ingenious Housekeeper . . . let Will take seven whites of Eggs to put into shoe Blacking – Rather Extravagant.'; LRO, DDB/81/17 (1772), f. 96: 'Miss Nanny Nutter left a candle burning all night in the Nursery'; LRO, DDB/81/37 (1780), f. 225: 'My wise housekeeper let off the head of the last night's milk and the other also, so she has been the Destruction of the Milk of eight cows at one do.'

81 Raffald, Experienced English Housekeeper, iii.

82 See L. Pollock, With Faith and Physic. The Life of a Tudor Gentlewomen: Lady Grace Mildmay, 1552-1620 (1993), pp. 92-142. For other examples, see Hole, English Housewife, pp. 79-98.

83 PRO, ASSI 45/25/2/98, Northern Circuit Assize Depositions, 1754; W. S. Lewis and R. M. Williams (eds.), Private Charity in England, 1747-1757 (New Haven, 1938), p. 41; Stirling, Annals of a Yorkshire House, I, pp. 97-8. Anecdotal evidence on the remedies favoured and dispensed by eighteenth-century ladies can be found in Bayne-Powell, Housekeeping in the Eighteenth Century, pp. 149-59. Recipes are in The Ladies Dispensatory.

84 Gentleman's Magazine, 23 Aug. 1753. On public awareness of rabies, see C. Mullett, 'Hydrophobia: Its History in England to 1800', Bulletin of the History of Medicine, 18 (1945), pp. 44-65. On the Gentleman's Magazine's function as a medical talking shop, see Porter, 'Lay Medical Knowledge'.

85   Compare the prices revealed in the 'table of proprietary medicines', reproduced in
     Porter, 'Lay Medical Knowledge', pp. 166–8, with LRO, DDB/81/11 (1770), f. 99.
86   Diary entries indicate that Isaac knew how to make up the medicine. For reference to
     Mrs Shackleton making up the medicine herself, see LRO, DDB/81/31 (1777), fos. 91,
     107. The bequest of the recipe ('a true account how to make the medicine') is recorded
     in LRO, DDB/81/27 (1776), f. 43.
87   G. D. Lumb and J. B. Place (eds.), 'Extracts from the Leeds Intelligencer and the Leeds
     Mercury, 1777–1782', *Thoresby Society Publications*, 40 (1955), p. 19.
88   YAS, MD335/Box 95/xcv/1 (1769–73), Letters from Mrs Beatrix Lister, Gisburn Park,
     and her daughter Miss Beatrix Lister to their son/brother Thomas Lister, Oxford and
     London.
89   Wigan Record Office, EHC, 51/M820, (1718–23), Scarah Accounts, fos. 99–101, 109,
     and loose sheet.
90   LPL, MS 8752 (1776), fos. 40, 74; LPL, MS 8753 (1778), fos. 14, 58, 78, 92, 102; LPL,
     MS 8754 (1779), fos. 9, 31, 47; LRO, DDPd/17/1 (16 April 1786), J. Pedder, Lancaster,
     to J. Pedder, Blackburn; and LRO, DDPd/17/1 (6 June 1786), same to same. In
     addition, see LRO, DDPd/7/1, Proposals for Building for Mrs Pedder.
91   LRO, DDB/72/215 and 297 (1768), B. Ramsden, Charterhouse, to E. Shackleton,
     Alkincoats.
92   LRO, DDB/72/201 (April 1767), B. Ramsden, Highgate, to E. Shackleton, Alkincoats;
     LRO, DDB/72/132, 139, 152 (1754–6), J. Scrimshire, Pontefract, to E. Parker,
     Alkincoats.
93   LRO, DDX 510/8 (1804), Dolly Clayton's Diary, last page; LRO, DDX 510/9 (1805),
     last page; LRO, DDX 510/11 (1807), penultimate page. Farming notes can be found
     on LRO, DDX 510/4 (1798), frontispiece.
94   LRO, DDWh/4/27 (12 Aug. 1813), E. Whitaker, Edgeworth, to C. Whitaker, Roefield;
     LRO, DDWh/4/107 and 110 (1820–21), W. St Clare, Preston, to E. Whitaker, Roefield;
     LRO, DDWh/4/23 (26 Oct. 1812), N. Bishop, Roby, to E. Whitaker, Roefield.
95   LRO, DDB/72/1506–7 (1817–21), E. Parker, Selby, to E. Reynolds, Colne.
96   LRO, DDGr C3 (21 July 1819), S. Tatham, Southall, to Mrs Bradley, Slyne.
97   For instances, see HL, HM 31201, Mrs Larpent's Diary, III, 1799–1800, f. 150, facing
     f. 154 and facing f. 157.
98   HL, HM 31201, Mrs Larpent's Diary, VIII, 1810–13, f. 40.
99   Chapone, *Improvement of the Mind*, p. 93. For similar exhortations, see Pennington,
     Unfortunate Mother's Advice, pp. 28–9.
100 LRO, DDB/81/37 (1780), f. 119.
101 Hall, *Miss Weeton's Journal*, I, p. 163.
102 Sarah Cowper's complaints are recorded in Brophy, *Women's Lives*, pp. 178–9. On
     the biblical distinctions drawn between a concubine and a wife, see Ezell, *Patriarch's
     Wife*, p. 139. On 'Egyptian bondage', see Haywood, *Betsy Thoughtless*, p. 442.
103 For examples of such cases in the Chester church courts, see CRO, EDC 5, Calkin v.
     Calkin and Lees v. Lees. For judicial outrage, see Hammerton, *Cruelty and Compan-
     ionship*, p. 98, also pp. 92 and 115. Moreover, the conventional acceptance of the
     female manager was exported to colonial New England. When Beatrice Berry faced
     the Salem Quarterly court in 1677, she recounted how her unreasonable husband had
     humiliated her by denying provisions for cooking, refusing her offers to help with his
     weaving and spurning her home-made beer. Evidently, the court was sympathetic to
     this thwarted housekeeper since Edmund Berry was fined for his 'abusive carriages
     and speeches': Ulrich, *Good Wives* (see n. 16, above), pp. 23–4. Ulrich further suggests
     that this dispute demonstrates 'the central position of huswifery in the self-definition'
     of this northern New England woman.
104 YAS, MD335/Box 95/xcv/1 (28 May 1773), Mrs B. Lister, Gisburn Park, to T. Lister,
     MP, London.

105 LRO, DDB Ac 7886/210 (24 March 1747), R. Parker, Alkincoats, to E. Parker, Browsholme. See also A. J. Fletcher, 'Honour, Reputation and Office Holding in Elizabethan and Stuart England', in A. J. Fletcher and J. Stevenson (eds.), *Order and Disorder in Early Modern England* (Cambridge, 1995), pp. 92–115, and Heal and Holmes, *Gentry in England and Wales*, pp. 76–7.

5 Elegance

1 Consumers of Gillows furniture include the Aspinalls of Standen, Barcrofts of Clitheroe, Claytons of Carr, Cromblehomes of Preston, Cunliffes of Wycoller, Ecroyds of Edge End, Listers of Gisburn Park, Moons of Colne, Parkers of Alkincoats, Parkers of Browsholme, Parkers of Cuerden, Parkers of Marshfield, Pedders of Preston, Sagars of Colne, Shackletons of Pasture House, Starkies of Huntroyde and Waltons of Marsden. See WPL, Gillows Collection, 344/52 ledger, 1776–80; 344/53 ledger, 1781–90; 344/54 ledger, 1790–97. On Gillow's design, read Nichols, 'Gillow and Company' (MA thesis), p. 9.
2 J. Gregory, *A Father's Legacy to His Daughter* (1774; Edinburgh, 1788), p. 24.
3 Balderston, *Thraliana*, I, pp. 336–7.
4 Harold Perkin's work provides an explicit example: 'At bottom the key to the Industrial Revolution was the infinitely elastic home demand for mass consumer goods. And the key to that demand was social emulation, keeping up with the Joneses, the compulsive urge for imitating the spending habits of one's betters.' See H. J. Perkin, 'The Social Causes of the British Industrial Revolution', *Transactions of the Royal Historical Society*, 5th ser., 75 (1968), p. 140. Neil McKendrick developed Perkin's thesis and went on to conceptualize this late eighteenth-century phenomenon as a consumer revolution. Thus, the consumer society was born, with recognizably modern advertising techniques exploiting a new propensity among the populace to consume in a self-consciously emulative fashion: McKendrick, Brewer and Plumb, *Birth of a Consumer Society*, pp. 9–194.
5 T. Veblen, *The Theory of the Leisure Class* (1925), p. 54.
6 McKendrick, 'Home Demand and Economic Growth', pp. 200, 209.
7 A. Ribeiro, *Dress in Eighteenth-Century Europe, 1715–1789* (1984), p. 116. A subtler treatment of contemporary commentary can be found in Buck, *Dress in Eighteenth-Century England*, pp. 103–19. Some dress historians are more explicit than others about the nature of gender costume. Witness the inimitable Cunningtons: 'feminine fashions . . . were less concerned than male fashions to express *Class Distinction*, being more intent on the display of *Sex Attraction*.' See Cunnington, *Handbook of English Costume*, p. 26. For practical tips, girls, read 'Costume as a Direct Method of Sex Attraction', in C. W. Cunnington, *Why Women Wear Clothes* (1941), pp. 41–76.
8 Weatherill, 'Possession of One's Own'.
9 P. Bordieu, *Distinction: A Social Critique of the Judgement of Taste* (1984); D. Hebdidge, 'Object as Image: The Italian Scooter Cycle', in id., (ed.), *Hiding in the Light* (1988), pp. 77–115; M. Poster (ed.), *Jean Baudrillard: Selected Writings* (Cambridge, 1988), pp. 119–48; M. Mauss, *The Gift* (New York, 1976); A. Appaduri (ed.), *The Social Life of Things: Commodities in Cultural Perspective* (Cambridge, 1986); M. Douglas and B. Isherwood, *The World of Goods* (1980); D. Miller, 'Appropriating the State on the Council Estate', *Man*, n.s., 23 (1988), pp. 353–72.
10 See J. Attfield, 'Inside Pram Town: A Case Study of Harlow House Interiors, 1951–61', A. Partington, 'The Designer Housewife of the 1950s', in Attfield and Kirkham, *View From the Interior*', and C. Steedman, *Landscape For a Good Woman: A Story of Two Lives* (1986).

11 LRO, DDB/72/19 (15 Aug. 1751), E. Parker, Browsholme, to R. Parker, Colne; LRO, DDB/72/43 and 45 (c.1756), R. Parker, York and Skipwith, to E. Parker, Alkincoats.

12 WYCRO, Leeds, TA 18/5 (31 Dec. 1753), W. Gossip, Askam, to A. Gossip, Skelton. See also TA 18/5 (17 Feb. 1747), W. Gossip, Nottingham, to same: 'you must therefore excuse me if I do not execute your commission about the stockings.'

13 LRO, DDB/72/125, 445, 132, 156 (1753–7), J. Scrimshire, Pontefract, to E. Parker, Alkincoats.

14 LRO, DDB/72/177 and 179 (1764), W. and B. Ramsden, Charterhouse, to E. Parker, Alkincoats.

15 For an approximate assessment of global accounting, see LRO, DDB/76/4 (1758–75), Trust Account of Thomas Parker. This account book registers income from rents and investments, plus disbursements on the children's upkeep, travel and tuition. However, it carries no information about John Shackleton's income, or that of Elizabeth Shackleton beyond her £140 p.a. jointure. Reference to total yearly expenditure is made once only, see LRO, DDB/81/3 (1764), f. 12: 'Spent including everything in 1762. £292.0.10. Spent including everything in 1763 £316.0.6.' The diaries contain no evidence of financial anxiety, nor extensive saving; the family appear to have covered ordinary expenditure with a modest margin. However, Elizabeth Shackleton experienced considerable difficulty raising apprenticeship fees of £300, see LRO, DDB/81/14 (1772), fos. 8, 32, 38.

16 Compare WPL, 344/7, Wastebook, 1779–80, fos. 639, 649, 720, with LRO, DDB/81/35 (1779), fos. 51a and 202.

17 LRO, DDB/81/13 (1771), f. 57.

18 By the terms of her first husband's will, Elizabeth Parker was charged with co-guardianship of the three Parker children, and, by her settlement of 1751, entitled to an annuity of £140 a year. After her second marriage she continued to receive her jointure in her own name and managed the children's trust accounts until they came of age. From 1765, however, the trust accounts bear John Shackleton's signature, alongside those of the other trustees. Occasional remarks indicate that a Parker–Shackleton marriage settlement was drawn up, but it has not survived. Refer to LRO, DDB/80/29 (1757), Will of Robert Parker of Alkincoats; LRO, DDB/78/13 (1751), Marriage Settlement of Elizabeth and Robert Parker; LRO, DDB/76/4 (1758–75), Trust Account of Thomas Parker, see entries for 1765–75. For reference to the existence of a second settlement, see LRO, DDB/81/27 (1776), fos. 62–3.

19 See M. B. Norton, *Liberty's Daughters: The Revolutionary Experience of American Women, 1750–1800* (Toronto, 1980), pp. 157–63, and Midgeley, 'Women Anti-Slavery Campaigners in Britain' (Ph.D. thesis), chap. 2.

20 Men's gifts from Birmingham, Sheffield, Skipwith and Chester are recorded in LRO, DDB/81/14 (1772), f. 13; LRO, DDB/81/22 (1774), fos. 3, 45. The enthusiastic consumption of waistcoats is a major theme of the following letters: LRO, DDB/72/322, 328 and 331 (1773–7), J. Parker, London, to T. Parker, Alkincoats.

21 LRO, DDB/72/185 (30 April 1765), W. and B. Ramsden, Charterhouse, to E. Parker, Alkincoats.

22 LRO, DDB/81/35 (1779), f. 51a.

23 LRO, DDB/72/683 (1796), E. Parker, Clitheroe, to T. Parker, Alkincoats.

24 This impression is confirmed by Clifford, 'Parker and Wakelin' (PhD thesis), p. 243. Parker and Wakelin's customers between 1766 and 1777 were made up of 257 men and 43 women. The women's purchases were almost invariably confined to the smaller less expensive items, like individual pieces of teaware, snuff boxes and paste and silver jewellery. Only three woman made large orders for investment goods, such as entire tea services or gold and precious stone jewellery. See also Lippincott, *Selling Art in Georgian London*, pp. 66–9. Wealthy and noble women made up a quarter of the customers of Arthur Pond, the painter and art dealer. However, their average

individual expenditure was in most cases lower than men of the same rank; only two women spent more than £50 and none exceeded £100. 82 per cent of these female consumers made only one purchase as opposed to 62 per cent of the men.

25 A complete breakdown of Elizabeth Shackleton's consumption by individual commodity can be found in Vickery, 'Women of the Local Elite' (Ph.D. thesis), pp. 264–76.

26 See LRO, DDB/72/74 (n.d.), B. Ramsden, Charterhouse, to E. Parker, Alkincoats; LRO, DDB/72/86 (21 March 1754), A. Pellet, London, to E. Parker, Alkincoats.

27 Consult Nichols, 'Gillow and Company', p. 9.

28 See LRO, DDB/72/123, 134, 137 (1753–4), J. Scrimshire, Pontefract, to E. Parker, Alkincoats.

29 LRO, DDB/72/223 (15 March 1768), B. Ramsden, Charterhouse, to E. Shackleton, Alkincoats. By contrast, Ann Pellet who was older and lived a more retired existence, satisfied herself with 'great inquiries' into the 'reigning fashions' on her niece's behalf, LRO, DDB/72/92 (11 June 1754), A. Pellet, London, to E. Parker, Alkincoats.

30 LRO, DDB/72/257 (18 Sept. 1772), B. Ramsden, Charterhouse, to E. Shackleton, Alkincoats; LRO, DDB/72/192 (31 May 1766), W. Ramsden, Charterhouse, to same.

31 LRO, DDB/72/280, 284 (1775), B. Ramsden, Charterhouse, to E. Shackleton, Alkincoats; LRO, DDB Ac 7886/256 (17 Dec. 1748), A. Pellet, London, to E. Parker, Browsholme; LRO, DDB Ac 7886/24 (n.d.), A. Parker, Royle, to E. Shackleton.

32 LRO, DDB/81/36 (1780), 21 April.

33 LRO, DDB/72/184, 280 (1765–75), B. Ramsden, Charterhouse, to E. Shackleton, Alkincoats.

34 LRO, DDB/72/92 (11 June 1754), A. Pellet, London, to E. Parker, Alkincoats; LRO, DDB/72/285 (n.d.), B. and W. Ramsden, Charterhouse, to same; LRO, DDB/72/133, 147 (n.d.), J. Scrimshire, Pontefract, to same.

35 Home, *Upon Education*, p. 231.

36 See LRO, DDB/72/91 (1 June 1754), A. Pellet, London, to E. Parker, Alkincoats; LRO, DDB/72/123 (22 Oct. 1753), J. Scrimshire, Pontefract, to same; LRO, DDB/72/285 (n.d.), B. and W. Ramsden, Charterhouse, to same; and LRO, DDB/72/288 (12 Nov. 1776), B. Ramsden, Charterhouse, to same; WYCRO, Sp St 6/1/50 (1 May 1746), M. Barnardiston to Mrs Stanhope, Leeds. That women were capable of sustaining an interest in fashion throughout the life-cycle is confirmed by N. Rothstein (ed.), *Barbara Johnson's Album of Fashions and Fabrics* (1987).

37 LRO, DDB/74/5 (n.d), Poem 'Given Me by Mrs Parker of Marshfield'. Compare this with M. D. George, *Catalogue of Political and Personal Satires Preserved in the Department of Prints and Drawings in the British Museum* (1942), VII, 1793–1800, 8569, 8570, 9491.

38 WYCRO, Bradford, Sp St 6/1/50 (17 Aug. 1743), M. Warde, Squerries, to Mrs Stanhope; HL, HM 31201, Mrs Larpent's Diary, III, 1799–1800, f. 149.

39 WYCRO, Sp St 6/1/50 (1 May 1746), M. Barnardiston to Mrs Stanhope, Leeds; A. Buck, 'Buying Clothes in Bedfordshire: Customers and Tradesmen, 1700–1800', in N. B. Harte (ed.), *Fabrics and Fashions: Studies in the Economic and Social History of Dress* (1991), pp. 211–37.

40 Weatherill, 'Consumer Behaviour and Social Status', p. 191.

41 Hall, *Miss Weeton's Journal*, I, pp. 33, 253, 122.

42 LRO, DDB/72/191 (3 April 1766), W. and B. Ramsden, Charterhouse, to E. Shackleton, Alkincoats. See also LRO, DDB/72/133 (n.d.), J. Scrimshire, Pontefract, to same: 'I am sorry you have a tabby sac they do not make their Lustrings so genteel in negligées But don't ask my advice again *when the thing is over*'.

43 LRO, DDB/72/207 and 172 (1767), B. and W. Ramsden, Charterhouse, to E. Shackleton, Alkincoats. See also LRO, DDB/72/86 (21 March 1754), A. Pellet, London, to E. Parker, Alkincoats.

44 LRO, DDB/72/684, 686 and 689 (1806–12), E. Parker, Preston and Selby, to T. Parker, Alkincoats; LRO, DDWh/4/80 and 131 (1816), A. Robbins, London, to E. Whitaker, Roefield.

45 LRO, DDB/81/26 (1775), f. 106; LRO, DDB/81/33A (1778), f. 187; LRO, DDB/81/33A (1778), f. 53; LRO, DDB/81/35 (1779), f. 17.

46 These generalizations are supported by LRO, DDB/81/37 (1780), f. 191; LRO, DDB/81/13 (1771), f. 8; and LRO, DDB/81/35 (1779), fos. 14, 116, 123, 126, 213.

47 The ritual packing up of 'Bag and Baggage' is illustrated in LRO, DDB/81/13 (1771), fos. 32, 33, and LRO, DDB/81/35 (1779), f. 119. On the role of clothes as a bargaining tool, see LRO, DDB/81/35 (1779), fos. 83–4.

48 LRO, DDB/81/37 (1780), f. 308.

49 The flourishing second-hand clothes business is reconstructed in Lemire, 'Consumerism in Pre-Industrial and Early Industrial England'. Daniel Roche cites the Parisian trade in second-hand finery as evidence to support an emulation model of popular consumer behaviour. Predictably, covetous female servants are presented as the chief carriers of the emulation virus. See, *The People of Paris: An Essay in Popular Culture in the Eighteenth Century* (Leamington Spa, 1987). A more profitable approach to the issue of servants and clothes, considering the difficulties employers faced providing clothes that reflected both their own prestige and the dependent status of their employees, can be found in Buck, *Dress in Eighteenth-Century England*, pp. 103–19. For a tenacious servant, see LRO, DDB/81/29 (1776), f. 98: 'Susan Harrison came here for her cloaths said if I shod not [let] her her wages wages 15s She wo'd have a Warrant for me by four this afternoon.'

50 See respectively, LRO, DDB/81/33A (1778), f. 118; and LRO, DDB/72/310 (16 March 1777), E. Shackleton, Alkincoats, to R. Parker, London. See also LRO, DDB/81/35 (1779), f. 148: 'I am on this day 54 or 55 years old . . . I put on my new white long lawn Pocket Handchief mark'd E.2. red in Honour of this Good day.'

51 LRO, DDB/81/35 (1779), f. 73.

52 LRO, DDB/81/33A (1778), f. 223. See also LRO, DDB/81/35 (1779), f. 96, on the first use of 'new Japan night Candlesticks'.

53 LRO, DDB/81/35 (1779), f. 221.

54 LRO, DDB/81/37 (1780), fos. 154–5.

55 LRO, DDB/81/17 (1772), f. 85.

56 See LRO, DDB/81/33A (1778), f. 68; LRO, DDB/81/35 (1779), fos. 87, 225, 235; LRO, DDB/81/10 (1770), f. 66.

57 LRO, DDB/81/39 (1781), f. 16(6).

58 LRO, DDB/81/17 (1772), f. 34. She could not resist mocking the 'great talker' Mrs Cunliffe for her elaborate coiffure and even her friend Mrs Walton 'in high conceit with herself and long train', see LRO, DDB/81/33A (1778), fos. 179, 184.

59 LRO, DDB/81/23 (1774), f. 72.

60 LRO, DDB/81/39 (1781), fos. 31–2. Affected architectural features were a popular target for satire in this period, see Donald, 'Mr Deputy Dumpling and Family'.

61 LRO, DDB/81/30 (1777), fos. 8–9. See also fos. 32–3.

62 LRO, DDB/81/35 (1779), f. 77; LRO, DDB/81/25 (1775), f. 107; LRO, DDB/81/35 (1779), f. 196; LRO, DDB/81/28 (1776), fos. 53–4.

63 For example LRO, DDB/81/19 (1773), f. 71.

64 LRO, DDB/81/27 (1776), fos. 47, 97–8.

65 LRO, DDB/81/31 (1777), f. 102.

66 LRO, DDB/81/13 (1771), f. 63. For the social significance of exchanges of game in landed society, see D. Hay, 'Poaching and the Game Laws on Cannock Chase', in D. Hay, P. Linebaugh, E. P. Thompson (eds.), *Albion's Fatal Tree: Crime and Society in Eighteenth-Century England* (1975), pp. 244–53.

67 LRO, DDB/81/39 (1781), f. 166. The painting officially belonged to Elizabeth

Shackleton, given by John Parker in 1776: 'A more valuable gift he co'd not have bestow'd': LRO, DDB/81/27 (1776), f. 18.

68 LRO, DDB/81/33A (1778), f. 40.

69 LRO, DDB/81/35 (1779), f. 202.

70 LRO, DDB/81/37 (1780), f. 261.

71 LRO, DDB/81/30 (1777), f. 40.

72 See respectively LRO, DDB/81/30 (1777), f. 40; LRO, DDB/81/33A (1778), f. 15; and LRO, DDB/81/35 (1779), f. 213.

73 LRO, DDB/81/35 (1779), f. 74.

74 LRO, DDB/81/37 (1780), f. 78.

75 LRO, DDB/81/35 (1779), f. 209.

76 Pennington, *Unfortunate Mother's Advice*, pp. 34–5.

77 LRO, DDB/72/179 (15 June 1764), B. Ramsden, Farm Hill, to E. Parker, Alkincoats. Bessy Ramsden was sufficiently versed in the language of envy and emulation to joke about the social impact of the Duchess of Devonshire's wax fruit 'was I in a Longing situation I should certainly mark the little one with a Bunce of currance which I saw at the Milliners'. See LRO, DDB/72/280 (18 Dec. 1775), same to E. Shackleton, Alkincoats.

78 LRO, DDB/81/35 (1779), f. 116.

79 For example LRO, DDB/81/37 (1780), f. 263.

80 LRO, DDB/72/132 (16 May 1754), J. Scrimshire, Pontefract, to E. Parker, Alkincoats; LRO, DDB/72/254 (4 May 1772), B. Ramsden, Charterhouse, to same; LRO, DDB/72/122 (c.1761), A. Pellet, London, to same. On the remembrance of 'dead as well as living friends' and Mrs Pellet's ambition to raise a monument on the grave of her father, see LRO, DDB/72/94 (1754), same to same.

81 Jane Pedder of Lancaster minutely catalogued her son's possessions, enquired after the state of his shirts, promised him 'some little present that you may say this come from London', and charged him to preserve a book of pressed flowers exactly as his brother had left it, see LRO, DDPd/17/1 (29 Feb. 1786 and 16 April 1786), J. Pedder, Lancaster, to J. Pedder, Blackburn. An admirer of Miss Martha Barcroft's set a lock of her hair into a ring for remembrance and treasured the little box she had donated, see LRO, DDB/72/1407 (29 Sept. 1785), D. Lang, London, to M. Barcroft, Colne. Ellen Parker acknowleged the power of objects to plead remembrance in letters to her Colne aunts, see for example LRO, DDB/72/1194 (21 June 1817), E. Parker, Selby, to E. Moon, Colne, and LRO, DDB/72/1507 (29 May 1821), E. Parker, Selby, to E. Reynolds, Colne.

82 Hall, *Miss Weeton's Journal*, II, pp. 353, 331, 325.

83 Because of the lack of comparable case studies, it is as yet impossible to assess whether the attitudes here outlined are peculiar to the later eighteenth century. Similar research on the personal records of seventeenth- and nineteenth-century consumers might, after all, uncover similar findings. Gifts, for instance, were worn for the sake of the donor in the seventeenth century, see Crawford, 'Katharine and Philip Henry', pp. 52–3, and V. Sackville-West (ed.), *Diary of Lady Anne Clifford*, p. 44. Lady Anne Clifford also recorded re-threading a string of pearls given by her mother, the first day her daughter wore stays and later a coat, the associations of different rooms, and inviting a female visitor into her closet to look at her clothes, see pp. 42, 64, 66, 67, 82. Moreover, the evidence of wills suggests the sentimental associations of artefacts in the fifteenth century, see BIHR, Probate Register VI, fos. 227, 214; Register III, f. 523. I am grateful to Jenny Kermode for this reference.

84 This emerges from a comparison of men and women's wills from Birmingham, Sheffield and South Lancashire, 1700–1800 (personal communication from Maxine Berg), and from East Anglia in the sixteenth and seventeenth centuries (personal communication from Susan Amussen and Christopher Marsh). This pattern has also

been remarked by historians of eighteenth-century America. Gloria Main notes that women's wills often contained loving descriptions of artefacts in contrast to the male focus on land. If men dwelt on their personalty at all, their comments were confined to a favourite animal or gun: G. Main, 'Widows in Rural Massachusetts on the Eve of Revolution', in Hoffman and Albert, *Women in the Age of American Revolution*, pp. 88–9. The possibility of a distinctively female attachment to household goods has also been raised by novelists, see H. James, *The Spoils of Poynton* (1897), *passim*, and G. Eliot, *The Mill on the Floss* (Harmondsworth, 1986), pp. 280–95.

85   This pattern of testamentary behaviour has been widely observed on either side of the Atlantic, see Davidoff and Hall, *Family Fortunes*, pp. 276 and 511; S. Lebsock, *The Free Women of Petersburg: Status and Culture in a Southern Town, 1784–1860* (New York, 1984).

86   See Norton, *Liberty's Daughters* (see n. 19 above), pp. 396–7. Norton compared the claims for compensation made by loyalist men and women exiled during the American War of Independence with useful results. Although the men consistently placed a precise valuation on their house and land, very few of the women were able to do so. By contrast, men submitted inadequate inventories of household goods, such as furniture, tableware and kitchen utensils, while the women could produce minute accounts. To Norton the contrasting lists submitted by men and women suggest not only discrete fields of knowledge, but different material priorities.

6   Civility and Vulgarity

1   LRO, DDB/81/33A (1778), f. 167.

2   Quoted in Heal, *Hospitality in Early Modern England*, p. 6. This offers the most sustained and rigorous study of hospitality as a trope and a social practice. On the public aspects of the elite family in a patronage society, see Pollock, 'Living on the Stage of the World'. For an explicit statement about the family as a public institution, see Amussen, *Ordered Society*, p. 36.

3   On the alleged walling-off of the nuclear family from kin, their withdrawal from the community, and the creation of architectural privacy, see Stone, *Family, Sex and Marriage*, pp. 149–80, 245–6. The rise of modern privacy is the framing premise of P. Ariès, *A History of Private Life* (1989).

4   On eighteenth-century survivals, see Mingay, *English Landed Society*, pp. 205–32; Beckett, *Aristocracy in England*, pp. 324–73; Jenkins, *Glamorgan Gentry*, pp. 196–216; Howell, *Gentry of South-West Wales*, pp. 182–4; and, despite the contradictory assertions in his earlier book, see Stone, *Open Elite?*, pp. 307–10. A comparable study of the sociability of rich Virginia planters is D. B. Smith, *Inside the Great House: Planter Family Life in the Eighteenth Century Chesapeake Society* (Ithaca, 1980), esp. pp. 200, 217.

5   L. Colley, *In Defiance of Oligarchy: The Tory Party, 1714–60* (Cambridge, 1982), pp. 100, 129–30.

6   B. J. Harris, 'Women and Politics in Early Tudor England', *HJ*, 33 (1990), pp. 259–81; L. Barroll, 'The Court of the First Stuart Queen', in L. Levy Peck (ed.), *The Mental World of the Jacobean Court* (Cambridge, 1991), pp. 191–208; L. Colley, 'Things That Are Worth Naming', *London Review of Books*, 21 Nov. 1991; Jalland, *Women, Marriage and Politics*; M. Pugh, *The Tories and the People, 1880–1935* (Oxford, 1985).

7   Haltunnen, *Confidence Men and Painted Women*, pp. 92–123, and Kasson, *Rudeness and Civility*, pp. 173–81.

8   Dallet Hemphill, 'Men, Women and Visiting' (unpub.), pp. 2–3. She continues:

'Rather than an aspect of a private female sphere we are talking about either a female public sphere, if one adopts a broad definition of "the public sphere", or, at the least, a female social sphere, an intermediate sphere where both sexes could interact in a quasi-public, quasi-private fashion. Historians have long been aware of the ways in which northern white middle-class women stretched their domestic sphere into the public domain in the ante-bellum era through associational and reform activity. Perhaps we also need to recognize the ways in which they pulled public functions into their so-called private domain by acknowledging the existence of this intermediate social sphere.' (p. 10). For similar doubts about the usefulness of the public/private model, see K. V. Hanson, *A Very Social Time: Crafting Community in Ante-bellum New England* (Berkeley, 1996).

9   D. F. Bond (ed.), *Spectator* (Oxford, 1965), I, p. 44.

10   On the potential space for female debate, see Klein, 'Gender, Conversation and the Public Sphere', pp. 111–12, and the slightly less expansive Copley, 'Commerce, Conversation and Politeness'. For contrasting assessments of Addison and Steele, see Hunt, 'Wife Beating'; Shevelow, *Women and Print Culture, passim*, and Blanchard, 'Richard Steele and the Status of Women', pp. 325–55.

11   D. Goodman, *The Republic of Letters: A Cultural History of the French Enlightenment* (Ithaca, 1994), pp. 5–11, 53–89, 123–4; id., 'Public Sphere and Private Life'.

12   For an exceptionally lucid account of changing advice on manners, see Childs, 'Prescriptions for Manners' (D.Phil. thesis), pp. 45–130. But see also the informative J. E. Mason, *Gentlefolk in the Making: Studies in the History of English Courtesy Literature and Related Topics, from 1531–1774* (Philadelphia, Pa., 1935). More specific is L. Klein, *Shaftesbury and the Culture of Politeness: Moral Discourse and Cultural Politics in Early Eighteenth-Century England* (Cambridge, 1994). For the reception and application of English conduct literature in America, see R. L. Bushman, *The Refinement of America: Persons, Houses, Cities* (New York, 1993).

13   Childs, 'Prescriptions for Manners' (D.Phil. thesis), pp. 143–287, and Mason, *Gentlefolk* (see n. 12 above), pp. 253–90.

14   LRO, DDB Ac 7886/125 (*c*.1746), R. Parker, Alkincoats to E. Parker. On secrecy and the elite family, see Pollock, 'Living on the Stage of the World'.

15   See *Gentleman's Magazine*, 67 (1797), pt 2, p. 612: '[John Parker] from his education, rank, and habits of life, was well known and much respected in the circles of the polite and noble, on account of his great hilarity, benevolence and generosity, not to mention the hereditary characteristic of Browsholme – a boundless hospitality.' Consider also Edward Parker's obituary in *Gentleman's Magazine*, 65 (1795), pt I, p. 82.

16   WYCRO, Bradford, Sp St 6/1/50 (n.d.), loose sheet, M. Warde to M. Warde.

17   See, for example, LRO, DDB/81/35 (1779), f. 275.

18   See LRO, DDB/81/25 (1775), f. 10; LRO, DDB/81/29 (1776), fos. 33–4; and LRO, DDB/81/35 (1779), fos. 75, 214.

19   LRO, DDB/81/17 (1772), f. 73.

20   LRO, DDB/72/321 (2 June 1773), J. Parker, London, to T. Parker, Alkincoats. In a similar manner, John Parker recommended a Mr Sheridan to his acquaintance in 1778: LRO, DDB/81/33B (1778), f. 57.

21   LRO, DDB/81/20 (1773), f. 72.

22   LRO, DDB/72/305 (10 June 1775), E. Shackleton, Alkincoats, to R. Parker, London.

23   LRO, DDB/81/13 (1771), f. 77.

24   LRO, DDB/81/35 (1779), f. 47; LRO, DDB/81/32 (1777), f. 99.

25   WYCRO, Bradford, Sp St 6/1/50 (16 Aug. 1745), M. Clayton to M. Stanhope; HL, HM 31201 Anna Larpent's Diary, I, 1790–95, f. 20.

26   See Nash's 'Rules to be observed at Bath', of 1742, in Goldsmith, *Richard Nash*, pp. 31–3. See also WYCRO, Bradford Sp St 6/1/50 (6 June 1742), M. Warde, Squerries, to M. Warde, Hooton Pagnell: 'every day was employed in receiving or making visits, an

Intrusion I was rather sorry for . . . as a ceremonious visit sometimes interrupted us in schemes we had rather pursued en famille, as confining us to the house and fixing the tea table in the drawing room, which we had rather proposed following into a wood . . .'

27 See LRO, DDB/72/132 (16 May 1754), J. Scrimshire, Pontefract, to E. Parker, Alkincoats; LRO, DDB/72/101 (n.d.), A. Pellet, London, to E. Parker, Alkincoats. For a fascinating comparison with an earlier period, read Whayman's account of John Verney's laxity in making wedding visits in 1680 and the corresponding resentment of his relatives, in her 'Sociability and Power' (Ph.D. thesis), pp. 276–324. Parallel arguments for later eighteenth-century America about rituals of inclusion and exclusion can be found in Bushman, *Refinement of America* (see n. 12 above), pp. 49–52.

28 LRO, DDB/72/310 (16 March 1777), E. Shackleton, Alkincoats, to R. Parker, London.

29 Kin were predominant in the social life of Nathaniel Bacon of Stiffkey, Norfolk, in the sixteenth century and very close kin in that of Ralph Josselin in the seventeenth century: Macfarlane, *Ralph Josselin*, pp. 153–60, and personal communication from A. Hassell Smith.

30 LRO, DDB//81/39 (1781), f. 101.

31 LRO, DDB/81/37 (1780), fos. 187, 263.

32 It is widely recognized that mealtimes were in flux over the course of the eighteenth century. For a rather quaint, but well-illustrated discussion of eating habits, see Hole, *English Home Life*, pp. 108–13. A more socially specific account can be found in Cruikshank and Burton, *Life in the Georgian City*, pp. 27–45. All that can be said with confidence of gastronomic habits in the North, is that breakfast was taken early to mid-morning, dinner mid- to late afternoon and supper late evening. The advancement of the polite dinner hour was acknowledged by Elizabeth Shackleton when she talked of eating dinner 'at the fashionable hour four o'clock', and this was the time chosen by Thomas and Betty Parker for their celebration dinners, see LRO, DDB/81/ 33A (1778), f. 94.

33 See Cruikshank and Burton, *Georgian City*, pp. 40–43.

34 LRO, DDB/81/37 (1780), f. 35.

35 See above, pp. 168–9; Shammas, 'Domestic Environment'.

36 B. Kowaleski-Wallace, 'Women, China and Consumer Culture in Eighteenth-Century England', *Eighteenth-Century Studies*, 29 (1995–6), p. 165. See also id., 'Tea, Gender and Domesticity'.

37 LRO, DDB/81/35 (1779), f. 135.

38 LRO, DDB/81/22 (1774), f. 29; LRO, DDB/81/31 (1777), f. 44; LRO, DDB/81/33A (1778), f. 103.

39 These phrases are taken in sequence from LRO, DDB/72/445 and 127 (1754–55), J. Scrimshire, Pontefract, to E. Parker, Alkincoats; LRO, DDB/72/220 (12 Jan. 1769), W. Ramsden, Charterhouse, to E. Shackleton, Alkincoats; LRO, DDB/72/115 and 167 (24 Jan. 1757), A. Pellet, London, to E. Parker later Shackleton, Alkincoats.

40 LRO, DDB/72/225 (25 July 1769), W. Ramsden, London, to E. Shackleton, Alkincoats. Criticisms of female visiting can be found in a letter 'To a Very Young Lady on Her Marriage' by Dr Swift, in *New Letter Writer*, p. 60; and *Gentleman's Magazine*, 6 (1736), p. 390. A bubbling account of a female gathering over a singing tea kettle and the morning paper is reproduced in R. Lonsdale (ed.), *Eighteenth-Century Women Poets* (Oxford, 1990), pp. 425–6. John Brown linked tea drinking and defamation in 1708, see Ashton, *Social Life in the Reign of Queen Anne*, I, pp. 95–6. For a brief, but suggestive gloss on the complaint literature, see Childs, 'Prescriptions for Manners' (D.Phil. thesis), pp. 255–7.

41 LPL, MS 8752 (1776), 7 July; LPL, MS 8753 (1778), 1 May; LPL, MS 8754 (1779), 2 June.

42 LRO, DDB/81/33A (1778), fos. 250 and 208; LRO, DDB/81/35 (1779), fos. 235a, 236, 239, 240, 277–9.

43 See respectively, LRO, DDB/81/26 (1775), f. 96, and LRO, DDB/81/33A (1778), f. 143.

44 LRO, DDB/81/33A (1778), f. 191; LRO, DDB/81/39 (1781), f. 182. See also f. 23: 'I sent to let my own dear Tom know how ill I was. He said he expected Company to dine with him, but if he co'd make it convenient to him he wo'd come some time this day here for 1/2 an hour. Bad work. He came after dinner was rather sly did not take much notice of me. He did stay tea.'

45 LRO, DDB/81/22 (1774), f. 47. Thereafter, she refused to attend dinners where he was invited and once, coming upon him by surprise, called him a low-life rascal and threatened to spit in his face! See LRO, DDB/81/33A (1778), f. 89.

46 LRO, DDB/81/13 (1771), f. 59; LRO, DDB/81/33A (1778), f. 40.

47 Goldsmith, *Richard Nash*, p. 24. The absurdities of an undue ceremoniousness were often remarked on. Praise for a pleasing ease and gentility of behaviour contrasted with an affected formality can be found in the London journal of the Quaker Betty Fothergill in 1769: Brophy, *Women's Lives*, p. 119.

48 LRO, DDB/81/37 (1780), fos. 18, 23, 122; LRO, DDB/81/33A (1778), f. 184.

49 LRO, DDB/81/33A (1778), f. 198. On the loquacious gentleman as a comic trope, see Staves, 'Secrets of Genteel Identity'.

50 Childs, 'Prescriptions for Manners' (D.Phil. thesis), p. 220.

51 LRO, DDB/81/35 (1779), f. 37.

52 LRO, DDB/81/33A (1778), f. 91.

53 LRO, DDB/81/33A (1778), f. 173.

54 LRO, DDB/81/33A (1778), f. 2; LRO, DDB/81/22 (1774), f. 77.

55 LRO, DDB/81/22 (1774), fos. 115, 117.

56 LRO, DDB/81/13 (1771), f. 75.

57 LRO, DDB/81/22 (1774), f. 67; LRO, DDB/81/33A (1778), f. 180.

58 LRO, DDB/81/33A (1778), f. 142; LRO, DDB/81/20 (1773), f. 83.

59 LRO, DDB/81/20 (1773), f. 26.

60 LRO, DDB/81/37 (1780), fos. 187–8.

61 See Childs, 'Prescriptions for Manners' (D.Phil. thesis), p. 198.

62 LRO, DDB/81/37 (1780), f. 17.

63 LRO, DDB/81/37 (1780), f. 134.

64 LRO, DDB/81/39 (1781), fos. 174, 175.

65 LRO, DDB/81/33A (1778), fos. 120–21; LRO, DDB/81/17 (1772), f. 87; LRO, DDB/81/20 (1773), fos. 21 and 4; LRO, DDB/81/22 (1774), f. 37. She also despaired that 'his ways that of his family are Brutal': DDB//81/39 (1781), f. 175.

66 That anxiety about dishonest performance was always inherent in politeness is the argument of Carter, 'Mollies, Fops and Men of Feeling' (D.Phil. thesis), chap. 8. Childs elucidates the way that the early eighteenth-century concept of 'good breeding' became associated with outer manners at the expense of inner civility, leading to its replacement by the term 'politeness', 'Prescriptions for Manners' (D.Phil. thesis), pp. 102–28. Mason also documents the Augustan concern to achieve heart-felt civility rather than an empty formality, *Gentlefolk in the Making*, p. 263. A Republican critique of polite superficiality can be found in Bushman, *Refinement of America* (see n. 12 above), pp. 181–203. Kasson and Haltunnen both discuss American courtesy writers' uneasy attempts to distinguish false etiquette from a true feeling courtesy in the nineteenth century, Haltunnen, *Confidence Men*, pp. 92–123 and Kasson, *Rudeness and Civility*, pp. 173–81. Novelists also distinguished between 'the politeness of manner, formed by the habits of high life' and 'that which springs spontaneously from benevolence of mind.' See Burney, *The Wanderer*, p. 134.

67 *Lord Chesterfield's Letters to His Son* (1774; Oxford, 1992), p. 49.

68 Collier, a *Short View of the Immorality*, p. 7. This, of course, was part and parcel of his attack on the smuttiness of the stage. Why then, he continues, 'Do the Women leave all the regards to Decency and Conscience behind them when they come to the Play-House?'

69   Thompson, 'Patrician Society', p. 389.

70   LRO, DDGR C3 (6 Sept. 1774), R. Greene, Calcutta, to P. Greene, Slyne. By contrast, Lyndal Roper is persuaded that masculine excess is not simply destructive, arguing of male drinking and whoring in sixteenth-century Germany that as much as the councils railed against violence, they also needed to sustain it in case of war: 'Blood and Codpieces: Masculinity in the Early Modern German Town', in id., *Oedipus and the Devil*, pp. 107–24.

71   Westhauser, 'Friendship and Family'.

72   LPL, MS 8754 (1779), 24 Jan.

73   Quoted in Brophy, *Women's Lives*, pp. 178–9.

74   On their wide circulation, see Klein, 'Politeness for Plebes', *passim*.

75   Hall, *Miss Weeton's Journal*, I, pp. 177, 135–6, 217. She also asked her brother to jot down any rules of etiquette that she might have overlooked, sought out a pamphlet on the art of carving and showed awareness of the subtle distinction between a real invitation and an empty compliment. See pp. 212 and 111.

76   LRO, DDGr C1 (6 July 1765), T. Greene, Serjeant's Inn, London, to his mother, Slyne.

77   Beresford, *James Woodforde*, I, p. 86; Gibson, *George Woodward's Letters*, pp. 50, 73.

78   LRO, DDB/81/33A (1778), fos. 180, 201–2; LRO, DDB/81/35 (1779), f. 249.

79   LRO, DDB/81/23 (1774), f. 70.

80   Leheny, *The Freeholder*, p. 56. The term 'Hottentot' denoting a rude and uncivilized person persisted in the literature of etiquette and courtesy. In his *Never: A Handbook for the Unititated and Inexperienced Aspirants to Refined Society's Giddy Heights and Glittering Attainments* (New York, 1884), Nathan D. Urner ordered gentleman 'Never appear at breakfast, even in sultry weather, without your coat, waistcoat, collar and necktie. Are you a gentleman or a Hottentot?' Cited in Kasson, *Rudeness and Civility*, p. 279. William Ramsden also likened rude companions to Hottentots: 'I am sorry their Company was not *better* but there are *Hottentots* to be met with in many [parts] besides the *Cape of Good Hope*, and no where oftener [than] on a *StageCoach*.' See LRO, DDB/72/172 (29 Dec.), W. Ramsden, Charterhouse, to E. Parker, Alkincoats. Hottentots had some local celebrity however, since 'The Famous African' had been exhibited at York races in 1741. See J. Jefferson Looney, 'Cultural life in the Provinces: Leeds and York, 1720–1820', in A. L. Beier, D. Cannadine and J. M. Rosenheim (eds.), *The First Modern Society: Essays in English History in Honour of Lawrence Stone* (Cambridge, 1989), p. 491.

81   See respectively LRO, DDB/81/35 (1779), fos. 265, 186–7, 190.

82   LRO, DDB/81/33A (1778), f. 121.

83   For this and other reactions to the letters, see Mason, *Gentlefolk in the Making*, p. 106.

84   LRO, DDB/81/37 (1780), f. 178.

7   Propriety

1   WYCRO, Bradford, Sp St 6/1/50 (29 March 1741), M. Warde, London, to M. Warde, Hooton Pagnell.

2   LRO, DDB Ac 7886/267 (28 Feb. 1748/9), A. Pellet, London, to E. Parker, Browsholme. See Borsay, *English Urban Renaissance, passim*; Barry, 'Cultural Life of Bristol' (D.Phil. thesis), p. 245.

3   J. Habermas, *The Structural Transformation of the Public Sphere: An Inquiry into a Category of Bourgeois Society* (Cambridge, Ma., 1989), p. 25; quoted in J. Brewer,

'The Most Polite Age and the Most Vicious: Attitudes towards Culture as a Commodity, 1660–1800', in Brewer and Bermingham, *Consumption of Culture*, p. 343. Other essays which use Habermas as a point of departure are in Castiglione and Sharpe, *Shifting the Boundaries*.

4   This interpretation in political history can be traced to John Money's influential article 'Taverns, Coffee Houses and Clubs: Local Politics and Popular Articulacy in the Birmingham Area in the Age of American Revolution', *HJ*, 14 (1971), pp. 15–47. The local picture was developed in his own *Experience and Identity*, and translated into national terms in Brewer, *Party, Ideology and Popular Politics*.

5   For one Marxist historian, the growth of a reading public, the commercialization of leisure, educational improvements and the increased economic and cultural confidence of the eighteenth-century town all add up to, 'the gradual coherence of a self-conscious middle-class public, whose provincialism was less an embarrassment than an expression of buoyant creativity'. See Eley, 'Rethinking the Political', p. 428.

6   Bermingham, 'Introduction', in Brewer and Bermingham, *Consumption of Culture*, p. 10.

7   R. J. Morris, 'Clubs, Societies and Associations', in F. M. L. Thompson (ed.), *The Cambridge Social History of Britain, 1750–1950* (Cambridge, 1990), III, p. 397. See also Hall, *White, Male and Middle Class*, pp. 75–93.

8   See J. Walkowitz, *City of Dreadful Delight: Narratives of Sexual Danger in Late Victorian London* (1992), pp. 41–80, on the 'new urban female style of being at home in the city' (p. 46).

9   Langford, *Polite and Commercial People*, p. 109. Barry also sees an enhanced role for women in eighteenth-century Bristol, see his 'Cultural Life of Bristol' (D.Phil. thesis), p. 170. And women are centre stage in the rich description of provincial assemblies in Girouard, *The English Town*, pp. 127–44. The importance of platforms for female refinement is emphasized in J. Brewer, *The Pleasures of the Imagination: English Culture in the Eighteenth Century* (1997), pp. 56–122.

10   WYCRO, Bradford Sp St 6/1/50 (10 June 1739), M. Warde, J. Warde, T. Warde and T. Duckworth, Squerries, Kent, to M. Warde, Hooton Pagnell; LRO, DDB/72/223 and 284 (n.d.), B. Ramsden, Charterhouse, to E. Shackleton, Alkincoats.

11   LRO, DDPd/17 (19 March 1786), J. Pedder, Lancaster, to J. Pedder, Blackburn.

12   W. M. Thomas (ed.), *Letters and Works of Lady Mary Wortley Montagu* (1893), II, p. 298, and Richardson, *Sir Charles Grandison*, p. 22. For similar examples, see Klein, 'Gender and the Public/Private Distinction'.

13   Brewer, 'Most Polite Age', p. 355.

14   B. van Muyden (ed.), *Foreign View of England in the Reigns of George I and George II: The Letters of Monsieur Cesar De Saussure to his Family* (1902), p. 44. For elaboration, see R. O. Bucholz, *The Augustan Court: Queen Anne and the Decline of Court Culture* (Stanford, Ca., 1993), pp. 202–48.

15   WYCRO, Bradford, Sp St 6/1/50 (28 May 1740), M. Warde, Squerries, to M. Warde, Hooton Pagnell.

16   LRO, DDGr C3 (23 Sept. 1765), T. Greene, London, to Miss Greene, Slyne.

17   See LRO, DDB/72/192 and 263 (1766–73), W. Ramsden, Charterhouse, to E. Shackleton, Alkincoats; LRO, DDGr C3 (n.d.), Anon., to Miss Greene, Slyne.

18   See the excellent W. Weber, 'L'Institution et son public: L'Opera à Paris et à Londres au XVIIIe siècle', *Annales*, 6 (1993), pp. 1519–39, and Weber, 'Opera and Nobility' (unpub. paper). I thank the author for allowing me to quote from this. See also C. Taylor, 'From Losses to Lawsuit: Patronage of the Italian Opera in London by Lord Middlesex, 1739–45', *Music and Letters*, 68 (1987), pp. 1–26.

19   Earl of Bessborough (ed.), *Georgiana: Extracts from the Correspondence of Georgiana, Duchess of Devonshire* (1955), p. 104.

20   C. B. Hogan, *The London Stage, 1660–1800* (Carbondale, Il., 1968), 'Part 5: 1776–

1800', p. xxvii; Burney, *Evelina*, pp. 38, 91; Conolly, 'Censor's Wife at the Theatre',
p. 58.

21   For example, in 1746 Jane Pellet reported, 'Operas are so bad nobody will go but
plays are more in fashion than they have been for several years that is they are better
Acted but they tempt me very little as they are all Tragedians': LRO, DDB Ac 7886/
130 (2 Dec. 1746), J. Pellet, London, to E. Parker, Browsholme. In 1771 Thomas Noel
reported 'it is quite the ton to go to' plays: M. Elwin (ed.), *The Noels and The
Milbankes: Their Letters for Twenty-Five Years, 1767-1792* (1967), p. 31.

22   The London stage and its public is a subject too massive to do justice to here. For
further discussion, see Price, *Theatre in the Age of Garrick*; Donahue, *Theatre in
the Age of Keen*; Nicholl, *The Garrick Stage*; and Pedicord, *By Their Majesties'
Command*; Brewer, *Pleasures* (see n. 9 above), pp. 325-423.

23   Conolly, 'Censor's Wife at the Theatre', pp. 53, 56.

24   LRO, DDB/64/14 (c.1808), Ellen Barcroft's Journal, f. 5.

25   Burney, *Evelina*, p. 25; LRO, DDPd/25/16 (c.1786), Margaret Pedder's Views of a
Journey to London, f. 4; H. Phillips, *Mid-Georgian London: A Topographical and
Social Survey of Central and Western London about 1750* (1964), p. 154; *The Connoisseur*, 43, 21 Nov. 1754, p. 255. When the Ramsdens went to 'Mrs Abbertsons
Benefit', they found the pit and the boxes so full, that they had to repair to the gallery,
where they could catch no sight of Garrick: LRO, DDB/72/284 (n.d.), B. Ramsden,
Charterhouse, to E. Shackleton, Alkincoats. Haywood's reckless heroine exposed
herself at the playhouse 'sitting in the third row' with a woman of ill-repute and had
to take the consequences. Ineffectually, she protested 'Pish . . . I went to see the play,
not to be seen myself': Haywood, *Betsy Thoughtless*, pp. 201, 202, 204.

26   Avery, 'Shakespeare Ladies Club'; M. Dobson, *The Making of the National Poet:
Shakespeare, Adaptation and Authorship, 1660-1769* (Oxford, 1992), pp. 147-58.

27   A. W. McDonald, 'The Season of 1782 on the Yorkshire Circuit', *Theatre Notebook*,
37 (1983), pp. 104-9, and id., 'The Social Life of the Performer on the Yorkshire
Circuit, 1766-1785', *Theatre Survey*, 25 (1984), pp. 167-76. For a parallel circuit, see
S. Rosenfeld, *The Georgian Theatre of Richmond, Yorkshire and its Circuit:
Beverley, Harrogate, Kendal, Northallerton, Ulverston and Whitby* (1984), and for a
wider context consult, id., *Strolling Players and Drama in the Provinces, 1660-1765*
(Cambridge, 1939).

28   G. D. Lumb (ed.), 'Extracts from the Leeds Intelligencer and the Leeds Mercury,
1769-1776', *Thoresby Society Publications*, XXXVIII (1938), pp. 60-3.

29   Abigail Gawthern saw Mrs Jordan act at the Nottingham playhouse in Garrick's *The
Country Girl* in 1790 and thought 'she performed delightfully'. She saw Mrs Siddons
act in *Macbeth* (1623), Garrick's *Isabella: Or the Fatal Marriage* (1757) and Otway's
Venice Preserved: Or A Plot Discovered (1735) at the same theatre in 1807: Henstock,
Diary of Abigail Gawthern, pp. 52, 131. Charlotte Dickson was awed by seeing Mrs
Siddons in Centlivre's *The Gamester: A Comedy* (1705) in 1795: 'I never saw a
countenance so strikingly expressive': LRO, DDB/72/1489 (7 July 1795), C. Dickson,
Berwick, to E. Barcroft. Ellen Weeton enjoyed a comfortable front seat in the gallery
of the Liverpool theatre in 1809. Though 'wonder struck' by Sarah Siddons as the
sleep-walking Lady Macbeth, she thought the witches and ghosts laughably banal:
Hall, *Miss Weeton's Journal*, I, p. 175. Charles Whitaker went to see one of Kemble's
last performances as Macbeth in Edinburgh: LRO, DDWh/4/55 (7 May 1814),
C. Whitaker, Edinburgh, to E. Whitaker, London.

30   On the rage for private theatricals, see Rosenfeld, *Temples of Thespis*, p. 118. On the
ambiguities of acting, see Crouch, "Attitudes towards Actresses' (D.Phil. thesis), pp.
98-132. The narrative possibilities inherent in amateur performance were seized on by
novelists, but assessments of the morality of female exhibition differed. Fanny Price
piously refuses to take part in *Lover's Vows*, which redounds to her credit: Jane

Austen, *Mansfield Park* (1814; Oxford, 1970), pp. 109–76. The pure and perfect Caroline Percy declines an invitation to take part in *Zara*, which in the event demonstrates the vanity of her rival, yet Caroline remains a sympathetic member of the audience: M. Edgeworth, *Patronage* (1814; 1986), pp. 346–69. On the other hand, the 'incognita' is allowed to give a dignified performance as Lady Townley in *The Provoked Husband* (1728), which convinces many in the audience of her gentility: Burney, *The Wanderer*, pp. 70–96. I am indebted to Charlotte Mitchell for alerting me to these preoccupations.

31 Russell, *Theatres of War*, p. 125. See also Rosenfeld, *Temples of Thespis*, p. 38.

32 On gentry performances, see Russell, *Theatres of War*, pp. 129–31, and Rosenfeld, *Temples of Thespis*, p. 8. Though there is no indication that the northern families studied here mounted private theatricals themselves, their fascination with the fabulous productions of the fashionable is evident. When Lord Stanley and his friends performed the play *Tancred and Sigismunde* (1745) in gorgeous costumes at the Preston Playhouse in October 1773 at least two of Elizabeth Shackleton's friends wrote letters describing the scene in full detail: LRO, DDB/72/1581 (24 Oct. 1773), E. Parker, Preston, to E. Shackleton, Alkincoats, and LRO, DDB/81/18 (1773), f. 81.

33 Borsay, *English Urban Renaissance*, pp. 122–3. For Leeds performances, see Lumb, 'Leeds Intelligencer and Leeds Mercury, 1769–1776' (see n. 28 above), pp. 16, 21, 70. For women's attendance at music meetings and oratorios in London, York, Pontefract, Preston and Nottingham, see LRO, DDPd/25/16 (*c*.1786), Margaret Pedder's Views of a Journey to London, f. 10; LRO, DDB/72/1198 (1 Oct. 1823), E. Parker, Selby, to E. Moon, Colne; LRO, DDB/72/142 (25 Dec. 1754), J. Scrimshire, Pontefract, to E. Parker, Alkincoats; Henstock, 'Diary of Abigail Gawthern', pp. 28, 105, 145. The analogue to public listening was private performance. Musical accomplishment was sprinkled across the networks. Mary Warde of Hooton Pagnell played the harpsichord in the 1730s and 1740s, Deb Scrimshire learned the spinet in the 1750s, Abigail Gawthern took music lessons from a Nottingham organist in the 1770s. On female musical accomplishments in general, see R. Leppert, *Music and Image: Domesticity, Ideology and Socio-Cultural Formation in Eighteenth-Century England* (Cambridge, 1988), pp. 28–50, 147–75. The world of amateur music-making is reconstructed in J. Brewer, 'The Harmony of Heaven: John Marsh and Provincial Music', in id., *Pleasures* (see n. 9 above), pp. 531–72.

34 LPL, MS 8754 (1779), 27 March; WYCRO, Leeds, TA, Box 22/1 (18 Aug. 1729), S. Gossip, York, to W. Gossip.

35 WYCRO, Bradford, Sp St 6/1/50 (31 Jan. n.y.), M. Barnardiston to Mrs Stanhope.

36 'Forgery Unmasked'. This trial engrossed the viewing and reading public in 1775. Anne Pellet reported that 'all conversation is I think turn'd now wholly on the infamous Mrs Rudd and her two accomplices. And may refer you to the Publick papers': LRO, DDB/72/168 (13 July 1775), A. Pellet, London, to E. Shackleton, Alkincoats. For her part, Mrs Shackleton was in no doubt as to guilt and innocence, noting in her diary the sufferings of the Perreau brothers at hands the of 'that Infamous Vile Woman Margaret Caroline Rudd': LRO, DDB Ac 7886/324 (1775–6), f. 31.

37 *Trials for Adultery*, I, title-page.

38 LRO, DDB/72/283–4 (1776), B. Ramsden, Charterhouse, to E. Shackleton, Alkincoats.

39 See Borsay, *English Urban Renaissance*, pp. 336–49; 'Leeds Intelligencer and the Leeds Mercury, 1777–1782', p. 6; *Oxford English Dictionary*, 'Assembly'.

40 *Notes from the Records of the Assembly Rooms of Edinburgh* (Edinburgh, 1842), quoted in Morris, 'Clubs, Societies and Associations' (see n. 7 above), p. 403. See also H. G. Graham, *The Social Life of Scotland in the Eighteenth-Century* (1909), pp. 98–9; J. Ellis, 'On the Town: Women in Augustan England', *History Today*, XLV, no. 12

(Dec. 1995), p. 22; J. Timbs, *Club Life in London* (1866), I, p. 316 and 88.; P. Egan, *Life in London* (1821), pp. 295–6.

41 In Westmorland it was noted that assemblies included both tradesmen and gentry, while at Tunbridge it was reported 'all ranks are mingled together without distinction. The nobility and the merchants; the gentry and the traders': Langford, *Polite and Commercial People*, pp. 101, 102. But in Derby it appears that 'trade' (by which I imagine they meant retail) was excluded. Similarly, a protest was raised in Romsey when the Southampton organist (and reportedly a shoemaker's son) took out a subscription to the local assembly in 1769: Brewer, *Pleasures* (see n. 9 above), p. 549. On dancing-masters' balls, read Fawcett, 'Dance and Teachers of Dance', and also his 'Provincial Dancing Masters'.

42 See WYCRO, Bradford, Sp St 6/1/50 (19 Jan. 1742), I. Crompton, Doncaster, to M. Stanhope, Horsforth; LRO, DDGr C1 (27 Sept. 1762), B. Wiglesworth, Townhead, to M. Greene; LRO, DDB/81/37 (1780), fos. 67, 69; and LRO, DDB/72/1490 (29 Oct. 1795), C. Dickson, Berwick, to E. Barcroft, Otley; LRO, DDB/72/687 (16 July 1807), E. Parker, Preston, to T. Parker, Alkincoats; LRO, DDB/72/223 (n.d.), B. Ramsden, Charterhouse, to E. Shackleton, Alkincoats.

43 WYCRO, Bradford, Sp St 6/1/50 (1 Dec. 1740), M. Warde, Squerries, Kent, to M. Warde, Hooton Pagnell.

44 Haywood, *Female Spectator*, I, p. 298.

45 Quoted in Jackson, *Hull in the Eighteenth Century*, p. 269.

46 T. Smollett, *Advice: A Satire* (1746), p. 5, n. 30.

47 LRO, DDB/64/14 (*c*.1808), Ellen Barcroft's Journal, f. 25.

48 Ashton, *Old Times*, p. 217; W. Boulton, *The Amusements of Old London* (1901), I, pp. 93–4; Phillips, *Mid-Georgian London* (see n. 25 above), pp. 277 and 91. On the disturbing associations of the masquerade, see Castle, *Masquerade and Civilization*.

49 LRO, DDB/72/251 (30 Jan. 1772), W. Ramsden, Charterhouse, to E. Shackleton, Alkincoats.

50 LRO, DDB Ac 7886/218 (30 April 1748), J. Pellet, London, to E. Parker, Browsholme.

51 WYCRO, Bradford, Sp St 6/1/50 (4 Oct. 1742), M. Richardson, Bierley, to M. Warde, Hooton Pagnell; W. A. Abram, *Memorials of the Preston Guilds* (Preston, 1882), p. 81. The Richardsons of Bierley were an established county family in the West Riding.

52 On the Lascelles's masquerade, see G. D. Lumb and J. B. Place (eds.), 'Extracts from the Leeds Intelligencer and the Leeds Mercury, 1777–1782', *Thoresby Society Publications*, XL (1955), p. 73. For Pontefract, see LRO, DDB/72/445 (2 Jan. *c*.1755), J. Scrimshire, Pontefract, to E. Parker, Alkincoats.

53 Browsholme Letters, Browsholme Hall, Clitheroe, Lancs, uncat. (7 July 1743), J. Pellet, London, to E. Parker, Browsholme.

54 W. Wroth, *The London Pleasure Gardens of the Eighteenth Century* (1896), p. 206.

55 LRO, DDB Ac 7886/273 (25 April 1749), A. Pellet, London, to E. Parker, Browsholme.

56 WYCRO, Bradford, Sp St 6/1/58 (29 Aug. 1749), J. Spencer, Middle Temple, to M. Stanhope, Leeds.

57 Wroth, *Pleasure Gardens*, p. 201.

58 Borsay, *English Urban Renaissance*, pp. 350–54.

59 Van Muyden, *Letters of De Saussure* (see n. 14 above), p. 48. For further commentaries, see Phillips, *Mid-Georgian London* (see n. 25 above), p. 45.

60 Girouard, *English Town*, p. 146.

61 R. Bayne Powell, *Travellers in Eighteenth-Century England* (1951), p. 180.

62 Van Muyden, *Letters of De Saussure* (see n. 14 above), p. 81.

63 Quoted Cruikshank and Burton, *Life in the Georgian City*, p. 23.

64 LRO, DDB/64/14 (*c*.1808), Ellen Barcroft's Journal, loose page.

65 LRO, DDB/72/308 (9 May 1780), E. Shackleton, Pasture House, to R. Parker, London.

66 Halsband, *Letters of Lady Mary Wortley Montagu*, I, p. 75. That in the 1880s women

contested established notions of the public and private, seizing urban pleasure in unprecedented ways, is the founding premise of Walkowitz, *City of Dreadful Delight* (see n. 8 above); E. D. Rappaport, 'The Halls of Temptation: Gender Politics and the Construction of the Department Store in late Victorian London', *Journal of British Studies* (1996), pp. 58–83, is also built on the assumption that shopping was not a legitimate public pursuit for respectable women before the 1880s. Doubtless the prospect of the female consumer out and about in the early to mid-nineteenth century raised considerable cultural anxiety, as female pleasure and consumerism had for centuries, but it would be mistaken to infer from this that respectable women had therefore abstained from shopping for fear of being taken for prostitutes. On the sophistication of shops in the eighteenth-century metropolis and the widespread recognition of shopping as a female cultural pursuit, see Walsh, 'Shop Design and the Display of Goods', and Bayne Powell, *Travellers* (see n. 61 above), pp. 60–61.

67 Tucker, *Instructions for Travellers* (1757); Berchtold; *Essay to Direct and Extend the Inquiries*. For elaboration, see Ousby, *Englishman's England*, and Andrews, *Search for the Picturesque*.

68 Consult LRO, DDB/81/4 (1765), f. 86; LRO, DDB/81/19 (1773), f. 59; LRO, DDB/81/26 (1775), fos. 132–7; LRO, DDB/81/33A (1778), f. 191.

69 LPL, MS 8752 (1776), 11 Jan. and 26 March, LPL, MS 8753 (1778), 14 May, 2 June, 19 Nov.; LRO, DDPd/25/16 (*c.*1786), Margaret Pedder's Views, fos. 5, 6, 10, 15; LPL, MS 8757 (1793), 3, 9, 15 Jan., 5 Aug.; LPL, MS 8758 (1796), 27 June, 30 July, 28 Oct.; and LPL, MS 8759 (1797), 25 Sept., 22 Nov., 31 Dec.; LRO, DDB/64/14 (*c.*1808), Ellen Barcroft's Journal, fos. 8, 23 and loose sheets; LRO, DDWh/4/34 (1 Nov. 1813), A. Wright, London to E. Whitaker, Roefield.

70 Pennington, *Unfortunate Mother's Advice*, pp. 15–16. On the same topic, see Wilkes, *Letter of Genteel Advice*, p. 41. However, I do not deny the reality of piety for many and, of course, female religiosity is a subject in itself. Consider P. Crawford, *Women and Religion in Early Modern England* (1993); D. M. Valenze, *Prophetic Sons and Daughters: Female Preaching and Popular Religion in Industrial England* (1986); G. Malmgreem (ed.), *Religion in the Lives of English Women, 1760–1930* (Bloomington, Ind., 1986). None the less, the absence of religious fervour amongst northern Anglicans is striking and has been noted by experts in the field (personal communication Jan Albers). When Charles Whitaker reported 'The Scotch appear uncommonly religious', he betrayed an indolent Anglicanism common to many: LRO, DDWh/4/55 (7 May 1814), C. Whitaker, Edinburgh, to E. Whitaker, London.

71 See respectively WYCRO, Leeds, TA 22/1 (1 May 1731), S. Gossip, York, to A. Gossip, Bath; LRO, DDB/81/11 (1770), f. 71; LRO, DDB/81/32 (1777), f. 103; LRO, DDB/81/33B (1778), f. 34; WYCRO, Bradford, Sp St/6/1/50 (4 Jan. 1749), M. Warde to M. Warde, Hooton Pagnell; LRO, DDB/72/47 (n.d.), R. Parker, Little Harwood, to E. Parker, Alkincoats: 'Miss Clayton . . . yet has hopes of Mr Faulkner and her sister . . . tells me he looks at her in church and very complaisant'; *The Connoisseur*, 43, 21 Nov. 1754, p. 255.

72 Henstock, 'Diary of Abigail Gawthern', p. 119; LRO, DDWh/4/49 (3 April 1814), B. Addison, Liverpool, to E. Whitaker, Roefield.

73 YAS, MD 3,35/Box 95/xcv/i (*c.*1773), B. Lister, Gisburn Park, to T. Lister, House of Commons. Although the unconventional governess Ellen Weeton thought that women should be encouraged to study divinity, she herself wondered 'who would listen to a female divine, except to ridicule? I could myself almost laugh at the idea.' See Hall, *Miss Weeton's Journal*, i, p. 197.

74 Andrew, 'Female Charity in an Age of Sentiment'; Andrew, *Philanthropy and Police: London Charity in the Eighteenth Century* (Princeton, NJ, 1989); Heal, *Hospitality in Early Modern England*, pp. 178–83.

75 NYRO, ZBA 25/1. In York, a Mrs Faith Gray and a Mrs Catherine Cappe were

instrumental in the establishment and superintendence of a Spinning School (1782), a Grey Coat School for Girls (1785), and a Female Friendly Society (1788), see Gray, *Papers and Diaries of a York Family, 1764–1839* (1927), pp. 54, 60, 67. The Carlisle Female Visiting Society was set up in 1803, and members engaged to search out the abodes of the wretched and supply their inhabitants with comforts. An Infant Clothing Society was set up in the same town in 1811. Similarly, Workington had an Infant Clothing Society (1811), A Blanket Society (1819) and a Dorcas Society (1818) which distributed 600 garments a year 'mostly wrought by the fair hands of the contributors to this excellent charity'. See W. Parson and W. White, *History and Directory of the Counties of Cumberland and Westmoreland* (1829), pp. 308–9. In Hawkshead, a Female Union Society was instituted in 1798: LRO, DP 384/8 Rule Book of Female Union Society. Whalley boasted a Sisterly Love Society active from at least 1818: LRO, DDX 680/2/3. A Female Sociable Society was active in Wadsworth from at least 1810: WYCRO, Bradford, Tong MS 6/6, Membership Certificate. A society was active in Leeds from at least 1801: WYCRO, Leeds, Leeds Female Benefit Society, 6, and in Wakefield from 1805: WYCRO, Wakefield, C 281/7/10, Rules of the Wakefield Female Benefit Society. Chester had a lying-in charity founded in 1798: CCRO, DNA/1, Minutes of the Chester Benevolent Institution. Liverpool boasted a Ladies Charity for the Relief of Poor Women in Childbed (1796), The Female School of Industry (1818), The Friends' Female Charity School (1818) and The Ladies Branch of the Liverpool Auxiliary Society (1818).

76 LRO, DDGr C3 (21 July 1819 and 6 April 1820), S. Tatham, Southall, to Mrs Bradley, Slyne.

77 HL, HM, 31201, Anna Larpent's Diary, XI, 1820–21, f. 2, facing f. 4, facing f. 7, facing f. 13, f. 45, facing f. 51, f. 71 and f. 130.

78 F. K. Prochaska, 'Philanthropy', in F. M. L. Thompson (ed.), *The Cambridge Social History of Britain, 1750–1950* (Cambridge, 1990), III, p. 386.

79 Kimber, *Life and Adventures of Joe Thompson*, II, p. 7. For further discussion, see Borsay, *English Urban Renaissance*, pp. 133–7; Morris, 'Clubs, Societies and Associations' (see n. 7 above), *passim*; Money, *Experience and Identity*, pp. 98–152.

80 Andrew, 'London Debating Societies', pp. 79, 383. Andrew finds that the societies of the 1770s concentrated on political and theological questions, with just a few topics of wider cultural concern. Morals, emotion and matrimony became more popular as debating topics later in the century, but the interest in religion and the state persisted.

81 *The Times*, 29 Oct. 1788, quoted in Andrew, 'London Debating Societies', p. xi. On the suppression of political debate, see D. Andrew 'Popular Culture and Public Debate: London 1780', *HJ*, 39 (1996), p. 421, but see generally pp. 405–23.

82 Beverley Lemire notes that the wife of a middling Manchester family attended a conversation club in the 1770s, see id., *Fashion's Favourite: The Cotton Trade and the Consumer in Britain, 1660–1800* (Oxford, 1991), p. 110, and Catherine Hall finds evidence of women's participation in debating societies in the Midlands, but sees this as a fleeting phenomenon: Hall, 'Victorian Domestic Ideology'. In Bristol, ladies were known to prefer morning to evening lectures: Barry, 'Cultural Life of Bristol' (D.Phil. thesis), p. 135. In Bath there was a house by the pump room where the ladies could read the news and enjoy 'each other's conversation', a 'female coffee-house' where they could withdraw after general assemblies, plus lectures on arts and sciences laid on to amuse the 'People of Fashion', Goldsmith, *Richard Nash*, pp. 43, 45, 46. Smollett's Lydia Melford said the young were not admitted to the ladies coffee house at Bath, 'inasmuch as the conversation turns on politics, scandal, philosophy, and other subjects above our capacity; but we are allowed to accompany them to book-sellers shops, which are charming places of resort; where we read novels, plays, pamphlets and news-papers, for so small a subscription as a crown a quarter': Smollett, *Humphry Clinker*, p. 40.

83 LRO, DDWh/4/78 (1 May 1816), A. Ainsworth, Bolton, to E. Whitaker, Roefield;
    LRO, DDWh/4/74 (4 Aug. 1816), 'A. B.', Preston, to same.

84 In this manner, she lent out R. Nelson's *Feasts and Fasts*, B. Kennet's, The *Lives and
    Characters of the Ancient Grecian Poets* (1697), Echard's *Roman History*, J. Potter,
    Archaelogia Graecae: Or the Antiquities of Greece (1699), Fielding's, *Tom Jones*
    (1749), *The Curiosities of the Tower* and numerous copies of *The Spectator*. For her
    part, she recorded borrowing the first volume of Smollett's *Expedition of Humphrey
    Clinker* (1771) from Owen Cunliffe, two volumes of *Don Quixote* (1615) from Miss
    Beatrix Lister, four volumes of Richardson's, *Clarissa: Or the History of a Young
    Lady* (1748) from Mrs Walton and Shakespeare's history plays from her daughter-in-
    law Betty Parker: LRO, DDB/81/6 (1767), fos. 2, 71; LRO, DDB/81/7 (1768), f. 105;
    and LRO, DDB/81/22 (1774), f. 2.

85 WYCRO, Bradford, Sp St 6/1/50 (29 March 1741), M. Warde, London, to M. Warde,
    Hooton Pagnell; LRO, DDB Ac 7886/272 (28 March 1749), A. Pellet, London, to E.
    Parker, Browsholme; LRO, DDB/72/132 (16 May 1754), J. Scrimshire, Pontefract, to
    E. Parker, Alkincoats; LRO, DDB/72/197, 173, 271 (1762–7), W. and B. Ramsden,
    Charterhouse, to E. Shackleton, Alkincoats.

86 Women in the Parker network who came of age in the 1740s and 1750s made no
    reference to a past schooling or old school-fellows. Nevertheless, Jane Scrimshire and
    Elizabeth Shackleton were clearly literate, literary and both spoke French; Bessy
    Ramsden on the other hand possessed only a rudimentary grasp of spelling and
    grammar. The writings of the two former suggest that, at the very least, they had
    benefited from the ministrations of a tutor or governess. When it came to the educa-
    tion of her own children, Jane Scrimshire recorded her young sons first day at school,
    but made no such reference for her daughters. Similarly, while Bessy Ramsden's sons
    were eventually enrolled at Charterhouse School, it appears her daughter Betsy was
    too useful around the house to be spared. A younger friend, Mrs Cooper of London,
    did write of sending her daughter Susan to school in the 1780s, though she resolved to
    keep her other daughter Kitty at home with her, specifically to serve as a personal
    companion. Outside the Parker network the same pattern is detectable in this period.
    No mention of formal schooling was made by Mary Warde of Squerries, Anne
    Stanhope of Leeds or Anne Gossip of Thorp Arch, although all three wrote well in the
    1740s and 1750s, and Warde delighted in the London literary scene. While Jane
    Pedder of Lancaster sent her son John to Blackburn to be apprenticed to an attorney,
    her daughter Margaret continued to reside at home. As the daughter of a clergyman,
    Margaret doubtless had some access to a semi-formal education. In all probability,
    her trip to London in 1786 had a didactic function. Certainly, the journal she wrote of
    her visit has the unenthusiastic air of an exercise book. Of course, home tuition was
    not necessarily deficient relative to institutional schooling. The possible scope of an
    education acquired at home is demonstrated by the diaries of the Lancaster Quakeress
    Mary Chorley. From at least 1776 to 1779 the Chorley sisters received tuition six days
    a week from an unnamed 'master' and later 'a mistress'; ordinarily, half the day was
    given over to lessons, the rest to chores and play. From the age of ten Mary learned
    history and geography; subjects taught by rote with the aid of a globe and lesson cards
    ('Now we dream to get of our History of England cards', 'I said my geographical cards
    to my Aunt Lydia'). On a less systematic basis, she was also taught biology, logic and
    arithmetic. She read Roman texts in translation, sermons, edifying treatises, trav-
    elogues and novels. That the Chorley curriculum was such a hybrid of modern and
    classical learning is probably a function of the educational liberalism of old dissent.
    Yet mainstream femininity was reinforced in three key respects. Mary Chorley was as
    preoccupied with sentimental novels as any little Anglican; the fostering of genteel
    tastes and skills ran in parallel with her academic training; and lastly, female identity
    with the home and housekeeping was not broken. The available commentary from

the early nineteenth century gives the impression that a higher proportion of elite families were sending their daughters out of the house to school. By the 1820s the number of local academies for girls had mushroomed: Baines's Lancashire directory for 1824 registers the existence of two such schools in Clitheroe, one in Colne, four in Blackburn, one in Preston and six in Lancaster. Six schools for ladies in Bradford were advertised in Baines's Yorkshire directory of 1822, yet this development seems to have had only a very limited impact. No expansion in intellectual content is detectable in women's letters, while polite accomplishment is still in abundant evidence. Girls still remained in closer association with home than their brothers and were never sent as far afield to school. On girls' education in general, see S. Skedd, 'Women Teachers and the Expansion of Girls' Schooling in England, c.1760–1820', in Barker and Chalus, *Gender in Eighteenth-Century England*, pp. 101–25.

87   Houston, 'Development of Literacy'. On the proliferation of magazines, see Fergus, 'Women, Class and the Growth of Magazine Readership', pp. 41–56; id., 'Eighteenth-Century Readers in Provincial England', Michaelson, 'Women in the Reading Circle'; Ballaster, et al.

88   See LPL, MS 8754 (1779), 29 April; NRO, 2 DE/39/3/7 (19 Jan. 1771), Sophia Delaval, Grosvenor House, to Lady Susannah Delaval, Seaton.

89   Ramsden's efforts are recorded in LRO, DDB/72/213 and 193 (1766–8), W. Ramsden, Charterhouse, to E. Shackleton, Alkincoats. Mrs Shackleton mentioned periodicals in LRO, DDB/81/3 (1764), f. 49, and LRO, DDB/81/7 (1768), fos. 26, 32. A report on Mrs Shackleton's rabies medicine can be seen in Lumb and Place, 'Extracts from the Leeds Intelligencer and the Leeds Mercury, 1777–1782' (see n. 52 above) p. 19. It was the Whig *Leeds Mercury* which carried comment on her potion. For Mrs Shackleton's political reading, see LRO, DDB/81/11 (1770), f. 48; LRO, DDB/81/26 (1775), f. 8; LRO, DDB/81/37 (1780), f. 128.

90   LRO, DDB/72/168 (13 July 1775), A. Pellet, London, to E. Shackleton, Alkincoats.

91   WYCRO, Bradford, Sp St 6/1/50 (25 July 1740), M. Warde, Squerries, Kent, to M. Warde, Hooton Pagnell.

92   WYCRO, Leeds, TA, Box 22/1 (26 Oct. c.1730), S. Gossip, York, to W. Gossip, London.

93   LRO, DDB/72/137, 154 (1756), J. Scrimshire, Pontefract, to E. Parker, Alkincoats.

94   WYCRO, Bradford, Sp St 6/1/50 (4 Oct. 1742), M. Richardson, Brierley, to M. Warde, Hooton Pagnell; LRO, DDB Ac 7886/24 (13 July), A. Parker, Royle, to E. Shackleton, Alkincoats.

95   On spa seasons, see Borsay, *English Urban Renaissance*, pp. 139–42.

96   WYCRO, Leeds, TA 18/5 (11 June 1746), W. Gossip, Buxton, to A. Gossip, Skelton, and WYCRO, Leeds, TA 18/5 (20 June 1746), W. Gossip, Buxton, to same; and Lumb, 'Extracts from the Leeds Intelligencer and the Leeds Mercury, 1769–1776' (see n. 28 above), p. 75.

97   WYCRO, Bradford, Sp St 6/1/42 (9 July c.1727), B. Stanhope, Scarborough, to J. Stanhope, Bradford. Noted sea-bathers included John Shackleton, Tom Parker, Mary Chorley, Ellen Weeton and Charles Whitaker. For holidays in the 1750s the newly married Parkers of Alkincoats confined themselves to family visits to Browsholme, Skipwith and Pontefract. In the same decade the Scrimshires of Pontefract took holidays at Harrogate and Scarborough on health grounds and enjoyed frequent sojourns with their relatives the Tempests of Tong Hall, Bradford. In the 1760s and 1770s, the Ramsdens spent their summer vacations from Charterhouse School either touring the southern counties and coast in a post-chaise, or in rented accommodation in Dulwich, Enfield, Highgate or Islington. Letters written in the Barcroft and Whitaker networks reveal the ground gained by the seaside holiday in the early nineteenth century. In the 1800s Betty Parker booked the 'best front lodging rooms' in Blackpool for the month of August. In the same decade the newly married Mr and

Mrs Reynolds decamped to the Isle of Wight. In the 1810s the Whitakers and St Clares took summer lodgings at Lytham, the Ainsworths and Horrockses at Blackpool, and the London-based Robbins family at Sandgate. In the 1820s Edward and Ellen Parker took their Selby brood to lodge at Cleethorpes and Scarborough.

98   Cited in Corfield, 'Class by Name and Number', p. 44; LRO, DDB/72/1190 (11 May 1806), E. Reynolds, Bristol, to E. Moon, Colne.

99   LRO, DDB/81/20 (1773), f. 36; LRO, DDB/81/32 (1777), f. 8; LRO, DDB/81/33A (1778), f. 207; LRO, DDB/81/35 (1779), f. 6; LRO, DDB/81/37 (1780), f. 51.

100 LRO, DDB/81/27 (1776), f. 50; LRO, DDB Ac 7886/56 (8 and 9 Aug. 1776), 'Memoirs of Oratorio'; LRO, DDB/72/286 (12 Oct. 1776), W. Ramsden, Charterhouse, to E. Shackleton, Alkincoats.

101 See, for example, Howell, *Gentry of South-West Wales*, pp. 175–7, and Jenkins, *Glamorgan Gentry*, pp. 241–4.

102 LRO, DDB/72/330 (Feb. 1775), Mr E. Parker, Otley, to Mr T. Parker, Alkincoats. On the Listers' sojourn in Pall Mall, see LRO, DDB/81/7 (1768), f. 35 and the Claytons in Bath, LRO, DDB/81/33A (1778), f. 14.

103 Goldsmith, *Richard Nash*, p. 21.

104 See, for example, LRO, DDB/72/684–5, 687, 690–91 (1804–14), E. Parker, Preston, to T. Parker, Alkincoats and Newton Hall; LRO, DDB/4/87 (20 Sept. 1816), W. St Clare, Preston, to E. Whitaker, Roefield.

105 LRO, DDGr C3 (22 April and 28 July), D. Ridsdale, Winsley, to Mrs Bradley, Slyne.

106 LRO, DDB/72/1496 (20 March 1800), B. Wiglesworth, Townhead, to E. Barcroft, Otley; Gibson, *George Woodward's Letters*, p. 73.

107 See respectively LRO, DDB Ac 7886/130 (2 Dec. 1746), J. Pellet, London, to E. Parker, Browsholme; LRO, DDB Ac 7886/286 (18 July 1749), A. Pellet, London, to same; LRO, DDB Ac 7886/145 (7 March 1746/7), E. Parker, Piccadilly, to R. Parker, Alkincoats.

108 See respectively LRO, DDB/72/102 (24 Oct. 1755), A. Pellet, London, to E. Parker, Alkincoats; LRO, DDB/72/174 (16 Sept. 1762), B. Ramsden, Charterhouse, to E. Parker, Alkincoats; LRO, DDB/81/6 (1767), f. 28; LRO, DDB/81/32 (1777), f. 8.

109 Day, *Correspondence of Mary Delany*, p. 195. However, Fanny Burney noted in August 1768 at the age of sixteen, 'I never was at a public assembly in my Life, at [school] balls I have been often, and once at a private Ball at an Acquaintance, where I danced till late in the morning'. See Troide, *Early Journals and Letters of Fanny Burney*, I, pp. 25–6. By contrast, in the 1770s the young Cornelia Knight enjoyed 'the boisterous gaiety of Plymouth' from as young as thirteen, but then 'She was so very tall for her age that people tended to treat her like a young lady instead of a child, and at the assembly rooms she was obligingly partnered by her father's brother officers'; see B. Luttrell, *The Prim Romantic: A Biography of Ellis Cornelia Knight, 1758–1837* (1965), p. 35 (I thank Joanna Innes for these references). Similarly, in Haywood, *Betsy Thoughtless*, p. 17, the heroine's adventures began when she was 'just entering into her fourteenth year, a nice and delicate time, in persons of her sex; since it is then they are most apt to take the bent of impression, which, according as it is well or ill-directed makes or marrs, the future prospect of their lives.'

110 Defoe, *Tour Through the Whole Island*, pp. 215–16.

111 LRO, DDB Ac 7886/82 (7 Jan. 1745–6), J. Aspinall, Preston, to E. Parker, Browsholme; WYCRO, Bradford, Sp St/6/1/58 (n.d.), J. Spencer, Cannon Hall, to Mrs Stanhope. Similarly, Mr Walmsley wrote from Carlisle in 1745, 'Here is A Good Match for you . . . if you are not promised': LRO, DDB Ac 7886/86 (18 Jan. 1745), R. Walmsley, Carlisle, to E. Parker, Browsholme.

112 LRO, DDB Ac 7886/211 (24 March 1747), Edward Parker, London, to R. Parker, Alkincoats; Robert Parker's annotations to LRO, DDB/72/483 (23 Aug. 1739),

Edward Parker, London, to R. Parker, Colne; LRO, DDB Ac 7886/286 (18 July 1749), A. Pellet, London, to E. Parker, Browsholme.

113 WRO, D/D st C5/2 (8 Nov. 1727), R. Standish, Ingalstone, to Lady P. Standish, Standish Hall, Wigan.

114 An amorous advertisement in the *London Chronicle* for 5 Aug. 1758, wherein a young gentleman appealed to a young lady seen listening to the orchestra at Vauxhall is reproduced in Boulton, *Amusements* (see n. 48 above), II, pp. 27–8. Another example, from the *Public Advertiser* in 1761, purporting to be from a woman to a young gentleman spied at a ridotto is cited in Bayne-Powell, *Travellers* (see n. 61 above), p. 179. For Wortley Montagu's aside, see Halsband, *Letters of Lady Mary Wortley Montagu*, I, p. 201.

115 Stirling, *Annals of a Yorkshire House*, pp. 156, 158–9.

116 WYCRO, Bradford, Sp St 6/1/50 (6 June 1742), M. Warde, Squerries, Kent, to M. Warde, Hooton Pagnell; Browsholme Letters, uncat. (7 July 1743), J. Pellet, London, to E. Parker, Browsholme.

117 Gibson, *Woodward's Letters*, p. 63.

118 Wollstonecraft, *Vindication*, p. 289.

119 Coventry, *Pompey, the Little*, p. 16; Haywood, *Betsy Thoughtless*, p. 11; Anon, *Mixing in Society: A Complete Manual of Manners* (1869), pp. 137–8; LRO, DDB/81/32 (1777), 'Introduction'.

120 WYCRO, Bradford Sp St 6/1/50 (22 May 1743), M. Warde, Squerries, to M. Stanhope, Horsforth; YAS, MD335, Box 26 (1789), List of the nobility and gentry who appeared at the assembly rooms in York.

121 LRO, DDB/72/224 (2 May 1769), W. Ramsden, Charterhouse, to E. Shackleton, Alkincoats.

122 See, for example, HL, HM 31201, Anna Larpent's Diary, VIII, 8, 1810–13, facing f. 19, facing f. 33, f. 36, f. 39, facing f. 46, facing f. 51, facing f. 52, facing f.63; and XI, 1820–21, f. 2, facing f. 3, f. 58, facing f. 122.

123 Goldsmith, *Richard Nash*, p. 33; F. C. Laird, *The Beauties of England and Wales*, XII, pt. 1 (1812), Nottinghamshire, p. 149, quoted in Henstock, 'Diary of Abigail Gawthern,' p. 20.

124 Henstock, 'Diary of Abigail Gawthern', pp. 98, 93 and 49. See also pp. 94, 95, 97, 103, 105, 109, 113, 135, 145.

125 See respectively, LRO, DDB Ac 7886/84 (Jan. 1745/6), A. Pellet, Browsholme, to J. Pellet, Preston; LRO, DDB Ac 7886/286 (18 July 1749), A. Pellet, to E. Parker, Browsholme; LRO, DDB Ac 7886/267 (28 Feb. 1748/9), A. Pellet, London, to same; LRO, DDB Ac 7886/304 (16 Oct. 1749), A. Pellet, Ealing, to same.

126 Elizabeth Parker did not accompany her first husband to meetings of the Colne vestry, the Blue Bell turnpike, the Slaidburn court, or the Clitheroe land tax assessment. Similarly, she remained at home when her second husband John Shackleton sat on the grand jury at Lancaster assizes or rode into the West Riding in fulfilment of his duties as a commissioner on the Blue Bell turnpike. Letters written in the same period by Jane Scrimshire of Pontefract, reveal her solitude during the frequent absences of her solicitor husband on the northern assize circuit. To her dismay, he was even obliged to be at York assize at the time of her third confinement in 1756. A similar pattern of male movement emerges from the later manuscripts. John Barcroft of Noyna and Foulridge, father to the Miss Barcrofts, was steward of Clitheroe Castle, and keeper of the manorial court in the 1770s. Ellen Barcroft's husband Edward Parker was not only a practising solicitor in Selby, but also a deputy lieutenant for the county and a Justice of the Peace for both Lancaster and York. Consequently, their family holidays in the 1820s had to be engineered to fit with his attendance at the quarter sessions. A corresponding picture emerges from the records of the Whitaker network. Eliza Whitaker's father Samuel Horrocks was an MP, and her husband Charles Whitaker

was a Justice of the Peace for the county of Lancaster, although he turned down the office of high sheriff in 1816.

127 Cohen, 'The Grand Tour'.

128 The grouse moors above Colne were famed across Lancashire and Yorkshire. 'Moorgame Day' (12 August) and 'Partridge Day' (1/2 September) were sufficiently significant to be designated in Elizabeth Shackleton's diary. The Stanhope brothers, who rubbed shoulders with Robert Parker on the grouse moor in the 1750s were both considered hot shots. Michael and Jane Scrimshire attempted to lure the newly married Parkers to Bradford by offering tantalizing descriptions of the woodland shooting opportunities: 'here is Hares, Partridges and Woodcocks in Plenty. They want nothing but shot to bring them to the table . . .': LRO, DDB/72/153 (21 Oct. 1756), J. Scrimshire, Tong, Bradford, to E. Parker, Alkincoats. Robert Parker's alacrity was matched by that of his successor John Shackleton and his eldest son's 'levelling skill among the partridges' drew comment in the 1790s: LRO, DDB/72/842 (13 Oct. 1794), E. Parker, Browsholme, to T. Parker, Alkincoats. Enthusiasm for shooting burned bright in the early nineteenth century. Charles Whitaker's bloodthirst was proverbial knowledge across the county: LRO, DDWh/4/112 (n.d.), W. St Clare, Preston, to E. Whitaker, Roefield: 'I suppose he will be busily engaged dealing death and destruction amongst the moor game.'

129 N. Scarfe (ed.), 'A Frenchman's Year in Suffolk', Suffolk Records Society, 30 (1988), p. 41.

130 Halsband, Letters of Lady Mary Wortley Montagu, I, p. 110; WYCRO, Bradford, Sp St 6/1/50 (26 Sept. 1742, 22 Oct. 1739, 16 Sept. 1741, 4 Dec. 1740), M. Warde, Great Cressingham, to M. Warde, Hooton Pagnell.

131 Lady's Magazine, 14, p. 114; Wollstonecraft, Vindication, p. 80.

132 LRO, DDB/81/22 (1774), f. 109. See also LRO, DDB/74/5 (n.d.), Hunting Poem made by the Gentlemen belonging to the Colne Hunt; LRO, DDB/74/3 (n.d.), Hunting Poem of Pendle, Colne, Marsden and Trawden; and LRO, DDB/74/4 (n.d.), Hunting Poem of Pendle, Downham, Wiswell and Bolton.

133 LRO, DDB/81/26 (1775), f. 18; LRO, DDB/81/33A (1778), f. 82.

134 WRO, D/D St C5/3 (17 Nov. 1727), R. Standish Howard, London, to R. Standish, Standish Hall.

135 LRO, DDB Ac 7886/324 (1 Jan. 1775–1 March 1776), f. 4.

136 Thus complained Sophia Curzon in 1778: Elwin (ed.), The Noels and the Milbankes, p. 103.

137 Haywood, Betsy Thoughtless, p. 37.

138 Macky, Journey Through England and Scotland, II, p. 41; A. Allardyce (ed.), Scotland and Scotsmen in the Eighteenth Century (Edinburgh, 1888), II, pp. 60–61, quoted in Langford, Polite and Commercial People, p. 109.

139 Heal and Holmes, Gentry in England and Wales, pp. 289–318, note that the elite relieved the tedium of life in their country manors with long-stay visits, hunting and hawking. Indoor diversions included music, drama and gaming. The provincial towns offered the society of the inn, the bowling green, the racecourse and the cockpit.

140 LRO, DDB/72/687 (16 July 1807), E. Parker, Preston, to T. Parker, Alkincoats.

141 LRO, DDWh/4/78 (1 May 1816), A. Ainsworth, Bolton, to E. Whitaker, Roefield; E. C. Gaskell, The Life of Charlotte Bronte (New York, 1857), p. 51.

142 C. Midgley, Women Against Slavery: The British Campaigns, 1780–1870 (1992), pp. 73–4. Furthermore, Midgley finds that there were at least seventy-three ladies' antislavery associations founded between 1825 and 1833 (p. 47).

143 Summers, 'A Home from Home', pp. 42 and 33.

144 Marylebone Gardens closed to the public in 1776. Ranelagh House and the Rotunda were demolished in 1805. Bagnigge Wells became known as a lower-class resort from about 1810. Vauxhall had numerous fashionable galas and firework displays in the

1800s and 1810s, but went downhill rapidly from the 1840s and closed in 1859: Wroth, *London Pleasure Gardens* (see n. 54 above), pp. 21–2, 64, 324. See also HL, HM 31201, Anna Larpent's Diary, III, 1799–1800, f. 247: 'Thursday at past 9 went with Seymour and John to Vauxhall where I had not been some years the evening was very delightful – but it was very thin. home about one.' And Henstock, 'Diary of Abigail Gawthern, p. 95: 'To Ranelagh [in June 1802]; very few people there; much disappointed, having seen crowds of nobility and well dressed people there, the fireworks the best I ever saw . . . Ranelagh is now quite forsaken and talked of being taken down or converted into some manufactory.' On the 'carriage airing' and social parade at the nineteenth-century seaside, see A. Dale, *Fashionable Brighton, 1820–1860* (1947), pp. 16–17.

145 Girouard, *English Town*, p. 144.

146 Wilkinson complained that a Mr Gawood of the Low Church, Hull, had pronounced in January 1792 that anyone who entered a playhouse would be damned along with actors for all eternity. Another preacher, a Mr Lambert, claimed that the late seventeenth-century plague was God's punishment on the people for their excessive love of the playhouse. In 1794–5, a Mr Dykes banished from his chapel all those who had been to plays. With some exasperation, Wilkinson declared 'It would be easier I believe to make a convert of a violent democrat to an aristocrat, than to make a methodist like the playhouse'. See Wilkinson, *Wandering Patentee*, I, p. 111, II, p. 122, IV, pp. 97–9, 201. For Larpent's reactions, see HL, H.M., 31201, Mrs Larpent's Diary, III, 1799–1800, facing f. 4.

147 M. Nava, 'Modernity's Disavowal: Women, the City and the Department Store', in M. Nava and A. O'Shea (eds.), *Modern Times: Reflections on a Century of English Modernity* (1996), p. 43; Walkowitz, *Dreadful Delight* (see n. 8 above), pp. 68–9; K. Dejardin, 'Etiquette and Marriage at the Turn of the Twentieth Century: Advice on Choosing One's Partner', in J. Carré, *The Crisis of Courtesy: Studies in the Conduct Book in Britain, 1600–1900* (Leiden, 1994), p. 175. On commercial spectacles, see R. Altick, *The Shows of London* (Cambridge, Mass., 1978), esp. pp. 141–210, and T. Richards, *The Commodity Culture of Victorian England: Advertising and Spectacle, 1851–1914* (Stanford, Ca., 1990). On the space for female consumption, see Rappaport, 'Halls of Temptation' (see n. 66 above); G. R. Dyer, 'The 'Vanity Fair' of Nineteenth-Century England: Commerce, Women and the East in the Ladies Bazaar', *Nineteenth-Century Literature*, 46 (1991), pp. 196–222.

148 Hall, 'Refashioning of Fashionable Society' (Ph.D. thesis), pp. 93–51.

149 With blatant didacticism, Burney's Evelina was drawn down one of the dark walks at Vauxhall, possibly the notorious Lovers' Walk, where she importuned by parties of lewd, impertinent men. Even worse, at a mismanaged fireworks display at the unimpressive Marylebone Gardens, she got lost in a crowd and to her inexpressible horror found she had taken refuge in the company of prostitutes: Burney, *Evelina*, pp. 193, 195–6, 232–3. Pleasure gardens became emblematic of fashionable dissipation and the capricious lifestyle of metropolitan youth. The worldly Mary Warde confessed that she deserved the 'excessive bad Cold' she caught in May 1743, having 'contrived to make the whole tour of Ranelagh and Vauxhall by Water . . .' in a bitter north-easter: WYCRO, Bradford, Sp St 6/1/50 (22 May 1743), M. Warde, Squerries, Kent, to Mrs Stanhope, Horsforth. Ranelagh and Vauxhall were also blamed when the apprentice Robert Parker contracted a dangerous fever in 1773: 'and Considering how most of the young folks of London live, I wonder they are ever well. The Misses when at home muffled up warm as if was winter and perhaps in the very same Evening you meet 'em at Ranelagh and Vauxhall half naked. The young men are violent in their Exercises and heedless when over. Mr Plestow seem'd to think R's fever was got in this Manner: but this I hope will be a warning to him': LRO, DDB/72/260 (15 Jan. 1773), W. Ramsden, Charterhouse, to E. Shackleton, Alkincoats.

150 Samuel Richardson, for his part, consistently criticized the masquerade ball, having his *ingénue* Harriet Byron abducted outside one in her glaring costume: 'But surely, I was past all shame, when I gave my consent to make such an appearance as I made, among a thousand strangers, at a Masquerade!' and his exemplary gentleman Sir Charles Grandison pronounce 'Masquerades . . . are not creditable places for young ladies to be known to be *insulted* at them'. Consult Richardson, *Sir Charles Grandison*, pp. 183 and 143. While a crude warning to parents was issued by Eliza Haywood when she described an innocent brother and sister at a London masquerade, who 'no sooner enter'd than both were bewilder'd amidst the promiscuous Assembly – the strange Habits – the Hurry'. Inevitably, the pair were separated in the confusion and the sister was abducted and raped: Haywood, *Female Spectator* (1745), I, bk I, p. 49.

151 Goldsmith, *Richard Nash*, p. 48.

152 Haywood, *Female Spectator*, I, bk 5, pp. 299–300; Pennington, *Unfortunate Mother's Advice*, pp. 20–21; J. Gregory, *A Father's Legacy to his Daughters* (1774; Edinburgh, 1788), p. 21; Richardson, *Sir Charles Grandison*, p. 180. Haywood also reiterated this point in *Betsy Thoughtless*, p. 438: 'I would not have you deprive yourself of those pleasures of life which are becoming your sex, your age, and character; – there is no necessity that because you are a wife you should become a mope: – I only recommend a proper medium in these things.'

153 Barry, 'Cultural Life of Bristol' (D.Phil. thesis), p. 195, Sekora, *Luxury*, *passim*.

154 Harrison, 'Gossip Family' (unpub. paper), pp. 7–8.

155 LRO, DDGr C3 (8 July 1776), T. Greene, Grays Inn, to Miss Greene, Slyne. Similarly, Jane Pellet archly wrote 'Let [your father] know I have not been at either play or Ridotto since I left Browsholm and he very well knows I was not at any whilst there. The inference I wo'd have you *draw is that I am very prudent*': Browsholme Letters, Browsholme Hall, Clitheroe, Lancs, uncat. (1745/6), J. Pellet to E. Parker.

156 LRO, DDB/72/308 (9 May 1780), E. Shackleton, Pasture House, to R. Parker, London.

157 The first quotation is drawn from Sophia Curzon's complaint about Ranelagh, see Elwin, *The Noels and the Milbankes*, p. 103. For the second, see Smollett, *Humphry Clinker*, p. 37.

158 Barry, 'Cultural Life in Bristol' (D.Phil. thesis), p. 211.

159 HL, HM 31201, XVII, Methodized Journal of Anna Margaretta Larpent, facing f. 10, facing f. 23, f. 24, f. 38 and f. 30. Similarly, Miss Betsy Thoughtless had 'her head turned with the promiscuous enjoyment, [of plays, balls etc] and the very power of reflection lost amidst the giddy whirl', and almost an entire novel passed 'before she could recover it to see the little true felicity of such a course of life'. Consult Haywood, *Betsy Thoughtless*, p. 18.

160 WYCRO, Bradford, Sp St 6/1/50 (25 July 1740), M. Warde, Squerries, Kent, to M. Warde, Hooton Pagnell.

161 LRO, DDGr C1 (27 Sept. 1762), B. Wiglesworth, Townhead, to Mr Greene; LRO, DDB/72/141 (2 Nov. 1754), J. Scrimshire, Pontefract, to E. Parker, Alkincoats; WYCRO, Bradford, Sp St 6/1/50 (12 Sept. 1740), M. Warde, Great Cressingham, to M. Warde, Hooten Pagnall; CRO, D/Lons/L1/1/67, I. Carr, London, to Sir J. Lowther. Similarly, note LRO, DDB Ac 7886/186 (18 May 1747), A. Lister, Broughton, to E. Parker, Browsholme: 'I can tell you the Country looks charmingly pleasant, and realy you can Scarce imagine how comfortable a little retirement seems after so much hurry as we have been in lately . . .'; LRO, DDWh/4/77 (28 April 1816), S. Whalley, Rocke Court, Fareham, Hants, to E. Whitaker, Roefield: 'Bath certainly was very pleasant but I cannot regret its dissipated amusements in the contemplation of my more rational system and the prospect of revisiting our own best country in the course of this month.'; LRO, DDB/72/1188 (4 June 1805), E. Reynolds, to E. Moon, Colne: 'She has I think spent a very gay time and I dare say has nearly [tasted] of all

the amusements that town affords but she says she would not live in London for all
the world.'

162   See respectively, WYCRO, Bradford, Sp St 6/1/50 (30 Dec. 1742), E. Winn to M.
Stanhope, Horsforth; and LRO, DDGr C3 (20 May 1820), L. Boynton, 55 Burton
Crescent, to Mr and Mrs Bradley, Slyne. On 'Otium', see Rostvig, *Happy Man*. On
women and intellectual retirement, consider Perry, *Celebrated Mary Astell*, pp. 126–
9 and Scott, *Millenium Hall*.

Conclusion

1   J. Vanbrugh, *The Provok'd Wife* (1697; Manchester, 1982), p. 143, act 5, scene 2.

2   For political and social links between new wealth and old elites in Manchester and in
north-east Lancashire, see V. A. C. Gatrell, 'Incorporation and the Pursuit of Liberal
Hegemony in Manchester, 1790–1839', in D. Fraser, *Municipal Reform and the
Industrial City* (Leicester, 1982) and Joyce, *Work, Society and Politics*, pp. 1–50.

3   Myers, *Bluestocking Circle*, p. 207. I am indebted to Joanna Innes for this reference.

4   Wilberforce, *Practical View*, p. 434.

5   Home, *Loose Hints*, p. 228.

6   LRO, DDB/72/119 (14 Oct. 1757), A. Pellet, London, to E. Parker, Alkincoats.

7   LRO, DDB/72/104 (28 Dec. 1755), A. Pellet, London, to E. Parker, Alkincoats; LRO,
DDWh/4/117 (n.d.), A. E. Robbins, London, to E. Whitaker, Lark Hill, Preston.
These sentiments seem quite conventional, even amongst the nobility. For instance in
1790 Lady Sarah Napier wished for another daughter 'to comfort me in my old age,
when my boys are gone to school', and Elizabeth Amherst confided 'For my part, I
believe I shall like girls best as they stay at home': Lewis, *Family Way*, p. 65 and
Brophy, *Women's Lives*, p. 42.

8   LRO, DDB/72/115 (24 Jan. 1757), A. Pellet, London, to E. Parker, Alkincoats. See also
LRO, DDB/72/161(a), (17 Nov. 1757), J. Scrimshire, Pontefract, to E. Parker,
Alkincoats; LRO, DDB/72/227 (29 Nov. 1769), W. Ramsden, Charterhouse, to same;
LRO, DDWh/4/69 (6 June 1814), M. Whitehead, London, to E. Whitaker, Roefield.

9   LRO, DDB/72/273 (7 Feb. 1775), B. and W. Ramsden, Charterhouse, to E.
Shackleton, Alkincoats.

10   HL, HM 31207, Methodized Journal of Anna Margaretta Larpent, unfol.; see entries
for 1773; LRO, DDB Ac 7886/205 (9 Jan. 1747), J. Pellet, London, to E. Parker,
Browsholme.

11   LRO, DDB/81/33A (1778), f. 183; Burney, *The Wanderer*, p. 249.

12   NRO, 2DE/39/1/21 (c.1777), Sir John Hussey Delaval to Lady S. H. Delaval at
Grosvenor House. Samuel Richardson was critical of Miss Grandison's desire to get
married in her chamber and had his heroine Harriet Byron marry the irreproachable
Sir Charles Grandison in full view of the community: 'that all our neighbours and
tenants may rejoice with us. I must make the village smoke. No *hugger-mugger* doings
– Let private weddings be for doubtful *happiness*.' Refer to Richardson, *Sir Charles
Grandison* (1986), IV, p. 336, VI, pp. 192–3. I thank Charlotte Mitchell for this
reference.

13   Hughes, *North East*, p. 387.

14   On private families, see for example, Haywood, *Betsy Thoughtless*, p. 18: 'Never did
a mistress of a private family indulge herself, and those about her, with such a
continual round of publick diversions. The court, the play, the ball and opera, with
giving and receiving visits, engrossed all the time could be spared from the toilet.' Also
p. 534: 'when the affairs of a family are laid open, and every dispute between the

husband and the wife exposed before a court of judicature . . . The whole becomes a public talk . . .' (I thank Naomi Tadmor for these references). Consider also Burney, *Evelina*, p. 116: 'I only speak in regard to a public and dissipated life; in private families, we may doubtless find as much goodness, honesty and virtue, in London as in the country.'

15 A. Carlyle, *Anecdotes and Characters of the Times* (1973), p. 3. Similarly, Austen's retiring hero Edward Ferrars 'had no turn for great men or barouches. All his wishes centred in domestic comfort and the quiet of private life.' See, id., *Sense and Sensibility*, p. 16. William Ramsden also suggested that a Charterhouse schoolmaster could not sustain a social life in the public eye: 'We live here out of the world. I know little what is doing in it till the papers tell us.' See LRO, DDB/72/261 (1 April 1773), W. Ramsden, Charterhouse, to E. Shackleton, Alkincoats. In addition, Betty Fothergill, the daughter of a reputable Quaker physician, noted of an unaffected gentleman caller in 1769: 'though he is not formed to make a brilliant figure in the theatre of life, he will shine perhaps in its private domestic scenes'. See Brophy, *Women's Lives*, p. 119.

16 YAS, MD 335/Box 95/xcv/i (28 May 1773), Mrs B. Lister, Gisburn Park, to T. Lister, MP.

17 As Atterbury observed, 'a good magistrate must be endowed with a publick spirit, that is with such an excellent temper, as sets him loose from all selfish views, and makes him endeavour towards promoting the common good.'; cited in S. Johnson, *A Dictionary of the English Language* (5th ed. London, 1784), II, 'Publick, adj.' For more on men and public service see the excellent Langford, *Public Life and the Propertied Englishman*.

18 *Gentleman's Magazine*, 23 Aug. 1753.

19 E. Chalus, 'That Epidemical Madness: Women and Electoral Politics in the Late Eighteenth Century', in Barker and Chalus, *Gender in Eighteenth-Century England*, pp. 151–78; L. Colley, 'The Female Political Elite in Unreformed Britain' (unpub. paper delivered to the Eighteenth-Century Seminar, Institute of Historical Research, 25 June 1993); J. S. Lewis, *Sacred to Female Patriotism: Class, Gender and Politics in the Age of Revolution, 1760–1832* (forthcoming).

20 Halsband, *Letters of Lady Mary Wortley Montagu*, II, pp. 135–6.

21 Jupp, 'Letter-Journal of George Canning', pp. 118 and 283–4.

22 Midgley, *Women Against Slavery*, p. 20.

23 L. Colley, *Britons: Forging the Nation, 1707–1837* (1992), p. 281.

24 J. Ruskin, 'Of Queen's Garden's', in *Sesame and Lilies* (1907), pp. 71, 60.

Appendix 1

Research Design and Sources

AT THE HEART OF THIS BOOK lies a study of elite women in Georgian Lancashire, a county noted in the period for an expanding manufacturing base, a growing service sector and numerous gentry. The research for the book was designed specifically to avoid the shortcomings of a number of previous studies of elites in the period, discussed in the introduction and chapter 1, which have too often taken for granted a crude distinction between an upper landed class and a middle class of professionals and businessmen. Rather than question the utility of this distinction, these studies have simply isolated the gentry, or the professions, or the commercial middle class as their subject of inquiry. Once a study is defined in this way, the links and parallels between these groups are inevitably played down, while differences between them are endowed with an analytical significance that is rarely subtantiated by direct empirical comparison. The research for this book was designed to avoid these pitfalls by examining *all* letters and diaries that survive for privileged women between about 1730 and about 1825 in the Lancashire Record Office at Preston, irrespective of whether the family's wealth came from land, the professions or business. This record office serves the post-1972 county of Lancashire, covering the central and most of the northern part of the old county of Lancaster, but excluding Furness and the southern plains, where the modern conurbations of Manchester and Liverpool lie. Supplementary archival material for the modern county of Lancashire and its fringes was found at the Wigan Record Office and the Lancaster Public Library. Equivalent material was then examined in other northern archives, particularly the Yorkshire Archaeological Society at Leeds, the branches of the West Yorkshire Record Office at Bradford and Leeds, and the branches of the Cumbria Record Office at Carlisle and Kendal. The purpose of extending the study in this way was twofold: to follow up the non-Lancashire friends and kin of the Lancashire families already examined, and to provide a broader perspective on the experience of genteel women in the north of England. It emerged that the sources examined in northern archives contained important evidence about women in London. It was decided to establish a fuller picture of the lives of genteel women in the metropolis by examining a selection of appropriate manuscripts at the Guildhall Library London, the Corporation of London Record Office, the Essex Record Office and the Huntington Library, San Marino, California. Although this exploration of London manuscript sources did not amount to a comprehensive review of the kind undertaken for Lancashire, it has served, at the very least, to counteract any tendency to ascribe excessive autonomy to developments in the north which were in fact national in scope and had their origins in London.

Appendix 2

Biographical Index

Correspondents of Elizabeth Parker (1726–81) and her first husband Robert Parker of Alkincoats (1720–80), including those who wrote to Elizabeth during her widowhood and her second marriage to John Shackleton (1744–88). An asterisk indicates the person concerned corresponded with Robert Parker only.

*James Aspinall, Burnley, Lancashire
A solicitor. Brother of John Aspinall, below.
MS: single letter LRO, DDB Ac 7886/285. Another letter from him to John Stanhope is preserved the Spencer Stanhope collection in WYCRO, Leeds (MS span: 1749).

John Aspinall, Preston, Lancashire (d. 1784)
A gentleman barrister on the northern circuit, later Serjeant-at-Law. His seat was the austerely impressive Standen Hall, Clitheroe, Lancashire. When he wrote he was clearly an admirer of the young Miss Elizabeth Parker, in Preston like himself to attend the assemblies. Years later, however, he incurred her wrath when he opposed the interests of the Parkers and Listers in the disputed Clitheroe election of 1781: 'He *within* these 30 years wo'd have esteem'd it a *Great* Honour and been Big of the application of being styl'd recorder of Clitheroe. What a wretch to behave so vilely to his most obliging, generous, worthy neighbours, Browsholme and Gisburne park . . . [He] most probably thinks Mr Curzon's Purse will enable him to make a Portico or add a Venetian window to the Beauties of Standen. What nonsense is he.' Like most of the Lancashire elite, Aspinall was a customer of Gillows of Lancaster.
MS: single letter LRO, DDB Ac 7886/82. For the diary reference, see LRO, DDB/ 81/39 (1781), fos. 31–2 (MS span: 1745/6).

Elizabeth Assheton (née Assheton), Broughton, Lancashire
One of the Asshetons of Cuerdale and Downham, who married a cousin, Richard

Assheton, brother of Sir Ralph Assheton of Middleton. Downham was one of the nearest gentry seats to Browsholme, so, unsurprisingly, Elizabeth Assheton was long-standing friend of Elizabeth Parker's; her sister Mary Witton was another of Elizabeth Parker's correspondents; her brother Ralph Assheton of Cuerdale was a trustee to Elizabeth Parker's settlement.
MS: single letter LRO, DDB Ac 7886/303 (MS span: 1749).

*Henry Blackmore, Lancashire
This man wrote to solicit Robert Parker's intervention in a local dispute.
MS: single letter LRO, DDB/72/481 (MS span: 1749).

James Bulcock, 85 Borough High Street, Southwark, London
The Bulcocks were a large trading family who descended from an ancient yeoman family in north-east Lancashire. The older Bulcocks still resided in Colne and owned land in the area, while the younger Bulcock brothers appear to have been double registered in contemporary directories as both Colne tailors and London haberdashers.
MS: six letters LRO, DDB/72/299–302, 305, and DDB Ac 7886/54. For landholding data, see LRO, DDB/59 Bulcock papers, and LRO, DDB/62/239, Map (MS span: 1765–76).

Robert Bulcock, Bishopsgate, London
A London-based wholesale haberdasher who sold (among other things) John Shackleton's callimancoes. His business was advertised in London directories for 1763 and 1777, and in the UBD I. He offered hospitality to the Parker children when schoolboys, and helped place John and Robert Parker as apprentices. In return, Elizabeth Shackleton supervised the education of his niece Nancy Bulcock. After a brief schooling with a Miss Wells of Bradford and a set of dancing lessons, Nancy became a milliner. She eventually married a hosier and hatter, a Mr Burbidge of Borough, Southwark, London.
MS: two letters LRO, DDB/72/450; DDB Ac 7886/64 (MS span: 1772–3).

*Miss Elizabeth Carleton, Appleby, Yorkshire
Status unknown. A one-time acquaintance of Miss Parker's enquiring about her whereabouts.
MS: single letter LRO, DDB Ac 7886/198 (MS span: 1747).

*Thomas Cockshott, Marley, Bingley, Yorkshire
This gentleman rented the Marley estate from the Parkers. He was married to a Mrs Hardy, the widow of a Horsforth attorney. The Cockshotts were long-standing friends of the Parkers and Shackletons, exchanging regular gifts of game and produce in the 1770s. They also purchased the Parker rabies medicine and communicated information about prospective servants.
MS: single letter to R. Parker LRO, DDB/72/64 (MS span: 1757).

M. Cookson (née Dawson), Leeds, Yorkshire
Daughter of the gentleman William Dawson Esq. of Longcliffe Hall, Settle. Wife
to a prominent Leeds merchant, Thomas Cookson (1707–73), who was elected to
the corporation in 1742 and resigned 1744. Cookson's father, William, was briefly
imprisoned in 1715 for alleged Jacobite sympathies; and was three times Mayor of
Leeds.
MS: single letter LRO, DDB Ac 7886/254 (MS span: 1748).

Mrs A. Cooper, Southampton Buildings, London
The precise social status of this worldly correspondent is unknown.
MS: single letter LRO, DDB/72/73 (MS span: 1781).

James Cowgill, Cambridge
This cleric was the son of the vicar of Downham and subsequently Clitheroe,
Lancashire. He went up to Emmanuel College, Cambridge, in 1732, and became
a fellow in 1739. He was another admirer of the unmarried Miss Parker of
Browsholme, and fancied himself as a poet. By 1743 he was appointed Vicar of
Clitheroe. However, other letters of the period report him pursuing a small college
living near Winchester, where it was said the fruit of the apricot tree growing by
the house amounted to more than the yearly value of the living. His poverty was
something of a running joke amongst the network: 'Mr Cowgill is prouder and
prouder since she [his wife] proves with child I fancy he is to do the office of a
midwife for it will save money.'
MS: single letter LRO, DDB Ac 7886/89 (MS span: 1745).

Miss Elizabeth Cromblehome, Preston, Lancashire (d. 1817)
An exceedingly wealthy heiress, she was probably the granddaughter of the
William Comblehome of St Michaels on the Wyre, who was ordained deacon by
the Archbishop of York in 1723. There is no evidence to link her with the Preston
corn merchants of the same name who registered in Baines's directory of 1825. She
purchased furniture from Gillows of Lancaster. Later, through her residence at
Churchtown, she became acquainted with the clerical Pedder family.
MS: single letter LRO, DDB/72/459. On her fortune, see DDPd/46 Cromblehome
trusteeship, and on her furniture, see WPL, 344/51 Gillows Ledger, 1769–75 (MS
span: 1773).

William Curron, Carleton, Yorkshire
An officer of the vestry of the parish church of Carleton, who wrote concerning
the mooted enclosure of Carleton Common. His occupational status is not
divulged.
MS: single letter LRO, DDB/72/451 (MS span: 1767).

Benjamin Ferrand, St Ives, Bingley, Yorkshire (1730–1803)
Only son of Benjamin Ferrand of St Ives (1676–1731) and Sarah (d. 1785),
daughter and co-heiress of Thomas Dobson of the vicarage near Bingley.
Benjamin Ferrand junior was lord of the manors of Cottingley and Oakworth,

among others in the West Riding. He was a zealous turnpike trustee, a major in Sir George Saville's battalion of militia, Deputy-Lieutenant and Justice of the Peace for the West Riding of Yorkshire. Elizabeth Parker gave Ferrand the courtesy title of gamekeeper for the manor of Harden in 1764. Thereafter, he sent her a brace of moor game every season. Although a match was suspected between Ferrand and Beatrix Lister in 1774, it came to nothing and he never married. He was taxed on three male servants in 1780.
MS: two letters LRO, DDB/72/449–50 (MS span: 1764).

Margaret Fielden, Manchester, Lancashire
Mantua-maker based in Burnley, who travelled in the course of her business.
MS: three letters to Elizabeth Shackleton LRO, DDB Ac 7886/20, 44, 68 (MS span: 1776–78).

Robert Frankland, Browsholme, Yorkshire
Steward to John Parker, father of Elizabeth Parker.
MS: single letter LRO, DDB Ac 7886/150 (MS span: 1747).

*****William Hill**, Ormskirk, Lancashire
This correspondent is credited with the original recipe for the Parkers' rabies medicine. After Parker's death, Hill went into partnership with a Mr James Berry, selling the potion in Berkeley Square, London. His son, Master Hill, was apprenticed to an attorney in Warrington in 1771. Hill's niece, Miss Smith, was a longstanding friend of Elizabeth Parker's. In the 1770s Miss Smith was forced into mean lodgings in Wigan and Ormskirk, and later into an unhappy marriage with a drunken tradesman, a Mr Knowles of Prescot.
MS: two letters LRO, DDB/72/56 and 475. The London business is referred to in LRO, DDB/81/10 (1770), f. 82 (MS span: 1748–54).

*****Henry Hubbard**, Emmanuel College, Cambridge (c.1708–1778)
This cleric was the son of an Ipswich cabinet-maker. He went up to St Catharine's College, Cambridge, in 1724, became a fellow in 1730 and a fellow of Emmanuel in 1732, where he was tutor for many years. He also served as Taxor (a college officer responsible for the regulation of weights and measures) and Registrar. Among other posts, he was ordained deacon of Lincoln in 1730. Hubbard's standing was such that he was painted by Gainsborough. His letters to Robert Parker itemize the young man's college accounts.
MS: five letters LRO, DDB/72/468–72 (MS span: 1744–5).

Anne Lister, at Chapel Thorp, Wakefield, Yorkshire, and Broughton, Lancashire (1722–55)
This woman was one of the powerful Listers of Gisburn Park, although in her letters she regretted not living at the family seat as in her father's day. It appears that she lived as a guest of various prominent and powerful northern families, such as the Asshetons of Broughton and the Curzons of Kedleston in Derbyshire. The

Listers of Gisburn Park were taxed on six male servants in 1780. They also bought their mahogany from Gillows of Lancaster.
MS: two letters LRO, DDB Ac 7886/186 and 270 (MS span: 1747–49).

*Lawrence Ormerod of Ormerod**, Burnley, Lancashire (d. 1758)
A gentleman, the son and heir of the Ormerod estate. He was married to Margaret Ormerod of Tunstead, Rossendale, and had four children. He was buried at Burnley. He was taxed on two male servants in 1780.
MS: single letter LRO, DDB Ac 7886/199 (MS span: 1747).

Anne Parker, Cuerden Hall, near Preston, Lancashire
The self-confident wife of Robert Parker of Cuerden, born Anne Townley of Royle who was on visiting terms with the titled and the fashionable. The Parkers of Cuerden were also customers of Gillows of Lancaster.
MS: six letters LRO, DDB Ac 7886/18, 19, 21, 22, 23, 24. (MS span: c.1776).

Barbara Parker (née Fleming), Browsholme, Yorkshire (d. 1813)
The daughter and co-heiress of the baronet Sir William Fleming of Rydal Hall, Westmorland. In 1754, in Lancaster, she married Edward Parker of Browsholme (Arthur Devis painted this couple in 1757). Thereby she became Elizabeth Parker's sister-in-law. Through the Fleming sisters, the Parkers associated with the Wilsons of Dalham Tower and Lord and Lady Leicester of Tarporley, Cheshire.
MS: single letter LRO, DDB Ac 7886/75 (MS span: c.1754).

Miss Elizabeth Parker, Preston, Lancashire
This woman was undoubtedly one of the Parkers of Preston and Cuerden. She was either the sister of Robert Parker of Cuerden (1727–79) or his daughter by Anne Townley of Royle. If the daughter, then she died in 1775. Robert Parker of Cuerden was taxed on six male servants in 1780. He also patronized Gillows of Lancaster.
MS: single letter LRO, DDB/72/1581 (MS span: 1773).

Edward ('Ned') Parker, Farm Hill, Waltham Abbey, Essex (b. 1725)
Robert Parker's cousin. His early successes in manufacturing enabled him to establish his Essex estate. Yet in 1773 he went bankrupt (being registered in the *Gazette* of that year as a bay maker, dealer and chapman.) He married his first wife, Frances Jones of Holborn (Fanny) in 1749, when aged twenty-four, but was widowed in 1763. In 1767 he married his second wife, a Miss Monat of New Bond Street. The Monats were grocers, said to be worth ten thousand pounds, although gossips reported with surprise that the couple never left their counter.
MS: thirty letters LRO, DDB/72/53, 58, 63, 71–2, 474, 476, 478–80, 485–6, 490; and DDB Ac 7886/1–7, 118, 138, 160, 183, 203, 206, 211, 214, 223, 283. For his first marriage, see Guildhall Marriage Licences, 1746–50. On the bankruptcy, refer to *London Gazette* (1773), items 11376, 11392 (MS span: 1745–58).

Edward Parker, Browsholme, Yorkshire (1731–94)
Elizabeth Parker's only brother. He was educated in Bury St Edmunds, Suffolk, and Cambridge. In adulthood he was Bow-Bearer of the Forest of Bolland and patron of the churches of Bentham, Ingleton, Chapel le Dale and Waddington. Edward Parker's letters date from the 1740s. He broke off personal communication with his sister from 1765 until c.1775 on account of her marriage to John Shackleton, although the instrumental contact was maintained through his wife, his steward and Elizabeth's sons, of whom Edward was co-guardian. The Parkers had only one surviving son, John Parker, who married Beatrix Lister. In his obituary of 1795, he was applauded for the 'dignity and hospitality of an ancient English baron'. Like his sister, he purchased his mahogany from Gillows of Lancaster.
MS: fifteen letters LRO, DDB Ac 7886/80, 81 and 149, 151, 154, 163, 169, 178, 182, 215, 237, 249, 250; LRO, DDB/72/66–7; three letters to Robert Parker LRO, DDB/ 72/57, 487 and 489. Letters survive from Barbara and Edward Parker to their nephew Thomas Parker of Alkincoats, see, for example, LRO, DDB/72/330, 941 and 943. See also, BIHR (1795), Will of Edward Parker, and *Gentleman's Magazine*, 65 (1795), p. 82 (MS span: 1746–95).

John Parker, Browsholme, Yorkshire (1695–1754)
Father to Elizabeth Parker. John Parker is designated linen-draper in his daughter's baptismal register, see G. W. G. Leveson Gower (ed.), *The Registers of St Peter's, Cornhill, 1667–1774*, Harleyan Society Registers Section, IV (1879), p. 35. Freedom records reveal that he was initially trained as a mercer. In 1713, at the age of eighteen, he was apprenticed for seven years to a Thomas Riley, citizen and mercer of London, at a cost of two hundred pounds: CLRO, Freedom Records, CF1/420. He married Elizabeth Southouse, the daughter of an Essex merchant (Henry Southouse of Manuden is described as a wire-drawer in 1723, see CLRO, Freedom Records, CF1/432). In 1728, however, John Parker inherited the Parker family estate through a half-brother and so became master of Browsholme Hall in the West Riding, close to the Lancashire border, and of a substantial estate in Ingleton. Despite their promotion, the family did not remove immediately to Yorkshire; certainly they were still resident in Cornhill when Elizabeth's brother Edward was born in 1731. Exactly how much longer the Parkers remained in London is unclear, although they stayed long enough for their daughter to be confirmed into the Anglican Church by the Archbishop of Canterbury at the Tower of London. Mrs Elizabeth Parker died before her daughter came of age, so Miss Elizabeth Parker was for some years sole mistress of Browsholme and the estate, worth almost five hundred pounds in annual rent. All of John Parker's letters were written as a widower.
MS: twenty-nine letters LRO, DDB Ac 7886/76–9, 87, 102, 146–7, 152–3, 155–6, 217, 222–6, 229, 231, 233, 234, 245, 247–8, 251–2, 291, 293, 297, 300, 306 (MS span: 1747–54).

*****Robert Parker**, Pall Mall, London
A London merchant by repute, he was almost certainly the father of Ned Parker,

Thomas Parker and Bessy Ramsden, and therefore the uncle of Robert Parker of Alkincoats.
MS: single letter to Robert Parker LRO, DDB/72/488 (MS span: 1755).

*Thomas Parker, London (d. 1767)
Robert Parker's first cousin and brother of Bessy Ramsden and Ned Parker. He was a stationer and printer. Although none of his letters to Elizabeth survives, her diaries reveal that he furnished her with London newspapers until his premature death in April 1767 of kidney disease.
MS: single letter to Robert Parker LRO, DDB/72/52. His death is mentioned in LRO, DDB/72/202 (29 May 1767), W. Ramsden, Charterhouse, to E. Shackleton, Alkincoats (MS span: 1751).

Thomas Parker, Winchester, Hampshire (1754–1819)
Eldest son of Elizabeth and Robert Parker of Alkincoats. Writing here from school. As the heir, Parker came into the Alkincoats estate upon his majority in 1775. Despite a mooted career in the church or the army, he took up no profession. Upon his marriage in 1779 to the nineteen-year-old heiress Betty Parker of Newton Hall, Yorkshire, his mother removed definitively to John Shackleton's newly built mansion, Pasture House at Barrowford. An extraordinary amount of the correspondence he received is preserved. Among numerous others, he got letters from Betty his wife, his brother John Parker, his uncle and aunt Edward and Barbara Parker of Browsholme, his cousins John and Beatrix Parker of Marshfield, his children Eliza, Edward and Thomas, and from families such as the Cunliffes of Wycoller, Claytons of Carr, Carrs of Langroyd and Stackhouse, Starkies of Huntroyde, Whitakers of Simonstone, St Clares of Preston and Grindleton, Towneley Parkers of Cuerden, Ferrands of Bingley, the Wiglesworths of Townhead and Thorp, etc.
MS: single letter LRO, DDB Ac 7886/64. For letters to him, see LRO, DDB/72/311–85, 492–979 (MS span: 1768–1819).

Ann Pellet (née Southouse), London (d. 1776)
Elizabeth Parker's maternal aunt, the daughter of the merchant Henry Southouse of Manuden, Essex, and the widow of Dr Thomas Pellet (?1671–1744), president of the Royal College of Physicians (1735–9). Mrs Pellet was stepmother to Thomas Pellet's daughter from his first marriage, Jane Scrimshire (née Pellet), but it appears that none of her own children survived infancy. Her marital home was in Henrietta Street, Covent Garden. During over thirty years of widowhood, she lived with her longtime servant, secretary and companion a Miss M. Bowen. They boarded with quiet, genteel families, many of them relatives, in Ealing, Brentford, Kensington and Westminster. Despite her conscious retirement, Mrs Pellet received visits from Lady Fleming of Rydal and Lady Leicester of Tarporley. At her death Ann donated twenty guineas to Elizabeth Shackleton and various monies to her numerous Southouse nephews, nieces and godchildren. She also bequeathed pieces of silverware to the Scrimshire children, the contents of a cabinet to the Duchess of Kensington, a sable tippet and the crimson damask furniture to

her niece Patsy Box, a mourning ring to her friend Frances Cole, ten pounds to be distributed to 'the fittest objects of charity' and all remaining clothes and furniture, plus an annuity of fifteen pounds a year to Miss Bowen.
MS: ninety-six letters LRO, DDB/72/76–122, 162–71, 446; DDB Ac 7886/96, 98–9, 113–14, 128, 133, 137, 143, 162, 170–71, 193, 201, 207, 213, 222, 227, 236, 239, 241, 246, 256, 264, 267, 272–5, 279, 284, 286, 294, 304, 313, 316. Also three letters to Robert Parker LRO, DDB/72/54, 59, 62. See also PRO, 11/1016, Will of Mrs Ann Pellet. For professional information, see W. Munk (ed.), *The Roll of the Royal College of Physicians of London* (1878), ii, p. 56 (MS span: 1746–75).

R. Pudsey, Bolton, Yorkshire
The Pudseys of Bolton by Bowland were an established Yorkshire gentry family, related by marriage to the Dawsons of Langliffe Hall. This woman wrote thanks for civilities received at Browsholme.
MS: single letter LRO, DDB Ac 7886/165 (MS span: 1747).

'MR'
Although this woman's status is unknown, she probably belonged to a local family of substance, as she entertained a great deal company and mentioned her husband's ('C:R') journeyings to the assizes.
MS: letter LRO, DDB Ac 7886/170 (MS span: *c*.1747).

Bessy Ramsden (née Parker) and William Ramsden (1718–1804), Charterhouse Square, London
Bessy was Elizabeth Parker's cousin. She was the daughter of Robert Parker of London, sister of the manufacturer Ned Parker and the stationer Thomas Parker. She married William Ramsden some time in the late 1750s. Before her marriage, she lived with her brother Ned and later boarded with a 'genteel family in Aldersgate street'. After her marriage her brother Ned demanded retroactive rent and refused to comply with the terms of Bessy's marriage settlement. Reverend Ramsden was the son of John Ramsden, Master of Penistone School, Yorkshire. Educated at Barnsland near Halifax; usher at Worsborough School, Yorks, 1737–8; BA Cantab. 1742; MA, 1745; PDD Lambeth, 1779; usher at Bishops Stortford School, 1741–8; usher at Charterhouse School, 1748–78, Master 1778–1804; Revd of Balsam, Cambridgeshire, 1779–1804. This cosy couple had four children, Billy (b. 1763), Betsy (b. 1764), Tommy (b. 1768) and Dick (b. 1770). Elizabeth Parker was godmother to the eldest boy.
MS: 129 letters LRO, DDB/72/74–5, 172–298. For professional information, see R. L. Arrowsmith (ed.), *Charterhouse Register, 1769–1872* (1974), p. 420 (MS span: 1760–77).

Robert Sclater, Clitheroe, Lancashire
This man acted as a political agent for the Listers of Gisburn Park; and was also a witness to the codicil to John Parker's will. A local land deed identifies him as a gentleman, but he was almost certainly a lawyer as well.
MS: three letters LRO, DDB/72/452 and 484; LRO, DDB Ac 7886/276 (1749). For deed, see LRO, DDB/80/116 (MS span: 1749–68).

Jane Scrimshire (née Pellet), Pontefract, Yorkshire
Daughter of Dr Thomas Pellet of London by his first wife. She met Elizabeth
Parker through her stepmother Mrs Ann Pellet, and was a frequent visitor to
Browsholme Hall in her youth. Unconventionally, she left her stepmother's establishment in 1748 and set up in rooms on her own in Pontefract with her servant
Betty ('a House of my own was always my Inclination and I think a Cottage to
oneself is preferable to a Palace of anothers'), where she met her husband Michael
Scrimshire, a local lawyer. He practised as an attorney in Ropergate, Pontefract,
but had property in Micklegate, York, and also appears to have followed the
assize around the northern circuit. The Scrimshires were related by marriage to
the Tempests of Tong Hall, Bradford, and therefore spent many summers in
this vicinity. (Michael's sister Elizabeth Scrimshire was married to Captain John
Tempest of Nottingham, younger son of Sir George Tempest of Tong. The title
passed to his family after the death of his two older brothers in the 1750s.)
The Scrimshires had three children: Jenny (b. 1752), who was born blind, Tom (b.
1753) and Deborah (b. 1756). Among many godparents, Sir George Tempest was
named godfather to the baby 'Deb'. Deborah Scrimshire married a Mr Green,
'citizen', in 1773, while Tom Scrimshire died abroad in 1774.
MS: forty-three letters before marriage LRO, DDB Ac 7886/88, 91, 94, 100, 105,
120, 127, 130, 134, 139, 171, 190, 194, 202, 205, 208, 218, 232, 235, 238, 240, 243,
253, 255, 257, 263, 265, 266, 268, 271, 287, 288, 289, 290, 292, 296, 298, 302, 305,
314, 317, 318, 320. Forty-one letters to Elizabeth after her marriage, LRO, DDB/
72/123–61, 445 and 447. Two letters to Robert Parker LRO, DDB/72/55 and 61
(MS span: 1745–57).

G. Seedall, Alkincoats, Lancashire
In the 1750s this woman was employed as nurse to the three Parker children, but
it is unclear whether she served in the capacity of wet-nurse or nursemaid.
MS: two letters LRO, DDB/72/69–70 (MS span: 1756).

Edward Southouse, Wax Chandlers Hall, London
Elizabeth Parker's maternal uncle. By his connections and address it was assumed
that he was a merchant. Given his commercial association, he was probably a
soap-maker like his brother Henry.
MS: single letter LRO, DDB Ac 7886/312 (MS span: 1749).

Henry Kynaston Southouse, Sidney Sussex College, Cambridge (c.1728–1773)
Cousin to Elizabeth Parker. The son of Henry Southouse and Mary
Kynaston. He was admitted to Sidney Sussex college in 1745 aged seventeen. He
matriculated in 1745 and gained his BA in 1748–9. His ultimate occupation is
unclear.
MS: single letter LRO, DDB Ac 7886/104 (MS span: 1746).

Jane Southouse (née Parker), London (b. 1702)
Elizabeth Parker's paternal aunt, who married the draper Samuel Southouse Esq.
of Manuden, Essex, son of the merchant Henry Southouse of Manuden, Essex.
She lived for a time in Leadenhall Street.

MS: five letters LRO, DDB/72/60, 68; DDB Ac 7886/92, 187, 262. See also CLRO, Freedom Records, CF1/432, 1723 (MS span: 1723–55).

Mary Southouse (née Kynaston), London (*c.*1702)
Elizabeth Parker's maternal aunt. She was born Mary Kynaston and in 1722 married Henry Southouse of St Giles, Cripplegate, London, a soap-maker 'being unfortunately one of the worst and most unprofitable trades in England'. At her husband's early death in 1729, she lived off the rent of various properties in St Martins-in-the-Fields, plus the residue of the estate after legacies. She was executor to his will.
MS: single letter LRO, DDB Ac 7886/90. See also CLRO, Freedom Records, CF1/390, June 1720, and ERO, D/Dc 27/1010 (1 Nov. 1729), Probate of will of Henry Southouse (MS span: 1720–45).

Sam Southouse, Temple Cloisters, London
Sam was Ann Pellet's nephew, named executor of her will. He inherited the portraits of his aunt and uncle. From his address and the content of his letter it is assumed that he was a lawyer of some description.
MS: single letter LRO, DDB/72/304 (MS span: 1776).

*****John Stanhope**, Horsforth, Yorkshire (1701–69)
A leading barrister on the northern circuit: 'Old friend Lawyer Stanhope' joined Robert Parker on the grouse moors in the 1750s and sent gifts of venison. Mr and Mrs Stanhope were also friends of the Scrimshires of Pontefract. Presumably the gentlemen worked together on the northern circuit. He is discussed below with the Spencer Stanhopes (see pp. 374–5).
MS: single letter LRO, DDB/72/482. One of his wife's letters to him is recorded in Stirling, *Annals*, pp. 85–112, but others are collected with the Spencer Stanhope manuscripts in WYAS, Bradford, below (see pp. 374–5). (MS span: 1749).

Thomas Stirling, Browsholme, Yorkshire
From 1757 to 1775 Thomas Stirling helped Elizabeth Parker administer the Alkincoats estate, in his capacity as steward of Browsholme. They enjoyed very amicable relations, exchanging advice and gifts of produce for over two decades.
MS: five letters LRO, DDB/72/448, 453–7 (MS span: 1763–70).

Miss Fanny Walker, Whitley, Yorkshire
This woman shared many northern friends and acquaintances with Elizabeth Parker. She writes while a house-guest in a substantial Yorkshire household, talking of the bell ringing for dinner, fine London company staying ('three of the longest chinned familys that ever was seen'), dancing every night and be-diamonded guests. However, the source of her family's money is unclear.
MS: LRO, DDB Ac 7886/280 (MS span: 1749).

Dr R. Walmsley, Carlisle, Cumberland
An army doctor, stationed near the border during the 1745 rebellion, whose flirtatious tone suggests he was an admirer of Elizabeth Parker.
MS: LRO, DDB Ac 7886/86 (MS span: 1745).

Mrs Walton, Skipwith Hall, Yorkshire
A gentlewoman. The wife of Banastre Walton of Skipwith and Marsden. Her
letter concerned her inoculation. The Walkers were taxed on eight male servants
in 1780. They, too, patronized the rising Gillows of Lancaster.
MS: single letter LRO, DDB Ac 7886/57 (MS span: 1773).

E. Webster, Croston, Lancashire
The status of this married woman is unknown.
MS: single letter LRO, DDB Ac 7886/311 (MS span: 1749).

***Thomas Whitaker** of Simonestone Hall, Lancashire (1701–66)
The Whitakers of Simonstone were an ancient gentry family.
MS: LRO, DDB Ac 7886/228 (MS span: 1748).

***Henry Wiglesworth** of Townhead, Slaidburn, Yorkshire (b. 1724)
Son and heir of Henry Wiglesworth of Slaidburn, Yorks. He was born at Colne,
his mother's home. Educated at Slaidburn School and Cambridge, he was
admitted to the Middle Temple on 6 May 1741. The Wiglesworths were
well-acquainted with the polite families of north-east Lancashire and owned
land in the area through the female line. Henry corresponded with Robert
Parker regarding livestock. The Wiglesworths were taxed on two male servants in
1780.
MS: two letters LRO, DDB/72/482, LRO, DDB Ac 7886/244 (MS span: 1748–9).

Mrs Mary Witton (née Assheton), Chapel Thorp, Wakefield, Yorkshire
One of the Asshetons of Downham and Cuerdale, whose first husband was the
Revd John Witton of Lupet Hall (1691–1754). John Witton was the son of a
Wakefield barrister, educated at Wakefield School and Cambridge. He was
ordained priest in 1722, was Rector of Houghton in Huntingdonshire, 1726–32,
Vicar of Throcking Northumberland 1740–54, and Prebendary of York 1743–52.
Despite the limited financial rewards of a clerical career, this family still appeared
one of social substance. They possessed a coach, were friends of the Listers
of Gisburn Park, escorted the unmarried Miss Parker to the Wakefield races
and were seen about town in York in the 1740s. They also had the wherewithal
to undertake building work on a new house, Birthwaite Hall, in the same
decade. Mary Witton's second husband was Peregrine Wentworth of Tolston
Lodge.
MS: three letters LRO, DDB Ac 7886/307–8, 310 (MS span: 1749).

BARCROFT CORRESPONDENCE NETWORK, 1785–1826

Correspondents of five sisters: Miss Martha Barcroft (b. 1757), Miss Mary
Barcroft (b. 1766), Miss Barbara Barcroft (b. 1762), Mrs Ellen Moon and Mrs
Elizabeth Reynolds.

Captain Ambrose Barcroft (1759–95)
Brother of Barbara, Ellen, Elizabeth, Mary and Martha. Married Eleanor Duffy, of whom nothing is known. He died by shipwreck leaving a daughter Ellen. Curiously, his will of 1793 makes no mention of a wife or daughter. As a young man he was known to Elizabeth Shackleton.
MS: four letters he wrote to his sister 'my dear Beth', LRO, DDB/61/34, and LRO, DDB/72/1486–8. Financial information can be gleaned from LRO, DDB/70/8 (1793), Will, and LRO, DDB/252 (1793–4), Account of Captain Barcroft's rents. His majority and military career are mentioned in Elizabeth Shackleton's diary, LRO, DDB/81/37 (1780), f. 34 (MS span: 1785).

Mrs Mary Barcroft, Bradford, Yorkshire
This woman was sister-in-law to the Miss Barcrofts, the widow of John Barcroft (1764–99), who died at Bradford. Although, by his father's will, John Barcroft inherited an interest in his mother's land in Trawden, Lancashire, how or whether he supplemented his landed income is unknown.
MS: four letters LRO, DDB/72/1500–3 (MS span: c.1803).

Joseph Bateman, Lancaster, Lancashire
Bateman communicated information to the sisters about a legal dispute they were embroiled in. Unfortunately, no data as to his occupation can be found.
MS: single letter LRO, DDB/72/1417 (MS span: 1819).

Mary Cunliffe (née Oldham) Wycoller, Lancashire
'Molly' was the daughter of a wealthy hat-manufacturer, Adam Oldham of Manchester, and was reportedly an heiress. In August 1775 she married Henry Owen Cunliffe (1752–1818) at the collegiate and parish church of Manchester. The Sheffield-born Henry Owen had inherited Wycoller Hall and its estate from his uncle Henry Cunliffe in June 1773. He was educated at Bolton Abbey School and for a time at Oxford. Upon his sudden promotion, he took his uncle's name, joined the Lancashire militia and set about rebuilding the hall. Despite extensive renovations and the purchase of mahogany furniture from Gillows of Lancaster, Wycoller could not throw off the nickname of the 'haunted house'. Cunliffe made abortive efforts to lease Ackworth Park near Pontefract and later a house near Addingham, but eventually in 1802 he rented Chapel House in Wharfedale, Yorkshire. Thereafter, he only returned to collect rents, shoot grouse and explore the possibilities of mining the coal on his estate. Mary Cunliffe may have been a Methodist, she was certainly accused of being such in Elizabeth Shackleton's diary. Moreover, it was the Cunliffes who rented out land in Colne upon which the first Methodist congregation built their chapel. They had no children.
MS: single letter LRO, DDB/72/1363. For examples of Henry's penmanship, see his letters to Thomas Parker LRO, DDB/72/836, 861, 933 (MS span: 1814).

Miss Charlotte Dickson, Berwick upon Tweed
This doctor's daughter met the Miss Barcrofts at Otley. When her father

retired from practice in the 1790s, she and her sister removed with him to the borders. Charlotte, however, continued to regret the loss of 'the amiable ladies at Manor House', filling her letters with queries about the West Riding social scene.
MS: five letters LRO, DDB/72/1489–91, 1495, 1499 (MS span: 1795–1801).

J. Hartley, Colne, Lancashire
This correspondent aided the Miss Barcrofts in the procurement of lodgings in the Colne area when they left Otley. He was certainly an able writer and businessman in the loosest sense. He may have been the superior cotton-manufacturer John Hartley of Colne or the gentleman-merchant Joseph Hartley of Colne, both of whom appear in local parish registers.
MS: single letter LRO, DDB/72/1494 . See also Spencer, *Baptism Register 1790–1812* (MS span: 1800).

Thomas Johnson, Eshton, Gargrave, Yorkshire
His son was named as executor to the Miss Barcrofts' estates along with Edward Parker of Selby and Captain Thomas Parker of Alkincoats. By his associations, he is believed to have been a gentleman.
MS: single letter LRO, DDB/72/1418 (MS span: 1822).

Anna Kendall, Leathley, Yorkshire
This woman befriended the unmarried Barcroft sisters during their residence at Otley. Her status is unknown.
MS: single letter LRO, DDB/72/1485 (MS span: 1784).

Mr E. King and Mrs Henrietta King, Leyland/Chorley, Lancashire
The one surviving letter from this woman was addressed from holiday accommodation, in Sydenham, London, but she was almost certainly a Lancashire resident. Her husband did not want occupation, but whether his labours were commercial or professional is not stated. The husband's letter announces her death and relates his attempts to re-establish a smooth-running household.
MS: two letters LRO, DDB/72/1504 and 1492 (MS span: 1786–96).

D. Lang, London
An ardent friend of Miss Martha Barcroft. Her social background cannot be ascertained.
MS: single letter to Martha Barcroft LRO, DDB/72/1407 (MS span: 1785).

Edward Parker, Selby, Yorkshire (1786–1865)
Second son of Thomas Parker of Alkincoats. He practised as a solicitor in Selby and lived there with his wife, Ellen, until 1832, when he inherited Alkincoats and Browsholme through his elder childless brother Captain Thomas Parker. His four surviving sons all took up a profession; one became a barrister, one a solicitor, one an infantry officer and one a clergyman. Meanwhile, of his three surviving daughters, one remained a spinster, one married an infantry officer and one a Colne gentleman.

MS: six letters LRO, DDB/72/1199, 1203, 1375, 1419, 1509, 1532. See also LRO, DDB/71/4 (1803), Apprenticeship to Richard Swallow of Selby. In addition, ten letters survive written by Edward's sister Eliza Parker to their father Thomas Parker of Alkincoats and Newton, see below (MS span: 1823–26).

Ellen Parker (née Barcroft), Selby, Yorkshire (c.1794–1866)
Daughter of Eleanor Duffy and Captain Ambrose Barcroft. After the death of her father in 1795, Ellen was raised by her aunts, the Miss Barcrofts. She attended school at Avenham, Preston, in the 1800s. In 1816 she married Edward Parker (see above, p. 366) and set up home in Selby. She bore eleven children, of whom seven survived: Ambrose, Thomas-Goulbourne, Edward, Robert, Elizabeth, Ellen and Barbara.
MS: forty letters LRO, DDB/72/1191–8, 1200–2, 1204–9, 1365–74, 1376–80, 1415, 1505–8, 1527–9. It also appears that Ellen wrote the journal LRO, DDB/64/14 (c.1808), whose authoress is styled simply 'Miss Barcroft' (MS span: 1808–25).

Thomas and Ambrose Parker, Selby, Yorkshire
Children of the solicitor above, these were great-nephews of the Miss Barcrofts.
MS: LRO, DDB/72/1420, 1530–31 (MS span: 1823–6).

Revd Samuel Payne, Weymouth, Dorset
Rector of Weymouth, writing an account of Ambrose Barcroft's funeral.
MS: single letter to 'Miss Barcroft' LRO, DDB/61/42 (MS span: 1795).

Mr B. Reynolds, London
Husband of Elizabeth Reynolds (née Barcroft), he wrote to his sisters-in-law from Newington, London. Because of his considerable leisure and prosperity, combined with an absence of any mention of professional commitments, he is assumed to have been a gentleman.
MS: letters LRO, DDB/72/1413 (MS span: 1807).

Mrs D. Ridsdale (née Wiglesworth) Park Gate, Leeds, Yorkshire
The sister of Barbara Wiglesworth. When the Miss Barcrofts moved back to Lancashire, Mrs Ridsdale felt bitterly 'the loss of so many social hours and friendship dish of chat'. Although Mrs Ridsdale was gentle by birth, her husband was a scion of the mercantile family of Ridsdale. Ridsdale and Company of Leeds were registered in national directories, see *UBD*, III, p. 540. Interestingly, this woman also appears in the Dawson–Greene network. However, the letters preserved in the Dawson–Green collection record a later period after her husband's Leeds business had failed (c.1813), when they had retired to a small farm in Winsley near Ripley loaned by Wiglesworth kin.
MS: two letters to the Barcrofts LRO, DDB/72/1362, 1497 (MS span: 1800–5).

Surgeon-Lieutenant W. E. Sharpnell, Weymouth, Dorset
Fellow-officer of the late Ambrose Barcroft.
MS: twelve letters LRO, DDB/61/41, 43–53 (MS span: 1795–6).

Mr John Tennant Esq., Chapelhouse, Leeds, Yorkshire
John Tennant was distantly related to the Miss Barcrofts by marriage. His sister, a Miss Jane Tennant of Grassington, Yorkshire, married the elderly John Barcroft of Clitheroe Castle in 1774, thereby becoming stepmother to the Miss Barcrofts. Mr Tennant was almost certainly a merchant, a John Tennant, tea-man, was registered in the *UBD*, III, p. 540.
MS: single letter LRO, DDB/72/1409. See also the Barcroft–Tennant marriage settlement, LRO, DDB/62/211, to which John Tennant was a signatory, guaranteeing his sister an annuity of thirty pounds per annum. (MS span: 1789).

Miss Barbara Wiglesworth of Townhead, Yorkshire
Almost certainly the daughter of James (1725–1807) and Barbara Wiglesworth (1733–1802), a couple who were particularly close to the Parkers of Browsholme. Barbara Wiglesworth was named a witness to the will of Edward Parker of Browsholme in January 1790, while James Wiglesworth was named trustee. Miss Barbara Wiglesworth married a Mr Bromley of Leeds, *c*.1800. While betrothed, she wrote of the reduced circumstances and quiet social life she envisaged after marriage, which suggests that Bromley was a struggling business-man or impoverished professional. Unfortunately, he fails to surface in any local directories.
MS: four letters LRO, DDB/72/1408, 1493, 1496, 1498 (MS span: 1797–1800).

Miss Ellen Wilson, Otley, Yorkshire
This gentlewoman was the Miss Barcrofts' first cousin. She was the daughter of Martha Barcroft of Foulridge (d. 1819) and Matthew Wilson of Manor House, Otley (d. 1826), only son of Revd Roger Wilson (1711–89), the curate of Colne parish church. Matthew Wilson was a captain in the 4th Royal Lancashire Militia, and served as a Deputy-Lieutenant for both Lancashire and Yorkshire. The Wilsons were a substantial family, related by marriage to the Butlers of Kirkland Hall, Lancashire, the Tennants of Chapelhouse, Yorkshire, and the Wiglesworths of Townhead, Yorkshire.
MS: single letter to Barbara Barcroft, LRO, DDB/72/1381 (MS span: 1826)

Miss Martha Wilson, Otley, Yorkshire
Sister to Ellen Wilson and a cousin to Miss Barcrofts. Martha and Ellen Wilson jointly executed their father's will of 1815, by which the unmarried sisters inher-ited substantial real estate in Otley, Burley, and Newall with Clifton, Yorkshire.
MS: two letters to Martha Barcroft LRO, DDB/72/1414, 1416. See also LRO, DDB/70/9, Will of Matthew Wilson of Otley (MS span: 1812).

WHITAKER CORRESPONDENCE NETWORK, 1812–21

Correspondents of Eliza Whitaker (1790–1860) and Charles Whitaker (1790–1843) of Roefield, Clitheroe, and later Simonstone Hall, Padiham, Lancashire.

Elizabeth Addison (?née Aspinall), Lodge Lane, Liverpool, Lancashire
Almost certainly the wife of merchant Richard Addison of 14 Lodge Lane, Toxteth Park, Liverpool, and later 19 Nile Street. Listed in Liverpool directories for 1805, 1823 and 1825. The Addisons made bulk purchases of provisions (wine and sugar) on behalf of the Whitaker's direct from the ships. They were probably related to the Addison family of Preston. Eliza Parker of Alkincoats recorded attending a 'hop' given by the Addisons in the 1814 Preston season. John Addison Esq., 8 Winckley St, was registered as a notable inhabitant of Preston in 1824.
MS: seven letters LRO, DDWh/4/40, 49, 56, 64, 72, 89, 124 (MS span: 1814).

Alice Ainsworth, Moss Bank, Bolton, Lancashire
By 1824 this correspondent was registered in Baines's Directory as a notable inhabitant of Preston, probably widowed, living at 68 Fishergate. She had married into a Bolton family of gentleman farmers. The Ainsworths were known to the children of Thomas and Betty Parker of Alkincoats and Newton.
MS: two letters LRO, DDWh/4/78, 120 (MS span: 1816).

N. Aspinall, Liverpool, Lanashire
Probably a relative of Nicholas Aspinall of Liverpool, younger son of John Aspinall Esq. of Standen Hall, Clitheroe.
MS: single letter LRO, DDWh/4/37 (MS span: 1814).

Mrs AB, Preston, Lancashire
A young matron who wrote of her babies and book society, though sadly mentioned nothing of her husband or her income.
MS: single letter LRO, DDWh/4/74 (MS span: 1814).

N. Bishop, Roby, near Liverpool, Lancashire
Because this woman wrote of estate management and inhabited the genteel residence of Roby Hall, it is assumed that she belonged to the lesser gentry.
MS: single letter LRO, DDWh/4/23 (MS span: 1812).

Mrs D. Bowyer, Bedford Row, London
Little is known of this London correspondent, but that she was a friend of Eliza Whitaker's aunt, Anne Eliza Robbins. After Robert Robbins's sudden death, Mrs Bowyer supervised the Robbins children, while their mother was prostrate with grief. Mr Bowyer's profession is not revealed, though it seems likely that he was a lawyer, like Robert Robbins. In any case, the families were on warm terms and their children were playmates, as an affectionate note to the 'dunce' Percy Robbins from his 'dear little sweetheart' Ann Bowyer confirms.
MS: single letter LRO, DDWh/4/68. Ann Bowyer's letter is LRO, DDWh/4/129 (MS span: 1814).

Mrs E. Daunsey, Bashall Lodge, Lancashire
Although this woman wrote from her sister's home in Lancashire, she had her own house in London. Like her sister Mrs Johnson, Mrs Daunsey was a widow. She

was clearly on friendly terms with east Lancashire families such as the Whitakers and St Clares, but unfortunately, her late husband's occupation is unknown.
MS: three letters LRO, DDWh/4/47, 63, 133 (MS span: 1814).

S. Greaves, Lincoln's Inn Fields, London
Another friend of Anne Elizabeth Robbins, perhaps like Ann, the wife of a lawyer. She was closely involved in the drama surrounding Robert Robbins's premature death in 1814. Her own husband's occupation is unknown.
MS: single letter LRO, DDWh/4/42 (MS span: 1814).

C. Harrison, 'Penrose', Lancashire
Since this woman wrote of relaying servants and messages, she was undoubtedly a Lancashire neighbour of the Whitakers. She was obviously an employer, though further information about her status cannot be found.
MS: single letter LRO, DDWh/4/93 (MS span: 1817).

Alice Horrocks, Shenstone, Worcestershire (b. 1799)
Fifth daughter of Samuel and Alice Horrocks. At the time of writing she was unmarried, although she subsequently wed the Revd James Streynsham, rector and canon of Chorley, rural dean. They were married at the parish church of St John's, Preston, in 1825 by the bridegroom's uncle Revd Robert Masters. At her father's death in 1842 she inherited eight hundred pounds cash and, with her husband, ten thousand pounds in trust.
MS: single letter LRO, DDWh/4/84 (MS span: 1816).

Jane Horrocks, Lark Hill, Preston, Lancashire (b. 1795)
Third daughter of Samuel and Alice Horrocks. At the time of writing she was unmarried. Her first husband was Thomas Monkhouse, who died in 1825, leaving one daughter Mary Elizabeth (b. 1822); she married secondly Paris Dick MD.
MS: two letters LRO, DDWh/4/46, 94 (MS span: 1814).

John and Jane Horrocks, Edgeworth, Lancashire
Grandparents of Eliza Whitaker, this couple began their married life as rather humble Quakers.
MS: single letter LRO, DDWh/4/41 (MS span: 1814).

Mary Horrocks, Lark Hill, Preston, Lancashire (b. 1798)
Fourth daughter of Samuel and Alice Horrocks. She moved briefly in the Lakes circle of Samuel Coleridge, Sarah Hutchinson et al., among whom she was known as 'the daisy'. She married Revd William Birkett, rector of Great Hasely, Oxfordshire, in 1824. At her father's death in 1842 she inherited eight hundred pounds cash and, with her husband, ten thousand pounds in trust.
MS: single letter LRO, DDWh/4/90 (MS span: 1816).

Samuel Horrocks, Lark Hill, Preston, Lancashire (1766–1842)
Eliza Whitaker's father also wrote from London, when attending parliament and doing business at the Bread Street office.
MS: seven letters LRO, DDWh/4/24, 26, 35, 48, 50, 80, 86 (MS span: 1812–16).

Sam Horrocks, Bread Street, London (1797–1846)
The Horrocks heir Sam attended preparatory school in Parsons Green and Eton, and then went into the London end of the business, becoming a junior partner. In 1827 he married Eliza Miller, the daughter of his father's business partner Thomas Miller. The newlyweds' fashionable address was 9 Winckley Square, Preston. From 1827 Sam was a full partner in the firm; in 1839 he was appointed deputy lieutenant of Lancashire; in 1842 he became Preston Guild major and served as the head of Horrocks and Co., 1842–6. At his father's death, he inherited the Lark Hill estate on trust for his lifetime. He had no legitimate offspring, though his will refers to 'his natural daughter' Mary Standing, for whom he ordered an investment of five hundred pounds. Most of the letters used in the book were written when Sam was still a rather hypochondriacal bachelor, undergoing his initiation in business at the London office. In this period, he fulfilled his sisters' fashionable commissions and communicated news of their London kin. Two later letters were written from Lancashire when Sam was enjoying the grouse shooting.
MS: eight letters LRO, DDWh/4/39, 43, 66, 67, 70, 75, 118–19 (MS span: 1813–14).

Sarah Horrocks, Lark Hill, Preston, Lancashire (b. 1792)
Second daughter of Samuel and Alice Horrocks. She appears to have managed the Lark Hill household in the 1810s, but still enjoyed a lively social life in Preston and Liverpool. In 1825, at the age of thirty-two, she married Dr William St Clare junior, at the parish church of St John, Preston. At her father's death in 1842 she inherited eight hundred pounds cash and, with her husband, ten thousand pounds in trust. Eventually, she lived out her widowhood in Bath.
MS: five letters LRO, DDWh/4/44, 51, 54, 122, and 129 (MS span: 1814).

Mrs M. Johnson, Bashall Lodge, Lancashire
The precise social position of this Lancashire widow cannot be established. She wrote in the first shock of bereavement, supported by her sister, a Mrs E. Daunsey of London.
MS: single letter LRO, DDWh/4/58 (MS span: 1814).

Jennette Leighton, address unknown
Little can be discovered about this woman, since no address or kin are named. Miss Leighton was a Horrocks family friend, who was to be met with regularly in London. She may have resided in north-east Lancashire, as her own letter to Eliza talks of a shared walk to Clitheroe. At the very least, she must have had friends or relatives in the area.
MS: single letter LRO, DDWh/4/123 (MS span: c.1814).

Mrs M. C. Martin, Enfield, Middlesex
Comments in her letter suggest this woman was Lancashire born, though she rarely visited the north because her husband had 'such a *horror* of Lancashire and its environs'. She maintained direct contact with the London-based Horrocks clan.

She herself had married into a professional family and complained of the lack of romantic initiative displayed by her spinster sisters, finally packing them off to board with another family.
MS: single letter LRO, DDWh/4/79 (MS span: 1816).

Eliza Molyneux, Alkincoats, Lancashire
Probably the sister of Mary Molyneux of Liverpool who in 1824 married Captain Thomas Parker, eldest son of Thomas Parker of Alkincoats and Newton. Captain Parker was a great friend of Charles Whitaker and Sarah Horrocks. His disastrous amours were widely discussed among the Whitaker network.
MS: single letter LRO, DDWh/4/121 (MS span: c.1824).

S. Mortimer, Cuerden Hall, Lancashire
This woman (probably a wealthy widow or young heiress) enjoyed some means, being in a position to chose at leisure where she wanted to settle. She was welcomed into the homes of the greater Lancashire gentry for long visits and was probably herself a member of the lesser gentry.
MS: two letters LRO, DDWh/4/25, 57 (MS span: 1812–14).

Margaret Nichols, Bewdley, Worcestershire
This sophisticated correspondent shared a great many of female acquaintances with Eliza Whitaker, many of whom were designated by nicknames and surnames, such as 'La Camea', 'Bisby', 'Tom', 'Knighton', all of which suggests the two women were former schoolfellows. Margaret Nichols considered herself one of the fashionable set, but the source of her income remains obscure.
MS: single letter LRO, DDWh/4/73 (MS span: 1814).

E. Nuttal, Overleigh Hall, Chester
This woman was a 'business' acquaintance of Eliza Whitaker; they corresponded concerning the employment of servants.
MS: single letter LRO, DDWh/4/45 (MS span: 1814).

Anne Eliza Robbins (née Horrocks), 23 Lincoln's Inn Fields, London (1786–1825)
Daughter of John Horrocks of Edgeworth, sister to Mrs Mary Whitehead, the enterprising John Horrocks of Preston and to his successor Samuel Horrocks of Lark Hill, Preston. The aunt of Alice, Eliza, Jane, Mary, Susanna and Sarah Horrocks. Her first husband, Robert Robbins, a barrister, died tragically when she was pregnant with their fifth child. (Children: William, George, Percy, Caroline, Elizabeth.) She remarried 1818 Revd Cornelius Pitt, Rector of Rendcombe, Gloucester. Convention has it that Mr Pitt senior, builder of Pittville, Cheltenham, opposed the match and disowned the couple. Together they had yet more children.
MS: seven letters LRO, DDWh/4/36, 38, 88, 117, 125, 131–2. See also LRO, DDWh/4/22 (11 Oct. 1812), R. Robbins, Radnorshire, to Samuel Horrocks, Preston (MS span: 1813–16).

Dr William St Clare, 4 Fishergate Hill, Preston, Lancashire (b. 1784)
The second son of Dr William St Clare of Blackburn, who was educated at Christ Church, Oxford (BA 1805, B.Med. 1809, D.Med. 1812). The family owned considerable property in Preston and Grindleton, Lancashire. Like his father before him, St Clare was regarded as a fashionable professional, treating most of the county's genteel families, including the Horrockses of Lark Hill, Starkies of Huntroyde, Whitakers of Simonstone and Roefield, Parkers of Alkincoats and Newton, and so on, but also worked in the Preston dispensary opened in Fishergate in 1809 supported by voluntary contributions. He stood as a witness at Eliza Whitaker's wedding in 1812 and was named godfather to her first son. In 1825 he married Eliza's younger sister Sarah Horrocks.
MS: twenty-one letters LRO, DDWh/4/87, 91–2, 95–7, 99–115. Compare with LRO, DDWh/4/12 (6 July 1789), W. St Clare, Preston, to Mrs H. Whitaker, Rosegrove, and LRO, DDB/72/492–507 (1780–1812), W. St Clare, Preston, Newton, Burnley and Grindleton, to Thomas Parker, Alkincoats and Newton. See also the 1812 will of William St Clare senior, LRO, DDWh/3/110 (MS span: 1816–21).

Miss ?Sarah Whalley, Rocke Court, Fareham, Hampshire
Since this unmarried woman referred to Lancashire as 'our own best country', it seems safe to say that she met Eliza Whitaker in the north in her youth. She was godmother to Eliza's eldest son Charles. From her contacts, conversation and residence, it is assumed that she belonged to the lesser gentry. She was probably one of the Whalleys of Hampshire and Somerset, who possessed an ancestral right to the lordship of the parish of Whalley, Lancashire.
MS: single letter LRO, DDWh/4/77 (MS span: 1816).

Mary Whitehead (née Horrocks), Winckley Square, Preston, Lancashire (d. 1858)
Eldest daughter of John and Jane Horrocks of Edgeworth, sister of Anne Eliza Robbins and therefore aunt to the seven Horrocks sisters. Her husband, the Prestonian John Whitehead, was a merchant of some description, though in 1802 he went into partnership with his brothers-in-law Samuel and John Horrocks. After his death in 1810 his widow continued to live in the fashionable residential area Winckley Square, though she made frequent visits to her sister Mrs Robbins in London, her mother and father at Edgeworth, and to other relatives at Ainsworth Hall. She had at least one child, Walter Whitehead.
MS: single letter LRO, DDWh/4/69 (MS span: 1814).

Elizabeth Wiglesworth, Townhead, Slaidburn, Yorkshire (1762–1820)
First wife of Henry Wiglesworth 'the Bold Rector of Slaidburn' (1758–1838). He was educated at Sedburgh School and at Sidney Sussex College, Cambridge. Despite his long clerical career, he was famed principally for his love of hunting and pack of hounds. Mrs Wiglesworth seems to have found her own diversion in her hothouse and garden.
MS: single letter LRO, DDWh/4/83 (MS span: 1816).

Mrs A. Wright, 54 Lower Brook Street, London
The exact status of this metropolitan correspondent is unknown, however she and
her husband were clearly wealthy enough to undertake lengthy national tours.
MS: two letters LRO, DDWh/4/34, 128 (MS span: 1813).

SELECTED CORRESPONDENTS FROM THE
STANHOPE NETWORK, 1727–1769

John Spencer, Middle Temple, London
The eldest son of the Spencers of Cannon Hall, he was educated at Winchester and
Oxford before he qualified at the Bar. His younger brothers were sent to Mr
Watt's Mercantile Academy in Little Tower Street, London, to learn arithmetic,
book-keeping and good handwriting. One of them at least, Benjamin Spencer,
went on to work as merchant in London.
MS: scattered letters to him, from his sister A. M. Graeme of Sewerby, from his
brother-in-law Walter Stanhope, and from his sister Anne Stanhope. Letters by
him to the Stanhopes are also preserved: WYCRO, Bradford, Sp St/6/1/55, 64, 65,
66, 72 (MS span: 1748–57).

Anne Stanhope (née Spencer), Leeds, Yorkshire
One of the Spencers of Cannon Hall, Cawthorne, Barnsley, a substantial landed
family active in the exploitation of the mineral reserves on their estates. In R. G.
Wilson's view 'they were as much industrialists as Landowners. Much of their
wealth was derived from their interest in a group of furnaces, forges and slitting
mills scattered throughout South Yorkshire', Wilson, 'Three Brothers', p. 115.
In 1749 the twenty-seven-year-old Anne Spencer married the widower Walter
Stanhope of Horsforth. Theirs was a successful partnership. Her letters date from
after her marriage, when they set up home in a commodious house in High Town,
Leeds. After her husband's death in 1759 she retired to the vicinity of Cannon Hall.
MS: scattered letters to her brother John Spencer, her husband Walter Stanhope,
as well as plentiful correspondence she received from friends and kin: *inter alia*
WYCRO, Bradford, Sp St/6/1/55–9, 69, 70, 75–7, 80, 92, 94–5, 101 (MS span:
1748–*c*.1767).

Barbara Stanhope (née Cockcroft), Horsforth, Yorkshire
A Bradford heiress, Barbara Stanhope is the least literate woman whose letters
survive in this study. She seemed pitifully subservient to the pleasure of her
husband John Stanhope of Horsforth. She produced no children and took the
waters at Scarborough in the 1720s, presumably in quest of a cure.
MS: six letters to her husband: WYCRO, Bradford, Sp St/6/1/42 (MS span:
c.1727).

John Stanhope, Horsforth, Yorkshire (1701–69)
Son of John Stanhope II of Horsforth JP and Mary Lowther, educated at
Bradford Grammar School and University College, Oxford. Stanhope was the

leading barrister on the Northern Circuit in the 1760s, recorder at Doncaster from 1766 and an influential promoter of the scheme to cut the Leeds–Liverpool canal. He refused to accept a judgeship or to move to London to advance his career. At his death Stanhope received a glowing obituary in the *Leeds Mercury* (19 Sept. 1769). MS: numerous letters sent to and received from family, friends and business aquaintances. The earliest letters he received are from Hannah Beale of York: *inter alia* WYCRO, Bradford, Sp St/5/2/24, 30, 35; Sp St/6/1/31, 54, 57, 76, 85, 90, 99, 102 (MS span: 1697–*c*.1769).

Walter Stanhope, Leeds, Yorkshire (1703–59)
The second son of John Stanhope II of Horsforth, Walter was educated at Bradford Grammar School and after apprenticed for seven years to a prominent firm of Leeds woollen merchants, Croft and William Preston, for the princely fee of £230. Thereafter, Stanhope set up in business on his own in the Upper Headrow at Leeds and in 1731 was elected to the merchant-dominated Leeds Corporation. Subsequently, however, he relaxed his grip on commercial success. He resigned from the corporation in 1738 and never managed to establish a grand merchant house. He left the day-to-day management to Cavendish Lister, the son of a Leicestershire gentleman, taken on as apprentice in 1752. He married comparatively late, wedding first Mary Warde of Hooton Pagnell in 1742 and second Anne Spencer of Cannon Hall in about 1748. He enjoyed field sports, and made long visits to Cannon Hall and Sewerby to indulge his passion. At his death in 1759 his capital and assets added up to £3,685. The neighbouring gentry and the Leeds merchants were presented with scarves; his servants, clothiers, cloth-dressers and local innkeepers were given gloves.
MS: six letters to his second wife from Bath, and numerous letters he received: *inter alia* WYCRO, Bradford, Sp St/6/1/68 (MS span: 1756–7).

Walter Spencer Stanhope, of Horsforth and Cannon Hall, Yorkshire (1749–1821)
The only son of Walter Stanhope of Leeds, he assumed the additional surname and arms of Spencer, as heir to his uncle John Spencer. He was educated at University College, Oxford (1766–70). In 1783, after a supremely romantic courtship, he married Mary Winifred (b. 1850) daughter and heir of Thomas Babington Pulleine of Carlton Hall, Co. York. They had seven sons and seven daughters. He was MP for Carlisle 1775–80, Haslemere 1780–84, Hull 1784–90, Cockermouth 1800–2, Carlisle 1802–12.
MS: five letters to his mother and to his uncles, while at Bradford Grammar School and Oxford WYCRO, Bradford, Sp St/6/1/75, 77, 85, 90, 102 (MS span: 1757–*c*.1767).

Mary Warde, Hooton Pagnell, Doncaster, Yorkshire (*c*.1747)
The daughter of Patience Warde of Hooton Pagnell and Anna Harvey of Wormersley. On the 21 December 1742, she married the handsome Leeds merchant Walter Stanhope Esq. She was said to be pretty and brought him £1,400 as a marriage portion. However she was dead within five years and her children died in infancy.

MS: forty-seven letters she received, mostly before her marriage, but some after: WYCRO, Bradford, Sp St/6/1/50 (MS span: 1733–46).

Mary Warde, Squerries Court, near Westerham, Kent (b. 1760)
The first daughter of John Warde of Squerryes Court purchased in 1731. Warde himself was the son of a Lord Mayor of London, and was wealthy enough to entertain an estimated 7,000 of his country neighbours on strong beer to celebrate reports of Admiral Vernon's success at Cartagena in 1741. Mary Warde's letters present her as the archetypal young woman about town in the 1730s and 1740s, enjoying plays, opera, masquerades, ridottos, pleasure gardens and the latest publications. Out of season she took country tours with her brothers, visiting grottoes and cascades and riding to hounds in the winter. She was a cousin to her namesake Mary Warde of Hooton Pagnell. In 1745 she married William Clayton (c.1718–83) of Harleyford Manor, near Marlow, Bucks, MP for Bletchingly (1745–61) and Great Marlow (1761–83). He was the second son of a baronet, Sir William Clayton MP. Mary Clayton died in January 1760, leaving a daughter and heir who eventually married John Lord Howard de Walden, KB. She was painted several times, once by Wootton, once by Hudson and once by Dandridge. Her brother George Warde was a bosom friend of the young General James Wolfe.
MS: sophisticated letters sent to her cousin Mary Warde of Hooton Pagnell, before and after marriage: WYCRO, Bradford, Sp St/6/1/50 (MS span: 1733–46).

SELECTED CORRESPONDENTS FROM THE GOSSIP NETWORK, 1731–1813

William Gossip (1704–72), Anne Wilmer (d. 1780) and sons
William Gossip's father was a West Riding mercer who had amassed a considerable fortune and died a 'gentleman', bequeathing his son land in Hatfield, York and Beverley. William Gossip was educated at Wakefield and later Kirkleatham Grammar School, and Trinity College, Cambridge (1722–9), where he hoped to take the post of college librarian. After Cambridge he decided not to pursue a career in the Church or the wine business, but chose to manage his father's affairs and live as an independent gentleman. In 1730 he became one of the twelve directors and the treasurer of Burlington's glittering York assembly rooms. The next year William Gossip was advantageously married in York Minster to Anne Wilmer, the daughter and co-heir of George Wilmer of York, who brought him further estates in Helmsley, Yorkshire, and Sible Hedingham, Essex, and about two thousand pounds-worth of stock in the South Sea Company. At first the couple lived with William's parents in Petergate, York, and then just his mother Susannah after his father's death in 1733. In 1734 they bought a house in Ogleforth, York, with a coach house fit for six horses, and William Gossip was appointed Justice of the Peace in the same year. In the 1740s the Gossips kept their York town house and tenanted Skelton Hall near York, but by 1756 they had established their growing family at Thorp Arch Hall, designed by the soon-to-be-fashionable architect John Carr (1723–1807). The 1,100 acre estate lay between

York and Leeds, on the River Wharfe, and brought with it the lordship of the manor, and thirty tenants. Gossip's prestige was confirmed by the appointment to the office of deputy lieutenant for the West Riding in 1757. Thereafter, he purchased a post-chaise and took on a postilion-cum-groom. His marriage was exceedingly happy and the couple were painted by Mercier. Anne Gossip bore him eleven children between 1732 and 1745, but, harrowingly, only one outlived her: William (1732–54), George (b. and d. 1734), George (1735–75), John (b. and d. 1734), Ann (b. and d. 1738), boy (still-born 1739), John (1740–51), Wilmer (1742–90), Randall (1743–69), Thomas (1744–76) and Anne (1745–6). Of the boys who survived childhood, William, the eldest, went to Edinburgh University to study medicine (where he died aged twenty-one), while the younger boys George, Randall, Wilmer and Thomas were all apprenticed to hosiers in Leicester. George Gossip, now the heir, proved a sad disappointment to his father: feckless, wrongheaded and indebted, he hurled away his father's good opinion when he secretly married Maria Copley, the daughter of a Halifax mantua-maker, in 1762. He was disinherited for his pains. Thereafter George and Randall left hosiery and went into the army. George Gossip's attempts to follow Clive to India came to nothing and he stayed a lieutenant in the 3rd Regiment of Foot. Eventually the bulk of the Thorp Arch estate passed to Wilmer and subsequently (since he died without issue) to his brother Thomas's children. Thomas Gossip (1744–76), apparently the only steady son, married in 1770 Johanna Cartwright (d. 1825), the daughter and heir of Richard Cartwright of Evington, Co. Leicester, and widow of Richard Cook. They had two sons, William (1770) and Randall (1774).
MS: plentiful family correspondence: WYCRO, Leeds, TA 11/4, 12/3, 18/5, 18/6, 22/1, 13/2. See also G. W. Foster and J. J. Green, *History of the Wilmer Family* (Leeds, 1888), pp. 128–34; Harrison, 'Thorp Arch Hall, 1749–56'; Harrison, 'Servants of William Gossip'; Harrison, 'Gossip Family of Thorp Arch' (MS span: 1731–1813).

SELECTED CORRESPONDENTS FROM THE DAWSON–GREENE NETWORK, 1762–1821

This collection is based on the letters sent to Mrs Elizabeth Greene of Slyne and Miss Margaret Greene, later Mrs Bradley of Slyne. Many of their female correspondents have remained socially anonymous despite exhaustive researches, including Sarah Tatham, of Southampton Street, and later Southall (MS span: 1812–21); Martha Simpson of Walton (MS span: 1770); Eliza Greenhow, Slyne (MS span: 1763); and Lydia Boynton, 55 Burton Crescent, London (MS span: 1820). Other correspondents included the wife of a bankrupt merchant, Mrs Ridsdale of Winsley (MS span: 1813), who also corresponded with the Miss Barcrofts, as well as Anne Wiglesworth of Leeds (MS span: 1790) and Elizabeth Wiglesworth of Townhead (MS span: 1813), both members of the gentry-clerical family discussed in the Barcroft network.

Mrs Margaret Bradley (née Greene), Slyne, Lancashire
Daughter of Thomas Greene I Esq. of Slyne and Elizabeth Barker of Rampside,

Lancashire. She married Robert Bradley of Slyne and was known to her friends as Peggy.

MS: letters she received from her brothers Thomas and Richard, her son Richard Greene Bradley and Lydia Boynton her daughter-in-law: LRO, DDGr C3 (MS span: 1762–*c*.1821).

Mrs Elizabeth Greene (née Barker), Slyne, Lancashire (1708–81)
Daughter of George Barker of Rampside, Lancashire, wife of Thomas Greene of Slyne (1681–1762). She had at least six children: Thomas the heir, Margaret, Mary who died in 1746 aged six, George who died in 1758 aged eighteen, William who died in 1762 aged sixteen, and Richard who died in the East Indies in 1776 aged thirty.

MS: letters she received from her son Thomas Greene, LRO, DDGr C1 (MS span: 1765–76).

Mrs Martha Greene (née Dawson), Gower Street, London (1754–1843)
The Lancastrian widow of Thomas Greene II. Sister-in-law to Mrs Bradley of Slyne, to whom her letters are addressed. Her son Thomas Greene III married the baronet's daughter Henrietta Russell in 1820, and Martha Greene proved a very affectionate mother-in-law as well as grandmother.

MS: LRO, DDGr Box C3 (MS span: 1820–21).

Thomas Greene, London (1737–1810)
A Lancastrian lawyer based in London, son and heir of Thomas Greene I of Slyne. He was in partnership with Mr Baynes who, at his death in September 1779, left a legacy of fifty pounds and five hundred pounds in a codicil. He wrote from Gray's Inn, Serjeant's Inn and the Inner Temple to his mother and sister in Slyne. In 1792, at a mature fifty-five, he married Martha, the second daughter and co-heir of Edmund Dawson Esq. of Warton, Lancashire.

MS: letters to his mother, sister and brothers, LRO, DDGr C1 (MS span: 1762–79).

PEOPLE OUTSIDE THE SIX CORRESPONDENCE NETWORKS

Mary Chorley, of Lancaster (b. 1766)
This motherless girl was raised by her aunts, the Miss Fords. Her father John Chorley of 54 Hanover Street, Liverpool, she saw only intermittently. He was a merchant named in the town's directory in 1774. The fact that the Chorleys and their aunts were on tea-drinking and visiting terms with Lord and Lady Fleming of Rydal and the Wilsons of Dalham Tower indicates that, although Quakers, they were nevertheless *personae gratae* in local polite society.

MS: diaries LPL, MS 8752–5 (MS span: 1776–81).

Mrs Dolly Clayton of Lostock Hall, Lancashire
Although this gentlewoman lived for most of her married life four miles outside Preston, occasional remarks in her pocket diaries suggest she hailed from Derby-

shire. She enjoyed a wide acquaintance and counted many titled gentry among her friends.
MS: thirty-one pocket diaries within the time-frame of this book: LRO, DDX 510/1–30 (MS span: 1773–1833).

Miss Sarah Ford, Lancaster, Lancashire
Probably the daughter of the Quaker Mary Chorley and her cousin John Ford. In the 1790s the family were still in contact with the Wilsons of Dalham Tower and the Listers. Like her mother before her, Sarah was educated at home and kept a pocket diary in her girlhood.
MS: four pocket diaries LPL, MS 8756–9 (MS span: 1792–7).

Mrs Abigail Gawthern (née Frost), Nottingham (1757–1822)
The daughter of a Nottingham grocer and tallow-chandler, who in 1783 married a white-lead manufacturer, her cousin Francis Gawthern. They had four children, the two youngest of whom died before the age of three. After her husband's death in 1792, Mrs Gawthern managed the business until her son's majority in 1807. She was registered as a white-lead manufacturer in a Nottingham directory for c.1793. She also managed considerable properties in Nottingham and the surrounding countryside, inheriting yet more from her parents in 1801. Mrs Gawthern's circle incorporated both Nottingham manufacturers and Nottinghamshire gentry. Her only surviving daughter Anna married Captain William Sleight of the 100th Regiment of Foot in 1812 in London. Abigail's son Francis abandoned the lead works a year after his majority. In 1812 he married his cousin Mary Frances Marriott of Askham, Yorkshire.
Source: A. Henstock (ed.), 'The Diary of Abigail Gawthern of Nottingham, 1751–1810', *Thornton Society Record Series*, 33 (MS span: 1751–1810).

Mrs Anna Larpent (née Porter), London (1758–?1829)
This woman is far and away the most cosmopolitan figure in this study. The daughter of Sir James Porter, a British diplomat, and a minor European aristocrat, she was born in Pera, Turkey. In 1782 she married the widower John Larpent, who was seventeen years her senior. He was a successful civil servant, and throughout the marriage was the Inspector of Plays in the Office of the Lord Chamberlain. It is clear that Anna Larpent collaborated with her husband on the collection, indexing and censoring of submitted plays. She had sole responsibility for the censorship of Italian opera since she was fluent in the language (as well as French) while her husband was not. Mrs Larpent brought up two children of her own and one stepson. She was a pious, serious-minded Anglican, who was active in good works from soup kitchens to Sunday schools in the early nineteenth century.
MS: HL, HM 31201, XVII, 1773–87, Anna Margaretta Larpent's Methodized Journal; HM 31201, Mrs Larpent's Diary, I, 1790–95, III, 1799–1800, VIII, 1810–13, XI, 1820–21. See also G. Larpent, *Turkey its History and Progress from the Journals and Correspondence of Sir James Porter . . .* (1851), I, pp. 3–14; L. W. Conolly, *The Censorship of English Drama* (San Marino, Ca., 1976), pp. 4–7,

34–5, 42–5, 81, 109–13, 154–9; Conolly, 'Censor's Wife at the Theatre'; Brewer, 'Reconstructing the Reader' (MS span: 1773–1821).

Beatrix Lister of Marshfield, Settle, Yorkshire (b. 1749)
Only surviving daughter of Thomas Lister of Gisburn Park (1723–61), MP for Clitheroe, and Beatrix Hulton (1723–74). Sister to Thomas Lister (1752–1826), the future Baron Ribblesdale, MP for Clitheroe 1773–90, and High Sheriff for Yorkshire in 1795. She had a reputation for accomplished elegance, which reached the pages of the *Gentleman's Magazine*, 65 (1795), p. 82. In 1777 she married John Parker of Browsholme (1749–97), and thereby became niece by marriage to Elizabeth Shackleton. John Parker was MP for Clitheroe 1780–82 (he resigned his seat to settle a dispute between the Lister and Curzon factions) and bow bearer of Bowland Forest in the Duchy of Lancaster 1794–7. His obituary of 1797 drew attention to his rententive memory and 'the hereditary characteristick of Browsholm – a boundless hospitality', see *Gentleman's Magazine*, 67 (1797), p. 612. They set up married life at Beatrix's elegant villa, Marshfield House in Settle, where she remained until 1811. She bore eight children between 1779 and 1790, six of whom survived infancy. The Parker and Lister families had long been close social and political allies, they reputedly shared Jacobite sympathies and together dominated the borough of Clitheroe. Elizabeth Shackleton was a regular visitor to Gisburn Park throughout her lifetime; the Listers were regular consumers of the famous Alkincoats rabies medicine; Beatrix's uncle Nathaniel Lister (MP for Clitheroe 1761–73) kept Elizabeth supplied with franks (a form of free postage enjoyed by MPs) for years; and her diary records that she maintained a correspondence with Beatrix Lister and her mother, although none of these letters has survived. However, the strong links between Browsholme and Gisburn Park were jeopardized in 1789. In that year, the families quarrelled over Thomas Lister's marriage to an Irish heiress, Rebecca Fielding. Beatrix reputedly slighted her sister-in-law and thereby precipitated 'the Parker Scandal'. Like Elizabeth Shackleton, the Parkers of Marshfield and the Listers of Gisburn were customers of Gillows of Lancaster.
MS: YAS, MD 335/95 (1768–75), letters from Mrs Beatrix Lister and Miss Beatrix Lister, Marshfield, to Thomas Lister, Brasenose College, Oxford, and London; YAS, MD 335/80, letters concerning 'the Parker Scandal'; LRO, DDB/74/6 (n.d.), 'Poem given me by Mrs Parker of Marshfield'. Consider also the letters Beatrix wrote to her cousin by marriage, Thomas Parker of Alkincoats, LRO, DDB/72/ 859, 916, 930, 937, 951. For furniture accounts, see YAS, MD 335/11 (17) (MS span: 1786–9).

Betty Parker (née Parker) of Newton (1757–1808)
Betty was the only daughter of Edward Parker of Newton Hall, Co. York, and Elizabeth Goulbourne of Manchester. Betty was the heiress of John Goulbourne of Manchester. She married Thomas Parker of Alkincoats in Manchester in June 1779 and bore him at least seven children, of whom five survived childhood. She suffered at least one miscarriage.
MS: two of her letters survive, one in the Whitaker collection, the other in the

Parker collection among her husband's papers, see respectively LRO, DDWh/4/18, and LRO, DDB/72/839 (MS span: c.1790–93).

Eliza Parker of Alkincoats, Colne, Lancashire (1781–1842)
Only surviving daughter of Thomas and Betty Parker of Alkincoats and Newton. Sister of Edward Parker of Selby. She married Captain John Atherton of the 6th Foot Regiment. In her twenties, in Preston, she knew and discussed many of the individuals in the Whitaker network, e.g. the Horrockses, Addisons and St Clares. MS: ten letters LRO, DDB/72/683–92 (MS span: 1796–1813).

Jane Pedder (née Bowes) of Lancaster, Lancashire (d. 1790)
Jane Bowes was born into a Lancaster mercantile family. In June 1757 she married James Pedder, vicar of Churchtown, Garstang, Lancashire, the younger son of Richard Pedder, a substantial Preston merchant. Her brothers-in-law Edward and Thomas Pedder were also Preston merchants and were named in Elizabeth Parker Shackleton's manuscripts. Her husband Revd James Pedder died in 1772, whereupon Jane and her daughter Margaret removed to Bridge Lane, Lancaster. By the 1780s her son John Pedder was living in the household of Revd Starkie of Blackburn. By all appearances he was undergoing a legal apprenticeship; his mother certainly was relieved that his studies were 'both instructive and pleasant without any danger attending', unlike some of the young overseas merchants of her acquaintance. Members of the extended Pedder family also bought Gillows mahogany.
MS: fourteen letters: LRO, DDPd/17/1 (1786), Jane Pedder, London and Lancaster, to John Pedder, Blackburn. Journals: LRO, DDPd/25/16 (c.1786), Miss Margaret Pedder's 'views of a journey to London and back'. See also LRO, DDPd/16/3 (1795), Furniture accounts of Revd John Pedder of Lancaster (MS span: 1786).

Ellen Stock (née Weeton), of Upholland, Lancashire (1776–?1844)
Ellen Weeton's social position was an ambiguous one, as she felt most sorely. Her mother was the daughter of a Preston butcher who had served as a lady's maid to the Houghtons of Walton Hall marrying eventually the captain of merchantman in the West Africa slave trade. (Her sisters married a Preston silk mercer and a Wigan solicitor.) Ellen's parents established themselves at Church Street, Lancaster, where Mrs Weeton took in lodgers to supplement her income while her husband was at sea. She bore four children, of whom only Nelly and her brother Tom survived. When Mr Weeton was killed at sea in 1782 the family was allegedly defrauded of his prize-money and forced to remove to Upholland, where they set up a school. Tom was educated at Mr Braithwaite's school nearby and was later apprenticed to the attorney Nicholas Grimshaw of Preston. Just qualified, he married the daughter of a Wigan factory owner. After the death of Mrs Weeton in 1797 Ellen ran the school singlehanded without a servant. Once the school was given up, she boarded with her brother and in mean lodgings in Liverpool. In 1809 she was employed as a governess by Edward Pedder of Doves Nest, Ambleside (another member of the mercantile family of Preston), and later by the Armitage

family at Milnsbridge, near Huddersfield. In 1814 she married the near-bankrupt manufacturer Aaron Stock of Wigan. Despite the birth of a beloved child, Mary, the marriage was an utter disaster, ending in a deed of separation in 1822. Thereafter, Ellen eked out an existence in lodgings, spending her time writing memoirs, taking modest walking holidays and struggling to maintain contact with her daughter.

Sources: E. Hall (ed.), *Mrs Weeton's Journal of Governess, 1807–1825* (1925), 2 vols, based on WRO, EHC 165, History of the Life of Nelly Stock/Occasional Reflections E. Stock (MS span: 1807–25).

Appendix 3

Members of the Parker Family
Mentioned in the Text

See genealogical tree on following page.

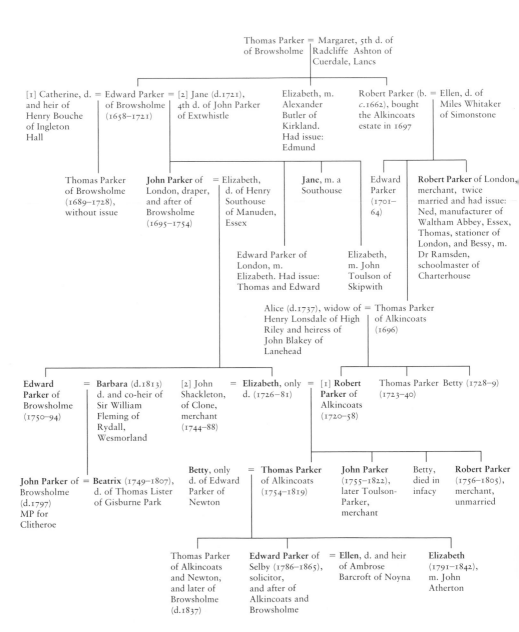

Thomas Parker = Margaret, 5th d. of
of Browsholme | Radcliffe Ashton of
Cuerdale, Lancs

[1] Catherine, d. = Edward Parker = [2] Jane (d.1721),   Elizabeth, m.   Robert Parker (b. = Ellen, d. of
and heir of   of Browsholme   4th d. of John Parker Alexander   c.1662), bought   Miles Whitaker
Henry Bouche   (1658–1721)   of Extwhistle   Butler of   the Alkincoats   of Simonstone
of Ingleton   Kirkland.   estate in 1697
Hall   Had issue:
                                                        Edmund

Thomas Parker   John Parker of   = Elizabeth,   Jane, m. a   Edward   Robert Parker of London,
of Browsholme   London, draper,   d. of Henry   Southouse   Parker   merchant, twice
(1689–1728),   and after of   Southouse   (1701–   married and had issue:
without issue   Browsholme   of Manuden,   64)   Ned, manufacturer of
                    (1695–1754)   Essex   Waltham Abbey, Essex,
                                                                                   Thomas, stationer of
                                                                                   London, and Bessy, m.
                                    Edward Parker of   Elizabeth,   Dr Ramsden,
                                    London, m.   m. John   schoolmaster of
                                    Elizabeth. Had issue: Toulson of   Charterhouse
                                    Thomas and Edward   Skipwith

                            Alice (d.1737), widow of = Thomas Parker
                            Henry Lonsdale of High   of Alkincoats
                            Riley and heiress of   (1696)
                            John Blakey of
                            Lanehead

Edward   = Barbara (d.1813)   [2] John   = Elizabeth, only = [1] Robert   Thomas Parker Betty (1728–9)
Parker of   d. and co-heir of Shackleton,   d. (1726–81)   Parker of   (1723–40)
Browsholme   Sir William   of Clone,   Alkincoats
(1750–94)   Fleming of   merchant   (1720–58)
                Rydall,   (1744–88)
                Wesmorland

                                                Betty, only = Thomas Parker   John Parker   Betty,   Robert Parker
                                                d. of Edward   of Alkincoats   (1755–1822),   died in   (1756–1805),
John Parker of = Beatrix (1749–1807),   Parker of   (1754–1819)   later Toulson- infacy   merchant,
Browsholme   d. of Thomas Lister   Newton   Parker,   unmarried
(d.1797)   of Gisburne Park   merchant
MP for
Clitheroe

                        Thomas Parker   Edward Parker of = Ellen, d. and heir   Elizabeth
                        of Alkincoats   Selby (1786–1865), of Ambrose   (1791–1842),
                        and Newton,   solicitor,   Barcroft of Noyna   m. John
                        and later of   and after of   Atherton
                        Browsholme   Alkincoats and
                        (d.1837)   Browsholme

Names in **bold** indicate people for whom letters survive.

Appendix 4

The Social Networks Database

THE MATERIAL USED IN CHAPTER TWO on Elizabeth Shackleton's social interactions is derived from the information provided in her five diaries, for the
two years 1773 and 1780 (LRO, DDB/81/18–20 and DDB/81/36–7). The phrase
'social interaction' is used to denote the whole range of possible contacts with
people resident outside her household, extending from the indirect, such as letters,
messages or gifts, to the direct, like calls, meals or extended visits. The two chosen
years are ones for which the density of information in the diaries is particularly
high, but they are not in any strict sense representative. They fall, however, within
two markedly different phases in Elizabeth Shackleton's later life: 1773, in the
period before Thomas Parker's majority, and 1780, in the period after Elizabeth
Shackleton had completed her move from Alkincoats to Pasture House.

All diary entries for these years which record interactions with individuals other
than resident servants and resident kin were analysed. (Of the total 1,131 diary
entries, 1,010 record Elizabeth Shackleton's personal involvement. The residual
121 entries describe those social encounters from which she was excluded, i.e.
those involving only her sons and husband.) The interactions were entered into a
computer database. Supplementary information on the people involved was then
compiled from a range of local primary and secondary sources. The information
was entered into ten fields as follows: (1) the date of the interaction, (2) the quarter
during which the interaction took place, (3) the name/s of the people involved, (4)
whether or not they were related to Elizabeth Shackleton, (5) their gender, (6) their
occupational status, (7) their residence, (8) the type of activity, (9) the location of
the interaction (if appropriate), (10) any miscellaneous information.

The most difficult problems of categorization arose with occupational status.
The categories employed were landed gentry, professional, upper trade, lesser
trade, tenant, farmer, servant, labourer and unknown. Not only is it difficult to
track down occupational information on late eighteenth-century individuals,
but it is also difficult to achieve clear distinctions, given the existence of multiple
occupations and the imprecision with which terms like 'gentleman' and 'yeoman'
were used. The main losers here were probably the categories upper and lesser

trades, because information on business activity was particularly difficult to secure. The chief beneficiary was probably the farming category: included in this category were all non-tenants for whom there is evidence of landholding, but no indication of involvement in trade or claim to gentility. Women were classified according to the status of their nearest male relative, usually that of her father before marriage and her husband after. Spinsters and widows often had to be labelled as status unknown, because although obviously wealthy and socially acceptable, they did not inhabit a recognized gentry seat and the source of their income is unknown.

The total number of interactions in the two years was 1,011, but it should be borne in mind that each recorded interaction could involve more than one type of activity and more than one individual. A letter might accompany a gift; several guests from a variety of occupational backgrounds might be invited to a dinner. Nevertheless, in most cases the results of analysis of the database are expressed as percentages of a figure for the number of interactions. This is because the question which has been asked of the database is what proportion of interactions involved certain categories of people, or certain categories of activity.

Basic genealogical data has been gleaned from Spencer, *Parochial Chapelry of Colne; Marriages from 1654–1754*, and Spencer, *Parochial Chapelry of Colne; Register of Baptisms and Burials, 1774–89*. Occupational data is recorded in Spencer, *Parochial Chapelry of Colne; Baptism Register, 1790–1812*. Additional information is in PRO, 11/wills and BIHR, wills.

Appendix 5

Elizabeth Shackleton's Servant Information Network, 1770–1781

Letters sent or received by Elizabeth Shackleton when attempting to procure rvants for Alkincoats and Pasture House

DATE	NAME	ADDRESS	STATUS/OCCUPATION	PURPOSE OF LETTER
Aug. 1770	to Mr Hill	Ormskirk, Lancs	gentleman merchant	follow up to first enquiry
Sept. 1770	from Mrs Barker	Cononley, Yorks		recommends a servant
5 Sept. 1770	to Marjorie Suttle			enquiry
o Nov. 1770	to Miss Cockshott	Marley, Keighley, Yorks	gentlewoman	enquiry
o Dec. 1770	to Miss Cockshott	Marley, Keighley, Yorks	gentlewoman	enquiry
1 April 1771	to Miss Cockshott	Marley, Keighley, Yorks	gentlewoman	enquiry
7 Nov. 1771	to Mrs Barbara Parker	Browsholme, Yorks	gentlewoman	enquiry
7 Nov. 1771	to Thomas Stirling	Browsholme, Yorks	steward	enquiry
1 Mar 1772	to Bulcocks	Heyroyd, Lancs	tradespeople	enquiry
1 May 1772	to Miss Swinglehurst	Trawden, Lancs		enquiry
3 July 1772	from Mr Garforth	Skipton Mill, Yorks	miller	recommends a servant
r Oct. 1772	from Mrs Fielden	Scartop and Burnley, Lancs	mantua-maker	recommends a servant
r July 1773	from Miss Windle	Barnoldswick, Yorks		recommends a servant
2 Dec. 1773	from Betty Hartley	Colne, Lancs	shopkeeper	recommends a servant
5 Dec. 1773	to Miss Cockshott	Marley, Keighley, Yorks	gentlewoman	?enquiry

DATE	NAME	ADDRESS	STATUS/OCCUPATION	PURPOSE OF LETTER
24 Feb. 1775	to Miss Wells	Bradford, Yorks	schoolmistress	enquiry
7 March 1775	to Thomas Stirling	Browsholme, Yorks	steward	enquiry
21 March 1775	from Mrs Hargreaves	Bradford, Yorks	shopkeeper	recommends a servant
22 March 1775	from Betty Hartley	Colne, Lancs	shopkeeper	?recommends a servant
19 Nov. 1775	to Mr Scholes	Talbot, Halifax, Yorks	innkeeper	enquiry
6 Dec. 1775	from Mrs Jane Altham			response to enquiry
18 March 1776	from Miss Briggs	Preston, Lancs		recommends a servant
12 May 1776	to Mrs Fielden	Burnley, Lancs	mantua-maker	enquiry
6 Sept. 1776	to Mrs Booth	Keighley, Yorks		enquiry
7 Sept. 1776	to Mrs Howarth	Clitheroe, Lancs	doctor's wife	enquiry
7 Sept. 1776	to Mrs Barbara Parker	Browsholme, Yorks	gentlewoman	enquiry
7 Sept. 1776	to Thomas Stirling	Browsholme, Yorks	steward	enquiry
7 Sept. 1776	from Miss Smith	Prescot, Lancs	?tradesman's daughter	recommends a servant
23 May 1777	to Mrs Barbara Parker	Browsholme, Yorks	gentlewoman	follow up to first enquiry
19 Feb. 1779	to Mrs Fielden	Burnley, Lancs	mantua-maker	enquiry
19 Feb. 1779	to Miss Cockshott	Marley, Keigley, Yorks	gentlewoman	enquiry
23 Feb. 1779	to Mrs Barbara Parker	Browsholme, Yorks	gentlewoman	enquiry
4 March 1779	from Miss Betty Parker	Newton Hall, Newton, Yorks	gentlewoman	recommends a housekeeper
12 Jan. 1780	to Betty Hartley	Colne, Lancs	shopkeeper	enquiry
12 Jan. 1780	from Mrs Richard Ecroyd	Edge End, Colne, Lancs	gentlewoman	gives a character
22 Aug. 1781	from Mrs Knowles (née Smith)	Ormskirk, Lancs	tradesman's wife	recommends a servant

B Letters Elizabeth Shackleton sent to or received from other employers seeking servants

22 July 1770	to Mr Wilkinson			reply to an enquiry
28 Sept. 1771	from Miss Beatrix Lister	Gisburn Park, Yorks	gentlewoman	reply to a suggested servant
22 Nov. 1772	from Miss Cromblehome	Preston, Lancs	gentlewoman	requests a reference
2 Dec. 1772	from Miss Cromblehome	Preston, Lancs	gentlewoman	asks after servant's terms

DATE	NAME	ADDRESS	STATUS/OCCUPATION	PURPOSE OF LETTER
11 June 1774	from Mrs Foulds	Trawden, Lancs	gentlewoman	thanks for enquiries &c.
19 Oct. 1777	from Mrs Viger	Manchester		enquiry
25 Oct. 1777	Mrs Johnson	High St, Manchester		requests a reference
9 June 1779	Lady Houghton	?Walton Hall, Lancs	noblewoman	requests a reference
24 Oct. 1779	Mrs Beatrix Parker	Marshfield, Yorks	gentlewoman	?enquiry

C   Servants seeking character references

11 July 1774	Hugh Wood	Local	chaise driver	seeks a reference for himself
?May 1778	John Nutter	Hey, Lancs	tenant farmer	requests reference for daughter
9 June 1779	Peggy Smith	Priestfield, Lancs	cloth-dresser's wife	requests reference for daughter

Appendix 6

Purchasers of Parker Rabies Medicine, 1767–1777

DATE	QUANTITY/TYPE	PURCHASER	ADDRESS	AGENT
16 March 1767	10 dogs	Sir James Lowther	Lowther, Westmorland	Mr Blades, Kendal
3 July 1767	3 pigs			Mr Blades, Kendal
23 Jan. 1768	4 cows			Mr Blades, Kendal
23 Jan. 1768	12 cattle	John Walton's cowman	Marsden, Lancs	
18 July 1768	2 cows, 1 pig			Mr Blades, Kendal
19 Oct. 1768	12 dogs	Matthew Carr Esq.	Ryhope, Sunderland	letter and New-castle carrier
14 Jan. 1770	unspecified	Lawrence Ridehalgh	Marsden, Lancs	
13 Feb. 1770	unspecified	6 Parker servants	Browsholme Hall, Yorks	
31 April 1770	1 horse	Mr Varley	Burnley, Lancs	
31 April 1770	3 dogs	Mr Lister	Gisburn Park, Yorks	by letter
9 July 1770	2 humans	Mr Cockshott and son	Park, Colne, Lancs	
13 July 1770	1 horse	Mr Moore	Slaidburne, Yorks	via 'a Middup man'
23 Sept. 1770	32 for dogs, horses and cattle	unspecified	Haindup, Gerard, Scotland	
29 Sept. 1770	1 man, 1 woman	William Foulds and sister	Trawden, Lancs	
29 Sept. 1770	unspecified	John Cockshott and his dog	?Marley, Yorks	
22 Oct. 1770	unspecified no. for humans	100 people	Roughlee, Lancs	
22 Oct. 1770	unspecified no. for humans	many people	Richard Elliot's, Swinden, Yorks	

DATE	QUANTITY/TYPE	PURCHASER	ADDRESS	AGENT
22 Oct. 1770	3 humans	John Woodyear's servants	Crookhill, Doncaster, Yorks	
6 Nov. 1770	2 men	(sent by Mrs Lister)	Gisburn Park, Yorks	
11 Nov. 1770	2 men	John Woodyear	Crookhill, Yorks	by letter and waggon
13 Nov. 1770	2 humans	Mr Lister and manservant	Gisburn Park, Yorks	
24 Nov. 1770	2 dogs, 2 men, 2 women	Mrs Lister	Gisburn Park, Yorks	by letter
4 Dec. 1770	1 horse, 6 men, 2 women	Mr Dunston	Nottingham, Notts	Huthwaite, Nottingham
14 Dec. 1770	1 woman	Mr Slack for his wife	White Bear, Colne, Lancs	
21 April 1771	4 unspecified	Miss Lister	Gisburn Park, Yorks	by letter
20 May 1771	unspecified	4 Lister tenants	Rimmington, Yorks	
25 June 1771	30 livestock, 20 dogs	Mr Shuttleworth	?Gawthorpe Hall, Lancs	by letter
11 July 1771	8 'Xtns', 40 horses, cows, dogs	Mr Turner	Kirkleatham, Yorks	via his servant
30 Aug. 1771	7 unspecified	unspecified	Gisburn Park, Yorks	
15 Sept. 1771	1 child	Mrs Woodyear	Crookhill, Yorks	
15 Nov. 1771	120 for hounds	Lord Strafford		sent his servants
16 Nov. 1771	2 men	Lord Scarborough	?Sandbeck Castle, Yorks	via his huntsman
21 Nov. 1771	1 man	George Smith	Selby, Yorks	
22 Nov. 1771	2 men and 10 for 'Christians'	Lord Scarborough's servants	?Sandbeck Castle, Yorks	
13 Jan. 1772	enquiry	Mr Turner	Kirkleatham, Yorks	by letter
7 Feb. 1772	1 dog	Mr Cockshott	Bracewell, Yorks	
16 Feb. 1772	1 dog	Mr Lister	Gisburn Park, Yorks	via butcher's man
28 March 1772	unspecified	A number of people	Chipping, Lancs	
29 May 1772	18 'Xtains'	Mr Paulmer	Skipwith, Yorks	sent his servant
13 July 1772	unspecified	Mr Garforth	Skipton Mill, Yorks	
12 Jan. 1773	26 dogs, 2 men	Mark Milbank		sent his servant
26 Jan. 1773	6 men and boys	Mrs Lister	Gisburn Park, Yorks	sent a lad
10 March 1773	6 humans	unspecified		
12 March 1773	1 boy	Ned Clayton's son	?Carr Hall, Lancs	
15 April 1773	unspecified	Betty and Alice Foulds	Wycoller, Lancs	
19 May 1773	1 human	Young Booth	Cottingley, Yorks	
29 May 1773	1 human	Mr Garforth	Steeton, Yorks	
22 June 1773	1 dog	'Poor Shadrach' (their dog)	Alkincoats, Lancs	

DATE	QUANTITY/TYPE	PURCHASER	ADDRESS	AGENT
24 June 1773	unspecified no. for humans	Mr Busfield	Myrtle Grove, Yorks	delivered by Shackleton
30 June 1773	3 dogs	Miss Cockshott	Marley, Yorks	delivered by Shackleton
2 July 1773	30 humans	30 persons	Bradford, Yorks	delivered by Will
19 July 1773	13 humans	'All the Elliots'	?Swinden Hall, Yorks	
19 July 1773	humans	Mrs Conyers and children		
19 July 1773	humans	Tom Brindle, wife and child	Colne, Lancs	
19 July 1773	humans	6 Nutters	Sabden, Lancs	
23 July 1773	1 man	Harrison	?Colne, Lancs	
16 Oct. 1773	humans	Mr and Mrs Heber		
16 Oct. 1773	1 woman	Mrs Coulthurst		
16 Oct. 1773	1 woman	Miss Salisbury		
16 Oct. 1773	humans	3 servants		
16 Oct. 1773	1 man	Kester Carr	Gargrave, Yorks	
16 Oct. 1773	1 man	Mr Parker	Dunholme, Cheshire	
17 Oct. 1773	humans	'All Mrs Coulthurst's servants'		
18 Oct. 1773	30 humans	30 people	Gargrave, Yorks	delivered by Shackleton
6 Nov. 1773	a dog	Mrs Foulds	Trawden, Lancs	
6 Nov. 1773	a cow	Hudsons	Trawden, Lancs	
7 Nov. 1773	1 human, 1 dog	Mr Midgely and his servant	Stunstead, Lancs	
9 Nov. 1773	1 man, 1 boy	'Poor Jack and the boy'	Alkincoats, Lancs	
23 Dec. 1773	44 for 'Xtains'	Mrs Bewley	Kendal, Westmorland	
1773	2 unspecified	Duke of Leeds' gamekeeper	Hornby Castle, Yorks	Mr Smith, Almondbury
18 March 1774	1 man	Mrs Cockcroft	Stocks, Yorks	via huntsman
19 March 1774	24 dogs	Sir George Saville, MP	Rufford, Notts	sent his servant
19 March 1774	unspecified	Day and his daughter		
20 March 1774	1 man	unspecified	Halifax, Yorks	
12 April 1774	1 man	Squire Holden's servant	Palace House, Burnley, Lancs	
14 April 1774	1 man	Townley Parker's huntsman	Cuerden, Chorley, Lancs	
15 April 1774	4 dogs	Revd Mr Robinson	Seaham, Durham	by letter and carrier
20 April 1774	unspecified	Holden family	Palace House, Burnley, Lancs	
22 April 1774	1 unspecified	Robert Elliot	?Swinden Hall, Yorks	
26 April 1774	unspecified no. for children	a number of children	Whalley, Lancs	

DATE	QUANTITY/TYPE	PURCHASER	ADDRESS	AGENT
12 June 1774	1 man	Mr Whitaker	Holme, Lancs	
14 June 1774	6 dogs	Matthew Carr Esq.	Ryhope, Sunderland	letter and New-castle carrier
9 July 1774	30 cattle	'A man'	Scotland	
28 July 1774	14 cattle	Mr York	Auton Place	sent his servant
31 Aug. 1774	8 servants, 2 dogs, 1 ox, 2 unspecified	Mr Parker	Browsholme, Yorks	via Peter Molyneux
12 Oct. 1774	44 hounds	George Hargreaves	Mansfield, Nottingham	
13 Oct. 1774	1 man	John Shackleton	Alkincoats, Lancs	
6 Dec. 1774	unspecified no. for girls	Smith's little girls		
23 March 1775	unspecified	'A waggon load of people'	Ripon, Yorks	
1 July 1775	unspecified	'A number of people'	Sawley, Lancs	
3 Aug. 1775	3 men, 3 dogs	William Fenwick Esq.	Bywill, Newcastle	by letter and carrier
3 Aug. 1775	3 men, 3 dogs	George Baker Esq.	Ellimere, Durham	by letter and carrier
6 Oct. 1775	1 man	James Hargreaves	Carr, Yorks	
7 March 1776	5 dogs and unspecified no. of children	Rothwell	?Colne, Lancs	
15 May 1776	1 child	Little John Nutter	Blako, Lancs	
1 June 1776	several for a family	Mr and Mrs Cockshott	Bracewell, Yorks	
3 June 1776	several for adults	Cockshott's servants	Bracewell, Yorks	delivered by Shackleton
13 June 1776	unspecified	Mr Ridehalgh	Marsden, Lancs	delivered by Isaac
18 June 1776	3 humans	Mrs Wilkinson and 2 boys	Gisburn Park, Yorks	
15 Jan. 1777	1 man, 10 dogs	Lord Holderness's servant		
18 Jan. 1777	23 dogs	Mr Houghton	Holroyd, Yorks	
18 Jan. 1777	5 men, 5 dogs	Mr Ascough		
20 March 1777	1 man, 1 woman	Mr Rothwell and his maid		
9 April 1777	unspecified	Harrison	?Colne, Lancs	
26 June 1777	26 for humans and livestock	Mrs Strickland	Sizergh, Westmorland	by letter
18 July 1777	1 man	Mr Moon	Colne, Lancs	
22 July 1777	42 dogs	Duke of Hamilton	?Ashston Hall, Lancs	sent his servant
3 Aug. 1777	10 people, 5 cows, 5 pigs, 5 dogs	Mr Strickland	Partington, Cheshire	
4 Dec. 1777	5 humans, 1 horse, 5 dogs	Henry Owen Cunliffe	Wycoller, Lancs	

Table 1

Participants in Elizabeth Shackleton's Social Interactions, as Recorded in Her Diaries for 1773 and 1780

	ALL		LANCASHIRE RESIDENT		YORKSHIRE RESIDENT		LONDON RESIDENT	
	No.	%	No.	%	No.	%	No.	%
Landed gentry	380	38	210	41	163	77	12	5
Professional	171	17	95	19	9	4	53	23
Upper trade	276	27	85	17	11	5	170	73
Lesser trade	93	9	71	14	7	3	2	1
Farmer/tenant	49	5	44	9	1	0	0	0
Labourer, artisan, servant	44	4	13	3	23	11	0	0
Unknown	73	7	52	10	7	4	1	0
Kin	381	38	127	25	84	39	161	69
Non-kin	633	63	384	75	131	61	72	31
Female	322	32	148	29	122	57	48	21
Male	531	53	225	44	69	32	181	78
Mixed	158	16	138	27	24	11	4	2
Total number of interactions	1011		511		215		233	

The number column gives the number of interactions in which people of the particular category participated.

The % column gives the percentage of the total number of interactions represented by the figure in the number column. The totals sum to more than 100% because some interactions involved more than one individual.

For sources and occupational classification, see Appendix 4.

Table 2

The Parker, Whitaker and Barcroft Correspondence Networks

	CORRESPONDENTS MENTIONED IN ELIZABETH SHACKLETON'S DIARIES FOR 1773 AND 1780		CORRESPONDENTS IN ELIZABETH SHACKLETON'S SURVIVING LETTERS		CORRESPONDENTS IN ELIZA WHITAKER'S SURVIVING LETTERS		CORRESPONDENTS IN BARCROFT SISTERS' SURVIVING LETTERS	
	No.	%	No.	%	No.	%	No.	%
Kin	13	17	12	31	10	33	10	43
Non-kin	63	83	27	69	20	66	13	57
Landed gentry	25	33	12	31	4	13	7	30
Professional	14	18	10	26	4	13	8	35
Upper trades	18	24	7	18	10	33	3	13
Inferiors	9	12	4	10	0	0	0	0
Unknown	10	13	6	15	12	40	5	22
Lancashire	23	30	10	26	18	60	4	18
Yorkshire	27	36	13	33	1	3	12	52
London	18	24	10	26	5	17	3	13
Other	8	11	6	15	6	20	4	17
Female	35	46	21	54	26	87	11	47
Male	41	54	18	46	4	13	12	53
Total number of correspondents	76		39		30		23	

For sources and occupational classification, see Appendices 2 and 4.

Table 3

Elizabeth Shackleton's Social Encounters at Home, 1773 and 1780

	DINNER		SUPPER		TEA		BREAKFAST		VISITS	
	No.	%	No.	%	No.	%	No.	%	No.	%
Landed gentry	37	44	3	7	12	30	5	42	19	22
Professional	11	13	9	22	6	15	2	17	18	21
Upper trade	28	33	9	22	10	25	2	17	9	10
Social inferior	14	17	18	45	12	30	3	25	33	38
Unknown	18	21	10	25	6	15	3	25	13	15
Male only	49	58	34	85	13	32	9	83	64	74
Female only	11	13	3	7	17	42	2	17	17	20
Mixed	24	29	3	7	10	25	1	8	6	7
Kin	29	35	5	12	10	25	0	0	9	10
Total number of encounters	84		40		40		12		86	

The number column gives the number of encounters in which guests of the particular category participated.

The % column gives the percentage of the total number of encounters represented by the figure in the no. column. The totals sum to more than 100% because many encounters involved more than one individual.

For sources and occupational classification and basis of calculation, see Appendix 4.

Select Bibliography

Manuscripts

National Archives

Public Record Office
  PCC, Prerogative Court of Canterbury, wills
  C 234, Lord Chancellor's Fiats for Commissions of the Peace
  ASSI45, Northern Circuit Assize Depositions

Local Archives

Borthwick Institute of Historical Research, York
  York wills
  Probate registers

Cheshire Record Office, Chester
  EDC 5, Consistory court papers, 1744–1809
  DNA/1 Minutes of the Chester Benevolent Institution

Corporation of London Record Office
  CF1, Freedom Records

Cumbria County Record Office, Carlisle
  D/KEN.3/56/1, Conduct letter written by E. Kennedy
  D/Lons/L1/1/67, Love letters to Sir James Lowther 'Wicked Jimmy' from his
    mistress Isabel Carr

Essex Record Office, Chelmsford
  D/Dc, D/Du, D/DB, Documents relating to the Southouse Family

Guildhall Library
  London Marriage Licences

Kent Record Office, Maidstone
  U 1823/35, A3, Daybook of a Draper and Haberdasher

Lancashire Record Office, Preston
  DDB, Parker of Browsholme collection
  DDB, Barcroft of Noyna collection
  DDGr, Dawson Greene collection
  DDPd, Pedder of Finsthwaite collection
  DDX 1–38, Dolly Clayton Memoranda
  DDX 390, Account book of Thomas Stirling
  DDX 680/2/3, Rules of the Whalley Sisterly Love Society, 1818
  DDWh, Whitaker of Simonstone collection
  QSC, Commissions of the Peace
  QSQ, Militia

Lancaster Public Library
  MS 8752–5, Mary Chorley Diaries
  MS 8756–9, [Sarah] Ford Diaries

Northumberland Record Office, Newcastle
  2DE, Delaval Collection, family letters

North Yorkshire Record Office, Northallerton:
  ZBA 25/1, Rules of the Bedale Ladies Amicable Society, 1783

Tyne and Wear Record Office, Newcastle
  Misc Accessions 1431/1, Daybook of Goods bought by D. & W. Wholesale
    Drapers of Newcastle

Westminster Public Library
  Gillows Collection

West Yorkshire County Record Office, Bradford
  Sp St, Spencer Stanhope collection
  Tong MS 6/6, Female Sociable Society Membership Certificate, 1810

West Yorkshire County Record Office, Leeds
  TA, Gossip of Thorp Arch collection
  Leeds Female Benefit Society, 6, 1801

West Yorkshire County Record Office, Wakefield
  RT 13/5, Minute Book of the Bradford–Colne Turnpike Trust, 1755–1823
  C 281/7/10, Rules of the Wakefield Female Benefit Society

Wigan Record Office, Leigh
  D/DZ EHC, 165, History of the Life of Nelly Stock
  D/D St C5/8, Standish Howard Letters
  EHC, 51/M820, Scarah Accounts

Yorkshire Archaeological Society, Leeds
  MD 335, Bradfer-Lawrence collection

International Archives

Huntington Library, San Marino, California, USA.:
  HM 31201, XVII, 1773–87, Anna Larpent's Methodized Journal
  HL, HM 31201, Mrs Larpent's Diary, I, 1790–95, III, 1799–1800, VIII, 1810–13,
    XI, 1820–21

Printed Primary Sources

Unless otherwise stated, the place of publication is London.

The Accomplished Letter-Writer; or Universal Correspondent (1779)

J. Aikin, *A Description of the Country from Thirty to Forty miles round Manchester* (1795)

T. Allen, *A New and Complete History of the County of York* (1828–31), 3 vols.

M. Astell, *A Serious Proposal to the Ladies, for the Advancement of their True and Greatest Interest by a Lover of her Sex* (1697)

J. Austen, *Sense and Sensibility* (1811; Oxford, 1990)

E. Baines, *History, Directory and Gazetteer of the County of York* (Leeds, 1822), 2 vols.

E. Baines, *History, Directory and Gazetteer of the County Palatine of Lancaster* (Liverpool, 1824), 2 vols.

K. Balderston (ed.), *Thraliana: The Diary of Mrs Hester Lynch Thrale* (Oxford, 1942), 2 vols.

Baldwin's New Complete Guide (1768)

P. Barfoot and J. Wilkes, *Universal British Directory* (1791), 5 vols.

L. Berchtold, *An Essay to Direct and Extend the Inquiries of Patriotic Travellers* (1787)

J. Beresford (ed.), *The Diary of a Country Parson: The Revd James Woodforde, 1758–81* (Oxford, 1924), 5 vols.

J. A. Blondel, *The Power of the Mother's Imagination Over the Foetus Examine'd* (1729)

D. F. Bond (ed.), *Tatler* (Oxford, 1987)

F. Burney, *Evelina; Or a Young Ladies Entrance into the World* (1778; Oxford, 1992)

F. Burney, *The Wanderer: or Female Difficulties* (1814; Oxford, 1991)

A. Carlyle, *Anecdotes and Characters of the Times* (1973)

H. Chapone, *Letters on the Improvement of the Mind Addressed To A Lady* (1773; 1835)

K. Coburn (ed.), *The Letters of Sara Hutchinson, 1800–1835* (1954)

J. Collier, *A Short View of the Immorality and Profaneness of the English Stage* (1698)

A Compleat Guide to London (1740)

A Complete Guide to London (1755)

A Complete Guide to London (1758)

A Complete Guide to London (1763)

A Complete Guide to London (1768)

The Complete Letter Writer or Polite English Secretary (10th ed., 1765)

The Complete Letter Writer or Whole Art of Polite Correspondence (Glasgow, c.1840)

The Court of Adultery: A Vision (1778)

F. Coventry, *The History of Pompey, the Little: or the Life and Adventures of a Lap-Dog* (1751; Oxford, 1974)

A. Day (ed.), *Letters From Georgian Ireland: The Correspondence of Mary Delany, 1731–68* (Belfast, 1991)

D. Defoe, *Tour Through the Whole Island of Great Britain* (1724–6; 1974)

R. Edgecombe (ed.), *The Diary of Frances, Lady Shelley, 1787–1817* (1912)

M. Elwin (ed.), *The Noels and The Milbankes: Their Letters for Twenty-Five Years, 1767–1792* (1967)

The Fashionable Letter Writer (Haverhill, Mass., 1823)

J. Fiske (ed.), *The Oakes Diaries: Business, Politics and the Family in Bury St Edmunds, 1778–1800* (Woodbridge, 1990), vol 1.

Gentleman's Magazine

'Forgery Unmasked or Genuine Memoirs of Two Unfortunate Brothers Rob. and Daniel Perreau, And Mrs Rudd', in *The Trials of Robert and Daniel Perreau* (1775)

M. D. George, *Catalogue of Political and Personal Satires Preserved in the Department of Prints and Drawings in the British Museum* (1942)

D. Gibson (ed.), *A Parson in the Vale of White Horse: George Woodward's Letters from East Hendred, 1753–1761* (Gloucester, 1983)

O. Goldsmith, *The Life of Richard Nash Esq.* (1762)

E. Gray, *Papers and Diaries of a York Family, 1764–1839* (1927)

[HN], *The Ladies Dictionary, Being a General Entertainment for the Fair Sex* (1694)

E. Hall (ed.), *Miss Weeton's Journal of a Governess, 1807–1825* (1939), 2 vols.

R. Halsband, *The Complete Letters of Lady Mary Wortley Montagu* (Oxford, 1965)

R. Halsband and I. Grundy (eds.), *Lady Mary Wortley Montagu: Essays and Poems* (Oxford, 1977)

E. Haywood, *The Female Spectator* (1745)

E. Haywood, *The History of Miss Betsy Thoughtless* (1751; Oxford, 1997)

A. Henstock (ed.), 'The Diary of Abigail Gawthern of Nottingham, 1751–1810', *Thornton Society Record Series*, 33 (1980)

H. Home, Lord Kames, *Loose Hints upon Education Chiefly Concerning the Culture of the Heart* (Edinburgh, 1781)

S. Johnson, *A Dictionary of the English Language* (5th ed., 1784)

P. Jupp (ed.), 'The Letter-Journal of George Canning, 1793–1795', *Camden Society*, 4th series, 41 (1991)

H. Kelly, *Memoirs of a Magdalene: Or the History of Louisa Mildmay* (1767; 1782)

E. Kimber, *The Life and Adventures of Joe Thompson: A Narrative Founded on Fact* (Dublin, 1750), 2 vols.

The Ladies Dispensatory: Or Every Woman Her Own Physician (c.1770)

The Ladies Miscellany (1731)

J. Leheny (ed.), *The Freeholder* (Oxford, 1979)

G. Leveson Gower (ed.), *The Registers of St Peter's Cornhill, 1667–1774, Harleyan Society Registers* (1879), IV

The London Directory for the Year 1780 (1780)

R. Lonsdale (ed.), *Eighteenth-Century Women Poets* (Oxford, 1990)

B. Luttrell, *The Prim Romantic: A Biography of Ellis Cornelia Knight, 1758–1837* (1965)

I. Macky, *A Journey Through England and Scotland* (1714–1729), 2 vols.

T. Marriot, *Female Conduct, being an Essay on the Art of Pleasing to be Practised by the Fair Sex* (1759)

J. D. Marshall (ed.), *The Autobiography of William Stout of Lancaster, 1665–1752* (1967)

Mixing in Society: A Complete Manual of Manners (1869)

J. Nelson, *An Essay on the Government of Children, under Three General Heads: viz Health, Manners and Education* (1753)

The New Letter Writer, or the Art of Correspondence (Whitehaven, 1775)

The New Complete Guide to London (1772)

The New Complete Guide to London (1774)

The New Complete Guide to London (1777)

Lady S. Pennington, *An Unfortunate Mother's Advice to Her Absent Daughters* (1761)

F. A. Pottle, *Boswell's London Journal, 1762–1763* (1950)

E. Raffald, *The Experienced English Housekeeper* (Manchester, 1769)

S. Richardson, *Sir Charles Grandison* (1753–4; Oxford, 1986)

V. Sackville-West (ed.), *The Diary of Lady Anne Clifford* (1923)

G. Savile, Marquess of Halifax, *The Lady's New Year's Gift: Or Advice to a Daughter* (1688)

N. Scarfe (ed.), 'A Frenchman's Year in Suffolk', *Suffolk Records Society*, 30 (1988)

S. Scott, *Millenium Hall* (1762; 1986)

[John Shirley], *The Accomplish'd Ladies Rich Closet of Rarieties or the Ingenious Gentlewoman & Servant Maids Delightful Companion* (169–)

T. Smollett, *Advice: A Satire* (1746)

T. Smollett, *The Expedition of Humphry Clinker* (1771; Oxford, 1984)

W. M. Spencer (ed.), *The Parochial Chapelry of Colne; Register of Baptisms and Burials, 1774–89* (Colne, 1969)

W. M. Spencer (ed.), *The Parochial Chapelry of Colne; Baptism Register, 1790–1812* (Colne, 1970).

W. M. Spencer (ed.), *The Parochial Chapelry of Colne; Marriages from 1654 to 1754* (Burnley, 1975)

A. M. W. Stirling, *Annals of a Yorkshire House: From the Papers of a Macaroni and His Kindred* (1911), 2 vols.

S. Stone, *A Complete Practice of Midwifery* (1737)

Trials for Adultery: or the History of Divorces being Select Trials at Doctor's Commons for Adultery, Fornication, Cruelty, Impotence, &c (1781), 7 vols.

L. E. Troide, *The Early Journals and Letters of Fanny Burney* (Oxford, 1990), 2 vols.

J. Tucker, *Instructions for Travellers* (1757)

T. D. Whitaker, *An History of the Original Parish of Whalley* (4th ed., 1872)

T. D. Whitaker, *The History and Antiquities of the Deanery of Craven* (1878)

W. Wilberforce, *Practical View of the Prevailing Religious System* (1797)

W. Wilkes, *A Letter of Genteel and Moral Advice to a Young Lady* (1744)

T. Wilkinson, *The Wandering Patentee; or a History of the Yorkshire Theatres, from 1770 to the Present Time* (York, 1795) 4 vols.

[Hannah Woolley], *The Accomplish'd Lady's Delight in Preserving, Physick, Beautifying, Cookery and Gardening* (1719)

M. Wollstonecraft, *Vindication of the Rights of Woman* (1792; Harmondsworth, 1982)

T. Wright (ed.), *Autobiography of Thomas Birkenshaw in the County of York, 1736–1797* (1864)

Printed Secondary Sources

Books

S. Amussen, *An Ordered Society: Class and Gender in Early Modern England* (Oxford, 1988)

M. Andrews, *The Search for the Picturesque: Landscape Aesthetics and Tourism in Britain, 1760–1800* (Stanford, Ca., 1989)

P. Ariès, *Centuries of Childhood* (Harmondsworth, 1962)

R. L. Arrowsmith (ed.), *Charterhouse Register, 1769–1872* (1974)

J. Ashton, *Social Life in the Reign of Queen Anne* (1882)

J. Ashton, *Old Times: A Picture of Social Life at the End of the Eighteenth Century* (1885)

J. Attfield and P. Kirkham (eds.), *A View From the Interior: Feminism, Women and Design* (1989)

E. Badinter, *The Myth of Motherhood: An Historical View of the Maternal Instinct* (1981)

E. Baines, *The History of the County Palatinate and Duchy of Lancaster* (rev. ed. Manchester, 1888)

H. Barker and E. Chalus (eds.), *Gender in Eighteenth-Century England: Roles, Representations and Responsibilities* (1997)

W. J. Bate, *From Classic to Romantic: Premises of Taste in Eighteenth-Century England* (Cambridge, 1946)

R. Bayne-Powell, *Housekeeping in the Eighteenth Century* (1956)

J. V. Beckett, *The Aristocracy in England, 1660–1914* (Oxford, 1986)

D. Blake Smith, *Inside the Great House: Planter Family Life in Eighteenth-Century Chesapeake Society* (Ithaca, 1980)

P. Borsay, *The English Urban Renaissance: Culture and Society in the Provincial Town, 1660–1770* (Oxford, 1989)

P. Branca, *Silent Sisterhood: Middle-Class Women and the Victorian Home* (1975)

J. Brewer, *Party, Ideology and Popular Politics at the Accession of George III* (Cambridge, 1976)

J. Brewer and A. Bermingham (eds.), *The Consumption of Culture, 1660–1800: Image, Object, Text* (1995)

E. B. Brophy, *Women's Lives and the Eighteenth-Century English Novel* (Tampa, Fl., 1991)

A. Buck, *Dress in Eighteenth-Century England* (1979)

J. Burke and A. P. Burke, *Genealogical and Heraldic History of the Colonial Gentry* (1891–5)

J. Burke and Sir J. Burke, *A Genealogical and Heraldic Dictionary of the Landed Gentry of Great Britain and Ireland* (2nd ed., 1846–9), 3 vols.

M. Burscough, *The History of Lark Hill, Preston, 1797–1989* (Preston, 1989)

M. Butler, *Jane Austen and the War of Ideas* (Oxford, 1975)

B. Caine, *Destined to be Wives: The Sisters of Beatrice Webb* (Oxford, 1988)

C. Campbell, *The Romantic Ethic and the Spirit of Modern Consumerism* (Oxford, 1987).

J. Cannon, *Aristocratic Century: The Peerage of Eighteenth-Century England* (Cambridge, 1984)

J. Carr, *Annals and Stories of Colne and Neighbourhood* (rev. ed., Manchester, 1878)

D. Castiglione and L. Sharpe (eds.), *Shifting the Boundaries: The Transformation of the Languages of Public and Private in the Eighteenth Century* (Exeter, 1995)

T. Castle, *Masquerade and Civilization: The Carnivalesque in Eighteenth-Century Culture and Fiction* (Stanford, Ca., 1986)

L. Charles and C. Duffin (eds.), *Women and Work in Pre-Industrial England* (1985)

A. Clark, *Working Life of Women in the Seventeenth Century* (1919)

L. Colley, *Britons: Forging the Nation, 1707–1837* (New Haven and London, 1992)

N. F. Cott, *The Bonds of Womanhood: Woman's Sphere in New England, 1780–1835* (New Haven, 1977)

R. S. Cowan, *More Work for Mother: The Ironies of Household Technology from the Open Hearth to the Microwave* (1983)

D. Cruikshank and N. Burton, *Life in the Georgian City* (1990)

C. W. and P. Cunnington, *A Handbook of English Costume in the Eighteenth Century* (rev. ed., 1972)

L. Davidoff and C. Hall, *Family Fortunes: Men and Women of the English Middle Class, 1780–1850* (1987)

C. Davidson, *A Woman's Work Is Never Done: A History of Housework in the British Isles, 1650–1950* (1982)

J. M. Donahue, *Theatre in the Age of Keen* (1975)

J. Donnison, *Midwives and Medical Men: A History of Interprofessional Rivalries and Women's Rights* (1977)

P. Earle, *The World of Defoe* (1976)

P. Earle, *The Making of the English Middle Class: Business, Society and Family Life in London, 1660–1730* (1989)

P. Earle, *A City Full of People: Men and Women of London, 1650–1750* (1994)

A. Eccles, *Obstetrics and Gynaecology in Tudor and Stuart England* (1982)

M. Ezell, *The Patriarch's Wife: Literary Evidence and the History of The Family* (Chapel Hill, NC, 1987)

V. A. Fildes, *Breasts, Bottles and Babies: A History of Infant Feeding* (Edinburgh, 1986)

V. A. Fildes (ed.), *Women as Mothers in Pre-Industrial England: Essays in Memory of Dorothy McLaren* (1990)

G. Firth, *Bradford and the Industrial Revolution* (Halifax, 1990)

A. Fletcher, *Gender, Sex and Subordination in England, 1500–1800* (New Haven and London, 1995)

J. Foster, *Pedigrees of the County Families of Lancashire* (1873)

J. Foster, *Pedigrees of the County Families of Yorkshire* (1874), 2 vols.

J. Foster, *Alumni Oxonienses, 1715–1886* (Oxford, 1888), 8 vols.

M. George, *Women in the First Capitalist Society: Experiences in Seventeenth-Century England* (Brighton, 1988)

M. Girouard, *The English Town: A History of Urban Life* (New Haven and London, 1990)

P. J. P. Goldberg, *Women, Work and the Life Cycle in a Medieval Economy: Women in York and Yorkshire, c.1300–1520* (Oxford, 1992)

L. Gowing, *Domestic Dangers: Women's Words and Sex in Early Modern London* (Oxford, 1996)

C. Hall, *White, Male and Middle Class: Explorations in Feminism and History* (Oxford, 1992)

K. Haltunnen, *Confidence Men and Painted Women: A Study of Middle-Class Culture in America, 1830–1870* (New Haven, 1982)

A. J. Hammerton, *Emigrant Gentlewomen* (1979)

A. J. Hammerton, *Cruelty and Companionship: Conflict in Nineteenth-Century Married Life* (1992)

F. Heal, *Hospitality in Early Modern England* (Oxford, 1990)

F. Heal and C. Holmes, *The Gentry in England and Wales, 1500–1700* (Stanford, Ca., 1994)

H. Heaton, *The Yorkshire Woollen and Worsted Industries* (Oxford, 1965)

J. J. Hecht, *The Domestic Servant in Eighteenth-Century England* (1980)

B. Hill, *Eighteenth-Century Women: An Anthology* (1984)

B. Hill, *Women, Work and Sexual Politics in Eighteenth-Century England* (Oxford, 1989)

B. Hill, *Servants: English Domestics in the Eighteenth Century* (Oxford, 1996)

R. Hoffman and P. J. Albert (eds.), *Women in the Age of American Revolution* (Charlottesville, Va., 1989)

C. Hole, *English Home Life, 1500–1800* (1947)

C. Hole, *The English Housewife in the Seventeenth Century* (1953)

G. Holmes, *Augustan England: Professions, State and Society, 1680–1730* (1982)

R. Houlbrooke, *The English Family, 1450–1700* (Harlow, 1984)

R. Houlbrooke, *English Family Life, 1576–1716: An Anthology from Diaries* (Oxford, 1988)

A. C. Howe, *The Cotton Masters, 1830–60* (Oxford, 1984)

D. W. Howell, *Patriarchs and Parasites: The Gentry of South-West Wales in the Eighteenth Century* (Cardiff, 1986)

O. Hufton, *The Prospect Before Her: A History of Western Women, 1500–1800* (1995)

E. Hughes, *North Country Life in the Eighteenth Century: The North-East, 1700–1750* (Oxford, 1952)

E. Hughes, *North Country Life in the Eighteenth Century: Cumberland and Westmorland, 1700–1830* (Oxford, 1965)

M. R. Hunt, *The Middling Sort: Commerce, Gender, and the Family in England, 1680–1780* (Berkeley, Ca., 1996)

M. Ingrams, *Church Courts, Sex and Marriage in England, 1570–1640* (Cambridge, 1987)

G. Jackson, *Hull in the Eighteenth Century: A Study in Economic and Social History* (1972)

P. Jalland, *Women, Marriage and Politics, 1860–1914* (Oxford, 1986)

J. James, *History of the Worsted Manufacture in England* (1857)

P. Jenkins, *The Making of a Ruling Class: The Glamorgan Gentry, 1640–1790* (Cambridge, 1983)

P. Joyce, *Work, Society and Politics: The Culture of the Factory in Later Victorian England* (1980)

J. F. Kasson, *Rudeness and Civility: Manners in Nineteenth-Century Urban America* (New York, 1990)

N. Landau, *The Justices of the Peace, 1679–1760* (Los Angeles, Ca., 1984)

P. Langford, *A Polite and Commercial People: England, 1727–1783* (Oxford, 1989)

P. Langford, *Public Life and the Propertied Englishman* (Oxford, 1991)

T. Laqueur, *Making Sex: Body and Gender from the Greeks to Freud* (Cambridge, Mass., 1990)

A. Laurence, *Women in England, 1500–1760: A Social History* (1994)

J. W. Laycock, *Early Methodist Heroes of the Haworth Round* (Keighley, 1909)

D. Levine and K. Wrightson, *The Making of an Industrial Society: Whickham, 1560–1765* (Oxford, 1991)

J. Lewis (ed.), *Labour and Love: Women's Experience of Home and Family, 1850–1940* (Oxford, 1986)

J. S. Lewis, *In the Family Way: Childbearing in the British Aristocracy, 1760–1860* (New Brunswick, NJ, 1986)

L. Lippincott, *Selling Art in Georgian London: The Rise of Arthur Pond* (New Haven and London, 1983)

M. MacDonald, *Mystical Bedlam: Madness, Anxiety and Healing in Seventeenth-Century England* (Cambridge, 1981)

A. Macfarlane, *The Family Life of Ralph Josselin, a Seventeenth Century Clergyman: An Essay in Historical Anthropolgy* (Cambridge, 1970)

A. Macfarlane, *Marriage and Love in England, 1300–1840* (Oxford, 1986)

N. McKendrick, J. Brewer and J. H. Plumb, *The Birth of a Consumer Society: The Commercialisation of Eighteenth-Century England* (1982)

A. McLaren, *Reproductive Rituals: The Perception of Fertility in England from the Sixteenth Century to the Nineteenth Century* (1984)

A. P. W. Malcolmson, *The Pursuit of the Heiress: Aristocratic Marriage in Ireland, 1750–1820* (Belfast, 1982)

J. E. Mason, *Gentlefolk in the Making: Studies in the History of English Courtesy Literature and Related Topics, 1531–1774* (Philadelphia, 1935)

L. de Mause (ed.), *The History of Childhood* (New York, 1974)

S. Mendelson, *The Mental World of Stuart Women: Three Studies* (Reading, 1987)

C. Midgley, *Women Against Slavery: The British Campaigns, 1780–1870* (1992)

G. E. Mingay, *English Landed Society in the Eighteenth Century* (1963)

J. Money, *Experience and Identity: Birmingham and the West Midlands, 1760–1800* (Manchester, 1977)

W. Munk (ed.), *The Roll of the Royal College of Physicians of London* (1878)

S. H. Myers, *The Bluestocking Circle: Women, Friendship and the Life of the Mind in Eighteenth-Century England* (1990)

A. Nicholl, *The Garrick Stage* (Manchester, 1980)

I. Ousby, *The Englishman's England: Taste, Travel and the Rise of Tourism* (Cambridge, 1990)

S. Pearson, *Rural Houses of the Lancashire Pennines, 1560–1760* (1985)

H. W. Pedicord, *'By Their Majesties' Command': The House of Hanover at the London Theatres, 1714–1800* (1991)

R. Perry, *The Celebrated Mary Astell: An Early English Feminist* (Chicago, 1986)

M. J. Peterson, *Family, Love and Work in the Lives of Victorian Gentlewomen* (Bloomington, Ind., 1989)

I. Pinchbeck, *Women Workers and the Industrial Revolution, 1750–1850* (1930)

L. A. Pollock, *Forgotten Children: Parent Child Relations from 1500 to 1900* (Cambridge, 1983)

L. A. Pollock, *A Lasting Relationship: Parents and Children over Three Centuries* (1987)

R. and D. Porter, *Patients' Progress: Doctors and Doctoring in Eighteenth-Century England* (Oxford, 1989)

W. Prest (ed.), *The Professions in Early Modern England* (1987)

C. Price, *Theatre in the Age of Garrick* (Oxford, 1973)

F. K. Prochaska, *Women and Philanthropy in Nineteenth-Century England* (Oxford, 1980)

J. Rendall, *The Origins of Modern Feminism: Women in Britain, France and the United States, 1780–1860* (Basingstoke, 1985)

M. Reynolds, *The Learned Lady in England, 1650–1750* (New York, 1920)

R. Robson, *The Attorney in Eighteenth-Century England* (1959)

P. Roebuck, *Yorkshire Baronets, 1640–1760* (Oxford, 1980)

K. M. Rogers, *Feminism in Eighteenth-Century England* (Chicago, 1982)

L. Roper, *Oedipus and the Devil: Witchcraft, Sexuality and Religion in Early Modern Europe* (1994)

S. Rosenfeld, *Temples of Thespis: Some Private Theatricals in England and Wales, 1700–1830* (1978)

M. Rostvig, *The Happy Man: Studies in the Metamorphosis of a Classical Ideal* (Oslo, 1954), 2 vols.

G. S. Rousseau and R. Porter (ed.), *Sexual Underworlds of the Enlightenment* (Manchester, 1987)

G. Russell, *Theatres of War: Performance, Politics and Society, 1793–1815* (Oxford, 1995)

J. Sekora, *Luxury: The Concept in Western Thought, Eden to Smollett* (Baltimore, 1977)

K. Shevelow, *Women and Print Culture: The Construction of Femininity in the Early Periodical* (1989)

E. Shorter, *The Making of the Modern Family* (1976)

M. Slater, *Family Life in the Seventeenth Century: The Verneys of Claydon House* (1984)

J. Smail, *The Origins of Middle-Class Culture: Halifax, Yorkshire, 1660–1780* (Ithaca, NY, 1994)

S. Staves, *Married Women's Separate Property in England, 1660–1833* (1990)

L. Stone, *The Family, Sex and Marriage in England, 1500–1800* (1977)

L. Stone, *Road to Divorce: England 1530–1987* (Oxford, 1990)

L. Stone and J. Fawtier Stone, *An Open Elite? England 1540–1880* (Oxford, abr. ed., 1986)

L. Stone, *Uncertain Unions: Marriage in England, 1660–1753* (Oxford, 1992)

L. Stone, *Broken Lives: Separation and Divorce in England, 1660–1857* (Oxford, 1993)

J. T. Swain, *Industry Before the Industrial Revolution: North-East Lancashire c.1500–1640* (Manchester, 1986)

C. A. Temple, *Horrocks Memoirs* (1891)

E. Ten Broek Runk, *Barcroft Family Records* (1910)

E. P. Thompson, *The Making of the English Working Class* (1963)

R. G. Thorne, *History of Parliament: The House of Commons 1790–1820 1986*)

R. Trumbach, *The Rise of the Egalitarian Family: Aristocratic Kinship and Domestic Relations in Eighteenth-Century England* (1978)

J. and J. A. Venn, *Alumni Cantabrigienses* (Cambridge, 1924), 6 vols.

M. Vicinus (ed.), *Suffer and Be Still: Women in the Victorian Age* (Bloomington, Ind., 1972)

Victoria County History of Lancashire, W. Farrar and J. Brownbill, eds. (1966), 8 vols.

A. P. Wadsworth and J. de Lacy Mann, *The Cotton Trade and Industrial Lancashire, 1600–1780* (Manchester, 1931)

I. Watt, *The Rise of the Novel* (1957)

L. Weatherill, *Consumer Behaviour and Material Culture in Britain, 1660–1760* (1988)

A. Wilson, *The Making of Man-Midwifery: Childbirth in England, 1660–1770* (Cambridge, Mass., 1995)

R. G. Wilson, *Gentleman Merchants: The Merchant Community in Leeds, 1700–1830* (Manchester, 1971)

K. Wrightson, *English Society, 1580–1680* (1982)

A. Wrigley and R. Schofield, *The Population History of England* (Cambridge, Mass., 1981)

Articles and Essays

S. Amussen, 'Being Stir'd to Much Unquietness: Violence and Domestic Violence in Early Modern England', *Journal of Women's History*, 6 (1994), pp. 70–89

D. T. Andrew, 'London Debating Societies, 1776–1799', *London Record Society*, 30 (1993)

D. T. Andrew, 'Female Charity in an Age of Sentiment', in J. Brewer and S. Staves (eds.), *Early Modern Conceptions of Property* (1995), pp. 275–300

E. L. Avery, 'The Shakespeare Ladies Club', *Shakespeare Quarterly*, 7 (1956), pp. 153–8

R. Ballaster, M. Beetham, E. Frazer and S. Hebron, 'Eighteenth-Century Women's Magazines', in id.,*Women's Worlds: Ideology, Femininity and the Women's Magazine* (Basingstoke, 1991), pp. 43–74

J. Bennett, 'History that Stands Still: Women's Work in the European Past', *Feminist Studies*, 14 (1988), pp. 269–83

R. Blanchard, 'Richard Steele and the Status of Women', *Studies in Philology*, 26 (1929), pp. 325–55.

R. H. Bloch, 'Ideals in Transition: The Rise of the Moral Mother, 1785–1815', *Feminist Studies* (1978), pp. 101–27

P. Branca, 'Image and Reality: The Myth of the Idle Victorian Woman', in M. Hartman and L. Banner (eds.), *Clio's Consciousness Raised: New Perspectives on the History of Women* (New York, 1974), pp. 179–91

J. Brewer, 'Reconstructing the Reader: Prescriptions, Texts and Strategies in Anna Larpent's Reading', in J. Raven, N. Tadmor and H. Small (eds.), *The Practice and Representation of Reading in England* (Cambridge, 1996), pp. 226–45

I. Q. Brown, 'Domesticity, Feminism and Friendship: Female Aristocratic Culture and Marriage in England, 1660–1760', *Journal of Family History*, 7 (1982), pp. 406–24

A. Buck and H. Matthews, 'Pocket Guides to Fashion: Ladies' Pocket Books Published in England, 1760–1830', *Costume*, 18 (1984), pp. 35–58

M. Cohen, 'The Grand Tour: Constructing the English Gentleman in Eighteenth-Century France', *History of Education*, 21 (1992), pp. 241–57

L. W. Conolly, 'The Censor's Wife at the Theatre: The Diary of Anna Margaretta Larpent, 1790–1800', *Huntingdon Library Quarterley*, 35 (1971), pp. 49–64

S. Copley, 'Commerce, Conversation and Politeness in the Early Eighteenth-Century Periodical', *British Journal for Eighteenth-Century Studies*, 18 (1995), pp. 63–77

P. J. Corfield, 'Class by Name and Number in Eighteenth-Century Britain', *History*, 72 (1987), pp. 38–61

P. J. Corfield, 'The Rivals: Landed and Other Gentleman', in N. B. Harte and R. Quinault (eds.), *Land and Society in Britain, 1700–1914* (Manchester, 1996), pp. 1–33

N. F. Cott, 'Divorce and the Changing Status of Women in Eighteenth-Century Massachusetts', *William and Mary Quarterly*, 33 (1976), pp. 587–92

P. Crawford, 'Attitudes to Pregnancy, from a Woman's Spiritual Diary, 1687–8', *Local Population Studies*, 21 (1978), pp. 43–5

P. Crawford, 'Katharine and Philip Henry and their Children: A Case Study in Family Ideology', *Transactions of the Historic Society of Lancashire and Cheshire*, 134 (1984), pp. 39–73

P. Crawford, 'The Sucking Child': Adult Attitudes to Child Care in the First Year of Life in Seventeenth-Century England', *Continuity and Change*, 1 (1986), pp. 31–2

P. Crawford, 'The Construction and Experience of Maternity in Seventeenth-Century England', in V. Fildes (ed.), *Women as Mothers in Pre-Industrial England: Essays in Memory of Dorothy McLaren* (1990), pp. 3–38

R. Darnton, 'Readers Respond to Rousseau: The Fabrication of Romantic Sensitivity', in id., *The Great Cat Massacre* (1984), pp. 215–56

K. M. Davies, 'Continuity and Change in Literary Advice on Marriage', in R. B. Outhwaite (ed.), *Marriage and Society: Studies in the Social History of Marriage* (1981), pp. 58–80

N. Z. Davis, 'Women on Top', in id., *Society and Culture in Early Modern France* (1975), pp. 124–52

C. N. Degler, 'What Ought to Be and What Was: Women's Sexuality in the Nineteenth Century', *American Historical Review*, 79 (1974), pp. 1467–90

D. Donald, ' "Mr Deputy Dumpling and Family": Satirical Images of the City Merchant in Eighteenth-Century England', *Burlington Magazine*, 131 (1989), pp. 755–63

P. Earle, 'The Female Labour Market in London in the late Seventeenth and Eighteenth centuries', *Ec.H.R.*, 2nd ser., 42 (1989), pp. 328–53

G. Eley, 'Rethinking the Political: Social History and Political Culture in Eighteenth and Nineteenth-Century Britain', *Archiv für Sozialgeschichte*, 21 (1981), pp. 427–57

T. Fawcett, 'Provincial Dancing Masters', *Norfolk Archaeology*, 25 (1970), pp. 134–41

T. Fawcett, 'Dance and Teachers of Dance in Eighteenth-Century Bath', *Bath History*, 2 (1988), pp. 27–48

J. Fergus, 'Eighteenth-Century Readers in Provincial England: The Customers of Samuel Clay's Circulating Library and Bookshop in Warwick, 1770–72', *Papers of the Bibliographic Society of America*, 78 (1984), pp. 155–213

J. Fergus, 'Women, Class and the Growth of Magazine Readership in the Provinces, 1746–80', *Studies in Eighteenth-Century Culture*, 16 (1986), pp. 41–56

D. M. George, 'From Good Wife to Mistress: the Transformation of the Female in Bourgeois Culture', *Science and Society*, 37 (1973), pp. 152–77

D. Goodman, 'Public Sphere and Private Life: Toward a Synthesis of Current Historiographical Approaches to the Old Regime', *History and Theory*, 31 (1992), pp. 1–20

J. Habermas, 'The Public Sphere', *New German Critique*, 3 (1974), pp. 45–55

C. Hall, 'The Early Formation of Victorian Domestic Ideology', in S. Burman (ed.), *Fit Work for Women* (1977), pp. 15–32

C. Hall, 'Gender Divisions and Class Formation in the Birmingham Middle Class, 1780–1850', in R. Samuel (ed.), *People's History and Socialist Theory* (1981), pp. 164–75

B. Harrison, 'The Servants of William Gossip', *Georgian Group Journal*, 6 (1996), pp. 134–143

B. Harrison, 'Thorp Arch Hall, 1749–1756: "Dabling a little in Mortar"', Thoresby Society, 2nd ser., 4 (1994 for 1993), pp. 1–39

N. A. Hewitt, 'Beyond the Search for Sisterhood: American Women's History in the 1980s', *Social History*, 10 (1985), pp. 299–321

K. Hodgkin, 'The Diary of Lady Anne Clifford: A Study of Class and Gender in the Seventeenth Century', *HWJ.*, 19 (1985), pp. 148–61

B. A. Holderness, 'Credit in a Rural Community, 1660–1800', *Midland History*, 3 (1975), pp. 94–115

T. H. Hollingsworth, 'The Demography of the British Peerage', *Population Studies Supplement*, 18 (1965), pp. 1–108

R. A. Houston, 'The Development of Literacy: Northern England, 1640–1750', *EcHR*, 2nd ser., 35 (1982), pp. 199–216

O. Hufton, 'Women in History: Early Modern Europe', *P&P*, 101 (1983), pp. 125–41

M. Hunt, 'Time-Management, Writing and Accounting in the Eighteenth-Century English Trading Family: A Bourgeois Enlightenment', *Business and Economic History*, 2nd ser., 18 (1989), pp. 150–59

M. Hunt, 'Wife Beating, Domesticity and Women's Independence in Eighteenth-Century London', *Gender and History*, 4 (1992), pp. 10–33

J. E. Hunter, 'The Eighteenth-Century Englishwoman: According to the *Gentleman's Magazine*', in P. Fritz and R. Morton (eds.), *Woman in the Eighteenth Century and Other Essays* (Toronto, 1976), pp. 73–88

L. Kerber, 'Separate Spheres, Female Worlds, Woman's Place: The Rhetoric of Women's History', *Journal of American History*, 75 (1988), pp. 9–39

L. Klein, 'The Third Earl of Shaftesbury and the Progress of Politeness', *Eighteenth-Century Studies*, 8 (1974), pp. 186–214

L. Klein, 'Gender, Conversation and the Public Sphere', in J. Still and M. Worton, *Textuality and Sexuality: Reading Theories and Practices* (Manchester, 1993), pp. 100–115

L. Klein, 'Politeness for Plebes: Consumption and Social Identity in Early Eighteenth-Century England', in J. Brewer and A. Bermingham (eds.), *The Consumption of Culture, 1660–1800: Image, Object, Text* (1995), pp. 362–82

L. Klein, 'Gender and the Public/Private Distinction in the Eighteenth Century: Some Questions about Evidence and Analytic Procedure', *Eighteenth-Century Studies*, 29, no. 1 (1995), pp. 97–109

H. F. Killick, 'Notes on the Early History of the Leeds–Liverpool Canal', *Bradford Antiquary*, n.s., 1 (1900), pp. 169–238

B. Kowaleski-Wallace, 'Tea, Gender and Domesticity in Eighteenth-Century England', *Studies in Eighteenth-Century English Culture*, 23 (1993), pp. 131–45

V. Larminie, 'Marriage and the Family: the Example of the Seventeenth-Century Newdigates', *Midland History*, 9 (1984), pp. 1–22

M. Legates, 'The Cult of Womanhood in Eighteenth-Century Thought', *Eighteenth-Century Studies*, 1 (1976), pp. 21–39

B. Lemire, 'Consumerism in Pre-industrial and Early Industrial England: The Trade in Secondhand Clothes', *Journal of British Studies*, 27 (1988), pp. 1–24

D. Lemmings, 'Marriage and the Law in the Eighteenth Century: Hardwicke's Marriage Act of 1753', *HJ*, 39, 2 (1996), pp. 339–60

G. Lerner, 'The Lady and the Mill Girl: Changes in the Status of Women in the Age of Jackson', *Midcontinent American Studies Journal*, 10 (1969), pp. 5–15

J. Lewis, 'Domestic Tranquillity and the Management of Emotion Among the Gentry of pre-Revolutionary Virginia', *William and Mary Quarterly*, 3rd ser., 39 (1982), pp. 135–49

P. H. Lindert and J. G. Williamson, 'Revising England's Social Tables, 1688–1812', *Explorations in Economic History*, 19 (1982), pp. 385–408

N. McKendrick, 'Home Demand and Economic Growth: A New View of the Role of Women and Children in the Industrial Revolution', in N. McKendrick (ed.), *Historical Perspectives: Studies in English Thought and Society in Honour of J. H. Plumb* (Cambridge, 1975), pp. 152–210

D. McLaren, 'Nature's Contraceptive: Wetnursing and Prolonged Lactation: The Case of Chesham, Buckinghamshire, 1578–1601', *Medical History*, 23 (1979), pp. 426–41

D. Marshall, 'The Domestic Servants of the Eighteenth Century', *Economica*, 19 (1929), pp. 15–40

J. E. Mechling, 'Advice to Historians on Advice to Mothers', *Journal of Social History*, 9 (1975), pp. 44–63

S. Mendelson, 'Stuart Women's Diaries and Occasional Memoirs', in M. Prior (ed.), *Women in English Society, 1500–1800* (1985), pp. 181–210

P. H. Michaelson, 'Women in the Reading Circle', *Eighteenth-Century Life*, 13 (1990), pp. 59–69

M. B. Norton, 'Eighteenth-Century American Women in Peace and War: The Case of the Loyalists', *William and Mary Quarterly*, 3rd ser., 33 (1976), pp. 386–409

M. B. Norton, 'The Myth of the Golden Age', in C. Berkin and M. B. Norton (eds.), *Women in America: A History* (Boston, Mass., 1979), pp. 37–47

R. Perry, 'Colonizing the Breast: Sexuality and Maternity in Eighteenth-Century England', in J. C. Fout, *Forbidden History: The State, Society and the Regulation of Sexuality in Modern Europe. Essays from the Journal of the History of Sexuality* (Chicago, 1992), pp. 107–37

D. Peters, 'The Pregnant Pamela: Characterization and Popular Medical Attitudes in the Eighteenth Century', *Eighteenth-Century Studies*, 14 (1981), pp. 432–51

M. J. Peterson, 'No Angels in the House: The Victorian Myth and the Paget Women', *American Historical Review*, 89 (1984), pp. 677–708

B. Pidock, 'The Spinners and Weavers of Swarthmoor Hall, Ulverston, in the late Seventeenth Century', *Transactions of the Cumberland and Westmorland Antiquarian and Archaeological Society*, 95 (1995), pp. 153–167

J. H. Plumb, 'The New World of Children in Eighteenth-Century England', *P&P*, 67 (1975), pp. 64–93

L. A. Pollock, '"An action like Stratagem": Courtship and Marriage from the Middle Ages to the Twentieth Century', *HJ*, 30 (1987), pp. 483–98

L. A. Pollock, 'Living on the Stage of the World: The Concept of the Privacy among the Elite of Early Modern England', in A. Wilson (ed.), *Rethinking Social History: English Society, 1570–1920* (Manchester, 1993), pp. 78–96

R. Porter, 'Lay Medical Knowledge in the Eighteenth Century: The Evidence of the *Gentleman's Magazine*', *Medical History*, 29 (1985), pp. 138–68.

R. Porter, 'A Touch of Danger: The Man-Midwife as Sexual Predator', in G. Rousseau and R. Porter (eds.), *Sexual Underworlds of the Enlightenment* (Manchester, 1987), pp. 206–32

E. Richards, 'Women in the British economy since about 1700: An Interpretation', *History*, 59 (1974), pp. 337–57

M. Roberts, 'Sickles and Scythes: Women's Work and Men's Work at Harvest Time', *HWJ*, 7 (1979), pp. 3–28

N. Rogers, 'Money, Land and Lineage: The Big Bourgeoisie of Hanoverian London', *Social History*, 4 (1979), pp. 437–54

B. B. Schnorrenberg, 'Is Childbirth any Place for a Woman? The Decline of Midwifery in Eighteenth-Century England', *Studies in Eighteenth-Century Culture*, 10 (1981), pp. 393–408

R. Schofield, 'Did the Mothers Really Die? Three Centuries of Maternal Mortality in the World We Have Lost', in L. Bonfield, R. M. Smith and K. Wrightson (eds.), *The World We Have Gained: Histories of Population and Social Structure* (Oxford, 1986), pp. 231–60

J. Scott, 'Gender: A Useful Category of Historical Analysis', *American Historical Review*, 91 (1986), pp. 1053–75

P. Seleski, 'Women, Work and Cultural Change in Eighteenth and Early Nineteenth-Century London', in T. Harris, (ed), *Popular Culture in England, c.1500–1850* (Basingstoke, 1995), pp. 143–67

C. Shammas, 'The Domestic Environment in Early Modern England and America', *Journal of Social History*, 14 (1980), pp. 3–24

D. Simonton, 'Apprenticeship: Training and Gender in Eighteenth-Century England', in M. Berg (ed.), *Markets and Manufactures in Early Industrial Europe* (1991), pp. 227–58

M. Slater, 'The Weightiest Business: Marriage in an Upper Gentry Family in Seventeenth-Century England', *P&P*, 72 (1976), pp. 25–54

A. Hassell Smith, 'Labourers in Late Sixteenth-Century England: A Case Study from North Norfolk', *Continuity and Change*, 4 (1989), Pt. I, pp. 11–52; Pt. II 367–94

K. Snell, 'Agricultural Seasonal Unemployment, the Standard of Living, and Women's Work in the South and East, 1690–1860', *EcHR*, 2nd ser., 34 (1981), pp. 407–37

P. M. Spacks, 'Ev'ry Woman is at Heart a Rake', *Eighteenth-Century Studies*, 8 (1974), pp. 27–46

S. Staves, 'The Secrets of Genteel Identity in *The Man of Mode*: Comedy of Manners vs the Courtesy Book', *Studies in Eighteenth-Century Culture*, 19 (1989), pp. 117–128

J. Styles, 'Clothing the North: The Supply of Non-Elite Clothing in the Eighteenth-Century North of England', *Textile History*, 25 (1994), pp. 139–66

A. Summers, 'A Home from Home: Women's Philanthropic Work in the Nineteenth Century', in S. Burman (ed.), *Fit Work for Women* (1977), pp. 33–63

N. Tadmor, '"Family" and "Friend" in Richardson's *Pamela*: A Case Study in the History of the Family in Eighteenth-Century England', *Social History*, 13 (1989), pp. 289–306

N. Tadmor, 'In the Even My Wife Read Unto Me: Women, Reading and Household Life in the Eighteenth Century', in J. Raven, N. Tadmor and H. Small (eds.), *The Practice and Representation of Reading in England* (Cambridge, 1996), pp. 162–74

K. Thomas, 'The Double Standard', *Journal of the History of Ideas*, 20 (1959), pp. 195–216

E. P. Thompson, 'Patrician Society, Plebeian Culture', *Journal of Social History*, 7 (1974), pp. 382–405

E. P. Thompson, 'Eighteenth-Century English Society: Class Struggle without Class?', *Social History*, 3 (1978), pp. 133–65

M. Todd, 'Humanists, Puritans and the Spiritualized Household', *Church History*, 49 (1980), pp. 18–34

D. E. Underdown, 'The Taming of the Scold: The Enforcement of Patriarchal Authority in Early Modern England', in A. Fletcher and J. Stevenson (eds.), *Order and Disorder in Early Modern England* (Cambridge, 1985), pp. 116–36

M. C. Versluyen, 'Midwives, Medical Men and ' "Poor Women Labouring of Child": Lying in Hospitals in Eighteenth-Century London', in H. Roberts (ed.), *Women, Health and Reproduction* (1981), pp. 18–49

A. J. Vickery, 'Golden Age to Separate Spheres: A Review of the Categories and Chronology of English Women's History', *Historical Journal*, 36, 2 (1993), pp. 383–414

A. Wall, 'Elizabethan Precept and Feminine Practice: The Thynne family of Longleat', *History*, 243 (1990), pp. 23–38

C. Walsh, 'Shop Design and the Display of Goods in Eighteenth-Century London', *Journal of Design History*, 8 (1995), pp. 157–76

L. Weatherill, 'A Possession of One's Own: Women and Consumer Behaviour in England, 1660–1740', *Journal of British Studies*, 25 (1986), pp. 131–56

L. Weatherill, 'Consumer Behaviour and Social Status in England, 1660–1750', *Continuity and Change*, 2 (1986), pp. 191–216

B. Welter, 'The Cult of True Womanhood, 1820–60', *American Quarterly*, 18 (1966), pp. 151–74

K. E. Westhauser, 'Friendship and Family in Early Modern England: The Sociability of Adam Eyre and Samuel Pepys', *Journal of Social History*, 27 (1994), pp. 517–36

A. Wilson, 'Participant or Patient? Seventeenth-Century Childbirth from the Mother's Point of View', in R. Porter (ed.), *Patients and Practitioners: Lay Perceptions of Medicine in Pre-Industrial Society* (Cambridge, 1985), pp. 129–44

A. Wilson, 'William Hunter and the Varieties of Man-Midwifery', in W. Bynum and R. Porter (eds.), *William Hunter and the Eighteenth-Century Medical World* (Cambridge, 1985), pp. 343–69

A. Wilson, 'The Perils of Early Modern Procreation: Childbirth With or Without Fear?', *British Journal for Eighteenth-Century Studies*, 16, (1993), pp. 1–19

R. G. Wilson, 'Three Brothers: A Study in the Fortunes of a Landed Family in the mid-Eighteenth Century', *Bradford Textile Society Journal* (1964–5), pp. 111–21

S. Wilson, 'The Myth of Motherhood a Myth: The Historical View of European Child-Rearing', *Social History*, 9 (1984), pp. 81–98

Unpublished Theses and Papers

J. Barry, 'The Cultural Life of Bristol, 1640–1775' (D.Phil. thesis, Oxford University, 1985)

P. Carter, 'Mollies, Fops and Men of Feeling: Aspects of Male Effeminacy and Masculinity in Britain, c.1700–1780 (D.Phil. thesis, Oxford University, 1995)

F. Childs, 'Prescriptions for Manners in English Courtesy Literature, 1690–1760, and their Social Implications' (D.Phil. thesis, Oxford University, 1984)

H. Clifford, 'Parker and Wakelin: The Study of an Eighteenth-Century Goldsmithing Firm, c.1760–76, with particular reference to the Garrard Ledgers' (Ph.D. thesis, Royal College of Art, 1988)

K. A. Crouch, 'Attitudes Toward Actresses in Eighteenth-Century Britain' (D.Phil. thesis, Oxford University, 1995)

J. Hall, 'The Refashioning of Fashionable Society: Opera-Going and Sociability in Britain, 1821–1861' (Ph.D. thesis, Yale University, 1996)

B. Harrison, 'The Gossip Family of Thorp Arch in the Eighteenth Century' (paper presented to the Yorkshire Archaeological Society, 1996)

C. Dallet Hemphill, 'Men, Women and Visiting in Ante-Bellum Conduct Literature' (paper given to the Berkshire Conference, June 1993)

J. Holmes, 'Domestic Service in Yorkshire, 1650–1780' (D.Phil. thesis, York University, 1989)

M. Hunt, 'English Urban Families in Trade, 1660–1800: The Social Relations of Early Modern Capitalism' (Ph.D. thesis, New York University, 1986)

T. Meldrum, 'Domestic Service in London, 1660–1750: Gender, Life Cycle, Work and Household Relations' (Ph.D. thesis, London University, 1996)

C. Midgeley, 'Women Anti-Slavery Campaigners in Britain' (Ph.D. thesis, University of Kent, 1989)

S. Nichols, 'Gillow and Company of Lancaster, England: An Eighteenth-Century Business History' (MA thesis, University of Delaware, 1982)

J. Raven, 'English Popular Literature and the Image of Business, 1760–90' (Ph.D. thesis, Cambridge University, 1985)

J. Smail, 'From the Middling to the Middle: Class Formation in Halifax, Yorkshire in the century before the Industrial Revolution' (Ph.D. thesis, Stanford University, 1988)

A. J. Vickery, 'Women of the Local Elite in Lancashire, 1750–c.1825' (Ph.D. thesis, University of London, 1991)

W. Weber, 'Opera and Nobility in Eighteenth-Century London and Paris' (work in progress)

S. Whayman, 'Sociability and Power: The World of the Verney's, 1660–1720' (Ph.D. thesis, Princeton University, 1993)

R. G. Wilson, 'Towards an Economic History of Country House Building in the Eighteenth Century' (seminar paper, Eighteenth Century Seminar, Institute of Historical Research, London University, October 1988)

Plates and Acknowledgements

Index

Note: Page references in *italics* refer to illustrations and their captions. Page numbers in **bold** type indicate persons listed in the Biographical Index (Appendix 2).

social networks   89–90, 368–74
and sport   347 n.128
Whitaker, Eliza (née Horrocks)
and child care   116, 121
and housekeeping   131, 157
marriage   23, 61, 68–70, 71, 373
and pregnancy and childbirth   97, 99–101,
315 n.55
and public life   254, 258, 265
and schooling   304 n.51
and servants   321 n.23
social networks   29–31, 89–90
Whitaker, Thomas   364
white lead   33, 379
Whitehead, Mary   88, 372, 373
widows
and fashion   175, 177
and material culture   163
status   22, 24
Wiglesworth, Barbara   265, 318 n.115, 368
Wiglesworth, Elizabeth   283, 373
Wiglesworth family   24, 301 n.32
Wiglesworth, Henry   364
Wiglesworth, James   301 n.34, 302 n.36
Wilberforce, William   289
Wilkes, John   260
Wilkes, Wetenhall   57, 72
Wilkinson family   28, 303 n.45, 304 n.54
wills   64, 190, 194
Wilmer, Anne   61, 63–4, 63
Wilson, Adrian   95
Wilson, Ellen   368
Wilson, James   215, 303 nn.45, 47, 49
Wilson, Martha   368
Wilson, Matthew   368
Wilson, R. G.   33, 34, 36, 374
Witton, John   364
Witton, Mary   355, 364
Wollstonecraft, Mary   12, 83, 269, 274
women
behaviour   198
see also covetousness; frivolousness;
idleness; obedience; propriety; prudence;
sauciness; virtues; visiting
and the body see childbirth; illness;
infertility; menstruation; pregnancy
freedoms and constraints see chaperonage;
law, and legal status; mobility; modesty;
property rights; violence

life-cycle   8, 265–6
see also age; childbirth; courtship;
marriage; pregnancy
and petitioning   49–52
and power   9–11
see also authority; courtship; expertise,
female; heiresses; patriarchy; politics;
tears; tyranny
recreation see assemblies; conversation;
entertainment; sport
and responsibility   3, 8–9, 285, 293–
4
roles see chaperonage; consumerism;
daughters; girls; hostesses; housekeeper;
motherhood; nurses
roles see public figures; widows
see also authority, female; charity; chastity;
dignity; duty; elegance; fortitude;
modesty; propriety; submissiveness
Woodeforde, Parson, and servants   138, 142,
219
Woodward, George   219–20, 268–9
wool
household manufacture   150
manufacturers   15, 17, 20, 28, 30, 73, 140,
303 n.47, 355
woollen drapers   73, 375
Wootton, John   376
John Warde and his Family   274
work
female   2, 4
male see officeholding
managerial see estate management;
household
worsted manufacturers   15, 16, 30
Wotton, Henry   195
Wright, Mrs A.   374
Wrightson, Keith   60, 86, 312 n.17
Wycoller Hall   24, 204, 365

York
assembly rooms   239, 240, 261, 270,
376
and female clubs   256
and public life   116, 267
season   261, 265–6
and shopping   168
and trials   237–8